THE LONG
NIGHT
OF DARK
INTENT

THE LONG
NIGHT
OF DARK
INTENT

A HALF
CENTURY
OF CUBAN
COMMUNISM

IRVING LOUIS HOROWITZ

Routledge
Taylor & Francis Group

LONDON AND NEW YORK

First published 2008 by Transaction Publishers

Published 2017 by Routledge
2 Park Square, Milton Park, Abingdon, Oxon OX14 4RN
711 Third Avenue, New York, NY 10017, USA

Routledge is an imprint of the Taylor & Francis Group, an informa business

Library of Congress Catalog Number: 2008014366

Library of Congress Cataloging-in-Publication Data

Horowitz, Irving Louis.
 The long night of dark intent : a half century of Cuban communism / Irving Louis Horowitz.
  p. cm.
 Includes bibliographical references and index.
 ISBN 978-1-4128-0879-8 (alk. cloth)
  1. Cuba—Politics and government—1959-1990. 2. Cuba— Economic conditions—1959-1990. 3. Cuba—Politics and government-- 1990- 4. Cuba—Economic conditions—1990- 5. Communism—Cuba. 6. Cuba—Military policy. 7. United States—Foreign relations--Cuba. 8. Cuba—Foreign relations—United States. 9. Cuba—Social condi- tions—1959- 10. Cuba—History—20th century. I. Title.

F1788.H573   2008
972.9106'4—dc22   2008014366

ISBN 13: 978-1-4128-4224-2 (pbk)
ISBN 13: 978-1-4128-0879-8 (hbk)

"It looked as if a night of dark intent was coming, and not only a night, an age … Someone had better be prepared for rage. There would be more than ocean water broken before God's last *Put out the Light* was spoken."—Robert Frost, *Once by the Pacific*, 1928

Contents

Preface:
The Long Night of Dark Intent:
50 Years of Cuban Communism

I chose as a title *The Long Night* for the simple reason that in the case of Fidel Castro's Cuba we are looking at a half century of rule, plus another earlier four years of guerrilla warfare and random incendiary incidents all dedicated to first achieving the aim of the revolution—the seizure of power. The Cuban Revolution did not start with the grand entrance of the guerrillas into the streets of Havana in the first week of January, 1959. That event simply and poignantly culminated several years of armed insurrection against the Batista Regime. Nonetheless, it was a benchmark of triumph and a harbinger of tragedy to come. Rather than herald a new era of Cuba joining the world community of nations as a paragon of democracy, as so many fervently hoped and believed at the time, it became a bellwether, or better a beachhead, of communist rule in the Western hemisphere. This strange amalgam of the proverbial "man on horseback," military rule as a consequence of guerrilla insurgency, and iron-fisted party rule evolving from near anarchic movement politics defined Castro's Cuba at the outset; and with a bow to the single-minded tenacity of the tyrant, has continued to do so for a half century.

Even those who doggedly continue to support the regime, or at least a search for normalcy between other nations in the West and the Communist regime in Havana, have come to the painful realization that the hopes and aspirations of the Cuban people were not fulfilled by the July 26th Movement that quickly morphed into the January 1st Movement of the Military. This collection of my essays, articles, and speeches over that long time frame is simply one person's odyssey of what I most emphatically believe to have been a collective national disaster. It is always a private trauma that does not go away, and will not go away, until the Cuban family dictatorship itself comes to termination.

Two astonishing facts define the past half century in Cuba: First is the capacity of a single individual to command and determine the fate of a nation, and do so with a minimum of opposition by agencies and figures thought to be dedicated to a democratic system. Second, there is the incredible reality that even those professing adhesion to democratic norms outside the grip of the dictatorship, far away from Cuba, are ready to forgive the dictator and damn the opposition. The aim of many of these essays, among other things, is to place in perspective the internal lack of opposition and the external support for the Castro family and its entourage. Even with the collapse of nearly all forms of European totalitarianism between 1945 and 1991, the ideology that underwrites such regimes and the utopia that fuels their support remain defining characteristics of the past half century in Cuban society. The trouble with much writing on this nation is that to explain is not to forgive, and to understand is not to celebrate. The capacity of extreme rule and continuous control is not something to celebrate. Indeed, it will be seen that survival techniuques are themselves a source of the problem of Cuban Communism.

Social historians have a fixation with temporal symmetry. It would arguably be aesthetically pleasing to speak of a half century in Cuban Communist history as dating from 1959. But while the entry into Havana by the Castro forces took place in the first few days of 1959, the seeds of that take over were well established in 1958. A concurrence of events took place—from the landing of the *Granma,* the frequent excursions and connections between Fidel Castro and his brother with the Soviet government prior to the seizure of power, the establishment of well disciplined military training camps in the Sierra Maestre mountain ranges, the ceding of large swatches of sparsely populated mountainous regions by the Batista government to the guerrillas, the inability or incapacity of the government's regular troops to seriously weaken much less destroy the guerrilla forces, the development of a firm military command structure under the aegis of Raul Castro, the completion of the trilogy of power with Ernesto Guevara taking on its ideological leadership, and the purging of rival factions within the insurgency. All of these elements made 1958 the year of decision, even though the start of 1959 represented the actual legitimizing control of state mechanisms. Major serious recent research confirms the decisive character of events in 1958. So the half century of celebration from within, and bereavement from without, is properly well underway.[1]

Now that the Preface to the book is complete, or what seems to me a Postscript at the start, is out of the way, let me make a confession, or in plain language, an admission. Although I have been writing on Cuba for a half century, I am not nor have I ever been a Cubanologist. Indeed, starting from a Latin American base for an even longer period, I am neither a Latin American expert either. Rather, the frame of reference that I developed for most of my life was as a developmentalist—someone for whom the forms of change vary over space and time, and that have particular nuances in area of the world subject to stagnation, corruption, exploitation, and the usual suspicions that accompany backwardness. To be sure, it is in that overall climate that the Cuban experience with dictatorship and socialism is best understood.

I admit to a hearty suspicion, bordering on disdain, that self anointed national or area experts in the social sciences are akin to medical specialists who are expert in the ailments of the pancreas or the liver or physical parts like the ear or the foot. They simply miss the whole, whether it is the social system or the human body. Of course, parts break down and require repair or at least close examination. But when parts of the body break down, the functional capacity of the whole is at risk. A great deal of this collection of essays and articles addresses such concerns. What is it about the whole, about Cuban Communism as such, that make its parts function poorly, erratically, or not at all. And why should it be that to even keep the whole intact, extraordinary measures are required: suppression of information, deprivation of elementary rights of criticism, and when all else fails, imprisonment or worse. In short, as in science, so too in society at large: specialization is the content of our everyday efforts, while generalization is its context. To make sense of the world, we thus need a double vision.

Such holistic generalities, derived in my case from a background in social philosophy and sociology of knowledge, may be a stimulant to thinking seriously about larger issues. But it is the anthropological act of travel that adds tasty foods to the dry bones of generalizations. Having spent the better part of 1958 in Buenos Aires, teaching at the Argentine national; university, was a way of looking up at events in Cuba rather than down or as the saying goes "ninety miles from home." For in post-Peronist, but militarily entrenched political centers, the drama of Castro was immediately felt. For the armed forces, Castro represents the anti-model, the ability to fashion a guerrilla movement with a small, ill equipped boat with 82 people, capable of overthrowing a fellow-military regime. But that same scenario unfolding as a melodrama, gave impulse to the pent up emotions of students who had endured a dozen years of Peronism followed by a timid insurrection, more a restoration than insurrection that restored civil authority more in name than in fact. The Cuban Revolution was this not a view from *The New York Times* correspondent, but from the essential forces that saw in that event the mark of the near future. In this, both opponents of Castro's and its student supporters saw the future correctly. But in opposite ends of the binoculars they were wearing.

To illustrate this point about a panoramic approach to a microscopic event, the Argentine military crackdown on student rebels and would be guerrillas was wildly out of proportion to their impact on the regime. But it was fueled in considerably measure by the ghost in the military machine—a movement dedicated to overthrow not just a regime but one capable of installing a system that promised more a rotating of military leaders. These fears in Buenos Aires about events in Havana were further fueled by eclectic heroes of the Argentine student movement: Jean-Paul Sartre, Régis Debray, C. Wright Mills, among others. Spanish may have been the official language of the nation, but the student vanguard was amazingly well versed in French and English. What else could one expect from the "Paris of Latin America"?

For the ruling elites, the Cuban developments before as well as after the seizure of the ruling elites, and before as well as after the seizure of power was a danger that could hardly be ignored. For the restless students, for whom social science was simply social theory without a purpose, the Cuban Revolution offered up a cause—communism, and a methodology, guerrilla insurgency.

Having myself grown up in a world of Jewish radicalism, in which the mythology of Soviet totalitarianism was the moral voice of the oppressed and downtrodden, whereas that of the Nazi totalitarianism was simply militarism and barbarism rolled into one, the siren call of Marxism Leninism seemed a perfect response to the evils of Wagner and Hitler. In some strange way, the Cuban response to events at the time was strikingly similar: the military of Batista was to be met by the military of Castro: bad armed forces would be conquered by good armed forces. In retrospect it is astonishing how few people took seriously the unity of totalitarianism as such, the sameness of military solutions to civil problems, whatever the parade of ideology dictated. Alas, Jewish radicals are hardly an exception.

The voices of Jacob Talmon and Hannah Arendt and Hans Kelsen were barely heard above the street demonstrations, the manifestations of popular solidarity as one end and military tenacity at the other. In short, the history of the Western Hemisphere as a whole was shaped in good measure by the emergence of the Castro Revolution. "History" may not have absolved Fidel, but it was the "God" that did not so much fail, as in Koestler, so much as the God that punished its followers with success. In short, the Cuban Revolution was the product of a Greek God rather than a Christian God. Perhaps that is why so many of the early revolutionaries who abandoned revolution for exile became so bitter. They helped bring about a revolutionary future that was not so much beautiful as downright ugly.

The Cuban Revolution has long held a curious fascination for me, since, along with Robert Dahl, I believe that democracy is a system best operational in small chunks. It must be thus, since the larger the nation or the region the smaller the chance was of direct participation or intervention in impacting the whole. Small nations, like small people (not masses) carry the burdens of civilization; they define the limits and possibilities of civility. One person who represents himself or herself is somehow a truer test, or so I believed, of the democratic vista, than one person who represents hundreds of thousands. "Representative" government is perhaps the modern equivalent of the division in political labor rather than a statement of democratic potentials. At least so it seemed to me in the late 1950s. The hint of anarchism translated into the actions of the guerrillas in Cuba.

In that environment, little nations like Cuba and Israel, and later, Armenia and Austria, carried the weight of the democratic credo—something that transcended the rhetoric of socialism, liberalism, or what have you. That each of these nations had different characteristics that required different evaluations is easier to understand at this point in time than it was a half century ago. But the emphasis on Cuba, the clinical estimate of events over time, the same sort of disillusionment that many earlier followers of Castro came to realize early in the game, finally dawned on my consciousness.

Cuba became a test case of all that I believed was politically possible, and all that I knew was social improbable. So the half century of these writings is a journey—from disillusionment with a revolution to the consolidation of a belief in democracy—whatever the scale, personal or representative—that makes possible the concordance of theorizing about a national when in fact it is no less a coming to maturity about a self. That here we are, a half century later, still wrestling with the demons that we believed were the saviors, is the measure of revenge that history takes upon those who believe, and continue to believe, that the despot, the tyrant, the ideologue, can ever bring a nation and its people salvation. This personal odyssey is intended to demonstrate that this is not the case. Freedom is found as often in the shout as in the artful whisper, better yet, in the capacity for resistance no less than the rationality of acquiescence. Personal and political decisions have consequences as well as causes. This is perhaps the best reason for examining the career of leaders no less than the behavior of masses.

A final note on the organization of this volume: Rather than select a tried and tested social scientific approach, one that is found in all eleven editions of *Cuban Communism*: the division of the system into five points of light: economic, politics, society, military, and ideology, I have opted for a more traditional approach. The work starts with an early attempt at general theory and closes with a final review of the dictator's own self-analysis of his life. Just what "factors" actually define situations is not an apriori matter, nor is it a dogmatic declaration supported by hoary theories of world history. Just who or what "determines" events and decisions is the stuff of real history. Precisely due to the variability in causal chains in society as in life generally, we have considerable variance in levels of predictability. The chronological approach seems best to tease out what is important from what is trivial, what is permanent from that which is transient in political analysis.

In the long years of writing on Cuban affairs I have been struck by special methodological considerations in doing was has come to be called research in "nation-building". I take the liberty of sharing my juggling act with those who come later and do better.

It is an area that requires exact attention to the details of a nation, its leaders and its people, while at the same time a sensitivity to the broader global context in which a nation operates. This is especially the case with smaller, and hence more vulnerable territories. The quality of that balancing act often determines the worth of the analysis as such.

To study a nation is not simply to look at its political leadership; doubtless, the most reported aspect of nations. It is to look at bottom up no less than top down. And to do so effectively means to take seriously economic, sociological, psychological, military, and cultural factors, no less than the political system.

Finally, to look at a nation is to look at a composite, a collectivity. Hence, many of the real or imaginary idiosyncrasies of personal behavior are washed away in the process. That makes the study of a nation, where accurate and honest, arguably far simpler than the examination of individuals.

In all three propositions we find the need for balance, for integration of parts into a whole, and a willingness to suspend judgment until there are a sufficient number of parts to provide a mosaic, a pattern as well as a structure to make the whole a meaningful unity. I hope and believe that my work on Cuba's half century of communist dictatorship performs this larger task.

The Cuban Revolution gives strong evidence for such an approach. The unlikely capacity of 82 men landing in a small boat, in which casualties were sustained, to end up ruling a nation is improbable, yet the ideological impulse is such that the event was turned into a blueprint for manufacturing revolutions elsewhere—with disastrous human and social consequences. A half century later, the pure certainty of the decline or death of a leader led to wild and premature celebrations, not to mention a myriad of "scenario designs" that were as fatuous as they were premature. To wish and to want is one thing, to examine and experience is quite another. If nothing else, the Cuban Revolution should have taught all concerned—from natives to exiles, from radicals to reactionaries, what the world of fact conspires against the fabrication of theory. And with that sobering lesson from the history of ideas we can proceed to the heartbreaking lessons of a single island nation in the Caribbean.

I chose as a title *The Long Night* for the simply reason that in the case of Fidel Castro's Cuba we are looking at a half century of rule, plus another earlier four years of guerrilla warfare and random incendiary incidents all dedicated to first achieving the aim of the revolution—the seizure of power. Robert Frost put matters best in his 1928 prescient poem, *Once by the Pacific*: "It looked as if a night of dark intent was coming, and not only a night, an age." Frost goes on to say that "Someone had better be prepared for rage. There would be more than ocean water broken before God's last *Put out the Light* was spoken." Frost spoke well for the century. The Castro Era is perhaps the last hurrah of a devastating century.

Dividing the universe or any part thereof into decades is a dangerous and mechanical act. No serious entity, and nations are serious entities, can establish policies by decennial calendars; and no brief and highly personal overview will satisfy all experts and commentator. That said, systems of power have rhythms. And much as dictatorships in particular like to make claims of eternal survival, the facts speak otherwise. They undergo life cycles, and they have origins, growth, high points, low points and then death. It is the truth of change that is at one and the same time proclaimed by totalitarianism states in theory and denied by these same states in practice. But in each nation such changes take place unevenly and as a result of human interest or as the case may be disinterest.

The amazing continuity of a dictator and his dictatorship for a half century is itself a test case of the above truisms. The very assertions of longevity that touches upon issues of immortality only heighten the public awareness that such categories are beyond the range of human life, and hence beyond the capacity of any single regime to retain power forever. The secret, great strength of democracy is its modesty, its awareness of the grandeur of the natural order of things, and the feeble, tentative nature of the social order imposed on things by those who would be gods.

The half century of the Castro regime in Cuba will not and should be neither forgotten nor memorialized. It is a reminder that small nations may commit large tragedies. It is not the size of a nation that defines its worth, but the worth of its people and values of its leaders than determines its size. I suspect that the Cuban people always knew this to be the case. It is a lesson that

Fidel Castro and his revolutionary cohort never quite learned. The absurd egotism involved in slogans such as "history will absolve me" is the stuff of tragedy without substance. History does little to prove or disprove the behavior of one or another absolutist. What it does achieve is to let it be known that absolutisms—modern and ancient—have a history of defeat.

Irving Louis Horowitz

Acknowledgments

In acknowledging the assistance provided in getting this book to market, I find myself taking a trip down memory lane rather than implicating those who now help. Indeed, how could it be otherwise in a work examining a fifty-year time span over the last forty years of personal life? But before I acknowledge some of the people who influenced the outcome, if not really the input, let me note that this is by no means a "collected works" effort. In deciding what to exclude, no less what to include, I felt that many of the reviews, congressional testimonies, prefaces to other work (including the eleven editions of Cuban Communism) and a variety of encomiums and dedications tendered along the way, simply do not work in such a focused account. As result, any written remarks that appear in retrospect to be digressive have simply been omitted. This is after all not a celebration of my writings but an examination over time of the most extraordinary revolution in Cuba lead by a dedicated and single minded leader.

Let me start with an appreciation to C. Wright Mills. As his outstanding student at the time, Rose Goldsen noted, when she worked with him on *Puerto Rican Journey*, he had the ability to pin point with precise insight the importance of national events without necessarily exercising the best of judgment about the political or moral importance emanating from such events. It was that initial circle of friends, including John Gerassi, Pablo González Casanova, and Carlos Fuentes among others, that stimulated me to think about Cuba in a hemispheric rather than strictly American or for that matter European context. The prodding by my dear friend and lifetime mentor in Buenos Aires and then later at Harvard, Gino Germani, was a big factor as well. Gino urged me to write a work on Cuba that paralleled his own efforts on the *Social Structure of Argentina*. Alas, that ambitious undertaking never came to pass, nor is it ever likely to, so this must serve as a poor man's substitute.

As for the actual work in progress over the years, in the earlier period the support of Julius Jacobson at *New Politics*, Jaime Suchlicki at the *Journal of Interamerican Studies and World Affairs*, and Morris Janowitz and Charles Moskos at *Armed Forces & Society* were especially important. They provided a significant and broad based forum for the expression of my unpopular views on totalitarianism and militarism in Cuba during its early, formative stages—topics that were neither popular nor for that matter welcome. Arguably, in some quarters they probably still fail to elicit much enthusiasm. I confess that they shared the pain of losing friends and colleagues for taking independent stands on their own, but they were unique in their editorial courage no less than there sense of professional responsibilities.

There were many wonderful scholars and colleagues along the way who were of great help and assistance. People like Ernesto Betancourt, Carmelo Mesa-Lago, and Edward Gonzales who were unfailing in support—and criticism when called for. People like Frank Calzón of the Free Cuba Committee, David Rohnfeldt at RAND Corporation, Michael Ledeen at American Enterprise Institute, and countless others who over the years provided me with a forum to express my views. Taken as a whole, the academic and policy persons alike gave backbone to the strong belief that the social sciences, when performing their tasks fairly and honestly provide a bulwark against, and not a rationale for, the worst infections of dictatorship. Ideas as such do not topple the ideological beasts, but they serve to make decent people weary and leery of them.

Special thanks are due to the University of Miami which, in granting me the Emilio Bacardí Visiting Professorship for 1994 gave me the time and space I needed to think of Cuba in less episodic and more historical terms. The results of those lectures are very much a part of this volume, as they were at the time in which they were initially presented. By the same token, the many people who contributed to the eleven editions of *Cuban Communism* over the years, and especially Jaime Suchlicki, who co-edited the final three volumes with me, merit deep appreciation. Every one of these contributions was prepared without payment, and without prodding. The task of steadily reconsidering this collection served to maintain my focus on Cuba even as other tasks pre-empted much of my time.

Finally I want to thank the people who have helped immensely in assembling this volume. First and foremost is my current assistant at Transaction, Jeffrey Stetz, whose fine editorial and technical skills made it possible to assemble a huge amount of material in record time. Along the way, editors such as Andrew McIntosh, Laurence Mintz, and Patrick Ivins, were immensely helpful. I know that over time I will come to a painful recollection of persons who were especially supportive in tough times with respect to my writings in this and related areas, and I ask that they forgive me for this oversight. If a second edition ever comes to pass, such personal derelictions will hopefully be remedied.

I was most fortunate to have the editorial advice and support of Angel L. Soto. It is one thing to perform copyediting services for a new book, quite another to do so for a volume that reflects a time period almost as long as the half century it attempts to depict. Stylistic variations in grammar, spelling, and punctuation over so long a time and for work appearing in a variety of places is hard enough to fine tune. Add to that the need to avoid repetitions and infelicities that reflect passions of the moment, and the editorial chores involved become a challenge to the intellect. I am grateful for his assistance and it is not to be unnoticed. For errors and shortcomings that remain, the standard caveat is very much in order. They are entirely my responsibility.

Irving Louis Horowitz
March 28, 2008

1960s: Guerrilla Dictatorship

The early years of the 1960s began with an extraordinary pair of events: the attempt to topple the Castro regime with a skeleton group of Cuban exiles with clumsy and unsteady American support at The Bay of Pigs, while at the other side, a no less clumsy and even more risky effort to place Soviet long range missiles with nuclear potential in Cuba with the full knowledge of the Castro regime and the furtive approbation of the Khrushchev regime in the U.S.S.R. While both efforts failed, their consequences were to place the Cold War on a permanent footing 90 miles from American soil; with a small nation in possession of big power pretensions as a resolute enemy.

In retrospect it seems strange and yet inevitable that a revolution that started life as a guerrilla adventure with a Marxist-Leninist ideology would evolve in a trajectory in which power remains lodged in the military and in the party. The phrase "guerrilla dictatorship" tries to capture the dorsal spine of the Cuban Revolution. It rested on the destruction or disintegration—whichever came first—of all sectors of civil society. Legislative, judicial and administrative elements of society continued to exist, as legitimating shadows of the past. But all power rapidly moved from civil to military instruments and to a party that performed all essential roles of civil society without the encumbrance of democratic exchange. Little wonder that Stalinist techniques of rule early became apparent in the conduct of the leadership no less than in the structure of Cuban society.

The opening essays on the Stalinization of Cuba reflect my own work with Mills on The Marxists; although it takes that collection in a direction that I can hardly attribute to Mills! If a certain caution and trepidation to criticize the regime is ap-

parent, the origins of the statement itself, prepared in the dark days of the Vietnam War, perhaps help explain, if not necessarily excuse, certain ambivalence toward the Castro regime, and for that matter, to the place of Cuba in a global context. Then again, so many of the leading opponents of the Castro regime also began life as revolutionists and defenders of the 1959 seizure of power. I too came to a realization that totalitarian regimes have a certain unity; a tragic sameness at that.

No such reservations appear in the remaining essays written in the 1960s as a whole. Indeed, as the critique of the Stalinization of Castro makes clear, the vague rhetoric of socialism, a third way, Marxism-Leninism etc. gives way to a blunt statement and characterization of the regime as such. The Revolution of 1950 was not the conventional golpe de estado, *or the sort of rotation of power undertaken by political and military elites. For this transgression on my part, the loss of friends and colleagues on the so-called Left became inevitable and almost immediately apparent. Indeed, the piece, responding to a Canadian social scientist, was drafted with a full understanding that my negative view of the Cuban dictatorship needed a response. From that point forward, that is from 1965 to the present, whatever the errors in judgment of American foreign policy, my position on dictatorship and democracy, informed as it was from a long study of European totalitarianism, became unequivocal and firm.*

1

The Stalinization of Fidel Castro

The first thing to clarify is what "Stalinization" means. We are now so distant from the Stalin period in Russia that it is easy to mistake Stalin for an earthly assistant of the Devil, for the modern reincarnation of Ivan the Terrible or for a generalized specter which haunted the Soviet Union. But the emotive use of the term will herein be eschewed. Stalinization refers to specific forms of social and political behavior and institutions.

First, Stalinization historically meant the bureaucratization of the Communist Party machinery which in turn signifies severe limits to inner party disputes and the termination of the period of factionalism. In broader terms it means the subordination of society to the Party State. Second, Stalinization means the emergence of a leader and his small coterie as exclusive spokesman for the Communist Party. The nation reduces *itself* to *himself*. The Party State is subordinated to the Party Leader. Third, Stalinization means the promotion of inner political struggle as a substitute for class struggle. The politics of the purge and the passion for development displaces the politics of debate and the passion for socialist democracy. Fourth, Stalinization means the elimination or at least abandonment of all roads to socialism save one: the economic growth road determined and defined by the maximum leader. Fifth, and most characteristic of Stalinism, is a nearly exclusive concentration of energies on national rather than international problems. This might be called the domestication of the revolutionary movement under the above conditions.

This definition of Stalinism is introduced in order to make plain what appears to be a new stage in the development of the Cuban Revolution. This stage, in comparison to the first seven years, represents an utter simplification of the sociological problem; that is to say, we have the "advantage" of being able to pay attention to what the leader says and having it stand for what the nation ostensibly believes. There no longer is a problem of pluralization: alternative spokesmen, alternative newspapers, or even of alternative responses to selective problems. There no longer is an empirical problem—a world to be interpreted on the basis of information—only an ideological problem—a world to be acted upon on the basis of imaginary demands by outside forces. The task of political interpretation and analysis is remarkably simplified, since access to the ideas of the leader becomes equivalent to the national essence no less than the political truth.

Within the first months of 1966 there have been three proclamations issued by Fidel Castro which, I submit, bear out my contention that Fidel Castro has become a Stalinist. Given the ideological assumptions of the leading players in the international power game, Castro perhaps had little alternative than to become what he became: as Stalin himself claimed, must is must. But whether the deterministic framework out of which Castro operates is a consequence of social forces or personal ideology is at issue. For the assumptions he now makes about the condition of the world deserve further scrutiny.

First, there is the stated need for rapid development and the internal obstacles to such development—the counter-insurgency forces operating with United States support in Camagüey, Matanzas and Las Villas provinces, the rise of absenteeism and slower work schedules developing among even the loyal workers. These require military effort in the first instance and repressive legal measures in the second. Second, there is the belief that Cuba is surrounded by hostile forces, led by the United States.

And that this ring of bases makes impossible the normalization of trade and aid agreements with the capitalist bloc generally or with other "captive" Latin American nations. Third is the growing dissatisfaction with any other "roads to socialism," particularly those of the more extreme variety such as China; hence the continued emphasis on independent forms of political expression invariably creates the base for leadership ideology derived from within rather than from international Communist leaders such as Mao Tse-tung. In other words, the "socialism in one country" slogan is not so much a cause as a consequence of Stalinization.

It should now be said that the denunciation of the Tri-Continental Meeting (Africa, Asia and Latin America) by all member nations of the Organization of American States (including the usually recalcitrant Chileans and Mexicans) has seriously missed the vital political point. Behind the talk of hemispheric revolution is a deep transformation. The rhetoric of world revolution adopted at the Tri-Continental Meeting disguises the intense nationalism of the Castro revolution, a disguise which fails to conceal its growing criticism of other Latin American revolutionists—if not yet revolutions. The Tri-Continental Conference recently held in Havana is the debut of a new Cuba, one which no longer has confidence in hemispheric revolution and one which in fact has transformed itself from the first stage of a high-risk *Latin American* Revolution into the conduct of a low-risk *Cuban* Revolution.

This is not simply a gaming analogy. There is as major a difference between a Latin American Revolution and a Cuban Revolution in the 1960s as there was between a world revolution and the Bolshevik Revolution in the 1920s. The Lenin period was characterized by a faith not so much in a Russian Revolution but rather a Soviet Revolution. Stalin transformed its character from a working class Soviet movement to a national Russian movement. The *degree* of terrorism, if not the fact of it, is a secondary consideration, whatever its human import. Just as fascism is not defined by the number of Jews killed, Stalinism cannot be defined by the number of people in Asian concentration camps. Those are historical variations in the slaughter and blood of the innocent, but not the essence of a definition.

The core of the Stalinist system is, first, left wing nationalism, or the rightward drift of revolutionism. Furthermore, it successfully pervades the society, as can be seen in the loyalty which the Russian people manifested for their homeland during the Nazi attacks, and that the Cuban people displayed during the American supported invasion at Playa Girón (Bay of Pigs). In other words, paradoxically, the survival of the revolution in Russia and Cuba depended in some measure on the abandonment of certain internationalist pretensions or ambitions. However, the rhetoric of internationalism is so firmly established in the socialist tradition that at the very period the Russian Revolution was being nationalized, international organizations such as the Comintern Bureau were hatched. The same seems to be the case with the Cuban Revolution. The more conservative its practices, the more noisy are its ideological pronouncements.

The various maneuverings within the Cuban Party system, while ostensibly an effort to "balance" old and new Communist militants, is at its core an effort on Castro's part to shape the Party system in his image. It is reminiscent of Stalin's technique in dealing with "right" and "left" wings within the Soviet Communist Party.

There are four clearly demarcated stages in the political transformation of Cuba's political party life. First was the *movement stage* in which the July 26th Movement was to have performed party tasks without the party bureaucracies. Second was the *united front stage* in which the Communists from the urban centers and revolutionists from the rural sectors were fused in the *Organizaciones Revolucionarias Integradas.* Third was the *socialist stage* which, while hastened by the internal machinations and intrigues of the various factions of the United Front groupings, was inevitable in light of the socialist-Marxist ideology in the name of which Cuba came to be ruled by the fifth year. Fourth came the *communist stage* in which the name of the party was changed to *Partido Comunista de Cuba*. While this final stage was accelerated by internal organizational dilemmas, the clear evidence is that the PCC. is a direct reflection of Castro's personal will and charismatic authority. The decline of internationalist pretensions, meshed as it is with the growth of a tight-knit political party bureaucracy, characterizes the new Castro regime just as assuredly as it did the pre-war Stalin period between 1929 and 1941.

What do we find in Cuba leading to this conclusion, and what are the unique conditions of the Cuban situation which give its form of Stalinism special properties? Most important is that Cuba is a small nation dependent on the world economy, dependent on a single group and above all simply dependent. By contrast, Russia in 1918 was relatively advanced industrially as well as being a politically sophisticated nation. Geographically, Russia dominates Europe while Cuba is dominated by the Americas. Given these conditions plus the fact that Cuba is engaged not in forced industrialization but in forced collectivization, the possibilities of liberalism in the Cuban situation are minimized.

The actual pattern of political growth in Russia was from totalitarianism to authoritarianism. No one can equate the Soviet Union of 1966 with that of 1946. Industrialism coupled with balanced urban growth opened up tendencies of pluralization and diversification in the Soviet Union. The Cuban situation, on the contrary, lacking at this point the basis of industrial diversification or even the possibility of land diversification, has collectivization in place of industrialization as the essence of its economic program.

The desperate efforts at crop diversification, while they serve to support the Cuban economy in a more meaningful way than a continued emphasis on sugar and tobacco, do not solve the Cuban dependence on the international economy—especially on the Soviet Union. The social ecology and geography of an island economy, which puts severe limits on natural resources also places sharp limits on any heavy industrialization process.

Even were these natural barriers to industrialization overcome, there remain the sociological barriers: peasant dominance, the absence of a strong proletarian tradition, the flight of professional and commercial expertise along with the other "remnants of the bourgeois past." The strain on the Castro regime produced by these problems suggests even harsher political repression. The steady rise of police informants and a street-by-street spy system is an augury of things to come. This is particularly significant since internal political and cultural repression is taking place at precisely a point in Cuban history when anti-Castro guerrillas are at low ebb of activity and when oppositional influence has been drained off by the "airlift" arranged with the United States.

Due to the possibilities of pluralization at the economic level are far more restricted than in Stalinist Russia that the potential for extreme repression increases rather than decreases over time. The collectivization of a single-crop economy is necessarily a more severe act than industrialization. In Russia the destruction of the kulak class was designed to break the back of the agricultural class as part of a campaign for industrialization. This industrialization did, in fact, enable the country to flower in economic ways, even in a severely repressive political atmosphere. That is one reason why the Stalinist system had sufficient resilience to outlive its tormentor. It is doubtful whether the same could be held in the Cuban situation. Were the United States, for example, to relax its pressures, the result might be more disastrous for Castro than any other tactic the United States might pursue.

Let us turn from the economic to the political consequences of having the first such system in the Western Hemisphere organized in one of the smallest and least representative of nations. One would have to say that the most singular fact of the revolution taking place in Cuba is that it raises the ante of revolutions everywhere else. Revolution becomes more expensive in every other country of the Americas, and at the same time the impotence of the first socialist republic itself becomes more manifest.

Bearing out this contention, it could be said that the United States action in the Dominican Republic was an opening salvo informing the Latin American nations: "We are here in the Dominican Republic. The Cubans are not. Nor will they come. Their revolution, you see, is not a Latin American revolution. They are impotent, and we are not." That lesson was not lost. Quite the reverse, the invasion of the Dominican Republic has already had immense value for the United States in terms of the schisms and splits that resulted throughout the rest of Latin America; particularly in Cuba.

What does this mean? Simply that many revolutionists have brought to the attention of Cuba that it was indeed impotent during the invasion of the Dominican Republic by the United States. Castro's response to this criticism was immediate and vigorous: that such action would have been precipitous, costly, and would have opened up Cuba to immediate invasion from the United States. This is likely to have been the case and, hence, calls for joint participation in revolutionary action were prime examples of adventurism. The next phase of the dialogue went something like this: That may very well be the case, a Cuban intervention to save Juan Bosch's regime would have been a form of adventurism, but if Cuba cannot do that for its Caribbean neighbor, what can it do for anyone else?

What then becomes the character of the Latin American Revolution except a kind of pathetic slogan that every nation has to come to its own revolution in its own way, in its own time? Indeed, if the Cuban Revolution raises the cost of starting a revolution, then not only has it failed in its stated task to assist revolutionary movements elsewhere, but its very existence jeopardizes other forms of revolutionary activity in the hemisphere. Cuba becomes a paper tiger which makes the real tiger ever more alert. The Cuban response to this, as Castro put it, is the accusation of "Trotskyism."

What Castro means by "Trotskyism" is not clear in his pronouncements. Dotted throughout the documents, especially the most important document—the closing session of the Tri-

Continental Conference—are attacks on all sorts of left-wingers who up to now have been identified with the Cuban Revolution. Adolfo Gilly is singled out as a Trotskyist in a four-page attack before an international meeting. Leo Huberman and Paul Sweezey—two original supporters of the Cuban Revolution in the United States—were criticized. Mexican leftists were also denounced as Trotskyists. What is the dispute about?

On inspection, it turns out that Castro strongly resents the call for revolution as a permanent entity; at least until the entire Latin American area is liberated from the American imperialists. There is a further rejection of the idea that the Cuban Revolution must have as an aim the revolution of the hemisphere as a whole or the Cuban "stage" will become bureaucratized and corrupt; an idea reminiscent of Trotsky's view of the Russian Revolution in his years of exile. Castro's response is much the same as was Stalin's.

The role of Cuba as a springboard for international revolution may be tactically halted, but its function as an exemplary case of a nation breaking its links with the colonial past is said to remain firmly intact. In this sense, Cuba is said to remain a model for Latin American revolutionaries. What this approach tends to underestimate drastically is that a "model" for revolutionists can also serve as a warning for the established order. It leads to a heightened emphasis on counter-revolutionary programs. The Stalinist concept of the Soviet Union as a "model" for Western Europe to follow quite obviously proved a failure. Yet, underlying Stalin's response to advocates of the permanent revolution is the mere existence of the Soviet Union to serve as a rallying point for European revolutionists. In this respect Stalinism was as erroneous in its theory as it was conservative in its practice. To the extent that Castro seems bound by similar ideological patterns, there is rightful doubt that it will have more success.

Evidence of this Stalinization process is not only known by indirection, such as the case of the Dominican Republic, but directly, as in the case of "Che" Guevara. Whether Guevara lives or not; whether he is in the mountains of Peru or a sanitarium in Mexico is not the major issue. The decisive fact is that he is not in Cuba. Guevara's role was obviously that of the surrogate Trotskyist. He was the gray eagle of the Cuban Revolution because what he primarily believed in was total revolution in the hemisphere. Trotsky, too, believed in revolution in Europe and not just in Russia. Thus the roles of the two exiled leaders are remarkably striking. Their parallel demises are likewise striking. The thought of both Trotsky and Guevara ending up in Mexican sanitaria is so painfully symbolic that the only amazing thing is that no one has drawn attention to the parallel.

An event of some moment is Castro's recent attack on China. It is extremely important to keep in mind that for the orthodox Communist Parties, China, in its ideological approach, represents not Stalinism but Trotskyism; that is to say, the Chinese position supports the necessity of world revolution, not just of any revolution, but of socialist revolution. This is one reason why the Chinese have encountered difficulty in Africa, because there the hue and cry is—we have had our revolution. What are they talking about, these Chinese? They must mean another revolution. The concept of the permanent revolution is embodied in the Chinese doctrine. From the point of view of ideology, Castro's attack on China was yet another attack on Trotskyism, in its most "insidious" form, Chinese Communism.

Interestingly enough, at the same time Castro openly broke with China, the Soviet ideologists were resuming their condemnation of "Trotskyism." Particularly striking are the subtle hints relating Trotsky to the Chinese position. The title itself of a recent feature article in *Pravda* indicates this: "Behind the Red Dragon Mask of Trotskyism." But lest the analogy be lost on the reader's imagination, Trotsky's position is described unmistakably in Chinese terms: the falsity of the claim that socialism cannot be built in one country (especially the U.S.S.R.), the falsity of any concept of permanent revolution; the falsity of the claim that peaceful coexistence entails class capitulation. The concluding point in the Soviet attack on "Trotskyism" is a reference to the *Maoist* position

held by *Frente Obrero* (Uruguay) on the need to "prepare for
nuclear war or preparing a preventive war before imperialism
unleashes it." Given the increased reliance of the Maoists upon
non-Party organs, there can be little doubt that the critique of
Maoism will increasingly be linked to the "bankrupt" Fourth
International established by Trotsky.

The severity of the Castro critique can best be appreciated by
keeping in mind that it is harsher in tone than any *Soviet* document ever released on the question of Chinese Communism.
"From the first moment we understood the obvious opportunistic position taken by China in trade relationships.... A much
more important and fundamental question than food is whether
the world of tomorrow can assume the right to blackmail,
extort, pressure, and strangle small peoples." This comment
by Castro, directed as it is toward China, can be viewed as a
response of those who believe in legality and dignity, a Latin
American rather than a Communist response.

It cannot be said that Castro's critique makes economic
sense. His critique is not going to get Cuba the necessary rice.
In bartering agreements one cannot make the assumption that
direct political attack is an effective method for gaining national
ends. From an economic point of view Castro's attack on China
is hopelessly absurd. There are two ways of interpreting his pronouncement. First, that it represents an outcry of a poor nation
against a wealthy nation. Second, it represents a rejection of the
notion of permanent revolution, i.e., therefore it is an extension
of the Stalinist perspective. The idea that Castro's critique is a
psychological phenomenon can be accepted only as a last resort.
One may end with a theory of personal madness, but political
analysis cannot start with it. Cuba has been exploited in many
ways with equal impunity by the Soviet Union—but there have
been no parallel attacks on Russian propagandists, on Russian
trade practices, or on the Russian abandonment of Cuba during
the missile crisis. Further, whether China can be considered even
remotely a "rich" nation is dubious. Thus, to assume that Castro's
anti-China declaration is the response of someone who believes

in law ignores his capacity previously to suppress commentary on departures from "socialist legality."

Let us take one step further in our survey, and examine Castro's attitude toward revolutionists elsewhere in the hemisphere. This, after all, is a decisive test of Stalinism. What is the attitude of Castro toward other Central American revolutionists? It turns out that it is of two kinds: patronizing and censorious. Patronizing when the revolution agrees with the Cuban position and censorious when it does not. The closing address to the Tri-Continental Conference by Castro is largely taken up with a critique of the leader of the guerrilla movement in Guatemala, Yon Sosa. Ironically enough, the attack is not much different from the attack of the Communists against Castro when he was a guerrilla leader in the mountains: Yon Sosa is a romantic; he doesn't know revolutionary strategies; he doesn't know how to win the people. He has allowed himself to be captivated by agents of imperialism, by Trotskyists. The arguments that were presented by the official Communist Party of Cuba prior to 1959 are now trotted out by Castro against Yon Sosa. The man he defends is Turcios, who represented Guatemala at the Tri-Continental Conference meeting. Simultaneous with the attack on Yon Sosa, Luis Augusto Turcios was upheld as the "orthodox" revolutionist, believer in the national rather than in the socialist character of revolution.

The attack on revolutionary romanticism, which up to now has been limited to revolutionists in Latin America, when generalized becomes an attack on any other hemispheric revolutions as premature or adventuristic. The United Front position taken by the Soviets during the 1930s has now become Castro's tactic—for revolutions being fought elsewhere.

A special characteristic of Castro is his growing reliance on nepotism, on familial contacts as political leaders. The steady rise in position of his brother Raúl Castro and the influence of other members of his extended family, all serve to surround Fidel with non-threatening figures. Personalism in Latin America has traditionally served to enhance the direct link of the Leader to the People. In the case of Fidel it enables him when necessary to bypass the only stable party apparatus remaining in the country—the Communist Party. By this tactic he is striving to make the image of the party his own.

Indeed, Castro even has his alter-ego as President—Osvaldo Dorticós—much as the late Joseph Stalin could boast of his in the person of Klementi Voroshilov. The trusted political lieutenant serves to legitimize the remarks of the *caudillo*. The Lieutenant provides the slogans; the Leader provides the cement linking doctrines to slogans.

Related to this emergent nepotism is the increased demand for proletarian Puritanism. First, in 1965 there was a concerted attack on alleged examples of homosexuality among government officials (featured by a "parade" of deviants in Havana); and in 1966 this was widened to include all those engaged in "antisocial activities." The dismissal of Efigenio Ameijeiras as Armed Forces Vice Minister, and his pending court martial along with several dozen others in Government life "for activities contrary to revolutionary morals," indicates that such Puritanism has the dimensions of a full-scale purge. The fusion, or rather fudging, of personal and political aspects of behavior has served to justify an increased politicalization of the military and, no less, of the diplomatic corps. Changes in the Army Chief of Staff, Commander of the Navy, and of leading posts in the Foreign Ministry, represent not simply a tightening of the political net, but an increased penetration by the Maximum Leader into middle echelons of power. For with each series of dismissals the actual power lodged in both civil and military agencies seems to become correspondingly weaker; the replacements are less able (or willing) to make decisions independently.

What do we make of this Cuban position at the Tri-Continental Conference meetings? The most important thing is that it announces that Castro is no longer a significant threat to the United States. Any government bent on national redemption, on the national road to salvation, on national socialism, on a concentration upon internal problems, can hardly threaten the international position of the United States. The meetings of the Tri-Continental Conference, far from announcing a new stage of struggle against the "imperialists," in fact announced that a condition of national sovereignty now prevails. It is not that Castro is seeking a rapprochement with the United States any more than Stalin was interested in obtaining such a rapprochement with Europe. This is a *realpolitik* phase. Rapprochement would be neither sought nor spurned. But it would be no more shocking to have an agreement between Johnson and Castro than it was to have one between Molotov and Von Ribbentrop. It may be viewed as shocking from the point of view of the Latin American revolutionists and their expectations (just as the Russo-German Pact of 1939 shocked and chagrined the world Communist movement) but not from the logic of the Stalinist position.

The period of Cuban-United States relations now being entered is a period of self-imposed isolation for both nations. The Cubans hope to make this a period of national economic growth. A newspaper headline every January First will announce the unswerving allegiance of the Castro regime to an anti-imperialist alliance; and July 26 will headline the celebration of the anniversary of the revolution embellished by rhetorical anti-imperialist vows. Other than that I would expect to see little in the way of Cuban action or Cuban behavior at the international plane. In this, Castro is not only pursuing a Stalinist position, but also a classical Latin American disregard of hemispheric needs as a whole. The Revolution of 1959 announced that Latin America will become a generalized reality; the Tri-Continental meetings of 1966 announced a return to 20 nations.

The differences between Stalin and Castro—both as ideologists and personality types—can hardly be minimized. Stalin was bureaucratic, and Castro is charismatic. Stalin was enmeshed with all phases of Soviet cultural life, while Castro has thus far limited himself to platitudinous comments on the scientific and cultural apparatus. Stalin was, above all, a figure of immense international significance, and Castro has little possibility of performing a similar world role. There are indeed other aspects indicating difference. But beneath the military tunic of Castro is a man concerned with consolidation and absolute loyalty—the same properties which made "socialism in one country" the rallying party slogan in the Soviet Union for over two decades and served to weld the military and political elites into a united phalanx for economic development.

This is not to deny in any way that the Cuban Revolution is an authentic revolution; only it has little chance of becoming hemispheric in character. The Cuban Revolution is of such major consequence that no leader can capture it, not even a man as powerful as Castro or the whole Castro family. The restoration of the Cuban bourgeoisie is neither warranted nor possible. It is inconceivable that there can be a restoration of Cuban barracks revolutionists, since democracy of arms still exists. The Cuban Revolution represents a total rupture with the past. There is no gainsaying that. Castro led as complete a revolution as ever took place in Europe. What is at stake is the character and purpose of that revolution; the strategy of Stalinism versus that of Trotskyism. What we are observing is the consolidation of a socialist Cuba and an indefinite postponement of a socialist Latin America.

The Stalinization of Cuba should occasion small comfort for Washington "Castrologists." As in so many aspects of political life, the degeneration of socialism in Cuba was sharpened and accelerated by an American hard-line, by support to counter-insurgency operations, however disreputable; by a virtual embargo on basic industrial and consumer goods; by constant violations of Cuban air and sea space; and above all, by the manipulation of the international economy to the disadvantage of Cuba. "War Communism" has indeed come to an end in Cuba—replaced by two steps backward and one step forward. But whether the new turn in Castroism would have taken place without the emergence of "War Capitalism" in the United States is impossible to say.

References/Notes

1.   Robert Daland, *Brazilian Planning: Development, Politics and Adminis-tration* (Chapel Hill, NC, 1967).
2.   Fidel Castro, "Speech in the Ceremony to Commemorate the Centennial of the Birth of V.I. Lenin," *Granma Weekly Review,* May 3, 1970, pp. 2-5.
3.   René Dumont, *Cuba est-it socialiste?* (Paris, 1970); and K.S. Karol, *Les Guérrilleros au pouvoir* (Paris, 1970).
4.   Fidel Castro, *Betrayal by Chinese Government of Cuban People's Good Faith* (Havana, February 6, 1966).
5.   Castro, "Speech in the Ceremony. . . ," op. cit., pp. 2-5.

Source and Original Title: "The Stalinization of Fidel Castro" in *New Politics,* Vol. 4, No. 4, 1965, pp. 61-69. Reissued with modifications as "The Political Sociology of Cuban Communism." *Revolutionary Change in Cuba,* edited by Carmelo Mesa-Lago. Pittsburgh, PA: University of Pittsburgh Press, 1971, pp. 127-41(notes are from this reissue).

2

Castrologists and Apologists: True Belief in the Service of False Sentiment

To begin his critique of my article on "The Stalinization of Fidel Castro," as C. Ian Lumsden does, with a complaint about analytical weakness and internal inconsistency is one thing. But to fail utterly to deliver even a reasonable not necessarily true (only reasonable) optional model, is quite another. Were the rhetorical aspects of Mr. Lumsden's remarks to be discounted, and we were to ask just how he perceives the present Cuban social system. The answer necessarily would be not very differently from the picture provided for within my own comparative analysis.

On my point that in Cuba there is a subordination of society to the Party State, my critic must say: "This feature is undoubtedly present in Cuba today. It has been recognized for the last few years as one of the weaknesses of the Revolution, and was surely the essence of the 1962 Escalante affair."

On my point that Cuba witnesses the emergence of a leader and his small coterie as exclusive spokesman for the Communist Party, my critic must say: "Indeed, one of the less pleasant aspects of the Revolution has been the glorification of the maximum leader as reflected in the slogan: *'Comandante en Jefe, ordene'* which began to appear all over Havana as long ago as 1962."

On my point that Cuba reveals the promotion of inner political struggle as a substitute for class struggle, my critic makes
reference to the apolitical character of various purges. Mysteriously enough, he fails to mention the complex struggle between
party and movement (and the host of figures therein involved).
Even more mysteriously, he fails to see any political significance
whatsoever in the two-year absence of Ernesto "Che" Guevara.
His "absence" is dismissed by a bland and meaningless assertion
that he was not an alternative leader of the Revolution.

On my point that the passion for development displaces the
politics of debate and the passion for socialist democracy (which
is what I said in the article, and not the simplistic phrase "dominates all political activity in Cuba" as is improperly ascribed to
me), my critic must say: "Admittedly, public debate has diminished
with the exit of Guevara." Yet, he finds no peculiarity in adding that
"Cuba continues to make progress toward a socialist democracy."
As evidence, he cites new municipal and regional administrations.
Clearly, Lumsden cannot distinguish between *civics* (which is
what such local reform entails) and *politics* (which is what public
debates, including "fiery public polemics") is all about.

On my point that Stalinization of Cuba has brought to a
halt discussion of alternative strategies for economic development, my critic must say: "This statement appears to be the one
nearest to the mark," with the gratuitous addendum, "at least
superficially." And if Mr. Lumsden's follow-up remarks pass for
profundities, then heaven help us all. "Guevara's permanent
legacy to his adopted land is the simultaneity of socialism and
communism." May we be preserved from the puerile. My point
on single crop socialism stands on the evidence of seven years of
economic stagnation. No profundities can eliminate the dreary
reports on Cuba made plain in the United Nations *Statistical
Yearbook-1965.* The downward trends, not only in comparison to
pre-Revolutionary periods, but with respect to the highs reached
in the 1962-63 "Che period" are amazing.

On my point that Stalinization in Cuba has meant the nearly
exclusive concentration of energies on national rather than

international problems, my critic must say: "It would not be surprising if this were, indeed, the case, for Cuba can hardly expect the Soviet Union to keep on subsidizing its economy indefinitely." Aside from obvious misinterpretation, since my point had to do with political consolidation and not with economic mobilization, the brute fact is that Cuba's agrarian economy is in rough shape. Droughts and hurricanes are Caribbean constants, the shifts and twists of Cuban agricultural policy are not. And it is political indecision, confusion and just plain technical ignorance that accounts for the present economic dilemmas, and not geographical, climatic factors.

Just what is it that has so upset my critic? Here we come not to matters of fact (although we shall address ourselves to some points raised in this connection later on), but to matters of sentiment. This use of science in the service of sentiment is made plain only late in his piece, when he writes: "In the face of inadequate information one would have expected Horowitz to have given Castroism the benefit of the doubt, rather than to subject it to an analysis which draws parallels with one of the most savage regimes known to mankind." My critic keeps talking about the "obligations" of socialists, my interests are the "obligations" of understanding the mechanisms of the Cuban social system, not a false patriotism. It has been my impression that terrorist practices or the absence of them do not determine one's attitudes toward a regime. Once people make up their minds about the good or evil of a regime (as my critic has about Cuba), they tend to take their terrors in stride—as historically necessary events, as really quite mild in comparison to other terrors. Such comparative judgments on the amount of terror used may be heuristically justifiable, but they hardly justify turning one's mind away from obvious historical parallels.

I take a very different moral tack: scientists and socialists have a double obligation (not half an obligation)—to ascertain the facts as accurately as possible, and to make moral judgments as firm and as binding as the facts allow. Would Mr. Lumsden argue, for example, that the regimes of Castelo Branco in Brazil or Juan Carlos Onganía in Argentina are not as bad as they appear to be, and that we ought to suspend judgment until all the information is available? Does one have to exhume the corpses before facing the likelihood that things are as bad as they seem to be—or perhaps even worse. My critic makes mention of the fact that I have the temerity to compare Cuba to Stalin's Russia. Surely, he is neither adolescent nor addled and should realize that for decades criticisms of Stalin were blunted and stymied in much the same fashion. The supporters of the Communist movement in the thirties took exactly the position that it would be temerities and dangerous to compare Stalin to Hitler, that such comparisons would be outrageous and a travesty upon the facts (meaning *ideology*). Now, in 1966, it is quite fashionable not only to make the linkage between them, but to stretch their similarities even though differences were indeed very real.

What I am trying to point out to Mr. Lumsden, hopefully in a not too indelicate manner, is that chores of social science and of socialists may not always be compatible. Priorities of the former over the latter might lead to serious examination of Castro's Cuba on factual grounds, which in turn might or might not stimulate equally probing examination on moral grounds if we start from a socialist standpoint. I did not urge a puritanical position toward Cuba in my paper. Indeed, I bent over backward not to take a position that rested on the quantum of terror as uniquely defining the social system. Lumsden's distortions on this point are classic: he confuses a necessary ingredient for explaining Stalinism with a sufficient explanation. In this light, his remarks that terror is intrinsic to Stalinism are meaningless. Terror was used by Stalin. But terror has also been used in various sizes and shapes by all dictators developmentally oriented or otherwise. My definition sought to move beyond terror as in explanatory device either for what Stalinism is or for what Castroism is. I addressed myself to basic structural features of the polity and the economy. Regrettably, my critic failed to do likewise.

Mr. Lumsden so utterly and completely misses the thrust of my remarks that were it not for the audience beyond him I would not try everyone's patience by restating my position. It is simply that socialist Cuba finds itself in a double bind (what some might insist on terming a dialectical situation). On one hand, it is being subject to *strangulation* from external sources, primarily the United States; and suffering *stagnation* as a result of internal sources, primarily the oligarchical political elite directed by Premier Fidel Castro. My concluding three paragraphs make this explicitly evident. I point out that the Cuban Revolution is an authentic one. The process of Stalinization should provide small comfort for Washington Castrologists, since, by the destructive nature of the United States policy toward Cuba, the worst possible features of the Cuban regime came to the fore.

I emphasized the internal rather than the external characteristics of the Castro regime. The reason for this should be evident: namely, that whatever the external conditions Cuba is confronted with, its internal response is the measure of the regime's worth. After all, few new social systems come into the world in pristine innocence and with *ancien regimes* singing the praises of the *nouveau regime.* To chalk up all errors made by a social order to meet the external threat would simply be evasive. Cuba might have responded in a far more rational and morally worthy way were this island surrounded by good neighbors providing wise counsel. My point is, it should have responded rationally and morally precisely because such ideal typical conditions were not present. This is the point of my concluding remarks. To ignore this is simply to blot out of consideration what was actually written in my essay.

It is written that "Horowitz has failed to contribute to the analysis of Cuban politics, while unfortunately leaving the sour traces of an emotive evaluation which he had claimed to eschew at the outset." It must first be stated that I made no such pretentious claim to eschew an emotive position. I clearly have emotions about Castro and have expressed them. What I actually said was quite different: "The emotive use of the term (Stalinism) will herein be eschewed." It is quite possible to be precise about a term, and emotive about a subject matter. And to this I plead guilty. The first part of the phrase, which I fail to contribute to the analysis of Cuban politics, I leave for others to judge. If I am wrong, this will soon enough become apparent. What I attempted was a difficult argument by analogy. Even with the safeguards listed in my article distinguishing and separating Castro from Stalin, it rests on an argument by historical analogy. Clearly, the argument by analogy is not the strongest framework for casting theories. But it is at least a framework. It takes on added weight when one realizes that Castro is guiding an ideological State, along lines laid down by Marxism-Leninism. This very fact makes the analogy not a creation of my imagination, but quite evidently, a set of guidelines within which, and through which, Castro desires to realize his goals—such as they may be. If my attempt "fails," it will take considerably more than an eclectic critic climbing on my back to prove it!

My critic does not like Stalinism. On the other hand, it is even plainer that what he does not know about Stalinism can fill (and has) many volumes. This is neither the time nor place for a dress review on the nature of Stalinism. But if one compares two sentences in a single paragraph the muddle-headed quality of my critic's remarks become manifest. First, he says "I too have observed an increasing conservatism and bureaucratization of Cuban socialism." But this is utterly unconnected to the next statement: "What still holds Cuban communism together is, to a surprising extent, the charismatic appeal of Fidel Castro." Anyone with a remotely compassionate disposition of mind would have understood my piece as an effort to bridge these apparent incongruities between charismatic and bureaucratic forms of rule that leave my critic so puzzled. This I did by showing how, in a Weberian context, the Stalin-Castro phenomenon has a shared basis organizationally in patrimonial restorationism. The revolution is conducted in the name of collective leadership principles, but the charismatic element, far from being enveloped by the bureaucratic organization, becomes transformed into a super-government. Traditional Latin American personalism resolves itself in private government. From this stems the social origins

of terrorism of the socialist type. The parallel structures of social system and state system are parallel in name only. In fact,
the superstate system mediates the claims of all social sectors.
In this way, the forms of legality are kept intact, but the actual
conduct of affairs is channeled into totalitarian directions. One
may, as Lumsden does, give his approbation to Castro's *jefatura*
principle, but to talk of him as leading a march toward democracy
is something else again.

Lumsden's capacity for irrelevant banalities is endless. He
proves the case for Cuban internationalism by "the solidarity of
the Cuban people with Vietnam"; something, we are told, that is
"genuine and deep felt." This rhetoric is supposed to stand as a
reply to various aspects of the nationalization of the Cuban Revolution I adduced: the impotence to assist the Dominican Republic
(whatever the subjective intentions), the outrageous imperial
attacks on the Guatemalan revolutionary movement, and the
utterly spurious condemnation of men long loyal to the Cuban
socialist cause. Just how the case for Castro's "revolutionary integrity" can be supported by the attitude toward the Vietnam war
is hard to fathom. Was Stalin's revolutionary integrity preserved
because of his support for the Spanish Republican cause in the
1936-39 period? At least, Stalin could justifiably claim to have
played an integral role in the Spanish Civil War. Can Castro make
any similar claims for the Vietnamese Civil War? Obviously this
whole point about internationalism is a rubric without meaning.
The support for democracy and freedom *abroad* is a traditional
ploy of dictatorships of the Left. When they do likewise at home,
Mr. Lumsden's point will take on some relevance.

The final *chutzpah* is Mr. Lumsden's self-appointment as
keeper of the facts about Cuba. You would think that at least
here he would be sure to get the record straight—if only to score
some much needed points. But he does not much bother.

What are my "serious factual errors?"

(1) I refer to counter-insurgency forces operating in Cuba's
central provinces, when according to my critic "they were virtually wiped out by 1964." Now, while I do not place much faith

in the importance of such counterinsurgency operations, that they exist is beyond a doubt the case. In 1965 (at least a year after Mr. Lumsden had wiped them out) the following *confirmed* engagements took place: an air attack on sugar producing facilities in Pinar del Rio province; the capture of guerrilla leader Eloy Gutiérrez Menoyo along with several of his comrades; a center of military opposition was stamped out in the port of Nuevitas. Also, an unconfirmed (but undenied) report, in mid-1965 concerned the military plot to overthrow Castro. While the plot was thwarted, it was reported that 350 officers and soldiers were arrested. Later in the harvest season, acts of sabotage were widely reported. As for United States complicity in these acts, the Cuban government itself spoke of the Central Intelligence Agency as masterminding sabotage efforts. The likelihood is that there has been an increase rather than a decrease in counter-insurgency. The question of new tactics was raised by the Revolutionary Recovery Movement during 1965. The new sophistication at least involved the shutdown of training camps in Central America under CIA sponsorship, and the commencement of indigenous and self-directed operations.

(2) An example of my critic's argument by innuendo is his remark that "Marxism-Leninism became the official ideology of the Revolution in 1961, not 1963." I never even raised, much less contested this point. In fact, I pointed out the socialist stage in Cuba corresponded to the adoption of the Marxian ideology in 1961. What did happen in 1963 were the beginnings of the Communist stage. The *Partido Comunista de Cuba* became pre-eminent in an attempt to resolve the organizational dilemmas posed by the loose affiliative and participatory type of system still present in the early 1960s. I could hardly care less when Marxism-Leninism became orthodox—unless it relates directly to the organizational structure of the Cuban political system.

(3) The third factual "error" is my passing comment on the absence of a strong factory proletariat in Cuba, and the reliance on the peasant-agrarian sector for Cuban economic well-being. First, Lumsden makes the frequent mistake of equating industrialization with urbanization. Just because 57 percent

of the population is urbanized (measures of urbanization are themselves subject to examination), has little to do with the degree to which a nation depends on industrialization. Correlations between the two broad indicators of modernization vary extensively. In Cuba, there is a relatively low correlation between urbanization and industrialization. Indeed, one might argue that this is itself an important element in the cause of the revolution. The fact that under Batista there was a high degree of unionization only indicates organizational strength, not sizes, or for that matter effectiveness. The factory workers of Havana no more made the Cuban Revolution than the factory workers of Shanghai made the Chinese Revolution.

It is plain to all concerned that Cuba is primarily an agricultural society. Sugar is the most important single item in the economy. And as I pointed out in my article, while the role of sugar was downgraded in the early 1960s, when various industrialization programs failed to lead to diversification, the role of sugar was once again made central. After sugar, comes tobacco, coffee, cacao, corn, rice, and potatoes. Despite the stagnation in this sector, the powerful agricultural base provided a great deal more in the way of a self-sustaining economy than the imagined benefits of rapid industrialization. To examine the *Statistical Yearbook* of the United Nations, is to be struck by the even greater stagnation of industrial production. Not only is there a seeming absence of production increase, but an equal absence of growth of new plant equipment. At the same time, it is interesting to note the increase in the national budget. The pressures on the Cuban economy compelled the reestablishment of agricultural preeminence in the economic sector, *i.e.*, of a return to single-crop socialism. The size of the Communist Party under Batista, or the degree of trade unionism in the fifties, is as irrelevant to a serious general characterization of the economy, as these two factors were to a general characterization of the polity at the time of the Castro revolution.

(4) I provided no "implication" that Cuba has failed to attempt to trade with capitalist countries. Indeed, I made much of the

power of the international economy to thwart just such attempts on the part of Cuba to increase its dollar yield. I wrote: "Cuba is a small nation dependent on the world economy, dependent on a single group, and above all, simply dependent." I further made quite clear that simple increase in crop sizes would be of no avail, since the manipulation of the world price of sugar is controlled by the United States. It is difficult to estimate trade by Cuba with other nations. One thing is clear, Mr. Lumsden is incorrect to assert that "in 1964, more than a third of its trade was with the non-socialist countries." All that can be said on this score is that one third of its *cash* transactions (this is the meaning of trading within the limits of dollar reserves) were with the non-socialist bloc. But since so large a portion of Cuban trade is now made within a barter framework, and such barter terms are nearly exclusively worked out with Communist bloc nations, the actual degree of trade conducted with the capitalist sphere (Spain, Japan, Canada) is much less than one third of its total exports.

(5) Finally, the fact that I mention a nepotistic tendency in Castro, and more important, his humiliation of old-line associates—and their displacement either by himself or by nonentities, is made light of. The family power held by Fidel Castro, Raúl Castro, Vilma Espín, is dismissed despite the fact that Raúl and Vilma, along with Dorticós, are about the only visible faces left in the new Cuba. But the politics of the purge, the dismemberment of any possible opposition, is so clear that one wonders about the purpose of Mr. Lumsden's dismissal of the evidence. The *purging* of Aníbal Escalante, Joaquín Ordoqui, Edith García Buchaca, Juan Marinello, Manuel Luzardo, Lázaro Peña, had nothing to do with their collective competences, but simply with their politics.

My critic chides me for drawing attention to various purges in Cuba. He does not deny their existence, only their magnitude and their political character. Indeed, he adds a Robespierrist note: that "many, many more junior officials could be 'purged' on grounds of inefficiency or lack of revolutionary integrity." The resignation of Carlos Rafael Rodríguez as head of the National Institute of Agrarian Reform (INRA) can hardly be considered a non-political event. The fact that Castro himself assumed this post is illustrative of his organizational concentration of power in his self. Further, the appointment of a military man, of Major Raúl Curbelo—Chief of the Air Force—as Vice President of INRA indicates the general militarization of Cuban society which I alluded to in the article.

My critic has no obligation to accept the interpretation of the Castro reaction to Trotskyism and Maoism which I presented. But since he seems so certain that my explanation is incorrect, one might imagine he would put forth an alternative explanatory device. But no. What we get instead is a display of Mr. Lumsden's fuzziness. "Castro's criticisms of the Latin American Trotsky-ists are not easy to understand unless they were really directed against the sectarian Posadist faction. Nor is the severity of his denunciation of China readily explicable. . ." The ready-to-hand explanation: that the distinction between Trotskyism and Mao-ism has intentionally been made ambiguous, since *both* represent a redirection of foreign affairs along the lines originally stated by Guevara, is too obvious, and evidently true, for my critic even to test, much less take seriously. Unless the evidence I adduce for this thesis is seriously confounded, my explanation remains at least worthy of application to concrete events.

What I find particularly depressing about my critic's position is that he insists that my "article does more to aid the enemies of the Revolution, than to facilitate its comprehension." This is where I came in. Precisely this sort of genteel fanaticism is ad-duced to prevent scholars from expressing their outrage at politi-cal evils in Vietnam, the Dominican Republic, or elsewhere. "Do not speak up, perhaps you are right, but mortifyingly, you may provide aid and comfort to the enemies of the United States," Of those who have spoken against the war in Vietnam, prob-ably including Mr. Lumsden himself, how many actually know an the facts, or even most of them. Yet, even though there is an abundance of information to indicate that Cuba sails on troubled waters, it is urged upon me to adopt either a judicious posture or silence altogether.

Let me say, in all fairness to Mr. Lumsden, that I did give very serious thought to being silent on the Cuban catastrophe, precisely on grounds he indicates. I did not want my work to provide comfort to professional reactionaries. But ultimately, I decided that the real comfort to reaction is silence. For silence now, often means embarrassment later. This has been the history of the Left in America. Tailoring and temporizing with events are among the defining characteristics of sections of the old Left. If we, as radicals, have not learned the dangerous aspects of unreflective support for errors which seem congenial, we will scarcely be spared the wrath of error which in fact is uncongenial.

Source and Original Title: "Castrologists and Apologists: A Reply to Science in the Service of Sentiment." *New Politics,* Vol. 5, No. 1, 1966, pp. 27-34.

3

Cuban Communism and
Marxist Revisionism

It is the specter of the Organization of Latin American Solidarity, and this specter is causing insomnia among the reactionaries, imperialists, henchmen, *gorilas* [militarists], and exploiters." In fact, however, the Fidelista specter seems to be more haunting and daunting to the communists of the Western world. For Castro's remarks promptly elicited a stinging response from a leading Chilean communist, Luis Corvalán, a response that appeared in *Pravda,* the leading newspaper of the Soviet Communist Party. Corvalán warned: "Any effort by communists to impose their views on other ranks of the anti-imperialist forces does not help the achievement of unity." He added, "Lenin warned against the danger of adventurism, which as a rule results in the loss of precious lives of revolutionaries and the retreat of the movement." What is more, the roster of those absent from the OLAS meeting is striking. Along with Corvalán, other old-guard Chilean communists boycotted the convention, as did veteran Communist Party leaders from Venezuela and Argentina. Even some old Cuban party-liners were conspicuously absent. Despite the meeting's name, then, solidarity was *not* its leitmotiv.

Less than a decade ago, Fidel Castro was the idol of Latin America's communist leaders. Why has he now become a focus of intra-party factional divisions? An even more urgent question deals with Cuban policy, which—like the Chinese—remained relatively prudent from 1962 to 1966. Just what has led to this immense tactical shift toward belligerency? Clearly, these two questions are related, for it is Cuba's shift toward belligerency that has, in large part, estranged her from other communist parties in other countries.

Some of the answers to both questions are suggested in the works of Régis Debray and those imputed to Che Guevara. Debray, a 26-year-old philosophy professor and self-declared authority on guerrilla warfare, was absent from the OLAS meeting, having been detained by the Bolivian military on a charge of practicing guerrilla warfare. Despite his arrest, U.S. readers learned from reviews in *The New York Times* (July 26) and elsewhere that Debray's analysis of the Cuban process, *Revolution in the Revolution?*, is now available in English. Ernesto Guevara was also away from the meeting, and the officially, and unofficially, encouraged explanation was that Che was off spreading the revolution on other stages—although it should be noted that the style of Guevara's recent pamphlets is noticeably lacking in either the sophistication or humanism that characterized his earlier writings. At the conference, the OLAS delegates named him Honorary President *in absentia.*

The writings of Debray and Guevara are key documents in the history of the Cuban Revolution. Their writings follow the pattern established by the two previous major communist revolutions, for Stalin—once victory had been consolidated—proceeded to rewrite universal history in terms of the experience of Russia's Communist Party, and Mao did likewise for the Chinese party. Now Guevara, and more recently Debray, is reinterpreting traditional communist doctrine, and it is their "revisions" that have evoked the wrath of conventional communists. And because Debray and Guevara have revised traditional communist doctrine to conform to the actualities of Cuba's past and present, let us now examine these actualities.

Ever since Castro's movement started 14 years ago, the Communist Party has played an ancillary role. As an ideology, Castroism began with a charismatic leader and a band of dedicated nationalists. It moved from that point to a series of insurrectionary successes, which compelled the leader to form a movement—the July 26th Movement. Then victorious revolt surprisingly took place, which ultimately compelled him to form a party, the Communist Party. The corresponding organizational stages were:

- The pre-Revolutionary phase (1953-59), during which Castro's politics operated outside the communist movement and its bureaucracy;
- The united-front stage (1959-62), when the communists from the urban centers and the revolutionaries from the rural sectors were fused into the *Organizaciones Revolutionarias Integradas;*
- The popular-class stage (1962-65), as Cuba came to be ruled by socialist-Marxist ideology; and
- The communist stage (1965-), during which the name of the party was changed to "Partido Comunista de Cuba." Internal organizational strife, it is true, speeded the attainment of this most recent stage. Still, it is clear that the Partido Comunista de Cuba is a direct reflection of Castro's will and charismatic authority. Domestically, during this stage the old-line Cuban communist leaders were purged; internationally, this stage witnessed Cuba's ideological separation from old-line Latin American communist parties. And this separation constitutes the substance of the Cuban "revolution in the revolution," positing a commitment not merely to the Cuban Revolution, but to a revolution throughout Latin America.

The break with the old-line communist parties, as well as the commitment to a concept of permanent revolution, was demanded by the dynamics of Cuban society—and by the original ideals of the Cuban Revolution.

After the July 26th Movement had crushed the forces of Batista, the new regime quickly became committed to Marxism-Leninism and to Soviet patronage. Next, Cuban politics took a nationalistic, inner turn: The Fidelistas would consolidate their power, while building their economy along industrial lines so as to free the nation from her dependence on commodity imports.

This course had two grave weaknesses. The attempt at industrialization proved suicidal: Cubans, still dependent upon agriculture, badly needed income from their sugar and tobacco crops. Further, this program of autarchy made in the name of independence in fact threatened to result in Cuba's economic dependence upon the Soviet Union and Cuba's domination by a traditional communist party apparatus.

As early as 1963, when Castro denounced Aníbal Escalante, an old-time Cuban communist and a symbol of old-time Cuban communism, Castro had begun to realize that the old Communist Party constituted an assault upon the ideals of his revolution, and for the following reasons:

- The centralization of the Communist Party would elevate Havana to a supreme place in the bureaucratic hierarchy, thus depriving Castro of the *rural* mystique so vital to his outlook.
- The party bureaucracy threatened the charismatic basis of Castro's leadership.
- If orthodoxy were victorious, Castro would be saddled with not only material but ideological dependence upon the Soviet Union.
- Orthodox communists threatened Cuba with isolation from other Latin American revolutionaries. Like Stalin, these old-time communists were afraid that every other revolution would be "premature," "lacking in basic historical conditions for change." Finally,
- Castro felt that orthodoxy would be likely to smother the revolutionary "will," that human quality that had overcome so many hardships and had actually made the Cuban Revolution possible.

Consequently, Castro felt he had to reinvigorate the revolutionary will. This meant emphasizing the immediate creation of revolutionary situations in the Hemisphere. A new stress was laid on "exporting revolution"—the Cuban model. And the success of this campaign rested upon a rejection of all who challenged the Cuban experience—by treachery, advice, comparison, or any of the tricks played by intellect upon the act. The recalcitrant, orthodox communist machinery was either to be captured by the *guerrilleros,* or—failing this—transcended, bypassed, and even reviled as a non-revolutionary force.

This new militancy underscores the doctrinal independence of Castro's Communist Party: It is charismatic rather than bureaucratic. This is the ineradicable heritage of the days in the Sierra Maestra Mountains. Guerrilla activity gave Castro faith in will rather than in doctrinal blueprints. "The school of war," Fidel told farm-machine workers on February 20, 1967, "taught us how men can do many things, how they can accomplish many tasks when they apply themselves in a practical way. This was the school of war, where a small nucleus of combatants developed into an army without bureaucracy. Without bureaucracy! It went to war, waged war, and won the war without bureaucracy.... And war taught us what man can do when he dedicates himself to working with enthusiasm, interest, and common sense."

The revolution in the revolution *is* also meant to describe the revolutionizing of party organization, for in Cuba the traditional communist order of priorities has been transformed. As Régis Debray formulates it, there must first be the guerrilla group; second, the ripened social class; and only third will there be the authentic revolutionary party. The guerrilla movement is the party apparatus in gestation. In March of this year, Castro defined the party's prime goal: "To us the international communist movement is in the first place just that: a movement of communists, of revolutionary fighters. And those who are not revolutionary fighters cannot be called communists. We conceive of Marxism as revolutionary thinking and action." Castro has thus found a way to differentiate his brand of communism from European and Asian modes—without going outside the framework of Marxism. The Fidelistas have made it clear that Marxism is the *heuristic principle for making revolution,* rather than what lies at the end of the revolutionary rainbow.

But how does one build a new political party? Clearly the mass base, the popular front, the urban compromises, the bait dangled before representatives from all social sectors—the features common to the organizational base of the conventional communist party—all these are anathema to the Fidelistas. For them, the traditional bureaucratic communist party can be a downright liability, frustrating rather than fomenting revolutionary action. In this sense, the current stress on rural revolution abroad may turn out to be Castro's last hurrah—the final settlement of accounts and the ultimate nostalgic bow to the new generation. The question is, Can the revolution survive its own faith in its adolescence?

What this would require, in part at least, is the retention of the heroic image of the Cuban Revolution. That revolution and the Chinese are the two outstanding indigenous socialist revolutions in the post-World War II era. Each, by virtue of its autonomy, felt under few constraints to the Soviet model of 50 years ago. Consequently, Castro's revolution in the revolution goes beyond rebellion against the orthodox dominion of the communist party. It is an all-out effort to use the communist party and the communist ideology as a springboard for recruiting activists. In this sense, the pained if sterile cries of the communists that the Cuban revolutionaries are urging the "liquidation" of the party are right. If the party is to become the refuse heap of the old and the infirm, if it is to give up its manliness, then Castro will indeed enforce its liquidation.

Castro's unconventional view of time and age has led him to other revisions farther and farther from the Marxist-Leninist doctrines. Lurking in the background is what Debray posits as a Manichaean struggle between "socialist guerrillas" (the good guys) and "political commissars" (the bad guys). Debray's juxtaposition is sharper than any made by either Castro or Guevara, but all three support this heresy.

As long as economic conditions in Latin America continue as they are now, or deteriorate relative to the United States and Western Europe, Castro's insurrectionary romanticism, his idealization of will over ideas, will displace the traditional communist long-range view that ultimate victory is expressed by history rather than action: a faith in the ultimate deterioration of the capitalist economy and in the long-range tendencies of capitalist nations to conflict with one another. The short range is thus an expression of discontent with and disbelief in the "historically determined" processes assumed to guide society. The long-range view, that history determines structural change, becomes suspect—as if history itself is a cloak for cowardice and inaction.

A counterpart of Castro's unorthodox position on determinism versus free will is found in the problem of the relationship between *his* person and the party. For although his rule is undoubtedly based on overwhelming popular support, he must still face the problem of succession—of the transfer of power from self to society. Sporadically during the past two years, Castro has announced that in the future the mass slogan will be transformed from "Everyone *with* Fidel" to "Everyone with the Party." This *is* one transformation that has not taken place. Because Castro is still relatively young (40), the matter is eased but not eliminated. The legitimacy of the revolution requires some demonstration of the capacity of the social system to survive the original revolutionary group. It requires that some decision-making machinery be set up. This has not yet been forthcoming; instead, the Fidelistas have launched sustained attacks on the rational decision-making machinery of conventional communist parties.

The specter of personalism, *caudillismo,* continues to haunt the Cuban Revolution, and in this sense Fidel's role is rooted in Latin American tradition. For the *caudillo* the boss of a province who angles, often successfully, to become dictator of the nation—is the Latin American embodiment of personalism. This in itself is a form of the love-hate relationship of serfs in bondage to the *chief* (or *jefe)* who played an essential role in the transition from pre-industrial to modern societies. The Cuban Revolution was a military revolution and required the *caudillo* figure to offset the traditional role of the regular army. A good case can be made that this kind of leadership was indispensable in the context of Cuba, which is undergoing socioeconomic transformations not unlike those sponsored by the more "enlightened" *caudillos* of past times, such as Obregón in Mexico or Quiroga in Argentina. But if the nineteenth-century *caudillo* had contempt for the masses he served and remained responsive to the machinations of the middle-class parties, the new-style *caudillo* has only love for the masses and seeks to eradicate the apparatus of electoral politics merely because it is cumbersome.

A symptom, if not a consequence, of *caudillismo* is the rather widespread existence of nepotism throughout the governing ranks. This is especially characteristic of Castro. In picking political leaders, he leans heavily toward longtime cronies and familial contacts. Because of his brother Raúl's steady rise to power (following his appointment in 1959 as heir to the leadership) and the influence of other members of Fidel's extended family, he is surrounded with non-threatening figures.

The *caudillo* spirit in Latin America has traditionally served to enhance the leader's direct link to the people. In Fidel's case it enables him to bypass, when necessary, the only stable "bureaucratic" apparatus remaining in the country—the Communist Party. Castro even has his alter ego in the post of President—Osvaldo Dorticós—much as Stalin could boast of his in the person of Kliment Voroshilov. The trusted political lieutenant serves to legitimize the remarks of the *caudillo*.

Castro's tendency to nepotism reveals itself most decisively in his humiliation of old-line associates and in his replacing them either with himself or with nonentities. The family power held by Fidel Castro, Raúl Castro, and Vilma Espín (Raúl's wife) cannot be underestimated. Raúl and Vilma, along with Dorticós and Juan Almeida (an old Sierra Maestra companion, now Minister of Labor), are about the most visible leaders in the new Cuba. This is the politics of the purge, the dismemberment of any possible opposition. The purging of a score of veteran Cuban Communist Party leaders—including Aníbal Escalante, Joaquín Ordoqui, Edith García Buchaca, Juan Marinello, Manuel Luzardo, and Lázaro Peña—had nothing to do with their competence, but simply with their politics. One of the inner-directed aspects of the revolution in the revolution is the elimination of the old party cadre. The ouster of Carlos Rafael Rodríguez as head of the National Institute of Agrarian Reform (INRA) in 1965 is the best example of the nexus between personal style and potential ideology. The fact that Castro himself assumed this post is a sign of his increasing concentration of power in his own presence.

Further, the appointment of a guerrilla cohort—Major Raúl Curbelo, Chief of the Air Force—as Vice President of INRA is only one instance of the continued militarization of Cuban society. Only Brazil has a larger army, and only the combined strength of the Argentine armed forces equals the regular armed force size of Cuba. The fusion of personal and political aspects of behavior has served to justify an increased politicization of the military and, no less, of the diplomatic corps. The replacement of the Army Chief of Staff, Armed Forces Vice Minister, Commander of the Navy, and leading officials in the Foreign Ministry represents not simply a tightening of the political net but an increased penetration by the *Líder Máximo* (Maximum Leader) into middle echelons of power. With each series of dismissals, the actual power lodged in civilian agencies seems to become correspondingly weaker; the replacements are less able (or willing) to make decisions independently. Thus, the general militarization of the Hemisphere has had its Left-wing reflex in Cuba.

For the Hemisphere, in turn, these transformations evoke their own terrors. Since it is the impression of most foreign observers that Cuba today is being placed on a wartime footing and is in a state of permanent mobilization, the external ramifications of the revolution in the revolution cannot be dismissed casually.

Restlessness and righteousness have undoubtedly combined to produce the new look in Cuba's foreign policy: the abandonment, to a large extent, of the prudence or caution Castro practiced in the 1962-66 period. This transformation represents responses on three distinct levels: Castro's realization of the dangers attendant on conservatism and bureaucracy, which could obstruct efforts to consolidate the Cuban Revolution; the frustration stemming from Cuba's hemispheric isolation. Indeed, the list of military-sponsored, right-wing *golpes de estado* (*coups d' état*) since 1959 is awesome.

Third, the international crisis created by the Vietnam conflict.

The first problem is largely a domestic concern, and it has been dealt with above in terms of Cuba's internal contradictions. It remains only to add that, when Castro threw out prudent foreign policy, he also threw out the baby. The nation-building phase in Cuba came to an end in 1966, and with it ended a certain belief in the viability of a strictly Cuban solution.

In the first years after the Cuban Revolution, its leadership went through the euphoric phase of thinking that Latin American social revolution was on the march. In a sense, the Fidelistas behaved much like the Leninists following their victory after the conclusion of World War I. So certain were the Leninists that the revolution would spread at least to Germany that they made no contingency plans for problems that might emerge from a frustration of communist ambitions. The collapse of international communism in the 1920s helps explain Stalin's single-minded foreign policy. The similar collapse of Latin American communism in the 1960s helps to explain Castroism. For up to 1966, Castro seemed bound by a similar belief that the Cuban revolutionary model projected a unique radiant energy that would power other hemispheric revolutions.

Yet during this time, the Cuban revolutionaries helplessly watched the utter disarray of Latin America's Leftists. In 1964, Goulart's Brazil went down to crashing counterrevolutionary defeat, and in 1965 Cuba could not mount even a token effort to prevent the Dominican Republic from being restored to a former Trujillo henchman. Throughout Latin America, the image of a mighty torrent of 200 million oppressed peons crushing all obstacles flickered and faded.

Nevertheless, Guevara and his disciples continued to press for total revolution in the Hemisphere. In 1964, Guevara made his "Colonialism Is Doomed" speech before the United Nations. He warned of a "wave of heightened fury, of just demands, of rights that have been flouted, which is rising throughout Latin America." Even after Che left Castro's side, in 1965, the assault on nation-building continued, and by 1966 any strict tendencies toward internal economic development had been repudiated.

In some measure the new turn in Cuban ideology, away from nation-building to continental communism, represents the politics of desperation. For while there are hundreds of thousands of students and workers who share the Cuban perspective, the guerrillas throughout Latin America cannot be numbered even in the thousands. *The New York Times* places the figure at about 750 men. Further, no governments have fallen as a result of the guerrilla activities. In fact, in Colombia, Bolivia, and Venezuela, the guerrilla menace has boomeranged, producing a united front from above—an opposition fusion of military and civilian sectors otherwise often at odds. If this lack of revolutionary victories has stirred the Cubans and their followers to new heights of forensics, it has also, and more substantially, permitted the old-line communists to announce the "bankruptcy" of the new turn.

Castro's retort to these frustrations throughout the Hemisphere constitutes the second level of the transformation of his foreign policy. Its organizational expression is the Organization of Latin American Solidarity, an obvious response to the Organization of American States, from which Cuba was expelled three years after the revolution. This expulsion, taken enthusiastically by the foreign ministers of the United States and reluctantly by those of Latin American states, isolated Cuba solely from the *governments* of other hemispheric nations—and did that only partially. The governments of Canada and Mexico continued to maintain diplomatic and trade relations with Cuba, and all sorts of private organizations and institutions elsewhere in the Hemisphere continued to provide Cuba with Hemispheric links. Indeed, special tours from Montevideo to Havana are constantly arranged despite the absence of formal diplomatic ties. There is, in fact, a dramaturgical conflict between government and people, with the Castro forces in the vanguard of the latter.

What cannot be lost sight of is that the very existence of the OAS serves to legitimize the OLAS If an organization can be used for the sole effective purpose of preventing "communist penetration" of the Hemisphere, as is indicated by the Declaration of Caracas, then on a *quid pro quo* basis there is no reason why a parallel organization to rid the Hemisphere of "imperialism" should not also be set up. The OLAS's ambiguous situation arises from the fact that the United States is the acknowledged leader of the OAS, though whether this leadership function is welcomed by the Latin Americans or imposed upon them is a moot point. But Cuba has not even been accepted as the leader of the Latin American revolutionary forces. And given Cuba's dependent economic status and diminutive size, it is hard to imagine that Castro can impose the same sort of authority on the "communists" of the Hemisphere as the United States can on its "capitalists." This is a clear example of the price paid for having the first socialist revolution in the Hemisphere conducted by one of its smallest nations.

But Castro still holds a few trump cards—one of them, the simple fact that he has made a socialist revolution in an underdeveloped nation. What characterize revolutions in underdeveloped areas are their discontinuities with the European experience, and even more with the North American experience. The prevailing political framework in Latin America is a juridical delight, a world of laws and orders that employs the forms of constitutionalism without realizing the substance of democratic politics. From the days of the Spanish viceroys, leaders were men who made rules, not those who abided by them. Despite their access to power, the Latin American middle classes have failed to convert their political compassion into affluence for all. Therefore, Castro attacks all sectors of society—including the communists—that affirm their devotion to European political traditions without a corresponding reformation of the social structure.

Régis Debray flatly admits that the bourgeoisie cannot be challenged on the Electoral terrain with any hope of victory—at least not in the majority of Latin American countries. In such circumstances, armed struggle must replace parliamentary cretinism. This is the "new dialectic" to which the revolution in the revolution has given rise. "It is possible," Debray declares, "to move from a military *foco* ["center of operations," or focus] to a political *foco*, but to move in the opposite direction is

virtually impossible." Debray points out that, expressed sche-
matically, the fundamental lesson of the Cuban Revolution
is that it represents the progression "from the military *foco*
to the political movement." Thus, at the ideological level the
revolution in the revolution represents the transformation of
guerrillas into *gorilas*) into advocates of the total militarization
of Latin America. This seems to incorporate Rightist doctrine
into a Leftist framework. Indeed, for Debray, the physical symbol
of the new Left is the military tunic; his heroes, in addition to
Fidel, are Ho Chi Minh, Mao Tse-tung, and Ernesto Guevara.
But is not the physical representation of the old Right also the
military tunic?

There is no plausible reason for equating fascism with Castroism. But the fusion of militarism with revolutionary minoritari-
anism has no more place in it for classical socialist politics than
it has for classical bourgeois politics. Actually, the revolution
in the revolution is not so much a call for sheer militancy or a
reflection of new class alignments as it is a call for the primacy
of the military.

Debray calls the primacy of the military *foco* a "classic involu-
tion." However, what it more nearly represents is a return to the
politics of radical irrationalism characteristic of French insurrectionary socialism from Babeuf to Sorel. The present stage of the
Cuban Revolution represents an unparalleled romantic outburst,
but this is very much in keeping with the Latin (French as well as
Spanish) ethos. Its romanticism is certified by dead heroes—young
soldiers who did not fade away, but died or were captured by
the enemy (as Debray was). It is intellectually and emotionally
underwritten by Marxism of free will to replace the Marxism of
historical determinism. Real men instead of impersonal man once
again make history. This exaltation of flesh-and-blood heroes
comes through most clearly in remarks published in the magazine
Tricontinental, in April 1966, and attributed to Guevara: Tribute
is paid to the "martyrs, who will figure in the history of Our
America as having given their necessary quota of blood in this
last stage of the fight for the total freedom of man."

The resurrection as well as the death is also certified by individuals. As Castro noted earlier (1967) this year: "The active mobilization of the people creates new leaders; César Montes and Yon Sosa raise the flag of battle in Guatemala; Fabio Vázquez and Marulanda in Colombia; Douglas Bravo in the western half of the country; and Américo Martín in *El Bachiller* direct their respective fronts in Venezuela. New uprisings will take place in these and other countries of Our America, as has already happened in Bolivia; they will continue to grow in the midst of all the hardships inherent in this dangerous profession of the modern revolutionary."

The case of Yon Sosa demonstrates how even the concept of romanticism has been transformed by Castro in line with his new turn in ideology. At his closing address to the January 1966 Tri-Continental Conference; Castro devoted considerable time to a critique of Yon Sosa's conduct in Guatemala. He charged that Yon Sosa was a romantic; he did not know revolutionary strategies; he did not know how to win the people. He had allowed himself to be captured by agents of imperialism, by Trotskyites. Ironically enough, Castro's attack was not much different from the attacks the official Communist Party of Cuba made against Castro himself when he was a guerrilla leader in the mountains.

The man Castro defended at the Tri-Continental meeting was Luis Augusto Turcios, who represented Guatemala. Turcios was upheld by Castro as the proper sort of guerrilla revolutionary, a believer in the national rather than in the socialist character of revolution. Since Turcios' death late in 1966, however, criticism of Yon Sosa has been muted, and (as we have seen) this year the Cuban regime restored him to leadership status—in the interests of a common Latin American revolutionary front. Nothing could better indicate the militant turn in Cuban foreign policy.

Cuban romanticism is partially a function of the scale of the revolution and of the nation. Castro today repeatedly harks back to the simpler, purer air of the Sierra Maestra, where an inspired handful of men came down from the mountains to defeat the Goliath in Havana. In assuming the spiritual leadership of the

Hemisphere, Castro almost makes a nostalgic appeal for his adherents to go tell it on the mountains. Speaking to Lee Lockwood, a U.S. photographer and journalist, earlier this year, Castro said: "Had we been men with little faith in the Revolution we would have given up the fight following our first setback at the Moncada Garrison [in July 1953], or when our little army landed from the *Granma* [the boat Castro used in December 1956 for his landing from Mexico] only to be dispersed three days later, and only seven of us were able to reunite. Thousands or rather millions of reasons could have been used as a pretext to say that we were wrong, and that those who said that it was impossible to fight that army, those great forces, were right. However, three weeks later, on January 17, we who at the end of December had barely reunited our forces carried out our first successful attack on an army post, killing its occupants."

In the same vein, Debray expresses the romantic revolutionary irrational in claiming that "For a revolutionary, failure is a springboard. As a source of theory it is richer than victory. It accumulates experience and knowledge." The young French philosopher clearly learned his lessons well from such irrationalism radical predecessors as Sorel, Peguy, and Bergson. He is, in fact, more a product of *fin de siècle* France than post-revolutionary Cuba.

Of course, Castro has been forced to convert his liabilities into assets, and he has done so very shrewdly. An irreversible fact that he must contend with is Cuba's physical limitations. The major socialist revolutions in Europe and Asia were concluded within the largest land masses in the world (Russia and China). Each had the potential for economic independence, for sustained takeoff, for inducing a restructuring of the economic balance of power within their respective spheres of influence. But what could Cuba, the first socialist revolutionary regime in Latin America, do on this score? She was a debtor nation; she could offer no viable economic assistance to revolutionary regimes in trouble.

Paradoxically enough, while Cuba's smallness may be a liability as far as her revolutionary potential is concerned, she has retained intact her function as an exemplary case of a nation breaking her links with the colonial past. But this is a two-edged weapon. The Cuban leadership tends to underestimate the fact that a model for revolutionaries can also serve as a warning for the established order. In fact, the United States has already stepped up its counterrevolutionary programs in the Hemisphere. And the absence of socialist victories since the Cuban Revolution can scarcely be dismissed as happenstance.

But the happenstance that the first socialist system in the Western Hemisphere has been organized in one of the smallest and least representative nations has clear consequences in political cost accounting. It has raised the cost of revolutions anywhere else. Revolution has become more "expensive" in every other country of the Americas at the very time that the impotence of the first socialist republic became manifest.

In this equation, the United State's intervention in the Dominican Republic in 1965 paid dividends. It unmistakably informed the Latin American nations that the North Americans were in Santo Domingo; the Cubans were not. Nor could they come. Through this action the United States succeeded in defining the Cuban Revolution as something less than a total Latin American revolution. That lesson was not lost. Quite the contrary. Schisms and splits erupted throughout the rest of Latin America, particularly within Cuba.

In Castro's reaction to the stinging taunts about his inaction during the Dominican crisis, righteousness was the keynote. In 1966 he attacked guerrilla insurgents throughout Latin America. In 1967 he generalized his attacks, challenging the right of major non-Hemispheric communist nations, as well as of communist parties in the Hemisphere, to dictate the character of resistance to the United States. In attacking other communist parties, Castro made it plain that their right of leadership had been abrogated. Here restlessness at his impotence began to seep in. Cuba now proclaimed herself the unique model for guiding revolutionary destinies in resisting the United States. In this way Cuba laid the groundwork for a position as a Third Force within the communist world and within the Third World—a grandiose ideological presumption that again takes advantage

of the very smallness of Cuba's base, geographically, demo-
graphically, and economically. For underlying this presumption
is the profound conviction that Big Power communism is also
Big Power chauvinism. The highhanded conduct of the Soviet
Union during the missile crisis is a sore point in Cuba today.
This is plain in Castro's statement to Lee Lockwood earlier
this year: "Khrushchev had made great gestures of friendship
toward our country. He had done things earlier that were extraordinarily helpful to us. But the way in which he conducted
himself during the October crisis was to us a serious affront....
After the missile crisis, while the Soviet Union was pressing
for the withdrawal of the remaining Soviet military personnel in
Cuba, the subversive activities of the United States were growing
increasingly frequent. In Central America a series of bases had
been organized in order to promote aggressions against us. All
of which, from our point of view, justified the position we had
taken at the beginning of the crisis..... The subsequent climate of
distrust [between Khrushchev and Castro] could never be completely overcome."

This "climate of distrust" is even more overt in Castro's attitude toward China, despite the many surface resemblances
between the two countries. In its first phase, Castro's critique
of the Chinese Communist Party could be viewed as a rejection
of both foreign domination and also of any unnecessary foreign
entanglements. Today, Cuba believes that China also represents
Big Power chauvinism.

The basic dilemma of the Cuban revolution in the revolution is
whether communism is a national movement or an international
movement. Now, for the orthodox communist parties, China's
ideological approach represents not Stalinism but Trotskyism.
This schism has in fact plagued communism from the first days
of its success. At the start of World War I, German and French socialists were faced with a choice between working-class solidarity
and nationalism. Naturally, they chose nationalism. A decade later,
the Russian Bolsheviks had to choose between "socialism in one
country" (the nationalist focus on building and industrializing) and

"permanent revolution" (based on the notion of the international solidarity of workers). The path chosen was the former—Stalin's road. Leon Trotsky, the Gray Eagle of the Revolution, was sent into ignominious exile.

The Chinese Revolution has been facing much the same dilemma, but in this case the outcome remains unclear. The young and the old revolutionaries have forged a united front against the Soviet-trained, nation-building, middle-aged generation. Since the old and the young have the upper hand now, China supports the necessity of world revolution—not just of any revolution, but of socialist revolution.

From the orthodox ideological point of view, Castro's attack on China may seem yet another attack on Trotskyism, in its most "insidious" form—Chinese communism. But from the perspective of the recent internal transformation of Cuban ideology, it is an attack on Big Power chauvinism, its rationale and its revolutionary pretenses. From this, even the potential perpetual revolution of the Chinese is not exempt. Then too, one cannot forget that Cuba's bitter assaults on China date from the time it became clear that China could not fulfill her promises of lavish aid.

However severe are Cuba's attacks on Chinese revisionism, they are caresses compared with the attacks on "Yankee imperialists." Régis Debray has again made the official formulation: "No one can avoid seeing that in Latin America today the struggle against imperialism is decisive. If it is decisive, then all else is secondary." What is painfully absent from Debray's work, and from any Cuban pronouncements, is any operational analysis of what "imperialism" is all about. It is almost as if subtlety and sophistication would jeopardize the single-minded assault on the enemy.

Cuba has thus carved out for herself a peculiarly hemispheric role—one in which both Russia and China are denied much of a voice. If the United States defined the Western Hemisphere as off-limits to the European and Asian powers in terms of the Monroe Doctrine, Castro—despite his sensitivity to confrontation—seems to have drawn the same geographic limitations, but in terms of a "Bolívar Doctrine."

In implementing his program for the Hemisphere, Castro faces three essential strategies of change that are now current in Latin America: The United State's strategy—concentrating on developing a national politics of a multi class variety, the Soviet model—developing a politics of an industrial-class variety in a predominantly urban setting, and the Chinese model—developing politics on the basis of mass peasant movements.

The difference between the first and the second and third is nothing short of a choice between reform and revolution. The second and the third differ in that they are two tactics for making revolution. And any knowledge of socialist history will make clear that, once reformist options have been dismissed, the tactical and strategic disputes between revolutionary factions become awesome and fierce. One needs look no further to understand why Corvalán and many other Latin American communist leaders boycotted the OLAS meeting in the summer.

Castro openly supports the revolutionary guerrillas in Venezuela, Guatemala, and Colombia. At the same time, he makes scarcely veiled attacks on the communist leaderships in these countries. The revolution in the revolution, he notes, "acts within revolutionary forms and respects those forms," but this does not prevent "practice coming first and then theory." This practice demands support for the guerrillas as a prime form of foreign relations. Castro indicates that even diplomatic recognition of other hemispheric nations will not be forthcoming "until there are revolutionary governments leading those countries."

Castro's relations with other, older communist parties in the Hemisphere reached a boiling point in March. With brimstone and vitriol, he lashed out at the Venezuelan party's rejection of the primacy of the guerrilla tactic as "defeatist." In unmistakable terms, he served notice that he would at no time be bound to a "Rightist, capitulationist current" simply because it is bureaucratically promoted "in the name of the international communist movement." At stake here is not merely the course of Venezuela's revolution. In time-honored communist technique, these words cloak a deeper design. Venezuela serves Castro as a surrogate for expressing not simply his frustration at the inaction of socialism elsewhere in the Hemisphere, but also for expressing his claim to ideological leadership in the Hemisphere.

The bitterness of the exchange reveals with terrible clarity the rapid disintegration of the party monolith in the Hemisphere. The current debate is only the latest episode in the long history of controversy within Latin American communism. In the 1940s and 1950s, the pro-Perón and anti-Perón Communist Party factions in Argentina disputed how the party could exploit the dictator's opportunistic swings between Moscow and Washington. During the Goulart epoch, there was the equally critical antagonism between the Chinese-oriented and the Soviet-oriented wings of the Brazilian party. But the Cuban-Venezuelan competition for loyal revolutionists has an especially acrimonious tone, since it involves the interference of a foreign communist party into the affairs of another communist party. Within the OAS, the doctrine of nonintervention has generally paralyzed action—despite fervent arguments by the United States for solidarity. Among communists, sovereignty is no less hotly contested. But once Castro adopts the view that his revolution is only the advanced phalanx of a hemispheric army, no country is foreign to him, none of his revolutionary activities can be defined as "intervention."

In Castro's attack on the Venezuelans, the Righteous Revolutionary did not even entirely spare his Soviet benefactors: "You see how the Venezuelan puppets talk, with their demands that the U.S.S.R. withdraw from the Tricontinental organization, that the U.S.S.R. do no less than virtually break with Cuba, the 'dead-end street,' to enter through the wide, expansive, and friendly door of the Venezuelan Government, the Government that has slaughtered more communists than any other on this continent!" Castro then introduced a defiant note: "As for us, we are Marxist-Leninists. Let others do as they please. We will never re-establish relations with such a government!" In an obvious challenge to Soviet leadership, Castro concluded with a barbed understatement: "All is not rose-colored in the revolutionary world. Complaints and more complaints are repeated because of contradictory attitudes. While one country [Romania] is being condemned for reopening relations with Federal Germany, there is a rush to seek relations with oligarchies of the sort run by Leoni [President of Venezuela] and company. A principled position in everything, a principled position in Asia, but a principled position in Latin America, too."

The Venezuelan Communist Party responded with immediacy and savagery, which can in some measure be attributed to the Soviet Government's certain displeasure at Castro's open and unprecedented challenge to its Latin American policy. Curiously, the Venezuelan response was less a rejoinder than an exposure. Castro, too, was called an opportunist: The Cuban regime, while calling for a "principled" stand in the Hemisphere, trades and carries on diplomatic negotiations with the fascist Franco regime. And, to justify its own position, the Venezuelan Communist Party invoked the classical contest between polity and morality. In 1966 Castro took virtually the same moralistic tack in criticizing China's actions: "From the first moment, we understood the obvious opportunistic position taken by China in trade relationships.... A much more important and fundamental question than food is whether the world of tomorrow can assume the right to blackmail, extort, pressure, and strangle small peoples." This year, at Cuba's instigation, the OLAS meeting adopted an astoundingly harsh resolution condemning the U.S.S.R. and other East European states for trading with the oligarchic regimes of Latin America. These are clearly idiosyncratic Latin American responses, for the accepted role of the sovereign state is to conduct foreign policy in the best interests of its own people. The substitution of moral absolutes for such a practical goal must seem as suicidal to communist politicians as to bourgeois politicians. In sum, the Cuba-Venezuela dispute has tangled somewhat the threads of national self-interest and international solidarity among communists. Ideological disputes are not unresponsive to nationalist sentiments, particularly in Latin America, where such sentiments are powerful among the

Left as well as the Right. And if the Fidelistas have moved closer to "permanent" Hemispheric revolution since the Tri-Continental Conference, the Venezuelans, in the wake of their activist guerrilla wing's bitter defeats and the internal disaffiliation of their Armed Forces of National Liberation, have moved further toward intense nationalism and political accommodation.

The tone of the Venezuelan response to Castro makes clear the "classical" nature of the contest. In a sharp rebuke, the response noted that "the aberration in the Castro position is that it makes him unable to pronounce the word 'peace.' It does not constitute a renunciation of any principles to urge the formulation of a democratic peace for Venezuela-particularly at a time when the most rapacious sectors of the ruling class are interested in gathering excuses for a policy of violence, and when a policy of violence has been repudiated by the majority of the country." The Venezuelan party further reasserts the primacy of organization over will: "It is necessary to point out that we are not attempting to provoke communist insurrections or create pure communists. We are attempting to prepare and organize a national revolutionary movement capable of opening new pathways of independent development for our nation. In this sense, it is imperative that the CPV organize a vast movement, with the workers and peasants in a mutually reinforced alliance, which also has the potential for including those sectors of the middle class and those national patriots able and willing to put an end to colonization and underdevelopment." Teodoro Petkoff and his fellow leaders of the CPV put the matter of Cuban assistance bluntly: "We will never accept agents of Cuba in Venezuela—as if they are the only true communist party in the world. We are Venezuelan communists, and we cannot accept tutelage under anybody." The declaration added tauntingly that "if there are small revolutionary groups that are eager to come under the tutelage of Fidel Castro, that is their business, not ours. The CPV will never accept such subordination."

Underneath the rousing rhetoric emanating from Cuba and Venezuela is a sociological disagreement. The orthodox communist position holds that a genuine national politics can emerge only when industrial classes within the cities perceive themselves as linked to the peasant masses in the rural area. It follows that the forces that control the cities control the nation. The catch is that today the aspirations of the organized working classes are much more nearly those of the middle sectors than those of the peasant masses. Urbanization and modernization have cut the ground from under traditional communist prescriptions. In Castro's almost pathological disdain for big-city politics, there is more than a hint of the nostalgic yearning for an age of peasant innocence, untouched by the corruption of the monstrous secular city.

The alternative position presented by Castro is an adaptation from Mao Tse-tung: The peasant mass surrounds the cities and overwhelms the urban-based sectors. At least in the initial guerrilla phase, those who control the rural countryside control the nation. The supreme difficulty of this approach in Latin America is the heavy concentration of the population in the coastal regions—the result of the masses' reliance upon migration rather than insurgency to obtain their goals. Castro's emotional response, inconsistent with his long-run aim of industrialization, is to identify urbanism with bureaucratic corruption.

In many parts of Latin America, moreover, the peasant masses may be unwilling to play their assigned role; many remain so tied to a semi feudal culture that their primary allegiance is to the *latifundistas* (big landowners) rather than to the revolutionaries. The recognition of this social variable by Debray, Guevara, and others has led to a view of guerrilla insurgency as dependent less upon the rural peasant than on the mountain terrain. This shift from a class approach to an ecological approach contributes to making romanticism a far more profound ingredient of present-day guerrilla insurgency in Venezuela, Guatemala, and Colombia than it ever was in the actual forging of the Cuban Revolution. In this sense, the revolution in the revolution can be seen as an attempt to transcend the actual empirical situation and return to the very theorizing Castro shows such contempt for on other grounds.

One more cause of Castro's new boldness in foreign policy is his reaction to the war in Vietnam, a reaction that links his hemispheric ambitions with his pretensions to Third World leadership. It also brings this small socialist state into a confrontation with the United States. Again it is Che Guevara who announces the theme. In the *Tricontinental* article presumably written by him, he defined Cuba's Third Force approach in relation to Vietnam. He pictured Vietnam as the primary ally of Cuba. As an outpost of socialism in Asia, Vietnam's position is parallel to Cuba's in the Western Hemisphere: "This is the sad reality: Vietnam—a nation representing the aspirations, the hopes of a whole world of forgotten peoples—is tragically alone.... The solidarity of all progressive forces of the world with the people of Vietnam today is similar to the bitter irony of the plebeians urging on the gladiators in the Roman arena." Guevara is quite precise on this point. "It is not a matter of wishing success to the victim of aggression, but of sharing his fate; one must accompany him to his death or to victory. When we analyze the lonely situation of the Vietnamese people, we are overcome by anguish at this illogical fix in which humanity finds itself. U.S. imperialism is guilty of aggression—its crimes are enormous and cover the whole world. We already know all that, gentlemen! But this guilt also applies to those who, when the time came for a definition, hesitated to make Vietnam an inviolable part of the socialist world; running, of course, the risks of a war on a global scale, but also forcing a decision upon imperialism. The guilt also applies to those who maintain a war of abuse and maneuvering—started quite some time ago by the representatives of the two greatest powers of the socialist camp."

Guevara then called for many Vietnams throughout Latin America. This exhortation, he asserted, is a consequence of the general impotence and shortcomings of China and the Soviet Union. Unsparingly he described the masculine, apocalyptic warfare and warriors these Vietnams would require: "Relentless hatred of the enemy impels us over and beyond the natural limitations of man and transforms us into effective, violent, selective, and cold killing-machines. Our soldiers must be thus; a people without hatred cannot vanquish a brutal enemy. We must carry the war as far as the enemy carries it: to his home, to his centers of entertainment, in a total war. It is necessary to prevent him from having a moment of peace, a quiet moment outside his barracks or even inside; we must attack him wherever he may be, make him feel like a cornered beast wherever he may move." Guevara concludes with a call to arms: "What a luminous, clear future would be Visible to us if two, three, or many Vietnams flourished throughout the world."

Not to be overlooked is the belief shared by the Cuban political leadership that an end to the fighting in Vietnam would signal the beginning of a United States offensive to "rid the Hemisphere of communism." Cuba sees the opening of this crusade in the Venezuelan Government's complaint to the Organization of American States that Castro is supplying and providing men for the anti-Government guerrilla movement.

If the best defense is an offense, then the Cuban leadership is performing correctly. The regime refused to disclaim any knowledge of the three Cubans in a landing party of revolutionists caught by Venezuelan Government forces. Instead, Havana declared on May 18, 1967, that "Cuba is lending and will continue to lend aid to all those who fight against imperialism in whatever part of the world." This commitment, in turn, rests on a profound conviction that a more active insurrectionary role would not harm Cuba—and would probably yield heightened respect in those sectors of the Latin American Left most disillusioned and disheartened by Cuba's prudent response to the U.S. intervention in the Dominican Republic.

The question of morale remains an important constituent of Castro's thinking. Guevara has cautioned: "We must not underrate our adversary; the U.S. soldier has technical capacity and is backed by weapons and resources of such magnitude as to render him formidable. He lacks the essential ideological motivation which his bitterest enemies of today—the Vietnamese soldiers—have in the highest degree." Castro's newly radical foreign policy itself seems to rest on the belief that no matter what the United States-dominated OAS orders, the people of Latin America will never willingly fight Cuba. Furthermore, there is a tacit belief that the Soviet Union will never willingly stop supporting Cuba, at least to the extent of underwriting her sugar crop, no matter how resentful orthodox Latin American communist parties may become—or, for that matter, the Soviet Union itself. It is doubtful whether this will be enough to fuel Castro's ambitions, however. In defending his passivity during the Dominican civil war, Castro pointed out (perhaps inadvertently) the purely defensive nature of the Cuban armed forces: "Cuba has weapons to defend herself, but in relation to the imperialists, they are infinitely inferior. Cuba has defensive arms."

Nevertheless, the new Cuban ideology downgrades the role of weaponry. In the romantic rationale, technology cannot halt the human agent of social change. On April 19, 1967, the sixth anniversary of the Bay of Pigs landing (now a Cuban national holiday), Castro reasserted his willingness to have Cuba serve as the Vietnam of the West, a kind of Second Front within the Third World. Plainly referring to the United States, he warned that "the firepower and combat capacity they would find here is equivalent to more than three times the firepower of the revolutionary combatants of South Vietnam. . . . As to the rest, let them find out for themselves should the time come. The imperialists must confront Vietnam, plus the several Vietnams that are developing on this continent, plus the Vietnam that they are going to find here if they attack us."

Even with the final prudent proviso, "If they attack us," the unabashed and uninhibited defense of guerrilla combat, along with the clear willingness to flout existing diplomatic truces, could well be the opening gambit in a Cuban maneuver to provoke the United States into a line of action that would once and for all crystallize the polarization of the United States and Latin America.

Amazingly, this Cuban programming of U.S. foreign policy may succeed. Castro now seems to have the United States military programmed to adopt a form of precipitate behavior that might well induce a second Vietnam. While on the surface this appears to be a Cuban invitation to attend her own suicide, there are several factors operating for Castro in Cuba that did not exist in any country where the United States previously intervened. Cuba is fully mobilized and prepared, militarily and psychologically, for attack. The Cuban population's support of the regime appears solid enough to rule out the possibility of any immediate collapse of the regime. Finally, in any future invasion, the United States—unlike its hands-off posture in the Bay of Pigs expedition—would have to draw on its own heavily committed armed forces. It could not rely on exiles to perform Hessian services.

If this analysis is correct, then there has been a profound transformation in the Castro regime: not merely an abandonment of the prudent policy that characterized the first eight years of the regime's existence, but more than that the possibility of a belligerent policy that could invite full-scale American military operations "only 90 miles from home."

There is monumental tragedy in this prospect—for Castro, for the United States, for the Hemisphere. The revolution within the revolution proposes a transcendence of the party organization through a reassertion of personality. The *true* party, in contrast with the established party, would be manned by symbolic leaders of proved revolutionary capacity, organizing for the great push outward against Big Powers and Big Brothers. At the psychological level, the new turn in Cuban ideology calls for liberation from the dominance of the bureaucratic party and instead the exaltation of the individual. At the political level, the new turn calls for a redefinition of victory as a hemispheric issue rather than a national issue. Marx observed that when history repeats itself, what tragedy returns was as comedy. In Hemispheric history, under Castro's impact, the classic tragedy of the schism between organization and humanism, internationalism and nationalism, may return not as comedy, but as calamity.

References/Notes

Studies on Cuba continue to grow, but their quality has declined markedly ever since the inundation of an apologetic and tendentious literature. Still, there are a number of recent works in English that deserve careful attention.

Revolution in the Revolution? by Régis Debray (New York: Monthly Review, 1967). The famed study by the French philosopher-guerrilla fighter who has sought to provide ideological backbone to the new turn in Cuban politics.

Castro's Cuba, Cuba's Fidel by Lee Lockwood (New York: The Macmillan Company, 1967). A remarkable set of interviews with Fidel Castro, providing the most up-to-date account of the Cuban Premier's beliefs and attitudes.

Revolutionary Politics and the Cuban Working Class by Maurice Zeitlin (Princeton, NJ: Princeton University Press, 1967). The first significant sociological field-study of post revolutionary Cuba, The attitudes of the masses expressed, though based on data obtained in 1962, remain unquestionably correct.

Source and Original Title: "Cuban Communism: Revolution within a Revolution." *Transaction/Society,* Vol. 4, No. 10, October 1967, pp. 7-15, 55-57.

4

The Missile Crisis: A Decade in United States-Cuban Relations

It has quite properly been said that the Cuban missile crisis stands as a watershed of the Cold War and in the history of the contemporary international system.[1] Not unexpectedly, the effects of this watershed on Cuban affairs have been submerged in a larger context of American-Soviet relations.[2] While it would be a mistake to claim Cuban centrality in this affair, the consequences for Cuba have been considerable. Paramount in this regard is the negation of the Monroe Doctrine, which prior to 1959 guaranteed American political dominion in the Western Hemisphere. What should be understood in retrospect is that Americans and Soviets alike suffered defeats and gains as an outcome of the Cuban missile crisis.

One would have to start from the premise that this mutuality of perceived assets permitted a pacific settlement of the crisis to take place. The big gain for the United States was to keep the Caribbean free of nuclear missiles in any hemispheric nation hostile to its geopolitical interests. The big loss for the United States was de facto acceptance of a nation with a social system entirely at variance with its own. The big gain for the Soviet Union was the maintenance of a socialist type of bridgehead sympathetic to its interests in the Western Hemisphere. The big loss for the Soviet Union was the sharp and clear delineation of its operational military range.[3] Without minimizing the risks entailed in confrontational politics, the very ambiguity of outcome spread out over time made possible a resolution which was held up for the past 14 years.

Given the general context of the political situation of the defense establishment, it is important to reexamine the Cuban missile crisis in its specifics. The services and the Defense Department expressed different strategic interpretations of the Cuban crisis in the congressional appropriations hearing of 1965. General Curtis LeMay, Air Force chief of staff, expressed the Air Force position:[4]

> We must maintain a credible general war force so that lesser options may be exercised under the protection of this general war deterrent. It is the general war strength of aircraft and missile forces which place an upper limit on the risks an aggressor is willing to take, and which deter escalation into an all-out conflict. In the Cuban crisis, this limit was tested.... I am convinced that superior U.S. strategic power, coupled with obvious will and ability to apply this power, was the major factor that forced the Soviets to back down. Under the shelter of strategic power, which the Soviets did not dare challenge, the other elements of military power were free to exercise their full potential.

This version of strategic theory is clearly beneficial to the long-run interests of the Air Force. The Air Force's answer to the problem of how to deter minor "aggression" is to play "chicken" with the air-force-delivered general war force. Posvar's comments on the Cuban crisis,[5] though brief, are consonant with their force position. General Earle Wheeler, army chief of staff, expressed the army position in his statement:

> In my opinion, the major lesson for the Army in the Cuban situation lies in the demonstrated value of maintaining ready Army forces at a high state of alert in order to equip national security policy with the military power to permit a direct confrontation of Soviet power. As Secretary McNamara pointed out to the NATO ministers recently, "the forces that were the cutting edge of the action were the nonnuclear ones. Nuclear force was not irrelevant, but it was in the background. Nonnuclear forces were our sword, our nuclear forces were our shield." I wholeheartedly agree with this statement. In the Cuban situation, the Army forces were alerted, brought up to strength in personnel and equipment, moved and made

ready for the operations as part of the largest U.S. invasion force prepared since World War II.[6]

The Air Force interpreted limited war and limited "aggression" as capable of being deterred by strategic nuclear forces and the credibility of its threatened use, while the army viewed strategic nuclear forces alone as insufficient. The Kennedy administration clearly leaned to the latter point of view.

A circumstantial argument for the influence of strategic expertise could be made if the position of the RAND Corporation coincided with the strategic interpretation of the Air Force, its sponsor. A staff-initiated RAND study noted as early as 1957 that "in the case of a sharply limited war in Europe, tactical forces have renewed utility, with strategic Air Forces complementing tactical forces as the necessary enforcers of weapons limitations."[7] In at least a dozen other studies of limited war before the crisis, the RAND Corporation developed the same theme. Because of the strategic balance of power, "neither side could expect to use its strategic capabilities to enforce a level of violence in the local area favorable to itself." A limited war capability was needed because "we shall not be able to rely on our strategic forces to deal with limited aggressions."[8] These studies clearly supported the army doctrine on limited warfare and contributed to the estrangement of RAND and the Air Force. The Defense Department, however, became quite interested:

> In early 1962, a large contract was consummated between the RAND Corporation and the Office of the Assistant Secretary of Defense for International Security Affairs (ISA). The ISA contract involved analytic studies of a variety of defense problems, including the counterinsurgency and limited war questions, and the annual funding under the ISA contract for a two-year period amounted to over $1,000,000. The ISA contract frightened the Air Force ... because many Air Force officers felt that some of the civilians in the ISA were contemptuous of military professionalism.[9]

The standard interpretation of this complaint by the new civilian militarists (NCM) is the masking of a lack of understanding and competence in strategic theory. Air force officers correctly perceived a threat to their position in the defense establishment—a more plausible explanation. The NCM theory would similarly attribute the Air Force's failure to implement the RAND-generated expertise on limited war to a lack of understanding. This theory would not explain why bureaucratic incompetence was limited to the Air Force, and was not also a fault of the army or Defense Department. The NCM theory of expertise equates lack of enthusiasm with ignorance and incompetence. One might argue that the Air Force neglected RAND's contribution because they did not know about it; Smith's account of the implementation of the strategic bases study shows that the communication of research findings is a long and complicated process. Furthermore, this NCM objection does not explain how the army and Defense Department positions coincided with the RAND position—they knew about RAND's work. The Air Force refused to understand because RAND's expert judgment benefited the army to the detriment of the Air Force.

Implementation of policy depends not only on the validity of game theory but also on the question of who benefits. The above emphasis on conflicts within the defense establishment neglects the consensus on two articles of faith: ideological perspective which divides the world into communists and anticommunists and coercion as the only mode of intercourse between the two.

Careful perusal of the military definition of game theory reveals that gaming strategy is the "science" of coercion. Anything that is not coercive is irrational from a strategic frame of reference. Anticommunism, too, is deeply rooted in strategic analysis. A RAND study notes that if limited wars occur, "they should be looked at as a local and limited manifestation of the global struggle between Communist and the Non-Communist World."[10] These two articles of faith pervade not only the strategy community and the defense establishment but also the rest of the government involved in the crisis, so that even if the strategy community had no influence over anyone else, it is questionable whether there would be any substantial difference in policy.[11]

While this analysis has emphasized political and social aspects of gaming analogies, experts themselves often emphasize the truth and rationality of war games. As de Sola Pool puts matters:

"That is essentially policy based on social science."[12] Traditional political concerns vanish in this hygienic version of social science. The claim of truth is a powerful way to legitimize authority, but it is also an exclusive way. The claim to social science expertise renders other decision criteria illegitimate on the basis of ignorance and bureaucratic incompetence. There is also a claim that the failure to perceive the role of expertise as a weapon in the political conflict within the defense establishment and between the latter and civilian groups against militarism weakens U.S. military "posture" abroad. Thus game theory serves as an organizational weapon of military terror—even when its strategies may go awry, as in the Cuban missile crisis.

The United States used war game strategies, while the Soviet Union used conventional Marxist rhetoric. And yet the latter managed to walk away with at the very least a stalemate, and in some Soviet interpretations the full victory. In exchange for the withdrawal of long-range missiles, the Soviet Union guaranteed the long-term Soviet presence in the Western Hemisphere. It might be argued that conventional diplomacy might have netted the United States far greater results: the maintenance of diplomatic ties between Cuba and the United States. Direct negotiations with Castro rather than negotiations with the Soviets about Castro would have prevented the Soviets from maintaining a long-range presence and would not have strengthened Cuba's sense of sovereignty any more than it already is. But this would have subjected the military to pressures of a historical, geographic, and cultural variety that they reject almost instinctively. War game theory is a model of simplicity: it supplies a two-person situation—even if it does sometimes select the wrong players; it structures outcomes—even if it does leave out of the reckoning the optimal sort of outcome; it resolves problems—even if it does so by raising the ante of the problem beyond its initial worth.

The sociological explanation of the functional role of war game theory for the military is still in its infancy.[13] Only a final word need be said about the symbolic role of war game theory, namely, the comfort provided by a world of psychological neatness in which the behavior of whole nations is reducible to the decisions of a single person or small group. In this sense war game theory is the ultimate expression, not only of the military ethic but also of the elitist and etatist mentality. Yet the management of political crisis is made more complex by the new military technology. The danger is that military leaders have chosen to ignore this and respond simplistically, precisely as the world of politics and ideology grows more problematic and complicated.

The Cuban missile crisis remained throughout a conventional war game built on coercion and threat, and not a model of a game premised on a mechanism of reinforcement built on consensus and compromise. Nor am I prepared to argue the merits of the claim that consensual game models reduce to conflictual models anyhow, thus eliminating the need to study "milder" forms of game theory. Consensual models only seemed to penetrate the decision-making apparatus when some sort of stable equilibrium was reached between the Soviet Union and the United States in the post-missile crisis period. War game theory is not so much an independent input in decision making as it is a sophisticated rationalization of decisions already taken.

One elusive step further brings us to the role of war game theory as a legitimizing device for whatever crude military strategy has been decided upon. A tautological aspect emerges: If the decision to blockade Cuba is taken, war game theory is appealed to as ultimate arbiter; if the decision to lift the blockade is taken, the same appeal to war gaming is made; and since any complete holocaust would "terminate the game" and "eliminate the players," there is no real possibility of disc on firming the "theory on which the decision is ostensibly reached."

Under such a wonderful protective covering of ex post facto legitimation, and with every strategic decision confirming anew the worth of war game theory, it is extremely difficult to reach any final estimate of the theory as such. The examination of real events—particularly military retaliations—may be the clearest way open to analysts for evaluating the potency, or as is more usually the case, the paucity, of war game strategies.

What has been described belongs partly to history rather than to current politics. And this is as it should be, because when a particular strategy becomes elevated to the level of military theology, the clear and present danger to human survival soon becomes apparent. In the shock surrounding the Cuban missile crisis—the delayed awareness that the world stood still for a week while games of strategy were permitted to run their course—war game theory had its proudest moment and yet its last moment.

It was not long after the Cuban missile crisis that the "game of chicken" was abandoned in favor of conventional forms of political accommodation. This came about through the mutual realization of the Soviet Union and the United States that Cuba was not a pawn or an ace-in-the-hole, but a sovereign power in its own right. The Castro revolution was both national and hemispheric; it evolved its own brand of socialism to meet the challenges of a single-crop island economy. The Cuban regime was a system that had to be dealt with in traditional political terms of how sovereign states with differing social structures related to each other. When this dawning took place, the Cuban crisis was really solved, by surrendering the notion that this was a behavioral situation reducible to the moves and countermoves of the world's two big military powers. Yet as long as such repudiation of strategic thinking remains informal and ambiguous, the dangers in a repetition of such forms of crisis management through games of change remain ever-present. What first appeared as tragedy may return not so much as comedy, but rather as absurdity—the absurdity of total mutual annihilation.

Retrospective analysis has tended to minimize the degree to which the Cubans forged an independent or intermediary strategy in the missile crisis. This can be measured by Castro's behavior during the height of the crisis. At no time did he even hint at a compromise solution. He was quite willing to see the extermination process commence in the name of revolutionary solidarity and anti-imperial correctness. First, Castro placed Cuba on a war footing in October 22, 1962, asserting that his nation had a right to all the arms, nuclear and conventional, it thought necessary to defend itself. Second, he rejected the UN offer of U Thant to mediate the dispute and call for a halt to further work on making the launching pads for the atomic weapons operation. Finally, Castro violently rejected Premier Khrushchev's offer to negotiate on the basis of representative Scali's proposals, i.e., the U.S. offer to trade off the state of military nonintervention in exchange for Cuba as an atom-free territory.[14] Thus the erratic behavior of third "players" was extremely difficult to control, which itself helps to explain a central purpose of détente: to prevent small power adventurism through big-power management.

The effects of détente and Cuba involve very much the same parameters as the issue of deterrence and Cuba. In any international dramaturgy the essential issue is the relationship between the United States and the Soviet Union. In the brief history of Castro's Cuba, the larger relationship has always determined the smaller relationship in terms of foreign policy posture. That is why the Cuban Revolution can well be described as authenticity without autonomy; it can develop a legitimate national polity, but no corresponding international or foreign policy.

Cuba is a reflection of a special sort of barometer of the Cold War. The impulse toward détente, while clearly an effort at rationalization of the world system and universality of treatment of nations by the big two, is at the same time a special outcome of the earlier collapse of deterrence policy. The policy of deterrence which failed completely at the Bay of Pigs, was followed by a decade of isolation which can only be characterized as political immobilism. Only now is the impact of détente being extended to Cuba.

Détente with respect to Cuba is somewhat different than with respect to the Soviet Union, albeit an outgrowth of that larger condition. It signifies the end of the Monroe Doctrine in legal and military terms. The normalization of relations with an alien socialist force is something American policy makers could barely have tolerated, much less advanced, in the past. One can expect that the movement toward detente, however genuine in relation to Cuba, will be done with reserve and in a spirit of caution.

Cuban leadership has not been unduly concerned about Soviet normalization of relationships with the United States. It has derived the benefits of a break of the U.S. stronghold in the hemisphere without the necessity of altering even slightly its militant ideological postures. It can trade with U.S. firms as long as they have overseas outlets, and it can get just about any kind of supplies, medical, military, and otherwise, from every country in the hemisphere and from Europe as well. In addition, by minimizing détente, the Cubans have been able to maintain a communist support base, a feeling of constant engagement with an imperial enemy, and hence a capacity to mobilize the population to continuing economic sacrifices.

The extent to which Cuba has been able to maintain its guerrilla image can be attested to by its sending a 300-500 crack tank corps cadre to aid Syria on the Northern front during the 1973 Yom Kippur War with Israel, and again by its reputed sending of 3,000 troops to aid the Soviet-supported liberation forces in Angola. Presumably, a protracted state of détente should produce a lesser use of Cuban military forces in troubled foreign areas. However, the extraordinary degree of animosity which Castro and Cuba's leaders manifest for the United States is likely to delay any wide-ranging implementation of détente, at least on a hemispheric level.

Any genuine détente poses considerably more problems hemispherically than internationally. If U.S. problems are diplomatic, namely, admittance of heterogeneity rather than homogeneity in Western economies, admittance of the United States back into Cuba via trade-and-aid necessarily collapses the spirit of supreme militancy and anti-imperialism characterized by the rhetoric of Cuban communist leadership.

The Soviet Union probably stands to benefit the most from the new turn of events. Its constant flow of monetary and material aid to Cuba can be lessened through detente. The final chapter of the Cuban missile crisis can then be written, crowned with success that Cuba's legitimacy has been finally accepted by an American government, on terms favorable to Cuban socialist survival not deemed even remotely possible a decade ago.

From an American vantage point both deterrence and detente are not so much policies as strategies employed for limiting and isolating the Cuban communist regime, first through the whip of invasion and then through the feather of aid. Deterrence and detente are also techniques for moving Cuba back into the family of the OAS, but making Cuba appear once again as a small banana republic with a structure not unlike that of neighboring countries. The policy of isolation failed to achieve that end. The policy of detente is calculated to gain that same end. But the likelihood of a completely pacific Cuba seems presently limited.

The United States is compelled to face the existence of more than one million Cuban exiles within the shores of the United States, who function to drastically limit, if not entirely destroy, any change of policy calculated to accept Fidel Castro and the communist leadership as legitimate. The Cuban refugees are that wild card, that imponderable and irritating phenomenon that clearly confines, if not defines, American posture toward Cuba.

In a strange sense, the Cuban exiles function like the Cuban communists with respect to the Soviet Union. They limit decision-making capacities no less, albeit in a rather different way, f than the earlier policy of deterrence. What begins as a simple extension of bilateralism between the United States and the Soviet Union to rationalize their respective world empires, comes directly into confrontation with smaller variables which at the same time have an enormous sense of vested interest that cannot be easily assuaged or dissolved. One should expect a lengthy period of normalization, but at the same time, continued ideological debate between Cubans and Americans. The policy of deterrence failed to remove the Cuban communist presence. The new policy of detente has serious limits that can also lead to failure, a failure to maintain a distinction between toleration of a Cuban regime less than democratic and more than bellicose, and promotion of a foreign policy that still distinguishes between freedom and tyranny abroad and at home.

References/Notes

1. James A. Nathan, "The Missile Crisis: His Finest Hour Now," *World Politics* 27, no. 2, January 1975, p. 257.
2. Robert F. Kennedy, *Thirteen Days: A Memoir of the Cuban Missile Crisis* (New York: New American Library, Signet, 1971), pp. 30-38.
3. Cf. Richard J. Barnet, *The Economy of Death* (New York: Atheneum, 1969), pp. 84-85; and John Spanier, *Games Nations Play: Analyzing International Politics,* 2nd ed. (New York: Praeger, 1975), p. 484.
4. Curtis LeMay, *Hearings before the Committee on Armed Services, U.S. Senate, 88th Congress, 1st Session* (Washington, D.C.: Government Printing Office, 1963) pp. 888-96.
5. Wesley W. Posvar, "The Impact of Strategy Expertise on the National Security Policy of the United States," in J. Montgomery and A. Smithies (eds.), *Public Policy* 13 (Cambridge, MA: Harvard School of Public Administration, 1964).
6. Earle Wheeler, *Hearings before the Committee on Armed Services, U.S. Senate, 88th Congress, 1st Session* (Washington, D.C.: Government Printing Office, 1963), p. 507.
7. M.W. Hoag, "NATO Deterrent vs. Shield," RAND Corporation, RM1926-RC, June, 1957, p. 13; and idem, "On Local War Doctrine," RAND Corporation, p-2433, August 1961, p. 26.
8. H.A. DeWeerd, "Concepts of Limited War: An Historical Approach," RAND Corporation, 2352, November 1961, p. 17.
9. Bruce Smith, *The RAND Corporation: Case Study of a Non-Profit Advisory Corporation* (Cambridge, MA: Harvard University Press, 1966), p. 127.
10. DeWeerd, p. 17.
11. Cf. H.S. Commager, "Can We Limit Presidential Power?" *New Republic* 158, February 1968, pp. 15-18.
12. Ithiel de Sola Pool, "The Necessity for Social Scientists Doing Research for Government," in Irving L. Horowitz (ed.), *The Rise and Fall of Project Camelot: Studies in the Relationship between Social Science and Practical Politics* (Cambridge, MA: MIT Press, 1967), p. 268.
13. Cf. Philip Green, *Deadly Logic: The Theory of Nuclear Deterrence* (Columbus, OH: Ohio State University Press, 1966); and Horowitz, pp. 339-76.
14. Andrés Suárez, *Cuba: Castroism and Communism, 1959-1966* (Cambridge, MA: MIT Press, 1967), pp. 167-71.

Source and Original Title: "United States-Cuban Relations: Beyond the Quarantine." *Transaction/Society*, Vol. 6, No. 6, April 1969. Reprint (revised and expanded). "Deterrence, Détente, and the Cuban Missile Crisis." *Cuban Communism*, third edition, edited by Irving Louis Horowitz. New Brunswick, NJ: Transaction Books, 1977.

1970s: Consolidation of Communism

The second decade of Castro's rule not only entailed the consolidation of personal power but also the institutionalization of party power. This took place at the expense of the guerrilla movement and the polycentric varieties of power sources that evolved in the first phase of the Cuban dictatorship. There has been a good deal of continuing discussion of when Castro embraces Communist doctrine. In truth, given the strains of hardened policy decisions on either side, this is a secondary and perhaps never to be completely answered question—at least not until the Cuban administrative and military archives are open for examination. Of far more profound concern is how the communist apparatus, its creaky past notwithstanding, and despite the justifiable concerns Castro had of its functioning during the Batista Era, came to serve his needs far better than the disparate movement with whom he came to power. The power had that capacity because it uniquely embraced organized sources of intimidation and disposed of the need for administrative apparatus such as the bureaucracy and the professional classes as such.

Many of the essays that I wrote in that period aimed to expand on the earlier statements that sought to explain a drift toward totalitarian rule. I attempted to make clear that Castro and his close advisors were determined not to fall prey to ordinary modalities of internal corruption, or to the blandishments of foreign powers. And they were successful on both fronts. Indeed, despite the regime identification in Havana with the interests of the Soviet bloc, a certain distance also materialized. Castro envisioned himself to be superior or at least unique in doctrine and in conduct to his Soviet counterparts. He was even more certain of his doctrinal superiority to the Chinese variety of Maoism. But the ideological vortex in which he traveled was evident; Marxism-Leninism.

The Castro regime, like the earlier forms of Leninism in Russia, saw an opportunity to export its revolution, and make good the threat of Bolivarism, or some form of nationalist concordat on a hemispheric basis. Its adventures extended from Venezuela and Bolivia, and strangely enough, these bore a certain fruit in the first decade of the new century. Less satisfactory were the adventures of Cuba in Africa and the Middle East—which themselves exhibited patterns of nationalism and revolutionary behavior foreign to Cuban volunteers and no less strange in terms of the orthodox tenets of Marxism-Leninism. Still, even in such far away places, the Cuban regime constantly boasts of its support—less military these days, but no less in terms of health and welfare measures. The medical and health personnel continue to serve as the Praetorian Guard of Cuban Communism.

5

United States Policy toward Cuba in a Latin Context

United States policy toward Latin America has been discussed so often one might be led to believe a policy exists. This is more fancy than fact; while major U.S. decisions often drastically affect affairs in Latin America, they do not flow from the overall design or consistent hemispheric posture to qualify as *policy* decisions. To the contrary, the beginning of all wisdom about United States policy for the hemisphere is an awareness of the schism between action and doctrine—a schism that becomes exceedingly dangerous to both North Americans and Latin Americans precisely at the point when it is forgotten that foreign policy serves national interests and not moral imperatives.

Confusion between foreign policy and foreign aid is also rampant. The United States does engage in heavy dosages of foreign aid, at both the civilian and military levels. Whether such aid adds up: to a foreign policy is something else again. Foreign aid has served many and diverse purposes of United States interests. In the 1940s, its primary purpose was European recovery along capitalist and democratic lines. In the 1950s, foreign aid served the purposes of mutual security—this was the period during which most aid and trade pacts were negotiated with Latin American countries. In the 1960s, foreign aid was tied to the tasks of economic development, specifically to making the Development Decade successful; in Latin America this meant underwriting certain activities in the public sector to act as a countervailing force to private sector imperialism. In the 1970s, aid programs are increasingly showing signs of being linked to an improved human and physical environment. In every period it is probably correct to say that such foreign aid was more often linked to the needs of what is euphemistically termed the cosmopolitan center of the client nations than to their colonized periphery.

Justification and rationalization of foreign aid differs in each period. In the 1940s, aid was to create a world safe for capitalism. In the 1950s, it was a world safe for democracy, or at least safe from Soviet expansionism. In the 1960s, foreign aid was justified primarily by the gap between wealth and poverty or, better, by the narrow wealth band in the temperate zones surrounded on each side by a wide mass of impoverishment. And as the 1970s, unfolded it is clear that the orientation is toward problem programs rather than, national areas. For example, more attention is being directed to problems of demography and urban explosion than to overseas nations as a whole. These shifts in emphasis have all been responses to situations, not part of an overall grand plan of imperialism. In fact, so little federal programming is directed toward specific private sector needs that one must wonder whether the tasks of imperialism have not been given over, once again, to the North American corporate sector.

The Nixon Doctrine of Action for Progress for Latin America follows closely the recommendations of the Rockefeller Commission of 1970. Basically, it argues that business and private investment funds are once more to become the exclusive instrument for promoting development. After 20 billion dollars and an Alliance for Progress program that failed to alter any fundamental relationships, the foreign policy posture is turning once more to private rather than public sector solutions. However, as the Special Latin American Coordinating Commission (CECLA) made clear in its Viña del Mar meetings, the problem is neither private nor public funding, and therefore the solution is something else again. In fact, listing what CECLA holds to be the main problems makes clear that the tactic of emphasizing private sector over public sector investment simply is wide of the mark.

Among the major obstacles facing Latin America that would otherwise enable it to carry out a coherent, progressive series of reforms in economic and trade relations with the United States, CECLA lists the following: restrictions which seal off equitable or favorable access for Latin American exports to other world markets; the continuing deterioration of the volume conditions and means of international financial assistance, aggravated by the need to repay high interest rates on existing debts; imposed difficulties which impede the transfer of technology to the nations of Latin America, thus delaying the modernization of its research and development facilities; the discouragement of multinational trade and aid pacts that would break the cycle of dependence inculcated by bilateral pacts. In many ways, the United States government has avoided facing these challenges by going backward rather than forward; that is to say, by putting the entire matter of foreign aid back in the hands of entrepreneurs doing business in Latin America. The United States has abdicated what little policy leverage it once had (which was precious little indeed), and is returning the hemisphere to the source of its ills, private investors, rather than address itself to the cure of such ills.

The motivation behind what is known as United States foreign policy is complicated not only by the rising preeminence of the Third World as an independent force, but by rational decision-making itself. For example, to what degree is United States foreign policy shaped by fear of the loss of its 16 billion dollars in corporate assets throughout the Third World, and to what extent by fear of Soviet communist militancy? In the case of Latin America at least, it is clear that the investment portfolio is dominant, since the behavior of the Soviet Union has been either revisionist or counterrevolutionist. Ironically, the requirements of its own foreign policy have compelled the Soviet Union to pursue a conservative approach serving as a major brake on radical social change. But the Chinese communist movement has stepped into this void and has radicalized Latin American communist behavior in countries such as Brazil, Uruguay, and Chile.

United States foreign policy toward Latin America is not a simple one-to-one relationship, but often filtered through a grid of Soviet and Chinese aspirations on the one hand, and its own internal entrepreneurial aspirations on the other. What occurs is a conflict at the level of policymaking between military sectors which believe in the need to respond always and everywhere to socialist and communist threats; State Department sectors which tend to advocate a benign approach based upon tolerance and respect for sovereignties as long as business interests are not menaced, and Department of Defense orientations which view intervention as a subtle matter based on generating civic action and counterinsurgency programs. In short, the complexities of the world order make the various formulators of United States policy toward Latin America either substantially or downright self-contradictory.

To be sure, the end of World War II, and the Chapultepec Conference that followed, not only failed to signal the end of Latin American distrust of the United States, but brought to the surface differences buried by the war, and ended the profits Latin American businessmen made from it. Differences of opinion emerged on every major question after World War II and remained unresolved: tariff protection, foreign capital domination in Latin American enterprises, government intervention in economic affairs, the need for multilateral finance mechanisms in place of existing bilateral mechanisms. In addition, there was a strong difference of emphasis on the crucial subject of planning and the public sector.

The aim of every American president from Truman to Eisenhower to Kennedy to Johnson and, finally, Nixon has been the same: to abolish Latin American economic dependency on non-American producers and to establish Latin American dependence upon the United States. Insofar as this is a policy, the United States has a policy. But in establishing such a model of dependency certain tactical problems arose. Should the United

States base its foreign policy on an economic model of free enterprise and private property; or should it place its bets on a military model of government assistance? The private enterprise versus the military appropriations approach has become the crucial divide among U.S. policy makers interested in formulating a Latin American policy. Obviously, such problems will ever remain unresolved to the extent that Latin America has moved beyond a dependency model.

Men like Spruille Braden and John Foster Dulles institution of private property alongside religion and the ranked the family as a bulwark of civilization. Needless to add, their beliefs were translated into the cornerstones of American foreign policy. In contrast, George C. Marshall, Bernard Baruch, Will Clayton and Averell Harriman, began to note that the real problem was military control and not economic control. As the military situation tightened up throughout the Third World, the Pentagon began to win out over The Brookings Institute in forming a strategy for Latin America. Later agreements, such as the Rio Pact, began to stress the role of the military—not as an international check against communism, but as an internal check against unsponsored social change. The Bogotá Conference of 1948 went even further toward securing political concessions from Latin America in exchange for slender economic concessions from the United States.

With the emergence or re-emergence of nationalism in Bolivia in 1952, Guatemala in 1954, Cuba in 1959, the Dominican Republic in 1965, Peru and Bolivia again in 1968, and Chile in 1970, the idea of imperial military solutions or military solidarity broke down. The Latin American military increasingly became attached to middle class nationalist aspirations and decreasingly attached to overseas American commitments. As a result, Nixon's Action for Progress looks much more like the earlier Roosevelt Good Neighbor Policy emphasis on private investment and private initiative. United States foreign policy, whatever its overall consistency at the level of principles, is badly polarized at the tactical level between economic *laissez-faire* doctrine and military interventionist policies. The resolution of this policy dilemma no longer lies within the power of the United States, but rather is a function of the internal dynamics of Latin American social classes and political movements on one side and of the changing character of industrial ownership and management on the other.

The multinational corporations, although still largely dominated by United States industrial units, clearly illustrate how limited the federal foreign policy role has become. The existence of international combines in the fields of petroleum, chemistry, and electrical energy stimulates direct contacts between the corporate structures and the political leadership of Latin American nations. Venezuela sets agreements with Standard Oil, Chile deals directly with Anaconda Copper, and Peru arranges meetings with the Council for Latin America, Inc. (a collectivity of more than two hundred United States firms representing more than 90 percent of our investments in the area). The Nixon Doctrine of maintaining a "low keyed profile" in the hemisphere is directly connected to the reemergence of the entrepreneurial hard sell. Whatever this might signify in the larger context, a return to neo-isolationism or simply faith in the supremacy of capitalism, with or without democracy, it is evident that at this juncture United States foreign policy counts for considerably less than at any time in the twentieth century, or certainly since the Presidency of Herbert Hoover. In sum, the United States foreign policy clout is limited by the rise of nationalism politically and the emergence of multi-national corporativism economically.

The presumed beacon light of United States policy toward Latin America has been anti-communism. At the Tenth Inter-American Conference which met at Caracas in March 1954, the United States intervention into Guatemalan affairs was anticipated on the basis of forging "a clear cut and unmistakable policy determination against the intervention of international communism in the hemisphere." Congress later ratified intervention in the case of Guatemala on the ground of "the existence of strong evidence of intervention by the international communist movement in the state of Guatemala." Somewhat later, in August 1960, at the Foreign Ministers meeting of the Organization of American States at San José, it was noted that "all members of the regional organization are under obligation to submit to the discipline of the Inter-American system." And in January 1962, at the Punta del Este meetings of the OAS in Uruguay, this discipline was spelled out: "The adherence by any member of the Organization of American States to Marxism-Leninism is incompatible with the Inter-American system and the alignment of such a government with the communist block breaks the unity and solidarity of the hemisphere." The assertion of such broad-ranging jurisdictional rights thereby provided the rationale for unqualified intervention into the affairs of the Cuban nation, just as it had eight years earlier in Guatemalan affairs, albeit with far different consequences.

Despite the seeming ideological consistency of American hemispheric policy, the functional diversity of Latin America created deep inconsistencies at the policy level: Cuba became the first socialist regime in the hemisphere, Peru and Bolivia have now declared strong nationalist aims counter to United States policy, while the recent elections brought Allende to power thus making Chile the second avowed socialist regime in the Western hemisphere. The smashing force of political pluralization has struck the hemisphere. The United States' response was to attempt to adjust realities to its ideological posture, which in part at least accounts for American advocacy of interventionist policies. But it is extremely doubtful that the same sort of interventionist maneuvers can be maintained in this decade.

United States foreign policy with respect to Latin America remains relatively inflexible at the ideological level, and relatively accommodating at the institutional level. In Mexico, Guatemala, Cuba, the Dominican Republic, and Brazil, where efforts to end colonialism and institutionalize nationalism took place, the United States applied economic boycott, sanctions, military invasion, and defense of corporate interests.

Latin American policy toward the United States has accommodated this dangerous polarity in United States policy-making. Mexico is a bourgeois one-party state, relatively friendly but clearly nationalistic. Cuba is a peasant-proletarian one-party state, flatly hostile to the United States, nationalistic, anti-imperialistic and friendly to the Soviet Union. Chile represents a socialist front coalition, nationalistic, anti-imperialistic—but maintaining strict neutrality with respect to the United States and the Soviet Union. It shows a national policy rather than a hemispheric policy toward problems of socialist development. Argentina under Perón was a coalition between middle echelon officer corps, trade-unionist and déclassé elements. It was nationalistic, but quite ready to cooperate with the imperial powers of Europe and America by playing them off against each other. In general, then, Latin Americans have carefully avoided offending North American ideological sensibilities, but have nonetheless gone about their business without much thought to the self-declared interests of the United States.

The matter of perception and perspective is crucial. The United States has never had any but a distorted sense not only of its international priorities (witness Vietnam and Southeast Asia generally), but a drastic underestimation of Latin American nationalism. Not even the Castro Revolution seems to have shaken the American faith that Latin American nations are merely an additional 20 states. Lyndon B. Johnson in particular tended to put his arm around Latin American Presidents as if they were governors, with appropriate and respectful knee slapping, before the inevitable question: what can I do for you today—as if, dignitaries of Ecuador or Mexico are simply state representatives sent from the folks back home with petty squabbles needing arbitration.

This regional approach has always added a special dimension to the United States relationship to Latin America. Every rebellion has appeared as treason, and every unreconstructed revolutionary nationalist seemed to come across as a Robert E. Lee seeking to take his state out of the Union. In other words, the very proximity in geography and history has led to a special sort of policy-response—a response based on the assumption that what Latin American did was part of domestic policy. It has taken Castro in Cuba, Allende in Chile, and the military *golpistas* of Peru and Bolivia, to make it clear that things have changed in the Western hemisphere and in the world; and that the nations of Latin America do not wish to become part of a Statehood or Commonwealth program. Even little Puerto Rico, long a United States satrapy, is now discontented with its role as a special charge of the United States. Indeed, the very shock of recognition that Latin America, left, right or center, is not part of the United States, may finally lead to an appropriate foreign policy posture.

If the question of imperialism could be resolved by diplomatic maneuver or popular acclaim, United States interests in Latin America would long since have been eliminated. But the process of nationalizing industry raises as many problems as it resolves. First, there is the matter of compensation or direct expropriation. If it is the former, the burdens of repayment may simply not be worth the costs and, as in Chile, mixed companies might be superior. If it is the latter, the expropriating procedures might so alienate the former colonial power that it would deny the Latin American nation access to First World banking credit, cut off the supply of capital goods and technology, and in addition put pressure on the other advanced countries to deny the expropriating nation any international development loans. What adds salt to the wound is that, again as in the case of Chile, the denial of the copper yield to the United States may prove meaningless—since Chilean copper mainly supplies the needs of Western Europe and Japan. Again, just what United States foreign policy can do in such a situation is problematic—at the most it can support the claims of its own capitalist entrepreneurs or, at the least, it can work out the equitable grounds for the transition from foreign to domestic ownership of mineral wealth and factory produce.

The issues generated by United States foreign policy in and toward Latin America are of a magnitude calculated to increase frustration and ferocity, but hardly reason or relaxation. For one economist, the United States is simply the center of an imperial domain under growing pressure to be the international monopoly to formulate and implement political and economic policies which will create an attractive investment climate in Latin America and the Third World. Economic development is thus desperately pushed for by the United States as a means for seeking outlets for its economic surplus. For another economist, the promotion of economic development by the United States is one of the noblest experiments in selfless giving—an attempt to create a climate of business and industrial stability with which to ward off the thrusts of totalitarianism. Thus, foreign aid as an instrument of United States foreign policy is the most mature expression of American ethics.

What does one do with conflicting interpretations of the same events? How does one measure such factors as dependence and independence, investment made from altruistic motives and investment based on egoistic motives? The analyst of United States foreign policy is faced with the problem of two cultures: one a line of structural analysis which places the blame for Latin American underdevelopment squarely on the external variable called imperialism; the other based upon an analysis which places the blame for underdevelopment on internal variables—such as religion, traditionalism, climate, race, etc. Nor does it suffice to say that the truth is some admixture of the two—since this form of question begging does not come to terms with the existence of special problems affecting Latin American relations with the United States. If imperialism is omnipotent, why is there such a differential response country by country? If culture and sociological factors like race and religion are so powerful, why does there seem to be such a strong connection between the problems of Latin America as a whole and the penetration of United States capital. In other words, the answers given seem to be a function of the interests of the examiner more than intrinsic to the nature of what is being examined.

There is a widespread belief that United States foreign policy toward Latin America is both more rigorous and more extensive than it is toward other parts of the Third World. The argument claims that there is a special tutelary relationship between the United States and Latin America, and hence a much tougher stance toward our hemispheric neighbors than toward other areas. This is not entirely true. What does in fact exist is a tough corporate policy of American giants of industry toward Latin America. That is to say, after years of struggle against foreign corporate interests, the United States has emerged as the strongest of foreign investors in the private sector. General Motors has ousted Fiat and Peugeot in the automobile sector; Pratt & Whitney has ousted Rolls Royce in the aircraft engine market, Ford-Philco dominates the television field over Phillips of the Netherlands, Colgate-Palmolive Peet is supreme in the bathroom supply field, etc.

These United States corporate interests were powerful long before the United States forged a unified policy toward the Latin Americans. Thus, the federal foreign policy sector has become the tail being wagged by the corporate dog. If there is precious little to United States foreign policy in general, its absence in Latin America is downright notorious. At every turn, United States policy has been dictated to and overruled by its own corporate interests: oil interests in Mexico dictated United States foreign policy to the point of collapsing the Good Neighbor policy of the New Deal period. International Telephone and Telegraph, incensed over attempts to expropriate its interests in Brazil, promoted an intense United States hostility toward the Goulart regime. Similarly, the Anaconda and Kennecott copper interests have done more to dissuade the United States government from establishing friendly relations with the new Chilean regime than any other single factor. What we have then of a foreign policy is more the creature of private corporations than of federal authorities.

What makes the relationship between the United States and Latin America unique and foreign policy parity so difficult is that the United States is dealing with people, many of whom identify more strongly with the Western World rather than a Third World syndrome. The interests of Latin America, Asia and Africa coincide far less frequently than revolutionary rhetoric would imply. To say that they all suffer from imperialism and colonialism is simply insufficient; especially if imperialism is itself a differential response revealing changing tactical requirements.

With a long tradition of constitutionalism, bourgeois economic control, ultra-nationalistic quests and countervailing demands for: world power, Latin America today is far from the responsive mechanism it once was. Whether we are dealing with bourgeois or socialist regimes, democratic or undemocratic regimes, Latin America displays a much more powerful clustering of nations, a more forceful presentation of national self-interests, than do other parts of the Third World, Moreover, the continuing warfare of the United States on Southeast Asia has had the uniform effect of hardening attitudes and of making it clear somehow that the age of gunboat diplomacy has seen its last. The United States which only managed to gain a military draw in Korea in the 1950s and was defeated in Vietnam in the 1960s can hardly expect acquiescence from even the most subservient Latin American regime. Indeed, the very bottleneck that Vietnam represents for the United States has merely served to underscore the absence of an overall United States policy; an overextended approach to the Asian conflict has necessarily shrunk its commitment to Latin America.

There is a vocabulary of motives that divides Latin America from the United States that no amount of revision in foreign policy on either side can or will remove. What, for the United States, is the containment of communism is, for most Latin American governments, pure and simple intervention. What the United States sees as dangerous tendencies toward socialism as a result of expropriation, for Latin Americans may simply be a half-way house of nationalization of basic industry. What for the United States is a matter of assistance is for Latins containment and even intervention. A further complication is whether Latin Americans want the products and results of development or control of the actual process for gaining development. More simply: do Latin Americans prefer first rate pots and pans, to second rate products of domestic manufacture? Is national production and national pride the key to a revision of attitudes, and hence the basis of a foreign policy posture?

Such questions are beyond the scope of empirical answer. Any powerful nation, whatever its motivations, will be hard put to convince the recipients of aid or trade of the special nobility that permits one nation to be in a superordinate role, while 20 nations remain in a subordinate role. There is a sense in which the fundamentals of social psychology rather than the fundamentals of economics hold the key to foreign policy and its reception elsewhere. What we are dealing with is the undulation of power and discontent, of superordinate and subordinate relationships. And it is hard to deny the conclusion that as long as nations behave as surrogate persons, assuming the characteristics of power and powerlessness, no complete resolution of the policy questions can occur.

Once again, we must understand that the problem is one of perception: can any small or medium sized nation feel secure and in a condition of equity when confronted by a super-power such as the United States? Can any set of actions or pronouncements be greeted with anything less than universal suspicion? I rather suspect that the emotive drive behind the charges of imperialism stem, in considerable part, not from the conduct of specific policies, but from the implicit clout behind the nation asserting its priorities. In this, we have ample precedent, not just ill the history of European colonies; but in the present period as well. There is Cuba's hostility to China; Algeria's response to France; Rhodesia's response to England; and Yugoslavia's response to the Soviet Union. It is not that red oppression does not exist. The outbursts of small powers against big powers are often based on hard fact. The main point is that as long as super-powers exist, to that degree will resentments based on disequilibrium of power and wealth remain a constant fact of political contact between nations.

Source and Original Title: "United States 'Policy' in Latin America." *New Politics,* Vol. 9, No. 1, Whole No. 33, Spring 1970, pp. 74-83.

6

Capitalism, Communism, and Multinationalism

A well-known party is looking for revolutionary ideas may come as a surprise, but the communists are no longer claiming they've invented every good idea under the sun. On the contrary, they're eagerly hoping that Westerners may have invented a few before them. The fact is that the communists—in particular the East Europeans—are building a broad consumer society. They're in a hurry. And they're in the market for advanced technology that East European countries need; you could work out some highly profitable arrangements. Sell technology to the communists? Can it even be done? The answer is that today it finally can be done, and is being done. In fact, over the past couple of years, major American corporations have been doing it with increasing frequency. Naturally, the technology must be non-strategic. Exactly how do you go about it? You go about it with infinite patience. As you can imagine, selling American technology in Eastern Europe is a highly complex economic, political and technical problem. Obviously, it's absolutely crucial to develop the right contacts and the right communication. That's where we, World Patent Development Corp. come in. For years now, we've maintained close technological contacts with the proper governmental agencies in all East European countries. Because of our unique position, we've been able to locate markets and negotiate licensing agreements for the sale of almost every kind of technology. Conversely, we're also presiding over the transfer of East European technology to the West. In fields ranging from synthetic copolymers to pollution control equipment. From advanced textile equipment to natural cosmetics.

The preceding ad, placed by the World Development Corporation in the *New York Times* (October 1, 1972), is a far cry from Cold War rhetoric; and helps place in perspective the obvious thaw *cum* rapprochement reached between Nixon and Kissinger for the American side and Brezhnev and Kosygin for the Soviet side. For the emergence of the multinational corporation is the paramount economic fact of the present epoch, and helps to explain current trends in the political sociology of world relations.

The struggle for supremacy between capitalism and communism has been the overriding ideological posture of the twentieth century. Now, however, the struggle has been broken by two developments: first, the rise of a Third World in Africa, Asia and Latin America, accompanied by a pluralization of economic forms, political systems and social doctrines; and second, the rise of multinational corporations which are primarily loyal to industrial growth and financial profitability, rather than to any-one national regime. Multinationalism has had an extraordinary impact on relations between capitalist and socialist states, taking us beyond a model premised on a showdown struggle between old capitalism and new communism.

The Nature of Multinationalism

Definitions of the term "multinational corporation" vary. Nonetheless, there is general agreement on the following operational guidelines:

- Multinationals are corporations that operate in at least six foreign nations.
- Multinationals are corporations whose foreign subsidiaries account for at least 10 to 20 percent of its total assets, sales or labor force.
- Multinationals have annual sales or income of more than $100 million (which effectively reduces the number of firms we are dealing with

to about 200, of which roughly 75 percent are primarily affiliated
with the United States).
* Multinationals have an above-average rate of growth and profit
  margins when measured against exclusively national firms.
* Multinationals are found most often in high technology industries,
  specifically those that devote a high proportion of their resources
  to research, advertising and marketing.

Many firms, such as Singer Sewing Machines, National Cash
Register, Unilever, General Motors and others, have been conducting overseas business for many years; it is, however, the
fusion of these older firms with more basic (high-level-technol-
ogy-producing) industrial firms, such as Xerox Corporation,
International Business Machines, British Petroleum, Phillips of
the Netherlands, International Nickel and others that has tipped
the balance within them from national to international corporate
participation. Since each of these giants of industry reveals annual sales that exceed the individual gross national product of all
except several dozen nations, the political and economic power
they wield is obviously potent, although highly diffuse.

That which is new about multinationals can be summarized
as follows. Firms which in the past maintained classical imperial
relations, that is, imported raw materials and exported finished
commodity goods at superprofits, have new arrangements,
forced partially because the old system was so limited that the
masses were barred from participation and reacted accordingly.
National liberation and socialist movements of various types and
structures simply invalidated the classical mode of colonialism.
Now multinational firms share research and development findings and patent rights distribution; manufacture in the economic
periphery at lower costs rather than producing the same goods in
the cosmopolitan center (which has the additional payoff of quiet-
ing nationalist opposition); develop profit-sharing arrangements
between local firms and foreign firms, which involve training and
tooling. Beyond that, one finds a reverse multinationalism, one
based on raw materials rather than on finished goods. Thus, the
oil-rich countries of the Arab Middle East form a bargaining col-

lective to do business directly with major oil companies of the West. National governments, such as the Arab oil states, joined by Venezuela, Iran, Nigeria, Indonesia, and other members of OPEC, barter and bargain with private-sector multinationals like the powerful oil corporations of America and Western Europe, thus bypassing governmental agencies of the big powers.

What is new about the multinational is not simply the transcendence of the nation-state boundaries to do business, an old ploy of corporations in wealthy nations but, more profoundly, a reduction in profits through increased payment of high prices for raw materials (like petroleum) and the acceptance of lower prices and hence less profit for finished manufactured goods (such as automobiles). This is the aspect of multinationals which most sharply points to the need for a modification of classical and new forms of Marxism-Leninism alike, since the very essence of politics as a reflection of national and economic exploitation is reversed. What we have now is economics as a managed, manipulated form of political exploitation and domination.

The multinationals help to bridge the gap between revolutionary nationalism and establishment internationalism by acquiescing to the symbolic demands of nationalists and revolutionists, while satisfying the very real economic demands of the conservative middle-sector elements in Third World societies.

Buying of Western Capitalism by Eastern Socialism

The post-World War II thrust of nationalism prevented any undue optimism about the capacity of socialism to triumph as a world system and as an international ideology. So intense did nationalist sentiments become in Third World areas of Asia, Africa and Latin America that the Soviets, after much hesitation, had to readjust their policy and ideology, and finally recognize a third way, something more than capitalism and less than socialism; a cross between a Keynesian economic mechanism and a Leninist political machinery. But in that act of recognition, the dream of an international proletarian revolution, with or without a Soviet vanguard, gave way to more parochial dreams of peoples' democracy and socialist republics that would no more dare try to transcend nationalist sentiments than would the older capitalist regimes in Western Europe. Between 1945 and 1970, the nationalist thrust profoundly diminished belief in a socialist utopia.

When internationalism finally did make its move, it did so in corporate rather than proletarian guise. The multinational corporation, pointing to an international brotherhood of the bourgeoisie and the bureaucracy, to a transcendent class loyalty beyond the national aspirations of even the United States or other principal capitalist social systems, discredited the socialist utopia no less than had the earlier nationalist phase. The multinationals offered a basket of commodity goods that the socialist states, no less than the Third World states, desire. The relative ease with which such multinationals of the capitalist sector penetrated the societies and economies of the socialist sector stands in marked contrast to the difficulties involved in concluding the most elemental treaty arrangements between East and West at the policy and political level. Doing things in a businesslike way has become as much a touchstone for rational efficiency in the Soviet Union as in the United States. The culture of multinationalism permeated Eastern Europe and the Soviet Union long before the actual economic penetration, with the mass consumer demands of the Soviet public following the Stalinist period. Multinationalism like nationalism in an earlier era, has stymied the socialist utopia, at the very same time that it has improved the commodity conditions of the socialist nations.

One need only consider the extensive trade agreements reached between the United States and the Soviet Union in September 1972, to gauge the velocity and the extent of multinational penetration. Not only do these trade agreements solve fiscal imbalances by intensifying internal shortages; they also place both major powers in a financial mosaic that can hardly be described in conventional terms of capitalism or socialism. As *U.S. News and World Report* indicated,

White House adviser Henry Kissinger, negotiating in Moscow between September 11 and 14, achieve substantial progress in trade talks with the Soviet Union.... On September 14, the U.S. Department of Agriculture confirmed a private sale of 15 million bushels of American wheat to Communist China, the first to that nation in many years. A few days earlier, the Boeing Company announced sale of 10 of its 707 jetliners to the Red Chinese for 125 million dollars in cash. The chairman of Occidental Petroleum Corporation, Armand Hammer, said in Moscow on September 14 that details of the trade pact his firm had signed in June with the Soviet Union were being arranged. Among other things under consideration, said Mr. Hammer, were sales of chemical fertilizers and construction of a 70-million-dollar U.S. trade center in the Russian capital, complete with a 400-room hotel ... reports from Moscow indicate that the overall trade agreement now being negotiated could increase business between the two countries to as much as 5 billion dollars a year by 1977. At present, U.S.-Russian trade amounts to about 220 million dollars annually. That figure, however, does not include around a billion dollars in purchases by the Russians of American grain in recent weeks.... Agreement also was reported near on a maritime pact that would guarantee to U.S. and Russian merchant ships at least a one-third share each of the cargoes involved in the billion-dollar grain sale to Russia.

The question then becomes: Can the Soviet Union maintain its basic commitment to production development rather than to consumption modernization in the face of foreign business penetration? Obviously, the Russians and to a lesser degree the Chinese think the answer is affirmative, However, the inexorable logic of consumer orientations is toward satisfying utilitarian needs of a social sector able to pay, rather than delaying such gratifications in favor of long-range moral goals of economic equality at home, and certainly rather than fulfilling ambitious political goals of national liberation abroad.

The political potential of multinationals, even those dominated by the United States, is revealed by their use in East European nations like Rumania and Hungary. One finds Pepsi-Cola Corporation, Hertz Rent-a-Car Agencies, Pan American and ITT-supported hotels in the center of Bucharest, and of course the most conspicuous multinationals in such a country, Western-dominated commercial airlines. This serves a double purpose: it permits Rumania to become the Switzerland of the East—the meeting place of Chinese, Russians, Israelis, Arabs and others, and it also weakens the socialist doctrine of development as a unique function of bootstrap industrialization. There can be no doubt that a number of East European regimes (Yugoslavia, Rumania and Poland, in particular) are fully aware of both the risks and possibilities in multinationalism.

Such firms, which do business on a licensing basis in East Europe, open up channels of communication to the West. If the socialist republic's dependence on the Soviet Union is lessened more symbolically than in reality, it nonetheless has the effect of displaying the physical presence of the West in Eastern Europe, It also permits higher numbers of international conferences at which Westerners participate and interact with participants from China and the Soviet Union, In short, the multinational firm provides a much-needed meeting place for the East Social- ist bloc; a place where Israelis, Albanians, Russians and Chinese interact freely and to the greater benefit of the open-ended social- ist regime. In the East European setting, national sovereignty is strengthened rather than weakened by the existence of the multi- national corporations. This is, of course, at considerable variance with the impact of multinationals in a Western European context. For example, the combined power of Dutch multinationals (Royal Dutch Shell, Unilever, KLM Airlines, Phillips) is much stronger than the standard vehicles of political life in the Netherlands. Holland shows how national sovereignty can be weakened rather than strengthened by multinationalism.

Raymond Vernon, in *Sovereignty at Bay: The Multinational Spread of U.S. Enterprises*, has indicated his own belief that labels of socialism will do as much to promote as to dissuade multina- tionals from penetrating the socialist and Third World sphere.

The fact that many less-developed countries associate themselves with some form of socialism needs no detailed documenting. The number may even have increased somewhat in the course of time. It is not clear, however, just what that espousal means for the role of the multinational enterprise. During recent years, several genuinely socialist countries have been exercising enormous ingenuity to find a way of assigning a role to foreign-owned enterprises in their economies. The Yugoslavs, of course, have moved furthest in this direction; by 1970, foreign-owned enterprises were in a position to negotiate for rights that were the de facto equivalent of those available in such non-socialist states as Mexico or Brazil.

Many other less-developed countries—for example, Pakistan, Tunisia, and Iraq—though committed to socialism of some sort, have nevertheless cultivated a certain deliberate ambiguity over the future position of multinational enterprises in their economies. As India edges her way toward national identification with socialism, it is not at all clear that the country's policies toward foreign investors will grow any more restrictive. Besides, the actual shift of less-developed countries toward state ownership of the means of production has not been irrevocable-witness the cases of Indonesia and Ghana. Neither is it clear that the countries that do not yet see the future in these terms will eventually make the shift. Mexico, with her abiding coalition of local big business, bureaucracy, and a single party of ambiguous ideology, seems as likely a model as Guinea; Yugoslavia, with her bent for improvisation and pragmatism, seems no less likely a model of the future than Cuba.

The idea of a single world market has so deeply permeated Soviet socialism, that the Soviet Union is now in the position of accepting as part of its own economic codebook the rules on any given day of the much-reviled free market economy. The recent "wheat deal" between the superpowers indicates an increasing sophistication by Soviet "business" in these areas of market management and manipulation. Twenty Soviet buying teams negotiated independently and without any apparent coordination, yet the actual high level of commercial orchestration enabled the Soviet Union both to fulfill an agrarian internal need for wheat, and to buy a low-cost surplus for high-profit resale on the world market. In this way the Soviets have become part of the "paper economy"—for the wheat deal involves the movement of money no less than the transfer of a basic crop.

The Soviets have done as well in the area of natural gas as in wheat negotiations. In 1966, they negotiated with Iran to purchase gas that had previously been flared off in the fields because there was no market for it. In turn, the Iranians received Soviet financing and assistance to construct the necessary pipelines and associated equipment as well as a steel mill. While the Iranians gained a valuable steel plant, the Soviets began negotiating its sale of the Iranian gas to both East and West European nations.

These deals culminated in sales equal to the total Iranian gas supply. The Soviet purchase price from Iran for the natural gas was 19 cents per thousand cubic feet, while its sale price was nearly double that price, or 37 cents. This deal, profitable as it was to the Soviets, was equally advantageous for the United States, who without this gas arrangement, would have had to pay 87 cents per thousand cubic feet to Algeria for such gas purchases, or similarly high prices to Middle East nations in the near future. The rise of sophisticated multinational dealings across East-West boundaries clearly services the major powers at the expense of Third World nations.

Huge trading blocs for shares of corporations are now developing. This gradual emergence of a single world market for securities rationalizes relationships between East and West. The increasing concentration of capital in the West permits a movement from multinational corporation to an interrelated fiscal network which readily connects up to the Soviet interrelated fiscal network.

Selling of Eastern Socialism to Western Capitalism

The fundamental antagonism within the socialist bloc has been the development of an industrial society without a corresponding modernized society. The Soviet Union can mount trips to outer space, but cannot satisfy consumer demands for automobiles; it can launch supersonic jet aircraft; but cannot supply the accoutrements of personal satisfaction to make such travel enjoyable. It can mass-produce military hardware, but cannot individualize stylistic consumer components. In every aspect of socialist society, the duality between industrialism and modernism has emerged as a central factor. In this the socialist sector is the opposite of the Third World where modernization is purchased at the cost of development, where production is increased with relatively low technology inputs, and product is exchanged for commodity goods produced in the advanced capitalist sector. Both the Second World (socialist nations) and Third World need and want consumer goods from the First World (capitalist nations). The Third World pays for such consumer goods with agrarian goods, while the Second World wants to pay for such consumer goods with industrial products.

The lessening of tension since the end of the Stalin era in 1952 has taken the form of opening consumption valves in the Soviet Union, consequently maintaining tight political, statist controls. The assumption was that: as the valves were opened wider, and as more demands for immediate consumer gratification were met, the stability of the socialist bureaucratic regimes would also increase. So far, this theory has proven correct. Protest in the socialist bloc has been limited to a narrow stratum, of intellectuals who have been declared malcontents or madmen in the face of the general satisfaction of consumer demands of ordinary people. Whatever the long-term secular trends may be, and whatever the consequences to socialist legitimacy and class interests, the fact remains that consumer orientations have worked. Multinational penetration must therefore be seen as part of a general commitment of the Soviet leadership to political quietude through economic gratitude.

The most obvious commodity that the Soviets have to sell is not agrarian products, and certainly not consumer goods—both of which are in profoundly short supply within the socialist orbit. However, it does have a high technological sophistication, built up over more than 50 years of emphasis on industrialization at the expense of nearly every other economic goal. To an increasing degree, American companies looking for ways to reduce costs in their own research and development are buying the latest Soviet technology. The trend is most apparent in the metallurgy field.

Since consumer goods are purchased largely through Western-dominated multinationals, the character of international banking communism has drawn closer to international banking capitalism, in short to the essence of banking principles, profits from interest on loans secured by equity arrangements. Coming into existence is a banking network that has the capacity to rationalize multinational exchanges. Banking capitalism links up with banking socialism precisely because banks are involved in similar international activities and investment in profitable enterprises. In the absence of direct industry-to-industry contacts, given East-West structural constraints at the manufacturing level, the banking system is the fluid which pumps life into an East-West economic detente. This detente permits arms reduction negotiations to take place in an atmosphere of political entente cordiale.

Fusion of Capitalism and Socialism as Social Science Ideology

The multinationalist framework has already demonstrated a cultural impact on an East-West accommodation beyond any level reached in the past. Led by the United States and the Soviet Union, scientific academies of a dozen nations have set up a "think tank" to seek solutions to problems created by industrialization and urbanization of societies. Such problems as pollution control, public health and overpopulation are to be studied by an International Institute of Applied Systems Analysis with overseas headquarters in Vienna, Austria. Even the broad composition of this new knowledge industry reflects multinational thinking: Its director will be a professor of managerial economics at Harvard, and its council chairman will be a member of the Soviet Academy of Sciences, Jerman M. Gvishiani, the son-in-law of Premier Aleksei N. Kosygin. In this remarkable display of East-West fusion, representatives from Czechoslovakia, Bulgaria, Poland and East Germany will be joined by representatives of Japan, Canada, Great Britain, West Germany and Italy. The director of the program, Dr. Howard Raiffa, indicated that the accumulated findings of management techniques, particularly as these have evolved in the aerospace industry, would be applied to a wide variety of health and welfare problems in Eastern Europe. This international think tank will be technocratic and non-ideological in nature; in short, the perfect cultural and educational coefficient to the rise of a multinational framework.

The rise of a multinational cultural apparatus has been made possible by the widening exchange of contact between scientists, scholars and performers from East and West alike. Underneath such widening contacts, in reality its presupposition has been the declining fervor of ideology. Both Marxism and Americanism have yielded to considerations of efficiency and effectiveness and have cooperated in a vigorous effort to provide methodological guidelines that will provide accurate and exchangeable data. The new technology, with its potential for simultaneous translation and rapid publication, has also served to bring East and West together. This coalescence occurs precisely in areas of intellectual activities relatively uncontaminated by inherited ideological sore points. Hence it is that such diverse subjects as futurism, computer technology and machine learning by virtue of their newness permit widening contact points. Of course it is precisely these areas that are most significant from the viewpoint of multinationalist exchanges of goods and services.

Reemergence of Proletarian Internationalism as a Function of Multinationalism

The strangest, or certainly the least anticipated, consequence of the multinational corporation is the reappearance of militant unionism. The emergence of worker resistance to the multinationalist attempt to seek out the cheapest supply of labor as well as raw materials, wherever they are available, is still in an infant stage, but clearly on the rise. High-paid West German optical workers must compete against low-paid workers from the same industries in Eastern Europe. Auto workers in Western Europe find themselves competing against workers in Latin America producing essentially the same cars. Chemical plants of wholly owned U.S. subsidiaries are put up in Belgium and England, to capitalize on the cheaper wage scales of European chemical workers and to gain greater proximity to retail markets. Even American advertising agencies are protesting the manufacture of commercials in Europe. Such stories can be repeated for every major multinational firm and every nation.

One can well appreciate the rationale offered by the multinationals. They can take advantage of the protectionist system of closed markets in the United States while pursuing an antiprotectionist approach for trading abroad. They can thereby derive the payoffs of having the American workers as a customer at high price, while employing overseas workers at low wages. Investment abroad is also a way to get beyond antitrust laws that apply fully within the United States but scarcely at all in other countries.

This new situation, whatever the merits or demerits of the rationalizing capacity of multinationals, has created a partially revivified working class that, in contrast to earlier periods, shows greater class solidarity than cross-class national solidarity. Certainly, in the major wars of the twentieth century, the working classes have lined up solidly behind nationalism and patriotism; and in so doing have frustrated just about every prediction made on their behalf by left-wing intellectuals. Now, precisely at the moment when so much left-oriented rhetoric has itself become infused with an anti-working-class bias, we bear witness to the emergence of proletarian militance, this time as a function of self-interest rather than lofty ideology.

The organization of working-class life is still along national lines; but when confronted with middle-class internationalism, as represented by the multinationals, it must either create new trade union mechanisms or revitalize old and existing ones. According to Gus Tyler,

> foreign resentment against U.S. multinationals flares up most dangerously when these corporations do to the workers of other countries what they have been doing to American workers all along: shut down a plant for company reasons. Within two weeks, General Motors closed down a plant with 685 employees in Paris, because of Italian competition, and Remington Rand closed down a plant with 1,000 employees to relocate in Vienna. The French government—then under Charles de Gaulle—decided to get tough with the U.S. multinationals; so GM opened a plant in Belgium instead of France and proceeded to ship the product into France—duty free.

It is intriguing to note how a relatively insular trade union movement such as the British Trades Union Congress has vigorously responded to multinationals as a threat. It has put forth demands for making union recognition a precondition for setting up foreign subsidiaries in the United Kingdom; and likewise to have organizations such as the Organization for Economic Co-operation and Development serve as an agency for funneling and channeling working-class demands on wider multinationals.

While British responses have been legalistic and proffered through government agencies. European workers on the mainland have become more direct and forthright in their dealings, engaging in strike actions and corporate lockouts led by international unions. According to John Gennard,

> The International Federation of Chemical and General Workers Union has acted as a coordinating body for different unions in various countries in negotiations with St. Gobain, a French-owned glass manufacturing multinational. Some success for international action coordinated through International Trade Secretariats has been achieved; for example: In 1970, strikers at May and Baker, a British subsidiary of Rhone-Poulenc, won a 16 percent pay rise "largely due to large-scale international intervention" at the company's French headquarters and at other May and Baker plants in the Commonwealth. Peugeot workers in Founee threatened a 15 minute stoppage in 1968 to back 1,000 workers suspended in an Argentinean subsidiary. After two days, the company agreed to take back nearly all the suspended workers.

This renewed working-class activity has had a stunning effect on East-West trade union relations. It is axiomatic that socialism does not tolerate or permit strikes since, in the doctrine of its founders, socialism is a workers' society, and a strike against the government is a strike against one's own interest. That such reasoning is a palpable hoax has never been denied, and the leaders of Poland, Hungary and other East European states have become quite sensitized to such mass pressure from below. Yet the impact of this reasoning is that strike actions have been rare, and met most often with repressive measures. The concept of working-class international action between laborers in "capitalist" and "socialist" countries has been virtually non-existent. Nevertheless, such is the force of multinationalism that even these deep political inhibitions are dissolving. We may be entering an era of working-class collaboration across systemic lines, perhaps resembling the coalescence between the bourgeois West and bureaucratic East.

Several important features of this special variant of proletarian internationalism must be distinguished. (1) It cuts across national lines for the first time in the twentieth century. (2) It cuts across systemic lines, being less responsive to Cold War calls for free labor or socialist labor than at any time in the post-World War II period. (3) The vanguard role in this effort is being assumed by the workers in the better paid and better organized sectors of labor; in the specialized craft sector more than the assembly-line industrial sector. (4) While new mechanisms are being created to deal with multinational corporations, the more customary approach is to strengthen the bargaining position of available organizations, such as the International Metal Workers Federation and the International Federation of Chemical and General Workers Unions.

What we have, then, is intensification of class competition, but on a scale and magnitude vastly unlike the conventional national constraints. It is still difficult to demonstrate or to predict whether such class struggles can be as readily resolved short of revolution in the industrial areas as the previous epoch was resolved in the national areas. In effect, if Marxism as a triumphal march of socialism throughout the world has thoroughly been discredited, it manages to rise, phoenix-like, out of the bitter ashes of such disrepair. The intensification of class struggles at the international level remains muted by the comparative advantages of multinationalism to countries like Japan and the United States. But if such comparative advantages dissolve over the long pull of time (and this is beginning to happen as less developed nations play catch-up), then the quality of class competition might well intensify.

The Theory of Big Power Convergence and Multinational Realities

Multinationalism has served to refocus attention on the theory of convergence that set of assumptions which holds that over time, the industrial and urbanizing tendencies of the

United States and the Soviet Union will prevail over systemic and ideological differences, and form a convergence, or at least enough of a similitude to prevent major grave international confrontations.

The evidence for the convergence theory has been generally made much stronger by the rise of multinationals. Without entering into an arid debate about whether capitalism and socialism can remain pure and noble if this can take place, the empirics of the situation are clear enough: the United States (whatever its economic system can be called) and the Soviet Union (whatever its system can be called) have shown a remarkable propensity to fuse their interests at the economic level and collapse their differences at a diplomatic level, for the purpose of forming a new big power coalition that dwarfs the dreams of Metternich for a United Europe in the nineteenth century. Indeed, we now have a situation in which the doctrine of national self-interest has been fused into one of regional and even hemispheric areas of domination by the two major world superpowers.

The issue of systemic convergence is certainly not new. The existence of commonalities between the major political and economic powers has long been evident. Geographical size, racial and religious similitudes, even psychological properties of the peoples of the United States and the Soviet Union, all conspire to fuse American and Soviet interests. What has been in dispute is whether such root commonalities would be sufficient to overcome long-standing differences in the economic organization of society, ideological commitments and political systems of domination. This argument remained largely unanswered and unanswerable as long as the mechanism, the lever, for expressing any functional convergence remained absent. The unique contribution of multinationalism to the debate over convergence between the major superpowers is precisely its functional rationality; its place in contemporary history as the Archimedean lever lifting both nations out of the Cold War. Multinationals take precedence over political differences in prosaic but meaningful ways. They serve to rationalize and standardize international

economic relationships. They demand perfect interchangeability
of parts; a uniform system of weights and measurements; common auditing languages for expression of world trade and commerce; standard codes for aircraft and airports, telephonic and
telegraphic communications; and banking rules and regulations
that are adhered to by all nations. Convergence takes place not
so much by ideological proclamation (although there has even
been some of this) but primarily by organizational fiat; that is, by
seeming to hold ideological differences constant, while rotating
every other factor in international relations.

Multinationalism has played a major role in breaking the Cold
War struggle between capitalism and socialism. Indeed, doing so
has profoundly lessened the bargaining power of smaller nations
vis-à-vis the superpowers. The position of radical states such as
Cuba must find their way by navigation rather than emphasizing
autonomy. They are forced to choose big power allies on an essentially pragmatic basis, but they cannot simply claim a special
status as a Third World leader. But whatever problems this leaves
in its wake for smaller nations, this movement toward consensus
between East and West at least makes possible a more realistic
international political climate.

Pax Americana Plus Pax Sovietica:
The Politics of Multinationalism

The politics of multinationalism is not so much an illustration
of convergence as it is an example of pragmatic parallelism. Michael Harrington points out that, underlying the Nixon-Kissinger
position, there is a shared metaphysical belief that the division
of the world is both necessary and desirable.

> Internationally, then, Nixonism has a profoundly conservative, shrewd yet
> utterly flawed approach. It seeks a Metternichian arrangement among the
> superpowers, capitalist and communist, according to which change would
> be relegated to controllable channels. In pursuit of this goal it is, unlike the
> moralistic policy of Dulles, willing to strengthen the power of its enemies
> if only they will accept the model of a global equilibrium. Nixonism is rhe-
> torically dedicated to the virtues of the global division of labor but actually

committed to utilizing America's state power to socialize the enormous advantage of our corporations on the world market.... Capitalist collectivism, in other Words, wants to make a deal with bureaucratic collectivism to preserve the status quo.

Edward Weisband and Thomas M. Frank, aside from assigning causal priority to this doctrine to the West, assert nonetheless the similitude of the Brezhnev approach toward peaceful coexistence as big-power sovereignty over smaller areas.

> The Brezhnev doctrine, which continues to govern the policies of the Warsaw Pact governments, to some degree represents a tradeoff or division of the world by the Soviet Union and the United States into spheres of influence or "regional ghettos." Not that our policy makers in Washington planned it that way: little or no evidence has been adduced to show that the U.S. government ever willfully intended to trade control over Latin America for recognition of absolute Soviet dominance over Eastern Europe. Nor can it be said that any actions we have taken in relation to Latin America are the same as Russia's brutal suppression of Czechoslovakia.... What we do wish to assert is that virtually every concept of the Brezhnev doctrine can be traced to an earlier arrogation of identical rights by the United States *vis-à-vis* Latin America ... it is important to realize that the search for new norms in the world must begin with a clear understanding that we, as much as the Russians, bear responsibility for conceptualizing the Brezhnev norms.... In the Soviet view, regional determination and prerogatives take precedence over those of the international community including the United Nations.

Curiously enough, the connection between international politics and the rise of multinationalism was not clearly articulated, even by the above prescient commentators on international affairs. Lesser analysts seem to prefer to think of the new Nixonism as some sort of magical mystery tour; a transformation of high spiritual beliefs into policy matters. My contention is that the current foreign policy initiatives of Henry Kissinger derive precisely from a new American policymaking realization of changes in corporate relationships as necessitating an end to the Cold War, and establishing a new detente based on economic realities. Throughout 1972 President Nixon clearly articulated such a geopolitical realignment based on economic realities.

As early as January 1972 Nixon articulated the point of view which he sustained on his diplomatic initiatives in Moscow and Peking.

We must remember that the only time in the history of the world that we had any extended periods of peace is when there has been a balance of power. It is when one nation becomes infinitely more powerful in relation to its potential competitor that the danger of war arises. So I believe in a world in which the United States is powerful. I think it would be a safer world and a better world if we have a strong, healthy United States, Europe, Soviet Union, China, and Japan, each balancing the other, not playing one against the other, an even balance.

The peculiar linkage is China, since it alone has yet to participate fully in the multinational system. Further, it can be said to be by far the poorest of the countries with which power balance has to be sought. But with that admittedly crucial exception, and this can be argued to be a requirement of political tradeoff preventing an undue Soviet impact on the Western world and an undue Japanese presence in the Eastern world, what Nixon has outlined is quite clearly the politics of multinationalism, and not of capitalism triumphant or socialism defeated. The trade and aid agreements between East and West during this period serve to confirm the accuracy of this appraisal. Even China is entering the multinational race with its increased sale of specialized consumer goods to the United States and its purchase from Boeing Aircraft of an international fleet of advanced jets.

This new Metternichian arrangement among the superpowers is precisely a repudiation of the earlier moral absolutism of anticommunism and anticapitalism. In a sense, and one step beyond an acknowledged end of the Cold War, is the fact that such a geopolitical redistribution also serves to solve a major problem of the multinational corporation, its transcendence of the limits and encumbrances placed by national sovereignty. By an international linkage of the superpowers, the problems of multinational regulation, which loom so large in the established literature can be rationalized, if not entirely resolved, by appeals to commercial rationality rather than to political sovereignty.

The thesis presented by George Kennan that the end of the Cold War came about as a result of a series of victories of the United States over the Soviet empire, is simply untenable. The plain fact is that Soviet foreign policy has remained consistently legalistic whatever its resort to extra legalities and terrorism internally. Beyond that, the Soviet Union has neither dissolved nor shrunk. Current Soviet policy, especially as it affects Eastern Europe, can only be described as extremely aggressive. It is precisely the absence of victory, of a thoroughly stalemated situation, that led the major powers to reconsider their collision course—a course that could threaten both empires at the expense of outsider factions in the Third World, China and even nonaligned nations like India, waiting in the wings to pick up the pieces.

Arms control agreements, direct executive rapprochement, new trade and purchasing agreements, exchanges of research and development technology in basic fields have all been instituted in rapid succession. These have signaled the real termination of the Cold War. Multinationalism, in its very extra-nation capacities, has served to rationalize this new foreign policy posture on both sides. Terms like "have" versus "have-not" states have come to replace and displace an older rhetoric of capitalism versus socialism, not simply as an expression of the uneven international distribution of wealth, but as an indication of the current sponginess of any concept of capitalism or socialism. It is precisely the inability of the Cold War to be resolved through victory that has led to a feeling on the part of the leadership in powerful states that the coalition of the big against the small, of the wealthy against the impoverished, and even of white-led nations against colored-led nations, that can best guarantee the peace of the world, and the tranquilization of potential sources of rival power like China in the East or Germany and France in the West. With one fell swoop the mutual winding down of the Cold War settles the hash of rival powers and determines the subordinate position of the Third World for the duration of the century. The cement for this new shift in fundamental policy is the multinational corporation. An end to ideology? No. An end to capitalist and communist rhetoric? Possibly. An end to the Cold War epoch? Yes.

Source and Original Title: "Capitalism, Communism, and Multinationalism." In *The New Sovereigns: Multinational Corporations as World Powers*, edited by Abdul A. Said and Luiz R. Simmons. Englewood Cliffs, NJ: Prentice-Hall, 1974, pp. 120-138.

7

The Militarization of Guerrilla Communism

This is not an essay on Cuba in general, but an examination of the status of the Cuban military in the light of the past pretensions and present performances of the Cuban Communist regime. This simple disclaimer is a necessary prerequisite since the ideological suspicion of "partisanship" is particularly prevalent in the case of Cuba. There is scant doubt that if the focus were the educational reforms or health measures of the regime, a positive appraisal might ensue. However, even at the level of health, education and welfare, the dominant requirements of a highly militarized and mobilized State make themselves felt. Given the publication of a splendid study of the antecedents of Cuban guerrilla militarism (Bonachea and San Martin, 1974), a considerable amount of background information on the pre-revolutionary build up can be taken for granted.

Guerrilla movements are, first and foremost, military movements in the making. They require organization, leadership, discipline, obedience and a command structure that is understood by the rank and file. As in any military organization, properties of courage, fortitude and daring must be combined with youth, masculinity, and intelligence. As in any regime that is a consequence of military engagements—whether it is that of General Franco in Spain or Comandante Fidel in Cuba—a sense of the necessary ingredients of military victory is carried over and perpetuated in the post-revolutionary epoch of reconstruction and reconsolidation. Hence, to speak of the military sociology of Cuban communism is to deal with a characteristic that defines revolutionary forces from the outset, not those which are simply grafted onto the revolution after its assumption of political power.

Several years ago I wrote a study on the "Political Sociology of Cuban Communism" (Mesa-Lago, 1971:127-41). It was essentially an examination of the morphology of political power; the transformation of the revolutionary regime from a mass movement to an elitist party apparatus. This paper should be understood as a complement to that earlier effort, focusing now on the military sociology of Cuba in terms of the shift from a guerrilla movement to a highly professionalized armed force. The results of the military side of the Castro regime have taken longer to work out than their political aspects; but the consequences are just as profound, and indeed could not have taken place were it not for the prier consolidation of State power in the hands of the revolutionary armed forces.

Antecedent Theories of the Cuban Revolution

The area of Cuban affairs invites ideological polarization. As a consequence, any analysis is suspect and is scrutinized from the standpoint of the analyst instead of how well it explains the realities of the Cuban system. Without intending to be *ad hominem*, it is instructive to examine fundamental views on post-revolutionary Cuba. Upon inspection, these early theories of the Cuban Revolution appear impoverished, so barren of originality that they invariably led to severe theoretical as well as practical confusions.

The early writings that emerged immediately after the Cuban Revolution were a veritable political Rorschach test; one perceived the revolution much the way he wanted to see it.

C. Wright Mills wrote *Listen Yankee*, which appeared in 1960, immediately following the revolution. In that work the revolution emerges as a connection, a therapeutic device for linking dreams and reality. Beyond that, Castro is spoken of as an experimentalist, someone dedicated to the tasks of national reconstruction and social rejuvenation. Fidel is described as both tough-minded and tenderhearted, a frontier democrat of pragmatic proportions (cf. Horowitz, 1964: 26-27). The theme of moral economy had only barely emerged in the new humanism of Guevara and Castro, but it was immediately translated by Mills into the essence of Cuban communism. The moral athlete of William James was converted, sub-rosa, into the armed political athlete of Fidel. This, in turn, was vouchsafed by the military source of revolutionary ethics. In retrospect, it is clear that Mills had little vision of the Cuban Revolution; he rather had a personalist vision of Fidel. He had a keen vision of the man, but not the system. This, too, is a highly Jamesian interpretation of political reality; a world in which good populists do battle with evil bureaucrats.

The Millsian framework, as it finally emerges in *Listen Yankee*, reduces itself to a notion that the revolution is the leader. That was the essential truth that Mills' work carried within its hyperbolic excesses. By the close of that brief work, Mills shifts from euphoria to considerable fear and concern lest anything happen to the maximal leader, the democratic Fidel (Mills, 1960: 179-189). He so identified the revolution with the leader that he all but declares that the revolution dies the minute Fidel dies. Mills did fear that something would happen, not to the Cuban Revolution, because he really did not understand it, but rather to the thin leadership strata that led the revolutionary forces to triumphant military victory.

If in Mills we witnessed the vision of the Cuban Revolution, in Jean-Paul Sartre we observe its mystification. His is a curious picture of the Cuban Revolution; in retrospect, even a bit shocking. His collection of papers, published as *Sartre on Cuba,* considers the revolution as essentially a romantic encounter with reality. Cuba shows how socialist "praxis" can triumph over both communist dogma and bourgeois corruption. Cuba was compelled to confirm the third stream approach to politics taken in *Les Temps Modernes.* The struggle, as he puts it, between the ideology of bourgeois individualism and the humanistic ideology of the people.

In contradistinction to Mills, Sartre saw the revolution as attacking individualism in both its bourgeois and proletarian forms. He viewed the Castro leadership as highly collectivist albeit preserving a humanist direction. Sartre even describes the revolution as the first restoration of pure radicalism in the twentieth century, the first concrete expression of popular revolution as opposed to bureaucratic revolution. To those who, like Sartre, were discontent and disenchanted with the Soviet Revolution, the rise of the Cuban Revolution seemed absolutely enthralling. The Sartrian vision of the Cuban Revolution was apocalyptic; above all, for him it represented the restoration of moral radicalism, of socialist practice that created political mobility in a world of European socialist immobilism.

Both Mills and Sartre, in their own way, reacted with fervent passion to the Cuban Revolution, in part due to their shared faith in something beyond the elitist and etatist consequences of the Russian Bolshevik Revolution. Castro helped to erase the memories of Stalinism. The sense that the leadership was concerned about ordinary people, the exotic romanticism of the revolution with respect to goals for Cuba, has a considerable amount to do with why Cuba restored faith in the revolutionary process among disenchanted intellectuals. Revolutions might take place outside the framework of the Communist Party system. Cuba spelled the remarriage of socialism and nationalism, and a break with the Communist International. In that very fact the Cuban experience fulfilled the terms of revolution as an act of integrity. Cuba uniquely satisfied the neo-Trotskyist impulses behind both Mills and Sartre. Their writings on the Cuban Revolution in many ways organized the thinking of the New Left in the early 1960s on the Third World.

The next significant analyses of the Cuban Revolution were made by social scientists. In a sophisticated extension of the pragmatic thesis of the Cuban Revolution, Richard Fagen (1972: 68-80) pointed out that the material advantages of Cuban society prior to the revolution endowed the revolutionary leadership with vast advantages and possibilities denied to most other new revolutionary regimes in underdeveloped areas. Fagen shrewdly observed that once the nationalist pivot was firmly adopted and certain infantile adventurist tactics were abandoned, the pre-revolutionary advantages of the Cuban leadership would begin to assert themselves. The theme of "a revolution for internal consumption only" became a new way to describe the experimental nature of the regime. The difficulty with such an approach was the implicit assumption that the special features of Cuba somehow disallowed general laws of development for both capitalist and socialist societies. In a sense, every revolution can be said to be exceptional, or made without a blueprint. Indeed, most are made in direct violation of a blueprint since a model is not something leaders slavishly emulate, but simply a guideline for instruction.

This kind of revised pragmatic vision, while marking a considerable advance over Mills' original formulation, leaves unanswered the basic question of social structure; i.e., after "exceptions" and "exemptions" are allowed for, what indeed are the essential characteristics of the Cuban Revolution? This, alas, remains shrouded in the mystery of specificity uninformed by any general theory of development. As a result, a positive sentiment toward the revolution remains the essential content, rather than just the moral backdrop of Fagen's kind of analysis.

It would be a mistake to claim that the work of Maurice Zeitlin was simply a more sophisticated extension of the efforts of Sartre. While it is true that Zeitlin is clearly more deeply immersed and more knowledgeable about European new-Marxian currents than Fagen, he shares with his fellow American compatriot a keen sense of the empirical and the concrete. He does, however, show that the nationalism of Fidel was but a stage and a phase of Cuban Socialism; and in this sense, goes beyond the pragmatic revolution hypothesis.

Zeitlin (1972:81-92) has claimed that the Cuban Revolution was essentially a national revolution, but that this "revolution without a blueprint" became a socialist revolution because it had no real stability as a spontaneous movement. Thus nationalism led to a kind of socialist and communist coalition because there were no available bourgeois alternatives. That is to say, what began in all integrity as a movement for national renovation, ended as a socialist revolution. This occurred not by design, not because Castro was a covert Marxist in his guerrilla period, but rather as a consequence of both inner political dynamics within Cuba, and the United States economic quarantine of Cuba from the rest of the hemisphere. Zeitlin, and his coworker of the early 1960s, Robert Sheer, raised some extremely important issues that remain very much on the agenda. They long ago noted that one major factor in the bitter antagonism between Cuba and the United States is the collapse of the latter as a viable role model for Latin American leftist regimes. A parliamentary system is abstractly satisfactory, but it carries within itself the germs of restorationism. And for that reason cries about electoral norms or democratic process proved less than persuasive to the Cuban revolutionaries. In the light of the Chilean experience with electoral socialism under Allende, it is hard to fault either the Castro posture at that time or, for that matter, the Zeitlin-Sheer analysis of the limits of reform tendencies after the revolution.

Beyond that, Zeitlin and Sheer (1962: 261-63) provided the basic rationale for the Cuban Revolution, not only moving beyond the "revolution without a blueprint" thesis, but asking why it so rapidly adopted a revolution with a definite bought and borrowed blueprint; namely, the Soviet model of mobilization and legitimation.

> At the same time, while the United States seems to be unable to offer Cuba any meaningful example for her own development, Soviet institutions based on government ownership of the means of production and a planned economy, must appear relevant. There is much in Soviet society that is relevant to Cuba: certain techniques of public planning and management, concern for the provision of social goods and the satisfaction of broad community needs, a dynamic state involvement in the extension of education and culture to the people. In these areas the Soviet Union has been a vital innovator and is worthy of emulation. The danger is that because of U. S. policies, the Soviet impact may be greater than necessary that Cuba will adopt Soviet institutions wholesale and uncritically. The revolutionaries were receptive to the consideration of diverse radical traditions and forms of socialist and Marxian thought. The question is, how long can they continue to be so, faced with U. S. pressure, Communist influence and the reliance on the Soviet bloc that was forced on them?

The inherited dangers pointed to by Zeitlin quickly materialized. Whether the Cuban Revolution was national or international, bourgeois or Marxian in origins, innovative or imitative, the impact of the growing authoritarianism of the Cuban system was overpowering.

With the series of events culminating in the institutionalization of the Communist Party in place of the July 26th Movement; and with the hardening of the regime's political arteries in general (cf. Horowitz, 1965:62-70), the nature of analysis quickly shifted from undiluted support to restrained acquiescence.

Cuban communism increasingly was defined by its leadership in terms of its ideal pretensions rather than its actual achievements. Just as Stalin, in his last days, announced that the basic law of political economy in the USSR was the "law of maximum happiness," so too, as the Cuban revolutionary arteries hardened, Castro announced the moral basis of Cuban economy and the end of bourgeois egotism. Prior emphasis on material incentives were declared reactionary while moral incentives (whatever they happened to be) were said to be progressive. Soon thereafter, social science analysts absorbed this theme of morality versus utilitarianism and stitched this argument into whole cloth: the idealization of the revolution.

It has been argued that the tendency to adopt the language of moral incentives has less to do with idealist tendencies than the Cuban political structure, and more to do with economic necessities of an island economy under siege (cf. Silverman, 1971: 3-28).

It is the case that Cuba, throughout the late 1960s, suffered from a lack of material goods but, in part, this lack rested on a set of policy decisions concerning military over civilian priorities and was not simply an imposed consequence of the embargo. However, the conversion of necessity into choice by administrative fiat is itself a characteristic of the Cuban political process.

This idealist interpretation of the Cuban Revolution emerged essentially from a number of programs that Castro himself advocated over the years in relation to the regime. Rather than face the weaknesses and limits of single crop socialism, Castro insisted that Cuba made a revolution based on the premise of making a new man and not just a new system. This constant emphasis on the tradition of the new, on the new humanism of the new man, originally a useful device for combating the bureaucracy, ultimately led to a general theory of moral incentives. Castro and Guevara raised certain tendencies in Leninism and Stalinism to a level of theory. It was claimed that people work either for money (for the purpose of converting money into material-utilitarian goods), or in terms of future goals (an incentive with ethical purpose). The theme of the moral athlete in pragmatist terms was wedded to that of the moral economist in Marxist terms. This was enunciated in the social science literature by Bernardo (1971) and later by Kahl (1972). Basically they argue that the Cuban Revolution cannot be measured simply by standard economic units, since its drive shaft is basically the ability to raise productivity through moral incentives rather than through costly commodity incentives.

The profound difficulty with all doctrines based on moral incentives is not only in the term "moral," but in the nature of incentives. Admittedly, rewards can be in terms of satisfaction as well as payment, and the Cuban regime had every right to frame its goals in terms of the increased satisfactoriness of the labor process under Socialism. However, such increased rewards must be recognizable to the laborers themselves, and this can be done through a variety of ways: mechanizations, new forms of job sharing, new ways of distributing produce, etc. But in the absence of any real fundamental changes for the labor masses, both in work styles or in material rewards, moral incentives were underwritten first by the party vanguard, and when this incentive by example approach fell short of the mark, through outright coercion. As a result, what started out as an experiment in alternative work styles, ended up as a demand by the regime to meet quotas arbitrarily and artificially set by the leadership without regard to world commodity prices or inter national grain conditions. This elitist definition of moral incentives, rather than the concept itself, thus became a characteristic of Cuba as it passed from a political to a military phase.

Kahl and Bernardo focused upon the role of ideology and morality in driving Cuban economic planners toward fundamentally negative decisions about the nature of market relationships, decisions that in turn have led to a series of problems which seem to presage an even greater series of catastrophes. Questions about the use of moral incentives in stimulating economic growth can be summarized as follows: Can a society have moral incentives under conditions of economic scarcity? More specifically, can a single-crop economy be designated as socialist in any but the most desultory sense? In a broader context, does not the Cuban emphasis on moral incentives violate classical economic rules concerning the market determination of prices and profits, and even the Marxist notion of the labor theory of value?

The problem may be one of causation rather than ideology. The Marxist theory of moral incentives to labor presupposes the solution of problems of material incentives. Only when ego needs are fully gratified, only when a material abundance is available for all to share in, does the Marxist doctrine of moral incentives come into play. In effect, the neo-Marxist doctrine moves up the timetable of economic development; that is, it accelerates the doctrine of moral incentives so that the reasons for effort and labor are related to the political survival of the system rather than the economic abundance created by that system. In some strange way, the Cuban economy has responded to the role of political ideology by noting that the essence of planning is not so much economic growth as it is political mobilization. And in this sense the theory of moral incentives has had a binding value on Cuban society far in excess of any economic profitability or losses occasioned by the premature disavowal of market incentives to labor. For Silverman (1971:20) the fundamental rationale behind the movement to increase overtime hours worked without compensation is the Marxian idea of primitive accumulation. "Were moral incentives to fail, the obvious necessity of using coercion to produce the economic surplus would have to be faced." And indeed, moral incentives have collapsed by Castro's own admission and the resort to increased military pressures on, the populace has been the consequence of this new turn toward economic realism.

One might say that the Cuban economy took an enormous gamble by assuming that there would be enough non-material incentives to maintain a stable state within the economy. Whether this is so or not of course depends not only on the state of mind of the Cuban working class, but on the levels of production and consumption of Cuban society as a whole. Obviously, if the question of economic incentives were one of simply monetary purchasing power, unemployment rates, absenteeism and even labor sabotage would be considerably higher than in fact they are. But how long can a society substitute moral fervor for consumer satisfaction? The Christian-Marxist doctrine of men living not by bread alone ignores the fact that there is an intermediate stage between matter and morals—what might be called comfort and well being. Here is where the vital trade-off between economy and morality takes place. Whether or not Cuban society can sustain sufficient fervor for the regime to permit the continued growth of the GNP at the expense of consumer fulfillment is extremely difficult to predict.

A balance-sheet view of the situation shows that the moral economy has succeeded in achieving a high degree of egalitarianism as a byproduct of Cuban productive organization, and there can be no doubt that Bernardo and Kahl are correct in observing that this was achieved largely by the use of the allocation system of moral stimulation. It is also clear that the price of this egalitarianism is a high demand for material goods—and the choice is limited among those goods. It is also true that the theory of moral stimulation alters old relationships and ends the exaggerated separation of supply and demand for money and goods. Wage differentials are reduced; price differentials are reduced; leisure and labor are flattened out; and in general, there is a definite complementarity between moral and material incentives in such a system. But again, the problem is whether in fact there are such things as moral incentives, or whether the doctrine is not simply a disguised way of defining unpaid labor time, or labor time paid at reduced wages for the purposes of increasing the gross national product.

An orthodox, rather than a revisionist Marxian view, might be taken. Indeed, common sense dictates that we should average in unpaid labor time with paid labor time to arrive at the actual earning power of Cuban labor. In point of fact, the theory of moral incentives is a way of maintaining a socialist economy in a single-crop situation with a minimal amount of inflationary spiraling and pressures for trade union reform.

The anomaly is that Cuban leaders have in effect spiritualized problems of economic production and allocation. They seem to be the first true idealists to emanate from the Marxist-Socialist tradition. Perhaps this philosophical outcome should not have been unexpected since the Cuban Revolution always seemed to be a matter of will and a problem in decision theory, rather than a matter of determinism or a matter of history.

In a sense the post-revolutionary Cuban leadership has carried forth this volitional or idealistic theory of the revolution and has made the success of the socialist economy also a matter of will which, of course, ultimately involves questions of moral choice. Thus it is that the book by Bernardo provides a fascinating episode not just in the annals of political economy, but even more profoundly in political sociology: the way in which problems of political leadership and social class determine the struggle of society, and ultimately the structure of values which provide the ideological fuel for Cuban society.

It is significant that the most recent pronouncements on the subject of incentives by Castro indicate a genuine backing away from the idealistic implications of the moral incentives doctrine. As a result, the newest formulations tend to emphasize that both material and spiritual incentives are required within a system of socialist production. The utter chaos and confusion in the wake of the sugar crop failures convinced the Cuban leadership, if not always its overseas intellectual followers, that something more than moral incentives are required to make people work effectively. In this recognition, the passage from the theoretical to the practical is completed since we move from what is past to what is present; and beyond that, from the consolidation of Stalinism as a political factor to its implementation in Cuban reality as a military factor.

Cuba as Satellite: A Case Study in Dependency

The end of the age of innocence, of the doctrine of moral incentives, meant that the Cuban people would be provided with material goods as incentives, or, failing that, terrorist threat mechanisms as a necessary means of economic persuasion. The regime moved from moralism to militarism at the same time as it consolidated internal political power but failed to attain its ambitious goals of economic independence. As a result, the Cuban system was compelled to move, in lock-step to Soviet intentions; and this meant specifically that attentions and priorities were shifted from civilian to military areas.

As the Cuban regime evolved, scholars made increasingly serious and critical evaluations of its development. My own view, first articulated in 1965, was a variant on the dependency model: it assumed that as the Cuban economy became isolated from the Western capitalist orbit, and as its single-crop economy became absorbed into the Soviet system, its social and political system would also become isomorphic with Soviet needs. Beyond that, I argued that Cuban society would not only replicate Soviet needs, but had already begun to internalize Soviet forms of development (Horowitz, 1965: 61-69).

Specifically, my claims were that

> Cuban communism has achieved special dimensions: (1) there is a subordination of society to the party and the army; (2) there is in Cuba the emergence of a leader and his small coterie as exclusive spokesmen for the communist party; (3) there is the promotion of inner political struggle as a substitute for class struggle; (4) the passion for economic development displaces the politics of debate and the passion for socialist democracy; (5) the Stalinization of the Cuban regime has brought to a halt discussion of alternative strategies for economic development, letting the matter rest with single-crop socialism; (6) Stalinization in Cuba has meant the nearly exclusive concentration of energies on national rather than international problems. Like any model built upon analogy, there are notable exceptions in the linkage between the organization and ideology of Stalinism and the present political and social structure of Cuban communism. Yet this effort at fusing historical information with the actual functioning of the Cuban regime may permit scholars to achieve a fully integrated statement of the nature of Cuban communism, a task which has been tragically ignored by most specialists on international development thus far.

René Dumont, an outstanding developmental theorist, independently verified this line of analysis. In his terminology Cuban socialism evolved in four distinct stages: the focal stage, the movement stage, the socialist stage, and the communist stage. Beyond that, Dumont shows that Castro started out as a model of the romantic revolutionist, only to become transformed, under the exigencies of the tasks of rule, into the charismatic head of a bureaucratic state. Perhaps most important, Dumont shows how this bureaucratization process, despite overt attempts by the Fidelistas to avoid its worst consequences, was made possible by the strengthening of the military, that is by the transformation of Castro's guerrilla forces into a highly professional military cadre. (Dumont, 1970: 78-97).

Picking up the thread of this argument, K.S. Karol, in *Guerrillas in Power*, who was an early friend and advisor to the Cuban leadership, explains the process by which Cuban society became "sovietized." Beyond that, Karol discloses how Fidel has mechanically taken Stalinist slogans about backwardness, such as the need to make up ten years of backwardness in one year of production, and applied it to what turned out to be impossible sugar crop norms. The trouble with this transmutation and transfiguration of Stalinism is that "Fidel, unlike Stalin, cannot pretend that his policy is indispensable to the survival of world socialism" (Karol, 1970: 537). But Karol, like Dumont, is not entirely certain about the status of the Cuban military. That the regime could not simply be characterized as a people's democracy had long been obvious, but that it might be characterized as a military dictatorship seemed premature.

Other studies likewise began to cast doubt on the earlier euphoric characterizations, but more important, pointed a way toward more serious analysis. Maurice Halperín (1972) pictures the "rise" and "decline" of Castro as taking place between 1959 and 1964. However, he would have been better advised to restrict this judgment to Guevara. In point of fact, what had declined by 1964 was the Trotskyist pivot, or the notion that the Cuban Revolution would simply be a spearhead of revolution in Latin America as a whole. The collapse of a series of over seas thrusts—in Venezuela, Guatemala, ending in tragedy in Bolivia several years later, did represent a decline in the revolutionary aspect of the Cuban regime. It was Castro's wisdom, or simply his understanding of the limits of Cuban power, that converted the revolution into a nationalist struggle. The challenge to Cuba by the United States took its most direct form in the thrust into the Dominican Republic which served as the final act of American gunboat diplomacy, to which the Cuban regime could not and did not offer direct military response. Such as it may be, the changeover from a guerrilla regime to a communist nation took place for all to see. And while everyone noted the change, no one was quite sure what it signified.

A recent convert to the dependency thesis is Ian Lumsden, an erstwhile defender of the regime, who until 1973 vigorously opposed my characterization of the regime or of its leadership (cf. Lumsden, 1966: 20-26).

> Cuba has continued to make important investments in its basic infrastructure as part of its programme of national integration and geographic decentralization. Much of this, of course, has only been possible as a result of the extensive foreign aid that Cuba has received from the Soviet Union.

> But has this aid resulted in Cuba substituting a dependent relationship to the Soviet Union for its previous dependence upon the United States? If this is indeed the case, then of course it would follow that, however impressive the redistribution of income and the improvement in the welfare of the vast majority of the Cuban population since 1959, no permanent basis for development would have been established. On the contrary, the dependent situation of the economy might well begin to reproduce the socio-economic conditions that characterize peripheral capitalist countries.

> Castro's volte-face in supporting the Soviet intervention in Czechoslovakia, despite his accompanying criticism of Soviet-style communism, and the economic catastrophe of 1970, have reopened the question of Cuba's relationship with the Soviet Union—not without some justification. It is indisputable that Cuba now has much closer political and military ties to the Soviet Union, and that its economy is becoming more closely integrated with the Soviet-dominated Comecon economies. Nevertheless, Cuba may not have become irrevocably locked into a new dependent situation, first because the Soviet "socialist" economy is not in essence expansionary as are developed capitalist economies, and secondly, because Cuba has not yet developed a new internal dominant class whose status is primarily conditioned by the function it performs on behalf of external metropolitan interests. This may yet happen to the Cuban leadership, however, if it

persists in compensating for its own errors by relying upon the massive
Soviet aid to which it has become increasingly accustomed. Although it
may well be true that the Soviet Union's motives are primarily political
rather than economic, in the sense that it is unable to divest itself of its
identification with the fate of Cuba's Marxist-Leninist regime, the terms
of the 1972 Trade Agreement give cause for concern because they ensure
that Cuba will increase its dependence upon the export of unrefined sugar
and nickel in exchange for the import of capital goods from essentially one
source. Nothing in their relationship with the underdeveloped countries
since 1968 negates the basis of the criticisms made by Che Guevara and
Fidel Castro between 1965 and 1968 of the foreign policies and implicitly,
the motives of the Comecon countries. The possibility that the price of the
greatly increased Soviet aid to Cuba may be internal conformity with Soviet
hegemony over the communist camp (excluding China) can no longer be
discounted as easily as it once was (Lumsden, 1973: 547-549).

It is indisputable that Cuba now is irretrievably dependent
on the Soviet Union and that its economy is becoming totally
integrated with the Soviet orbit. This has resulted first, because
the Soviet socialist economy is not as capable of absorbing surplus
goods as is a capitalist economy and, second, because Cuba has not
developed a new bourgeoisie to place limits on the conditions for
exporting and importing goods and services. The Soviet economy is
highly expansive as is Soviet policy generally. An internal ruling class
does exist in Cuba, the bureaucratic military, and it does perform
functions on behalf of the external metropolitan sector. But that
notwithstanding, the price of greatly increased aid to Cuba may be
internal conformity with the Soviet style of communism.

Lumsden's support for the proposition that Cuba is part and
parcel of the Soviet satellite system is accurate, albeit belated. His
effort to date this dependency relationship after 1968 is clearly a
ruse to disguise his own earlier errors in judgment. It ignores the
structural features of single-crop socialism that plagued Cuba
from the outset of the Castro Revolution. Yet, quite beyond the
secondary literature, we have an increasing crescendo of commentary on the subject by Castro himself.

At the Fourth Conference of Nonaligned Nations in Algeria,
on September 7, 1973, Premier Castro delivered an address
presenting a thoroughly aligned position. His view has four

component parts: (1) that the world is divided into capitalist and socialist orbits, and is not a three-track system. (2) The doctrine of Soviet imperialism is erroneous, and there is only one imperialist center, that located in the United States. (3) The Soviet Union is not only exempt from the theory of two imperialisms; it is the vanguard of the international socialist movement. (4) All forms of national liberation efforts, whatever their stage of development, must be supported as the basic protest and opposition against American imperialism (cf. Castro, 1973:12).

> There has been talk at this Conference of the different ways of dividing the world. To our way of thinking the world is divided into capitalist and socialist countries, imperialist and neocolonialized countries, colonialist and colonialized countries, reactionary and progressive countries—governments, in a word, that back imperialism, colonialism, neocolonialism and racism, and governments that oppose imperialism, colonialism, neocolonialism and racism.
>
> The theory of "two imperialisms," one headed by the united States and the other allegedly by the Soviet Union, encouraged by the theoreticians of capitalism, has been echoed at times deliberately and at others through ignorance of history and the realities of the present-day world, by leaders and spokesmen of nonaligned countries. This is fostered, of course, by those who regrettably betray the cause of internationalism from supposedly revolutionary positions.
>
> There are some who, with patent historic injustice and ingratitude, forgetting the real facts and disregarding the profound, unbridgeable abyss between the imperialist regime and socialism, try to ignore the glorious, heroic and extraordinary services rendered to the human race by the Soviet people, as if the collapse of the colossal system of colonial rule implanted in that world up to World War II, and the conditions that made possible the liberation of scores of peoples heretofore under direct colonial subjugation, the disappearance of capitalism in large parts of the world and the holding at bay of the aggressiveness and insatiable voracity of imperialism.
>
> Some regret the fact that the first socialist state in history has become a military and economic power. We underdeveloped and plundered countries must not regret this. Cuba rejoices that this is so. Without the October Revolution, and without the immortal feat of the Soviet people who first withstood imperialist intervention and blockade, and later defeated the fascist aggression at the cost of 20 million dead, who have developed their technology and economy at an unbelievable price in efforts and heroism, without exploiting the labor of a single worker of any country on the fact of

the earth—without them, the end of colonialism and the balance of power in the world that favored the heroic struggles of so many peoples for their liberation, wouldn't have been possible.

This undiluted celebration by Castro of the Soviet position is a fundamental statement of Cuban foreign policy. It is a denial of the imperialist aspects of Soviet foreign policy, and ultimately a denial that the concept of nonalignment can be serviceable to Third World nations. A more serious and sober analysis of the sources of such Cuban militancy must extend far beyond the Stalinization of Cuba, into the militarization of Cuba.

References/Notes

Agüero, L. C., 1959, *Cartas del Presidio.* Havana: Editorial Let

Bernardo, Robert M., 1971, *The Theory of Moral Incentives in Cuba.* University of Alabama: The University of Alabama Press.

Bonachea, Ramón L. and Marta San Martin, 1974, *The Cuban Insurrection: 1952-1959.* New Brunswick: Transaction Books - E. P. Dutton.

Castro, Fidel, 1968, *History Will Absolve Me.* London: Jonathan Cape.

Castro, Fidel, 1972, "Interview with Andrew St. George" (February 4, 1958) in *Revolutionary Struggle: 1947-1958—Selected Works of Fidel Castro, Volume I,* edited by Rolando E. Bonachea and Nelson P. Valdes. Cambridge: MIT Press.

Castro, Raúl, 1973, Speech at Ceremony organized by the Revolutionary Armed Forces (FAR) on the occasion of the 55th Anniversary of The Founding of the Red Army, February 22, 1973. *Granma Weekly Review,* March 4.

Castro, Raúl, 1973, Closing Address establishing the Army of Working Youth. *Granma Weekly Review.* August 12.

Castro, Raúl, 1974, Speech to Vanguards of the Revolutionary Armed Forces (FAR). *Granma Weekly Review,* January 20.

Comités de Defensa de la Revolución, 1964, *Memorias de 1963.* Havana: Ediciones con la Guardia en Alto (Publicado por la Direccion Nacional de los CDR).

Debray, Régis, 1967, *Revolution in the Revolution?* New York: Monthly Review Press.

Debray, Régis, 1970, *Strategy for Revolution: Essays on Latin America.* New York: Monthly Review Press.

del Valle, Sergio, Blas Roca and Carlos Rafael Rodriguez, 1974, Excerpts from speeches at Third National Evaluation Meeting of The Committees for the Defense of the Revolution. *Granma Weekly Review,* February 17.

Dumont, René, 1970, *Cuba: est-il socialiste?* Paris: Editions du Seuil.

Fagen, Richard R., 1970, "Revolution for Internal Consumption Only: Transformation of Political Culture in Cuba," Stanford University Press: 68-80.

Ferrero, Guglielmo, 1968, *The Two French Revolutions: 1789-1796.* New York: Basic Books.

González, Edward, 1972, *Partners in Deadlock: The United States and Castro*, 1959-72. Los Angeles: Arms Control and Foreign Policy Seminar, June, 1972.
González, Edward, 1972, "The United States and Castro: Breaking the Deadlock". *Foreign Affairs*, Vol. 50, No. 4 (July: 722-737).
Guevara, Ernesto "Che", 1961, *Guerrilla Warfare*. New York: Monthly Review Press.
Guevara, Ernesto "Che", 1968, "Guerilla Warfare: A Method," in *Venceremos: The Speeches and Writings of Guevara*, edited by John Gerassi. New York: The Macmillan Company.
Halperín, Maurice, 1972, *The Rise and Decline of Fidel Castro: An Essay in Contemporary History*. Berkeley: University of California Press.
Horowitz, Irving Louis, 1964, "Introduction" *Sociology and Pragmatism: The Higher Learning in America*, by C. Wright Mills. New York: Oxford University Press.
Horowitz, Irving Louis, 1965, "The Stalinization of Fidel Castro," *New Politics*. Volume IV, No.4 (Fall: 62-70).
Horowitz, Irving Louis, 1966, "Castrologists and Apologists: A Reply to Science in the Service of Sentiment", *New Politics*, Volume 5, No. 1 (winter: 27-34).
Horowitz, Irving Louis, 1971, "The Political Sociology of Cuban Communism" in *Revolutionary Change in Cuba*, edited by Carmelo Mesa-Lago. Pittsburgh: University of Pittsburgh Press: 127-141.
Kahl, Joseph A., 1972, "The Moral Economy of a Revolutionary Society", in *Cuban Communism*, edited by Irving Louis Horowitz. New Brunswick: Transaction Books/ E.P. Dutton (second edition: 193-211).
Karol, K. S., 1970, *Guerrillas in Power: The Course of the Cuban Revolution*. New York: Hill and Wang.
Lumsden, Ian, 1966, "On Socialists and Stalinists: A Reply to Irving Louis Horowitz", *New Politics* Volume 5, No. 1 (winter: 20-26).
Lumsden, Ian, 1973, "Dependency, revolution, and development in Latin America". *International Journal*, Volume XXVIII, No.3 (Summer: 525-551.).
Mills, C. Wright, 1960, *Listen Yankee: The Revolution in Cuba*. New York: McGraw-Hill Publishers.
Sartre, Jean-Paul, 1961, *Sartre on Cuba*. New York: Ballantine Books.
Silverman, Bertram, 1971, "The Great Debate in Retrospect: Economic Rationality and the Ethics of Revolution" in *Man and Socialism in Cuba: The Great Debate*, edited by Bertram Silverman. New York: Atheneum.
Tang, P. and J. Maloney, 1962, *The Chinese Communist Input in Cuba: Washington Research Institute on the Sino-Soviet Bloc* - Monograph Series #12.
Zeitlin, Maurice and Robert Scheer, 1964, *Cuba: An American Tragedy* (rev. ed.). Harmondsworth, Middlesex: Penguin Books.
Zeitlin, Maurice, 1967, *Revolutionary Politics and the Cuban Working Class*. Princeton, New Jersey: Princeton University Press.

Source and Original Title: "Authenticity and Militarization: A Postscript on the Cuban Revolution." *Atlanta Forum on National and International Affairs*. Atlanta: Georgia Institute of Technology, pp. 7-9.

8

Military Origins of the Cuban Revolution

The concept of military organization as a basis for communist revolution was greatly enhanced by the Cuban revolutionary experience. Indeed, one theorist of the Cuban Revolution has elevated the guerrilla band to a prominence that subordinates, even denigrates, Communist party political organization.[1] How was a nonparty, guerrilla revolutionary model possible in Cuba, and how could those who made the revolution so easily become "communists?" First, the Cuban Revolution was carried out by a pragmatic and theoretically unself-conscious leadership which did not apply Leninist or Maoist precepts to a Cuban context. Consequently, military means of overthrowing the old regime could be advocated or employed without subjecting guerrilla actions to the discipline of a party. Second, the Cuban Revolution eventually brought about an alliance between two distinct leaderships—the revolutionary guerrillas' military band and the Communist party. Unlike any previous communist revolution, military and party leaderships did not overlap. Thus, the guerrilla leader could continue to see himself as a military man, not a political actor, even while coordinating action with the Communist party. Third, the primary revolutionary role of initiation and sustained insurrection was played by the guerrilla band, not by the Communist party. Ex post facto theorizing has elevated this fact to the level of a new revolutionary principle favoring the enlarged role of a popular military force in communist revolution-making.

Castroism can be located historically from July 26, 1953, the date of the unsuccessful attack on the Moncada army post in Santiago de Cuba, a year and a half after Batista's seizure of power. Fidel Castro emerged from this as an independent figure with a personal following. The July 26th movement gained some definition thereafter, although it remained broad and vague. During Castro's imprisonment on the Isle of Pines, from October 1953 to May 1955, he published "History Will Absolve Me."[2] It became the articulation of the reforms sought by the July 26th movement. There is little clear-cut ideology in it, aside from general pleading for reform and justifying militant action toward that end. Then, in a pamphlet published clandestinely in June 1954, Castro took hold of reform a little more firmly. He promised to restore Cuba's 1940 constitution, to hold popular elections, and to carry out land reform—which would include restriction of large landholdings and an increase in the number of smaller ones. He also promised vaguely-defined agricultural cooperatives. In 1954, he sent a number of letters to Luis Conte Agüero, an Ortodoxo leader and radio commentator, to whom he confided some thoughts about his developing movement.[3] On August 14, 1954, Castro thought that he ought to "organize the men of the 26th of July movement"; he wanted to unite them "into an unbreakable body" of fighters. They must constitute "a perfectly disciplined human nucleus" for the "force necessary to conquer power, whether it is by peaceful or forcible means." He pointed out that

> the indispensable preconditions of a genuine civic movement are: ideology, discipline, and leadership. The three are essential but leadership is most fundamental. I do not know if it was Napoleon who said that one bad general in battle counts more than twenty good ones. It is not possible to organize a movement in which everyone believes he has the right to issue public statements without consulting the others; nor can anything be expected of an organization made up of anarchic men, who, at the first dispute, find the easiest way out, breaking and destroying the machine. The apparatus of propaganda, or organization, should be so powerful that it would implacably destroy anyone who tried to create tendencies, cliques, schisms, or rebels against the movement.[4]

Of the three conditions, Castro was least concerned with ideology and most with discipline, especially leadership. "Leadership is basic" had the force of a first principle for him. Thus, Castro could freely espouse nonparty military or guerrilla rebellion, when the time came, with little concern for party rules, traditions, and doctrine.

Guerrilla warfare techniques and rationales came to him slowly. Neither he nor Guevara sought out the likely example Mao Tse-tung could have provided. The consistent failures of Cuban communists to produce a revolution, the spontaneous uprisings and romantic conspiracies, finally convinced Castro that he should consider guerrilla warfare and prepare for a protracted struggle. However, in the early months of 1957, not even Castro believed wholly in this plan. He had gone into the mountains still believing that he would merely harass the regime until a great urban strike paralyzed Batista and caused his downfall. In the course of battle, when his abortive "strike" failed, on April 9, 1958, Castro became convinced that guerrilla military operations were the path to power. Significantly, he began with little ideology, remained independent of the Cuban Communist party which was still thinking in 1917 terms, and learned from his experiences that total control over the insurrectionary process is a precondition for seizing power.

The Castro-Communist alliance was first realized in 1958. Some Castroites and some Communists may have labored for such an alliance earlier, but they were inhibited from working together so long as an important segment of the July 26th movement was anti-Communist in principle and the Communist leadership was anti-insurrectionist in practice. By summer 1958, the urban branch of the movement had suffered a major blow when it procrastinated about an urban strike which ultimately failed.[5] The Communist party in the meantime had partially come around to an insurrectionary policy. The dividing line between Castro and the Communists narrowed to the overall value of armed struggle. The Castroites could not give up this issue, but the Communists could assimilate it as "tactics." They crossed the line and switched to Castro's side in order to make an alliance possible.[6] This represented the final consolidation of the revolutionary forces in Castro's person as commander-in-chief.

At first Castro identified himself with a vague humanism, something distinct from capitalism or communism a third way that would involve meaningful citizen participation. Communists tried to avoid clashing with him over his humanist "vogue." Yet it gained some stature and especially frightened the older Communist party when the July 26th trade union section swamped the Communists in union elections on a humanist program. Aníbal Escalante criticized Castro's humanism as "ideological confusion," for which Castro never altogether forgave him, but Escalante prevailed for the moment. Castro dropped the term to preserve the alliance. The gradual extension of communist ideological influence on Fidel, which grew out of the exigencies of alliance, convinced him that he was carrying out a socialist revolution. In 1959, with victory, he could declare it so. Despite such influences, the July 26th movement and the Communist party remained distinct entities. By whatever degrees Castro came to accept communism, he never gave an inch on the matter of guerrilla insurrection.[7]

Escalante, then secretary of the Cuban Communist party, observed on June 30, 1959 in *Hoy* that Fidel had proclaimed that the revolution had entered its socialist phase. The first phase of national liberation and antifeudalism had been completed. The revolution had now entered into a new, higher stage of social development—the socialist stage.[8] Castro's ideological pliability enabled communists to make common cause with him. In a speech on December 20, 1961, Castro said: "We have acted in a Marxist-Leninist manner." He then went on to indicate that he had always been a Marxist-Leninist. "Of course, if we stopped at the Pico Turquino [a height in the Sierra Maestra] when we were very weak and said 'We are Marxist-Leninists' we might not have been able to descend from the Pico Turquino to the plain. Thus we called it something else, we did not broach this subject, and we raised other questions that the people understood perfectly."[9] In his speech of December 1, 1961, Castro claimed that he had been something of a Marxist-Leninist since his student days:

We began in the university to make the first contacts with the Communist Manifesto, with the works of Marx and Engels and Lenin. That marked a process. I can say an honest confession, that many of the things that we have done in the revolution are not things that we invented, not in the least. When we left the university, in my particular case, I was really greatly influenced—not that I will say I was in the least a Marxist-Leninist.[10]

He climaxed this speech with the cry, "I am a Marxist-Leninist, and I will be one until the last days of my life." Fidel lacked a strong ideological character. He could absorb Marxism-Leninism while viewing his earlier thinking as a process of evolution toward it, justifying his earlier belief in leadership and his "humanism" as youthful expressions of the mature communist. Yet earlier he had not appeared to display an understanding of Marxism-Leninism; as late as 1958, Castro opposed blanket nationalization and supported "the right kind of private investment—domestic and foreign."[11] He certainly never accepted or advocated the idea of a party-led revolution (definitely a "first law" for proper Leninists). Not even Ernesto Guevara, his revolutionary companion, whose communist sympathies were never in doubt, exhibited an ideologically defined personality, much less one accepting the strictures of Marxist-Leninism. Guevara's entire attention appears to have been occupied by an unorthodox concept of guerrilla action.

Far from unraveling the intricacies of Marxism-Leninism for the Cuban environment, Guevara was content to combine a practical "methodological" guidebook on guerrilla warfare with a simple revolutionary theory: (1) popular forces can win against a regular army; (2) one need not always wait for "objective conditions" appropriate for revolution, for the insurrectional focal point can create them; and (3) in Latin America, the countryside is the main locale of armed struggle.[12] Aside from offering some technical guidance for the "popular war," Guevara did little more than elaborate these points. Gone are the phases of class revolution we are accustomed to hearing from a Mao or a Lenin. Stages are merely conditions of closeness to or distance from victory. But importantly, though not for Guevara, the item which is the center of unorthodox rebellion against traditional

Marxism—the armed guerrilla band—is loosely and indiscriminately conceived as a popular vanguard. "The guerrilla band is an armed nucleus, the fighting vanguard of the people."[13] The guerrilla himself is conceived in such a way that he could have been mistrusted by a Lenin or a Mao as a romantic individualist with a muddled intellect, incapable of analyzing his society, his goals, his historic role.

> We must come to the inevitable conclusion that the guerrilla fighter is a social reformer, that he takes up arms responding to the angry protest of the people against their oppressors, and that he fights to change the social system that keeps all his unarmed brothers in ignominy and misery. He launches himself against the conditions of the reigning institutions at a particular moment with all the vigor that circumstances permit to breaking the mold of these institutions.[14]

And far from being so knowledgeable about the "stages of history" that he can master a "science of society," the guerrilla leader need know little more than what is required of a good man and soldier. The guerrilla needs a "good knowledge of the surrounding countryside, the paths of entry and escape, the possibilities of speedy maneuver, good hiding places." "Naturally," in all of this, he must "count on the support of the people." He should be willing to die for nothing more defined than "an ideal" and "social justice." Moreover, "whoever does not feel this undoubted truth cannot be a guerrilla fighter." It is not even a truth that men can know. The good revolutionary "feels" it as an overpowering force. There is much talk devoted to guiding the fighter through the countryside, the intricacies of his weapons, supplies, and so forth. But the mystic "feeling" is accompanied only by a practicality that verges on the misanthropic. Unlike Mao whose emphasis is on persuading, reeducating, or returning captured enemies, Che suggests that they "should be eliminated without hesitation when they are dangerous. In this respect the guerrilla band must be drastic."[15]

Mao attempted to exploit the contrast between an elitist Kuomintang army and a populist Red army. Guevara instead focused on the credibility of guerrilla power and the practical steps for enhancing it. The guerrilla need not trouble himself

with "contrasts" or party directives about his behavior toward
enemy or peasantry. He is stoic, saintly, a "teacher-fighter" ready
to make supreme sacrifices from the sheer intensity of his conviction. His rewards are violence and battle themselves: "Within the
framework of the combatant life, the most interesting event, the
one that carries all to a convulsion of joy and puts new vigor in
everybody's steps, is the battle." Indeed, the battle is "the climax
of the guerrilla life."[16]

Guevara may be criticized for romanticism, for a lack of analytic skill and vigor, for a lack of commanding style, for excessive preoccupation with the details of combat, for sketchiness,
and for a dangerous and unappealing simplicity of mind. But as
a voice expressing shifts in the conceptualization of communism
as a power-seizing formula, his is authentic. He shared with Fidel
a distaste for ideological stricture and a careless appraisal of the
ideological traditions with which the Cuban regime became associated through the party influences on it. Thus, Che could also
share with Fidel an abiding faith in the effectiveness of guerrilla
organization as a mode of acquiring power independent of party.
Guerrilla organization as a power-seizing instrument returned to
human will a capacity for shaping environment that was not inhibited by the timing of action according to historical law. Historical law
became merely a post hoc justification for an accomplished deed
and did not impose itself in the actual power struggle. Guerrilla
organization thus succeeded party organization, as will fully succeeded law, as an instrument of gaining power. The Cuban Revolution created alternatives to party-centered communist revolutions
that are potentially competitive with it (except where the mollifying
effects of "alliance" are fully exploited and appreciated).

Debray synthesized this tendency into a new ideology of
communist revolution. His is a bold effort consciously to sweep
away law, party, and history as obstructions to power seizure.
Debray is clear from the beginning—"the socialist revolution is
the result of an armed struggle against the armed power of the
bourgeois state."[17] Failure to grasp this "beginning" has plagued
Communist parties still living in the idealized world of the ac-

cidents of 1917. Each party, in each succeeding period, has been living parasitically off a victorious predecessor and has been saddled with its pet theories about seizing power. The leaders of the Cuban Revolution started with the focus of armed struggles as the basis for revolutionary policy formulation. They were not oppressed by costly party dogmas. Only late in the revolution did they discover the writings of Mao.[18] By then their tactics were already so well defined they could not be led to fruitless imitation. To their everlasting advantage, they were able to read Mao from a specifically Cuban standpoint and to escape the abstract devotion to party he counseled. Cuba could thus stand as a model for the Latin American continent, for it displayed the wisdom and courage of following no dogma; its antidogmatic character is its model. Cuba demonstrated the value of beginning with arms and developing theory only in the course of battle. The new revolutionary model is an antimodel. The initial commitment is a matter of picking up a gun; all else will follow, depending on conditions revolutionaries find in their own context of operations. Since the world is ready for "total class warfare" and total showdown, theories about who is acting according to historical law are inhibitions on what must be done. Older Communist parties are leavings of a "political age," when class struggle was still fully or partially a matter of political struggle for political advantages. That time is past; today is an age of "action in the streets"; compromises and coalitions are all fading into the communist past.[19]

The new context for struggle is set by the massive weaponry of bourgeois nations and by the exhaustion of old communist techniques.[20] Even the intellectual per se fails to illuminate our understanding of what has happened, for his perspective is by nature conservative. He is always aware of precedents, a past, other strategies, and high abstractions. These are useless; what is valuable are data-tactical data, drawn from battle experience. The seasoned guerrilla knows this. The intellectual thinks he does, but knows only his own political experience. This knowledge is not transferable to a battlefield where outcomes are determined.

A guerrilla not so beset by intellectual illusions, Guevara could carry on about the need for guerrilla bases after the manner of Mao. But Mao is insufficient. Che declares that it is necessary to strike and run; to rest, to worry about the "liberating areas," and to settle down to govern them is to risk destruction.[21]

Debray denies that urban politics is the center of revolutionary action. For communists, the countryside is supplementary to and dependent on city politics, as it is for everything else. The party counsels guerrillas to make contact with the city, to coordinate action with Communist party planning there. Debray claims that Castro suffered from this illusion for a while. Contact with the city party makes location and destruction of the guerrilla organization easier. At all costs, such contact must be avoided. Better to kidnap a country doctor to help the wounded than to go to the city for medical aid.[22] Dependence on the city is corrupting.

Debray is careful to say that military operations must have a political object, aim at political goals. Political and military goals are inseparable. But no party should be responsible for setting the political goals of the guerrilla organization. However, Debray cannot articulate what these may be aside from "total confrontation with a bourgeoisie." All parties, including the Communist party, are obsessed with "commissions, congresses, conferences, plenary sessions, meetings, and assemblies at all levels, national, provincial, regional and local."[23] Thus the party dwells on problems of its own internal cohesion. It socializes members into the going system by failing to direct energies toward seizing government power.[24] The party is an unfit instrument for power seizure; at best, its value is assistance in governing. Power seizure is inherently a military operation and requires an organizational apparatus suited to this end. Military discipline over a group of committed and armed men is needed—not party discipline suited to party demands. Political experience and its acquisition cannot justify party dominance in revolutionary affairs. Political experience can always be acquired. Military experience is difficult to acquire and must be deliberately sought. A military body can always gain in political experience on ascension to power. Thus, a vanguard military organization is more easily a ruling party in embryo than a party can be an effective military organization.[25]

Debray's work typifies the dangers of transforming a case into a model, the Cuban experience into a Latin American necessity. But even more practically, Debray's empirics are far from secure. From the outset, the Castro forces were thoroughly dependent on and connected to events in the cities. The very success of the revolution was signified by the New Year's march into Havana and not by any cumulative series of rural victories. Castro's early cautionary spirit was justified on the basis of conservative elements in peasant society. The search for a united front in the capital, organized by a vanguard party, made good sense in the context of Batista's regime. In the style of early enthusiasts, Debray romanticized the role of the peasantry. In so doing, he tended to ignore the specifically military aspects of the campaign that led to Castro's victory. It was more a requisite of revolutionary rhetoric that social change be made in the name of a social class than a reflection of the realities that a revolution can in fact be executed by a disciplined guerrilla cadre and then, as an afterthought, presume widespread class support. The rural/urban bifurcation was real enough. So was the gap between the July 26th movement and the Communist party. But ultimately, the issue of state power was settled by military force and not by adherence to class factors. The military origins of the Cuban Revolution profoundly affected its military outcomes.

The Cuban Revolution emerged from a set of circumstances in which a militant band of revolutionaries initiated armed action against city strongholds of government. Uncommitted to any given source outside themselves, they pursued the apparently fruitful pattern that involved independence from the Communist party—ignoring "history" and communist propriety. But alliance, being mutually useful, was effected between Castro guerrillas and Communist forces. The elements of the two organizations showed mutual influence, especially as the

Castro regime is committed to detaching Cuba from its traditional client position. But his insurrection stands as a model of independence and triumph of will over law, of nationalist initiatives over the internationalist Soviet party model.[26] Communists everywhere are able to consider military lines of action without surrendering their ideological convictions. In this way, outfitting an exclusively military (however "popular") organization for the seizure of state power meshes with the aims of the party. History calls, not for a reading of its latest manifestations, but for total showdown and the exertion of initiative and armed will. To abandon the wearisome politics of radical parties can connote, not betraying Marxism-Leninism, but fitting revolutionary aims to a modern context. The party of the Communists may be freely altered, and the political form itself may be set aside for considerations of military strategy and tactics.

Militarizing Aspects of the Cuban Revolution

Throughout the Third World and particularly in Latin America, the military increasingly represents the pivotal element in any ruling class. At the least, the military has the capacity to prevent anyone sector from maintaining power—even when, as an armed force, they are able to seize power. In most instances (e.g. Brazil, Chile, Peru, Bolivia, Paraguay) power has been taken by tacit agreement between a nervous bourgeoisie and a nationalistic military caste. In Cuba the bourgeoisie was not a contender for power. During the consolidation period there was a struggle for power between the civilian bureaucratic and the military bureaucratic sectors. The civilian sector increasingly came under the domination of the Communist party apparatus, the only surviving party in the postrevolutionary era and the only one approved by the Soviet Union. The civilian sector, like its bourgeois counterparts elsewhere in the hemisphere, proved less than efficacious in the tasks of economic industrialization and modernization.

During 1967-72, the civilian Communist party sector managed to maintain legitimacy and to absorb the full force of the
July 26th movement and various dissident socialist sectors.
This absorption was accomplished through Committees for the
Defense of the Revolution (CDRs), whose likes had not been
seen since the Committees of Public Safety and General Security during the final stage of Robespierre's Convention.[27] Led by
communists like Sergio del Valle, Bias Roca, and Carlos Rafael
Rodríguez, these committees absorbed the revolutionary fervor
of the early movement and harnessed its activities to those of the
Communist party. CDRs became a paramilitary factor in their
own right. By 1963 more than 90,000 separate CDR units existed.
The party's task was to organize CDRs on every block of every
city; coordinate CDR activities with police security forces; and
transform a mass organization into an arm of the Ministry of the
Interior.[28] The development of CDRs was greatly aided by the
Bay of Pigs invasion, which permitted the Cuban regime to cast
a wide net for "enemies." Now, more than a decade later, the term
enemies still exists. However, the tasks of CDRs have become
more broad-ranging, juridical no less than overtly military. They
provide the basis of "socialist legality" by administering and carrying out the Law of the Organization of the Juridical System
through Popular Tribunal. In Cuba, what in other societies is
decried as vigilantism is celebrated by officials as the "basis
of socialist legality."[29] These committees served to transform
what was in its origins a mass democratic movement into a
paramilitary elite with direct support of the party apparatus.
The structure of the Cuban armed forces is directly linked to
its defense strategy, and part of this strategy is the activity of
paramilitary mass organizations. Real threats did exist, but the
Castro regime responded with heightened security measures to
assert very early in the regime that political challenges would
be met in military rather than in civilian terms.

The structure of Cuba's Revolutionary Armed Forces (FAR)
ties into the country's defense strategy. As early as September
20, 1961, Fidel Castro projected three types of offensive over-

tures against Cuba that remain equally possible today: a formal or informal U.S.-sponsored Cuban exile invasion, guerrilla warfare, or a spontaneous uprising generated by elimination of the main revolutionary leaders. The last two alternatives were largely canceled out by the effectiveness of the FAR-MININT forces controlling mass organizations such as CDR, UJC, and the National Militias. Dependent paramilitary organizations can be instrumental in breaking up any urban underground, and since an internal uprising must be planned from inside, an urban underground movement must be developed first. As for irregular war or guerrilla warfare, the existence of an underground is a concomitant of any successful armed struggle. Because of organizational difficulties, the likelihood of this is remote.[30] A massive invasion, or one like the Bay of Pigs, is not at all impossible. FAR prefers to concentrate on this possibility.

One of the unique aspects of the Cuban Revolution is that FAR consolidated control of the state apparatus for the revolutionaries. As a result, the party, as early as 1960-61, became dependent on military decision making. The revolutionary cadre itself absorbed the bureaucracy and with it a technocratic work style, and then reverted to a military style characteristic of guerrillas in power. The old bureaucracy was either absorbed into the revolutionary process or fled into exile. The old military had been crushed. Thus a political apparatus could easily adapt itself to new military modes without opposition from competing elites, as was the case in the formation of the new nations of Africa. The double edge of a successful guerrilla revolution, on one side, and the voluntary exile of an entire bureaucratic stratum, on the other, gave the regime a superficial appearance of solidarity.

Inner tensions within the Cuban regime must be located within the military rather than in the customary Third World pattern of military versus bureaucracy. There are clear military conflicts among three groups of officers: (1) graduates of the Frunze Military Academy; (2) graduates of the Inter-Armas Maceo military academies in Cuba; and (3) veterans of Sierra Maestra. Within the last classification, tensions are also present among three different groups: (1) the *Raúlistas,* veterans of the II Front of Oriente (Frank Pais Second Front); (2) the *fidelistas,* veterans who fought under columns whose chiefs belonged to the general staff of the Rebel Army and who were active throughout Sierra Maestra, and the Third and Fourth Guerrilla Fronts; and (3) the veterans of the underground (here further definitions are necessary, reflecting the movements to which they belonged in the 1950s).

This stratification creates the ground for profound differences in power and status. Graduates of the Frunze military academy in the Soviet Union hold important posts in the administrative and military structure (*Armas Coheteriles*). Missile and radar bases, for example, are under the absolute control of the *frunzistas.* Graduates of Cuban military schools are placed in secondary and less strategic positions throughout the state's civilian or military agencies. Sierra Maestra veterans are placed in tertiary positions, being viewed as militarily unprepared, inefficient, and closer to party policies than to military strategy and tactics; the classic competition of military versus bureaucratic reappears. The reorganization of CDRs in 1973, the complete reorganization of the economic sector to reflect a demotion for Sierra veterans and a promotion for the Soviet-trained "officers," and the purges of the youth section of the party to reflect a more intense paramilitary orientation—all indicate the military's central role in the bureaucratic party machinery. Even the decisive sector within the bureaucracy (MININT) functions as a direct part of FAR, as an independent army unit, reporting only to Raúl Castro. The civilian sector attempted to establish control over MININT in 1972-73, but failed. The consequence of this failure was that the frontier battalions were also placed under direct military supervision. As a result, tensions between the civilian and military sectors have increased at almost every level of the state machinery. Passive resistance to high production norms is but the most dramatic reflection of the militarization of Cuba and the intensification of contradictions between the democratic ideals of the revolution and its military outcomes.

Failures in sugar production, crop diversification, cattle breeding, and so on made it apparent that the party was either incompetent or so much under the influence of a foreign power, in this case the Soviet Union, that both military and paramilitary units had to exercise their prerogatives, much as they had in other nations of South and Central America where civilian administrations had also failed to produce impressive economic results. The movement into militarization was less protracted in Cuba, because "bourgeois" democratic factions had long since been annihilated as a political factor. The very origins of the Cuban military, steeped in guerrilla folklore and in Communist party indifference to spontaneous mass action, made the transition from civilianism to militarism not so much a matter of national upheaval as an expected stage of national development.

The accelerated movement of the Cuban Revolution into militaristic forms reflects the multiple needs of the Cuban regime. First, the regime employed the military, in classic Latin American tradition, for internal police functions, through the CDRs. Second, it used the military to mobilize the population after the less than successful phase in which moral incentives were used to spur economic development. During this phase, the youth brigades in particular were converted into a paramilitary fight force subject to military discipline and at the same time able to perform as labor shock troops in the event of any decline in sugar production. Third, and perhaps most ominous, the regime encouraged the rise of a professional attitude in the military so that it could perform on international terrain with a competence dismally absent from Guevara's guerrilla efforts. The maintenance of internal security, the mobilization of economic production, and finally the creation of revolutionary conditions in other countries or support for revolutionary groups in future rounds of insurgency efforts, deserve some amplification, even if it does involve speculation about the future.

The critical year was 1973, when critical decisions were made to substitute material incentives for moral incentives and to satisfy minimum demands of economic growth by whatever means necessary, including coercion. It became the essential role of the armed forces to satisfy the need for growth and to avoid the disastrous civilian-oriented programs of 1968-72. Not only did 1973 represent a new stage in the militarization of Cuban communism, but it also witnessed the thoroughgoing displacement of Guevara as the number-two figure (even in death) by the orthodox military figure of Raúl Castro, brother of Fidel, and second secretary of the Central Committee of the Party and minister of the Revolutionary Armed Forces. Raúl's rise to a place second only to Fidel's, and increasingly paralleling Fidel's role in crucial state and diplomatic functions, can hardly be exaggerated. Raúl has become the spokesman for all things military and the heir apparent to the revolution itself. His orthodoxy extends to the cut of his uniform (in contrast to that of Fidel) and his insistence on creating ranks within the Cuban military that are isomorphic with military ranks elsewhere in the world.

The basic mechanism by which the military performs its internal police functions varies in Cuba from that of most countries in Latin America. Elsewhere, the standard operating procedure is to restrain the military from political participation. In Cuba, the situation is reversed. There is a direct linkage between the Communist party apparatus and the military apparatus. Not even the Soviet Union has so close an identification of party and military. Raúl himself has provided the one hundred percent isomorphism between Communist party activities and Cuban military activities in the officer corps:

In this year that has just concluded, the individual training of our officers and commanders has been improved and greater cohesion and efficiency has been obtained in command bodies, which, together with the level reached in the handling of combat equipment, make it possible for the FAR to successfully deal with any enemy attack and defend the great achievements brought about through the efforts of our working people in these 15 years of the Revolution. We are very proud that 100 per cent of you are members of the Party or the Young Communist League. To be exact, 78 per cent are members of the Party and 22 per cent of the Young Communist League.

There is more data which sheds light on the humane and revolutionary quality of this group of vanguards: the average age is 29 and the average length of service in the ranks of our Revolutionary Armed Forces is 11, demonstrating that our armed institution has become an extraordinary school of cadres trained in firm revolutionary and Marxist-Leninist principles, loyal to the homeland, the Socialist Revolution, the working class and its leader, Commander in Chief Fidel Castro.[31]

More directly, the military is used as the basic mechanism for economic construction and production. This involves, first, the fusion of regular military units with paramilitary units and the linkage of both with Communist party activities. Cubans have gone the Soviets one step further: the old Stakhanovites were factory shock troops in no way linked to the military, but the new Cuban economic shock troops are directly drawn from military sources. Again, Raúl explains the basis of this military mobilization with considerable frankness:

> The present Followers of Camilo and Che detachments must also become units of the Army of Working Youth, continuing their work in the construction of junior high schools. From now on, the Followers movement must come from the ranks of the army of Working Youth, being made up of the best young people, the vanguard workers, so that every contingent of Followers will not mean depriving the work centers of their best young workers, members and leaders of the Young Communist League.

> The Army of Working Youth, as a para-military body which is a branch of the Ministry of the Revolutionary Armed Forces, will include all young men who, having to do their tour of duty of active military service according to existing laws, are not drafted into the regular units of the Armed Forces, as well as to the post-graduates assigned to the Army of Working Youth in keeping with the Social Service Law.

> The Young Communist League and its National Committee have been assigned to handle political and ideological work at all levels in the Army of Working Youth, in a demonstration of the great esteem our Party has of the political work it did in the CJC. This will be done with the same organizational principles as those prevailing in the rest of the Armed Forces, that is, that of a single command structure.[32]

The final piece of the Cuban military puzzle is the professionalization of the armed forces. This has been accomplished largely with the assistance of resident Soviet military personnel and hardware. Cuban references to Soviet support are far more direct than are those of any other Latin American country *vis-à-vis* U.S. military support. This does not necessarily mean that Cuba is any the more potent; it does mean that any confrontation by force of arms in the Western Hemisphere involving Cuba could well become a surrogate struggle between the latest Soviet hardware and intelligence and that of the United States. The growth of Cuban armed forces represents a far more considerable input into hemispheric affairs than does the earlier romantic phase of international revolution. Raúl Castro makes this clear in his recent speech before the leadership of the Revolutionary Armed Forces.

> Our FAR has not only drawn on the experiences of the Soviet Armed Forces but that they are generously supplied by the Soviet people who are staunchly loyal to the principles of proletarian internationalism with the modern means of combat that are essential for defending the Revolution.
>
> We have been in close contact with that internationalist support for more than a decade, with those feelings of fraternity, solidarity and mutual respect. It has been passed on to us by the thousands of Soviet specialists who have worked in our units during these years and by the ones who have given us their knowledge in the U.S.S.R.'s schools and military academies. Extraordinary relations, a friendship and a fraternal spirit that is a fitting example of the ties existing between two socialist armies struggling for the same cause and ideal have developed between the military men of Cuba and the U.S.S.R..[33]

Cuba seems quite different than any other country in the hemisphere. The nature of its Soviet support, as well as the character of its anti-American ideology, emphasize its uniqueness.[34] By an entirely different series of measures, the Cuban experience is painfully similar to that of other Third World countries. First, Cuba is dependent on hardware supplies from a major advanced industrial nation, the Soviet Union; second, Cuba defines state sovereignty almost exclusively in terms of hardware potential; third, its people bear an enormous burden to support military regimentation. There is the same pattern of economic solvency through military rule that occurs in Brazil, Argentina, Chile, Peru, and many other countries of the hemisphere. Admittedly, the linkage between the military and the bourgeoisie that characterizes many of these regimes does not exist. Cuba exhibits an even more pure form of military control, by virtue of the fact that its military is capable of functioning as a direct aim of the bureaucratic elite not mediated by class claims or interests.

In recent years it has become fashionable to speak of Cuba as being governed in part by civic soldiers: armed forces dedicated to technical proficiency and developmental goals. This is partly correct since like all military of the Third World, the main tasks are economic integration and mobilization. However, it would be dangerous to speak of a gradual restoration of civilian rule in Cuba since there is no evidence of any such process taking place. The origins of the Cuban Revolution and guerrilla insurgency, the maintenance of military regimentation within political apparatuses, the growth of the military ethic, the institutionalization of rank corresponding to ranks around the world, and above all the growing penetration of Soviet armed might, all strongly suggest that any movement toward civilianization is more a wish than a possibility.

Problems of the Cuban economy are too serious for an excessive reliance on the armed forces. Its political costs are also too high. But as long as the Soviet government continues to underwrite such excesses, not to mention political totalitarianism, the cost factor can be absorbed without too much self-reflection or political soul-searching. The likelihood of the Cuban armed forces becoming the advance guard of voluntary labor rewarded in moral terms only, is again a dangerous oversimplification of the current state of Cuban military affairs. While it is probably true that increasing professionalization of Cuban bureaucracy will serve to pressure the Cuban military to reduce its mobilization capacity, outcomes probably depend more heavily on a decline in Soviet participation in internal Cuban affairs than on any formal interplay of class and bureaucracy within Cuban society.

The militarization of Cuba is significant not so much because it is unique but because it falls into a pattern of contemporary Latin American bureaucratic politics. The classic inability of any single economic class to govern successfully has led to a series of coups in nation after nation. Some have been overt, as in Brazil, Argentina, Bolivia, and Peru. Others remain covert, as in Uruguay, the Dominican Republic, and to a lesser extent in Mexico. Cuba, in its splendid socialist isolation, demonstrates the iron law of oligarchy, or better, the rise of the military as an independent and crucial "base" for orchestrating politics and allocating economic goods. The growing isomorphism of Cuba with the rest of the Latin American orbit has disappointed rather than attracted followers and adherents. The promise of socialism in Cuba was at the outset far nobler in intent than is the dreary replication, under special conditions of isolation from the United States and dependence on the Soviet Union, which has come to define the realities of Cuban social structure.

The greatest part of wisdom is the recognition that social and revolutionary change proceed slowly and undramatically. The revolutionary moment is one of enormous drama. The decades of anguish following that moment that are required to make the revolution work, even remotely, are less dramatic, more painful, and often include false starts. The mystification of the revolution has long since ended. Even those who are most exuberant about the Cuban Revolution must face the fact that what has been gained is socialism without abundance and mass mobilization without mass democracy. Limbo is not paradise; but neither is it hell.

References/Notes

1. Régis Debray, *Revolution in the Revolution?* (New York: Monthly Review Press, 1967).
2. Fidel Castro, "Interview Andrew St. George," in Rolando E. Bonachea and Nelson P. Valdés (eds.), *Revolutionary Struggle, 1947-1958: Selected Works of Fidel Castro,* vol. 1 (Cambridge: MIT Press, 1972), pp. 164-221.
3. Ibid., pp. 233-38.
4. L.C. Agüero, *Cartas del presidio* (Havana: Editorial Let, 1959).
5. Ramón L. Bonachea and Marta San Martín, *The Cuban Insurrection: 1952-1959* (new Brunswick: Transaction Books/Dutton, 1974), ch. 8.
6. Régis Debray, *Strategy for Revolution: Essays on Latin America* (New York: Monthly Review Press, 1970), pp. 31-46.
7. Irving Louis Horowitz, "The Stalinization of Fidel Castro," New Politics 4, no. 4, Fall 1965, pp. 62-70; and idem, "The Political Sociology of Cuban Communism," in Carmelo Mesa-Lago (ed.), *Revolutionary Change in Cuba* (Pittsburgh: University of Pittsburgh Press, 1971), pp.127-41.

8. P. Tang and J. Maloney, "The Chinese Communist Input in Cuba," Washington Research Institute on the Sino-Soviet Bloc, Monograph Series 12, 1962, pp. 2-3.
9. Ibid., p. 6.
10. Ibid., p. 10.
11. Castro, pp. 369-71.
12. Ernesto "Che" Guevara, Guerrilla Warfare: A Method," in John Gerassi (ed.), *Venceremos: The Speeches and Writings of Guevara* (New York: Macmillan, 1968), pp. 266-79.
13. Guevara, *Guerrilla Warfare* (New York: Monthly Review Press, 1961), p. 10.
14. Ibid., p.17.
15. Ibid., pp. 17-34.
16. Ibid., pp. 49-50.
17. Debray, 1967, p. 19.
18. Ibid., p. 20.
19. Ibid., p. 27.
20. Ibid., p. 20.
21. Ibid., p. 62.
22. Ibid., p. 69.
23. Ibid., p. 102.
24. Ibid., p. 103.
25. Ibid., p. 106.
26. Edward González, "Partners in Deadlock: The United States and Castro, 1959-1972" (Los Angeles: California Arms Control and Foreign Policy Seminar, 1972), p. 11.
27. Guglielmo Ferrero, *The Two French Revolutions:* 1789-1796 (New York: Basic Books, 1968), pp. 203-27.
28. Comités de Defensa de la Revolución, *Memorias de* 1963 (Havana: Ediciones con la Guardia en Alto, 1964), pp. 13-22.
29. Sergio del Valle, Bias Roca, and Carlos Rafael Rodríguez, excerpts from speeches at the Third National Evaluation Meeting of the Committee for the Defense of the Revolution, *Granma Weekly Review,* February 17, 1974, p. 3.
30. Bonachea and San Martín., p. 30.
31. Raúl Castro, speech to Vanguards of the Revolutionary Armed Forces (FAR), *Granma,* January 20, 1974, p. 7.
32. Raúl Castro, closing address establishing the Army of Working Youth, *Granma,* August 12, 1973, p. 3.
33. Raúl Castro, 1974, pp. 3-4.
34. Edward González, "The United States and Castro: Breaking the Deadlock," *Foreign Affairs* 50, no. 4, July 1972, pp. 722-37.

Source and Original Title: "Military Origins of the Cuban Revolution." *Armed Forces and Society,* Vol. 1, No. 4, August 1975, pp. 402-18.

9

Ideological Euphoria and Post-Revolutionary Cuba

Social science writing on Cuba, like the revolution itself, has become sober and solid. Gone is the euphoria of the first flush of revolutionary fervor and counterrevolutionary fever. The complications of the social and political world have reasserted themselves: a world in which socialism is declared but the class and ideological imbalances remain; a world in which Soviet revisionists are praised to the skies and Maoist radicals condemned as traitors; a world in which planning pronouncements are met by stolid peasant resistance or simple mass disbelief. If the regime itself has been slow on the upbeat, preferring military displays on the first day of January and May to serious political reform, exiled analysts of the regime have taken up the slack. If the end of ideology with respect to writings on the Cuban Revolution did not exactly usher in an age of reason, it at least made possible the penetration of social and political science into this void of domestic analysis. It is entirely possible that the Cuban regime will draw correct lessons from this 16-year-old journey. Those who celebrate are often quick to condemn. Those who dispassionately examine may prove irritating—but the product of such efforts has a much longer durability.

The area of Cuban affairs invites ideological polarization. Any analysis is suspect and scrutinized from the standpoint of the analyst instead of how well it explains the Cuban system. Upon

inspection, early theories of the Cuban Revolution appear impoverished, so barren of originality that they invariably led to
severe theoretical as well as practical confusions. The writings
that emerged immediately after the Cuban Revolution were a
veritable political Rorschach test; one perceived the revolution
much the way he wanted to see it.

Cuban communism was increasingly defined by its leadership
in terms of ideal pretensions rather than actual achievements.
Just as Stalin, in his last days, announced that the basic law of
political economy in the USSR was the "law of maximum happiness," so too, as the Cuban revolutionary arteries hardened,
Castro announced the moral basis of Cuban economy and the
end of bourgeois egotism. Prior emphasis on material incentives
was declared reactionary, while moral incentives (whatever they
happened to be) were said to be progressive. Soon thereafter,
social science analysts absorbed this theme of morality versus
utilitarianism and stitched this argument into whole cloth: the
idealization of the revolution.

The tendency to adopt the language of moral incentives has
less to do with revolutionary romanticism than with the Cuban
political structure and with economic necessities of an island
economy under seige.[1] Cuba throughout the late sixties suffered
from a lack of material goods, but it rested in part on a set of
policy decisions concerning military over civilian priorities, and
was not simply an imposed consequence of the embargo. However, the conversion of necessity into choice by administrative
fiat is itself a characteristic of the Cuban political process.

This idealist interpretation of the Cuban Revolution emerged
from a number of programs that Castro advocated over the years.
Rather than face the weaknesses and limits of single-crop socialism, Castro insisted that Cuba made a revolution based on the
premise of making a new man and not just a new system. This
constant emphasis on the new humanism of the new man, originally a useful device for combating bureaucracy, ultimately led to
a general theory of moral incentives. Castro and Guevara raised
certain tendencies in Leninism and Stalinism to a level of theory. It

was claimed that people work either for money (to convert it into material-utilitarian goods) or in terms of future goals (an incentive with ethical purpose). The theme of the moral athlete in pragmatic terms was wedded to that of the moral economist in Marxist terms. This was enunciated in the social science literature by Bernardo and later by Kahl.[2] They argued that the Cuban Revolution cannot be measured simply by standard economic units since its drive shaft is the ability to raise productivity through moral incentives rather than through costly commodity incentives.

The profound difficulty with doctrines based on moral incentives is not only in the term *moral* but in the nature of incentives. Admittedly, rewards can be in terms of satisfaction as well as payment, and the Cuban regime had every right to frame its goals in terms of increased satisfactoriness of the labor process under socialism. However, such increased rewards must be recognizable to laborers themselves, and this can be done through a variety of ways: mechanization, new forms of job sharing, new ways of distributing produce, etc. In the absence of any fundamental changes for the masses both in work styles or material rewards, moral incentives were underwritten first by the party vanguard, and when this incentive by example approach fell short of the mark, through outright coercion. What started out as an experience in alternative work styles ended up as a demand by the regime to meet quotas arbitrarily and artificially set by the leadership without regard to world commodity prices or international grain conditions. This elitist definition of moral incentives, rather than the concept itself, became a characteristic of Cuba as it passed from a political to a military phase.

Kahl and Bernardo have both focused upon the role of ideology and morality in driving Cuban economic planners toward negative decisions about the nature of market relationships—decisions that in turn have led to a series of problems which seem to presage an even greater series of catastrophes. Questions about the use of moral incentives in stimulating economic growth can be summarized as follows: Can a society have moral incentives under conditions of economic scarcity?

More specifically, can a single-crop economy be designated as socialist in any but the most desultory sense? In a broader context, does not Cuban emphasis on moral incentives violate classic economic rules concerning market determination of prices and profits, and even the Marxist theory of labor?

The problem is one of causation rather than ideology. Marxist theory of moral incentives to labor presupposed the solution of problems of material incentives. Only when ego needs are fully gratified, only when material abundance is available for all to share in, does the Marxist doctrine of moral incentives come into play. Neo-Marxist doctrine moves up the timetable of economic development; that is, it accelerates the doctrine of moral incentives so that the reasons for effort and labor are related to political survival of the system rather than economic abundance created by that system. The Cuban economy has responded to the role of political ideology by showing that the essence of planning is not so much economic growth as it is political mobilization. In this sense the theory of moral incentives has had a binding value on Cuban society far in excess of any economic profitability or losses occasioned by premature disavowal of market incentives to labor. For Silverman the fundamental rationale behind the movement to increase overtime hours worked without compensation is the Marxian idea of primitive accumulation: "Were moral incentives to fail, the obvious necessity of using coercion to produce the economic surplus would have to be faced."[3] And indeed, moral incentives have collapsed by Castro's own admission and the resort to increased military pressures on the populace has been the consequence of this new turn toward economic realism.

The Cuban economy took an enormous gamble by assuming that there would be enough nonmaterial incentives to maintain a stable state within the economy. Whether this is so depends not only on the state of mind of the Cuban working class, but on levels of production and consumption of Cuban society as a whole. If the question of economic incentives were simply one of monetary purchasing power—unemployment rates, absenteeism, and even labor sabotage would be considerably higher than they are. How long can a society substitute moral fervor for consumer satisfaction? The Christian-Marxist doctrine of men living not by bread alone ignores the fact that there is an intermediate stage between matter and morals—what might be called comfort and well-being. Here is where the vital trade-off between economy and morality takes place. Whether or not Cuban society can sustain sufficient fervor for the regime to permit continued growth of the GNP at the expense of consumer fulfillment is extremely difficult to predict.

A balance sheet view of the situation shows that the moral economy has succeeded in achieving a high degree of egalitarianism as a by-product of Cuban productive organization, and Bernardo and Kahl are correct in observing that this was achieved largely by use of the allocation system of moral stimulation. The price of this egalitarianism is a high demand for material goods—and the choice is limited. The theory of moral stimulation alters old relationships and ends the exaggerated separation of supply and demand for money and goods. Wage differentials are reduced; price differentials are reduced; leisure and labor are flattened out; and in general, there is a definite complementarily between moral and material incentives in such a system. But again, the problem is whether in fact there are such things as moral incentives, or whether the doctrine is not simply a disguised way of defining unpaid labor time, or labor time paid at reduced wages, for the purposes of increasing the GNP.

An orthodox rather than a revisionist Marxian view might be taken. Common sense dictates that we should average unpaid labor time with paid labor time to arrive at the actual earning power of Cuban labor. The theory of moral incentives is a way of maintaining a socialist economy in a single-crop situation with a minimal amount of inflationary spiraling and pressures for trade union reform.

The anomaly is that Cuban leaders have spiritualized problems of economic production and allocation. They are the first true idealists to emanate from the Marxist-socialist tradition. This philosophical outcome should not have been unexpected since the Cuban Revolution always seemed to be a matter of will and a problem in decision theory, rather than a matter of determinism or of history. Postrevolutionary Cuban leadership has carried forth this volitional or idealistic theory of revolution and has made the success of socialist economy also a matter of will, which ultimately involves questions of moral choice. Bernardo's book provides a fascinating episode not just in the annals of political economy, but even more profoundly in political sociology: the way in which problems of political leadership and social class determine the struggle of society, and ultimately the structure of values which provide the ideological fuel for Cuban society.

The most recent pronouncements on the subject of incentives by Castro indicate a backing away from the idealistic implications of the moral incentives doctrine. The newest formulations tend to emphasize that both material and spiritual incentives are required within a system of socialist production. The utter chaos and confusion in the wake of sugar crop failures convinced the Cuban leadership, if not always its overseas intellectual followers, that something more than moral incentives is required to make people work effectively. In this recognition the passage from theory to practice is completed, since we move from what is past to what is present; and beyond that, from the consolidation of Stalinism as a political factor to its implementation in Cuban reality as a military factor.[4]

We have come a long way from the writings on the Cuban Revolution which appeared during the first decade following the triumphal entrance of the *fidelistas* into Havana 15 years ago. The literature of the 1960s was alternatively euphoric and condemnatory. In the halcyon days of the revolution we were confronted with false alternatives: apocalyptic and unstinting praise that turned sour at the first sign of real political cleavage in Cuba; and homespun jingoistic journalism that operated within a conspiracy theory which assumed that behind every nationalist *cri de coeur* was a Marxist master plan. Present-day examination of Cuba has also gone far beyond an earlier generation's efforts to conduct empirical research employing attitudinal and behavioral measures which only proved the obvious: a real revolution had actually occurred with an attendant support base among the

Cuban masses. There are the uncomfortable suspicions that were a counterrevolution to occur; these same peasants would reveal similar loyalty and confidence in the new regime. Survey research rarely takes into account the accommodating tendencies of peasant masses. As noted, the early literature did not provide a general theory of the revolution. Because the Cuban revolutionary cadre and its supporters assumed that Cuba had undergone a model Marxist insurgency worthy of endless praise and emulation, one had to look outside the nation, certainly outside the regime, to establish even the rudiments of authentic theorizing. The problem was that earlier writers on Cuba were either too close or too remote from the Castro regime to reproduce a systematic vision of either the structure or process of the revolution.

A far more sophisticated analytical phase began with the second decade of the Cuban Revolution. Some of the cracks in the Cuban facade were revealed by the Castro regime itself; the more obvious shortcomings of earlier decisions in the agricultural and industrial sectors became evident. At this level, European journalists and historians such as Hugh Thomas, René Dumont, and K.S. Karol[5] took the lead. Surprisingly, even today few "officialist" American social scientists have made even a modicum of sense or given a decent burial to inherited nonsense about the Cuban Revolution. Politically sanctioned writings on Cuba are still mired in vague assumptions about the hemisphere as a whole or about Cuba as an exception to every rule of structural conduct. Apart from the forthrightness of European philosophers, most writers on Cuba must be dismissed either as propagandists of the revolutionary deed or purveyors of the obvious.

Of Cuban analysts themselves very little can be said. The revolution dismembered the ranks of authentic social scientists. This dissolution of "bourgeois social science" robbed critics of the regime of their voices and left a generation of handicapped intellectuals who could only recite a syllabus in praise of nationalism and socialism. Not since the infamous linguistics controversy in the Soviet Union during the early 1950s have the ranks of critical social scientists and historians been so depleted of homegrown talent.

So bereft of honest commentary has the Cuban regime become, that it has had to cultivate, even curry, social scientists in exile, born and partially raised and educated in pre-Castro Cuba. Not without irony, these much despised and vilified "worms" have carried the day; they represent *gusanos de la conciencia* for the regime. Mesa-Lago, González, and Suchlicki have carried the tradition of analysis into the Cuban heartland, symbolically and empirically. There we have it: North American social scientists and European journalists making brief, on-site inspection tours, competing with Cubans in exile, in an effort to describe a nation and an island which exported and exiled the talent it needed to explain itself.

Contributions to the study of Cuba by officialist U.S. social scientists read as if they have been produced by people looking through a telescope, or perhaps from an airplane 30,000 feet above sea level. They have more in common with the American passion for guerrilla and counter guerrilla scenarios than with the facts of the Cuban experience. One is led to wonder why radical criticism of Cuba has offered such weak resistance to orthodox interpretations. American interpretations as a whole are weak in quality rather than quantity. In part, they have dried up in disillusionment with the Cuban Revolution. Some critics believe the revolution has not gone far enough; others say it has gone too far. Another group is disturbed by Cuban foreign policy, particularly those with a shared faith in the Cuban and Israeli models and their presumed transcendental similitudes. This group has been stunned by the vitriolic anti-Israeli posture of the Cuban regime. Others, who saw the Cuban Revolution as an opportunity for independent socialist action apart from the Soviet Union, have been dismayed by the regime's increasing reliance upon Soviet aid. Of Course, there remains the usual "I was there . . .," "the people are Wonderful . . .," and "we shall win" literature. But even those sorts of inspirational tracts have seen better days. What we are left with is much more in the nature of quasi-policy studies concerning the United States than empirical studies examining Cuba without jaundice.

Two books, one edited by Luigi Einaudi for the RAND Corporation, *Beyond Cuba,* and the other by D.E.H. Russell, *A Comparative Study of Fifteen Countries,* emphasizing Cuba and South Africa, typify this new genre.[6] The work by Russell is rather painful to review because it is so well-intentioned. She seeks to establish a quantifiable basis for determining successful and unsuccessful revolutionary struggles. Since we have so little in the way of quantification of large-scale revolutions, this effort is certainly praiseworthy. Underlying the volume is a search for general laws which govern the conduct of revolutionary events. The key is the analysis of successful and unsuccessful rebellion with respect to the behavior of the armed forces.

The problem is: Which armed forces? Generally, the author refers to the established armed forces of the ancien régime. But as it turns out, the key is not a mathematical equation but a dialectical relation: the size and capability of guerrillas on one hand, and the resoluteness of regulars on the other. These vary so dramatically from nation to nation that a mathematical understanding of revolution and rebellion in Cuba or South Africa is hardly feasible. Even the author is led to observe that at one point, according to Hugh Thomas, there were only four square miles of territory under Fidel Castro's military control. But at that moment, the morale of the Batista forces dropped so badly that they were unable to launch the final thrust that would have eliminated the Fidel forces. So much for a simple mathematical model, and perhaps so much for models of inevitable guerrilla triumph.

An additional problem in Russell's work is her infelicitous choice of Cuba and South Africa. The rationale for this comparative analysis is capricious; there is no point in looking for comparisons without carefully stating control elements that might enable one to isolate factors for analysis. Russell's analysis of Cuba and South Africa, however well motivated, reveals a correlation between the two nations that exists more in her own mind than in political or military similitudes. Russell concludes that the South African regime, being more oppressive than the Cuban regime and more capable of generating what she calls "regime unity," is thereby less subject to penetration by guerrillas or overthrow by external forces. Those ubiquitous "other conditions," either missing or weakly stated, make the analysis tenuous at best and spurious at worst. Even the mathematical scaling is somewhat eccentric, since the "disloyalty score" for the Cuban rebellion of 1959 is 10.5 (a successful rebellion), whereas the disloyalty score for the Honduran rebellion of 1933 (which was singularly unsuccessful) is 10.0. Given such data, one can only conclude that either our mathematics or our social science is simply not up to the task of thoroughgoing quantification.

The volume edited by Luigi Einaudi is another kettle of fish, since it was produced with a direct policy imperative in mind. The original task was to analyze major trends in Latin America (in 1970) for the Department of State. The volume rests on the rather comfortable and certainly dubious proposition put forth by the State Department, that the surfacing of divisions among Latin American revolutionary groups after the Cuban Revolution, together with other changes in regional and international political contexts, render repetition of the Cuban experience elsewhere in Latin America improbable despite the continuing relevance of radical nationalist critiques of the status quo. This somewhat fatuous theme underwrites the volume, although there are considerable variations in the papers produced under Einaudi's general direction. Given the fact that this is not simply an edited volume, but one in which he either authored or coauthored no fewer than nine of the 15 papers included, we have a much more integral view than is customary in a reader.

It is hard to know what Einaudi is offering the buyers of this research. There is such an air of buoyant optimism that one wonders if this is the same Latin America we have heard about from other sources. We are told, in the paper on "Patterns of Civility and Military Rule," that "narrowly civilian or highly militarized ruling coalitions will prove to be inherently unstable" (p. 117); and that "even the most militarized regime in Latin America that of Peru has important civilian components." Aside from the fact that the most militarized regime in Latin America is not Peru (that honor would have to go to

Paraguay, Brazil, Chile, and Argentina, in that order, with Peru a distant fifth), the tendency toward military or quasi-military rule has become dominant. Coalition rule in Latin America is virtually absent, except for Mexico. Beyond that, the regime most capable of generating sustained economic growth is Brazil. Interestingly, the economic patterns of Brazil and Mexico appear to be closest, despite their differences in political/military regimes.

The Einaudi volume hopelessly clutches for straw men. It assumes that internal differentiation within Latin America will somehow prevent totalitarianism of a Cuban variety from emerging. Einaudi also seems to argue that a new regional consciousness will provide plurality within unity. But Cuba is somehow not dealt with in the context of emerging regionalism. It is not that the volume lacks insight. Einaudi and his associates in the Latin American section at RAND are extremely able and shrewd observers of the Latin American scene. Their optimism is pervasive, yet in the end rests solely on status quo and system-maintenance assumptions. Their five summary points indicate as much. Latin American Social and economic inequality, they say, will occasionally provide fuel for political thrust, but will not prevent overall institutional continuity. The presumption is that institutional continuity once really existed in Latin America, a point of view that I have long disputed, arguing instead that Latin America is based on norms of political illegitimacy rather than political institutionalization. It is probably true that governments and elites in Latin America are less subject to external manipulation than in the past. However, when the masses in the area rule, they may be subject to greater internal manipulation. This qualification is conveniently overlooked by Einaudi, since the Department of State could not care less about internal chaos unless it affects external stability. Their assertion that Latin American governments are likely to maximize industrialization in an age of food and energy shortage is also dubious. Export of crops and petroleum might prove an easier path economically, with fewer risks in terms of class struggles than revival of nationalism based exclusively upon an industrial model.

The Einaudi work handles the problem in a way that provides aid and comfort to those who paid for the research, but not necessarily the sort of analysis which helps us understand Cuba, or for that matter events beyond Cuba either spatially or structurally. For if Cuba is a model which cannot be emulated, and has no bearing on the future course of events, what is the meaning of the phrase *Beyond Cuba?* or of the subtitle *Latin America Takes Charge of Its Future?* Latin America's ability to take charge is in no small part a consequence of the Cuban Revolution.

When I first read René Dumont's volume in French, *Cuba: Est il Socialiste?*, I found his sublime ignorance of previous works on the subject of Stalinization in Cuba so irritating that I was inclined not to evaluate the intrinsic merits or demerits of his argument. The work of his colleague, K.S. Karol, which appeared at approximately the same time, demonstrated a higher level of intellectual penetration and practical understanding. Both the Dumont and Karol volumes are in the classic continental mold of critical social journalism.[7] Both offer sound, general, overall characterizations of the regime. In part, they accomplish this through periodization that is, breaking the Cuban Revolution into time frames and showing how they are connected with each other. Both Dumont and Karol employ popular history as the spine of their analysis of how the revolution progressed over time and through interaction of elite bureaucracies with mass organizations. If the analysis is imprecise, even loose, it does represent a welcome relief from the North American propensity to assume that a rank order correlation is tantamount to divine revelation. The French writers analyze Cuba on its own terms, not in relation to French foreign policy or any other foreign policy. If there are any explicit continental connections, they are the presumed linkage of revolutionary Cuba with the history of socialism as a European movement more than 125 years old. But that socialist framework gives both Karol and Dumont a level of sophistication and a penetration into Cuban society distinctly absent in the work of their American counterparts. It also separates their efforts from the social science traditions of middle-range observations and generalizations.

The work of Dumont, even more than that of Karol, suffers from insufferable conceit. Both presume that political decisions must be moral if they are to be legitimate. Castro's problems throughout his 15 years as premier have been rather practical, or as Carmelo Mesa-Lago would say, "pragmatic." The militarization and bureaucratization of Cuba, faith in maximum leaders, total breakdown in parliamentary behavior, are all real enough. The question is whether there are or ever have been genuine alternatives. Are there nonauthoritarian alternatives for socialism within Cuba or Latin America as a whole? The militarization of the island and the export of guerrilla insurgents to other nations reflected an intense period of hostility toward Cuban communism from hostile Latin American as well as North American states.

These kinds of issues are either entirely ignored or placed in a peculiar volitional context by Dumont. One would think only Fidel's spitefulness has led to the regime's problems. For Dumont, so colossal does the figure of Fidel loom that he falls only a hair's width short of claiming that the maximum leader uniquely determines the course of Cuban history. Even Fidel would not presume quite so magnificent a role. We are told, for example, that "in the final analysis, Fidel has confidence only in himself and is unable to delegate responsibility." One of the principal tenets and current concerns of Fidel is the institutionalization of the revolution and the creation of secondary and tertiary cadre capable of handling much greater responsibility than in the past. Power has become differentiated in Cuba, or at least remarkably polarized in terms of efforts toward militarization undertaken by Castro's younger brother Raúl, in contrast to efforts toward civil bureaucratization encouraged by Fidel. Simplistic formulations replace analysis by Dumont, such as "Castro would not accept control from below because he has enjoyed personal power too long to be able to give it up gradually." This is followed by meaningless exhortation to none other than Raúl Castro, Dorticós, Rodríguez, Armando Hart, and Bias Roca to have courage and "realize that the present personal dictatorship power structure threatens a series of difficulties that may lead to catastrophe."[8]

As Dumont fittingly concludes, generalization always leads to exaggeration.

Dumont finally exhorts Castro to think over his responsibilities and resign. This is either a form of arrogance beyond description, or foolishness equally difficult to measure. Whatever else Castro does, he is constantly thinking over his responsibilities. The difficulty with Dumont's book is that it really never answers the question, Is Cuba socialist? To say that "socialist elements are on the retreat," especially because of the military takeover of the economy, is not to take seriously the fundamental economic and structural components of Cuban socialism, beginning with its liquidation of the bourgeoisie as a social class in power. Certainly if Dumont wants to say Cuba is not socialist, it is incumbent on him to say what it is. The book comes to a grinding halt just when we need Dumont's help the most. The problem is not "that it is all too easy to write at an old Professor's desk in old Europe," as Dumont says, but rather he assumes that personalism is an ideology from which he thinks Fidel never emerged. We are left with characterizations of the personality of the leader, but with no parallel analysis of the regime. I seriously doubt Dumont's assertion that Cuba has become an island where "it is every man for himself," or that massive indulgence in thievery has become commonplace. It is imprudent to assume that the regime has such a degree of economic inflexibility that it cannot survive. In part, this error arises because of Dumont's exaggerations of personality characteristics at the expense of social structure, an epistemic problem almost inherent in journalistic analysis.

Yet it must be finally said that the honesty and forthrightness of both Dumont and Karol are extremely important to the current debate about Cuba. Both are voices from the Left, not as Castro apparently claims; agents of the CIA. Left-wing analysts have usually been characterized by a moral posture, far more sensitive to ethical coordinates than to political requirements. They make it plain that Cuba has lost much of its luster not as a result of American imperialism or foreign intervention, but as a consequence of authentic politics itself, a pedestrian politics of compromise and accommodation with the Soviet Union. However necessary this "stage" in the Cuban Revolution may be, it cannot help but lead to the appreciation that politics itself is a tarnished pursuit engaged in by tarnished men. In short, what Dumont and Karol really cannot understand about the course of the Cuban Revolution is that it has become pedestrian and prosaic—politics as usual. Were things to be otherwise, the regime would hardly have lasted 15 months, much less 15 years.

We next turn to the three contributions of the much hated *gusanos,* the "worms," the exiles. Feared by the Cuban regime, loathed by the American Left, these refugees in American institutions of higher learning have nonetheless provided the best analyses—with certain noteworthy exceptions—of contemporary Cuba. It is curious that despite the vilification that could easily turn individuals sour, Cuban exiles (in marked contrast to Soviet exiles) have remained remarkably evenhanded and fair-minded. I am not referring here to the ordinary nonpolitical exile, which established economic bases in Miami and recreated pre-Revolutionary Cuban society with its vested interest groups. I refer rather to that special breed of social scientist and historian whose sense of reality was heightened rather than distorted by the agonizing choice of exile. Such Cuban exiles remain convinced of the need for revolution, not restoration, and they remain Cuban, not American. Their continuing affection and respect for Cuba is never diminished by the ferocious criticisms they often provide. The sad truth is that Castro has never required such objectivity, and never has bothered to utilize it in the past 15 years of the Cuban Revolution. But the age of the sycophant may be coming to an end. Exiles are being treated civilly for the first time-some are even being invited to return as honored citizens. How the worms have turned into giants!

The work of Carmelo Mesa-Lago is especially impressive for its combination of economic and sociological understanding. This is the most concentrated, condensed, and valuable 150 pages of writing on Cuba between 1960 and 1975 that I have yet come upon. For the scholar about to disembark on the Camelotian island of Cuba, the one indispensable book is Mesa-Lago's.[9] The tabular outline divides the first 15 years of the Cuban Revolution into five stages which tell the story of the book in synoptic form. This chart should be required study for anyone giving or taking instruction in the regime as it now stands. *Cuba in the 1970s* provides a model for combining quantitative and qualitative analysis. Where Russell and Einaudi fail, Mesa-Lago succeeds in providing high levels of generalization enriched by empirical specification. The volume is an embellishment and a working out of those five stages and 16 factors emphasized in the charts.

Rather than simply present an outline of the book, it might be more useful to indicate problems economists have had in developing an appropriate, full-blooded characterization of the Cuban regime. The reader is given a most careful analysis of Cuba's political and administrative systems; it represents a schema of organization with which one can hardly argue. However, it presumes a rational model of government and society which does not exist in Cuba. To speak conventionally of the separation of government functions into an administrative and party apparatus is to ignore the fact that we are not dealing with just a social order, but also with a flow chart of power determined on an ad hoc basis. It is not simply that the armed forces are now characterized by a high degree of military professionalization, or that their necessary component was reorganization into a constitutional bureaucracy much like that in other parts of the world. Mesa-Lago is correct on this point. But the main point is that the overall direction of the regime has been toward militarization: even trade unions have become subject to military dominion.[10] That labor politics has become integrated into the armed forces, and that the overall direction of the economy has increasingly become subject to centralization as well as militarization, indicates that even the goal of democracy has been placed on the back burner by Fidel and his followers.

Under such military rank ordering it is a forlorn hope to speak of the Cuban regime as moving toward a slow transformation from socialist dependency to a democratic independent system.

Even given Mesa-Lago's analysis, a single-crop system on a small island is geopolitically and geographically incapable of bringing to fructification this dream of a better world of social harmony. Carmelo Mesa-Lago's suggestion that the movement will be in this democratic direction is naive and romantic. I am not suggesting that the Castro regime should not move in other directions. However, the call for greater autonomy and independence ultimately violates the high level of analysis Mesa-Lago offers throughout the analytic portions of his book. That as it may be, one must repeat that this book is a considerable achievement: a balanced appraisal of the Cuban Revolution that should be taken seriously by friend and foe of the regime alike.

The work of Edward González[11] more nearly typifies the efforts of an historian than of a social scientist, perhaps an appropriate reflection of his own Castilian as well as Cuban ancestry. Yet here too we have a book that is remarkably sensitive to the dynamics of revolutionary development, dedicated to a fair-minded evaluation of the Castro regime. The problem with the González volume is not so much the level of description, but rather the level of conceptualization. While one can hardly deny that *fidelismo* is an ideology unto itself, and that the man behind the "ism" represents a socialist caudillo, there are problems in reducing below life size the characteristics of the Cuban Revolution in terms of Fidel's larger-than-life deeds. His ability to produce remarkable and beneficial results such as agrarian reform, and his defense against the U.S.-assisted invasion at the Bay of Pigs, has given misplaced emphasis to leadership at the expense of membership. González's approach, for all of his intimacies with Fidel, ignores the central fact: Fidel has created a regime capable of surviving him. The greatest myth of all is the CIA myth of assassination: that somehow to destroy the leader is to destroy the regime or, even better, the system. Such thinking is palpably wrong, even dangerous. It leads to a mistaken over identification of personal leadership and regime survival.

Cuba is no longer committed to permanent revolution, but to national reconstruction. Even Fidel, that supreme agrarian moralist, is no longer dedicated solely to ethical regeneration, but equally to material incentives. Quite unlike the moral dogmatist Ché Guevara, Fidel is no longer concerned with rapid industrial development as an abstract prerequisite for national independence, but with aid and trade that will keep the regime going even if there is no industrial development. González comes to an understanding of this in his evaluation of the current period, in which he points out that populism could not vie successfully with socialism. Administrative reform, followed by regime rationalization, has made older forms of personalism obsolete. And no one knows this more keenly than Fidel himself. The shock to Fidel in the wake of the sugar harvest fiasco was that Cuba is indeed a small island and that the sort of autonomy he seeks is not only elusive but is made even more remote by posturing and pretending.

González designs three alternative futures for Cuba: Sovietized bureaucratic communism, populism based on Fidel's nationalism, and a tropical Titoism—none of which makes much sense in terms of the future. Soviet communism is closest to what Cuba is about now. Populism, based on Fidel's charismatic personality, is more like what initially inspired the Cuban Revolution. And tropical Titoism is the only future envisaged by González which is remotely possible, but even then one of many possibilities (even Balkan Titoism is getting hard to describe). But as González himself indicates, current Cuban leadership is so thoroughly dependent upon its Soviet patron that any major redirection of the Cuban Revolution would depend upon reestablishment of relations with the United States. Only in that way might democratization of Cuban socialism become remotely feasible. But to understand the social history of Cuba, and to fix the Cuban system within a context of race, class, and generational factors, one can hardly do better than to start with González's volume.

Jaime Suchlicki, an outstanding representative of the exile tradition, best explains why the Titoist option is unrealistic for Cuba:

> Although the Communist party of Cuba is organized along classic lines, there is a preponderance of military representatives in its higher echelons, particularly in the executive organs. Coupled with this is the exclusion of

"old-guard Communists" from leadership roles. The party is controlled by Castroites rather than pro-Soviet Communists. Eighty percent or more of the 100-member Central Committee consists of pro-Castro officers and comrades from the anti-Batista struggle. Castro, therefore, does not appear able or willing to become the Tito of the Western Hemisphere. His political style and ideology and his apprehensions about U.S. motivations make him more prone to deviate to the left than to the right of the Soviet line. His awareness of Cuba's vulnerability is reinforced by the hostile activities of Cuban refugees. The preservation of a radical position is therefore more desirable not only for the defense of the revolution but also to encourage the anti-U.S. struggle in Latin America.

This work was published several years ago, but was neglected with the rush of books at the time. Suchliki's volume, *Cuba, Castro, and Revolution*[12] has an American policy base as its center of gravity; but its understanding of Cuban political motives is higher than that set forth in the Einaudi volume. Perhaps that is because the Center for Advanced International Studies at the University of Miami is closer to Cuba than the RAND Corporation at Santa Monica. This geographical point is not made fatuously, but out of simple appreciation that proximity does lead to increased sensitivity. The Latin American Center at the University of Miami, along with similar centers at the University of Florida, represents the best Americans have in the way of systematic studies of Latin America, certainly of the Caribbean. The strong proximity of Hispanic culture and the interaction of North and Latin Americans help to explain this uniquely high level of achievement in the field of Caribbean studies.

This volume was a forerunner of current efforts to distinguish Cuban foreign policy from the nationalism in its leadership structure. Cuban foreign relations with the Soviet Union, its integration within the Soviet economic orbit, and finally, the unique challenge that Castro represents to Latin American communism of a more orthodox variety, are dealt with in a series of sensitive and insightful papers. The works of Leon Gouré, M. Michael Kline, and Sergio Roca are especially impressive.

The supreme merit of the book, despite its title, is to emphasize Cuban society rather than personalistic politics. For no matter how hard Castro has attempted to come out with a unique posture, he ultimately has had to negate his own "Third Way" in favor of Soviet aid. Third World, yes; third way, no. Throughout the 1970s dependency upon the Soviet Union has only increased. Every internal failure in Cuba has occasioned one more loss of sovereignty. Still, it must be said in admiration of Cuba that it is one of the few places on earth that can be considered geographically small yet ideologically and militarily is reckoned with in world historic terms. In that sense, the normal buoyancy and ebullience of the Cuban people, as exemplified by its leadership, will perhaps preserve it from the worst features of the Stalinist regime it has been forced to embrace.

James Nelson Goodsell (1975), Latin American desk editor of *The Christian Science Monitor,* has put together a most useful anthology in the Knopf series on Latin America. *Fidel Castro's Personal Revolution in Cuba:* 1959-1973[13] well illustrates the historicist and traditionalist biases of other volumes in the same series. Yet it would be unseemly for the editor of one anthology to raise too much of a ruckus with an editor of another such volume (although it is not asking too much to have the fact of other anthologies more candidly acknowledged by Goodsell). The intriguing aspect of this reader is the editor's thesis. Only personalism emerges strongly from his assessment of the Cuban Revolution: Castro's caudillo qualities and his complete domination of the national course. Why the implications of such totalitarian dictatorship are not drawn by Goodsell is hard to explain, stemming perhaps from a sentimental belief that the good done by the revolution in social affairs outweighs evils performed in a political context. Had he added this caveat, all would be saved.

Once again, we are forced to observe how many of the outstanding essays in this volume are by *gusanos:* Andrés Suárez, Jaime Suchliki, Carmelo Mesa-Lago, Boris Goldenberg, Edward González, etc., while the articles written in overt support of the revolution are provided by American and European writers: Lee Lockwood, Hugh Thomas, John Gerassi, Richard Fagen, etc. Contributions by Cuban *fidelistas* themselves are sparse and extraordinarily insipid. Only Fidel speaks with authority and comprehensiveness. This is clearly not a fault with Goodsell, whose knowledge of Cuban affairs is deep and intimate. The fact that even those few selections chosen from Cuban sources are an embarrassment must mean that something deeper is rotten in the state of Cuba.

The Cuban Revolution has created a generation of intellectual vacancies. No vilification of those who left the country can erase this fact. The very luster of the exiled social science communities attests to the abilities of Cubans as a people, but parenthetically, it serves to heighten the sense of tyranny in the regime. As any reader of *Granma* can well attest, careful analysis and sophistication have come to be viewed as enemies of the regime. If anyone cares to examine the consequences of Castroism as a hemispheric variant of Stalinism, one can stop right at Goodsell's anthology, with its tragic display of brilliant exiles and critics living abroad and its simpleminded and truly vulgar Marxist "scholars" living at home. This contradiction exposes a fatal flaw in the Cuban Revolution: its lack of respect for plain truths or honest criticisms.

At the risk of being labeled an inveterate enemy of the people who can be dealt with only by being tossed off the railroad car of history, I should like to end with a plea: may the social achievements of the revolution—social welfare, mass education, an end to inherited forms of class exploitation, a termination of imported mass ills such as prostitution and gambling, and a grappling with problems of race and sex at a level unparalleled by most other nations of Latin America—be matched with political and intellectual achievements of a similar order of magnitude. To date, that has not been the case. That such matters as civil liberties, intellectual freedom, and personal rights to dissent have not been forthcoming is the true agony of the present stage in the Cuban Revolution. In this, political sociology has badly lagged behind political reality.

An exaggeration of the costs of liberty is the inevitable outcome of being small and dependent. It is also a consequence of Cuba's former dependence upon the United States. Its mentors cared precious little for the sorts of social equities now present in Cuba; while current Soviet mentors care even less for the sorts of political and economic liberties becoming increasingly scarce in other parts of the Third World. It might be that the marriage of social welfare and political liberty is impossible as long as two major world systems running the global show have so little patience with either economic equality or political liberty respectively. While there is an easy impulse to suggest that small nations take the lead in this marriage of equity and liberty, the empirical problem remains that such small nations as Cuba lack the clout to make their own world-historic decisions. Until Cuba joins the Third World to which it rightfully, i.e., structurally, belongs, and surrenders the myth of independent socialism (as it was compelled by force of circumstances to surrender the myth of independent capitalism), it cannot serve as an hemispheric model. It must first rid itself of the burden of being the victim of current world-historic bifurcations.

References/Notes

1. Bertram Silverman, "The Great Debate in Retrospect: Economic Rationality and the Ethics of Revolution," in idem (ed.), *Man and Socialism in Cuba: The Great Debate* (New York: Atheneum, 1971), pp. 3-28.
2. Robert M. Bernardo, *The Theory of Moral Incentives in Cuba* (University: University of Alabama Press, 1971); and Joseph A. Kahl, "The Moral Economy of a Revolutionary Society," in Irving L. Horowitz (ed.), *Cuban Communism*, 2nd ed. (New Brunswick, NJ.: Transaction Books/E.P. Dutton, 1972).
3. Silverman, p. 20.
4. Horowitz, 1965; and idem, "The Political Sociology of Cuban Communism," in Carmelo Mesa-Lago (ed.), *Revolutionary Change in Cuba* (Pittsburgh: University of Pittsburgh Press, 1971).
5. Hugh Thomas, *Cuba: The Pursuit of Freedom, 1762-1969* (New York: Harper and Row); René Dumont, *Is Cuba Socialist?* Translated by Stanley Hochman (New York: Viking Press, 1974); and K.S. Karol, *Guerrillas in Power: The Course of the Cuban Revolution* (New York: Hill and Wang, 1971).
6. Luigi R. Einaudi (ed.), *Beyond Cuba: Latin America Takes Charge of Its Future* (New York: Crane-Russak Publishers, in cooperation with RAND Corporation, 1974); and D.E.H. Russell, *Rebellion, Revolution, and Armed Force: A Comparative Study of Fifteen Countries with Special Emphasis on Cuba and South Africa* (New York: Academic Press, 1974).
7. René Dumont, *Cuba: Est-if socialiste?* (Paris: Editions du Seuil, 1970); and Karol, 1971.
8. Dumont, 1974, p. 140.

9. Carmelo Mesa-Lago, *Cuba in the 1970s: Pragmatism and Institutionaliza-tion* (Albuquerque: University of New Mexico Press, 1974).
10. See Ramón L. Bonachea and Marta San Martín, *The Cuban Insurrec-tion, 1952-1959* (New Brunswick, N.J.: Transaction Books/E.P. Dutton, 1974).
11. Edward González, *Cuba under Castro: The Limits of Charisma* (Boston: Houghton Mifflin, 1974).
12. Jaime Suchliki, *Cuba, Castro, and Revolution* (Coral Gables: University of Mïami Press, 1972).
13. James Nelson Goodsell, *Fidel Castro's Personal Revolution in Cuba, 1959-1973* (New York: Knopf, 1975).

Source and Original Title: "Cuba Libre?: Social Science Writings on Postrevolutionary Cuba, 1959-1975." *Studies in Compara-tive International Development*, Vol. 10, No. 1, Fall 1975, pp. 101-23.

10

Authenticity and Autonomy in Cuban Communism

The literature on the rhetoric of revolution considerably out-weighs writings on the anatomy of revolution. The apparent fascination for ideological rather than morphological explanations can in part be attributed to the fact that those either in support or opposition to drastic social change must appeal to exhortation, whereas those in search of explanation must perforce attempt to demystify (and in consequence demystify) the revolutionary process. It might properly be argued that those asserting a natural history of the revolutionary process or party have a hidden ideological agenda of their own which underwrites their anatomical searchings. For if the process of revolution takes place in stages which are oblivious to the specifics of this or that revolution, it is hard to avoid the consequent belief that there is little point to commencing the process of revolution to begin with. If cyclical rather than causal explanation prevails the faster one runs, the more rapidly does one return to the original starting place.

While "dialectical" (read: causal) rather than "naturalistic" (read: cyclical) approaches have provided far less in the way of operational guidelines than one might have expected by this time, the former at least allow for revolutions having quite real consequences. As is so often the case, the truth is somewhere between the euphoria of dialectics and the pessimism of naturalism. This

Aristotelian caveat stated, we are still left in desperate need for a theory of revolution—one that provides an operational set of benchmarks by which we can determine what is an authentic revolution and what is a spurious form of political alteration, such as a *coup d'état*.

In the search for such an operational framework, I will restrict my statements to those internal (national) and external (international) factors which determine the authenticity of a revolution and the limits to its autonomy. I shall illustrate my contentions with references to the Cuban revolutionary experience from 1959 to the present. It is not that I believe the Cuban Revolution provides a model for revolutions elsewhere. The tragic consequences of Ernesto "Che" Guevara's adventures in Bolivia should caution against any presumptuous notion that a single national revolution in extremely special circumstances can serve as a model for big changes elsewhere and everywhere. Yet an intellectual balance must be struck. The Cuban experience illustrates the risks of revolution, but also its possibilities.

If the following five internal and five external factors listed are employed and expanded to measure revolutions, the authenticity and autonomy of the Cuban Revolution or others, can at least be measured against some basic, if not entirely exhaustive, standard measuring rods. It is hoped that computer technologists will begin to translate such qualitative indicators into the sorts of operational guideposts that will lead, not so much to predictions about conditions under which revolutions will occur, but at least some satisfactory intellectual statement that an authentic revolution has in fact taken place. This in itself might be considered as one giant step toward a political sociology of revolution.

The Cuban Revolution was first and foremost, in its original execution, a military revolution. As such, it was distinctly different from the Bolshevik revolution in Russia. The Bolsheviks organized and developed a revolution of class and parties in which there was a sense of mass political participation. The Bolshevik movement turned military only after the revolution. That is, the civil war phase took place after the seizure of state power. The Chinese Revolution had a quasi-military character. But it too began with a class model and only later developed into a peasant-military struggle with the ruling Kuomintang. The Cuban experience represents the highest development of manifest military politics.

The Cuban leadership denied that their revolution was without a class basis, without the necessary conditions for revolutionary change prescribed in Marxist theory. Despite their claims and the claims of those who have called it "a revolution without a blueprint," in fact it was a revolution with a military blueprint. This gave a particular character to the Cuban movement, a Third World character.

Aside from the fact that Fidel Castro and Che Guevara spearheaded a military revolution, Cuba witnessed an authentic revolution. What is a real revolution in contrast to a spurious *coup d'état*? Five conditions must prevail as necessary but not sufficient for a real revolution to have occurred.

First, the alpha and omega of a revolution is the destruction of a social class after the revolution. In Cuba, a social class, the bourgeoisie, was sentenced to exile. In the Soviet Union the bourgeoisie was destroyed in both economic and human terms. In Cuba the bourgeoisie was permitted to leave and regroup in Miami, New York, and other urban cities in the United States. But the consequences, while less bloody, were the same: the transference of economic power from one social class to another.

Second, reputed social evils, e.g. gambling, prostitution, and drug traffic, must be eliminated. Such hallmarks of "social deviance" were largely destroyed in Cuba, not only as a change in social style, but rather as an extirpation of classic "social evils." Other evils eliminated by a revolution are illiteracy and poverty.

The third necessary condition for an authentic revolution is that it should bring about mass education, mass social welfare, and all things connected with societal provisions for the citizens. Although Cuba achieved a low level of equality in economic terms, it did put an end to the scourges of noneducation, miseducation, and huge class differences in education. The Cuban

Revolution shifted onto the state and removed from the masses the responsibilities for employment, health, and welfare.

The fourth condition for a revolution, and very important within the Cuban context, is the elimination of racial supremacy. The old Cuban society allowed no leadership to emerge from that 40 percent of the population which was black. Now blacks have some leadership and are taking part in political administration, military affairs, and public health. Although the Cuban government is still predominantly white in character, the incorporation of the black masses proved as important as the destruction of a social class in the delineation of the revolution.

The fifth and final necessary condition for an authentic revolution is the direct substitution of state power for class power. This central importance of the revolutionary (and often military) state is the final condition of the Cuban revolutionary experience.

These five elements are necessary but not sufficient conditions in the definition of an authentic revolution. The Cubans have experienced these five conditions. They are therefore entitled to consideration as a nation which has undergone an authentic revolution. But the question yet remains: What are the limits to the autonomy of that revolution?

After one properly itemizes those features making for authenticity, hence satisfying even our relatively rigorous conditions for a successful revolution, we are still left with the problem of autonomy; or those factors which are beyond or outside the domain or control of the nation-state (especially a single-crop island). In the case of Cuba, this distinction between authenticity and autonomy becomes especially acute since most debates about the postrevolutionary situation (Cuban or elsewhere) is made in terms of autonomy more than authenticity. The emergence of antidependency ideologies as a general feature of the Third World is nowhere better observed than in Latin America. Hence any claims concerning the dependency of Cuba upon Soviet foreign aid, even in simple cash flow terms, not to mention more broad-gauged political terms, is doubly serious: it represents a basic compromise of its socio-economic autonomy, and in the long pull of time could conceivably compromise its revolutionary authenticity. Even if all five internal factors of an authentic revolution are satisfied, the mitigating force of external circumstances may deliver a crippling blow to autonomic aspects of the revolution and thus compromise the revolutionary process. This takes place not so much as a function of any "natural history," but the inability to even fulfill that cycle of natural history in order to satisfy the global requirements of a major power which at the same time is a major sponsor of the revolution.

The difficulty with the Cuban Revolution is that it happened on a small island. It quickly reached its zenith and proceeded on a path of political development more typical of Third World nations than of socialist nations. Cuba made a "social contract" in which a portion of its autonomy was traded off in exchange for protection of its sovereignty.

After the revolution, when all real problems begin, the Cuban government had to decide on the exact parameters of its revolution. Was it to be a socialist revolution with Cuba acting as a launching pad for establishing revolutionary regimes throughout the hemisphere? Or was it to be a national revolution which, besides acting as a model for the other nations of the hemisphere, would do nothing more than show through illustration and example its superiority to hemispheric capitalism? The first perspective was provided by Che Guevara, the second by Fidel Castro. As is now ancient history, the Castro faction won. Che Guevara went to Bolivia to die a hemispheric hero, while Fidel remained in Cuba to forge a nationalist revolution.

Like all revolutions that emerge victorious, the very fact of victory tends to blunt and turn the regime conservative. Still, the Cuban nationalist-socialist regime might nonetheless have succeeded in inspiring other nations in the hemisphere to do likewise but for the peculiar circumstances surrounding the Cuban Revolution. Cuba had an agrarian based, single-crop economy unable to maintain its independence from big powers. Thus it was compelled to move from the American orbit to the Socialist orbit with only a small fraction of its autonomy retrieved by the revolution.

Perhaps a fatal blow to the highest hemispheric power aspirations of the Cuban Revolution, was the collapse of the Goulart regime in Brazil early in 1964. The defeat of the labor-peasant revolution by a military coup d'état meant that the largest nation of the Western Hemisphere in Latin America fell under the sway of rightist rather than leftist impulse. As a result, the patterns established by the U.S.S.R. and China, in which the largest land masses on the continent of Europe and Asia went Left, were thwarted. In the Western world socialism came with a whisper rather than a loud boom.

Cuba's policy confusions in its earlier years isolated it not only from the United States but also from the rest of the hemisphere. Only now is it recovering from a policy of adventurism and romanticism that did more to frighten off hemispheric support than gamer new adherents. As a result, the Cuban Revolution became less socialist and more Third World oriented. It has become internally dependent on its military and externally dependent on Soviet foreign aid.

The alliances and allegiances entered into by the Soviet Union with the United States, as well as Soviet needs in the Western Hemisphere as a whole, serve to add a note of confusion, some might even say optimism, in the conduct of Cuban affairs. It must silence its criticism of the United States insofar as détente is part of Soviet policy, and it must join the Arab bloc in denunciation of Israel and Zionism if this too becomes Soviet foreign policy. As a result, the Cuban Revolution begins to identify increasingly with the needs of Soviet foreign policy, even though economically and militarily it acquires Third World rather than socialist characteristics.

As the Cuban revolution matures, inner-party and inner-group conflict becomes much more pronounced. Definitions employed by revolutionaries themselves concerning success and failure of the goals of the revolution begins to be heard. Even Castro was willing to assume the burdens of responsibility for the failure of the sugar quota and the inability to curb bureaucratic propensities within the Cuban administrative apparatus. In part, Cubans have been able to mute such internal criticism via the safety valve of exile. Yet as this becomes a decreasing possibility over time, one can expect the sorts of debates involving disillusionment over the revolution: artist debates, problems of freedom of expression, questions of deviance within Cuban society, and so forth. This final point about revolution involves the very concept of the revolutionary success and failure itself as defined by the makers of the revolution. These are the five essential external pivots which made the Cuban Revolution a moderate success rather than a rousing example.

The Cuban regime and its leadership are to be credited with an appreciation of the spiritual and economic dynamics of social change. The Cuban Revolution put into motion and to the test the question of moral incentives. The very definition of socialism was bound up with moral commitment rather than material gain. When this moral economy proved incapable of producing a gigantic sugar crop without disrupting the nation's global economy, when the moral economy degenerated into unpaid labor time, then a considerable amount of the "romance" of the revolution vanished, to be replaced by normal considerations of supply and demand and modernization versus developmental industrialization. Castro's recognition of this fact, his backing off from the implications of the moral economy and return to material incentives as a basis of production, served to deflate the vision of the Cuban Revolution as an exportable hemispheric project. On the other hand, it also made the Cuban Revolution even closer in its psychological dimensions and social structure to the Third World than to the Second World of socialism.

The fires of the Cuban Revolution have been dampened in some measure because it has been successful for the Cubans living on the island. And success, while it may be of sociological interest, is of little political interest to the outside world. Stability is not news—instability is. The lack of appeal of the Cuban Revolution is its very institutionalization. It is linked to intensification of central authority, growing militarization of the island, Communist party control over bureaucratic elites, and the Committees for the Defense of the Revolution and their control over all elements in the social infrastructure. All of this, while unquestionably having taken place, must be put in the context of a successful revolution. The tragedy is that so often we substitute the romanticism of a revolution for its authenticity. All revolutionaries have the problem of politics the day after the revolution ends, and the Cuban experience, while it may have lost its enchantment, has certainly not lost its excitement for those seriously concerned with social change and political development in the Third World.

The realities of the Cuban Revolution are not socialist and "pure" in character, but Third World and eclectic. The Cuban state has to deal with the institutionalization of nationalism no less than the single-party regime. Cuba must deal with the authority of the military and its captive bureaucratic sector. The Cuban Revolution is not exactly the beatification of socialism. But it is nonetheless a vindication of the Third World model for generating and sustaining a successful revolution in a big-power political universe.

There is a need to move beyond the descriptive "stages" and "cycles" approach in explaining the revolutionary process. One such avenue is to indicate those elements in a revolution, in contrast to a coup, that are universal. Five such indicators are provided: (1) destruction of a social class and the transferal of economic power to another; (2) elimination of communally agreed upon "social evils"; (3) qualitative changes in levels of mass education, communication, and social welfare; (4) drive toward social equity and overcoming inherited forms of racial and ethnic supremacy; (5) consolidation of state power by the political leadership of new social sectors.

While these universal characteristics may be the necessary conditions for defining a revolutionary process, they are not sufficient for defining a revolutionary structure. For this kind of analysis it is necessary to examine the unique aspects of each revolution. Among such indicators would be: (1) the relationship of civilian to military leadership in the composition of the new ruling class; (2) geographic and demographic components in a revolutionary process; (3) decision and policy making with respect to developmental and industrial priorities; (4) alliances and alignments at both national and international levels, which permit a revolution to be either consolidated or dismantled; (5) definitions employed by revolutionary groups themselves in determining the success and failure of the goals of the revolution.

A worthwhile political sociology of revolutionary conflicts must be both universal, that is examine the context of revolutionary structure and process; and unique, that is examine the contents of each specific national regime to determine the extent to which actual events shape the consolidation of revolutionary conflict. This is the essential path to be traversed if we are to move beyond the present inherited impasse of causal and cyclical explanations of revolution that can only go around and around.

Source and Original Title: "Authenticity and Autonomy in the Cuban Experience." *Cuban Studies/Estudios Cubanos,* Vol. 6, No. 1, January 1976, pp. 67-91.

11

Institutionalized Militarism of Cuba

Little more than ten years ago my article "The Stalinization of Castro" was published[1] and immediately criticized as bewildering and outrageous.[2] Subsequent events led my critics, several years later, to view the process therein outlined as commonplace, and finally to consider Sovietization (if not Stalinization) as an inevitable step in the evolution of Cuba.[3] Ten years later, I am again confronted with a critique of an article on Cuba. I am confident that my viewpoint will be considered commonplace, even inevitable, in an even shorter time span than the previous decennial go-round.

I take small comfort in my characterization of contemporary Cuba and its continuing militarization. I am willing to accept the determinist argument that given the alignment of hemispheric and international forces, the *fidelistas* and *raulistas* have little choice. But it would take an act of ostrich-like self-deception to assume that since 1970 Cuba has been in a process of demilitarization. Such a characterization even lacks support in the Cuban Marxist literature. If anything, Cuban leadership has become more bellicose over the last several years in claiming the righteousness of the decision to resort to the military as the underpinning of the state.[4]

Bringing to bear sociological analysis in an area charged with ideological passion is no simple chore in the best of circumstances. When it comes to Cuba, the task is made more complicated by the bitter clash of patriotism, nationalism, big-power relationships and, parenthetically, the constituency of seven million Cubans and one million exiles. The potential for hyperbole is always present in any discussion of Cuba, made infinitely more likely by the penchant of the Cuban regime and its opposite number abroad to impart exaggerated pronouncements, meaningless slogans, unfulfilled expectations, and banal exhortations. To insist that the analytic task must go forward even in this climate and that empirical characterization remains possible, even necessary, under such conditions can itself arouse hatred. There is a clear assumption that any kind of social science research on Cuba is nothing more than bourgeois objectivism and non partisan degeneracy. Yet the tasks of research remain with us, and the ever-present, if flickering expectation that truth will somehow be heard above the roar of competing ideological persuasions must sustain us.

With the fond hope that a dialogue on the nature of the Cuban social and political system will be stimulated rather than curbed by Mr. LeoGrande's remarks, I accept the challenge of his rejoinder to my essay on the militarization of Cuba.[5] In part, the difficulty in responding to his rejoinder is that LeoGrande presents four categories of criticism: first, he challenges my major premises concerning the militarization of Cuba, with a counter thesis concerning the demilitarization of Cuba; second, he criticizes the evidence on which my position rests; third, he presents a historical summary of Cuban labor and mass organization which mayor may not be correct, but which certainly has nothing to do with anything I have written to which LeoGrande is responding; and finally, he gives us a set of small items of a factual sort that again are largely irrelevant to my paper but to which I will nonetheless attempt to reply.

If LeoGrande wishes to comment on my work, and in so doing present his own viewpoints regarding the Cuban revolutionary experience, that is understandable and clearly not unique in the annals of Western scholarship. But I hope he realizes that I have enough troubles defending my own positions without concerning myself with his reading of mass mobilization in post revolutionary Cuba.[6] My position on the militarization of Cuba may seem

professionally harsh if one accepts at face value every exaggerated claim of the Castro regime to being a socialist system. Once
that system is examined in the light of overall mobilization and
militarization patterns of the Third World, my analysis seems
not simply plausible, but downright inevitable. My viewpoint
hinges on three interconnected ideas:

First, militarization is the fundamental attribute of politics in
Third World countries, just as economics dominated the origins
of Western capitalism and politics dominated the origins of soviet
communism. Third World nations came into existence with the help
of a military sub-class uniting bureaucratic and political networks
and creating class mobilization in nations where social classes themselves were not able to mobilize directly for social action. As I have
explained elsewhere, Cuba clearly fits such a tripolar model.[7]

A second assumption is that militarization is inevitable in Cuba
because the potential for civilian and bureaucratic control is limited
there, unlike the Soviet Union, by weaknesses imposed by single-crop
systems on the means of production and the evolution of industrialization. With single-crop export "socialism," militarization became
inevitable during a period of consolidation following the anti colonialist struggle. Cuban agriculture is entirely militarized. Workers have
been mobilized and organized into brigades. "They simply carry out
orders as though they were soldiers."[8] One might speak of the "export"
of military cadres to the civilian sector, but even the most optimistic
analyst must "conclude that there are no significant pressures from
within the Cuban Armed Forces to put the civic soldier to rest."[9]

My third contention is that the militarization of Cuba is a
consequence of the inner history of the Cuban Revolution. The
guerrilla struggles which overthrew the Batista regime were
above all military or paramilitary in character. The sources of
Castroism are military; the personnel who made up the regime at
the outset and continues to rule, has been military. In the 1970s
the Cuban military have a larger share of the Central Committee
of the Communist party than any other communist regime.

The contrast with the Soviet Union is important since the Red
Army came into being during the Civil War period, after the

political party apparatus of the communists seized power. The causal sequence in Cuba, the reversal of civil and military ruling cadres, is critical to an understanding of how deeply the Cuban experience is linked to that of the rest of the Third World, and how sharply it differs from the military professionalism exhibited by the Soviet Union.

To reply to questions as to why Cuba is a militarist regime one has to harken back to original premises and void arguments by extension, i.e.; that since Cuba's Communist party has grown four fold since 1969, military influence has dropped off. There are limits to reasoning by reference to the Soviet model. The similarity in rhetoric between Cubans and Soviets by no means insures an isomorphism in reality. The growth of the Communist party does not signify an expansion of civilianism; only that it is a paramilitary party in charge of managing dependent state machinery.

The central empirical point in contention is whether Cuba has become a militarized or a demilitarized regime, as LeoGrande claims. Curiously, he does not argue a third possibility asserted by Cuban authorities themselves, that Cuban militarization is justified as a counter-imperialist measure. This is the burden of Fidel Castro's own position. As he recently observed with regard to the Cuban role in Angola, pointing out the role of the United States and its foreign military involvement:

> The Yankee imperialists have hundreds of thousands of soldiers abroad; they have military bases on all the continents and in all the seas. In Korea, Japan, the Philippines, Turkey, Western Europe, Panama and many other places, their military installations can be counted by the dozens and the hundreds. In Cuba itself they occupy by force a piece of our territory. What moral and legal right do they have to protest that Cuba provides instructors and assistance for the technical preparation of the armies of African countries and in other parts of the underdeveloped world that request them?[10]

Having pored through volumes of official records, I do not see a single statement by a Cuban official willing to make any claim for Cuba's demilitarization. References bald facedly provided by Leo-Grande to numerous students of Cuban politics "who presumably share his view" do no such thing. Quite the contrary: nearly all share a position closer to that outlined in my paper, whatever their own political persuasion. This curious habit of citing information as if it somehow negated what I wrote, when in fact it either confirms my position or is irrelevant to the argument, is done with such alarming frequency that one can only hope that serious students of Cuban politics will review the evidence and make their own assessments.

LeoGrande's argument with me is not really over dates but over substance. In my paper I neither denied nor asserted that the militarization of Cuba began in 1968; I would probably date it somewhat earlier. It is my position that the military factor is endemic to the structure of the Cuban Revolution, spurred first, in response to U. S. pressures culminating in the Bay of Pigs; second, in response to Cuba's position as an outpost of the Soviet empire with the need to satisfy the Soviet Union; and third, by the nature of Cuban society as part of the Third World system. To speak of some magic demilitarization having begun in the 1970s is, to put it mildly, idiosyncratic. Militarization is not easily turned on and off at will. Even Cuban authorities have not asserted such an extreme voluntarist position concerning demilitarization.

Let us look more closely at the characteristics of militarization to clarify certain points which perhaps improperly were taken for granted in my earlier paper. There are three central characteristics of militarization: first, intervention by military means in the affairs of foreign nations; second, growth in professional specialization so that the military approach is clearly distinguished from the civilian approach in training procedures, control of instruments of destruction, and carrying out of the national political will; third, a basic measurement of militarization is levels and increments of hardware: expenditures for military purposes that have no purpose other than military ends. Cuba scores very high on each of these scales of militarization.

Let us omit discussion of earlier tendencies to intervention in Bolivia and Venezuela, assuming that Cuba has the right to foment change in sister Latin American nations (an argument that violates the notion of national sovereignty, but one that is at least arguable). Cuba also has a military presence outside the hemisphere in the following countries: Guinea-Bissau, Guinea,

São Tomé, Congo Republic, Mozambique, Tanzania, South Yemen, North Vietnam, and above all, Angola.[11]

The physical presence in Africa of what are euphemistically described as instructors and technicians underscores the role of Cuba as an agent of Soviet foreign policy. It also makes absolutely clear that at least with respect to participation in the affairs of foreign nations, Cuba scores higher than any nation in the Western Hemisphere other than the United States. If this does not necessarily excuse the United States, it does not add up to a vote of confidence for the demilitarization of Cuba hypothesis.

Carlos Rafael Rodriquez, deputy prime minister responsible for foreign affairs, pointed out that the intervention in Angola, where there are an estimated 15,000 Cuban troops, was undertaken because "the legitimate government" had asked for Cuban military aid and it was Cuba's "duty" to assist a Third World country where there was an internal threat to its survival.[12] Whether in fact there was a legitimate Angolan government to begin with or, as is more likely the case, the Cuban intervention itself legitimized Agostino Neto's regime, is a moot question for our purposes.

The argument—intervention to help a legitimate government—is exactly that used by other imperial powers, such as the U.S. intervention in Korea and Vietnam to maintain "legitimate governments" there. The spurious nature of this position is reflected in the fact that Fidel Castro later announced that Cuba had begun or would soon begin withdrawing 200 military personnel a week from Angola, and that further, Cuba had no intention of sending troops to other countries in Southern Africa or Latin America. Belatedly, he informed Olaf Palme, the Swedish prime minister: "I do not wish to become the crusader of the twentieth century."[13]

Cuban militarization is not simply a function of national ambitions, but of external compunction. According to a recent report, Castro has become so dependent upon the million dollars a day Soviet subsidy that he must do the Kremlin's bidding. At least one secret report claims that "he at first resisted getting involved in Angola and that it took Soviet pressure to induce him to send Cuban troops to Africa." And what the Soviets give they can take away. This same report notes that "Secret intelligence documents suggest that the Soviets actually ordered Fidel Castro to announce the gradual withdrawal of Cuban forces from Angola."[14] Those who have raised the cry of Latin American dependency upon the United States, might well ponder if the United States could presently extract the same levels of military commitment to fight its battles on other shores as the Soviet Union does from Cuba. Cuba exemplifies militarization as a process, and military dependence upon a foreign power as a structure.

A sobering aspect of Cuban overseas activities is in relation to the 500 *tanquistas* or armored corps troops who manned Syrian tanks during the October 1973 Middle East war.[15] The struggles between Syria and Israel did not involve an internal threat to the Cuban system, but a very definite threat by one sovereign nation to another. The participation of Cubans was unquestionably under Soviet instructions, since the Syrians only had Soviet tanks. The Cuban military role in the world as a whole is extraordinarily great for a nation with a population less than that of New York City.

The growth of military specialization is clearly evidenced by institutionalization of the Cuban regime. The whole concept of institutionalization has meant a brand new ruling coalition of civilian and military elites. The turn from an idiosyncratic personalistic style characteristic of Fidel in his more flamboyant earlier period reflects the intensification and certainly the persistence of militarization. The professional military values qualities of rationality, efficiency, and administrative order—also important for the civilian bureaucracy—which has become a hallmark of the militarization process. A recent piece by Edward González well reflects the trends toward militarization herein described.

> Fidel pulled nine senior or high-level officers from the Ministry of the Revolutionary Armed Forces who are loyal to him, or at least to his brother, and placed them in the expanded party Secretariat, in the newly-created Executive Committee of the Council of Ministers, and at the top of several ministries. This stratagem strengthened his power base in two ways. It prevented less reliable or hostile elements from the ranks of the old PSP from occupying these key positions in the party and government. In turn, the transfer of senior officers to civilian posts enabled the Castro brothers to promote still others to the top ranks, thereby further ensuring the personal loyalty of the FAR's

high command. Indeed, in December 1973 a new professional ranking system was introduced which provided the new senior officers with ranks equivalent to that of Major General (instead of Major).

Fidel, as Commander-in-Chief, and Raúl, as Minister of the Revolutionary Armed Forces, personally began courting members of the armed forces, not only at the senior level but also down to the troop and combat-unit level. In addition, veteran officers from the Sierra Maestra campaign reportedly assumed direction of the PCC organizational meetings within the armed forces. In brief, Fidel and Raúl made sure that they had solid support in the most institutional-ized, as well as the most powerful organ in Cuba today, the FAR.[16]

The degree to which the military has become a crucial variable in the Cuban Communist party (PCC) is indicated by the fact, as Fidel himself reported that 19 percent of the Congress delegates came from the military and security forces. But, as González has pointed out, even this figure considerably understates the influence of FAR delegates; they possess a higher level of education and technical competence than the general party membership.

The development of a professional specialization in the military is further vouchsafed by the growth of military training academies, training of Cuban military elites at the Frunze Military Academy of Moscow, evolution of military rank to correspond exactly with military indicia elsewhere in the world, sub specialization of a navy and air force—again corresponding to the general professional style of military in the Third World—and the emergence of compulsory military service.

So far have the 1970s moved in the direction of militarization that the Ministries of Defense or Army of nearly every country in Eastern Europe under Soviet dominion has visited Cuba. Fidel and Raúl Castro have reciprocated these visits clearly engaged in military missions. Beyond that, the 1970s have seen a new generation of hardware introduced into Cuba that has taken the country far beyond the initial equipment gained after the missile crisis when Cubans were armed with conventional arms as the price of removal of the atomic missiles themselves. Carmelo Mesa-Lago indicates how characteristic the military buildup in the 1970s has been:

Early in January the Cuban Navy received several Soviet missile-carrying launches that doubled its missile and anti-aircraft equipment. In April, the air force, in turn, received a flotilla of MIG-23s, the most technologically advanced Soviet aircraft, which modernized the Cuban stock of MiG-15s, MiG-17s, MiG-19s, and MiG-21s. For several months a team consisting of hundreds of Soviet military experts led by Lt. General Dimitri Krutskikn had been training Cuban personnel in the use of this equipment. The ceremony to present the airplanes received wide publicity; it was opened by Krutskikn, who was followed by the Soviet ambassador in Cuba, Nikita Tulubeev, and it was closed by Minister of the Armed Forces Raúl Castro, who said that the military aid was proof of Soviet confidence.[17]

Nor should this be viewed as a one-shot injection; between the four-year period of 1960-63, Cuba received $265 million worth of major weapons, mainly from the Soviet Union. These were the most sophisticated weapons in the region, including MiG-21s, Guideline and Atoll missiles, and Konar patrol boats armed with Styx missiles.[18] The Cuban missile crisis succeeded in limiting weapons of offensive potential; but it did not lessen emphasis on military approaches and solutions to political problems.

On all three items, foreign intervention, professional specialization, and increased levels of sophistication of hardware, Cubans have moved toward a military posture more rapidly than any other nation in the hemisphere. The one shred of evidence introduced by LeoGrande for a reduced role of the military in Cuba is the composition of the Central Committee of the Cuban Communist party. These two points need to be adduced: the number of military officers does not uniquely determine military influence. Indeed, the decline of paramilitary agencies of the earlier period is evident in the reverse direction; reorganization of the armed forces in the 1970s has reduced ranks, but in concentration on purely military activities the military has become increasingly specialized. As Carmelo Mesa-Lago has pointed out:

One reason for this reorganization was the need for centralization to avoid "the proliferation of mini columns that disperse and divert efforts, developing a structure parallel to that of the administrative leadership." Another was to institutionalize a selective process to strengthen the increasing professionalization of the army. The regular army will not be involved in production while the EJT will draft youngsters, who are neither fit for the army nor for study, into a three-year program of disciplinary training and work in agriculture.[19]

Even more revealing is an examination of the Cuban leadership. Here one detects the military origins of nearly all important leaders except Blas Roca and Carlos Rafael Rodríguez who are from the Socialist party (PSP). Nearly all others were drawn from the original guerrilla movement itself. If one examines party positions it becomes clear that rank within the armed forces corresponds with party position within the government itself. Raúl Castro is president of the Commission on Security and the Armed Forces, while Ramiro Valdés and Sergio del Valle are leading members of the same party position. Their parallel government positions are all linked to military activities: Raúl is minister of the Revolutionary Armed Forces; Valdés is deputy prime minister in charge of construction; del Valle is minister of the interior.[20] Nowhere else, not even in the Soviet Union, is isomorphism between military and government functions so powerfully integrated as in Cuba.

A series of smaller misinterpretations and misanthropisms made by LeoGrande require only passing comment. First, I do not have an "excessive reliance on the theories of Régis Debray." My critique of Debray as a Bergsonian mystic who fitted the needs of the Cuban Revolution at the earlier period and became dangerous during the consolidation period has been presented elsewhere.[21] Second, I drew the distinction between the Popular Socialist party and the new Cuban Communist party which emerged after 1965, and the importance of this event, as long ago as 1966. Indeed, this earlier phase in the institutionalization of the regime was the basis of my earlier studies of the "Stalinization of Castro." Third, my evaluation of the Committees for the Defense of the Revolution (CDRs) is drawn entirely from Cuban sources.[22] After the most careful review of the evidence and literature, as well as speaking to many people who were once participants in CDRs, I remain convinced that this is a vicious and pernicious instrument of mass terror. Fourth, I continue to believe that my understanding of the Cuban political hierarchy is sound. Since these last two points bear directly on main aspects of my paper, I shall burden the reader with further discussion and hopefully clarification.

Claims that CDR members comprise "90 percent of the adult population" should alert any serious social scientist that "mobilization" at such levels is, to put it mildly, a central characteristic of the totalitarian regime. I do think that LeoGrande is fudging his numbers. His claim is made for 4,800,000 members, or probably closer to 75 percent of the adult population.[23] The 90 percent figure he uses relates to the vote at Matanzas. In the words of Fidel, "it reflected the fact that while voting is not obligatory, we can see all this is outstanding. It is the outcome of the enthusiasm of the people."[24]

The role of CDRs is so important that while it is peripheral to my own remarks, it is not without significance to point out that at the fifteenth anniversary of the CDRs, when Fidel noted a rise in their membership from 100,000 to 4,800,000, one *Granma* photo caption shows "CDR members patrolling the block"—against whom, nobody knows. Fidel himself points to the "vigilance duties" involved in the CDR:

> The CDRs have fulfilled their vigilance duties and have helped solve various social problems. The CDRs have cooperated with our Armed Forces in the mobilization of reserves and in carrying out important military maneuvers through their support to production and services when, in a given region of the country, thousands of our workers have been called to take part in these maneuvers.[25]

One can only ask rhetorically: Vigilance against whom? Against the small minority by the overwhelming majority? What are those global interests other than one's own national interests? The interest of the international revolutionary movement? Does that mean that the CDR will become involved in foreign adventures and become part of that military effort abroad? Needless to say, answers to such questions are not forthcoming because, as Fidel is constantly reminding us; important matters are not fit for the ears of the enemies of the regime; only for the loyalists of the regime.

If there is a lack of documentation concerning the CDR, surely the fault is not mine. It is not customary for totalitarian regimes to reveal the inner workings of their private police force. One can only judge by public comments and in this case, the organizational blueprints cited in my earlier piece. To speak of a trend in Cuba, of either the Young Communists or the Communist party itself, or the Ministry of the Interior, as moving away from the paramilitary style characteristic of the late 1960s, is to do violence to what the regime's leadership itself points out. Take, for example, the speech made by José Abrantes, first deputy minister of the interior, commemorating the 13th anniversary of the Ministry of the Interior, in which he speaks of "absolute unanimity and the most complete support of the masses for the law enforcement agencies in the struggle to abolish crimes." It is the call for "constant on-the-job training, more perfect and complete investigatory and operative work, calling for the police to develop to the maximum their relations with the prosecutors to make the law more effective."[26] Differences between the Ministry of the Interior, the Armed Forces, and the CDRs shrink in the cohesion of organization and the consensus of ideological mission:

> Our Ministry is a part of the "people in uniform" of which the unforgettable Major Camilo Cienfuegos spoke; it is flesh of the flesh and blood of the blood of our revolutionary people, and we can say with the greatest satisfaction and pride that all the people look on it as their own, as something that exists to serve them and to defend their work and lives.[27]

Beyond that, I would argue that the Reserve Forces have really not been dismantled; that the national revolutionary militia has become a vast recruiting ground for the armed forces; that this national militia has adopted military values in style and in substance, not simply in terms of uniforms, but in terms of job specification. Raúl Castro reported in 1975 that over 5,000 officers had been promoted to higher rank. Further, 74 percent of the national revolutionary military are members of the Young Communist League or the Communist party. Such isomorphism between the military and the polity cannot possibly be squared with a move toward demilitarization.

One curious criticism by LeoGrande is that my study assumes that Raúl Castro has only recently become the second most important Cuban leader. This is clearly nonsense.

On the other hand, it is equally nonsensical to claim that Raúl has been second since 1962 when he was named second secretary of the National Directorate. It is surprising how thoroughly Ché Guevara has been purged from LeoGrande's rejoinder. Unquestionably Ché was second in command until his death in Bolivia. His demise took place long after 1962. This historical myopia is characteristic of LeoGrande's insinuations. His officialist vision would make it appear that because Raúl was named to a post with the designation "second secretary," he thereby became Number Two in the Cuban political hierarchy. Of such stuff is historical falsification made.

There is a greater falsification by omission than any presumed falsification by commission. Not a single statement in the entire rejoinder addresses itself to the Soviet Union, to the role of the superpower in the militarization of Cuba. As one quite moderate analyst notes: "The current Cuban leadership is tied to, and dependent upon, its Soviet patron to a greater extent than at any time in the past."[29] If there is to be demilitarization with the present climate and context of Cuban dependency, it will have to be called for by the Soviet Union. Just as the Soviets orchestrated the Cuban role in Angola, one must presume that they will likewise determine the extent of Cuban military efforts elsewhere. We are dealing here not simply with a militarizing regime, but with a nation entirely within the orbit of a major foreign power. It is fanciful to talk about Cuba as if it was an autonomous nation making its own policy decisions.[30] Cuba is a tragic example of an authentic revolution that failed to realize its autonomous development. This is not the first time small nations have felt the lash of super-power tyranny but it may be the first time that no one is permitted to bring this uncomfortable fact into public discourse.

One must speak frankly about the sociology of militarizing regimes. They have in common high levels of punitive treatment of political prisoners. In this, Cuba must unfortunately be placed second only to Chile as a regime that confuses the temporary suspension of civil liberties of dissidents during moments of turmoil, with the permanent detention and cruel punishment of opponents to the regime. No one denies that Cuba (again, like Chile) has 20 to 30 thousand prisoners detained on a long-term basis.

Now we have the report filed by the Inter-American Commission on Human Rights that Cuban political prisoners "have been victims of inhuman treatment." The 1976 report cites prisoners who have died from lack of adequate medical attention; who were denied any visitors' rights; and who were forced to remain in extremely uncomfortable cells for long period of time. The prisoners who suffer most are those who will not participate in Fidel's "rehabilitation program." Those "prisoners who refused to wear the uniforms of the rehabilitation program were allowed only to wear their underclothes."[31] Wherein does the difference lie between Pinochet's fascism and Castro's communism?

My purpose in this response is not to claim that every point made in my article is beyond reproach or above criticism, or that every fact which could have been adduced to support my argument was used. On the other hand, I am afraid that LeoGrande has really bigger game in mind. What he would like to do is delegitimize my position by the colossal jump of assuming that because a change in administrative leadership between 1965 and 1966 did or did not take place, or because Castro became a "Marxist-Leninist" in 1961 rather than 1959, my position on militarization of Cuba is not correct.[32] This he simply cannot do. The details are not there to support his position or for that matter to contravene my own. My point of view rests on the best available evidence, and draws the most coherent and reasonable conclusions. The admittedly ambiguous organizational transformations within various ministries hardly constitute evidence against my position. More to the point, LeoGrande's clutching at ideological straws reflects a scholarship of desperation. So intent on supporting the present regime and its evolution does my critic seem to be, that even the vaguest example of negative characterization is denied. What we would be left with is a propagandist *punto de vista* where Castrology reigns supreme.

The attempt to offer moral justification for the present militarization of Cuba is difficult enough to live with, but any effort to provide an ideological denial of what has become apparent to friends and foes of the regime alike must be considered entirely unacceptable.

References/Notes

1. Irving Louis Horowitz, "The Stalinization of Fidel Castro," *New Politics*, Vol. IV, No. 4 (Fall 1965): 61-69.
2. C. Ian Lumsden, "On Socialists and Stalinists," *New Politics*, Vol. V, No. 1 (Winter 1966): 20-26.
3. Irving Louis Horowitz, "Castrologists and Apologists," *New Politics*, Vol. V, No.1 (Winter 1966): 27-34.
4. Fidel Castro, *Angola-African Giron*. Havana: Editorial de Ciencias Sociales, 1976; and Fidel Castro, *Our Armed Forces are Firmly Linked to the People, to the Revolution State and to their Vanguard Party*. Havana: Political Editions, 1974, pp. 9-21.
5. Irving Louis Horowitz, "Military Origins of the Cuban Revolution," *Armed Forces and Society*. Vol. 1, No.4 (Summer 1975): 402-418.
6. Nonetheless, I am compelled to note that Mr. LeoGrande's remarks do not represent any noticeable improvement on the work of Nelson Amaro Victoria, "Mass and Class in the Origins of the Cuban Revolution," *Studies in Comparative International Development*. Vol. 4, No. 10 (1968-1969): 221-237.
7. Irving Louis Horowitz, "Authenticity and Autonomy in the Cuban Experience," *Cuban Studies/Estudios Cubanes*. Vol. 6, No.1 (January 1976): 67-74.
8. Rene Dumont, *Is Cuba Socialist?* (originally published in 1970) :96-97 New York: The Viking Press, 1974
9. Jorge I. Domínguez, "Institutionalization and Civil-Military Relations in Cuba," *Cuban Studies/Estudios Cubanos*. Vol. 6, No. (January 1976) : 39-65.
10. Fidel Castro, *Angola-Africa Giron*. Havana: Editorial de Ciencias Sociales, 1976: 26-270.
11. Joan Forbes, *The Christian Science Monitor,*1976. Reprinted in *Free Trade Union News*, published by the Department of International Affairs, AFL-CIO. Vol. 31, No. 2-3 (February-March 1976):15.
12. David Binder, "Cuban Aide Bars Role in Rhodesia," *The New York Times*. (May 21, 1976)
13. Craig R. Whitney, "Castro Says He Will Begin To Cut Forces in Angola," *The New York Times* (May 26, 1976).
14. Jack Anderson, "A Soviet Policy That Favors Ford?". *The Washington Post* (June 6) 1976.
15. Stanley Karnow, "Castro Rejects Reconciliation to Fight for The Cause." *The New York Times* (December 14) 1975.
16. Edward González, "Castro and Cuba's New Orthodoxy," *Problems of Communism*. Vol. 25, No.1 (January-February 1976): 1-19.
17. Carmelo Mesa-Lago, *Cuba in the 1970's: Pragmatism and Institutionalization*. Albuquerque: University of New Mexico Press, 1974. p. 14.
18. Stockholm International Peace Research Institute; *The Arms Trade With the Third World* (rev. edition). New York: Holmes & Meier, Publishers, 1975. pp. 259-260.

19. Carmelo Mesa-Lago, *Cuba in the 1970's: Pragmatism and Institutional-ization.* Albuquerque: University of New Mexico Press, 1974. p. 70.
20. Central Committee of the Communist Party of Cuba, "We Approve," *Granma*, Vol. 11, No. 1 (January 4, 1976) :12.
21. Irving Louis Horowitz, "Cuban Communism", *Transaction/Society* Vol. 4, No. 10 (October 1967):7-15. Reprinted in *Cuban Communism.* New Brunswick: Transaction Books, 1972 (second edition) 9-36. See also my chapter on "The Morphology of Modern Revolution" in *Foundations of Political Sociology.* New York and London: Harper & Row, 1972: pp. 253-281.
22. Comités de Defensa de la Revolución, *Memorias de 1963* Havana: Ediciones con la Guardia en Alto, 1964. This volume published with the supervision of the C.D.R. stated clearly and unambiguously its vigilante, quasi-legal character.
23. Fidel Castro, "Speech on the 15th Anniversary of the Committee for the Defense of the Revolution," *Granma*. Vol. 10, No. 41 (October 12, 1975): 2-3.
24. Fidel Castro, "Speech to Journalists", *Granma*. Vol. 9, No. 28 July 14, 1974): 2
25. Fidel Castro, "Speech on the 15th Anniversary of the Committee for the Defense of the Revolution," *Granma.* Vol. 10, No. 41 (October 12, 1975): 2-3.
26. Jose Abrantes, "Speech at Ceremony Marking the 13th Anniversary of the Ministry of the Interior," *Granma*. Vol. 9, No. 24 (June 16, 1974): 4.
27. Ibid.
28. Raúl Castro, "Speech at the Ceremony in Honor of Militia Day," *Granma*. Vol. 10, No. 17 (April 27, 1975): 3.
29. Edward Gonzales, *Cuba under Castro: The Limits of Charisma*: Boston: Houghton-Mifflin Co., 1974. p. 236. For a further and deeper analysis of Cuban military mobilization and combat readiness, see Edward González and David Ronfeldt, *Post-Revolutionary Cuba in a Changing World* (A report prepared for the Office of the Assistant Secretary of Defense/International Security Affairs). Santa Monica: Rand Corporation, R-1844-15A (December) 1975.
30. K. S. Karol, Guerrillas in Power: *The Course of the Cuban Revolution.* New York: Hill and Wang, 1971. pp. 490-550.
31. Inter-American Commission on Human Rights, "Cuba Scored on Prisoner Treatment" (Summary of Report). *The Washington Post* (June 6) 1976.
32. For example, Mr. LeoGrande assumes that because I use the word "climax" with respect to Castro's self-declaration about being a Marxist-Leninist in 1961, that this perforce means he closed the speech with this statement. Since I am also accused of being "dramatic", it is not inappropriate to note that at the end of a play is the denouement—the climax often takes place in the "middle." In any event, his quibble does nothing to settle the question of whether Castro embraced Marxism-Leninism in 1961, 1959—or, as some claim, much earlier, in 1956.

Source and Original Title: "Castrology Revisited: Further Observations on the Militarization of Cuba." *Armed Forces and Society*, Vol. 3, No. 4, August 1977, pp. 617-31

12

The Cuba Lobby: Supplying Rope to a Mortgaged Revolution

Aleksandr Solzhenitsyn, in his now famous address delivered in Washington, D.C. on June 30, 1975, reminded his listeners of an unusual Communist party meeting which took place in the early days of the Soviet revolution. "In a difficult moment, at a party meeting in Moscow, Lenin said: 'Comrades, don't panic; when things go very hard for us we will give a rope to the bourgeoisie and the bourgeoisie will hang itself.' Then, Karl Radek, who is a very resourceful wit, said: 'Vladimir Ilyich, but where are we going to get enough rope to hang the whole bourgeoisie?' Wherein Lenin blithely replied: 'they will supply us with it.'"[1]

This story, whether apocryphal or actual, is as revealing of post revolutionary Cuban foreign relations as it was in pre-Revolutionary Russia. For we have two parallel developments going at breakneck speed in opposite directions: the first, armed Cuban intervention throughout Africa; and, the other, an effort within the United States to legitimatize the restoration of diplomatic and cordial relations between Cuba and the United States.

Military Whips

It is apparent that there is an enormous armed Cuban intervention from one end of Africa to the other,[2] of such proportions that the president of Zambia, Kenneth Kaunda, has been forced to speak of "a plundering tiger with its deadly cubs now coming in the back door," a clear reference to Soviet manipulation of Cubans in the Angolan Civil War.[3] This was followed by the invasion of Shaba Province in Zaire, the heavy commitment in the Ethiopian/Somali conflict, and a second Shaba adventure. Only the most myopic would deny the role of Cuba in African intervention; only the most draconian would describe this involvement as humane.

The Cuban position on military participation is unambiguous: the regime has repeatedly asserted its right to intervene on behalf of "legitimate revolutionary governments." Carlos Rafael Rodríguez, one of the old war horses of the Cuban Communist party, in commemorating the founding of the 250th anniversary of the University of Havana, put the matter of Cuban interventionism in the sharpest focus and made it absolutely clear that diplomatic recognition would not alter what he refers to as "the Leninist position" on the two cultures—those of the dominant classes that refused to die, and the new culture whose advance is inexorable. Rodríguez' sense of what ought to live and die is underwritten by this new internationalism. "Internationalism means that we didn't wait for all of our aspirations to be realized or for all our people's needs to be met in order to help other peoples whose state of backwardness was greater than ours." He concludes his educational peroration by noting, "Every time our troops fought outside of our country they did so to defend the people who were being threatened and who had requested our help."[4] Whether such assistance had been requested by the regimes involved or by the Soviet Union is never made clear; and just what the Cuban troops are fighting against is equally ambiguous. That notwithstanding, there can be no doubt that the Cuban regime not only has an interventionist policy, but has an aggressive ideology well orchestrated to underwrite that policy. Only an itemization, a laundry list of interventions, remains to be provided.

Cuban interventions in Africa indicate that these involvements are coordinated with the larger aims of Soviet foreign policy.[5]

- The use of at least 500 crack Cuban tank corps troops to man the Soviet tanks shipped to Syria during the October Round Four of 1973; also, an assorted cluster of technicians and medical advisors.
- The participation of anywhere from 10,000 to 15,000 Cuban ground troops in the Angolan Civil War on the side of Augustino Neto's MPLA, and the retention of a great majority of these troops, plus 4,000 civilian technicians on permanent duty to prevent "counter-revolution," i.e., the forces of UNITA to emerge triumphant in the cities as they remain in the countryside.
- The participation of 10,000 or more officers, troops, and pilots, directly under Soviet military command in the Ethiopian-Somali dispute over Ogaden. Needless to say, Ethiopia represents the peoples' will, whereas the Somali regime, which until last year was also part of the Soviet sphere of influence, now represents the agents of imperialism. There are, in addition, an estimated 3,000 Soviet troops presently on location in Ethiopia.

This is a far cry from the Debray-Guevara early-1960s salad days of the "foco," wherein Cuban intervention was limited to support of native peasant and guerrilla movements in such Latin American nations as Guatemala, Venezuela, and above all, the fiasco in Bolivia. The Debray-Guevara theory was that Latin America is a unitary force, and Castroism a twentieth-century Bolivarism—with rights to march from the Rio Bravo to Tierra del Fuego. The new Castro theory (Raúl no less than Fidel) is simply that Cuba has a "revolutionary obligation," as defined by Soviet geopolitical strategies to support any regime anywhere in the world that calls for assistance in the unending anti-imperialist struggle. There is usually a brief spell of ambiguity during which time the Soviets puzzle out their position, followed by an absolute and fanatic devotion to the side finally chosen. Cuban troops have in this way become the mass battering ram of Soviet foreign policy from Angola to Ethiopia—and perhaps from Eritrea to Rhodesia in the next phase of struggle.

A relatively moderate critic of the Castro regime, Carlos Alberto Montaner, has made a series of interesting observations on the Cuban military that casts its interventionist posture in a broader but clearer light. He notes that for the past 15 years, at least since the Bay of Pigs, the Cuban military has been preparing for a confrontation with the United States. In the absence of that classic David and Goliath event, the Cubans were faced with a big military establishment filled with *Sturm und Drang* and nowhere to go—until the Soviet Union gave Fidel his marching orders. Montaner notes that this military corps represents the "dorsal spine" of the Cuban regime. It is a society filled with the imagery of militarism, not unlike the Prussian caste system of the last century.[6] Like many exiles, Montaner sees military adventurism in Africa as a potential source for the overthrow of the regime. Also, like many exiles, he does not fully appreciate the extent to which Cuba is part of a Third World model which, to put the matter bluntly, rests on highly authoritarian styles of rule in the absence of viable social classes or a powerful administrative apparatus detached from military power. But the long-term potentials of the Castro regime notwithstanding, the Cuban military has become the single most powerful sector of that society. This sector, under the direct leadership of Raúl Castro, has, in its obsession with sophisticated weapons and grand preparations for the great showdown with imperialism, fallen under the direct domination of the Soviet Union. This domination is made secure by a training network for the officer corps that established links between Cuban military personnel and Soviet training quarters far more extensive than any parallel relations between the other regimes of Latin America and similar American training quarters. In short, Cuban militarism is not simply a tactical concern, but represents the root and branch of present-day Cuban society.

Congressional Feathers

In contrast to this development is an extraordinary two-pronged effort by American politicians and business-people to urge the resumption of normalization of trade-and-aid between the United States and Cuba. Beyond that, there is an insistence that the regime's internal success more than compensates for its external adventures. The vanity of Congress and business-people is such that it takes little more than a casual wining and dining, and a midnight visitation, to turn the heads of the American guests of the Cuban leadership. Senator George McGovern, kingpin figure in the Cuba lobby, described Castro as "soft-spoken, wry, sensitive, sometimes witty, sometimes slightly ill at ease.... I frankly liked him and so did the rest of my party."[7] For McGovern (D-South Dakota), the parallels between Vietnam and Cuba are as obvious as they are important. He rarely misses the opportunity of noting that "Castro is something of a Ho Chi Minh of Cuba"; never is he described as a Quisling of Moscow. One congressional leader after another has succumbed to such blandishments. Senator Frank Church (D-Idaho) considers Cuba as a fact which only the United States fails to recognize.

> Tightly as we may cling to our blinders, the rest of the world has long since recognized that Fidel Castro's revolution is a *fait accompli.* Today, our embargo of Cuba isolates only the United States. Most other nations, Western Europe, Japan, as well as the socialist countries, trade freely with Castro, along with Canada and Mexico. Within Cuba today, one cannot help but see the signs of a spreading prosperity; despite the setback of rock-bottom sugar prices in the current world market. Not only the people in Havana, but people in the once-impoverished countryside are surprisingly well dressed and fed, their youngsters a picture of health. Modem schools—all built alike, to save money—are spread across the landscape. Here the children are boarded, each devoting 15 hours a week to work in the fields, with their weekends spent at home.[8]

The metaphysical pathos behind Senator Church's quite typical remarks is clear: the political instinct to get on a bandwagon underwrites much of the effort by the Cuba lobby. The syllogism is: If the current United States position leads to its isolation and isolationism is evil, then the way to break that isolation is to reestablish relationships with Cuba. But all kinds of questions remain—whether, in fact, such a legitimation of relationships would not indeed isolate the United States from other nations of the hemisphere, such as Brazil, Argentina, and Venezuela. With the exception of the 1974 harvest, Cuban foreign trade exhibited patterns of stagnation and even regression; imports now increasingly outweigh exports. True, schools *are* widespread, education *is* universal; but curiously, what is taught therein remains unreported. Children do indeed work 15 hours weekly in farm labor; but to celebrate child labor in Cuba hardly represents necessary or sufficient grounds for full diplomatic relationships. There was once a time when both critics and supporters or bourgeois civilization held child labor to be a vice, not a virtue.

The Cuba lobby embraces various types, ranging from those who believe that diplomatic recognition favors more normalized *political* relationships (and creates a potential for control of damaging situations), to those who encourage diplomatic recognition on *moral* grounds as well. One might say that the positions of Senators Javits (R-New York) and Church tend to be of the former sort, while Senators Abourezk (D-South Dakota) and McGovern, who see the Cuba question in precisely the same light as the Vietnam issue, hold the latter view. As McGovern puts it, we are "mean and vindictive," responding negatively toward "a tiny island of 10 million people for a revolution that happened nearly a generation ago."[9] There is a strong whiff of Vietnam that hangs over everything that McGovern says, and it leads to some facile formulas: tiny Vietnam, tiny Cuba.

Senator Church takes a more economic and less moralistic tack. His theme is that "the Cuban economy appears to be thriving." Senator Church appreciates the fact that diplomatic and trade relations will not alter the Cuban position with respect to military intervention in Africa, or close ties to the Soviet Union, or lead Cuba to pay in full for the expropriated properties of another generation and another regime. Church says bluntly that "those who believe this have simply exchanged one delusion for another."[10] Unfortunately, Senator Church's delusion, while more modest, is also real and equally grand; for while he views Fidel's role as liberator of Africa to be dangerously wrong, he also equates this to the United States' view of its intervention in South Vietnam. But how precisely such a mutuality of moral foul-up leads to a theory of diplomatic recognition is not spelled out. Once again, Senator Church holds out the carrot of high trade, of a share of rice, and of other commodities. In this way, he says we would also begin to exercise a moderating influence in Cuban affairs. But having already denied that we have that leverage, what moderating influence we could exert becomes difficult to assess.

Congressman Jonathan Bingham (D-N.Y.), issuing a report of his own 1977 study mission, made points similar to those of his Senate colleagues; but he decided to urge the recognition of Cuba in a more quaint manner. Bingham admitted that sending troops to all parts of Africa may not constitute the best use of Cuban manpower. However, he concludes that Cuba suffers most by such activities since "the net result is little time or energy for intimacy building with one's spouse."[11] Bingham goes on to offer a bizarre interpretation of Latin American law based on the premise that since Cuba does not have Anglo-Saxon law, it cannot be judged in the same way in terms of human rights.[12] It is almost too painful to point out that Romanic law is at least as concerned with human rights as Anglo law, or that the concept of evidence, juries, and trial records are more a matter of who is in power than the legal inheritance. But again, the carrot at the end of Congressman Bingham's stick is trade.

> Cuban officials indicated that as much as $1 billion a year of its trade with capitalist countries could be conducted with the United States. The United States, they noted, however, has lost the Cuban market through more than 16 years of embargo, and will have to work hard to regain it after the embargo is lifted.[13]

But, in the first place, less than 30 percent of Cuban trade is with capitalist countries; and any penetration by the United States of the Cuban market would be a fight for a fraction of that 30 percent. Castro has taken great pains to point out that "in the event the trade embargo is lifted, American businessmen would be competing for Cuban markets that now are linked to other Western countries rather than markets linked to the Soviet Union or other socialist countries."[14] Nonetheless, the Cuba lobby repeatedly urges an abandonment of political policy in favor of purported economic advantages. When one considers the minuscule character of those advantages in exchange for the acceptance of the very real presence of a worldwide military effort on the part of the Soviet Union enlisting the Cubans as their battering rams, the magnitude of the Cuba lobby as a pure political instrument becomes self-evident.

The survey research methods of the Cuba lobby are of a piece with the entire enterprise. For example, Senator Abourezk entered into the *Congressional Record* a rather modest and slender poll of 605 Minnesotans, from which one gathers that indifference was magically transformed into enthusiasm, and vague acceptance of Castro into celebration. But this poll, which indicates that 68 percent of the Minnesotans think the United States should reestablish diplomatic relations, actually indicates a low level of concern: only 4 percent have any interest in traveling to Cuba; only 9 percent some interest; and the rest, no interest or very little interest. At the same time, 44 percent said yes, Castro does take orders from Moscow. Perhaps the shrewdest observation of all was from one respondent who simply said: "The Cubans traded their freedoms for economics; it is better and worse."[15] Such is the myopia of the Cuba lobby (especially its South Dakota senatorial branch) that the intent of placing this item in the *Congressional Record* has obviated only the contents of the poll itself.

What then are the benefits seen by the Cuba lobby in a new diplomatic push? First, elevation of our standing in the eyes of Latin American and Canadian neighbors—this despite the fact that a majority of Latin American states and the Organization of American States have emphatically rejected unilateral diplomatic initiatives. Second, the canard about our own economic well-being by opening the way to a meaningful and two-way trade, although even the most optimistic amounts of exchanges would hardly yield anything more than the indirect trade presently going on through multinational subsidiaries. And finally, the belief that such a recognition would create a free flow of people between the two countries, although even Senator McGovern is hard put to offer anything other than the possibility that Cuban refugees in this country would benefit by the opportunity to visit their families still living in Cuba. There is not one iota of evidence that the Cubans would permit the free flow of traffic to the United States. Indeed, there is every strong indication that such free flow is a serious obstacle to the Cuban desire for diplomatic negotiations. It would almost inevitably raise the specter of a new migration, and hence the loss of much needed skilled manpower.

Political Point and Counterpoint

There exists, then, a parallel evolution—a heightening of the militarism of the Cuban regime, alongside demands for normalization of diplomatic relations between the United States and Cuba. In part, such demands are entirely understandable. It is, after all, preposterous to think of Cuba as being denied rights to normal diplomatic relations when we have precisely these relations with onerous right-wing regimes such as Paraguay and Uruguay, not to mention left-wing regimes the world over, far more removed from even the possibility of sanctions and controls of totalitarian behavior. But what is revealed by the congressional wing of the Cuba lobby is a belief extending far beyond reasons of state for diplomatic normalization. Its propositions can be summarized easily enough:

- That normalization of diplomatic relations will reduce military intervention in the affairs of other states. This belief persists as the cornerstone of the Cuba lobby, despite the evidence that the Cuban regime has quite the opposite intention.
- That the normalization of diplomatic relations will somehow provide for a return to pluralism in Cuba. Some writers and commentators have already spoken of Cuba as a place where "pluralism" can be expanded.[16] This despite the fact that along with Chile and Paraguay, Cuba is probably the most highly regulated and completely managed system in the hemisphere, containing the highest numbers of political prisoners.[17] And the advocates of normalization have forgotten the Stalinist canon that the more flexible a foreign policy, the more rigid the internal repression can become. My thesis on the Stalinization of Cuba, enunciated more than a decade ago, has unfortunately become a hardened reality. It is no accident that Soviet foreign policy, for periods such as 1937 through 1939 and again from 1949 through 1952, was remarkably flexible, postulating the theory of peaceful coexistence, first in terms of the Soviet Union and Nazi

Germany, and later between the Soviet Union and the United States. But the very success of this foreign policy led to a level of internal repression the likes of which has hardly been known elsewhere or even subsequently in the Soviet Union. There is no reason whatsoever to postulate internal freedom as an automatic consequence of diplomatic recognition.

• That there is in fact an enormous possibility of expanded trade between the United States and the multinationals on one side and Cuba on the other; that once the Cuban market is opened up, a whole new area for expansion will open to American business. In fact, however, the actual data reveal no such motion. Quite the contrary—Cuba's foreign trade, whether in terms of major trade groups or Cuban imports from noncommunist countries, has actually declined between 1975 and 1976.

• That the Cuban leadership can be weaned away from the Soviet Union by relinquishing the whip and applying the feather. Such soft strokes fail to reckon with the hurt, with the implacable determination of Castro to eliminate Guantanamo Naval Base as an American outpost, and beyond that, to ready a people to engage in combat not only against Africans, but against Americans if need be. It is furthermore a standing element in Fidel's ideology to see the Latin peoples in sharp racial and linguistic contradistinction to the North American peoples—to see them as implacable foes in historical terms. It is difficult to imagine how a simplified blueprint of diplomatic recognition would turn the tide in favor of the United States and against the Soviet Union.

Underlying a good many of the Cuba lobby's analytic shortcomings is a belief in Cuba as a socialist outpost on the level of Eastern Europe. It is a *Soviet* outpost. Cuba remains a single-crop economy and a single-party polity. As a Soviet tutelary, it does not have the capacity for diversification at the economic level, or the resolve for pluralism at the political level. It is indeed part of the Third World, a part of the militarized world, similar to other regimes in the hemisphere despite the patina of socialist rhetoric. True enough, the entrepreneurial class has been liquidated; but Latin America has a tradition of a middle class military; and in Cuba the military management of the economy has simply been taken one step further.

One theory often advanced is that the relative power of the United States and Cuba is so asymmetrical that Cuba's stake in improved relations exceeds considerably the American stake.

American diplomats should be in a position to produce a favorable balance in the process of compromise. Again, we have a liberal rhetoric abstracted from the liberal sensibility. For, in fact, what the Cubans perceive themselves to be is *both* a big power and a small nation. The sheer absence of size does not prevent the Cubans from seeing themselves as a major, if not *the* major, voice in the hemisphere. It sees itself in a condition of near-parity with, and not dependence on, the United States. Therefore, the imagined benefit that would come to the United States from lifting its embargo and working toward normal relations becomes vague at best.

A final caveat in the Cuba lobby position is that if we somehow cool the rhetoric, if we deny the political nature of differences between our two nations and systems, problems will go away in a glow of diplomatic immunity. Extensive reports, such as the Consultant's Report to the Ford Foundation, speak in general terms of improved communications, improved travel, and the usual abstract exchange of vague scholars.[18] But there are no specific sets of programs that would compel the Cuban government to move toward that kind of pluralism that wishful, liberal thinking has created around the Cuban system. The nonpolitical, bureaucratic style has added credibility and legitimacy to Cuba and its present rulers. But it has not served to open a new chapter in American-Cuban relationships.

It may be worth the risk to establish diplomatic relations and be in a better position to monitor actual events at a more intimate level. The Cubans already have this advantage through its mission at the United Nations. But to believe for an instant that such recognition by the United States of the Cuban claims will result in an immediate transformation of Cuban foreign policy would be a profound error. For the present, it might be worthwhile to consider the precise terms of negotiations of such a diplomatic exchange. It would also be fruitful if a foreign policy task force was charged with a review of the Cuban regime: the source of its economic trade practices, its overseas military involvements, its handling of political opponents. An authentic revolution is not necessarily an autonomous revolution. As a result, a clear distinction should be made between diplomatic recognition and ideological rationalization.

The Opposition

If there is a Cuba lobby, there is also an anti-Cuba lobby: one that seems plugged into the group of business concerns who demand settlement of U. S. claims against Cuba prior to the resumption of normal diplomatic relations and as a condition thereof. It would be a mistake to think that this group is without power, and one would have to say that recent events have probably strengthened the anti-recognition bloc, which has found its most forceful spokesman in Senator Robert Dole (R-Kansas).

The main thrust of the Dole position is that prior to the lifting of an embargo, and prior to the extension of formal diplomatic recognition, four main conditions must be met. Because these four conditions are the basis of the anti-Cuba lobby, it is worth presenting in some detail:

> First, Cuba must provide compensation for U.S. property confiscated when Castro came to power in 1959. I understand that the U.S. Foreign Claims Settlement Commission has established American losses in Cuba at $1.8 billion. Second, Cuba must withdraw its military troops and advisers from Africa. If Castro really wants to improve relations with the free world, it is time he stopped trying to export revolutions and bloodshed to developing nations. Third, Cuba must release from its prisons those citizens of the United States who are being held on political charges of a doubtful nature. In addition, we must see some substantial progress in observance of the human rights of Cuban citizens, especially those thousands who are imprisoned because of their political beliefs. Fourth, Cuba must reverse its stubborn attitude and agree to renew the 1973 anti-hijacking accord with the United States, which helps to discourage hijackings and to protect the lives of American citizens. On a related note, it is certainly time we are given guarantees on the future security of the U.S. naval base at Guantanamo Bay.[19]

Underlying Senator Dole's position which cautions diplomatic recognition is a conviction that the Cuba connection is not worth the candle. First, Cuba currently owes the Soviet Union $5 billion, and that indebtedness determines all other economic decisions it makes. Second, trade possibilities are seriously limited because Cubans would import from the West even if they lack cash reserves to do so. Third, the obstinacy of the Castro regime will only be intensified by a partial lifting of the embargo. Evidence for this last point is Cuba's rejection of a purchase of lifesaving medicines. Vice-President Carlos Rafael Rodríguez, addressing the East-West Trade Council, rejected the proposal as "a very, very narrow way of thinking as to our relations, and we are against this kind of approach."[20]

Another group of opponents to recognition have a heavy Cuban-exile constituency. For example, Senator Richard Stone (D-Fla.) is very much in the forefront of the anti-Cuba lobby, urging that all 700 U.S. citizens remaining in Cuba, who have applied to leave, be permitted to do so as a condition for diplomatic recognition.[21] Similarly, Congressman Harold Hollenbeck (R), representing the Ninth Congressional District in New Jersey, which probably has the second largest Cuban-exile community in the United States, constantly draws attention to the fact that Cuba is one of the biggest violators of human rights in the world, and ranks at the top of the list in terms of nations with political prisoners. Again, Congressman Hollenbeck attaches, as a condition for the restoration of trade, a special commission to study the ramifications of restored relations in the absence of political rights.[22] Probably the most articulate and blunt leader of the anti-Cuba lobby is Senator Barry Goldwater (R-Arizona) who sees the problem of Cuba as an essential watershed in American foreign policy. Like his opposite number, George McGovern, Goldwater uses the imagery of Vietnam:

> We do not seem to have learned much in our 200 years about the successful operation of foreign policy. I think it is mainly because we forget that there are instruments of national policy that can be used short of war. War is the ultimate and last instrument to which we have to resort. We have a political instrument, but the United States never has been politically strong here, because we have not been a country tending toward colonization. Therefore, we did not have lands to swap or other things to give.[23]

Senator Goldwater, however, somewhat tarnished his historical peroration on current history by noting in an off-the-cuff remark that "Our big mistake was when we did not make it [Cuba] a state after we captured it."[24] It is not the kind of statement that would endear him to the Cuban leadership or, for that matter, do anything but underscore the enormous gulf which still exists in congressional attitudes toward Cuba: On the one hand, there are those who think of diplomatic recognition as having nothing to do with moral or military risks and, on the other, those who would deny diplomatic recognition to those Western hemisphere states which do not have a subservient relationship to the United States. The search for a center that will hold continues.

Commercial Offerings

The Cuba lobby is comprised essentially of two elements—liberal senators and conservative businessmen—just as the anti-Cuba lobby is comprised of leading conservative senators and liberal businessmen. Thus, the current situation has led to coalitions across ideological lines, which probably has more to do with the present diplomatic impasse than any resolve—one way or the other—in the White House.

The interface between the business and political sides of the Cuba lobby is the offices of Kirby Jones and the organization he runs, called Alamar Associates. Jones himself is a veteran of the presidential campaigns of Kennedy and McGovern, having served as press aide in the 1972 election campaign. His partner is Norman Sherman, former press secretary to the late Senator Hubert H. Humphrey (Humphrey was instrumental in encouraging a group of 50 Minnesota business people to hire Alamar's services at $2,000 per company in 1977). A further linkage is through the offices of Frank Mankiewicz, formerly McGovern's campaign director, who along with Jones formed the National Executive Conference. This organization brought politicians and business leaders together in seminars, which led to the trips to Cuba and the introductory letters required for the businessmen to see Castro and his associates at the other end.[25]

Kirby Jones is closely aligned with northeast business interests seeking reintroduction to the Cuban markets, as well as

Midwestern firms seeking to penetrate Cuban markets for the first time. To this date, he has made 30 trips to Cuba and is on easy terms with important figures, such as Marcello Fernández, overseas minister of foreign travel. At the same time, when the Cubans established their interest section in the Czechoslovakian Embassy in 1977, it was Jones who helped the Cuban officials set up shop and make the necessary contact.

There are various types of firms interested in Cuba connections. One of these is Honeywell whose interests were capsized after Batista was overthrown in 1959. While their losses were minuscule, the feeling now is that profit margins could overcome and compensate for the earlier losses. John May, general manager of the Latin American region for Honeywell, speaks affectionately of Kirby Jones, but reserves his best words for Fidel Castro: "Always going through my mind was this same thought: Here is a guy who is a revolutionary leader talking to businessmen. I've never met anyone like that."[26]

There is nothing especially insidious about this, and certainly nothing unusual. However, the linkup does demonstrate that the business community knows no politics other than those of doing business, while, on the other side, the so-called political Left in the Senate has no problem whatsoever connecting to the business community or a set of conduits in dummy organizations that, in the words of Mankiewicz, "create something where there was not anything better."

Fifty firms have formed a committee called the Joint Corporate Committee on Cuban Claims Asking to be Reimbursed. Property worth $1.8 billion, with interest, would add $1.7 billion, or roughly $3.5 billion in total compensation. These firms, the *claims men,* are not so much interested in renegotiating the terms of reentering Cuba as they are in compensation. But the more aggressive group is the traders rather than the claims men who, remembering the almost $1 billion per year that the United States and Cuba traded before 1959, are eager to renegotiate such agreements. The multinationals in particular are less interested in earlier claims than they are in reactivating business. For these big firms, the earlier expropriations are of little moment, having been long ago written off as tax losses. Indeed, only 1 percent of the certified claimants have entered compensation complaints. The traders are therefore the paramount group. Coca-Cola, for example, has a $27.5 million claim against Cuba, but is more interested in renewing a business that would bring 300 million bottles of soft drink sales per year into Cuba. J. Paul Austin, chairman of the board of Coca-Cola, was a recent visitor, purportedly going as a special envoy from President Carter. [27]

General Motors and Ford fall in the same category, and indeed they have already enjoyed trade with Cuba through their Argentine subsidiaries. Then we have what might be called the industrial hardware group, including International Harvester, Minnesota Mining, Caterpillar Tractor, John Deere, Xerox, Boeing, and Dow Chemical. To the multinational group, the problem of compensation is distinctly secondary. Indeed, old claimants appear as a stumbling block to what they hope will be a small bonanza.

The problem with the bonanza theory is the Cuban economy itself: it is wholly mortgaged, with its indebtedness to the Soviet Union increasing by $2 million a day. It is thus a bankrupt economy living off political rather than economic capital, and cannot even purchase goods already licensed by the U.S. Treasury Department for the modest amount of less than $300 million. Its prospects are accordingly severely limited.

Even in tourism, which brought 272,000 Americans to Cuba in 1957, much has happened since the 1950s. The Caribbean region has been developed immensely, and Cuba cannot compete effectively. The hotels are old, used-up, and barely convenient in terms of middle-class U.S. styles. The Havana nightlife has all but been squeezed out. Unless one enjoys repeated visits to Hemingway's home, there is not much to do in terms of the American style of tourism. Moreover, the closed political system mitigates against a tourist boom. There is absolutely nothing in Cuban propaganda that would indicate a willingness to open the system to free motion in both directions, or for that matter, free movement within the island. Finally, as the Minnesota poll shows, Americans are just not interested in Cuba.

The Cuban government has embarked on a five-year develop-ment plan to once again make tourism a major industry. The plan calls for building a new Havana airport and two more elsewhere on the island, construction of 59 new hotels and resorts, and beefing up public rental cars and taxi and motor coach trans-portation. This will undoubtedly change a situation in which tourism remains tightly controlled. For the present, the biggest growth potential is in sports: boxers, gymnasts, basketball and baseball players—and the revenues from network television in broadcasting such fun and games. But the big trade prize still goes to the Soviets: after all, those who put forth risk and venture capital reap the rewards—even if they are taken in rubles.

Conclusion

The obsequious behavior and banal commentary of United States study missions, site visitations by congressional junkets, and missions from American businessmen have only reinforced the intransigence of the Castro regime. Fidel's position, and hence that of his subordinates has been unchanged: not a single concession on matters of principle, while at the same time every aggression is converted into a principle. Cuba claims the right to participate or aid in the fomenting of guerrilla insurgency throughout the world, and the shipment of military cadres and arms to all allies. The rhetoric of international solidarity thinly masks the total domination of Cuban foreign policy by Soviet interests. If Cuba is the mass battering ram of Soviet policy, it carries with it the potential of a small nation to acquire big-nation military and diplomatic status. If Cuba is the military state that serves as a proxy for Soviet intentions, this role permits Castro to continue a long-held revolutionary belief in the international solidarity of oppressed Latin peoples. For a brief spell, up to and including the Bolivian debacle of the mid-1960s, such a theory was put into practice. But what first appeared on the scene of history as hemispheric solidarity now returns as international bravura. The risk factor in Cuban foreign policy is virtually nil. It does not so much aid and abet nascent revolutionary movements as it comes to the rescue of Soviet client states in deep political trouble. It does not so much prompt revolution as prop up tottering or repressive regimes self-described as Marxist-Leninist in character. If the trade-off is virtually unavoidable, given Cuba's enormous debt and balance of payments situation, it has had the disastrous effect of depriving the regime of its earlier romantic imageries. Not even the Cuba lobby can restore the tarnished image of a revolution for sale.

But for the present, all discussion, by the Cuba lobby and its opponents alike, comes down to the question of diplomatic recognition: thorny, but hardly insoluble. From an operational viewpoint, the United States must make up its mind whether to withhold full diplomatic recognition because it finds the regime repugnant and hence unacceptable, or a direct military threat to American interests. I submit that using the first criterion is both implausible and dangerous. If agreement to principles of conduct were the basis of diplomacy, there would be little of it. It might be argued that even to open "interest sections" in each other's capitals has served to increase channels of communication and hence to normalize relations to some degree. Those who argue for withholding recognition as a form of punishment only postpone the settlement of outstanding differences—from troop deployment and expropriation payments to control of air space.

If, however, the question of diplomatic recognition is seen in a specific context of military adventurism, then the issue becomes far more difficult. From the missile crisis of the early 1960s, to the current troop deployments in Africa, Cuba has conducted an aggressive foreign policy, based on the principle that no nation is off limits as long as it is conducting an assault on imperialism (meaning the United States) and no price is high enough to warrant a more prudent policy. The real questions then become two: Do the adventures of Cuban troops in Africa directly assault United States political interests? Does the very existence of a Cuban military force serving as a Soviet proxy warrant non-recognition of this peculiar client state?

The participation of Cuban troops in Angola and in Ethiopia currently does not constitute a direct threat to United States interests. It is hard to image Somalia as more of a friend to the United States than Ethiopia in a nonbelligerent context; and while Somalia would be nicer to the UNITA forces than the Neto regime, this clearly does not represent a sufficient military basis to threaten direct United States interests. Further, should such adventurism take on aspects of direct contact with American troops or American supported nations, then diplomatic recognition can be revoked easily enough. The history of our relations with Asian countries shows clearly that diplomatic outposts can be opened and shut with remarkable alacrity.

The central concern that will not easily dissolve upon inspection is that the Cuban armed forces are being used as a proxy for the Soviet foreign policy, including such dangerous aspects as the deployment of Soviet fighter pilots in Cuba. The issue is essentially one between the United States and the Soviet Union: if the issues are grave enough, they will erupt as a direct confrontation between the two great powers, as they did during the Cuban Missile Crisis. If Cuba is a true client state, then it will act now as then-by responding to Soviet "requests" for dismantling its military war machine, or at least limiting its spheres of operations. But this too becomes a null hypothesis for denial of diplomatic recognition, since the essential leverage factor concerns the United States and the Soviet Union. Diplomatic recognition would finally place Cuba on the same status as any other small Caribbean nation, and deny it the moral force of its special pariah diplomatic status.

But all evidence would indicate that Cuba would not accept full diplomatic recognition with the United States at this point. Even if the United States accepts lifting all trade embargoes as a precondition for such diplomatic recognition, U.S. troops on Guantanamo remain a thorn. In February 1978 Castro indicated that nothing would be done, diplomatically, until the ratification settlement of the Panama Canal Zone treaties by the Senate. He said "there are political problems in treaties; and Carter knows them and he is trying to get the treaties through the Senate. Getting the treaties passed by the Senate takes precedence over normal-ization of relations." But the linkages between Cuban recognition and Canal Zone transference are tenuous. Normalization is not quite the same as full diplomatic exchanges of consular staffs, and Castro has never had such diplomatic relations high on his own list of political priorities. Without at least a tacit understanding on removal of U.S. troops from Guantanamo, i.e., from Cuban soil, it is difficult to imagine such a full-scale diplomatic effort taking place, unless there are compelling reasons for the Soviet Union to urge the Cubans to move in such a direction.

Diplomatic recognition in cases such as Cuba is better under-stood not in terms of who has the most to gain, so much as who has the least to lose. And in such a context, the answer might well be the United States. Part of the myopia of the Cuba lobby is its seeming inability to recognize how low on the scale of pri-orities diplomatic recognition is for the Cuban authorities. The lobby acts and speaks as if the simple lifting of an embargo will automatically yield the desired normalizations. But this does not contend with the host—the Cuban regime. That regime has made a reputation and built an ideology on anti-yanquism. It enjoys its special relations to the Soviet Union that might well be impaired in a normalized diplomatic climate. And it is faced with the prob-lems of any dictatorship: the need to mobilize and galvanize a population into action on the basis of supposed foreign threats. This might easily dissolve under the weight of normal relations; and with that, the regime itself might be imperiled-no small part of the current equation in Cuban-American relations.

Early adherents to Fidel's Cuba, often drawn from radical intellectual elements in search of the Holy Grail of a Pure Revolu-tion, are reduced to writing memos and pleas to the maximum leader. They implore Castro to reconsider his position on the condemnation of Israel, or revoke the arrest of homosexuals, or terminate the incarceration of writers, or end the unequal treatment of blacks in the officer corps. They are met either by stony silence or clear rebuke—silence by the leader and rebuke by the propagandists. Any proclamation or plea becomes itself a definition of the enemy, the degenerate act of foreign intellectuals who do not know better-Zionists cloaked as American academics, Gusanos disguised as Latin American revolutionaries, Trotskyists disguised as European politicians. The Latin Czar has sent a message to former adherents that scribblings and wall posters about democratic socialism cannot be permitted to interfere with the course of Soviet empire. From Sartre to Sheer, the old supporters have been reduced to a dreary silence. However, the new Cuba lobby is not made up of ideologues and intellectuals, but hard and tough politicos and entrepreneurs. They take up where the old celebrationists left off. These new types, not having many, if any, illusions about Castro's Cuba to begin with, and not being especially concerned with the fates or fortunes of poets, perverts, or politicians, see only an opportunity to do business as usual. Here we have that infinite supply of rope that was spoken of, but this time the rope comes to the satellite instead of the source.

References/Notes

1.   Aleksandr Solzhenitsyn, *Detente: Prospects for Democracy and Dictatorship.* New Brunswick, NJ: Transaction Books, 1976, 11-12.
2.   Angus Deming et al., "The Cubans in Africa," *Newsweek.* Vol. XCI, no. 11. March 13, 1978: 36-42; and also *U.S. News and World Report,* "Africa: A 'Vietnam' for Russia and Cuba?," February 6, 1978.
3.   Kenneth D. Kaunda, cited in Bayard Rustin, "Black African Independence: The Cuban Threat," *New York Times,* December 15, 1977. See also Graham Hovey, "Brzezinski Asserts that Soviet General Leads Ethiopia Units." *New York Times,* February 25, 1978.
4.   Carlos Rafael Rodríguez, "Closing speech at the 250th Anniversary of the Founding of the University of Havana," *Gramma: Official Organ of the Central Committee of the Communist Party of Cuba.* Vol. 13, no. 4. January 22, 1978: 9.
5.   Irving Louis Horowitz, "Castrology Revisited: Further Observations on the Militarization of Cuba," *Armed Forces and Society.* Vol. 3, no. 4. August 1977: 617-631.
6.   Carlos Alberto Montaner, *Informe Secreto Sobre la Revolución Cubana.* Madrid: Ediciones Sedway, 1976, 313-316.

7. George McGovern, "A Talk with Castro," *The New York Times Magazine*. March 13, 1977: 20 et passim.

8. Frank Church, "Chauffeured by Castro, Church Likes What He Sees." *News Release*. August 22, 1977.

9. George McGovern, "Statement," *Congressional Record-Senate*, June 16, 1977: S9986-S9987.

10. Frank Church, "Delusions and Reality: The Future of United States-Cuba Relations," *Report to the Senate Committee on Foreign Relations of the United States Senate*. Washington, D.C.: U.S. Government Printing Office, 1977 (August 8-11, 1977).

11. Jonathan B. Bingham, "Toward Improved United States-Cuba Relations," *Report of a Special Study Mission to Cuba, February 10-15, 1977*. Washington, D.C.: U.S. Government Printing Office, 1977, 11.

12. Jonathan B. Bingham, ibid., 9.

13. Jonathan B. Bingham, ibid., 12.

14. Fidel Castro, cited in the *Los Angeles Times*. February 19, 1978: 2.

15. James Abourezk, "Diplomatic Relations with Cuba," *Congressional Record-Senate*, June 27, 1977.

16. Patricia Weiss Fagen, "Toward Detente with Cuba: Issues and Obstacles," *International Policy Report*. Vol. III, no. 3, November 1977: 16-18.

17. Stephen Miller, "Politics and Amnesty International," *Commentary*. Vol. 65, no. 3. March 1978: 57-60.

18. Peter Winn, *Consultant's Report to the Ford Foundation*. Mimeograph Report issued on September 30, 1977.

19. Robert Dole, *Congressional Record-Senate*, June 16, 1977: S9976.

20. Jack Nelson, "Cuba Spurns U.S. Medicine Sale as Not Enough," *Los Angeles Times*. February 20, 1978: 20.

21. Richard Stone, *Congressional Record-Senate*, June 16, 1977:S9980.

22. Tom Sullivan, "Cubans tell 'Cap' a Thing or Two," *The Sunday Herald-News* (New Jersey), August 14, 1977: A-12.

23. Barry Goldwater, *Congressional Record-Senate*, June 16, 1977: S9981.

24. Barry Goldwater, quoted "Goldwater tips hat to Truman, Humphrey," *Washington Post-Los Angeles Times News* Service. October 13, 1977.

25. Karen deWitt, "Cuban Business? See Man Named Jones," *New York Times*, January 30, 1977: D1, D6.

26. Al Craig, "Rolling Up the 'Sugar Cane Curtain,'" *Passages: The Magazine of Northwest Airlines*. Vol. 8, no. 5. August 1977: 16-18.

27. Alfred L. Padula, Jr., "U.S. Business Squabbles Over Cuba." *The Nation*. Vol. 225, no. 13. October 22, 1977: 390-91.

Source and Original Title: "The Cuba Lobby." *The Washington Review of Strategic and International Studies*, Vol. 1, No. 3, July 1978, pp. 58-71.

13

Institutionalization as Integration: The Cuban Revolution at Age Twenty

Ever since the Cuban Constitution of 1976 was ratified, announcing the existence of a socialist republic with appropriate organs of popular power consecrated by a national assembly, academics have debated its meaning. Too frequently, arguments among Cuba analysts about institutionalization describe niceties, rather than substance. It is disconcerting to see perfectly capable scholars treat the words of a political leader as the gospel truth. It is inconceivable, for instance, that experts on the Soviet Union would argue that the actual arrival of communism in the first socialist state coincides with Leonid Brezhnev's announcement of a new constitution to replace the 1936 Stalin Constitution. It would be of equal absurdity to imagine a group of foreign experts on the United States taking for granted that Jimmy Carter's outline of New Foundations marked a turning point in American social economic affairs as a direct result of a declaration. Cuba experts—pro or anti regime—too often are exempt from skepticism or doubt.

Rather than use the space herein allocated to engage the views of others or defend the positions outlined in my work, I will discuss what institutionalization means, and in what sense it has arrived in Cuba. The one exception to this caveat is to correct a profound error in Azicri's summary of my position. My point is definitely not that "inner tensions within the Cuban regime must be located within the military rather than in the customary Third World pattern of military versus bureaucracy."[1] Indeed, it is actually the reverse: Cuban patterns of militarization are structurally quite similar to Third World patterns; that the fusion between armed forces, police forces, bureaucratic ministries, and vigilante surveillance at the mass level, tends to make Cuba resemble regimes that ideologically and even economically are quite different from it. I have claimed for at least 15 years that single crop systems and political dependency on a foreign power are characteristic of most Third World nations—whosoever they are dependent upon—and do not represent, except to the most draconian minds, an advanced form of socialism. The military pivot is the essence of internal control. If the boot of militarism fits the foot of dependency, then the Cuban regime will simply have to wear it; hygienic apologetics notwithstanding.

Essentially, I agree with Domínguez's recently stated view that "with very few exceptions, the people in power at the beginning of the 1960s remain in power in the 1970s." Further, such institutionalization represents "formalized politics as they already exist in Cuba."[2] My own starting point is that Castro is not simply concerned with the formalistic concept of institutionalization, but rather with insulating the Cuban regime against possible sources of a golpe. The best modern political science holds that party dominance is stabilizing whereas pluralism is destabilizing; and strong single party control (with or without mass support) has the best chance of survival.[3] In this area, "democratic centralism" better known as Stalinism, seems best suited for regime maintenance in Cuba.

Institutionalization as Independence

If institutionalization means independence, or serves as a measure of self-regulation, then the true course of institutionalization certainly has not run smoothly. Cuba is, by all odds and measured by every indicator, more dependent upon the Soviet Union than at any time in the past two decades. This is not to say that dependency in Cuba is any more "total" than elsewhere. Perhaps the most balanced and fair-minded appraisal recently offered is that by Jacques Levesque: "Cuba is indeed entirely dependent on the Soviet Union for a whole series of vitally important products, but it is obvious that dependence does not automatically become economic exploitation." But even if the economic levers and decisions remain in Cuban hands, the tendencies become crucial. And here Levesque must note that "although it was Cuba's choice to align itself with the Soviet Union, it is not at all certain that it would be able to return to its 1969-70 position of neutrality, even if so desired."[4] With the Cuban military serving as a battering ram of Soviet foreign policy, the quid pro quo might temporarily shift in Cuba's favor with respect to a favorable balance of trade or increased sophisticated military hardware. However, the intensity of dependency as measured by the militarization of Cuban society also becomes increasingly manifest.

A useful indicator of Cuban dependency upon the Soviet Union is an ideological hegemony that would be unthinkable in any Latin American nation similarly beholden upon the United States. It is not far fetched to say that *Granma* has become *Pravda* in the Spanish language. It might even be said that the editorial posturing and exaggerations in *Granma* on every issue from China to Israel to Kampuchea probably embarrasses soviet ideologues. The Cubans well illustrate political dependence in Latin America. Only Bulgaria in Eastern Europe appears to have the same ideological solidarity with its Soviet political support base, and they have a good excuse: geographical proximity. The level of ideological latitude and policy autonomy exhibited by Romania, Poland, and Yugoslavia is perceived as heretical among the Cuban political elite; i.e. breaking ranks with proletarian (Soviet) internationalism. Thus, whatever else institutionalization may signify; only those suffering from an irreparable case of political myopia would call it independence. As I have pointed out on many occasions: the Cuban revolution is authentic, but by no stretch of the imagination is it autonomous.

Institutionalization as Succession

A second meaning of institutionalization is that the process of political succession has been resolved, or at least addressed. A consensus builds after a long period of turmoil, in which the mechanism for transference of power is put in place. This is done in such a way as to forestall the possibility of violent upheaval, disaffection or unsponsored social change. In point of fact, institutionalization in Cuba has not faced any such shift in leadership; nor has it meant the infusion of new political parties; nor has it signified regulatory machinery whereby upon the death of the leader an orderly transfer of power takes place. On the contrary: at no point in Cuban history has the gap between top-echelon leadership and operational personnel been as pronounced. Given the fact that the leadership now in power made the revolution 20 years ago any possibility of testing institutionalization in this sense is clearly implausible. It is indeed the case that a middle-echelon leadership has been created and a corresponding economic infrastructure has emerged; but any view of this as institutionalization omits the question of political succession.

Since the men who made the Cuban Revolution were, for the most part, young, energetic and healthy, a postponement rather than a resolution of problems of institutionalization as succession has been made possible. But Fidel cannot indefinitely avoid the "Franco Problem"—or for those who prefer socialist analogues the "Mao Problem"—namely, how orderly transfer of power is to be insured. It might well be that a secular dynastic effect can be maintained, i.e., a shift from Fidel to Raúl. But this would only be a short term solution. The problem of succession looms larger in Cuba than in the Soviet Union, since the official Communist Party, the chief organ of political power, was not the vanguard but the tail of the Cuban revolution. Hence, its legitimacy as a ruling force cannot simply be institutionalized through fiat. One ancillary intent of the First Party Congress of December, 1975, and the Constitution which ensued, was to create legitimacy by decree. But a revolution born in armed combat, involving "foco" strategies and "movement" tactics, could not hope to simulate Soviet patterns of succession (which are hardly anything to brag about or inscribe in the annals of political systems as a model for a changing of the guard).

Institutionalization as Civilianization

Another meaning to the concept of institutionalization is the preeminence of civilian authority over military authority; in other words, a regime in which the military is legally subordinate to and carries out orders of an elected regime. Aside from the most gratuitous kinds of analysis, even those who are completely dedicated to rendering the regime favorably admit either that the military have increased their power, or that the line between civilian and military authority is so murky that it is virtually impossible to make a distinction between the two forms of authority. This is another way of saying that there are some police in uniform and others out of uniform, just as there are some authorities in uniform and others out of uniform. But this would severely weaken any notion of institutionalization as civil authority, since whether we are talking about the United States or the Soviet Union; institutionalization does entail a distinct separation between civilian and military powers not only in terms of function, but also of structure. In Cuba, quite the reverse: a strong sense of military preeminence prevails in everything from hardware to rank. Restoration of officer corps privilege would indicate that institutionalization does not mean civilianization.

Beyond the blurring of lines between civil and military authority is the repressive nature of the regime itself. There are considerable gradations to military rule. Militarism should not be viewed mechanistically as a front for the political system. Military forms of political rule are often covert. Militarism can assume the guise of maximum police power; or it can take the form of a civilian ruler fronting for a military junta. In the case of Cuba, for the moment it is more nearly a sharing of authority; an uncomfortable organizational equilibrium between Fidel's civilianism and Raúl's militarism. Some national development tasks are organized around administrative cadre; others are linked to paramilitary or directly military personnel. Some foreign policy involvement is based on civilian technicians; others (more frequently) are based on military intervention. The ambiguities of militarism notwithstanding, Cuba exhibits a higher degree of armed force preparedness and mobilization, not to mention overseas intervention and participation, than any other country in Latin America.

What then is the Meaning of Institutionalization of the Cuban Revolution?

Here we come upon the less attractive features of the regime. For what has been institutionalized is the political culture itself: a sense of the regime as no longer being experimental, but one locked into a Soviet model. This lock on innovation actually prohibits normalization. Admittedly, in theory institutionalization will provide for direct and indirect elections for provincial and national legislative assemblies, and provide for a separation of functions between the Cuban State and the Communist Party. In practice, it means an imposing division between politicized and the non-politicized sectors of society. Institutionalization is at root a depoliticization of the Cuban masses: the lodging of authority within the communist party and its military satrapies, the negation of mass political participation. With the exception of politics as circus, as a banal theatrical salute for visiting dignitaries, or as a series of nominations for approved communist party cadre, mass participation in political life is less than it was prior to the announced institutionalization.

Institutionalization means liquidation of old classes with a corresponding expansion of class struggle. The essence of the Stalinist system of terror is the assumption that older classes, through migration or expropriation, no longer exist; but that for Cuba to become a society of workers, peasants, and intellectuals it must liquidate old class "remnants" and "attitudes." Just as in the Soviet Union, there is an end to classes, but not class struggle. Behind this liquidation process is the emergence of a new technocracy, a modernized military, and a party apparatus that grows older and more integrated. This certainly is the essential framework of institutionalization. It presumes a lessening tension between a modernizing technocracy and a traditionalist polity. The operative meaning of institutionalization is regime consolidation. Institutionalization as regime integration is at the heart of the present stage in the Cuban Revolution. Involved is the rationalization of agencies and activities of the system and the total integration of social-political-economic-military subsystems. Whether the Cuban people can or will be so bridled remains a point to be decided by actual history, rather than political slogans.

When Division General Sergio del Valle commemorates the 20th anniversary of the National Police Force, he plainly notes the isomorphism between the police and the rebel army, an agency which constitutes a "powerful armed force of the working class," the fusion of a "new legal order" with a police-inspired "drop in crime," and the utilization of science and technology "at the service of a police force of a new type." "This offensive" against crime "has been taken up enthusiastically by every police officer, every member of the Ministry of the Interior, and has had the support of the Young Communist League, the Committees for the Defense of the Revolution, the Federation of Cuban Women, and Central Organization of Cuban Trade Unions and the social organizations."[5]

When Jesús Montané notes that the main function of the trade union is a "counterbalance," this is a neat way of saying that strikes are prohibited and antisocial.

This counterbalance is intended to "fulfill the technical and economic plan, to mobilize all the reserve forces.... The trade union's role as counterbalance is necessary above all for the union to contribute with full efficiency to the fulfillment of the technical and economic plan, to mobilize all the reserve forces of production and place at the disposal of the economy that inexhaustible resource of subjective factors—the workers' consciousness, spirit, organization, love for their work center and understanding of the importance of an ever greater quantitative effort." He too is noting the new integration of labor, management and state administration.

Raúl Castro, General of the Army, notes the "cooperation, technical assistance, solidarity and fraternal aid of the Party, Government, Armed Forces, and the people of the Soviet Union as represented in exemplary fashion by the Soviet military specialists who work among us."[7] This constant theme of administrative fusion indicates again that institutionalization means the integration, not the separation of military and civil functions, police and legal power.

When Fidel speaks of the integration of university life and working class participation, the channeling of university study efforts toward basic careers in technology, tying wages to production, acting firmly against irresponsibility, soft heartedness, and inefficiency, he ties it all together by insisting that managers not be "buddies" of workers, but that managers become "demanding." As for strikes Fidel is entirely emphatic: "Strikes? Who talks about strikes in a revolutionary process, a socialist process? Under capitalism all you hear about is strikes and more strikes at all hours and every day; and there's always something brought to a halt under capitalism. One day TV stations go on strike; another air control towers go on strike, and there's one catastrophe after another, there's chaos in the world, because flight controllers are out on strike. Such chaos and disorder are what is most commonplace in capitalist society."[8] Only capitalism apparently countenances "chaos and disorder." Institutionalization in this sense means quite clearly no tolerance for chaos, disorder, or anti-Senate behavior of any kind; in short total integration of administrative and political functions.

It is clear that institutionalization means quite simply authoritarianism. To those who prefer a rosier rhetoric, the new regime seeks integration, in which opposition is simply viewed as intolerable, a remnant of the old order. It might well be that such a concept of integration is no more and no less that what Cuban society seeks as it establishes its claims to survival as an authentic revolution. It might also be that other options are foreclosed, and that the repressive integration offered in the name of institutionalization is the only "choice" available. Then let this be understood and acknowledged by the academic community, by experts on Latin America, and by commentators on Cuba.

While the Cuban political leadership manages to speak in an abrasive, blunt, and at times an entirely distasteful manner—filled with political crudities and moral vulgarities, it does speak truthfully. Tragically, its intellectual epigones, those for whom the Cuban regime has shown little but contempt and condescension, prefer to speak in laundered language, with what Jean-Francois Revel has with sad precision termed "interiorized censorship"[9] filled with circumlocutions and circumspections, replete with sophistication and qualification. Unfortunately, they have failed to communicate the elementary forms of Cuban social realities. The current wave of intellectual junk food called institutionalization is sadly only the most recent example of political dogs wagging academic tails.

References/Notes

1. Max Azicri, "The Institutionalization of the Cuban Revolution", *Cuban Studies* (forthcoming) p.16 of manuscript version.
2. Jorge I. Domínguez, *Cuba: Order and Revolution*. Cambridge, Mass.: The Belknap Press of Harvard University Press, 1978, pp. 7-8.
3. Robert W. Jackman, "The Predictability of Coups d'etat", *The American Political Science Review*. Vol. 72, No.4. December, 1978, pp. 262-75.
4. Jacques Levesque, *The USSR and the Cuban Revolution: Soviet Ideological and Strategic Perspectives, 1959-77* (translated from the French by Deanna Drendel Leboeuf). New York: Praeger Publishers/Holt, Rinehart and Winston, CBS Inc., 1978, pp. 195-99.
5. Sergio del Valle, "On the 20th Anniversary of the Founding of the National Revolutionary Police", *Granma*. Vol. 14, No.3 (January 21) 1979. p. 4.
6. Jesús Montané, "14th Congress of the Central Organization of Cuban Trade Unions" (Speech delivered on November 29, 1978), *Granma*. Vol. 13, No. 52 (December 24) 1978. P. 5.
7. Raúl Castro Ruz, "In Honor of the 20th Anniversary of the Triumph of the Revolution...", (Speech delivered on January 2, 1979), *Granma*. Vol. 14, No.2 (January 14) 1979. pp. 4-5.
8. Fidel Castro, "Our Revolutionary Process Can Really Be Proud of the Role Being Played By Our Workers and Our Trade Union Movement." (Speech delivered on December 2, 1978), *Granma*. Vol. 13, No. 51 (December 17) 1978. pp. 6-7.
9. Jean-Francois Revel, "The Trouble with Latin America", *Commentary*, Vol. 67, No.2, February, 1979. pp. 47-50.

Source and Original Title: "Institutionalization as Integration: The Cuban Revolution at Age Twenty." *Cuban Studies/Estudios Cubanos*, Vol. 9, No. 2, July 1979, pp. 84-90.

1980s: Militarization of the Regime

In retrospect, the 1980s were the high point of the Castro Era. His regime was able to rid the nation of the potentially "counterrevolutionary" forces—numbering well over one million people, who left Cuba and the struggle within to more hospitable environs. The boatlift from Mariel to Miami may have tarnished the regime in world public opinion, and created a countervailing force in the United States, especially in the Florida region. This outward migration solidified Castro's hold on the working masses. It made opposition from within fragmented and reduced it to very limited proportions. The reticence of the advanced powers, especially the United States to enter into direct military confrontation was also a factor that played out in a Castro victory. Having the scars of Vietnam starting to heal from a decade of warfare, the West was neither ready nor capable of launching anything resembling a massive struggle.

The 1980s witnessed several major developments within Cuba: the receipt of massive aid from the Soviet Union and it satellites which stabilized the economy, and allowed it to grow modestly within the sugar-tobacco syndrome. Again, even if this meant that the economy could not build the sort of modern infrastructure envisioned by Castro and his economic advisors, it offered a sense of worldly participation in its struggles again the United States. This situation had a price: Cuban adventurism in the Third World, a destabilizing force performed on behalf of the Soviet Union with a low risk to the Bolshevik regime as such. What was required was the final transformation of the Cuban system from a civil to a military state. While the Communist Party quickly displaced the administrative apparatus of the Batista regime, the transformation of the military into the advanced guard of the regime was difficult. It was fraught with problems of resistance in the military to the regime, and even more, potential corruption from its special status in terms of the export of drugs and other illegal commercial activities. The so-called "Ochoa Affair"—and the court martial of the presumed military ring leaders involved in drug running activities, once and for all eliminated the armed forces as a source of independent or oppositional power and made it a force molded to and dedicated to the needs of the Castro regime. Were it not for transformations taking place elsewhere, the Castro dynasty seemed to be poised for a period of absolutism unequalled in Latin American history.

By the close of the decade, and continuing well into the following decade, this process was aided and abetted by the Cuban armed forces. This tightly knit elite sector was the most efficient, and perhaps the only effective element capable of exploiting the global economic marketplace. As was the case in many parts of Latin America in earlier periods, such as Argentina, Chile and Brazil, commercial activities managed by the armed forces have expanded to account for a significant portion of the Cuban foreign revenues and export earnings; including the critical tourist industry Efficiencies of size and scale exhibited in Cuba are managed by the military, which in effect serves as the bureaucratic arm of the Cuban regime, with little inclination to engage in barrack-style political golpes. *What began as a guerrilla insurgency matured into a military dictatorship.*

14

C. Wright Mills and *Listen, Yankee*

The Causes of World War Three was a negative book with a holocaust message: namely, prevent a war that nobody wants and that will perish from. What eluded Mills were the positive forces of change. He located this positive message with a vengeance in the Cuban Revolution. It came at a propitious moment. He was running out of time. Even the possibility of heroism within an American context seemed remote. Sociological analysis had failed to come up with the collective hero: neither the labor intellectual nor the inner-directed white collar worker nor undergraduate students nor Christian ministers would do. But this time Mills was not to be denied. The hero had come; the Messiah's name was Fidel Castro. Like the prophets of the Old Testament Castro led a crusade which seemed at first without hope (it was also without political dogmatism); and he led it to victory. By 1960, Mills wanted not just history, but victory.

Mills' love affair with the Cuban Revolution was many-sided. Initially, there was the personage of Castro. His identification with him gave Mills a sense of doing battle, first with Dwight D. Eisenhower and then with John F. Kennedy. In this way he was continuing his commitment to assault the bastions of power as he had in *The Power Elite.* The *bête noire* of his mind was to become President Kennedy, just as William James fifty years earlier had viewed Teddy Roosevelt as the quintessential imperialist. For

Mills, Castro was the essential pragmatist, the quasi-Marxist who got things done without regard to Communist dogma or a Communist party. If there was a touch of mysticism in this view, then at least it was one that gave substance to Mills's sense of Third Worldliness; his love affair with an exotic place, and an unformed movement within a downtrodden nation. In *Listen, Yankee* he wrote:

> You just have to come up with the facts about what kind of man Fidel Castro is, and what kinds of men the forty-or-so commandantes and the two-hundred-or-so capitáns of the Council of Ministers—all those who make up the revolutionary government of Cuba today—what kinds of men they really are. They have a real respect for the people and a real belief in the people. It's not some romantic idea. It's just something they know and something they are. These are the people—we revolutionaries think—and so you trust them. These are the people—and they can learn very fast what has to be done.

The key to *Listen, Yankee* is Mills's internalizing of the experiences of others. Mills writes manifestly and unabashedly as a partisan. The depersonalized "we" is really a generalized "I." This literary device was part of an ongoing effort by Mills to reach masses of people through the paperback medium. He never surrendered the eighteenth-century idea of Enlightenment: good ideas translate into a good society. He carried this vision one step forward and spoke as a partisan of those ideas—not unlike nineteenth-century advocates of the Socialist International.

> There is a worldwide competition going on, you know, and in this competition, we Cubans don't think you or your Government can avoid assuming that the advice and the aid we are taking from Russia, we are taking voluntarily. That happens to be the plain truth. We haven't done all this fighting to get from under one tyranny just to stick our necks into some other yoke—any other yoke. We're taking orders only from ourselves.

Mills received a great deal of advice on how to do *Listen, Yankee* from many people within the Cuban Revolution movement: above all Carlos Franqui, who as press attaché became a critical pivot in transmitting the Cuban message, and Juan Arcocha, who served as translator to Mills. What began for Mills as a series of interviews with Cuban leaders ended as the internalizing of the Cuban Revolution. The revolution which Fidel made became one which Mills vicariously lived through. His volume contains some blunt reminders of an earlier era in which the United States was branded, often accurately, as the main if not the only source of Latin American miseries. The Cuban Revolution became, like the Russian Revolution, a harbinger of things to come: the inevitable end of the American presence in hemispheric affairs. The differences in size between the Soviet Union and Cuba, and the distinctions at the level of industrialization, melted in a tidal wave of words, a rhetoric quite widely believed at the time.

> Latin America is a great world region; it is a continent, long and repeatedly plundered; and it is in revolutionary ferment. That it is now in such ferment is a heartening testimony to the will of man not to remain forever an exploited object. For over a century Latin American man has been largely outside world history—except as an object; now he is entering that history—as a subject, with vengeance and pride, with violence. The unilateral Monroe Doctrine is part of the epoch of Latin American isolation. The epoch, and with it the Monroe Doctrine, is now coming to an end.

The overview Mills offers, or rather voices, about Cuba with respect to the rest of Latin America now reads as high irony. Nations like Brazil, Venezuela, and Mexico are pilloried in *Listen, Yankee*. Argentina is said to have done "nothing of significance" to develop its wealth; Mexico's, great revolution is considered stalled and "just a series of memories"; Brazil is simply a "dual society," whatever that was meant to convey. The possibility that these societies and all others would actually fare great deal better than Cuba over time was simply incomprehensible to Mills. He failed to appreciate the meaning of Sovietization within a single-crop economy, or how an early rush to destroy the private sect; served to inhibit the very expansion of the developmental groups Cuba he was pinning so much hope upon.

Mills not only wrote about revolutionary euphoria in Cuba, he was a willing victim of that euphoria. Harvey Swados was correct in identifying the euphoria's source as the Cuban Revolution, which provided Mills with an "emotional home." Seemingly, Mills had in mind a model French Revolution. The day the revolution triumphs, begins the world anew. The big clock in the sky both measures and determines the seizure of power:

> We're starting out with all the disorder that we've inherited, and with what amounts to No Culture in Cuba. To bring about real cultural and intellectual establishments is one of our greatest and most difficult tasks. It is linked, as we've said, with our need for administrators and technicians in the new Cuba. But we want much more than that. We want poetry as well as physics. And we know you can't plan for poets as you can for engineers. You can only plan and construct cultural institutions, and then hope that poets, as well as engineers, will grow in them and do great work.

Throughout, we observe the theme of the society creating its poets and engineers, but little willingness to confront the way in which this Saint Simonian dream was transformed into a Platonic nightmare.

Mills was reacting to the first years of a revolution whose structure had not yet crystallized. Hope against hope, he was affirming, not just describing, a movement without a party; a leadership born and bred in guerrilla activities and not just parliamentary cretinism; a nation seeking to carve out its own destiny apart from the American empire formerly inhibiting that destiny. It is to Mills's credit that *Listen, Yankee* contains certain hesitations about events, even a cautionary spirit at the end. This helped him to put the brakes on the thrust of the work. The tract on Cuba reveals a curious dichotomy: When Mills spoke with his own voice he did so as the political sociologist he was; when he spoke in the collective voice, he just as clearly summoned up the ideologist he had become.

The ideology which emerges in *Listen, Yankee* is first and foremost a faith in populist Marxism; a polycentric vision of socialism breaking away from all orthodoxies. The belief rested on the fact that Cuba, at the least, represented a new Yugoslavia; like Tito's regime, Castro had earned his independence on the field of battle. In this way, the Cuban Revolution confirmed not only the end of American imperialism but the end of Soviet hegemonic control. It is not fruitful to speculate on how Mills would ultimately have come to view the utter dependency of Cuban society upon Soviet aid and support; one can only speculate that on the basis of his own commitment to pluralistic socialism he would have viewed the outcome as dismaying. Harvey Swados suggested that Mills's faith in Fidel had peaked by 1961. But Mill's interview "Listen Again, Yankee" showed only the reverse attitude: a pugnacity even less concerned with canons of evidence than it had been in the book.

Mills embraced the Cuban Revolution because it seemed to confirm his long-held pet theories about the decline of liberalism in the West and the growing embrace of democratic values by Marxist states. The do-it-yourself economics practiced by Cuba in 1960 was to Mills equivalent to the do-it-yourself pragmatism of the early New Deal days. In Mills's mind, the Cuban Revolution represented a victory for experimentation over and against the old American colonial yoke or the new Soviet ideological yoke. Even though he had moved far to the left of his earlier convictions, he remained adamant that the USA/USSR confrontation represented a singular evil-one best confronted by a "pluralized Marxism" rather than an emaciated liberalism."

Mills had no doubt that Cuba would become a hemispheric model. Adopting the official tone of a Cuban spokesman, he shouted a warning:

> We're talking sense to you, Yankee; listen to us, please. What will happen, for example, when the people of all those South American countries realize their enormous wealth, both the actual and what could be, and yet find themselves poor? When looking across to tiny Cuba, they see the Cubans are not poor? What will happen then?

The prospect that the rest of Latin America would do better economically than Cuba, that countries like Venezuela and Colombia would look across the Caribbean and see Cubans who were poor and a regime unable to exercise independence in foreign policy, simply never entered Mills's calculations. For him the course of events was clear: Since Socialist revolutions bring about nearly automatic new wealth and this largesse in turn is widely distributed, the Cuban nation would become a model for the hemisphere, and finally the whole hemisphere would engage in a thunderous revolt against its American masters.

That this scenario did not play out—and, it seemed at the time of Mills's death, would not play out in the near future—failed to deter his enthusiasm. The love affair Mills had with the Cuban Revolution had no hemispheric antecedent. In fact, it became a mutual love affair on the part of Latin American intellectuals with Mills. He became lionized by everyone from Fidel Castro to Carlos Fuentes; receiving the sort of flattery his colleagues in American sociology, especially at Columbia, had entirely denied him. In Cuba, Mills's sense of a revolutionary movement unencumbered by Stalinism was fulfilled, as were his own sense of self-importance and larger-than-life ego needs. The only thing that began to unravel was the Revolution itself.

If the reviews of *Listen, Yankee* were critical in the American press, the letters of support, especially from the Mexican Left, became thunderous. Arnaldo Orfila Reynal, at that time director of the leading publishing house of Mexico, wrote to Mills in strongly affective personal terms.

> In reading aloud your *Listen, Yankee* with my wife, we were deeply touched with the greatness you show in your sheer understanding of the root of the problems of our Continent. It is the exact essence of the Cuban Revolution. I want to express to you the profound satisfaction I feel to be able to diffuse your beautiful message to the Spanish-speaking world.

And a young scholar who had returned to Cuba to participate in the work of the Revolution, Armando Betancourt, wrote in a similarly effusive, mythologizing vein.

> Your name is already popular in all Cuba, to say Wright Mills sounds to say a friend. We thank you very deeply from the bottom of our hearts for having done that task, of telling our neighbors to the north the truth about this little island, little in size, but great in hopes, and spirit, and courage.

To someone long denied what he felt were his just academic fruits, the enormous popularity of *Listen, Yankee* was highly gratifying. Not that the correspondence was uniformly favorable. Indeed, the leader of the *Frente Revolucionario Democrático*, Salvador Ferrer, took umbrage no less than issue with Mills. That his statement could well have come out of the exile Cuban community in the 1980s, no less than in 1960, would have clearly disturbed Mills. Mills's marginalia proved that he was badly shaken by critical responses. Excerpts from Ferrer's letters are indicative of the polarizing impact, early on, of the Cuban Revolution—a development Mills, with his limited knowledge of the hemisphere, could hardly cope with:

> So Cuba was a "hungry nation" before Castro? We had Latin America's highest per capita production income and living standards. We were the Western Hemisphere's biggest producers of chrome, the second of nickel and manganese, the sixth of copper, ranked high in cattle raising, and led the world in sugar and fine tobacco. You say "only one school" was built in 58 years; our literacy ranked among Latin America's highest.... Our universities are barracks, with 750 professors ousted, and "students" drilling in uniform inside. Labor unions can no longer elect their leaders. The free, constitutional elections for which Cubans followed Castro; where are they? With Cuba's free press silenced, uncounted millions go for propaganda. In Havana for two years, thousands of Cubans daily have had the guts to defy Castro's guns to form four lines, in sun and rain, at the American Embassy. The fourth line is called the "life or death" line. Altogether, 300,000 have fled Castro, who says that only "the millionaires want to leave."

In any final evaluation of Mills' work on Cuba it is important to keep in mind that however Mills may have idolized, sentimentalized, and pragmatized the Cuban revolutionary experience, he never accepted totalitarianism as the proper outcome of this regime. *Listen, Yankee* is dotted by warnings and apprehensions about such a possibility. Cuba became part of Mills' final internal ideological struggle: his hatred of the American ruling class balanced only by his loathing of Soviet totalitarianism. Cuba was to be a third way, a new and independent variety of socialism. That his analysis failed to detect the utter impossibility of such a "Swedish" outcome within a Cuban context is less a reflection on Mills than on the backward state of hemispheric affairs prior to Castro's revolution.

The elemental decency of Mills (in contrast to Sartre's writings on Cuba) comes from the fact that Mills saw in Cuba practical, nonideological individuals—above all, people who admitted to confusion and doubt—whereas Sartre in his brief trip to Cuba saw only evidence of the Bergsonian *élan vital.* Sadly, as Régis Debray was later to make clear, it was mysticism, not pragmatism, which triumphed. The mystification of the Cuban revolution-ary experience stood at the other end of the pole for Mills. His pragmatic view of the Cuban experience was played out without regard to either Sartre's metaphysical predispositions toward existentialism or the fanaticism of Soviet-type Marxism. The revolution from early on was locked into a world structure quite beyond national control. But Mills did not know that—or worse, pretended not to know. On the contrary, he accepted the views expressed by Carlos Franqui and other Left-critics of the Cuban Communist party that saw the Cuban solution as the ultimate proof that one can have a revolution without it becoming cor-rupted or perverted by Communist forces:

> The plain fact is our revolution has outdone the Communists on every score. From the beginning up till today, always at every turn of event and policy, the revolution is always faster than the Cuban Communist Party, or individual Communists. In all objective facts, we are much more radical, much more revolutionary than they. And that is why we are using them, rather than the reverse; they are not using us. In fact they are being very grateful to us for letting them in on the work of the revolution.

One must only wonder what Mills's response would have been to the triumph of party over movement, of collectives over individuals, and of Soviet domination over autonomous devel-opment. But even during Mills's life it was already evident that questions were being asked about forced collectivization. Jules Dubois, in his review of *Listen, Yankee* on December 17, 1960, pointed out this fact bluntly. "When he states that 'the Cuban revolution, unlike the Russian, has in my judgment solved the major problems of agricultural production by its agrarian reform,' Mills is selling the American people a bill of goods that the facts fail to substantiate." And in a much more sympathetic review, Hubert Herring, reviewing the book for the *Herald-Tribune* a month earlier, made his own set of rejoinders in a quieter mode, which Mills failed to address.

The rejoinders to these points seem obvious. On Communism: the noises made by Fidel and Raúl and Che Guevara sound like noises from the Kremlin—it may be pure coincidence. Rockets:

those were mentioned by the master of the Kremlin. On the killing of thousands: no sober person has talked of' "thousands" executed without fair trial, the figure is about seven hundred. On "democracy and freedom": we can point to the long list of patriotic Cubans who have left Fidel Castro and gone into exile-or to jail—because they saw no hope for democracy and freedom.

The ideological climate in which Mills was writing must be kept in mind. There had emerged a widespread belief that the end of American civilization was at hand—or at least there was the absolute conviction that justice would be done only with the destruction of the American imperial enclave in the hemisphere. So incensed were Mills's radical Latin American supporters by the critical reviews he received that a group of leading Mexican cultural figures wrote a letter of protest. They reasserted the value of Mills's book and reaffirmed the absolute incorruptibility of the new Cuban order:

> "Listen, Yankee": We've been in Cuba. We've seen thousands of new schools, new hospitals, new roads, new housing, new symphony orchestras and theater groups, new popular priced books, new crops rising on the once-dead land of the huge estates. We've seen a people grown confident, proud, better off, consuming more than ever before—which accounts for the so-called "shortages" Dubois bandies about. We've seen the old order of privileges and exploitationary leaders. We've seen an incorruptible government at work. We've seen the wealth and the future of Cuba, for the first time, in the hands of the Cuban people. We've seen the hope of all Latin America in the faces of the new Cubans.

As this manifesto makes clear, Mills became part of the struggle of ideas in the hemisphere itself: an outcome he and others did indeed anticipate when the book was being written.

Mills's quick response to the Cuban Revolution was not simply a search for a new heroism; it also expressed a sense of identification with Latin people. Since the mid-1940s, when he had written essays on Mexican barrios in Los Angeles (which were followed, later, with research on the Puerto Rican communities of New York), Mills had had a special at-a-distance love affair with Latin peoples. He did have some personal contact, however marginal, with Mexican-Americans during his Texas years, but aside from a passing mention of drinking with them in San Antonio bars, there is no other real evidence of face-to-face contact. Certainly Mills neither pretended nor aimed to be a Latin American specialist. Latin Americans for Mills seemed rather to represent the "ideal-typical" oppressed region, whether in Spanish Harlem or in Playa Girón.

Mills became the writer seeking world historic vindication, and he tried to achieve it by violating nearly every canon of the sociological imagination he had urged upon others. *Listen, Yankee* ended up as his poorest effort in social analysis, a tract placed at the disposal of political forces he knew little of but cared much for. It contained banalities and hectorings which he personally loathed in others. From 1960 forward, his sense of self-doubt and failure overtook him. At the very point in time when the popularity of *Listen, Yankee* was highest, his sense of self-esteem was lowest. Mills's desperate search for workable ideals came to an end in this wishful portrait of a nation embodying the perfect model of the perfect revolution. Swados summed this up touchingly:

> In his last months Mills was torn between defending *Listen, Yankee* as a good and honest book and acknowledging publicly for the first time in his life that he had been terribly wrong. This would have meant not only caving in to the few whose opinions he valued . . . but returning to the United States and telling not only his enemies on the right, but the hundreds of thousands who had, so to speak, voted for him, that he was not a rough rider after all, but only a man of ideas who could be wrong, as men of ideas so often are. The tension was too much, the decline of the revolution, atop his personal pains, was too much.

With the publication of *Listen, Yankee* and its earlier excerpt in *Harper's* magazine, Mills achieved the celebrity status which had eluded him in the past. But the problem of Mills's limited knowledge of Cuba became dangerously apparent, especially when a debate on NBC television was proposed between himself and Adolf A. Berle, who, among his other talents in economics and diplomacy, had a lifelong commitment to hemispheric problems. Mills could scarcely back away from the confrontation, not only because of a sense of purpose and mission, but also as a means to broaden his own commitment to underdevelopment as a global cause. Mills spent the month prior to the scheduled debate with Berle soliciting information from a wide range of Latin Americanists, including Frederick Pike, Donald Bray, Ray Higgins, Waldo Frank, Ronald Hilton, and others. In each case, the letters asked for exact information on the hemisphere, on American military supports, and not least, on Berle himself.

Just how concerned Mills was about the forthcoming debate is indicated by the design of scenarios, i.e., what Mills would reply to queries and how much time each would spend on a variety of themes; Mills even solicited lists of individuals who might attend the debate, who could be called upon to ask the right questions at the right time. He viewed this debate as a career highlight, only slightly less significant than the publication of the Cuba volume itself. This contrasted sharply with Berle's downplaying of the event. But even Berle was caught up in the impact of a potential viewing audience of five million. "Mills' book, *Listen, Yankee*, written after a couple of months in Cuba, where he had never been, was derived from interviews in Spanish, which he does not know, with refusal to ascribe identity to the sources thereof; really a piece of noisy propaganda and not even good, so I was ready to plaster him."

But the debate never took place, at least not with Mills present. He suffered his penultimate heart attack just a few days before the debate was to be aired. Berle's response to the inability of Mills to participate was characteristically pugnacious: "C. Wright Mills has degenerated from being a capable though rather left-wing opinionated Professor of Sociology (Columbia) into a ranting propagandist. He was to have been the champion of the Castro regime, but he got a heart attack—partly I think because he was frightened—and had reason to be." If Berle was relatively calm and benign about the debate, he remained bitterly angered by Mills's presumptions. Still, Berle's imputation of cowardice, of a feigned heart attack, was simply wrong. Mills had sustained a series of heart attacks dating back to his University of Maryland days. Mills' penultimate heart attack was not in any identifiable way connected with the proposed Berle television debate. Quite the contrary, such public appearances came to increasingly sustain Mills in his last days.

In place of Mills, Congressman Charles O. Porter from Oregon was chosen. "The result was a not uninteresting debate with a lot of questions from the audience, mainly loaded. But it did not allow for really good presentation of the issues and one always feels a sense of frustration." And so ended this widely reported, incredible nonevent, occasioned by Mills' heart ailment.

Mills did an interview with the Mexican newspaper *Novedades* which in turn was translated into Spanish by Carlos Fuentes. The interview proved to be far superior in its command of Latin American materials and its sense of Cuba's place in hemispheric affairs. But it was also strident in its vision of American imperialism. Indeed, quite the reverse of expectations, Mills's view of the Cuban Revolution hardened rather than softened. By 1961 his defense of the revolution had been elevated into a direct assault on American social celebration. He went back to older pet hatreds, weaving them into the fabric of his new love. Liberals became sheer obfuscators, right-wingers in hiding. *Times* became viewed as the "weekly fiction magazine." The Cuban Revolution became "the great unmasking of American liberalism." This revolution became not only a cause for Mills but a vindication of his prejudices. The frustrations of earlier years came to fruition with Cuba.

In the end, the revolution was a political act of a small Caribbean nation, which could contain neither Mills's intellectual ambitions nor his personal pretensions. Mills the political ideologist ultimately betrayed Mills the social scientist. He identified with a regime and with a position without ever investigating the social and political structure of the other side. There is no record, no indication, that Mills ever took seriously the critics of Castro—no indication except frustration that the regime could not manifest its self-professed independence even in the short run. In July 1961, only nine months before his death, Mills felt no need to update *Listen, Yankee,* for he was sure that the events had vindicated him in every detail. He became more rasping, more convinced of the conspiratorial nature of the opposition and the institutional nature of the revolution. Increasingly, he turned his attack on the New Frontier, on President Kennedy, on Ambassador Adlai Stevenson, on all U.S. officials who would not listen to him. A number of Mills's commentators, like Swados, have tried to soften the blow by claiming that Mills was backing away from the more rabid of his statements in *Listen, Yankee*. But there is simply no evidence for this.

Mills became even more deeply enmeshed in what he saw as a one-against-one struggle with President Kennedy for the minds of Americans. Ultimately the revolution itself became a backdrop to a personal revivalism. The Bay of Pigs notwithstanding, what actually took place was neither the open warfare which Mills predicted nor the reconciliation between Cuba and the United States which he wanted.

Mills's great illusion about Cuba was that it could be a third way. It was an illusion he went to his grave believing. The Cuban Revolution today, after nearly twenty-five years of existence, with its initial leadership and inspiration intact, is the vindication of its own authenticity, as well as proof that Mills was correct in his perceptions of its importance. That the Cuban Revolution has failed to achieve its primary goal of political independence is an indication that what it achieved in authenticity it failed to achieve in autonomy. Hence one is left with an unhappy belief that Mills would have been confronted by Hobson's choice: to continue support for a revolution that had become bankrupt or to oppose that revolution and hence mock his own euphoria. One is reminded of Decoud's observation about Nostromo toward the close of Joseph Conrad's novel by the same name: "Here was a man that seemed as though he would have preferred to die rather than deface the perfect form of his egoism. Such a man was safe."

Source and Original Title: C. Wright Mills: An American Utopian. New York: The Free Press/Macmillan Publishers; London: Collier/Macmillan Publishers Ltd., 1983 pp 292-302.

15

The Role of Cuba in the Pacification
of Central America

My charge is to discuss how Cuba can be involved in the Caribbean peacemaking process. This is certainly not a topic of recent vintage. Since Fidel Castro came to power nearly a quarter century ago, diplomats from Latin America, politicians from North America, and academics from both hemispheres have been asking this question. More often than maybe warranted by evidence, they have assumed that Cuban interests are consonant with those of the other member states of the Caribbean region. To those for whom the word *interests* is too strong, has come a rhetorical barrage of arguments that at least a *modus vivendi* is possible. Cuban communism is a sore thumb not easily disposed of by appeals to use the opposite hand. To skirt the issue of Cuba is to insure either clumsy ad hoc arrangements or to avoid resolution of the very tasks with which the commission is charged.

From the outset of its revolution, Cuba viewed itself not only as bringing a message of truth and hope to the hemisphere, but as a revolutionary vanguard to be emulated and imitated. In the post-revolutionary phase of the early 1960s, Venezuela and Guatemala were rocked by Cuban "warrior-proletarian" insurgency movements. Even giants like Brazil found themselves warmly embracing the causes and purposes of the Cuban Revolution during the final gasp of the Goulart regime. For nations as remote as Chile and Bolivia, the Cuban model of revolution reared its head, weakly in some instances and intimately in others. But for all the contagion of the Cuban Revolution and the charisma of Fidel, the successes during the first 20 years of the Cuban Revolution were rather meager: promissory notes were issued without fulfillment, elites led without mass support, *foco* groups existed without grounded support. In the aftermath of the Bolivian adventure of the mid-1960s, the model itself was finally called into question with the shattering defeat and death of Ernesto "Che" Guevara in the Bolivian interior.

The second phase, which occupied most of the 1970s, witnessed the internationalization of Cuban foreign policy. Senator Daniel Patrick Moynihan, referring to Cuba's willingness to fight in far away places of Africa and the Middle East, called its troops the "Gurkhas of the Russian Empire." At the diplomatic level, Cuba took a central role in the various summit meetings of the nonaligned nations. On the economic front, Cuba focused demands for a New International Economic Order, pushing the argument that there is a natural alliance between the Third World and the communist camp, and an equally natural antagonism between the Third World and the West. But this strategy found its limits with the Cuban stalking horse isolating itself from Third World condemnation of the Soviet invasion of Afghanistan, which was crystallized by Cuba's failure to win support in its bid for a seat on the United Nations Security Council.

This set the stage, in turn, for a third phase in the 1980s, one in which the Cuban praetorian guard shifted its geographical focus away from Africa and the Middle East and toward the Caribbean Basin. Military adventurism was replaced by Cuban developmental aid programs; and concern for Latin America as a whole became much more highly focused on critical events in Central America. The Cuban vanguard has begun to develop a serpentine tail: the Sandinista uprising in Nicaragua, however indigenous in origin, soon took on Cuban features—from the organization of the military to the foreign policy of its leaders.

This was also true on the small island of Grenada where an indigenous change of regimes rapidly evolved into a powerful identification with Cuba as the center.

The scenario was expected to be similar in El Salvador. However, its people and politicians foiled the designs of history and, albeit imperfectly, chose a path of democratic realignment.[1]

What we have witnessed is the evolution of a grand strategy carried forth by a satellite, Cuba, on behalf of its major supporter and supplier, the Soviet Union. Revolution has forced us not simply to changes in our foreign policy but to a profound alteration in our strategic conclusions for what the hemisphere, and more specifically the Caribbean region, might become if Soviet grand strategy were allowed to play out its hand unimpeded.

Cuba is the willing, enthusiastic executor of Soviet designs. The wide level of tactical maneuverability granted to Cuba by the Soviet Union has given it a latitude of operations which can be easily misinterpreted as autonomy. Cuban latitude, its seeming indifference to the tactical styles of the Soviet Union, is what diplomats, politicians, and academics are responding to when they speak so casually of bringing Cuba into the Caribbean peacemaking process. Such figures often confuse tactical maneuverability with overall strategic conclusions. Cuban tactics are often pragmatic and home grown, but Cuban strategies are very definitely imported from the Soviets. It is the special mission of Raúl Castro in Cuba to insure a clear distinction between tactical maneuverability and strategic coordination.

The idea of a peace process implies an ability on the part of each national actor to act autonomously. But the history of Cuba over the past quarter century demonstrates that such independent behavior is no longer feasible when Cuba has become, to all intents and purposes, a satellite, surrogate, and sponsor of Soviet activities from Afghanistan to Angola. The revolution of 1959 was authentic; but the breakdown of autonomy in Cuban actions in 1983 is a reality. Cuba is simply not an independent actor. Hence determining how it can fit into a peace process depends heavily on the Soviet Union's immediate sense of its limits. Cuba is the weathervane for the long-range potential which the Soviet Union envisions for the Caribbean region. Although the latter is geographically remote, one must not think that the Soviet Union has no interest in the area or in the expansion of Cuban power. It would be as correct to suggest that because the Philippines are geographically remote from the United States, the United States has a flagging interest in Asian affairs. The world is too small to divide in neat geographic terms. Spheres of influence have become enlarged to the point where national concerns have become global in character. Nor is this particular question of autonomy and authenticity simply a function of Cuban foreign policy commitments toward the Soviet Union. The internal structure of Cuban national life conspires to sharply limit its Caribbean initiatives.

As one informed figure, Carlos Alberto Montaner, has pointed out, the dorsal spine of Cuban society is its armed forces. He speaks of the Cuban military as highly Prussianized.[2] I would modify this somewhat by pointing out that while the *Paraguayan* military is highly Prussianized, the Cuban military is highly *Russianized* by virtue of its elite training at Soviet military academies. The near-shuttle like trips of Raúl Castro between Havana and Moscow, along with the deepening sophistication and strength of Cuban hardware, conspire to make Cuba one of the most powerful armed forces in the hemisphere. In Caribbean terms its military might is greater than that of all other nations in Central America combined.

Since the mid-1970s, when Cuba intervened in Angola on a large scale and the Soviet Union began to modernize Cuba's armed forces, the Cuban military has evolved from a predominantly home defense force into a formidable power relative to its Latin American neighbors. The cost of Soviet arms delivered to Castro since 1960 exceeds $2.5 billion.

These arms deliveries, plus the annual $3 billion economic subsidy, are tied to Cuba's ongoing military and political role abroad in support of Soviet objectives. Cuba's armed forces total more than 225,000 personnel—200,000 army, 15,000 air force and air defense, and 10,000 navy—including those on active duty either in Cuba or overseas and those belonging to the reserves, subject to immediate mobilization. With a population of just under 10 million, Cuba has the largest military force in the Caribbean Basin and the second largest in Latin America after Brazil, with a population of more than 120 million. More than 2 percent of the Cuban population belongs to the active-duty military and ready reserves, compared with an average of less than 0.4 percent in other countries in the Caribbean Basin. In addition, Cuba's large paramilitary organizations and reserves can provide internal support to the military.[3]

The structure of the Cuban economy, again, does not suggest easy participation in Caribbean regional planning. The Cuban economy has extremely high dependence on the Soviet Union and Eastern Europe. Roughly 85-90 percent of its economic trade is with that region. Cuba does indeed share similar problems with the Caribbean region, a single-crop economy, relatively low levels of agrarian production, and the absence of accumulated savings and wealth. But while the problems of Cuba and the region may be similar in the sense of being outside the market economy and inside the planning economy, this places it in a unique position, one that not even Nicaragua comes close to emulating.

The Cuban economy remains heavily determined by outside forces over which its national leaders do not have significant control. The Soviet Union basically has the power to set prices, grant subsidies, and extend credit. A small part of Cuba's trade is still with market economies and hence the island is not totally removed from the international market in terms of price fluctuations and need of credit. Cuba remains a single-crop economy which exports a few raw materials to the Soviets and buys from them most of the needed intermediate and capital goods. The island has been unable to accumulate enough capital from domestic resources, has shown little progress in the expansion of the capital goods sector, and has been incapable of self-sustained economic growth. To keep its economy running, Cuba has had to borrow heavily and increasingly from the Soviets and from other socialist and market economies, thus dramatically increasing its foreign debt.[4]

The structure of Cuba's polity shows wide variances with the rest of the Caribbean region. It boasts a single Communist Party apparatus, lacks voluntary associations, its social life is depoliticized, its ideology is routinized and ritualized, and the same family has been in power since the onset of the revolution. Cuba has a great deal in common with some of the worst features of authoritarian regimes past and present in the Caribbean. One finds in Cuba the routinization of a revolution without its institutionalization. Events become regularized, expectations leveled, and any hope of dramatic changes in the system virtually eliminated. While a great show was made several years ago that this signifies the institutionalization of the revolution, it is evident that devices ensuring legitimacy (such as elections, oppositional parties, or a free press) are absent. What has been institutionalized is single-party rule and vanguard political domination. What have been routinized are professions of faith and loyalty to the revolution. Neither friends nor foes of the regime deny this. Explanations are another matter. At this level, cleavages show: Cuba is a country small in size and large in pretenses. It plays a considerable role in hemispheric affairs, Caribbean affairs, and even Third World activities. Cuba considers itself the leader of a hemispheric revolt against "Yankee imperialism"—a never-ending holy war of an island David with the Goliath of the north—while it has tremendous difficulty in coping with its own internal mundane problems.

What intensifies this sense of routinization, this depoliticization of Cuban life, is the continued existence in power of the original leadership. The same figures who made the revolution, at least some of them, retain power in that revolution. Although many original revolutionaries were purged, others are in exile, and still others died spuriously heroic deaths in foreign guerrilla insurgency activities, Cuba's leadership has endured over a quarter century—unbroken and intact.

The routinization of the Cuban Revolution is thus scarcely the same as asserting its normalization. What has been sadly routinized is not only an authoritarian substance but also a paranoid style. Nor is this meant invidiously: Richard Hofstadter was able to write one of his most brilliant essays on "The Paranoid Style in American Politics." Still, a sense of frenetic, ceremonial mobilization, combined with a peculiar inability to act on the presumption that Cuba may not always be at the center of world events (a malady suffered by other small nations also on a permanent war footing) is easily fed by random remarks. When Senator Barry Goldwater announced that Cuba would be best off as the fifty-first state in the Union, the response of the Cuban Communist Party was emblazoned across the banner of *Granma*: "Whoever tries to conquer Cuba will gain nothing but the dust of her blood-soaked soil—if he doesn't perish in the struggle first!"

It is not that threats are unreal, but that their quality is uniformly misread and misunderstood. Subtlety, humor, discounting rhetorical claims, has like so much else, fallen victim to a revolution that feeds on its own slogans; one in which complexity has become suspect and simplicity the essential tool of political analysis and social living.

The political functions of the paranoid style are numerous and complex, but above all can best be viewed as the essential mechanism of mass mobilization. Quite like the Stalinist doctrine of capitalist encirclement, Castro is able to present Cuba as an island of socialist probity in a hemisphere of imperialist aggression. Whatever the exactitude of such a definition, it has the effect of maintaining the Cuban people in a state of high military and paramilitary alert; providing a practical role for vanguard groups and a touchstone of regime loyalty. The danger with the constant pumping of the external threat syndrome is similar to the problem of apocalyptic religious cults: when the cataclysmic event fails to materialize, questions of the soundness of the leadership are raised among some (while others band even more tightly about their leader), followed by a cynical withdrawal from the political process. In the absence of market incentives based on consumption rewards, the regime is compelled to manufacture escalated threats of disaster and destruction.

While continuity seems to best characterize the most recent phase of the Cuban Revolution, this does not mean that stasis has set in. Tendencies have hardened into trends. As dialecticians would have it: quantitative changes have resulted in a qualitatively new situation. The most decisive development is intensified Cuban dependency on the Soviet Union. Single-crop socialism has had to confront a weak world sugar market and a series of natural disasters. To overcome this dual situation without disturbing current, relatively high, consumer levels, Cuba's trade with the Soviet bloc is fast approaching 90 percent. Soviet aid to Cuba is now at $4 billion annually, roughly 25 percent of the Cuban gross national product. The weakness of the Cuban export economy has driven up Cuba's debt to the hard currency nations of the West and Japan to such a degree that it can no longer pay the interest (much less the principal) due. It would take an extraordinarily naive view not to appreciate the extent to which Cuban communism in order to survive must become increasingly communist (in the sense of adherence to Soviet bloc politics and policies) and decreasingly Cuban (in the sense of developing a nationalist standpoint). The consequences for the Castro regime of such a transformation in its overseas patterns deserves close scrutiny.

Cuba is not China. It does not have a range of autonomous behavior which would permit the evolution of an independent foreign policy. This is not simply a consequence of Castro's wishes but of deep social structures. Its demands while quite real are developed within a larger context of Soviet policy requirements. On the basis of Cuban policy materials, five policy pivots emerge:

(1) Complete acceptance by the Caribbean regions, and above all by the United States, of the Sandinistas as the rightful, exclusive rulers of Nicaragua and that no support be provided for the opponents of the Sandinistas for such people as Eden Pastora, by Honduran authorities.

(2) Complete acceptance of the demands of the Farabundo group in El Salvador and the disposition and dismantling of the present regime. In other words, an El Salvador which would put the guerrillas in

power and provide them with a monopoly of military and political control.

(3) Cuban authorities would demand removal of any and all U.S. military presence in the area, starting with its Guantanamo Naval Base in Cuba and not ending until all U.S. troops, advisors, and other paramilitary elements were removed from the region.

(4) Free and unimpeded passage of weapons and hardware from the Soviet Union to Cuba, and if necessary from Cuba to other parts of the Caribbean region in the midst of insurgent struggles.

(5) Acceptance of guerrilla movements and Communist Party groups as legitimate heirs to Caribbean rule especially in Guatemala, which the Cubans perceive as the more immediately vulnerable Central American nation.

If the United States is willing to pay the price outlined above, or is able to coexist with such Cuban demands with respect to the political process in the rest of the Caribbean, Cuba could be brought into the peace process. But at that point, one is not examining a multilateral peace process with the region, but a bilateral process with the Soviet Union for the capitulation and surrender of any and all vital interests which the United States might deem important in the rest of the Caribbean region. On the presumption that such Cuban policy demands are an acceptance by the United States of humiliating defeat and are thus unacceptable, one must turn to other ways of discussing Cuba and the Caribbean.

The key issue in Central America is not war or peace, but rather varieties of political systems. The issue is between forms and varieties of democratic rule versus the singular form and absence of variety of totalitarian communism. The vulgar economic determinisms we inherited from the late nineteenth century have come to a crashing halt. The issue before American society is not the struggle between free market systems on one hand and planning systems on the other, but between free peoples and enslaved ones. We know enough to realize that nearly every nation, large and small, nominally communist or capitalist, has a whole range of mixes within its economic grasp, and that these are constantly shifted about: strong capitalist trends in China, worker-management trends in Yugoslavia, village handicraft socialism in India, high levels of public sector involvement in Mexico. The economic mix within which political systems operate is no longer novel and should no longer be fearsome. The United States should be capable of living with a whole variety of economic systems. But thus far it has found itself less able to deal with a declining variety of political systems.

Public opinion data on American attitudes toward Central America reveal an ambivalent pattern: fear of greater military involvement, a striking lack of information on the region, coupled with deep-seated beliefs that Cuba and Nicaragua are sources of regional destabilization and subversion.[5] Policy options must be framed in a flexible manner which both respects the tolerance of hemispheric differences and also recognizes the firm commitments of this people to democratic values and sovereign rights. The policy sector of the United States would be well advised to support popular movements for democracy wherever and whenever possible in the Caribbean. The touchstone of these regimes ought not to be the specifics of the economic production cycle but rather the specifics of commitments to democratic shift on one hand and a totalitarian effort on the other. The smoke screen of north/south-east/west all comes to the simple fact that the grave danger posed to peace by the Cuban regime is not a function of economic modes but rather of its political decisions. The political decisions made by the nations of the Caribbean—and not individual nuances and varieties of economics—must be the touchstone by which an American foreign policy for the region is measured. We are in a period of breakup not only of ideologies and systems, but also of the paradigm of what we consider base and what we consider superstructure.

Given the intricate network of foreign policy considerations it is naive to presume that Cuba can be dealt with by the United States strictly within the context of multilateral regional negotiations. While such an approach is abstractly preferable to the big stick of a big brother, the presence of a Soviet surrogate introduces big-power bilateral considerations through the proverbial back door. Any solution to United States participation in the stabilization of El Salvador or the destabilization of Nicaragua for that matter must entail the resolution of a longstanding Soviet presence, in both large-scale military manpower and military hardware terms, in Cuban life. The search for future autonomous forms of political organization and social systems should not be confused with present dependencies. Big-power interests are real and will not vanish as long as the threat persists that every new guerrilla insurgency entails the prospect of adding to Soviet power in the Caribbean.

There are two uncomfortable and quite risky policy conclusions that emanate from my remarks: first, that the Soviet Union, since it is evidently part of the problem must become part of any Caribbean peace process; and second, that the United States must avoid mechanistic parallels with post-world-war two Europe and thus overcome the notion that a Marshall Plan for Central America is a political cure-all; it may not even be an appropriate band-aid. Let us probe such a paired conclusion in greater depth.

There is a widespread feeling that if the Soviet Union joins a Caribbean peace process, the United States will thus be legitimating a role for the Russians in the region, and by so doing give them an easy victory. While this argument has some merit, it pales when confronted by the obvious, empirical fact that the Soviets already have made a significant penetration of the region through Cuba and Nicaragua (especially the former). To think that bilateral discussions are feasible in the Middle East or in Southeast Asia but not in Latin America is a dangerous illusion. One cannot isolate Soviet power by evasive diplomatic techniques.

The Contadora position is that it is "undesirable for Caribbean conflicts to be incorporated into the context of the East-West confrontation." However, since a key source of the present structures and processes in the region derive from that conflict, Contadora has been unable to extract anything but a general commitment to peace.

Since Cuba is laundered out of consideration, what Contadora can effectively negotiate is solely a diminution of United States influence in the region; the Soviet role remains conspicuously unexamined or unexplained. Thus, by a sheer act of omission, the Contadora Group would conduct negotiations as if Cuba has neither a role to play, nor losses to suffer in the event of an overall settlement. To bring the Russians into the negotiating process is to permit a serious policy discussion between the contending parties, i.e., it is to make clear that the massive Soviet presence in Cuba is at least as much an agenda item as the modest American presence in El Salvador. In so doing, the education of American public opinion can dovetail with the resolution of Central American issues of vital collective concern.

Large-scale economic aid to the region is a serious necessity. For example, Honduras has taken highly risky steps to inhibit an extension or even consolidation of the Sandinista forces in Nicaragua. Not to support their repeated, and thus far unanswered, pleas for fiscal aid is certainly to destabilize a crucial American ally in the region. But such supports are essentially bilateral in character, given quite bluntly, for real support rendered rather than the blackmail and threat that if such aid is not rendered, revolutionary upheaval is inevitable.

The economic needs of Central America are real and great: crop diversification, rational urbanization and industrialization, reduction of extremities in sectoral inequality and misdistribution of wealth. But to think that a Marshall Plan for Latin America, created in a political vacuum will have more than very short term palliative results is not to take the chronic history of the region seriously. It is better to accept systemic diversity in the economies of the region that attempt integration based on presumed free-market ideologies. Again, American public opinion will be happier to have such economic indigenization than economic rationalization from the top down.

Whatever specific policy options emerge from current United States reconsiderations of Central America they will be wiser, more prudent, and above all, more successful if the Soviet master and the Cuban proxy are factored in at all levels of analysis. Caribbean pacification clearly rests first on a cease and desist in the export of armed revolution or counterrevolution; second, the elimination of barriers to the free flow of peoples and ideas in the region; and third, respect for the autonomy and territorial integrity of all nations in the region. The limits of such premises, and of policy itself, are that these cornerstones do not necessarily comprise a tight fit. Hence building upon them becomes either an exercise in futility or an excruciatingly painful series of choices among worthy alternatives involving, more often than not, Draconian consequences. Yet the goal of Caribbean pacification is not of such significance that, contradictory elements notwithstanding, the struggle for a policy consensus within the context of new regional realities must go forward.

References/Notes

1. H. Michael Erisman, "Cuba and the Third World: The Nonaligned Nations Movement," *The New Cuban Presence in the Caribbean*, edited by Barry R. Levine. Boulder, Colorado: Westview Press, 1983, pp. 149-70.
2. Carlos Alberto Montaner, "Cuban Military Imperialism," *Secret Report on the Cuban Revolution*. New Brunswick and London: Transaction Books, 1981, pp. 29-37.
3. Christopher Whalen, "The Soviet Military Buildup in Cuba," *Cuban Communism* (fifth edition), edited by Irving Louis Horowitz. New Brunswick and London: Transaction Books, 1984.
4. Carmelo Mesa-Lago, "Evaluation of Socioeconomic Performance," *The Economy of Socialist Cuba: A Two Decade Appraisal*. Albuquerque: University of New Mexico Press, 1981, pp. 175-98.
5. Everett Carll Ladd, "Public Opinion on Central America," *Public Opinion*, Vol. 6, No. 4 (August/September) 1983, pp. 20-41.

Source and Original Title: "The Role of Cuba in the Pacification of Central America." Report of the National Bipartisan Commission on Central America (Appendix). Washington, D.C.: U.S. Government Printing Office, March 1984, pp. 617-32.

16

Fidel's "Soft" Stalinism

At a time of turmoil and transition in both Eastern Europe and the Soviet Union, when Soviet premier Mikhail Gorbachev is calling for "radical reform" of the economies of socialism, we find Fidel Castro reversing such gears, and demanding (and getting) an immediate closure of the free farmers' market: a network of incipient private initiative which at its maximum never impacted 4.9 percent of the agrarian sector. This seeming anomaly, this reversal of trends that are taking place in Communist lands elsewhere is no random measure. Indeed, I submit that it flows from the special internal tensions of Cuban society in the final phases of its founder's rule, reflecting the "autonomous" character of Castro's decision-making (within limits). But it also reflects his reactionary, Stalinist propensities.

In 1964, five years after Castro assumed power, I wrote an article for *New Politics* entitled "The Stalinization of Fidel's Cuba," In it, I indicated five characteristics of Stalinism that were evident early on in postrevolutionary Cuba. They are worth restating in light of current events and the lingering hopes among the die-hards that a democratic outcome is still feasible in Cuba under communism.

Elements in Fidel's Stalinism

There were—and remain still—six identifiable elements in Fidel's Stalinism. What is surprising, if not shocking, is how

rooted in concrete these elements have remained. Fidel's Stalinism indicates that (1) all aspects of civil society are subordinated
to the Party State; (2) the leader and a small coterie are exclusive
spokesmen for the Communist Party and state organs; (3) inner
political struggle, arbitrary purges and leadership rotation, replace efforts at social and class reintegration; (4) the passion for
economic development prevails over any concern for political
democracy; (5) control and terror are institutionalized, bringing
to a halt discussions of alternative economic strategies and policies; (6) national control at all costs is emphasized, even beyond
overseas adventures.

Fidel's Stalinism is nonetheless a dependent Stalinism—which
makes it uniquely ossified. Single crop socialism still prevails,
militarization of the system has intensified, and total fiscal
reliance upon Soviet support has now been institutionalized.
Indeed, although Chernobyl has exposed the vulnerabilities
of the Soviet nuclear program, Lazaro Hernandez, director of
Cuba's Export-Import Agency, declared "our confidence in the
scientific-technical development of the Soviet Union in the
energy and nuclear fields." This was at a time when the peoples
of Poland and other parts of Europe are still reeling from the
atomic reactor disaster at Chernobyl. But the key element in
Stalinism is, of course, dictatorship, a deep fear of any dissolution of absolute authority.

Radio Rebelde (the Cuban network) has reported (19 May
1986) that Fidel Castro called a halt to a six-year experiment with
free farmers' markets. This program, modeled after those in Poland
and Hungary, was aimed at providing farmers with an incentive to
increase production by allowing them to sell produce themselves
after satisfying government quotas. After two years, even with
the imposition of a twenty percent tax in 1982, this free-market
program served to stimulate the growth of intermediary sectors,
"middlemen," who moved from the countryside to cities the produce that otherwise would not have been grown.

Speaking with his customary certainty, Castro noted that the
free-market had become "a source of enrichment for neocapital-

ists and neobourgeoisie." The future is clear to him: "The peasant free market will pass without glory, leaving behind a great lesson, much damage and many millionaires." The psychological characteristic of Stalinism in both its pristine and reincarnated forms is its demand for purification through conflict and struggle—even at the risk of inventing a "parasitic" and "abusive" class. Its primary economic feat (and confusion) is any division of labor that detracts from the sharpest class struggle.

In true Stalinist fashion, Fidel notes that "the struggle against all kinds of exploitation and parasites is a struggle without truce, because such a deviation could damage the revolutionary cycle of the people. The free market became an obstacle to the development of the cooperative movement and was useful only for a group of intermediaries to get rich individually." Just what is or who ordains the "revolutionary cycle" is never examined. The muse of history apparently takes care of this by whispering great truths to the maximum leader's ears—the same leader who sanctioned the free agrarian sector to begin with.

Degrees of Repression

The decision to cut bait was clearly not taken lightly; for it implies a much higher degree of repression not only against intermediary classes of parasites but against proletarians and revolutionaries who had come to expect more results and less rhetoric from the Cuban economy. Neo-Stalinism's power in Cuba is based on levers of coercion that are so concretely centralized that decisions to introduce or cancel programs can be made with relative immunity from immediate political consequences. There is no question that the cancellation of the free market in foodstuffs will be met with roaring popular silence.

The serious problems come next: lower produce reaching the cities, decline in work output and potential demoralization of the production centers. All this is doubtless well appreciated by Castro—who must know that these negative consequences are the essence of the "revolutionary cycle of the people."

What does the maximum leader substitute for private incentives and a free market? The same, of course, as his intellectual mentor did after the New Economic Plan collapsed in the 1930s: call for an "eradication of errors in both the economic and planning sectors"; demand a renewed emphasis on "basic industry" (whatever that means in a Cuban context); and above all, point out, as in the July 4th issue of the official Communist Party paper, *Granma,* "that these are times for work, efficiency and sacrifice." One can only wonder how well such political platitudes went down on a special day in which millions of Cuban-Americans were sharing with all other Americans the festivities of Independence Day.

It is the strength of Stalinism to fine-tune the screws of oppression at will; it is the weakness of Stalinism that these screws choke the creative energies of the people, making the system surly, if not vulnerable. Stalinism did come to end, as will Castroism, but whether the Communist system can outlive the Cuban despot as it did his Russian predecessor is problematic. Cuba's dependency is after all not comparable to the USSR's relative independence. But this peasant crackdown should be watched for its impact on this, the final stage of Cuban Stalinism.

Source and Original Title: "Fidel's Stalinism." *Freedom at Issue,* Whole Nos. 92-93, November/December 1986, pp. 11-12.

1990s: Regionalization and Retreat

The critical edge of the 1990s took place in two stages: the collapse of the East European communist regimes in 1989 and the even more pronounced termination of the Soviet Union in 1991. These events spelled the end of the Cuban largesse and special status with respect to minerals, petroleum and commodities as a whole. It occasioned the emergency era, the special period in which there took place a drastic reduction in food and other rations. Hunger became a Cuban reality, with sugar a substitute for substance. The much vaunted health system was seen to be an empty vessel filled with sickly children and women. This special period lead to a popular disillusion, albeit of a quiet, apolitical sort. It also led to a modest opening of free market activities of the small shopkeeper sort. And even if was a window that was to close out prior to the close of the decade, it exposed the weaknesses of the administrative state run by a single party. By the close of the decade, the issue of Castro's demise—political if not personal—was on the Cuban agenda. And it is an issue that remains on the table.

The decade also revealed a shift in international tactics. The limitations of small powers that paraded about the global struggles of the time became transparent. And even if the rhetoric of the Cuban Revolution continued to trumpet the values of socialism and the inevitable triumph of communist values over capitalist venalities, the ability to sustain its place at the head of the Third World table sharply diminished. The Cuban adventures in Africa were resolved by death beds shipped back in late night flights. Allies such as China took a dramatic departure into free enterprise economics, and political supporters such as India were even less inclined to repeat shibboleths of previous decades. Religion and culture entered into places such as Yugoslavia, Iraq and even

Vietnam to disrupt the neat formulas inherited by Castro from the Leninist visions of the world.

It was also apparent that economic setbacks can take place while political systems maintain some semblance of equilibrium. And that was the case in Cuba. There was always a tendency in Castro to pull back from adventures overseas. The new situation in the world made this a necessity of communism's survival in Cuba. Castro was adroit enough to take advantage of these conditions. While retaining the drumbeat of his island communism, the rhymes pounded out served to realign his position with Latin American and Brazilian political changes, and sought a continuing role as anti-American par excellence, even as he mocked the failure of communism in Europe. While the results for the people of Cuba were hardly inspiring, they were sufficiently compelling to move Cuba into the new millennium without a collapse of the regime itself.

17

Small Nation, Global Pretensions: Fidel Castro Redux

Castro was reported to have recently said to a group of astonished diplomats in Havana: "If these changes go on in the USSR, they will soon be describing us as those madmen in the Albania of the Caribbean." Whether this is a piece of apocrypha or an actual interview, the fact is that Albania and Cuba remain, albeit for quite different reasons, hold-outs in the revolutions which have swept communist regimes from power in Eastern Europe, and have roiled the political process within the Soviet Union proper. It is entirely appropriate therefore for Georges Fauriol and Eva Loser to have explored the reasons for this apparent anomaly, in short, to locate the changing perceptions of Cuba throughout its thirty one year old history. They have assembled a group of high quality specialists to review the international dimensions of its hardened political arteries. This comes at a significant historical juncture, since Cuba as a "strategic outpost" and proxy for global power struggles explains much of what would otherwise appear as sheer aberrant political behavior.

The volume is graced not only by serious studies of the sort of bilateral relations one might well expect in a Fauriol project, but by a final section on functional policy areas that constitutes six of the fourteen chapters. This is fit, proper, and innovative. For in a series of excellent papers by Michael J. Mazaar, Constantine

Menges, Jorge Perez-Lopez, Jorge Sanguinetty, Paula J. Pettavino and Juan M. del Aguila we are moved beyond conventional versions of Latin American militarism and policy into the complex sources and mixed games of Cuban foreign policy; a policy now in a state of atrophy at best and shambles at worst.

One comes away from this text with an appreciation of the fact that Cuba is neither socialist nor Third World in the classical sense. Caudillismo is more prevalent in Cuba than in most Latin American societies; indeed, the caudillo image is probably truer for Cuban now then it has been in its past (pre-Castro) epoch. The armed forces (whether in the form of the internal ministry or the armed forces directly) have occupied a most favored status from the outset of the Castro regime some 31 years ago. This has been muted because the extreme left was able to define the situation, insisting upon casual designations of Cuba as socialist or communist. There was a presumption, entirely false with respect to Cuba at least, that radical regimes tend to undercut long-standing Latin traditions of the military figure on horseback. But the military man cum guerrilla is much the same thing. The key is not the horse nor the back pack, but the militarized character of the society—the carrier of Cuba's international dimension. The military is the only social force that has been institutionalized in contemporary Cuba. The analysis of Cuba's security apparatus by Michael Mazaar, herein contained is perhaps the best single paper on the neo-Stalinist characteristics of Castro-style militarism available.

A special part of Castro's "foreign policy" is the elimination of rivals through heavy outward migration. It cannot be overlooked that unlike East Europe, there is no "wall" or border, but an ocean between Cuba and the United States. Travel was difficult after the Cuban revolution, but for the impatient and insistent, entrepreneurs and convicts alike, it was continuous. As a result the most discontent and determined ended up in exile and not in armed insurrection against the regime. Castro in this sense learned well the lessons of sociology: permitting emigration is the functional equivalent of tranquilizing a discontented people.

Such a policy also tranquilized would-be critics of the regime; at least until events in Eastern Europe reminded scholars of the "Albanianization" of Cuba.

A key element permitting Castro a free-hand in forging foreign adventures no less than foreign policies is the remoteness of Cuba from the dorsal spine that links North and South America. External ideas and influences filter in only with difficulty, unlike, for example Poland to Hungary or Hungary to Romania. Cuba is an island society par excellence. As a result, Castro is capable of shutting down information, even from the USSR, at the whim of the leader. Insularity is built into the structure of Cuban geography no less than society. Local issues become global in perceived importance. Irritations, major and minor, that occur in nations which share common borders and uncommon social systems did not affect Castro's Cuba; at least not to any serious extent as a threat to regime stability or as a modifier of its foreign policy.

Despite all the signs of a coming crisis, the economic collapse of Castro's Cuba is prevented by continuing Soviet support. The papers by Jiri Valenta and Jaime Suchlicki make the character of such "core relationships" painfully evident. Unlike Poland and other nations of Eastern Europe that paid the USSR reparations and provided goods, the situation is reversed: the USSR pays Cuba roughly six billion dollars annually, or one fourth of its foreign aid, to remain in the communist fold. This is starting to change—but its full impact had not hit home yet at the time of the completion of this volume. While Soviet supplies to Cuba have slowed, and in reprisal, Cuban foodstuffs to the USSR have also slowed, these are still described in technical terms, i.e., a breakdown in shipping capacities, rather than a profound change in policies. There remains only limited evidence of a new policy as such over the long haul. But what several papers make clear is that Cuba is at a critical juncture in its foreign policy; especially as it effects its relations to the Soviet Union and the Eastern Bloc.

The character of what Jiri Valenta calls the Leninization of Cuba, or what I still prefer to view as neo-Stalinism, as an independent element in the survival of Cuban communism, cannot be overlooked. There are solid grounds for describing Castro as a Leninist, since unlike Stalin the genocidal potential of the regime has only sporadically been brought to bear on the Cuban citizenry. But the elements of continuity from Lenin to Stalin were brought into play: they include lawlessness of the system, lack of accountability (both to its own people and to outside powers), and secrecy in decision-making. In the absence of public accountability, actual foreign policy decisions often came as surprises to the outside world. The idea that Leninism is simply bare-boned repression misses the point. For as Valenta correctly notes, the foreign policy adventures serves in the short run to ease internal mechanisms of repression. Symbolic terror and the everyday social force of the Committees for the Defense of the Revolution are adequate to the task. It might be added that such quasi military cadres make it more likely that a bitter civil struggle as in Romania, rather than the benign outcome as in the rest of Eastern Europe, is perhaps more likely than the benign transition to a mellow socialism that a few of the participants in this volume envision, or at least hope for. It might be that the gradual transformation of Cuba from a totalitarian to an authoritarian state envisioned by Juan del Aguila will still take place, much in the fashion of the USSR under Gorbachev. But this seems less likely in an environment in which Cuba is the sole surviving communist state in the hemisphere, with a leader who has absorbed the pathology, but not the power of early communism—of being an island of communist probity in a sea of capitalist vice.

Dynastic communism as such enters the Cuban equation. While it shares many of the properties of neo-Stalinism, the familial features of the Castro regime has long been recognized as an element of its policy making unto itself. As Douglas Payne recently pointed out, capriciousness plays a role. "Castro's career has been marked by numerous sharp turns in both domestic and foreign policy. The possibility cannot be excluded that he might suddenly declare himself a champion of *perestroika* and swear, in typically egoistical fashion, his *perestroika* is the best. He would then demand immediate concessions from the United States, including an end to economic embargo, and would have the full support of Moscow." This is, of course, a possible (not inevitable) scenario; one anticipated by several contributors to this volume. Nonetheless, it indicates the hazards of even informed guesses of Castro's foreign policy directions in a political environment of near-total political illegitimacy. Perhaps a new law of political science or better, an equation, is that levels of predictability are a function of democracy. This is so because the caprice of a single individual is at least checked by the caprices of others. But in the absence of checks there are no balances, and without the latter, prediction becomes plausible in therapeutic rather than analytic terms. It is to the credit of the tone set by the editors of this volume that such intellectual risks are fully appreciated.

What then pushes the Cuban political process to the breaking point? Primarily the foreign overseas conditions in which Cuba finds itself. This begins with a profound and growing isolation of Cuba from the rest of Latin America, his crusades to muster support from Puerto Rico to Porto Alegre notwithstanding. Richard Ratliff and Ernest Evans clearly give expression in their respective contributions to this strange symbiosis between isolation at home and adventure abroad.

Then there is the dependence upon Soviet economic support, if not agreement with Soviet political policies, that fuels Cuban foreign policy; well noted in several papers. The complex relations of Cuba with Europe and Canada coupled with a declining interest on the part of former Eastern European allies like Czechoslovakia is well documented by Scott B. MacDonald. The question for now is whether the European "door" will in fact remain "half-open" or increasingly shut.

Then there is the willingness of the United States to let Castro simply continue to twist in the wind, coupled with a near breakdown in Cuba's ability to meet its own basic trade and sales obligations, even at the bartering levels. There is an increasing urgency in forcing the United States to say "what if..." with respect to a post-Castro Cuba. But thus far, this impulse to announce

scenarios in advance of actions has been resisted, and the laissez-faire approach described by Fauriol, and dominant since the
parallel crisis of the Bay of Pigs misadventure and the Missile
Base confrontation remains intact.

A new, potentially explosive factor, one that unfolded substantially after this volume was assembled, but which nonetheless is
critical to the conduct of Cuban foreign policy, is the emergence
in Nicaragua of the Sandinistas as a Gorbachev type of State,
which, now forced into opposition, functions in bold relief to
the Leninist or Stalinist (take your pick) system to be found in
Cuba. Daniel Ortega and the Sandinista National Liberation
Front took its appeals to the people, and lost decisively to the
broad democratic coalition headed by Violeta Barrios de Cham-
orro, leader of the National Opposition Union. The Nicaraguan
election campaign was conducted on broadly multi-party terms.
The electoral process, which is a harbinger of things to come
throughout Eastern Europe no less than Latin America, served
to institutionalize political legitimacy. The regime and opposition
alike in Nicaragua can now chart a democratic path, in a way that
Communism in Cuba has never been able to achieve, or even to
imagine. Beyond the political, Nicaragua never did completely
destroy the private sector, hence it was, and remains, in a position
to change the economic "mix" without a sense of severe rupture.
These developments in Nicaragua have taken place to the bitter chagrin of Fidel Castro. The impact of events in Nicaragua
will certainly exacerbate Castro's growing sense of hemispheric
isolation, and more dangerously, sense of desperation.

What these developments indicate is a continuing round of in-
stabilities in Cuba until some form of opposition can crystallize.
And that some opposition is now fusing becomes evident when
reports indicate that Cuban youth are talking of political change
openly and defiantly for the first time since the 1959 revolution.
This is after all a situation best described in processual terms
of when and not structural terms of whether. It takes little to
recollect that the late Premier of Romania, Nicolae Ceauşescu,
mustered a massive if sullen public rally only one week before

his demise. He had to face that same crowd in total opposition one week later. And one week later still he was tried, convicted and executed for crimes against the people. This volume was assembled prior to the shattering events of 1989 in most parts of Eastern Europe. Hence, its prognosis are for more benign (and slower) forms of change then seem to be taking place in the communist world of which Cuba is very much a part.

Still, we must remember the dangers in the Cuban situation. In Spain, Francisco Franco endured long after any utility, but there was a monarchist tradition which provided a key element in the transition to Spanish democracy in the 1970s. Such an element does not exist within Cuba proper. It is, however possible that the exile community may function in such a restorative capacity, at least to cushion the shock of transition during the early stages of a return to democratic norms.

That many of the contributions to *Cuba: The International Dimension* conclude in admittedly speculative terms indicates that some form of closure to the Cuban dictatorship is at hand—if not in 1990, then assuredly in the decade of the nineties, and probably in the early years. Castro is down to the bare bones of the family. The costs of his foreign policies are too high and the results too limited to enlist continuing Soviet support. The administrative infrastructure is demoralized, the earlier passion among the military cadres for international adventure has, as Juan Benemelis and Gillian Gunn point out, been sapped by battles in Africa and trials in Cuba, and the energy of the best and the brightest has long ago migrated to points North and West.

In any post-Castro context, it might well turn out that the most serious problems of reconstruction will be political rather than economic. The forces of a new turn in international affairs, whether administrative or military, have not yet emerged in identifiable form. Under such circumstances, what we have is best described as a continuing political tragedy, especially for the internal victims of Castro's foreign policy adventures. Rejoicing over any perceived foreign policy setbacks should be muted in the face of the calamitous outcome of this revolution;

one begun in high expectations and concluding with the near total paralysis of a major Caribbean nation. The great length of time under which Cuban people have suffered tyranny will make the task of democracy harder and the potential for disillusion greater. Fortunately, the quality of Cuba's people, their endurance, diligence and patience should serve to cut down the retooling time of the society in its effort to return to the family of democratic nations. Still, we would be well advised to think carefully on the heavy price paid by blind passions and a revanchist spirit in past efforts to improve the lot of the Cuban people and system. In so doing, we must start with curbing our own euphoria while passing along our current wisdom (without laundering past follies) to the next generation. The contributors to *Cuba: The International Dimension* helps us walk out from under the shadows of the past in an appropriately modest way. If the lessons of this collective portrait are properly understood, we can then hold open the prospects for a future in which Cuba will play a constructive, and much needed, foreign policy role in hemispheric affairs.

Source and Original Title: "Fidel Castro Redux: Old Revolutionaries Resisting New Revolutions." *Freedom at Issue,* Whole No. 115, July-August, pp. 12-15.

18

Revolution, Longevity, and Legitimacy in Communist States*

I

There can scarcely be any doubt, even two years after the events, that 1989 was equal to 1789 in its world historic dimensions. Cynics and sophisticates alike recognize that the ubiquitous and oft-maligned "people" have spoken. Not a week passes without another startling revelation cracking the mythology of the communist past; nor another mass demonstration or electoral disaffection rejecting the communist present; and finally, outpouring of resentment casting grave doubt on any communist future in any nation-state. Deserving of consideration is what exactly links these events; and further, what unites the revolutionary upheavals in nearly every single country from Central Europe, the Baltic states, onto Central Asia, in spirit if not always in exact consequences.

The impact of these events on more remote regions is hardly uniform. On one hand, there is the express curb in diplomatic relations by Czechoslovakia with Cuba; while on the other a definite schism between the new regimes of Eastern Europe and the few hard line states that remain, such as North Korea. Thus, in place of euphoria is a need to make clear what states resonate to the new turn in European ex-communist affairs, and which remain adamant in their adherence to totalitarian forms of power—and why.

In its simplest historical terms the breakdown of the Brezhnev Doctrine and the rise of Gorbachev's Perestroika provided Eastern Europe with a window of opportunity to break the shackles of an unwanted, oppressive regime. Only a short decade ago, the Soviet Union and its satellites were captive to the claim, one that united every regime since the time of Lenin, that once a people accept the mixed blessings of communism, they must forswear all other blessings, especially the blandishments of western capitalism. In slightly less metaphorical terms: to embrace the communist system was to cross over from the mythical bilateral world of capitalism to communism once and for all. With the "revolutionary seizure of power," any real politics ceased to be practiced, replaced as it were by circuses and caucuses dedicated to celebrating the new order.

The explosiveness of events is partially explained by the absence of routine politics in the communist world. After the concentration of power in the hands of party officials and government bureaucrats, organized opposition collapsed, or was crushed, in each East European nation. What emerged was an essentially apolitical opposition, drawn from a variety of fields and professions, but outside the framework of the communist party as such. What rapidly unfolded was a struggle between party officials without legitimacy that is in its simplest form, without a mass supportive base; and the emergence of non-political figures—from welders in Polish shipyards to poets in Czech bistros—who established solid support from broad sectors.

Symbolic of the new age of freedom we have the position of such former "iron-curtain" figures as Vytautas Landsbergis, Antanas J. Buracas, and Zigmas Vaisvila, president of the Lithuanian Reform Movement and members of the Lithuanian Supreme Soviet respectively, that national independence is inviolable; based on the principle of autonomy and self-determination—not within the greater Soviet Union, but outside of that Union. Indeed, Gorbachev and his military supporters have come to appreciate, and increasingly to fear the national character of this latest phase of East European revolutionary behavior. The

Baltic States illustrate the power of legitimacy as a factor in the ongoing revolutions of East Europe. Since Latvia, Lithuania, and Estonia all claim to be independent nations, and hence entitled to be viewed apart from internal struggles taking place with the U.S.S.R.. The recent votes in these nations to express support for national independence underscore the emphasis on legitimacy rather than insurgency as the path of greatest potential. Such political, rather than military struggles, also revealed a strategy of awaiting the total dissolution of communist power in the Soviet Union rather than taking the path of armed insurrection.

The impact of these movements provides an expression of life under communism. The problem of legitimacy, with which social scientists have long wrestled, has turned practical with a vengeance. More specifically, communist societies are confronting the absence of those elements within their orbits that bind people together symbolically in the face of troubles and turmoil. It is as if almost any practice will do if it can upset extant political and social landscapes. In its practical terms, legitimacy means rule with the consent of the governed, or doing things one's own way rather than the way of an imposed power. Legitimacy also entails a policy: if a social structure does not succeed, one does not have to punish or purge the leaders, or engage in ritualistic self criticisms within party cells. Instead, one goes to the heart of the matter: change policies, cadres, and even systems. In this sense, legitimacy at the optimal level is a process of democratization no less than a structure of legal succession over time.

Legitimate rule is established either through a democratic consensus, as in the evolution of Western democracies; or through a broad-based revolutionary movement, as in the case of Russia between 1905-1917 and China between 1910-1948. In both of these examples, the appeal to vox populi was broad based, whether on ballots or by bullets. Legitimacy can be eroded, as can personal trust, but not easily. At the outset at least, there is a direct sense of a stake in the running of government. Thus, neither royal abdications in England nor presidential assassinations in America remotely rocked the political boat. For that matter, major upheavals such as the death of dictators, like Stalin in Russia or Mao Tse-tung in China did not automatically result in a revolutionary, and certainly not a democratic, upheaval. Dramatic changes in both sets of systems do occur with leadership change. But prospects for the overthrow of the present political system in either Russia or China depend upon the diminution of legitimate rule—and these are functions of internal cataclysms rather than external impositions. Cuba under Fidel Castro has also laid explicit claim to this non-democratic, albeit authentic meaning of legitimacy. And the continuing hold of single party rule and dictatorial modes of political and bureaucratic modes would indicate the dangers in presuming that the events of Eastern Europe in 1989 will simply spill over to every other part of the communist world. This is a hard, Weberian lesson to deal with. But one that must be understood in its paradoxical fullness if we are not to fall prey to a dangerous sentimentality in assuming the automatic spread of democracy to China, Cuba, North Korea, Vietnam, Cambodia, and like minded places.[1]

II

In operational terms legitimacy entails a recognition of the mixed pattern involved with the slow introduction of the rule of law and parliamentary norms into the lives of ordinary people throughout the ex-communist world, rather than armed struggle or counter-revolution. This emphasis on legal norms is a critical factor in the present level of struggle throughout Eastern Europe, and no less, inside the Soviet Union. Among the more remarkable developments throughout the former communist orbit can be listed the following:

The right of physical movement of citizens without constraint, punishment, and with the right (even encouragement) of return.

Proposals to permit freedom of the press and prohibitions against government censorship and/or arbitrary removal.

Proposals to permit ownership of private property and retain surpluses owned in small enterprises or farming.

Laws which guarantee workers the right to strike for the first time in communist history since Kronstadt.

Legislation which give citizens of communist lands the unrestricted right
to choose their own religion.

Enabling legislation that permit the establishment of business cooperatives
unregulated by the central government.

Enactment of laws requiring all legislation be submitted to the people in
direct referendum before enactment.

Consideration of a multiple party system, in which the Communist Party
can be displaced or replaced by other parties, factions or alignments.

These developments, and many others like them, repudiate the
specter of the arbitrary tyranny of the past; and no less, indicate
the parliamentary shape of the future. In this sense, however
difficult it may be to provide causal explanations of the impact
of revolutionary changes in Eastern Europe and their impact
on the orthodox regimes of Cuba, North Korea and China, the
congruence of circumstances must itself be taken as evidence of
the importance of system legitimacy in the region as a whole.

Before the issue of the new legitimacy and their implications
are addressed, the question of political illegitimacy, or the absence of rule by consent of the governed, also needs far closer
scrutiny. It is this history of illegitimacy which links the current
upheavals in every nation of Eastern Europe; and which while
understated abstractly by social and political science, was missed
in the concrete in nearly every analyst's prediction about events
in Eastern Europe prior to the actual revolutions which took
place 1989. What follows is not so much an attempt at history
on the quick, but rather to appreciate the thread of legitimacy as
a factor in political change in the Eastern European sphere.

Illegitimacy takes many forms. In Rumania, as in North Korea,
strong elements of dynastic communism emerged during the
post-Stalin epoch. As some old Bolsheviks predicted, the rule
of the people moved quickly into the rule of the Party, and then
onto the rule of the ruler. Protection of that ruling elite becomes
a family repository, much like a modern political equivalent of

primogeniture. The basis of such a system was not principle but payoff. In Poland (under Jaruzelski) the bankruptcy of Communist Party rule was anticipated by a direct form of military nationalism, in which the armed forces ruled in the name of the Party but exercised authority apart from the Party.[2] In Hungary and Yugoslavia, albeit in radically different ways, local government agencies ruled apart from party instrumentalities. As a result, the stifling control of the Party apparatus was seriously and perhaps permanently eroded. In places like Bulgaria and East Germany, at least until the upheavals of 1989, Party rule was absolute. The model of control was a direct outgrowth of Stalinism; or as it is now being called in Sofia by the reformists, a variety of Czarist Communism. To be sure, such a thumb-nail sketch omits contextual limits to change that made Polish "military communism" tolerable at least in short run terms. It is also a fact that economic reforms, including opening the market, took place not only in Hungary but even in Bulgaria. Still, it is fair to say that the distinction between the restoration of legitimacy in the post-1989 context differs qualitatively from the pseudo-legitimacy of the decade which came before.

In none of these varieties of communist experience prior to 1989 was popular legitimacy either expressed or countenanced by the Soviet rulers. But they are, or were, so different from each other that the forms of political change in Eastern Europe, while superficially similar, are in fact radically different from each other. One need only consider ongoing struggles in Czechoslovakia, which is a nation with a far more democratic past than most areas in Eastern Europe, to appreciate the protracted nature of the struggles no less than the distinct characteristics of the outcomes. The search for unifying elements is neither simple nor as transparent as news headlines tend to assume. The end of totalitarian rule is but the start of the process of democratization.

Czechoslovakia is a model of the struggle between legitimate and illegitimate authority in Eastern Europe. Between 1918 and 1938, this nation was an exemplar of both industrial innovation and political freedom. Legitimacy of the Masaryk regime was never in doubt. Nor was its suspension with the invasion of portions of the Czech nation in 1938. But so integral was Czechoslovakia to the Western consensus that it became again part of the West after the Nazis were crushed. Between 1945 and 1948, legitimacy was restored, as was the industrial capacities of the nation. But again, this time with the active collusion of the Stalinist regime in the Soviet Union, democracy was aborted, and the Klement Gottwald puppet regime destroyed legitimacy in that nation. The mass effort to restore democracy in 1968 failed, but only in a temporal way. Events made possible a crushing of the Czech people only with outside military force, and in so doing exposed the illegitimacy of the communist rulers with a finality that was lost neither on the conquered nor the conqueror.

If France is the land of the "model" nineteenth-century revolutions: 1789, 1830, 1848, 1871, Czechoslovakia is the "model" of twentieth-century legitimacy: Frantisek Palacky and his disciple, Tomas Masaryk provided a framework which has endured through the present leadership: 1918, 1938, 1948, 1968, and 1989 are woven into the fabric of Czech life. This is not uniformly the case in Eastern Europe, as the volatile situations in Rumania, Yugoslavia and Bulgaria make clear. These differences notwithstanding, the arguments within Eastern Europe are no longer whether but when the market mechanisms shall displace the no longer functioning pricing mechanism of Comecon.[3] Such discussions entail a presumption of legitimacy; which, while still new, show remarkable sturdiness across Eastern Europe. Of course, the degree of success adaptation to new economic conditions will vary greatly; not the least major factor will be the antecedent levels of industrialization prior to the assumption to power of communist hegemony.

Experts assumed, falsely as it turns out, that longevity and continuity in the rule of individuals, such as with Erich Honecker in East Germany or Todor Zhivkov in Bulgaria is the same as system legitimacy. Indeed, one of the few writers on the GDR to call the shots right may have been David Childs, who in his book on Moscow's German Ally notes that East Germany is especially vulnerable to Western Democratic influences.[4] That protest movements have mushroomed most profoundly in regimes that were politically most repressive, such as Albania, often moving from hundreds to hundreds of thousands in a matter of weeks, gives vivid testimony to the volatility of change behind the now bent-iron curtain

East Germany is now dissolved and essentially reincorporated into Germany as such. The postwar regime was set up as a result of a four part division of the German nation. In the West, United States, England and France held sway; in the East, the Soviet Union dominated. Again the division was externally imposed, arbitrary, based on the twin principles: to the victors go war booty and reparations; coupled with the belief that a divided Germany would be less of a threat to world peace and stability than a united Germany. With the direct intervention of Soviet occupying troops after 1953, Berlin and its Wall became the symbol not only of a divided Germany, but of a sealed community, alienated from its own people, and not just from the West. As a consequence the governing body, lacking even a remote popular base, or any sort of differentiation one from the other, they had little choice but to derive their power from the Communist Party. The Government and Party have been so closely identified that calls for popular elections and a multi-party system threatened and eventually toppled both State and Communist authority at one fell swoop. The East German regime, whether under Honecker or Grenz, was faced with the same unpalatable choice: return to all out repression or resort to total resignation. Either option betrays the complete bankruptcy of the regime. So it came to pass that the convulsions in East Germany, starting with the resignation of Honecker and ending with the collapse of the Berlin Wall, quickly changed, restored would be more appropriate, the map of Germany and the fate of all Europe. These post-1989 shocks are part of a future chapter of a united Europe, and not of this particular moment of the restoration of regime legitimacy.

Poland, under the tireless, patient, decade-long leadership of the Solidarity movement serves as a prototype for developments throughout the region. It never wavered in its belief that parliamentary rather than insurrectionary solutions were key. And its very search for legitimacy, under the cautious leadership of Lech Walesa, placed Solidarity in sharp relief to the communist leadership which came to the leadership of Poland as a direct consequence of the Nazi-Soviet Pact and the World War Two outcome. The Communist party was doomed by its absolute acceptance of the division of Poland to suit the needs of the major players in the post-war epoch. The postwar border adjustments were at the expense of Germany (the nominal loser) and to the advantage of the Soviet Union, which effectively annexed the eastern portion of Poland. But these divisions and redivisions had nothing to do with an internal national consensus. In contrast, Solidarity developed, survived and thrived because of its consensual base. Whether that base can survive the transition from a controlled state to a free-market economy is another question. Still its emergence as the governing element resulted from a startling series of developments, brilliantly stage managed by Lech Walesa; and in part is an indirect consequence of the larger incapacity of the externally imposed inauthentic Soviet regime to impose its will on Poland indefinitely, whether in party or military guise.

In Hungary, the effective ruler of the nation was a Communist Party that underwent a national communist phase in 1956 only to be decimated by Soviet invasion and occupation. After that, it was evident that the Communist Party was a foreign imposition, one extending even to Soviet military advisors helping administer the Hungarian state apparatus. Thus, the negation of the Communist Party itself in 1989 was an understandable, and in retrospect, a natural consequence of the party's delegitimation. It is part of this search for a new style of governance that has led the Hungarian regime to petition for membership in the Council of Europe, that West European group founded in 1949 "to uphold the principle of parliamentary democracy." Of special interest is how, an essentially agrarian society, moved in the same democratic direction as more industrial portions of Eastern Europe. The question of the relative autonomy of political impulses still needs to be examined in depth.

In Czechoslovakia, we have a similar, if faster, paced natural history of mass protest. With the fusion of student protests, broad working class support, and the admission of communist party bankruptcy, the non-communist outcome resembled events in Poland, Germany, Hungary and elsewhere. But the form and the rate of democratization are quite distinct. The character assassination, and some claim physical elimination, of Tomas Masaryk put in place a Communist regime without a shred of legitimacy. It ruled until 1968, when a democratic movement within an authoritarian husk took place led by Alexander Dubcek, only to be crushed a year later by direct Soviet occupation. The present reemergence of Dubcek, like a phoenix from the ashes of past defeat, is itself a powerful indicator of democratic restoration in Czechoslovakia.

Only with massive and protracted opposition, did the dominance of hardliners within the Communist party cease to prevail. The government, itself a hostage to party factional ism, has been compelled to develop independent policies in the face of massive public disaffection from communist rule. This led to a strange condition in which the Soviet authorities warned its Czech supporters of the risks in their continuing press for power—to little avail. While protesters faced a far more severe challenge than one might have predicted based on the character of the regime or the levels of social and economic development. Regime continuity in Czech politics had been maintained only with the aid of riot police. With a political opposition led by a writer, and now president of the nation, like Václav Havel; and jazz critics like Karel Srp, the potential for a full-scaled political transformation proved to be both more difficult and potentially more profound than elsewhere. Václav Havel put the deep implications squarely on the line in asserting that his country was "at a historical crossroads," accusing the Communists of leading the nation to the bring of "spiritual, moral, political and economic catastrophe." He added that "we want to live in a free, democratic and prospering Czechoslovakia, returned to Europe, and we will never give up this idea."[6] In this nation with a strong democratic past, legitimacy requires plural parties no less than legislators unfettered by edict. And in Czechoslovakia such a prospect has materialized because, as I indicated earlier, legitimization is built into the fabric of its past history.

In some nations, such as Yugoslavia, which long ago broke from the Stalinist yoke in organizational terms, the character of opposition to the illegitimate Communist Party takes the form of separatist, nationalist movements, with six ethnic segments from Croatians to Albanians demanding a share of government, or a separate autonomous regional fate. Political leadership rotates not out of a clear sense of democratic participation, but as a consequence of full-scale and mutual mistrust. The relatively benign Communist movement of Yugoslavia, with its workers councils and regional associations, were enough to fend off Soviet blandishments, but could not establish political legitimacy any more than its Stalinist opponents. The Marxist myopia for nationalist movements made Yugoslavia more vulnerable to civil and regional warfare than other "hard line" communist states. Hence, the national and ethnic rivalries within Yugoslavia take on a special role in accelerating national disintegration, instead of national rebellion. As Harold Lydall notes, socialist self management coupled with ethnic federalism has created a "monstrous amalgam" resulting in enormous waste of human and material resources.[7]

Even in Bulgaria, a nation-State which had tied its fate and fortunes closely to the Soviet Union, has witnessed startling opposition to the conservative regime, with the now "normal cycle" of small protests, followed by large protests, followed by bold demands for democratization of the polity and opening up the economy, and finally ending with the resignation of Todor I. Zhivkov, the longest running dictator in the Soviet bloc (35 years) and his displacement with a moderate reformist, Petar T. Mladenov. And if perestroika, glasnost, and the new thinking has permeated Sofia, with its independent discussion clubs, demands for free elections in a multi-party environment, one can say in all frankness that the last vestiges of the Soviet Empire in Eastern Europe are under mortal siege.

When we turn to the strange case of Romania we see what Daniel Nelson describes as a textbook case in political immobility made possible by international isolation from the Eastern and Western blocs alike.[8] To that, one must add that Rumania shared with North Korea and Cuba, a communist party dominated by a family network. This sort of Mafia-style communism is probably the hardest to uproot. Its very organic intimacy makes it impervious to ordinary forms of pressure and protest. But such isolation, while reinforcing the pseudo-Stalinist pivot of Nicolae Ceausescu and his family in the sort run, lacked a capacity to resolve domestic conflict. Little wonder that the end of the dictatorship was nasty, brutish and violent. Familial dictatorship, lacking the mythic potentials of royal dynasties, is perhaps the least legitimate form of rule in the world. Hence it has only the capacity to postpone, but not resolve the problem of political legitimacy—one that has terrible consequences for the population in the short run but lacking any capacity for survival or growth in the long run. Dynastic communism has a special capacity to restrict decision-making to the private realm. Hence, even those forces within ordinary communist regimes: the army, the secret police, or special bureaucratic agencies, can be bypassed, or as happened in Cuba, manifestly purged. This is a source of the extremely difficult situation in which even when a revolutionary situation materializes, there are few, if any, social forces available to carry it to fulfillment.

Romania indicates how a carefully textured policy that cultivated a global image of being the "Switzerland" of the East, could yet be coupled with being a domestic variant of a Latinized Stalinism; or more exactly, a case of dynastic communism which is a special variant of the dictatorship of the proletariat, albeit in this case, the dictatorship of the extended family. And whatever weakness such dynastic varieties on the communist theme possess, they offer the political tightness, the sense of solidarity which was absent elsewhere in communist structures of Eastern Europe. Ceauşescu's formula of no capitalism and no democracy resonated well amongst the threatened Communist party cadres suffering an after shock of dispossession. Perhaps for this reason the old rulers of the Iron Guard made common cause with the recently deposed rulers of the Communist Party, and more tragically, nearly every shade of political opinion in between. Again, we see how the broad contours of the search for legitimacy are linked to the intimate textures of nation al histories of the region.

III

We then must turn to the problem of legitimacy in the Soviet Union and the Peoples Republic of China. For in these two nations, however imperfectly, we witness precisely the existence of a legitimate revolutionary upheaval and tradition. And if in both places, the destruction of despotic traditional rule also meant the disastrous bypassing of liberal democratic options, alternatives that were just beginning to emerge in the early decades of the twentieth century, one can hardly deny the social bases of revolutionary ferment.

In these two giant countries, the twin peaks of the communist world in the post-war epoch, the struggle for mass democracy and free economy takes on their most complex form. Essentially, the very organic nature of communism, in these two master nations makes the evolution of reform all the more difficult. For not only is the overthrow of an imposed administrative cadre involved, but the economic and social structures that came into existence after a huge amount of personal sacrifice and public turmoil.

In the U.S.S.R. every admission of guilt or responsibility comes with great difficulty. Decades of mythology and layers of ideology come unglued. Accepting responsibility for the Katyn Forest massacres involves a revision of Soviet history and a re-evaluation of the ethics of the Soviet armed forces *vis-à-vis* the Nazi Wehrmacht. Even Nazi atrocities as in the Babi Yar region of the Ukraine were long denied by Soviet authorities who denied by fiat the history of anti-Semitism in communist regions. The admission of secret pacts for the division of Poland and the Baltic States completely discredits the communist idea of international proletarian solidarity, showing the Soviet Union to be a venal state in the Machiavellian, or dare one say, Czarist mold. The continuing reevaluation of figures like Lenin and Stalin moves in fits and starts—with efforts to describe the death and imprisonment of 25 million Russian people (excluding the 20 million which are attributed to the Nazi invasion of the Soviet Union between 1941-1945) as "excesses" and "aberrations" within an otherwise perfect system, not something endemic to socialist development as such. Political assassinations are linguistically papered over by posthumous "rehabilitations" as a sort of communist-materialist bow in the direction of the province of immortality. Many old Bolsheviks are rehabilitated posthumously. Even those not honored are at least reviewed. Leon Trotsky, the villain of Stalinist ideology, is now routinely dealt with—warts and all.

As a consequence, the movement for reform in Soviet Russia takes place not as unadulterated regime liberalization but also as opposition to communism that is to broad demands for restoration of nationalist and traditionalist values. Democracy is one polar element in the Soviet reform movement, while ultra nationalism and totalitarian anti-Semitism is at the opposite pole. Public opinion surveys indicate this two sided nature of Soviet reform movements: a demand for more democracy and no less a demand that the state impose added restrictions to insure work and stability. In short, the very legitimacy of the Soviet State, its birth in a revolutionary situation makes the process of reform extremely volatile and taxing. As a consequence, Leninism no less than Stalinism has become the ultimate victim of Gorbachev's New Thinking, since appeals to self management and free markets, become tactics to encourage a break with the totalitarian tradition within a reform regime that has demonstrated little capacity to appeal directly to democratic political slogans.[9]

One finds a similar set of contradictory characteristics in China. Repression in Tiananmen Square was real, 2,600 dead civilians and 10,000 injured people attest to that. But the character of the opposition was massive enough to threaten stability, but not system legitimacy—certainly as measured by the loyalty of military cadres or urban citizens for example. On the other hand, reform precedes top down, with efforts to revive the pre-1989 movement for economic reform again picking up steam by fits and starts. The Chinese leadership itself is divided into pragmatic and hard line elements, as is evident by the change of leadership from Deng Xiaoping to Jiang Zemin. But while a myriad of economic and social reforms are permitted—such as the struggle against prostitution, political corruption, and currency speculation—they continue to take place amidst efforts to control their political pace and impact. Little real challenge to communist rule is possible at this point in time.

The Cultural Revolution was allowed to run its course in the late 1960s because it simply extended to a new generation the regime legitimacy of the Maoist revolution of the 1940s. This was not the case with events in 1989, which even introduced the symbols of Western democracy, such as the Statue of Liberty, to show the displeasure of largely young opponents to the old regime. But again, as in France in the late 1960s, the industrial working masses stood with the regime or remained passive against the blandishments of the reformers, as painful a reminder as that may be. Even if this mass support for the regime was essentially passive in nature, it was sufficient to insure the survival of the Deng regime in its time of crisis and in the aftermath of the massacre of students and dissidents.

However abortive, the events of 1989 are likely to mark the rise of Chinese society against the Communist state. The fissure within legitimacy is a permanent part of the Chinese landscape.[10] The Chinese people have a new sense of community, and no longer are they disenfranchised individuals dealing with an all-powerful state. This is precisely the subjective core of the weakening of legitimacy of the communist apparatus. Indeed, the events in Tiananmen Square call to mind Marx's famous opening lines on The Suppression of the June 1848 Revolution in France: "The Paris workers are crushed by superior force, they did not surrender. They are beaten, but their opponents are defeated. The momentary triumph of brute force is bought with the destruction of all illusions and images."[11] However such a transformation is slow and not likely to display East European characteristics of democratic revival. One has to reluctantly assume, as given in the postponed optimism of Winston Lord, that by "the end of the century, the Chinese may well enjoy a freer press, a more highly developed legal system and a more open political process than would have been the case without the dark phase now being endured."[12] This is so because the facade of legitimacy claimed by the heirs of the "the long march" has been impaired but not destroyed by the Tiananmen massacres. Internal mechanisms of repression persist, because support from the party elites and military cadres for the regime remain largely intact. And given the indifferent response to student appeals in the rural areas, no less than amongst the urban proletariat, it is fair, albeit painful, to say that the opposition elements exaggerated their base of support, and paid an extremely heavy price in human suffering and future political mobilization in this broad equation of Chinese and East European situations.

Without pushing parallels too far, it remains the case that the Castro regime in Cuba has increasingly distanced itself from events in Eastern Europe precisely on the grounds of legitimacy of the revolutionary regime; its sources and roots in mass participation and military populism. Fidel Castro and Carlos Rafael Rodríguez have repeatedly asserted that "authenticity" characterizes Cuba (as it did Russia and China earlier). And as result, "mistakes"—a euphemism for Stalinism—lead to corrections rather than corrosion of the national socialist Revolution of 1959.[13] The dangers within the Cuban situation is a willingness to sacrifice any number of people to an ideology deemed worthwhile precisely because it came about without direct Soviet communist participation. Hence, even in a period of contracting Soviet-Cuban relations the impulse to democratic change in Castro's world is thwarted, if not entirely stamped out.

I am not suggesting that the Soviet Union, China, or Cuba, are impervious to regime transformation.[14] Clearly, nothing could be further from the truth; a great deal of the impulse to the current stage of unrest and protest were made possible, if not artificially stimulated, by the Gorbachev and early Deng reforms. But the nature of those national systems must be reckoned quite differently from the small states of Eastern Europe precisely because legitimacy, or the consent of the governed, remain complicated by the quasi-legitimacy bestowed by their respective revolutionary and military origins. Thus, what is not true of Eastern Europe is still true of Russia, Cuba, and China: that their leadership has a basis, however tenuous, in legitimate authority, in this often passive consent of the governed. Only when military and police power is revealed as naked force can such legitimacy come under popular scrutiny. Indeed, the new parliamentary reforms in Russia and the far more modest political reforms in China giving increased power to regional heads and decentralization of authority generally, indicate an awareness within their leadership cadres of the unique opportunities no less than risks at this juncture for both communist super powers. The Cubans, for their part, have accepted Cambodianization as a last resort, a Pol Potist conversion of office workers into field hands, a solution to turmoil that is simply unthinkable in Eastern Europe or the Soviet Union even on an emergency basis.

We have already witnessed a serious transformation of Eastern bloc politics, a removal of most, if not all these nations from the political orbit of Soviet life. But there is a price to be paid. In exchange for internal democracy there is external neutrality; a certain amount of Finlandization, i.e., willingness of these nations to forego any sort of threatening or menacing role in foreign policy and military affairs directed at the U.S.S.R.. To be sure, this is partially disguised by the new liberalization tendencies of Soviet foreign policy itself. In domestic terms, there is a hiatus, a period in which old, unresolved problems of ethnic identity and national ambitions, compete with larger, less parochial goals of democratization and modernization. Within Soviet, Chinese and Cuban societies, Communist party rule will continue to be challenged, but with mixed results. The quasi-legitimacy of such communist systems can be overcome by largely parliamentary and judiciary networks. But these develop by fits and starts over time. And the force of arms instead of the force of law is a ready ally of totalitarian power.

IV

This is a unique moment within the history of twentieth century socialist and communist life; one that Western democracies can ill afford to miss. Every effort should be made to strengthen ties with reform elements in China and Russia, and even more, every opportunity seized to the present rulers in each of these master countries with real choices that would not threaten stability. For the process of displacing illegitimate with legitimate regimes in Eastern Europe is well underway; in certain cases, just about completed. The same process will take far different, longer, and more tortuous, complex forms in the great nations of Russia and China. It will take yet other forms in small nations like Cuba and North Korea. Cuban conditions are mitigated by a powerful exile community and blue-prints for a reincorporation of Cuba into a free market zone. North Korea has made a series of moves: from establishing limited ties with Japan, to integrating sports activities with South Korea. What we find is the resurgence of cultural factors, i.e., matters of language and religion for example, as possible sources for transforming regimes even when political legitimacy may have a firm and clear basis.

This speculative sketch of past events and present prospects in the Eastern bloc is not intended to replace careful study on a nation-by-nation basis. Nor would I wish to deny that each country has internal historical conditions that make their march to democracy tortuous, painful, uneven, and certainly unexpected. Beyond that, these remarks do not begin to address, much less resolve questions as to why these forces for basic change took place in 1989 and not in 1988 or 1990. It might well be that a certain "J-Curve" phenomenon was at work: 1989 being a period of moderate upswing in the economies of East Europe, but insufficient to meet the drum beat of much higher levels of expectations due to the diverging nature of Communist development between "material production" and "consumerism."

One can also speculate that what started out as a national reconsideration in the Soviet Union, quickly assumed global dimensions that were unforeseen even by the founding fathers of the New Thinking. Uncapping steam valves may lead to uncontrollable consequences. It is evident that in direct head-to-head economic competition, the Soviets fare poorly with respect to the Americans. But it is no less evident that the North Koreans fare poorly with respect to the South Koreans, the East Germans with respect to the West Germans; mainland China with respect to Taiwan. And in the larger scheme of things, systematic inadequacies of the East has led to a general feeling of relative deprivation throughout the Soviet empire, and in the Soviet Union as such. Even if one can make a case that conditions have improved within an Eastern European context, in comparative terms such changes have been slow in coming, costly in terms of taxation, and even more so in terms of personal deprivations.

The new Soviet thinking is largely driven by the new technology, not by classical liberalism. The mass media have served to highlight such polarities in the political economy; and the advances in everything from satellite television to computer work stations deprived the communist bloc of its previous insularity. In short, whatever measure one examines 1989, like 1789 in France, was neither the worst of times nor the best of times. Rather its very ordinariness pointed up the stagnation of the economy which along with the illegitimacy of the polity made the moment of change come together in far flung segments of the communist empire. Thus far, it is the inner sanctum of that empire that remains problematic.

Whatever the specific immediate factors that produced a combustible situation in so many nations at a single moment in time, the search for structural factors indicating commonalties is important, lest we view the revolutions of 1989 as sporadic, spontaneous or impervious to any deeper meaning. For beneath the intense rivalries between the Slavic and Romany, the Catholic and Orthodox forms of Christianity, agrarianism of Hungary and industrialism of Czechoslovakia, and a myriad of other factors that has made the term "Balkanization" synonymous over centuries with divisiveness and bald-faced competition, is a common thirst for freedom—even if it signifies the freedom to return to the old days of ethnic fratricide. As Walter Laqueur has recently reminded us, it would be a half-baked fantasy to assume that out of the rubble of communism will emerge pure, unadulterated western-style democracies.[15] The autocratic soil that nourished the current communist regimes is itself sufficient to prevent any ready-made solutions. But whatever emerges in Eastern Europe will, nay already has, restored a sense of regime authenticity, and hence the revival of political legitimacy, in the former empire of communism.

The recognition by policy analysts and politicians alike of the acute differences in historical antecedents, as measured by the illegitimate versus legitimate origins of each nation, and more adroitly, degrees of popular consent (past and present) involved in each of the nations now undergoing upheaval, will be a useful starting point in developing a proper retrospective on the events of 1989. But it bears repeating that historical longevity and political legitimacy are simply not the same. The efforts underway to distinguish legislative democracy from executive dictatorship is a deep structural recognition of this new condition through the world no less than in Eastern Europe. To ignore this most fundamental striving for democracy and against despotism is to be cast, along with the ex-Bolshevik vanguard, into its own widely heralded dust bin of history. In an intellectual nutshell, and certainly within the Eastern European context, Weber has persevered, while Marx has bitten the dust.

References/Notes

1. For a fuller discussion of my view of the interrelations between legitimacy and revolution, see Irving Louis Horowitz, *Foundations of Political Sociology* (New York and London: Harper & Row, 1972), pp.253-325; and for a somewhat more detailed consideration of those views, see my papers on "Political Legitimacy and the Institutionalization of Crisis," *Comparative Political Studies*. Vol.1, No.1, April 1968, pp.45-70; "The Norm of Illegitimacy," *Soundings: A Journal of Interdisciplinary Studies*. Volume 15,

No.1, Spring 1968; and "The Norm of Illegitimacy: Ten Years Later," in *Legitimization of Regimes*, edited by Bogdan Denitch (London and Beverly Hills: Sage Publishers, 1978), pp. 23-35.

2. Voytek, Zubek, "Poland's Party Self-Destructs," *Orbis: A Journal of World Affairs*. Vol.34, No.2 (Spring 1990), pp. 179-194.

3. Charles Gati, "East Central Europe: The Morning After," *Foreign Affairs*. Vol.69, No.5 (Winter 1990/91), pp.129-145.

4. David Childs, *The German Democratic Republic: Moscow's German Ally*. (Boston and London: Unwin & Hyman, 1988). For a brilliant journalistic study of the collapse of communist power in Germany, see Melvin J. Lasky, *Wortmeldung zu einer Revolution: Der Zusammenbruch de kommunistischen Herrschaft in Ostdeutschland*. Frankfurt and Berlin: Ullstein Sachbuch Verlag, 1990. 160pp.

5. Bogdan Nahaylo and Victor Swoboda, *Soviet Disunion: A History of the Nationalities Problem in the U.S.S.R.* (New York: The Free Press-Macmillan, 1990); and Lubomyr Hajda and Mark Beissinger, *The Nationalities Factor in Soviet Politics and Society* (Boulder, Westview Press, 1990).

6. Václav Havel, "New Year's Address," *Orbis: A Journal of World Affairs*. Vol.34, No.2 (Spring 1990), pp.253-261; and Alexander Kramer, "The New Czechoslovak Foreign Policy," *Uncaptive Minds: A Journal of Information and Opinion on Eastern Europe*. Vol.3, No.4 (Aug-Oct 1990), pp.31-33.

7. Harold Lydall, *Yugoslavia in Crisis* (New York and London: Oxford University Press, 1989).

8. Daniel Nelson, *Rumanian Politics in the Ceausescu Era* (New York: Gordon & Breach, 1988); and for a more recent and comprehensive picture, see Trond Gilberg, *Nationalism and Communism in Romania: The Rise and Fall of Ceausescu's Personal Dictatorship* (Boulder, Westview, 1990).

9. Among the most important works on the new situation in the Soviet world, one must single out Jacques Baynac, *The Gorbachev Revolution* (London: Oxford University Press, 1989); Jeffrey C. Goldfarb, *Beyond Glasnost: The Post-Totalitarian Mind* (Chicago: University of Chicago Press, 1989); Ilya Zemtsov and John Farrar, *Gorbachev: The Man and the System* (New Brunswick and London: Transaction Publishers, 1988); and the fine compendium edited by Jiri Valenta and Frank Cibulka, *Gorbachev's New Thinking and Third World Conflicts* (New Brunswick and London: Transaction Publishers 1990).

10. Ezra F. Vogel, *One Step Ahead in China: Guangdong Under Reform* (Cambridge: Harvard University Press, 1989); and for a useful starting point in understanding recent China events see the volume edited for the China Council of the Asia Society, by Anthony J. Kane, *China Briefing: 1990* (Boulder: Westview Press, 1990).

11. Karl Marx, *The Class Struggles in France* (The Karl Marx Library, On Revolution) edited by Saul K. Padover (New York: McGraw-Hill Book Company, 1971). pp. 154-242.

12. Winston Lord, "China and America Beyond the Big Chill," *Foreign Affairs*. Vol.68, No.4 (Fall, 1989), pp.1-27.

13. The series of reports filed by Howard W. French from Cuba indicate how dramatic the shift has been from building socialism to maintaining legitimacy. See: "Cuba, Hurt by Falling Soviet Imports, Makes Field Hands of Office Workers"; "Officials in Cuba Seem to Be on the Defensive." *The New York Times* (December 1-2, 1990), pp.3, 25.

14. While this article does not focus on Cuba, my appreciation of the practical implications of legitimacy derives from that country's experience. See Irving Louis Horowitz, "Cuba's Insular Revolution," Hemisphere: Latin American and Caribbean Affairs. Vol.2, No.3 (Summer, 1990), pp.22-26.

15. Walter Laqueur, *The Long Road to Freedom: Russia and Glasnost* (New York: Scribners-Macmillan, 1989); for a quite different appraisal, Zbigniew Brzezinski, *The Grand Failure: The Birth and Death of Communism in the Twentieth Century* (New York: Scribners-Macmillan, 1989).

Source and Original Title: This paper was delivered at the Conference on "Revolutionary Change in the U.S.S.R. and Eastern Europe: Its Impact on Orthodox Communist Regimes" held in Prague, between December 3rd-7th, 1990. The meeting was co-sponsored by the Institute of International Relations of the Czechoslovak Ministry of Foreign Affairs and the Graduate School of International Studies of the University of Miami.

Printed in: "Revolution and Counter-Revolution in 1989: Longevity and Legitimacy in Communist States." *Culture and Politics in China: An Anatomy of Tiananmen Square* (edited by Peter Li, Steven Mark and Marjorie Li). New Brunswick and London: Transaction Publishers, 1991, pp. 285-298.

* This paper was written and accepted for publication in the wake of events following the collapse of communist power in most states of Eastern Europe during 1989. It does not cover the events which led to the collapse of communist power in the Soviet Union during 1991.

19

The Dictator Who Would Be King

Thirty-two years after the seizure of State power in Cuba by Fidel Castro and his July 26th Movement, the same regime reigns. Tyrannies and their tyrants throughout the former communist empire have toppled at amazing rates. Indeed, it is an accepted canon that 1989 was as much a watershed year as 1789 in the liberation of humanity from the yoke of inherited oppressive regimes. But neither 1989 nor 1990 saw Cuba swept up in such a tide. Prophesies to the contrary notwithstanding; the iron grip of Castro remains the central fact of life for the Cuban people. Longevity is almost as fascinating a topic in political rule as legitimacy—and Castro repeatedly lays claim to both.

Even those regnant Stalinist regimes that survived the wave of popular rebellion that overthrew communism in Eastern Europe, and liberalized the Soviet regime at the heart of the empire have undergone substantial changes: Albania now has a two-party system and the start of popular rule; North Korea is involved in a slow series of moves that will lead to reintegration with South Korea; and even places like Cambodia and Vietnam show definite signs of political or at least diplomatic liberalization. But Castro remains more adamant than ever that he will not yield power, nor modify his direction. Thus it is that the last hurrah of Marxism-Leninism is in Havana not Moscow.

Such single-minded determination has a fascination whatever be the doctrinal vision. Fanaticism and fanatics have always been the source of good biography; and Fidel Castro is no exception. Single-minded determination, obstinacy, identification of his person with world history and ability to survive adversity; each of these are elements Castro shares with dictators who came before him. But it is the singular merit of Georgie Anne Geyer's *Guerrilla Prince: The Untold Story of Fidel Castro* that her work specifies not only the psychological characteristics of Castro, but links these to events and people who have made him a central player in hemispheric history of the twentieth century.

The books by Roberto Luque Escalona, *Fidel: El juicio de la historia*, and by Jacobo Timerman, *Cuba: A Journey*, while less substantial in coverage and range, each provide special angles of vision. Escalona, a self-described "man, and only a man," who seeks to confirm his machismo credentials by dedicating his book to the American heavyweight prize-fighter, Jersey Joe Walcott, was in fact born in 1936, trained in Law at the University of Havana, went to Mexico in 1958 to provide a support base for the Castro July 26th movement, pursued further studies at the National University of Mexico, and returned to Havana in 1961. His disillusionment with the regime began with Castro's supine support for the Soviet invasion of Czechoslovakia. By 1972 he ceased any positive involvement with the regime, becoming a copyeditor of the journal *Economía y Desarrollo* (Economy and Development).

Timerman, for his part, is one of the most famous figures in Argentine politics. He was editor of the Argentine newspaper *La Opinión*. He was incarcerated by the military authorities, where he remained a prisoner without a name in a cell without a number, between the years 1977-1979. In addition to his book on Cuba, he has written savage critiques of the Begin regime, *The Longest War: Israel in Lebanon*; and the Pinochet regime, *Chile: Death in the South*. Like Luque Escalona, Timerman makes much of his radical pedigree. Indeed, he holds such a commitment to the socialist Left as a moral center of gravity, from which all analysis must begin and end. It comes as little surprise, and gives nothing away, that such earnest, if ill-defined persuasions seriously weaken the impact of his work.

I find it fascinating that each of these three books, arguably the most important texts to emerge in recent years on Cuban Communism are written by people with strong journalistic roots. Timerman is a lifelong journalist, founding news magazines, serving as radio commentator, as well as editor of a key newspaper; Luque worked at Prensa Latina for two years after his return from diplomatic services; and Georgie Anne Geyer writes a thrice weekly column appearing in over one hundred newspapers. These three then are ethnographers of the common people—newspaper folks.

It must be recorded bluntly that the social scientists and policy analysts, especially those from "advanced nations," have provided little guidance to events, and much pettifogging. Even now, those researchers who once trumpeted Castro's revolution with a human face have fallen into stony, inhuman silence. The great advocates of "self-criticism" (for others of course) have managed hardly a peep—some simply turned their attention to the American Empire directly, others to places like Nicaragua and El Salvador. The best of them have at least had the decency to turn to other pursuits. There are those precious few who remain Castro loyalists, enthralled by the very presence of the masterbuilder. But these books are written in the spirit of reaching those with open minds, rather than offer hope for the hopeless.

Georgie Anne Geyer's book is written in the breathless style of a French chronique scandaleuse. And while most political figures do not easily fit the bill, in Fidel, she has a perfect foil. For behind the sociological rhetoric of exploring a "charismatic figure" is a psychological portrait of a figure who plainly does not want to be considered as a lover or a lout. Perhaps the cleverest of all ploys, Ms. Geyer's best decision, is to bring Fidel down to life size. By subjecting him to the vagaries of bad marriages, illegal children, and failed romances, Geyer does indeed show us "Fidel as a man and not just a myth." And if at times, there is a one-sided distortion in this examination, it does at least serve to redress the deadly dull exercise of taking Fidel at face value as the Bolivar of our times.

Guerrilla Prince is cleverly divided into two parts: part one is entitled "Fidel," and part two "Castro." It is the first part that will assuredly carry the freight for the sophisticated reader. For it is here that the pre-1959 period is fully explored in ways largely hidden from view by the mature ruler of Cuba. The vignettes about Fidel in New York buying a Lincoln Continental, and in Bogotá seeing first hand the assassination of Jorge Eliécer Gaitán and drawing lessons about the power of insurrectionary uprisings, walking about Havana with his copy of Hitler's *Mein Kampf*—all of this adds to a portrait of a young man as a budding old dictator.

And through it all, there is Fidel living on the edge of personal danger and risk—of women parading forth in his life (as they still do according to all reports) providing him with a sense of importance and validating his masculinity. There is something of a woman's insight in Ms. Geyer's book. I am not sure that a male author would so self-consciously tie in Fidel's sexual adventures and misadventures with his disregard for marital vows and parental responsibilities. The tone in such passages is engagingly disapproving, but if Fidel were in fact some sort of Puritan straight laced divine (or Russian variant of some such as Lenin) would the outcomes have been different? Ms. Geyer leaves us with a moot point. What we are left with is a sense of personal style Fidel offers when he becomes Castro, but not quite the smooth transition from guerrilla to ruler promised by the title.

Still, we do learn the extent to which contemporary dictator ships are fueled by personality cults. Living in a world where no one dares to say no, we have the portrait of a dictator whose ideology disguises every sort of excess, and enters into every area of public and private life—from theology to agronomy. And hence, the comparisons of Fidel with Mussolini, Hitler, Stalin, and in my view most tellingly, Francisco Franco, give us the sort of first hand view of Castro that friends and foes alike have thus far failed to bring forth: for the superman diminishes to life size no-where more rapidly than when confronted with the problems of ordinary mortals: friendship, love, betrayal, loyalty, and the myriad of human frailties that unbridled leaders seek to disguise whether they belong to the communist left or to the fascist right. Fidel can handle ideological disputation with impunity; but Ms.

Geyer's portrait of the dictator as a young man is likely to irritate him and undermine his authority in ways beyond the realm of the comfortably political.

And yet, there is a troubling aspect to this sort of Hollywood (trade publishing redux) treatment of Castro. The broad implication of an arrogant, awkward, explorative young man growing impatient with ordinary politics and hence moving to a grandiose, mostly illegal vision of guerrilla insurgency is accurate. However it does not allow for the fact that the strategies and tactics adopted were well suited to a regime, such as Batista's, ripe for insurrection, and unwilling to respond to modernizing norms. The personality of Castro, however important in the post revolutionary phase, is not necessarily a piece of evidence that political outcomes were especially determined by personality factors.

I rather suspect that the problem with Castro is better revealed in Robert Dahl's phrase: "After the Revolution, What" than Max Weber's oft-repeated, but little understood notion of charisma. Ms. Geyer forgets that many of the people whom she interviewed for this book were part and parcel of the Cuban revolution of 1959. The breaks with the regime that happened along the way had to do with public issues like economic systems and foreign policies, rather than private excesses like philandering and fornicating. The logic of dictatorship is to inexorably move toward heightening rather than curbing those features in all of us that prefer unquestioned obedience to consensus building and personalities adjusting to each other in the give and take of daily politics. Give absolute power to a saint and we have the Inquisition; give the same amount of power to a sinner and we have Committees for the Defense of the Revolution. In this context, we have six of one, and half dozen of another in the study of modern dictatorships.

Having said this, it is important to note Ms. Geyer's major breakthrough. This is an unauthorized biography. It is not controlled by Fidel, does not rest on his approbation, was not screwed up by late night "interviews" patently intended to give disinformation—as was the case with Tad Szulc and his tortured discussion of whether or when Fidel became a communist. As a result, it gives the reader a picture that is rounded precisely because it does not have the seal of approval of the dictator.

Characteristic of great dictators is their desire to control not only present worlds but future interpretations of their roles. Authorized biographies of Stalin reached the point where, in fact, no one could be entrusted with this task—so that biography became autobiography. Fidel in his endless series of interviews seeks to provide just such a self-portrait that would render him a unique authoritative source. Writing an unauthorized biography clearly was a complex decision for Ms. Geyer, who as a journalist doubtless would have preferred interview materials to surrounding the character Fidel with anecdotes and associates. But I think she made the wise decision, one that adds immeasurably to the authenticity of her book. After all, Barbara Walters' interviews with Fidel gave the dictator a forum more than it gave the viewer knowledge.

There is so much written on totalitarianism and so little written on the totalitarians who fuel the system, that this must be ranked a welcome book. For in its blunt appraisal of the man, we get a portrait of Castro as part of a network of cult figures of the twentieth century who have in common despotic rule far more than ideological consistency. As a result, the great chain of dictatorial beings—from Lenin and Stalin through Hitler and Mussolini—is established without ambiguity as a governing force in Castro's life. Most devastating of all is the portrait at the start and finish of the book linking Castro to Franco —as a mutual admiration society. Geyer notes that Franco greatly admired Castro's anti-Americanism, and Castro in turn declared a week of mourning upon the death of the Spanish dictator. One must wonder what the surviving members of the Abraham Lincoln Brigade who fought for the maintenance of the Spanish Republic, and even those younger generations of American who formed the backbone of the Venceremos Brigade, who fought for the maintenance of Castro, would think or could think upon learning that their personal hero was cut from such an alien neo-fascist cloth!

Only on the very last page of *Guerrilla Prince* do we learn the secret of the title and the section heads of the Geyer book. It is so well said that the author deserves this final moment with her readers: "In the beginning, the Cuban people had called him 'Fidel' in adoration, in salvation, in love, like a Spanish woman with her husband before marriage. After the magnificence of the Triunfo, they immediately began calling him 'Castro' in sobriety, in respect, in fear. In the end, they called him only 'El' or 'He'. For he had become finally not one of them but a differentiated creature away from them—that sun so hot that it burned to come close."

Alas, the two paragraphs which follow, concerning Fidel finally turning out to be a communist, the last Communist, has an anti-climactic ring—for the book reveals that labels like communism and fascism disguise rather than clarify the tragedy of our political times—the tendency of those who rule to frustrate and ultimately betray the source of their authority—the people. Still, problems of conceptual mapping aside, Georgie Anne Geyer has given us a fine book, a must book for those concerned with the fate of western politics, and no less the special character of an anti-western dictator with the staying power of a Franco and the vision of a Torquemada. She has made crystal clear how the "legacy" of Spain more than the "ideology" of Russia helps us to explain the soul and substance of Fidel Castro.

Jacobo Timerman's *Cuba* is best viewed as a sight-seeing foot note to Geyer's work. It is an extended essay—part polemic and part narrative. Despite its self-serving and rather superficial treatment, and no less, Timerman's continued animus toward the "United States aggression," this does offer glimpses into Castro's Cuba at this point in time that have a special cachet given the author's steady drumbeat of Left radical identification. "A man of the left, a socialist." Indeed, Timerman's self-elevation as a counterweight to the "rightist views" of Armando Valladares (an unpardonable slander against the man who exposed Cuba's prison system) is a conceit, but for those who can only hear or trust such a voice, this can be a useful book.

One must wade through piles of Timerman's rhetoric: his life long identification with revolution, his clashes with the American anti-Castro forces, his debates with the Cuban organizers of his trip. He has one foot in the life of the political pilgrim, but the other is firmly planted in a European sensibility filtered through Argentine life—not a bad combination for those trying to examine El Comandante. Finally, in the midst of this extended essay (on page 45) we get the core of Timerman's concerns: "Cuba's problem goes deeper than the deterioration of world economic conditions or the fact that Cuba is in the Caribbean and not on the Black Sea. The problem continues to be the limitations imposed by the impenetrable glass dome on Cubans' lives, their energies, and their innermost human nature."

But instead of following this sensitive appreciation with some tough analysis, the monograph veers into a study of cultural and literary clashes that curiously reflect Timerman's peculiar literary concerns. It is Gabriel Garcia Marquez and the ghost of Ernest Hemingway who seem to attract most of his energies. The colossal ego of a minor political actor (Timerman) becomes so overwhelming that the analysis of the colossal ego of a major political actor (Castro) simply gets lost in the process. Timerman even envisions Castro being wounded by his not setting up an interview. One paragraph begins with "I pause in my reading...", followed by another which begins "I ask Barnet...", then a third with "I have encountered..." and a fourth with "I visited a friend...", and finally "my meeting with the writers" (all this in the space of two pages (58 and 59)).

Little wonder that the shock of Cuba not realizing its development goals is played in low key by Timerman, while the screeching sounds are reserved for "CIA marionettes." It is the case that "no one believes it is possible for Cuba, via the armed forces and its security organs, to be a distributor of Colombian drugs without the Castro brothers' participation in the operation," but this counts for little compared to "the scant credibility of the United States government in its accusations against Cuba—often verging, no doubt on paranoia or on state terrorist tactics"—the evidence for which is a 1988 report on Time of Choice published by the Aspen Institute for Humanistic Studies—not exactly a Cold Warrior Center by any stretch of the imagination.

As a result, the sort of even-handedness in which dictators and democrats are made short shrift of—while left socialists like

Timerman parade his virtues—ends in a quagmire What he terms the "Jewish element" in journalism—irony and skepticism, leads to ambiguity and confusion. All that is left is the purity of Timerman—not quite enough to merit a protracted reading about his journey to Cuba. Without benefit of absolute moral fervor, as in his earlier essays, Timerman is simply a man revealed to be at loose ends. Castro will do that to critics. He makes the world of socialism uninhabitable for Western apologists; but he also convinces them that there are no democratic options.

When one turns to Roberto Luque Escalona's remarkable essay on *Fidel: The Judgment of History* one can see that the "glass dome" called Cuba is not quite as impenetrable as Timerman makes it out to be. There is after all a human rights movement on the island, there are disaffected students singing critical hymns, there are defectors from the armed forces, there are gentle forms of subversion of the forced conversion of city dwellers into rural moles. And there are the Marielitas—more than one million people who have made Cuban American an honorable as well as powerful conjunction.

Still living in Cuba, Luque also appreciates the gap between the process of revolution and the structure of a society. His historical narrative on the Machado dictatorship, the Batista years, and pre-rule years of Fidel and Che cover familiar territory; but do so in a lively way. He understands the naiveté and the limits of United States power at the time of Eisenhower and Kennedy—their preoccupation with other, mainly domestic, problems. Luque sees policy confusions rather than economic tentacles of the North Americans as responsible for many of Fidel's successes. Fidel was sagacious enough to understand this, precisely while employing the rhetoric of anti-colonialism.

Roberto Luque Escalona is no Carlos Alberto Montaner; still he has a similarly close reading of Castro characteristics. Like Geyer, Luque also emphasizes the "Gallego" or Spanish origins of Castro's name and person—but sees him as a "perverse Norman baron" or even a Robin Hood figure. He goes on to make the comparison with Melville's *Moby Dick*—the struggle of the heroic man and his obsession with the mystical whale. This is also the theme of other recent essays on Castro. Why should literary metaphor rather than political analysis seem to prevail? In part, the answer is the very longevity in office of Castro. The reduction of power to family, gives him a special dynastic place in the sun that is easier for students of Elizabethan plays to manage than postmodern policymakers to predict.

Luque basically argues that Cuba needs a period of reconciliation, to realize its potentials within some sort of mixture that the Cubans themselves create. And while he ferociously defends the honor of the exiles, this is not followed by any sense that they can or should play a role in the post-Castro epoch. He sees this as the unique task of those who endure, those who remain.

He asks rhetorically, if the United States and the Soviet Union can reconcile differences at fundamental levels, why should this not also be possible with Cuba? But Fidel (and for Luque it is always Fidel—past and present) is not the man for this role. Castro's megalomania, his preoccupation with world historic roles, prevents the sort of mosaic, a combination of colors that can lead Cuba into a future that does not require shedding blood or presuming missions.

Luque Escalona writes as he lives: a survivor in perilous waters. The silent grace of the tiger at home rather than the loud roar of the lion in exile guide his commentary. But that such writing is even possible from the belly of the whale is an encouragement that we need now; just as surely as we needed the searing prison memoirs of Armando Valladares, Against All Hope, in the last decade.

Whatever the strengths and weaknesses of these three books, they have in common an anti-official stance. These are not works written to please the standing dictator, but to inform the public. Beyond that, each passes judgment on Fidel. The verdict is clear: he is a colossal failure as a leader, but far worse, an enormous tragedy for the Cuban people.

Sources and Original Titles: Guerrilla Prince (Georgie Anne Geyer); *Fidel* (Roberto Luque Escalona); *Cuba* (Jacobo Timerman). Review essay in *The American Spectator,* Vol. 24, No. 6, June 1991, pp. 35-36.

20

New Beginnings and Familiar Endings

Until now, I have been extremely reticent to forecast the downfall of the Castro regime in Cuba. Indeed, I may well have saddened those friends who felt that such caution is a function of defeatism rather than serious analysis. Yet, even at this point in time, the dictator remains enthroned. My purpose is not to gloat over a correct prediction. Indeed, I profess to preferring error to accuracy in such prognosis. It would have been easier on the Cuban people had Castro expired on the day of the glorious thirtieth anniversary celebrations. But that blessed event did not happen, for reasons explained often and elsewhere.

Nonetheless, I now believe that the end is very much in sight. The survival of the current regime beyond 1992 is hardly likely—possible but unlikely. There is only a remote chance that the end can come elegantly in a mass movement of people as in the nations of Eastern Europe. The human resources needed for such an effort are scattered throughout this hemisphere and in Western Europe. A more likely scenario will be a death of the regime through exhaustion at the top, or even through the natural history of an aging leadership.

In a curious sense, this constant chatter about the end of Castro already presages the collapse of vitality of the old regime. The omnipresent risk of all dictatorships is that they invite speculation of downfall. The longer a regime is in power, unchecked by countervailing elements, the more arbitrary and capricious the character of its rule. At the same time, the broader will be discourses on how and when a regime will be transformed. In the process of such discourse, the energy of the regime is sapped, turned inward to the tasks of sheer personal survival, and away from chances at objective growth. The utter stagnation of the Cuban economic infrastructure attests to the truth of such political wisdom.

When the end of the Castro era does come it probably will be as if this 33-year period was like a dream, far more in relief than in celebration. At that point too, serious reflection will begin—for North Americans no less than Cubans. For how could it be that a proud, advanced and democratic people could be goaded into a despotic system—and with the active support of good people and true patriots? Perhaps one inhibiting element in the change-over from the Castro to a post-Castro regime will be the flood of self-reflections such new conditions will unleash.

Rather than continue in this abstract, perhaps even distracting manner, let me indicate five basic elements that exist within Cuban society that add up to a terminal political cancer for Castro. For it is these reasons that determine the inevitability of the end, even if, as in most forms of cancer, we cannot predict to a day the final denouement of Castro's Communism.

My first reason for claiming that the end is clearly in sight is the growth of humor about the regime. There is an old adage in American politics, whose origins I confess not to know, (although I suspect that it might be George Washington Plunkitt of Tammany Hall fame or Mayor Daley of Chicago), that when people start laughing at a politician, he is done for. This was certainly the case during the Army-McCarthy hearings. For when the jokes about the late, unlamented Senator became public knowledge, the sense of fear and fright that Joseph McCarthy conveyed, gave way to demands for his impeachment. Two of the many *chistes* making the rounds in Cuba illustrate the point nicely:

Fidel was delivering a speech to over one million people in Revolution Square when suddenly there was thunderous lightning. From behind a cloud appeared a resplendent beam of light. On it was Jesus Christ, slowly descending from Heaven. He approached the podium and whispered something into Fidel's ear. Fidel addressed the crowd on the microphone: "El compañero Jesus Christ wishes to make a suggestion to you." So Jesus Christ clutched the microphone and said: "People of Cuba! Does this man not have a beard like my own and did he not give the people the bread of knowledge like I did?" And the people responded: "Siiiiii!" After a pause, Jesus asked: "Is it not true that as I multiplied the breads and the fishes so that everyone could eat, this man invented the ration card so that all could eat alike?":—"Siiiiii!" "Has he not built hospitals and polyclinics for the sick like I healed them? And was he not betrayed by del Pino as I was by Judas"?:—"Siiiiii!" Looking sternly into the eyes of those before Him, Jesus asked: "Then what are you waiting for? Crucify him!"

The theme of death and crucifixion is too prevalent in Cuban street humor to be dismissed. It may not be mass struggle, but massive humor is no small factor in the life of the nation at this point. Here is a second illustration: "Two Cubans are talking and one asks the other: 'Listen, if you were to be crucified, under which system would you prefer it to happen—socialism or capitalism?' Without even giving it a second thought, the man replied: 'Chico, under socialism of course!' Astonished at the answer, the first one asks him why. 'It is very simple my friend. When they have the nails, they will not have the wood; when they have wood, they will not have a hammer, and when they have the nails, the wood and the hammer, then they will not have a permit to crucify me!'" This is not the first time around for such commentary, but the shoe still fits and the political barbs continue.

That both *chistes* have to do with death, Christ and crucifixion, well illustrates a point with which Luis Aguilar concludes his introduction to his slender but entirely worthy volume on Political Humor in Cuba: "Humor is a serious affair." And so it is. For the same political humor may be recycled from generation to generation, even nation to nation, But the object is always the same—a hatred for the despot and an early warning indicator that the end is in sight.

Such elements as humor and regime bashing are cultural reflections of what is taking place at the base of Cuban society. Here we come to the essential point of the present moment—the shift from political to economic struggles and antipathies. The hatred of a regime for its lack of democracy is a pleasant intellectual, but often middle class based vocation. However, the despondency over a breakdown of economic viability cuts through all sectors of Cuban society. As Lisandro Pérez reports after his trip to Havana in May of 1991, to be intellectually aware of a nation in dire straits is one thing, to see this collapse in person is quite another. "To see the bus stops packed with weary people, waiting interminably in the rain for infrequent buses that are also packed. To see the constant and slow-moving queues, at any time, in front of any place that serves food. To see the crumbling and buttressed buildings, the broken-down automobiles, the hassles and frustrations of daily life. It is a chilling experience to be in a country in which the entire material structure is literally falling apart." This is the cement of what remains the quiet opposition.

In this regard the Cambodianization of Cuba has now taken place, albeit not with the same intense levels of physical torture and genocide. For whatever else the Khmer Rouge represents, it did provide for the leveling of the society. This has been achieved in the new Cuba with disastrous consequences. In a recent report, one young employee at a Havana food processing plant, Jorge Luis Torres, who recently arrived in Miami put matters rightly: "Our (Cuba's) system is not something with a future. I made 350 pesos a month. That is not bad compared to some. But even if you work five years, you have nothing to show for it. A simple pair of pants, if you can find them, costs 50 pesos." The wage differentials that do exist, and that have been accentuated by Castro as a mechanism to stimulate work output have come to nothing. For whatever one earns, the fact that it can buy little of value serves to "level" the society, but at the expense of any sort of effort at high output and certainly at the risk of any sort of innovation. And in the world of an absolute per capita decline, questions of wage differential lose empirical meaning.

Given such a situation, Castro is faced with the choice of doing nothing to exacerbate the present mood of hopelessness and despair, or step up levels of repression to such an extent that coercion alone permits the preconditions of economic stability that cannot be accomplished by any positive incentives. Of course, that is the ultimate step of a hard Stalinism—a step that Castro is either unwilling or unable to undertake, more because of an inability to carry this out without massive turmoil than any moral scruples about the consequences it might have for ordinary people. In a revealing aside, a recent Associated Press report on the new waves of immigrants leaving Cuba for Florida in rafts, is most revealing. It seems that the Cuban Coast Guard is fully aware of such movements, but has chosen to do nothing to prevent such rafts from departing Cuban territorial waters. And this is hardly a military without the capacity to exercise force if called upon to do so. One suspects an erosion of will rather than the establishment of a benign policy to the new Marielitas.

Before leaving this second point of decomposition in the Cuban economy, one must take into account that in his efforts to raise hard currency, Fidel has had to do everything from expand the base of overseas tourism, to brokering the sale of expensive family jewelry in exchange for worthless vouchers in an effort to obtain hard currency. The results have been desultory. For example, as Carmelo Mesa-Lago pointed out: after a decade of effort, tourism is less than one half of one per cent of the total Cuban G.N.P. Such efforts have in fact only further emphasized the gap between Cuban nationals and foreigners. Special stores, diplomercados, that Robert Cox witnessed, are stocked with goods that can only be purchased by foreigners with hard currency, stand in marked contrast to supermercados aimed at ordinary people with little, sometimes nothing, to sell for the national money. Indeed, another recent visitor to Cuba, María Dolores Espino, reports that "for all practical purposes the dollar has become the only currency of value that circulates in Cuba. And it circulates freely. The dollar buys anything and everything; with pesos, there is nothing to be had." The search by Castro for hard currency to pay the national debt, while maintaining the last pure communist regime, has led to what Ms. Espino properly terms "a system of economic apartheid, separating foreigners from natives, or rather those with access to dollars from those who do not."

Castro is therefore faced with an impossible anomaly: if he argues the case for a pure communism, leveling tendencies will not only be supported but insisted upon. Yet every effort to garner hard cash to pay for much needed supplies from Soviet petrol to Canadian and Swiss pharmaceuticals more in a contrary direction. The capitalist sector, in which differentiating tendencies tend to multiply, are thus encouraged. With either option, Fidel is faced with a death notice to his regime—one which he can delay, even make more benign or repressive. What he cannot do is overcome the logic of his cancerous system.

The weakening of the Soviet support system has dramatically changed the Cuban equation. It is hardly a secret that the Soviets reduced its technical and specialized personnel by more than 50 per cent in 1990 with a further reduction in 1991. While trade remains at relatively high levels between the two nations, these are increasingly in line with world standards of goods, transport, and services. In addition, firm to firm rather than state to state mechanisms are now the norm; further weakening any sense of a special relationship between Cuba and the USSR.

The growing demand for repayment of the massive Cuban debt to the USSR in hard currencies does little to ease Castro's situation. The virtual collapse of trade with the smaller Eastern European nations only exacerbates an already difficult situation. The Soviet Union cannot go before the world community and ask for massive aid—from the IMF, the EEC, or highly industrialized nations like the United States and Japan—and then turn around and support Castro's Cuba with such funds. To be sure, the price of such economic assistance from the West to the Soviets will surely include commitments to lessen if not terminate support of dictatorial regimes in remote places. And from American and Soviet positions alike, Cuba is just such a remote place.

In this situation of growing economic isolation for the Castro regime, Cuba faces a deepening antagonism within its own population. If indeed Castro is willing to maintain his communist regime—"even if 98 percent of the Cuban people did not believe in it"—he must also be compelled to institutionalize repressive machinery beyond what the Cuban population has experienced in the past. The problem is the absence of machinery beyond the terrorist capacities of the CDRs, to implement such increased repression.

The armed forces remain in a state of a paralysis since the execution of General Ochoa and several of his associates on drug charges. In addition, defections like those of General Del Pino, only serve to further isolate the regime from its armed forces. It might well be that the military will remain quiescent during this period, but they hardly are a force for the repression of the populace. The resolution of the Angolan struggles without Cuban inputs into the final settlement has made such military adventures harder to sell to the armed forces. The elements in Cuban society that Castro can call upon in a time of dire emergency are now reduced to his personal security forces and elements of the CDRs. This only intensifies a sense of regime instability.

The experiments that have been conducted in the Cambodianization Process have largely failed. Citizens of Havana have viewed the period in the countryside as vacation time, and then some. Further, the process of such artificial mobilization is costly in economic terms and disruptive in social terms. The continuing round of shortages and rationing further inhibit the ability of the regime to provide a workable reward system to compensate for demands for increased sacrifice. Thus, neither repression nor reward offers the prospect of much improvement in the Cuban economy.

In such circumstances, the continuing ability of the Castro governance to endure is more a function of divided anti-regime efforts than any positive initiatives the system can generate. The émigré community remains sharply divided in its aims and policies. The fact that the Cuban middle classes are in Miami rather than Havana prevents economic or political opposition from crystallizing. Cuban exiles in Río Piedras, Paris, and Madrid have sharply different visions for a post-Castro Cuba than the exiles in Miami. Indeed, one might argue that even the gap between the Washington-based and Miami-based exiles remains noticeable; indeed has considerably sharpened in recent years.

Under such circumstances, the population of Cuba can have no point of union in opposition. It has become increasingly apparent that key sectors of the Cuban population, such as the young people, are becoming anti-political rather than anti-communist. Cynicism rather than activism becomes the mode of the day. And as Mark Falcoff has well understood, that sort of cynicism, permits the regime to continue, despite its obvious dysfunctionality to friend and foe alike.

Pamela Falk has outlined four possible forms of change: a popular uprising (impossible given the state of security); a military coup (unlikely but it could happen); Castro goes down with a sinking economic ship in a quiet manner (also unlikely); and Castro attempts to create a transitional government, in which he turns over formal reigns of political power to a neophyte but holds on to his domination as commander in chief. Hopefully, I have been fair to Ms. Falk's scenarios. She does not entertain scenarios that some have put forth in recent years: assassination of the maximum leader and his cohort; or for that matter, a renewed invasion attempt. Certainly, while unlikely, either scenario could take place. Such a development in turn would trigger the sort of wild search for new options everyone sees now as unlikely or improbable.

As I have said in other contexts, but want to now reiterate: the very fact that discussions are taking place about regime dissolution in Havana indicates its material bankruptcy. This extraordinary odyssey of the Castro regime in Cuba will soon end. One hopes that the restoration of Cuba to the community of nations will be both democratic in politics and free in economics. The next Cuban revolution is waiting to happen. It deserves repetition to note that the processes which Cuba is undergoing are no longer conjectural. It is not whether but when the end of the tyranny will come about, how it will take place, who will emerge as the new leaders, and what will be the consequences for the future of Cuba and its beleaguered people.

Since I started with a little bit of black humor from Cuba perhaps it is appropriate to end with a few tidbits of black humor from North America. In the first eleven days of June 1991, we have the spectacle of *The New York Times* running three pieces that call for diplomatic initiatives aimed at, or at least resulting in, support for the Castro regime. This is taking place in a context of continuing Castro support for the worst tyrants remaining in world affairs. From Manuel Noriega, formerly of Panama, to Saddam Hussein still of Iraq, the Cuban delegation to the United Nations provided succor for the dictators. All of this took place in a context of an emotive anti-Americanism lacking in any sort of objective meaning. But there is a variety of American political pilgrim who remains impervious to real world events.

The first is by Mark Feierstein, in which the author, described as "a specialist in Latin American politics," calls for a major league baseball franchise for Havana. In this scenario, George Bush visits the Havana dugout, Joe Garagiola is in the NBC broadcast booth, and Fidel Castro throws out the first ball. Clearly, Mr. Feierstein is not a specialist in the serious business of acquiring sport franchises. The second is by Jerome Rubin, a senior executive of the Times-Mirror Corporation, who traveled with a group of political pilgrims to Havana representing the Association of American Publishers, exploring publishing prospects in present day Cuba. Our intrepid publishers would, while offering a bland show of solidarity with human rights figures (unnamed) on the island, managed to remain completely silent as to the nature of the Castro regime. A third item is by Rebecca J. Scott of the history department at the University of Michigan, who assures us that in the absence of a contrite spirit and historic guilt for what North Americans did in Cuba between 1898 and 1902 (the inauguration of the first Cuban president) we should not expect anyone to take criticism of Castro seriously, nor should Americans dare adopt a negative posture toward him.

After reviewing these three pieces of contaminated iron-ore, I took great hope. For it was just such strange and desperate urgings from the fringes of American intellectual life that presaged the end of totalitarianism in Eastern Europe, and the removal from power of the Sandinistas in Nicaragua. In short, friends of democracy need not despair. The mindless rush to save a dying regime from the sheltered groves of academe is already well underway. As a result we can surely predict that the end of the tyrant of Havana is clearly in sight.

Source and Original Title: "Waiting for the End / Wondering about New Beginnings: Fidel Castro's Death and Transfiguration." Lecture presented at the North-South Center Conference on United States Latin-American Relations in the 1990s. June 13-15, 1991 at the Hotel Intercontinental, Miami, Florida. Sponsored by the North-South Center of the University of Miami.

21

Totalitarian Options in a Post-Communist World

The euphoria over the collapse of the communist regime in the Soviet Union is so great and widespread, that we are likely to ignore the imaginary lessons of history, but also the quite real lessons of bureaucracy—specifically Roberto Michels "Iron Law of Oligarchy." Agencies and institutions are not easily dissolved, even if they lose all semblance of the functions for which they were originally organized. For that reason, it is not only possible, but necessary, to examine the debris left from the collapse of the Bolshevik November 1917 Revolution. For unlike the death of an individual, the end of a system does not take place at once and irrevocably, but by fits and starts and if one be permitted to say so, by lurches and lunges.

Uneven decay is the situation with communist parties around the world; especially those in Western Europe, and even in the United States, where tightly knit, well disciplined institutional frameworks have been built up over seven decades. In the past, the communist parties have been for the most part, although not always, obedient servants of the USSR and the Stalinist International. That role of communism as a servant of a foreign national power is at an end. The virtual collapse of the Communist Party in the Soviet Union, combined with the extraordinary outburst of nationalist and regionalist sentiments, assures such an outcome. But so too are the constraints imposed by so centrifugal a force as the Soviet Union on its former satellites and acolytes.

There is also no question that in a larger context, the disintegration of the Soviet empire will enhance the forces of freedom wherever and whoever they are. The independence of the Baltic Republics, greater autonomy of the Russian Republics the decline in foreign adventures as in Afghanistan, all must be ranked a huge plus. The days have ended when a Berlin Wall or a Cuban Missile could compel humanity to hold its collective breath. But the global scene may have paradoxical outcomes in a variety of national contexts. No longer confined by the political requisites of Soviet power, radical organizations may permit nativism in the guise of populism to flourish. It is far easier to advocate radical alternatives when measured against utopian prospects than against Soviet communist performance or preference.

The equation of communism as an ideology with communism as a national system of the old Union of Soviet Socialist Republics is a profound mistake. Inherent in the history of Bolshevik domination has been a dualism of loyalties: to Russian national interests on one side and Communist class and party interests on the other. This dualism surfaced at critical times to roil the Party: the Stalin-Trotsky split in the 1920s, the non-aggression pact between Nazi Germany and Communist Russia in the 1930s, the Khrushchev revelations of Stalinist "excesses" in the mid-1950; and indeed, the emergence of Perestroika and Glasnost in the mid-1980s.

In each case, despite suffering substantial losses in party membership and electoral potency, the Communist movement remained a factor in advanced nations. While the current loss of a supportive base inside Russia is an enormous blow, it would be a deep mistake to think that this automatically translates into worldwide communist party defeat. Schisms, erosion, debates, defections, and struggles for power, these will occur nation by nation. But what could emerge is a highly radicalized, far more tightly knit set of groups, capable and willing to implement terrorist action across the board.

In this sense, the Shining Light, or Sendero Luminoso of Peru may be an example of what develops. Totally unconcerned about political struggles in European contexts, and loosely identifying with the military positions of Mao Tse-tung and Ernesto "Che" Guevara, such groups may actually be enhanced in their activities by the Russian search for democracy and legitimacy. They may well interpret the fumbling and stumbling inside the Soviet Union as precisely what a "real" revolutionary movement must seek to avoid, or at least overcome in its ranks.

In the wake of the collapse of Soviet communism, the Sendero Luminoso has stepped up its terrorist activities within Peru. Indeed, in a period of remarkable financial recovery based on free market premises, Peru is unique in its inability to develop—despite a President (Alberto K. Fujimori) dedicated to a rebirth of the market economy. Peru has become polarized in its infrastructure. The prisons may be filled with the Senderistas, but the inside of such prisons are owned and operated by the prisoners. Not only is the bloodbath of the bourgeoisie and the communist aftermath celebrated, but even individuals like Fidel Castro are denounced as revisionists and traitors to the cause of total and global revolution.

A similar hemispheric movement, with an even longer counter-insurgency tradition, is the Farabundo Martí Front for National Liberation (FMLN) of El Salvador. Armed with high technology weapons procured from semi-legal American and Soviet arms suppliers alike, such a movement hardly takes the time to respond to events in the Soviet Communist Party. And when it does, as did the so-called "pro-Moscow" leader of the FMLN, Shafik Handal, it is to reassert a role to play by the guerrillas "in this capitalist world," what is claimed to be "the next stage of world conflict." Another leader of the guerrillas, Mario Aguinaldo Carranza, sees events in the USSR as "serving Gorbachev right. He had been putting the Soviet people into destitution and selling their national sovereignty to the West." In short, the politics of confrontation in conjunction with the rhetoric of anti-Americanism, far from dissolving in these "front-line" states, actually shows signs of hardening.

Within well established Communist Parties, one finds a continuing struggle that shapes up precisely along such lines: sections advocating hard terrorism, versus those who believe in soft social democracy. The comments by at least one segment of the Spanish Communist Party are indicative. The Secretary General of Spain's Communist Party, Julio Anguita has already stated that "the Party will continue to defend revolutionary Marxism." And another member of its Central Committee, Antonio Romero, was quick to add that "the defeat of a dictatorial model does not mean the victory of the capitalist system or the defeat of the left." If this attitude can prevail in the Spanish Communist Party, one in which the very phrase "Eurocommunism" was introduced in the early 1970s by its long time leader, Santiago Carrillo, what can one expect from those countries that have proven to be slavish in their past devotionals to Moscow?

The answers have been quick in coming: The French Communist Party, far less innovative in recent years than either the Italian or Spanish variants, simply reasserted its orthodox positions. Georges Marchais accused the Soviet Union of "borrowing recipes of the most savage capitalism." He added that "We carry the name 'Communist' with pride and see no reason to renounce it." To be sure, the theme of the annual festival of the French Communists was "solidarity with Cuba." This was viewed as a noncontroversial slogan. But as the Fete de L'Humanite proceeds at La Courneuve Park in the outskirts of Paris, the Party itself slides from a mass party to a tiny elitist grouping. As Alan Riding reporting in the New York Times from Paris noted "From 1945 until the mid-1970s the [Communist] party routinely won 20 to 25 percent of the vote. By 1981 it was down to 16 per cent, in 1986 it won only 11 percent and today polls give it 7 percent. No less dismaying, many former Communist supporters have switched to the far right National Front." This is a telling shift, indicating the capacity of the Communist remnant to become more violent as it becomes smaller. Shrinking in size is not necessarily shrinking into oblivion. The French Communists clearly understand as much—which may account for their relative lack of concern over the end of Soviet Communism.

We also see this "new left" line being implemented in the United States. The pages of *The Nation* carry a series of pieces in its September 16th issue, in which we are placed on notice that (a) The Soviet union cannot claim to be democratic if it cannot tolerate a communist party; (b) Gorbachev failed to understand the potentials for a socialist option to the Communist Party; (c) Bush's New World Order demands the destruction of Marxist governments the world over no less than the dissolution of Soviet power (d) the Soviet counterweight to imperialism has now drifted into the hands of independent democratic popular fronts; (e) in these days of post communism we should all remember that Communism did some good things as well as bad things. Among the good things is support for the Cuban and Vietnam regimes in their time of crisis. The bad things—like the genocidal destruction of more than forty million Soviet citizens—will be discussed by the bourgeois press, so why bother giving the imperial "them" ammunition.

The hard-line echoes of peripheral responses to the Soviet debacle can be found in the official American Communist Party responses as well. Mr. Arva Justa "Gus" Hall, the leader of the American Communist Party, was quick to support the 72-hour coup, then even more rapidly distancing himself from the putschists. He now sees the efforts of the Russian people to rid themselves of the Communist yoke as a "new form of mass hysteria and McCarthyism." Indeed, Hall's regnant remnant saw events in the Russian Parliament as "Reactionary pro-capitalist forces in the Soviet Union, with the backing of transnational corporations, are exploiting the situation." Needless to say the specific capitalist interests of Soviet parliamentarians is not revealed, nor is any single case given of a single multinational donating even a dime to the effort of the Soviet Union to rid itself of its hideous single-party regime.

That events in the Soviet Union may further reduce the size of such a small party in the United States from 15,000 to 5,000 members is small comfort. Since for the enemies of democracy, numbers and procedures represent "parliamentary cretinism" in any event. As a result, the small size may actually prove attractive to the remaining hard core communists. Alessandra Stanley, in her *New York Times* write up of the Gus Hall press conference may be right to note that the erstwhile communist leader sounded like Chance Gardner in the novel *Being There*, but she might have remembered that fictional lunatic worked his magic into the boudoirs of the Executive Office before wandering off to greener pastures.

The juxtaposition of Soviet perfidy and Communist morality is likely to be a theme repeated a thousand ways in a hundred countries in which Communist cells exist. It is already the stated policy of the American communists who insist that "members of the Communist Party are not going to take this (presumably the attack on the Party's dominance in the Soviet Union) lying down." And underneath this idiotic formulation is a sober message: "Socialism is not an annual; it is a perennial." In short, the end of small tyrannies and petty tyrants is not yet in sight.

In the South African Communist Party, having roughly the same size (12,000 to 15,000 members) as the United States Communist Party, the process of response is different. Given the alliance of the Party for the past forty years with the far larger African National Congress, Communism in South Africa not only has a social bases but a political thrust denied it almost everywhere else in the world. And if its leader, Joe Slovo, can speak of "democratic socialism as the only rational future for mankind," its ideologists, such as Denis Goldberg and Ronnie Kasrils, see great things ahead for the South African Party. This is predicated on a world-wide cataclysm "that 50 years down the road, if we are not careful, we will find the same multinational corporations will still control the economy" while at the other end "we will still find the workers able to vote but living in squalor." How the Party plans to overcome this classical Marxist model of squalor to immiseration, or explain why the real squalor has taken place with the Soviet working class, remains a mystery. Still, one can again see the broad outlines of class struggle theory, in the guise of multinationals, reemerging even as the Party dissolves elsewhere.

In place of the Soviet Union and its monolithic Communist Party, is the Communist Party of autonomy and authenticity: small, mobile, capable of striking in military as well as in parliamentary terms. In short, a party of the Leninist type; or in contemporary terms, a party of the Castroist type. In this, the South African Communist ideologist, Jonny Steinberg, sets the tone with his statement that it is a "contradiction of classical revolutionary Marxism to endorse political pluralism and the various bourgeois democratic forms so scathingly rejected by Lenin." One can expect a return to the sacred texts of Lenin and Stalin in the years ahead. It will be a heady wine indeed, unencumbered as it is by the dismal performance of the Soviet Union in the field of economics. Communism has always thrived best when no empirical evidence of a contradictory sort can be adduced to measure its actual performance. This is hardly a comforting thought for those seeing world communism as a dissolving entity.

We must then factor into account the non-communist terrorists, those who, like Gadaffi in Libya and Hussein in Iraq, immediately came to the support of the Soviet Communist Putschists in the first 48 hours of the regime's seizure of power. They saw this counterrevolution as the restoration of international balance between the superpowers. It is highly unlikely that the revolt against autocracy within the Soviet Union will have a moderating impact on their global behavior. Again, as in the case of terrorist outfits ranging from the PLO to the IRA, the end of Soviet Communism is but the end of an illusion, and the prelude to a new round of fanatic quasi-military activities. These could actually come in short order, as a means to re-establish such authority as these extremists still possess.

There is also the network of surviving Communist Parties, such as China the big and Cuba the small, for whom events in the Soviet Union are declared to be essentially irrelevant, without merit; requiring a redoubling of efforts to maintain the totalitarian State machinery. Indeed, for Castro, developments in the Soviet Union only confirm the authenticity of the Cuban

Revolution of 1959. In the words of *Granma*, the Communist Party organ of the Cuban Central Committee: "We will not move away from the path we have chosen. We will continue with our independent, Cuban, socialist line." In these nations, and in others like North Korean and Vietnam, a curious politics of authenticity takes place. In which the argument is made—and indeed has often been made by people like Fidel Castro—that "our" (fill in the missing country) cannot be touched by events in the Soviet Union since the revolution "we" (fill in the founding heroes) have had when (fill in the missing year) was authentic and not dependant on Soviet support or invasion as in Eastern Europe.

Just how deeply embedded in this sort of abstract syllogism the orthodox Communists remain is indicated by the hysterical response by Castro on September 14th to the announcement of the Soviet pull-out from Cuba of its remaining 10-12,000 troops. Arguing that this is being done without consultation and in violation of treaty obligations and international norms—as if the original placement of Soviet troops on Cuban soil had such force of international approbation—Castro went on to argue that the Soviet Union has not only abandoned socialism, but has made the sort of equation concerning American troops at Guantanamo Bay with Russian troops in Cuba that only confirms big power chauvinism. To be sure, Castro sees in the threat of Soviet troop withdrawals the same sort of big power settlement that also took place in the 1962 removal of Soviet missiles. Nonetheless, it is evident that, lacking Soviet military support on the island, Castro becomes vulnerable to the sort of populist revolt that took place in the wake of the Communist-KGB putsch. For without external military support, continued support from Castro's elite cadres could begin to crumble—leaving the Communist Party vulnerable to destruction.

Just how that argument will resonate once people factor into account that the Bolshevik Revolution of 1917 was the mother of all Communist revolutions is another question. For example, in his report for *The Washington Post* filed from Hanoi, William

Branigin notes that the Vietnamese diplomatic community notes that Do Muoi, the Communist Party chief, was delighted with the coup attempt. The party leaders thought they were back to the good old days and could play the Soviet Union off against China again. Now, it was ruefully added, "the Vietnamese communists must go to see the Chinese 'emperor' completely naked. The risk is that Vietnam could become a political satellite of Beijing." In short, the politics of authenticity turns out to be largely illusory. It is more a trading of big brothers, indeed, where one can be still located.

It would be emotionally impossible to advise against the cel-ebration of the downfall of Communism in the Soviet Union, or minimize the world historic importance of the beginnings of a new democratic world order. Nonetheless, communism, as both organization and ideology, will not necessarily disappear. Individuals capable of accepting Enver Hoxha of the ill-fated Albanian Communist Party as their spiritual leader, or those who could transcend the "corruption" of pure communism in Deng Xiaoping's China or Gorbachev's Russia, are hardly likely to return to the normal, democratic range of political partici-pation for their activist thrills and ideological spills. For such individuals, victory is remote; the process alone is real. That is the tradition of radicalism in its revolt against reason in the fin de siecle of the 19th and 20th centuries alike. The devotees of the Fourth International, the so-called Trotskyists, have argued in precisely this fashion. They claim that the Soviet abandon-ment of internationalism, meaning the destruction of the free market system at any cost and in every place, long ago provided the underpinnings for the present transition in Russia from socialism to capitalism. Hence, such new developments, far from weakening the irrational elements within the far left may actually serve to strengthen them. Groups of ultra-leftists, long critical of the Soviet Union, can well emerge larger in numbers and bolder in tactics.

If we need a final cautionary note, it is the continuing power of communist ideology as reflected in the politics of discontent and retribution. The Nazis paid dearly for their contempt of "theory." When the thousand years of domination that Hitler built crumbled in a matter of twelve years, the ideology of racism on which it was built quickly lost any intellectual cachet it ever had. However, with the collapse of Russian communism after seven decades, and through its internal incapacities (not invading armies), the fanatics who run the ex-Communist apparatus were quick to establish a place in the future sun for Marxism-Leninism. It is as if the sins of real men could not be permitted to tarnish the beatification of a disgraced ideology. No sooner does Russian Communism collapse and debate begins on pulling Lenin's corpse from his Moscow Mausoleum and sending the remains to the family burial plot in St. Petersburg, then sociological "calls for papers" go out on the theme "The Future of Marxism." Surely, so tenacious an ideology, held on to for dear life by enthralled academics, must be the apple in the eye of "scientific" and "secular" fundamentalists.

There will be a strong tendency for critics of communism to dismiss splinter groups and marginal activities and their bizarre ideologies even more fulsomely than in the past. It would be wise to keep in mind that the early Nazis gathered in Munich Beer Halls a decade before the national socialists seizure of power. The idea of absolutism and its discontents goes deep into the sinews of western culture. It would be wise to assume that Communist marginal groups, sometimes meshing with Fascist splinter groups, and fusing around "issues"—i.e., the control of the world economy by the Jews; the invasion of white bastions of purity by the blacks; the power of multinationals in grinding down the people; etc. ad nausea—will still be with us long after Gorbachev's first name is forgotten (it is Mikhail by the way). The destruction of one "evil empire" when viewed in the long course of history, is a small dent in the struggle against political evil as such; especially one holding firm to an ideology with the force of a theology. In short: *la lutte pour la vie* continue.

In the meanwhile, the politics of exposure that reached its previous high point when *The Gulag Archipelago* by Alexander

Solzhenitsyn was published twenty years ago must now move forward toward an internal self-analysis. The archives of the Soviet Secret police, the KGB, must be opened; and the files of the communist conspirators lay bare. The millions of ordinary lives taken away by the communists no less than the Nazis must now be redeemed. It will not do to simply tear down monuments, destroy symbols, or move icons from mausoleums. That represents the anti-politics of the street, the mass psychology of frustrated victims, and the destruction of memory.

What is urgently needed in Russia, and from Russia, is commencing the politics of parties and recapturing the history of memories. Only on this dual track can we start to appreciate how it came to be that a deformed movement took root on the fertile soil of the Russian democratic imagination. To do less than this is to run the grave risk of a resurrection of national communism; with the same set of horrific consequences for human decency as national socialism created earlier in the century. The Russian peoples understood these lessons well. One must remain hopeful that the emerging Soviet leadership will remain untouched by totalitarian temptations, and repudiate the blandishments of old tyrants and old ways.

Source and Original Title: "Totalitarian Options in a Post-Communist World." *Freedom Review,* Volume 23, Number 3, May-June 1992.

22

American Foreign Policy toward Castro: Paradox, Procrastination, and Paralysis

Reviewing the range of academic and policy literature on Cuba as written by those who have played a role in creating United States policy is a fascinating exercise. It helps to explain, or at least place in focus, the immobility of the United States' responses to the final stage of Fidel Castro's regime. In recent years, policy analysts have focused so exclusively on meaningless questions, for example, trying to predict when Castro will die, vanish, or relinquish power that far more practical questions of United States foreign policy have been allowed to languish in the thick cloud of Cubanology.

Remembering the fate of Kremlinologists, who focused exclusively on matters such as where members of the Soviet Politburo stood on the May Day podium so that they could not make even rudimentary predictions of the actual state of Soviet affairs, should remind those of us who discourse readily on Cuban affairs not to presume too much or disdain the common wisdom too easily. One might even argue that there has been such a fixation on when Castro's regime would dissolve that his continued ability to hang on has contributed to a policy paralysis. For in the argument by analogy (announced by President George Bush at the end of 1991 and again by Defense Secretary Dick Cheney at the start of February 1992) that Cuban communism will go the way of Eastern Europe, we await events rather than take the initiative to forge policies. Waiting for Castro to step—or fall—down has turned out to be like waiting for Godot.

At the most general policy level, one sees a familiar pattern: The United States prefers to deal with established, stable powers and figures, even if they are venal and totalitarian. The extraordinary events in the Soviet Union and Eastern Europe took place despite U.S. policies, not because of them. Our sentiments were in tune with the demands of the people for democracy, but our policies remained attuned to traditional State Department patterns of realpolitik. In the Baltics, the independence movement was a *fait accompli* before we granted diplomatic recognition; in Yugoslavia, we upheld the principle of national self-determination long after it became evident that Croatia was not going to remain a part of Yugoslavia. And in the USSR, the American policy apparatus supported Mikhail Gorbachev against Boris Yeltsin—long after it was clear that Gorbachev lacked the support of his own people. Indeed, the encomiums heaped upon Gorbachev were far more pronounced in American policy circles than among Soviet experts.

Given the recent U.S. record, it is not surprising that the United States continues to maintain a cool but correct relationship with Castro's Cuba. This regime does, after all, present stability and continuity—elements which the Bush administration prizes above anything else except electoral votes. In an effort to preserve the status quo, that is to say, Castro in power, even such stalwart Cold Warriors as Ray Cline are said to be urging the president to lift the economic embargo and pursue ameliorative policy toward Castro. To be sure, we have it on the authority of J. Anthony Lukas, writing in *The New York Times* (January 20, 1992), that the Bush administration is said to be only an election away from pursuing a policy of consensus and perhaps even rapprochement with Castro. This predicted turnabout in U.S. policy comes at a time when leading Russian politicians have announced that each republic will strike its own trade deals with Cuba and that Castro no longer will receive petroleum on a favorable basis. Russian deliveries to Cuba of lumber, foodstuffs, and spare machine parts will have all but ceased with the start of 1992. Russia, rather than the United States, has become the implacable foe of Castro's regime.

There are deeper elements to the paradox of quiescent support for Castro's continuation. They reside in the character of hemispheric relations and the unspoken belief that the United States, because of imperialist pretensions and colonialist behavior at the end of the nineteenth century, lacks legitimacy to take action at the end of the twentieth century. A lingering feeling of historic guilt, rather than a theory of foreign policy, seems to prevail at the present. Monroeism has been replaced by Bolívarism. The idea that European powers would not be welcomed in the Western Hemisphere translated into the tacit assumption that regime change itself would be determined largely by American global interests. The new view, so well captured by David Scott Palmer in *Setting the North-South Agenda,* is that the United States' role is "reduced," and by so doing, "the way is opened to creating a new relationship of partnership in which the parties come together as equals, each seeking to derive some benefit from the relationship" (Palmer 1991, 86). The further evolution of such a view was expounded in a recent statement by Kenneth N. Waltz at the annual meeting of the American Political Science Association (APSA), at which he noted, "We cannot take America or any other country as a model for the world ... I believe that America is better than most nations; I fear that it is not as much better as many Americans believe" (Waltz 1991, 667-70). However one responds to such a statement, and I confess to astonishment that such remarks can be offered casually in 1992, it clearly signals commitment to a foreign policy of stasis and quiescence rather than activism.

It is almost as if the United States is bogged down in its own history, an inertia based on guilt as well as ignorance. George Quester, speaking at the same APSA forum on "America as Model for the World," noted that the 1960s produced a "major American disenchantment with foreign policy" (Quester 1991, 658-59). As premature as this disenchantment may have been, it was not simply a consequence of radical opposition from outside but a result of liberal self-doubt within the establishment. Such doubt can only be reinforced by Fidel Castro's announcement at the January 1992 conference in Havana, sponsored by Brown University's Center for Foreign Policy Development: "Times have changed. We have changed.... Military aid outside our borders is a thing of the past."[1]

That such pronouncements came at a time when military adventures would not be tolerated by any nation in the hemisphere does not alter the soothing balm of the message to those Americans, in both the Democratic and Republican parties, for whom isolationism has become not just a moral goal but an instrument of American foreign policy.

In addition to an overall foreign policy of *laissez-faire* toward Cuba, one must factor in ambiguities of the big power settlement after the so-called Cuban missile crisis. Castro's pride may have been wounded because of his exclusion from resolution of the crisis, but both President John F. Kennedy and Premier Nikita Khrushchev arrived at a trade-off. Soviet nuclear-tipped warheads in Cuba were eliminated in exchange for a firm policy of nonintervention by the United States. While its juridical outlines may be contested, this arrangement has been honored for more than 30 years. With the collapse of the Soviet Union, the policy haunts the United States, leaving the former Soviet Union indifferent, even embarrassed.

United States policy toward Cuba for the past 31 of 33 years of the Castro regime reveals paradox followed by procrastination, ending in paralysis.

- Should we invade or not invade?
- Should we support exiled guerrilla troops or punish them for violating the neutrality pact?
- Should we isolate Cuba diplomatically or open windows of diplomatic opportunity?
- Should we welcome refugees from Cuba as political freedom fighters or return them, or some of them, as criminal elements?
- Should we seal off the island from commercial activity or send commercial missions and diplomatic attaches to explore trade and aid?

Our Cuba policy papers offer a serious set of rifts that have plagued the Departments of State and Defense for more than 30 years and have produced ramifications in the executive office for the same length of time. When the heavenly book finally is closed on Castro, it will be seen that America stood fast at the ideological level but was in stasis at the policy level.

Castro's dogmatic posture has frustrated even his most ardent followers in the United States, as they attempt to influence U.S. policy. Such unbending admirers of Castro as Saul Landau have had to acknowledge a Cuban political climate of deepening repression, but, of course, this would all come to a magical end if the United States lifted its embargo and ended its "cold war hostility toward Cuba" (Landau 1992, 225-27). According to such experts, the United States has passed mysteriously from being an impotent force unable to contain the mighty tide of socialism to the only power in the world capable of preserving Cuba's socialist system.

Castro has offered enough tidbits along the way to prevent all-out hostility or a unified critical posture. At various times we have had hints of a private market, promises of a multi-party system, considerations for religious groups, vague declarations of free and unfettered elections, denials of drug involvement and offers of punishment, and willingness to consider reuniting family members. All of these "balloons" occurred as backroom gossip or in private, nonofficial, off-the-record meetings. But they were enough to stave off the hand of retribution. Flattery of vain and pompous minor government officials, pampering of wealthy businessmen, and cajoling of potential critics—all contributed to paralysis in American foreign policy toward Cuba. At this level, Castro's continuing political adroitness cannot be denied.

We see three distinct levels of U.S. political life that led to policy paralysis: (1) general U.S. disdain for intervention, especially in light of the Vietnam experience; (2) a hemispheric turn to Bolívarism and rejection of Monroeism, specifically, the belief that Latin American countries are in control of their own destinies and would solve the Cuban problem by cauterization; and finally, (3) an *entente cordiale* after the Cuban missile crisis, defining with great precision the limits of policy for the United States, along with the limits of arms dumping for the Soviet Union.

There is a fourth and final factor in the paradox of American foreign policy toward Castro's Cuba: the demise of Eastern European and Russian communism. Cuba is no longer the central cockpit for world communism. As a result, calls for an activist foreign policy toward Cuba, few as they had been, came to a crashing halt in 1991. The sense of urgency and the need for any sort of policy seemed to go by the boards. With the end of totalitarian rule in Europe came a widespread belief that Cuba would be forced to reject Castro if only because of shortages of fuel, food, or technology. The closest anyone came to an activist posture are statements by former National Security Council member, José Sorzano, "The beast is wounded." and "It's time to go in for the kill" (Sorzano 1991, 146-52). But metaphor is hardly a substitute for policy at this point in the endgame called Castroism.

It well might be that such calculated non-gambles provide the best opportunity for change without bloodshed in Cuba. Indeed, the emergence of independent states in the Baltic Republics, the liberation of Eastern Europe from the Soviet yoke, and finally, the collapse of the Soviet empire—all took place in the environment of an unambiguous United States policy of military neutrality, coupled with broad displays of ideological support for those seeking freedom in these areas. Talk is cheap, but it bought victories for the democratic camp at virtually no cost in American lives and precious little in economic aid.

Perhaps Castro's Cuba will be different. Perhaps policy paradox, followed by political paralysis, will have different results from those we have been observing in Latvia, Lithuania, or Estonia. After all, post-Tiananmen Square China indicates that a noninterventionist approach does not always yield favorable results. Nor does it seem to have worked with respect to North Korea and Vietnam. American political leaders talk as if Cuba is an extension of European communism, with barely a nod to the possibility that it might take the road of what the late Karl Witt-fogel called "oriental despotism" (Wittfogel [1956] 1981). Still, one must reckon that the Cuban people and the Latin culture will not be led easily down such a dangerous path.

As I have said and written often, Castro is perfectly able to initiate the Cambodianization of Cuba and force the populace to accept economic retreat and a variety of hardships in the name of communism. The so-called zero option is a mechanism for Castro's survival. The zero option reduces Cuba's threat abroad and increases repression at home. That, at any rate, is the theory behind the practice. The consequence of return to a preindustrial economy and a horse-and-buggy technology makes Cuba a nonfactor in world affairs. It also justifies nonintervention or nonaction as a style. While this may result in hardship for the Cuban population, it does not result in hardship for the American people. In this way, the absence of a Soviet threat actually may prolong rather than terminate Castro's rule, at least in the short term.

Increasingly, the United States sees itself as a power broker rather than a player in the post-Castro future. Bush has pro-nounced the end of Castro but was careful not to set forth how that anticipated demise was to be brought about, other than by the collapse of Castro's regime through economic self-strangu-lation. But that, too, depends on the viability of the European communist analogy, something that remains open to question.

At the subjective level, United States policy turns on the meaning of democracy, on employing a less pleasant rhetoric, or on the weakness of the American society. Who are we to tell anyone else what sort of society to have? This diffident attitude can be labeled anti-interventionist. However, it reveals at its roots a fear of the employment of power under any circumstances. The passive response to Cuba is thus best seen as a microcosm of overall American foreign policy ambiguity. Such sentiments often are followed by insistence that quiescence or silence is the only correct posture when it comes to revolutionary regimes like Castro's. This, in turn, is followed by insistence on active sup-port for Cuban totalitarianism or at least for the normalization of relations and letting bygones be bygones. In the absence of a Soviet threat, such a posture will gain adherents and acceptability in high places.

Such thinking yields a four-step policy process into oblivion: first, guilt over past adventures in the hemisphere; second, self-hatred for assuming the mantle of imperialism; third, policy quiescence or acquiescence in repugnant regimes to "make up" for past transgressions; and fourth, urging modification of totalitarian behavior by infusion of the best of the American liberal credo into the Castro bloodstream. Such subjectivism serves as the perfect complement to an objective side of policymaking: first, general commitment to noninterventionism or isolationism with respect to totalitarian regimes; second, extension of this to the Latin American environment, with a belief that democracy will overwhelm all adversaries; third, specific detente representing a residual from the Cuban missile crisis era; fourth and finally, an analysis that Cuba is no longer a vital United States interest because of the collapse of communism in Europe.

American foreign policy toward Cuba always has been highly reactive. Events are seen not as a consequence of American initiatives but in recognition that the United States essentially is not a key player in the current round of Cuban transformation. Such a self-effacing posture is reinforced by Cuban exiles in Paris, Toronto, and Puerto Rico, among other places, who assert a role greater than Miami's, each declaiming against American presence in the transformation of Cuban society after the fall of the dictator.

It is time for a new American policy. This policy must be based on

- the end of a theory of historic guilt;
- an end to the sort of informal diplomacy that has led to stagnation at the diplomatic front for 32 years; and
- recognition of the United States as a partially Latin nation and thus entitled to consider actions as insider rather than outsider.

We must translate changes in American demographics into changes in American policy. The United States remains oriented to Europe and Asia in near disregard of the actual population make-up of places like Los Angeles, Miami, New York, and San Antonio.

The reassertion of the United States' implacable opposition to Castro's tyranny—and a tightening rather than lifting of the embargo—may flow from a sense of being at least partially a Latin nation, over against the current tendency to perceive ourselves as an Anglo-Protestant nation with only marginal interests in events south of the North American borders.

The recent meeting in New York calling for an end to the war on Castro's Cuba is most likely the final demonic act of the American communist movement and its fellow travelers. To deny this group a victory will require more than opposition meetings. It will require a constant struggle against Castro, until the tyrant is overthrown. But this can be done only when the extent of our own Latinization is incorporated into the American ethos as well as into American policy.

At the moment, the battle lines are drawn. American intellectuals and lawyers argue the case for Castro, as they have for most of the 33 years of his reign. Cuban exiles, and now native-born Cubans, carry on the struggle for a free Cuba. If the latter are wondering about the character of American policy, they would be well advised to examine in detail the general reluctance of the United States to undertake any actions that are reminiscent of an earlier era of gunboat diplomacy. The rise of neo-isolationism, as articulated by Patrick Buchanan, only serves to provide a rightist gloss to leftist substance.

My conclusion is that, as long as the current malaise of policy exists, Castro, too, will persist. It is time to take a close look not just at economic deterioration within Cuba but at political demobilization within the United States, following the Gulf War and the collapse of the Soviet Union. Guilt has a high price, one that appears less dangerous because of the relaxation of global tensions.

Castro is no longer a pawn of the USSR. But it does not follow axiomatically that he is no longer a threat to hemispheric tranquility. "The wounded beast" of which Sorzano speaks might become doubly dangerous in the military arena, since Castro is now liberated from responsibility as the praetorian guard of Soviet communism. The situation in Cuba will remain desperate and fluid. For quite different reasons, the same words, "desperate" and "fluid," mark the current stage in American policy toward the last dictatorship in the hemisphere.

In the United States, a new constellation of forces, embracing the extreme right and the usual suspects from the ultra-left, urges immobility as a policy of nonintervention and an ethic of grand isolation. We have seen this strange new coalition at work, denigrating the effort to contain, not defeat, Saddam Hussein in Iraq. One sees the ideologues of extremes decrying United States' intervention and even sharing a worn rhetoric about a high loss of Iraqi civilian life, while virtually denying what led to United States involvement in Iraq to start with. The same forces are at work to deny the United States a role in any settlement of the Balkan crisis. Lawrence Freedman of King's College, London, has called this the "crisis fatigue" syndrome (Freedman 1992). However, there will be no European Community to come to the rescue of the United States in Havana as it did in Zagreb. With respect to the continued communist rule of Cuba, the essentially defensive posture of American foreign policy will be sorely tested and quite possibly be found wanting.

It would be foolishly naive to believe that this newly established coalition of extreme right and left would remain silent in the event of a U.S. decision to topple the Castro regime—even in conjunction with other nations of the Western Hemisphere. To be sure, the paradox of American power has long been its powerlessness in the face of internal forces that would prefer to define the United States as an island of national virtue in a sea of international troubles. It is worth remembering that under pressure, Fidel Castro, unlike Saddam Hussein, has a history of diplomatic flexibility rather than nationalistic dogmatism. Indeed, it might be that Castro's growing sense of frustration and isolation will, as it did with Saddam Hussein, provide the basis for U.S. action. But to await such a fortuitous event would be clutching at straws.

In any event, paradox and procrastination in U.S. foreign policy translates into an opportunity for Castro to stay, albeit temporarily, the hand of history. It will be intriguing to see whether an American policy of nonpolicy leads to a successful democratic resolution. Will the immediate period ahead signal an end to Cuban communism, as in Eastern Europe and Russia, or to a tightening of the vise of totalitarian rule, as in China and North Korea? I intend neither to arouse expectations nor to dash hopes. Rather, my concern is to instill a sense of sobriety among those who expect a radical shift in American policy and, no less, to arouse a sense of anxiety among those who believe that a policy of nonpolicy inevitably will have happy consequences for the forces of freedom.

Cuban communism will be an acid test of American foreign policy. The outcome in Moscow favored the democratic gods; the outcome in Beijing favored the totalitarian demigods. What takes place in Havana over the proximate period of time will tell us much about an American policy that simultaneously appears impatient to observe positive changes in Cuba and yet seems to be too exhausted by recent world events to help bring about such a desirable outcome.

Meanwhile, we should take comfort from José Martí's *Letter to a Cuban Farmer,* written one hundred years ago: "Mankind is composed of two sorts of men—those who love and create, and those who hate and destroy." Martí was too wise to predict which sort of person would win. But he did say, a decade earlier in 1881, "Life on earth is a hand-to-hand mortal combat ... between the law of love and the law of hate" (Martí [1881] 1980, 671). I suspect that Martí would have understood well that yielding to exhaustion, like surrendering to temptation, is to invite the victory of the despot. And that cannot be. In spite of momentary U.S. foreign policy indecision, a free Cuba will emerge because the struggle to foster relationships based on love and creativity—in the public as well as in the private realm—is indeed stronger than the inclination to maintain systems based on hate and destruction.

References/Notes

1. Fidel Castro's comments concerning an end to Cuban adventurism, while presumably off the record as is most of his policy statements directed at North American consumption, were made within earshot of both J. Anthony Lukas and Saul Landau (see the list of references). I also have had his remarks confirmed in a personal interview with Arthur Schlesinger, Jr. upon his return from the Havana Conference on the Missile Crisis in late January 1992.

Freedman, Lawrence. 1992. "Order and Disorder in the New World." *Foreign Affairs* 81(1): 20-37.

Horowitz, Irving Louis. 1991. "Fidel Castro Redux: Old Revolutionaries Resisting New Revolutions." *Cuba in the Nineties*. Washington, D.C.: Freedom House.

Landau, Saul. 1992. "Economic War on Cuba: Killing the Wounded Beast." *The Nation* (February 24):225-227.

Lukas, J. Anthony. 1992. "Fidel Castro's Theater of Now." *The New York Times* (January 20).

Martí [y Perez], José [Julian]. [1881] 1980. "Letter" Trans. James Nelson Goodsell. *Familiar Quotations*. Edited by Emily Morison Beck. Boston: Little Brown & Company, 671.

Palmer, David Scott. 1991. "Democracy and Change in Latin America." In *Setting the North-South Agenda*. Edited by Henry Hamman. Miami: North-South Center, University of Miami.

Phillips, James A. 1991. "Tracking Moscow's Activity Around the Globe: Cuba." *U.S.S.R. Monitor* 27 and 28 (November and December).

Quester, George H. 1991. "America as a Model for the World?" *PS: Political Science & Politics* (December) 24(4): 658-659.

Sorzano, José S. 1991. "United States Policy Toward Cuba." *Cuba in a Changing World: The United States, Soviet, Cuban Trianage.* (Hearings before the Subcommittees on Europe and the Middle East and on Western Hemisphere Affairs of the Committee on Foreign Affairs, U.S. House of Representatives). Washington, D.C.: U.S. Government Printing Office: 146-152.

Vargas Llosa, Mario. 1992. "The Miami Model" *Commentary* (February) 93:23-27.

Waltz, Kenneth N. 1991. "America as Model for the World? A Foreign Policy Perspective." *PS: Political Science & Politics* (December) 24(4): 667-670.

Wittfogel, Karl A. [1956] 1981. *Oriental Despotism: A Comparative Study of Total Power.* New York: Vintage/Random House.

Source and Original Title: "American Foreign Policy toward Castro's Cuba: Paradox, Procrastination and Paralysis" in *The Conscience of Worms and the Cowardice of Lions: The Cuban-American Experience, 1959-1992.* Miami: The North-South Center/University of Miami, 1993, 92 pp. p. 1-13.

23

The Conscience of Castrologists

My text for this chapter is derived from neither the prophet Isaiah nor from the apostle Peter. Rather, I have selected two statements: one from Max Weber, arguably the leading sociologist who ever graced our earth, and the other from Ivan Pavlov, the great Nobel Laureate in physiology. Both dared to take direct aim at the passionate partisanship for political ideologies. In the midst of a paroxysm of German rightist nationalism, Weber reduced the arguments of Gustav Schmoller to ashes. And five years after the assumption to power of the Bolshevik ultra-leftists, and on the eve of the consolidation of Stalinist power, Pavlov took apart the rubbish of Nikolai Bukharin and the *ABCs of Communism*. I hope that the reason for my choice of heroes will become manifest during this discourse.

Weber showed his ultra-nationalist critics and precursors to Nazism that it is one thing for teachers to state facts or even to determine the internal structure of cultural values. It is quite another to answer questions about the value of a culture or about how one should act with regard to the cultural community or in political associations. In Weber's exact words: "The primary task of a useful teacher is to teach his students to recognize 'inconvenient' facts—I mean facts that are inconvenient for their party opinions. And for every party opinion there are facts that are extremely inconvenient, for my own opinion no less than for others. I believe the teacher accomplishes more than a mere intellectual task if he compels his audience to accustom itself to the existence of such facts. Science contributes to the technology of controlling life by calculating external objects as well as man's activities. Science can contribute something that the greengrocer cannot: methods of thinking, the tools and the training for thought. We are in a position to help with a third objective: to gain clarity" (Weber [1918] 1946, 129-56).

For his part, Pavlov faced an even more challenging audience: He rejected all claims of communism to exclusive truth, to a quick road to culture through class analysis or party indoctrination dressed up as higher education. The communists, he said, instead of accelerating education, succeed only in debasing and lowering culture. In his final words, he directly confronted any linkage of science to dogmatism. "When you enter science, you will find that science and dogmatism are entirely different things. Science and free criticism, these are equivalent. But dogmatism is not suitable, and there is no need to bring up examples. How much was avowed truth? Take, for example, the indivisibility of the atom. Years have passed, and nothing has remained of this. And all science is saturated with these examples. And if you respect science, as it follows that you will if you become thoroughly acquainted with it, then in spite of the fact that you are communists, or members of workmen's schools set up by the Soviets, if you acknowledge that Marxism and communism are not absolute truths, that it is only a theory in which there may be a part of a truth, but in which there is perhaps no truth, then you will look on all life with freedom of view, but not with slavery" (Pavlov [1923] 1991, 466-75).

In some quite precise ways, those who address the Cuban Question, or more exactly, the status of Fidel Castro's 33-year-old regime, must confront the painful theme of science versus ideology to which both Weber and Pavlov allude. There is a profound crisis within social science, and how researchers have dealt with the Cuban Question demonstrates that the concerns of Weber and Pavlov are as valid today as in earlier times and places. Castro's Cuba is the perfect illustration of the notion of "partisanship" and "insurgency" in sociological theory: It was a revolutionary regime illustrating the potential for a fresh beginning and, as such, gave us a chance to evaluate a nation under virtually laboratory circumstances.

It was not a lost opportunity. Social scientists flocked to Cuba, as political pilgrims had earlier to the Soviet experiment. But the Castro regime yielded a devastating outcome for its subjects, and it became a palpable embarrassment for its acolytes. The early Cuban researchers were "armed" less with information and more with biases than anyone dared to admit at the outset. And now, thirty-three years after the fact, it is clear that their failure of scientific analysis and their collapse of moral nerve has left the social science community vulnerable to charges of pure and simple bias—and worse, just plain stupidity.

Marxist tradition boasts a little-used tradition of self-criticism. Historically, self-criticism was employed in Russia, China, and indeed in Cuba, to incarcerate, and when necessary, to liquidate enemies of the state. But it is time to put the tradition to better use and to review what, for the most part, has been a sad history of deception and self-deception on the part of those charged with the task of examining world systems.

The initial phase of the response to the Castro Revolution, from 1959 through 1962, was characterized by euphoria, a fatuous set of assumptions that Cuba would be the long-lost opportunity for socialism to show its invincible superiority to capitalism. In C. Wright Mills, one found a perfect expression of zealotry and anti-Americanism as in his last political tract, *Listen, Yankee.* Here a brilliant analyst of class and status in American society was reduced to a polemicist of the worst sort: blustering, ignorant, and certain. Worse, C. Wright Mills presented the example of a first-rank scholar declaiming against "hysteria as knowledge" while offering slogans delivered up by Castro's ministers of propaganda as his own observed truths.

Throughout this tract, poor Mills asked the right questions but came up with consistently wrong answers. In his conclusion, he asked, "Is it possible today to have a society that is economically just and sensible and at the same time politically fluent and free? This is an old question, an ultimate question, a continuing question—and no one knows the answer to it." But in direct violation of what I knew to be his better judgment, he answered, "I believe that Cuba does represent now a real chance for the development of one form of such a society." In place of reasoned analysis of the serious shortcomings that were apparent early on, the great polemicist of American sociology urged that we turn a blind eye to the exaggerations and passions of the Castro group. Americans "should behave with reason and civilized policies": since Cuba's "revolutionaries represent the hungry nation bloc" (Mills 1960, 282-304). Mills' pathetic confusion of Cuban history with the Sahel notwithstanding, he set the tone for the scientific distortions to come.

In the second phase, from 1963 through 1968, it became apparent that, for American intellectuals, every ailment Castro inflicted on his people was to be viewed through United States intransigence. In this, the fine historian William Appleman Williams took the lead, arguing in 1962 "there would be no missiles of any description or range in Cuba if the actions of the United States toward Cuba since 1898 had followed and honored its professions and promises." In other words, the placement of Soviet missiles was not a function of communist expansion but of nineteenth-century American imperialism. Indeed, Williams wrote an entire volume premised on the notion that every excess of Castroism is a function of American intransigence. He tells us it is the United States, "the state of the nation and the society," that deserves censuring, not Cuban communism (Williams 1962, 1-3).

Williams' analysis does not consider that Castro made a decision for communism nor the possibility that his alliances with the Soviet Union were proactive and not reactive, nor that the wave upon wave of guerrilla activities Castro launched were motivated by a desire to destroy the United States, or at least any semblance of hemispheric effort to seek foreign aid from the United States. While U. S. actions have not always been exemplary over time, Williams moves far beyond this position, chastising the United States for putting the world at risk in a nuclear holocaust. The themes of "historic guilt" and the attendant policy recommendations based on reparations and self-destruction have become familiar ones in a wide variety of contexts, but with respect to the radical view of United States-Castro Cuban relationships, it has been carried to a high art.

An interesting sidelight of this Marxist vision of the early 1960s is how dramatically it contravenes Oliver Stone's image of the late President John F. Kennedy and foreign policy toward Cuba. Kennedy is portrayed by Williams as having "acted unilaterally" in the Cuban missile crisis, failing to "respond to peaceful alternatives framed by Russia," and presuming "a missile as offensive before it is used to initiate an attack." This hardly describes a president who would give the CIA cause for planning his assassination.

For critics like Williams, only after the United States is destroyed by its adversaries, does it have a right to a policy or military response. Williams argued that "the Kennedy administration in effect has retaliated before any blow has been struck." Further, he declares Kennedy to be a war president in the category of Franklin Delano Roosevelt. "From being almost obsessed with fear of another Pearl Harbor, the United States under the Kennedy administration has moved perilously close to adopting the psychology that produced that attack" (Williams 1962, 168-75). Such is the rhetoric of radical isolationism—left-wing 30 years ago and right-wing today—that any posture other than capitulation to a tyrant is wrongheaded, and any action by the tyrant is an appropriate defense of the realm. That such approaches have gone largely unchallenged in the academic realm goes without saying. It is not a love of democracy, and certainly not Marxism, but anti-Americanism that has fueled this particular response.

This is made perfectly plain in the words of Thomas Morgan, writing in 1967: "Fidelismo is the result of the want of understanding and sensibility on the part of the United States facing the struggle against underdevelopment and misery. And so is Catholic Marxism among Brazilian students. They are the creation of your anti-communism which is unable to understand our hunger and thirst for peace." Morgan incredibly disqualifies the United States' ability to understand political and psychological values of backward societies, going beyond this to argue that even Fidel's ideology is a function of American guilt. "I don't think Castro was a communist until he was made desperate" (Morgan 1967, 26). In this way, anti-Americanism, which in fact had been a weak theme in classical Marxisms of Latin America, took front and center in the early stages of Castroism (Hollander 1992, 333-63).

The third phase in the parade of academic support for Castro and his regime was characterized more by a wave of pseudo-toughness than criticism. Even if things were not going well in the 1970s, even if dictatorship did not equate to high levels of productivity, the very existence of the regime was heralded. The guerrilla became a moral hero of our time. The Cuban Revolution was an act of moral purification and rectitude. The quintessential hero of heroes in this context was Ernesto Che Guevara rather than Fidel Castro. It was his picture that appeared in college dorms from one end of the United States to the other in the 1960s. His death in Bolivia came to symbolize the purity of a revolutionary heart, rather than an utterly botched effort to impose Castroism upon a country with a quite well-developed, indigenous radical history and spirit of its own.

John Gerassi captured the near-religious fervor of this attachment to the Cuban Revolution and its chief apostle of the cult of violence, Che Guevara. In his introduction to the speeches and writings of Guevara, his effusive praise is well worth quoting as illustrative of the temper of the times: "Che was first and foremost an activist himself. He thought hard and well, reading everything he could find, going into every problem as deeply as he could. He was, as Fidel has said, 'a communist revolutionary, a true Communist, he had boundless faith in moral values, he had a boundless faith in the conscience of man. And we should say that he saw, with absolute clarity, moral resources as the fundamental lever in the construction of communism in human society.' But he was primarily a doer, a revolutionary activist. That was what led him to Guatemala, to Cuba, to Bolivia. It is that faith and activism that lead the new Ches today, men who still believe in men, who are still convinced that we can build a decent society in which all men respect one another, and in which all men can communicate with each other as full-bodied human beings who are still persuaded that 'we can make it, that *venceremos!*" (Gerassi 1968, 22-3).

Politicians get drunk on power and make mistakes. Intellectuals get drunk on their own rhetoric and make ludicrous remarks. Too often, in such hands, death alone certifies the purity of revolutionary spirit. The Gerassi type of approach filled with emotive charge and mucho macho madness caught the spirit of the new age of Aquarius. The cult of Castro, mimicking the earlier cult of Stalin, began to reveal the underside of the Cuban Revolution—its totalitarian demands for complete abdication of the skeptical spirit of science. Amidst this rhetorical exaggeration, a sense of unease began to pervade even the unqualified but still rational supporters of the Cuban communism. The "Cantos a Fidel" with their pious rubbish about agrarian reform by the "ardent prophet of aurora" and their menacing assertion of the "sanitary operation against tyranny" made it evident that earlier views of Castro turning toward the United States and away from the Soviet Union were untenable at best and mendacious at worst.

When cracks in the regime began to emerge, between 1968 and 1973, social scientists turned apologists saw this as the beginning of restoration and reformation in the regime. Cuba became a testing ground of "things that needed doing" as Leo Huberman and Paul Sweezy put socialistic matters in Cuba. The new Cuba was to be characterized by "crop diversification, steadily expanding the range of industries, elimination of illiteracy and the expansion of technical personnel, better networking within Cuba of its diverse regions and a vast enlargement of transportation and communication." Indeed, Huberman and Sweezy insisted that all of these things were being done in a "healthy socialist" state instead of a sick capitalist one. For these two people, it was Havana rather than Miami that held out high purpose.

Huberman and Sweezy argued, without a shred of doubt or caution, that Cuban communism was a new humanism. Indeed, the doubts about Stalinism that had led them to establish *The Monthly Review* as a non-Party organ of Marxist opinion, gave way to a vision of a Cuba in a state of grace. Cuba could overcome

Soviet excesses because it would not have to cope with a Russian past. Every dogma inherited from the dissident communist past found its way into their thinking. Writing as they did long after the debacle of Stalinism, and after the ruthless invasion of Czechoslovakia, they still could declare a faith in communism uncorrupted by evidence. This was, after all, a revolution made by civilized people! Let us quote them:

> The experience of Cuba proves beyond doubt that a social revolution is an indispensable precondition for the initiation of economic growth and social development. The adoption of a planned economy is enabling Cuba to lay the groundwork for a balanced, healthy, educated, and eventually rich, society—a society in which the very nature of man himself may be transformed (Huberman and Sweezy 1969, 20-21).

In their wonderful world of Oz, there was no need for legal safeguards, legislative bodies, or electoral processes. Democracy somehow would take care of itself in the process of development. The old variety of developmental Stalinism never was discarded by such people, only moved from Russia to Cuba. In the mind of the other member of *The Monthly Review* triad, Paul Baran, no amount of suffering was too much if it produced growth. If *The Political Economy of Growth* now reads like a sick joke, it should be kept in mind that, at the time, Baran's equation of development and communism was viewed widely in academic circles as a healthy antidote to empirical research on actual varieties of modernization.

We find a far more sophisticated variety of political apologetics during the 1970s in the work of the European, K. S. Karol. For him, Cuba in its revolutionary purity has as its "destiny to reveal to the rest of the world the real nature of America's foreign policy ... and pierce the veil of the liberal and anti-colonialist rhetoric." Also in Cuba, "they laid bare the true nature of the Soviet bloc"—which turned out to be "treating the island as a pawn on the international chess board" (Karol 1970, viii-x). So it came to pass that apologists for Fidel now held that both the United States and the Soviet Union were enemies of the people. In this revisionist scenario, it was Trotsky, not Stalin, who would provide the blueprint for Cuban happiness.

Like others before and after him, Karol mistook writing about a revolution for making a revolution. Karol saw himself in dialogue with Castro (as indeed did C. Wright Mills and Jean-Paul Sartre, and yes, Barbara Walters and Bryant Gumbel after him). It never seems to dawn on these intellectuals and journalists that were they not residing in free countries, such dialogues never would have commenced or would have ended tragically in their imprisonment, exile, or worse. But such is the hubris of the intellectual class that they fail to detect forms of irony in their dialogues with dictators.

As he himself makes clear, Karol was more flattered than taken aback by Castro's open rejection of his "two varieties of imperialism" formula. Ironically, in mid-1992, Castro probably would be more than willing to accept such a two-devil formula. Yet despite all he knew about flaws in the regime and flies in the political ointment, Karol was able to declare that "my researches, whether of the past or the present, have been made in a spirit of solidarity with the Cuban Revolution." To be sure, Cuba had a unique revolutionary destiny for Karol. "I have the utmost sympathy for a country to which fate has reserved an outstanding historical role" (Karol 1970, 550).

That this historical role now has shriveled into nothingness should not obscure the fact that Karol, more than most of the radical intellectuals of the time, at least saw through the fatuous claims of the regime and into its contradictions. But poor Karol, dedicated as he was to "social justice" as well as the revolution as such, ended up by urging Cuba to forsake the developmental model advocated by Baran, Sweezy, and Huberman, calling appeals for increased foreign trade and industrial production "calamitous." Karol, instead, says that Cuban communists "still have the means to start on a road that will lead them to a free and equal society. One does not have to be a dreamer to think that this is, in fact, the road they will choose." But, of course, pleasant dreams are not the stuff of dictatorial systems. Democracy was not the road chosen. And this literary ballast reveals only the deep-seated utopianism that beats in the hearts and minds of unreconstructed "scientific" socialists. People like Karol were less interested in reporting events than in locating the human form of the new Trotsky, the new leader who would provide socialism with its long sought-after, non-bureaucratic human face.

When it became evident in the 1980s that the Castro regime was corrupt, unproductive, and unable to sustain its autonomy a part from Soviet aid, these apologists cum social scientists called for the restoration of normal ties with the West, a lifting of the economic embargo, and everything else possible to prop up the last dictatorship in the Western Hemisphere. As with Richard Fagen, this was done in the name of fairness, of sensing that there is weakness in both radical and liberal approaches to social change. As the nature of the Castro tyranny became clearer, more transparent, the social science apologists became more abstract, more remote in their analytic thinking—in short, more remote from actual events taking place in Cuba.

Fagen, perhaps the most sophisticated of this type, was able to appreciate the fact that, prior to the Castro Revolution, Cuba had the best medical facilities in the hemisphere outside the United States. It ranked among the top five Latin American nations in gross national product, commercial energy consumption, literacy of the population, newspaper circulation, radios and televisions per population, and students in higher education. In short, this was a modern, advanced country. But the spin given to this is that the distribution of such goods and services was unequal. That was true, but it hardly explains why one country has a revolution and twenty others do not. Instead, Fagen draws eccentric conclusions. In a nation of high literacy, he sees the campaigns against illiteracy as having "the ring of realism" (Fagen 1969, 45-69). Needless to say, he has never answered how a nation with such a remarkable set of pre-revolutionary indicators of growth could end up, thirty years later, at the bottom on nearly every indicator.

The same is true for Maurice Zeitlin, who saw the uniqueness of the Cuban Revolution as "the first socialist revolution to take place in a capitalist country—a country in which the owning class was capitalist and the direct producers were wage workers" (Zeitlin 1969, 38-42). Neither Fagen, for whom "there has never been anything quite like the Cuban Revolution in the entire history of Latin America," nor Zeitlin, whose pragmatic notion of Castroism is captured by his phrase "revolution without a blueprint," bothered to explain why nor how such a unique laboratory of socialist experimentation could end in such a disastrous series of economic consequences. Indeed, to all who would look, it was evident that dogmatism, not pragmatism, and blueprints cast in stone, not flexible policy-making, were at the heart of Cuban economic performance, or lack thereof. Such myopia among quality social scientists is a tribute to the power of ideology over science.

Fagen tells us that "the politics of the center and even of the 'democratic left' seem to be the politics of the status quo in Latin America." He presents this as an antidote to the simple alternatives of reform or revolution into which so many discussions of Latin America are cast. But while the antidote is clear, the source of the ailment remains a mystery. The socialist system goes unexamined for its colossal failures, and Cuba's negation of democracy is seen as a leverage point in the uneven battle with the United States. Fagen views Castro's "investing no more than a handful of its own citizens and a limited amount of its resources in the armed struggle abroad" as indicating that "the Cuban presence is of a different order than that of the United States" (Fagen 1970, 410-11). In short, Castro's guerrilla operations are equated with tourism and the technical aid programs of the powerful United States.

Equivocation about Castro's dictatorship came to prevail in accounts by political scientists and sociologists. The placebo of ostensible fair-mindedness, perhaps best expressed in the past writings of William LeoGrande, replaces earlier euphoria and manifest partisanship. Casting themselves as a middle ground between Castro apologists and exiled Cuban commentators, a sense of sweet reasonableness dominated social science analysis of Cuba in the 1970s. It was a clever, if transparent, mechanism to seize the intellectual high ground—while casting those old-fashioned apologists in the same net with the new crop of social scientists writing from the exiled community. But this rubric is a transparent disguise for a threadbare lack of substance.

As the crisis of Castroism deepened, apologists within the social science field found themselves retreating to an abstract realm in which criticism was unnecessary. Their level of discourse was twice removed: from the realities of Cuba and from the requirements of reviewing the data. Jockeying for a position to the right and left of nowhere became a replacement for serious analysis of the Castro regime. Only with the utter collapse of Eastern European and Soviet communism has this stratagem backfired and become intellectually uncomfortable, even absurd. In such a condition, the solitude of social science was a blessing for everyone.

Nowhere was this more widely evident than in the attempt to cope with Cuban militarization. Reams of paper were written denouncing every variety of military regimes in Latin America. But when the doyen in this area of research, Edwin Lieuwen, was asked how it was possible to write a text on militarism in Latin America, while failing even once to mention, much less examine, the phenomenon of Cuban militarization under Castro, the results were a loud and permanent silence; this from a major figure in the business of Latin American research. In one area after another, a strange sort of Cuban exceptionalism set in. Books on bureaucratic-authoritarian "models" were written with nary a word on Castro. For what really was disturbing to these researchers was not so much militarism or bureaucracy, but prospects of United States hegemony in the absence of military adventures. One could tolerate a frank discussion of issues comparing and contrasting Cuba with the rest of the region. Less tolerable was the myopia that denied the military, bureaucratic, and authoritarian nature of the regime in Havana (Lieuwen 1964, 1965; Rosenberg 1991, 72-92).

It has been characteristic of nearly every left-oriented social science researcher to denounce militarism and U.S. aid (which had dwindled to very little by the mid-1960s) while remaining utterly silent on the question of Cuban militarism or Soviet military support and manpower systems. This silence on questions ranging from racial discrimination in the status hierarchy of the party to declining levels of productivity in basic crops has devastating implications for social research. For such refusal to examine the interstices of the most totalitarian regime in the history of Latin America represents a subversion of social science in favor of covert political support for a dictatorship.

It would seem that no amount of reality checking can weaken the fervor of the converted. In their 1989 report on Cuba's socialist performance, Andrew Zimbalist and Claes Brundenius continue to use older data and make no effort to incorporate uncomfortable, recent post-1985 information on balance of payments and external debt for trade imbalances. Even against Cuban admissions, they hold that economic growth is real, that free enterprise zones exist, albeit on hold. This must appear as news to those who try to deal with data. These apologists argue that unqualified dependence on sugar as a crop is overestimated, that Soviet aid has been greatly exaggerated, and that the rectification process has been a great success. Zimbalist and Brundenius return to the theory struck 30 years earlier by Mills, that Cuba "favors greater pragmatism, eclecticism, and openness. There is widespread experimentation with both market and administrative decentralization" (Zimbalist and Brundenius 1989, xiv). The fact that the Cuban economy is in shambles is to be treated in two ways. First, it is a myth. Second, if true, the U.S. embargo policy is at fault.

When it further became evident that Castroism meant intervention in the affairs of other nations in the hemisphere and at large, the argument of social science apologists shifted to one of analog. After all, they claim, this indicates Cuba has an independent foreign policy. This is but an advanced praetorian guard of Bolívarism or hemispheric solidarity against American imperialism and hegemony. Despite Cuba's egregious support of every tyranny in the Third World, such social scientists continue to claim that support of Cuba is the best mechanism for integrating the hemisphere and for pulling Fidel toward a compatible foreign and domestic policy. Alas, as a result of Fidel's refusal to cooperate with this myth of the dictator turned democrat, this latest phase, openly predicated on normalization, fell flat.

The tendency in American social science has paralleled the growing desperation of an isolated left, a left that still lives, works, and dreams within categories derived from the Vietnam trauma. But it also has revealed an ongoing commitment of sociologists in particular to an underdog mentality, to a belief that Castro's Cuba was the hope of the world and the beacon of light to the poor. In point of fact, the work of social scientists on Cuba represents a fundamental betrayal of the critical tradition, one demanding examination of events based in a framework of analysis first and foremost and in a valuation framework last and tentatively. Such work also pitted domestic American sociologists against the new immigrants. And in academic life, unlike anywhere else, this older nativistic tradition was powerful enough to bloc routes of access to academic higher stations.[1]

The rise of centers like the University of Miami has been a direct consequence of blockage through the more established avenues of upward mobility in teaching and research. Because of the entrenched radicalization of older "Ivy League" centers of learning, it became difficult to establish a new wave of social science voices difficult but not impossible. Thus, in the late 1960s and early 1970s, we began to see Cuban scholars emerge in major public institutions such as Texas A & M, the University of Pittsburgh, Florida International, the University of California at Los Angeles, Georgetown University, and yes, Rutgers University.

Apart from things and places strictly academic, Cuban social scientists became increasingly involved in the U.S. policy apparatus, that is, in those agencies of government that specialized in questions of international development, economics, and demographic patterns. In part, this reflected pockets of population movement in the Cuban American community. But it also represented a fundamental, tenaciously held belief that the social sciences as science would provide the data as well as the theory necessary to combat the communist regime and the Marxist ideology that drives it. Younger social scientists, often trained in major centers within the United States, were the most likely candidates to pursue such applied research roles.

As a consequence of the Castro Revolution, and the attendant migration of a million souls who have created a virtual culture in exile, the United States has seen confrontation between two visions of social science. The field of Cuban studies is not unique; in field after field, we see examples of the glories and tragedies of social science. We also see vivid fissures in the sociology of knowledge and culture within North American life. A characteristic of these new Cubanologists was virtual silence on real Cuban history. And Marxist-Leninists, who pride themselves on paying attention to real history, managed to avoid any idea of Cuban history prior to Castro. After creating a demonology about Batista, who in retrospect was a pussy cat compared to the tyranny that now reigns, these apologists had nothing to say about the actual status of the island that was not sanctioned officially by Castro. The new history "absolved" the tyrant by denying real history.

The fact that before Castro Cuba was third in Latin America in rail and road construction, second in per capita income, and one of the leaders in health and welfare measures was dropped conveniently into the memory hole. Not that such data is necessarily an antidote to revolution. From the French Revolution to the Russian Revolution, we have recorded similar inconsistencies about the overthrowing of regimes—not at the point of worst performance, but precisely when their economies rebounded. Cuba was the perfect illustration of the "J-Curve" phenomenon deciphered by James Davis, but ideologists within social science preferred crude judgments to complex analysis.

Perhaps the use of past tense is still premature. In a volume issued in 1992, entitled *Work and Democracy in Socialist Cuba*, Linda O. Fuller has no difficulty in concluding that "glancing back over more than thirty years of production in Cuba, 1970 continues to stand out as a democratic watershed. Cuban workers had demonstrably more control over production in the 1970s and early 1980s than they did in the 1960s, and much of the explanation for this improvement lies in the politics through which socialism was instituted and consolidated on the island." And lest one think that such fantasies are about an earlier period, the author concludes by acknowledging the "revolutions of 1989 and 1990," and the mandatory assumption that whatever ills occur are "in the face of unremitting hostility from the United States." But whatever happens, whatever the fate of the Castro regime, we are reassured that such real-world events "cannot detract from the imaginativeness, the boldness, the diligence, and the commitment displayed in Cuba's attempts to counter command by the few and obedience by the many in the realm of production" (Fuller 1992, 200-201). A social science driven not by utopia but by myopia cannot long endure.

But there is a nasty corollary to this proposition: a totalitarian ideology driven by myopia can endure long after all evidence is collected and evaluated. Thus we have a new monograph on *Cuba and the USA* (Targ 1992, 113) arguing that despite "the collapse of the Socialist Bloc and the discrediting of one vision of socialism because of the former's failures, progressive people, poor people, people of color, women, workers, students, elderly persons, ecologists have been stripped of the historical ideal that has animated countless millions to act on behalf of social change." In other words, "appropriate criticisms of its [Cuba's] performance" notwithstanding, the author demands that "the Cuban revolution must be defended." Such demands for ideological purification have always been the stock and trade of true believers. With a seventy-five-year history of failure in Europe, and a parallel thirty-three-year history in Cuba, such vacuous demands in the name of the people are likely to fall on deaf ears of real people, especially the beneficiaries of such "ideals," the Cubans themselves.

When all is said and done, error and truth are both part of human nature. And in the case of the history of social scientific prognostication, error is perhaps the greater part of human nature. As a result, error can, and within a democratic society must, be forgiven, explained rather than punished. What cannot be forgiven, and what characterizes Castrologists as a group, is the sin of pride, the hubris of self-righteousness, and the animosity toward those with whom they disagree. Their motto inheres in their methodology: Deny all wrongdoing; attack those who have raised objections with ad hominem assault on their motives; demand levels of evidence beyond even the proverbial smoking gun; and, as a last resort, when the intellectual game is up, lapse into permanent, sullen silence.[2]

Once in a while, we will be told that "historical" circumstances have changed, but rarely that the scholar who makes grotesque errors has changed. The Castrologists use as their model Fidel's "rectification program." As did Castro, they fail to note that absolutely nothing has changed. The only blessing is that, finally, the political pilgrims are silent. The pictures of Che no longer stare down from the walls of the Castrologists.

The instinct for self-delusion, or perhaps simple reputational preservation, is so strong in these people that they use primitive arguments and apologetics to fend off further criticism. Now they argue for the immediate lifting of the economic embargo. They present analysis which presumes that the real culprit is George Bush, not Fidel Castro. They claim that Cuban communism is different from Soviet communism, since Cuba has "thousands of honest communist cadre" who have retained the love of the people. Rationalization is the stepchild of intellectual embarrassment.

To the bitter end, and perhaps after the end, we are faced by a group of people, daring to use the word "science," for which the only issue is right or left instead of right or wrong. We who live in this relatively sheltered world of social research must learn to look at ourselves critically. With greater depth and understanding, we must see the decomposition of the scientific grounds for policy research and social analysis within, as well as the decadence or decomposition of a communist regime without. "Reflexivity," for those who prefer such arcane language, begins at home.

At its deepest level, the problem of the American social scientific response to Castro is linked to the eternal search for paradise. This was especially true in the earlier phases. If ideology is the curse of the masses, then utopia is the bane of the intellectuals. The French intellectuals Jacques Merleau-Ponty and Raymond Claude Aron have understood this best in the postwar world, since they have had to contend with communism as an immediate danger to democracy from 1945 onward. Indeed, they also have had to contend with a higher level of chiliastic supporters of Castro—from Jean-Paul Sartre (Sartre 1961) to Régis Debray (Debray 1967)—motivated by intense hatred for democratic prospects in the West. Perhaps we in the United States have taken for granted an environment of free expression. The risks to our society and to our culture are not so remote that we can be unconcerned by a fevered few with enthusiastic responses to dictatorships. It is ultimately memory, not technique that will permit us to dig out of 33 years of a dictatorial tunnel called Castroism. Memory can be painful. But it is from this pain that a healthy social science and a new democratic political order can emerge in Cuba.

References/Notes

1. For a ringing critique of the "critical economics" and its apologetics, see Carmelo Mesa Lago, "Review Essay" in *Economic Development and Cultural Change*. Winter, 1991, 432-438.
2. When my article on "The Stalinization of Castro" broke the code of silence on the left (see *New Politics*, volume 4, number 4, 1964, 62-71), it unleashed a flood of vitriol best captured in the statement by C. Ian Lumdsen, a Canadian political economist, whose argument in "On Socialists and Stalinists: A Reply to Irving Louis Horowitz" essentially took the four-fold stage herein outlined (see *New Politics*, volume 5, number 1, 1965, 20-26). Needless to add, I still await, after 28 years, a simple acknowledgment that my response in "Castrologists and Apologists: Science in the Service of Sentiment" (see *New Politics*, volume 5, number 1, 1965, 27-34) further defining the Stalinization and militarization of Castro's Cuba did, in fact, take place.

Debray, Régis. 1967. *Revolution in the Revolution? Armed Struggle and Political Struggle in Latin America*. New York: Monthly Review Press, 126 pages.

Fagen, Richard R. 1969. *The Transformation of Political Culture in Cuba*. Stanford: Stanford University Press, 45-69.

Fagen, Richard R. 1970. "Conclusion." *Political Power in Latin America*, edited by Richard R. Fagen and Wayne A. Cornelius, Jr. Englewood Cliffs, N.J.: Prentice-Hall, 410-411.

Fuller, Linda O. 1992. *Work and Democracy in Socialist Cuba*. Philadelphia: Temple University Press, 200-201.

Gerassi, John. 1968. "Introduction." *Venceremos! The Speeches and Writings of Ernesto Che Guevara*. New York: Simon and Schuster, 22-23.

Hollander, Paul. 1992. *Anti-Americanism: Critiques at Home and Abroad, 1965-1990*. New York and Oxford: Oxford University Press, esp. 333-363. This is the best one-volume analysis of the global ideology that fuels many of the quasi-intellectual resentments characteristic of the early supporters of the Castro regime.

Huberman, Leo and Paul M. Sweezy. 1969. *Socialism in Cuba*. New York and London: Monthly Review Press, 20-21.

Karol, K.S. 1970. *Guerrillas in Power: The Course of the Cuban Revolution*. New York: Hill & Wang, viii-x, 550.

LeoGrande, William M. with Morris J. Blackman and Kenneth E. Sharpe. 1986. *Confronting Revolution: Security Through Diplomacy in Central America*. New York: Pantheon Books, 438 pages.

Lieuwen, Edwin. 1964, 1965. *Generals vs. Presidents*. New York: Praeger Publishers, 160 pages; and by the same author, *U.S. Policy in Latin America*. New York: Praeger Publishers, 149 pages. A more recent illustration of the same sort of anti-Americanism disguised as antimilitary orientation is found in Tina Rosenberg, 1991.

Mills, C. Wright. 1960. *Listen, Yankee: The Revolution in Cuba*. New York: Ballantine Books, 188-89. I have dealt at length with this in my biography, *C. Wright Mills: An American Utopian*. New York: The Free Press/Macmillan, and London: Collier-Macmillan, 1983, 282-304.

Morgan, Thomas B. 1967. *The Anti-Americans*. London: Michael Joseph Publishers, 26.

Pavlov, Ivan. [1923] 1991. "On Communist Dogmatism" [originally a speech at the Military Medical Academy in Leningrad in 1923]. *Minerva: A Review of Science, Learning and Policy*, Volume 24, Number 4 (Winter 1991), 466-475.

Rosenberg, Tina. 1991. "Beyond Elections." *Foreign Policy*, 84 (Fall), 72-92.

Sartre, Jean-Paul. 1961. *On Cuba*. New York: Ballantine Books, 160 pages.

Targ, Harry R. 1992. *Cuba and the USA: A New World Order?* New York: International Publishers, 112-113.

Weber, Max. [1918] 1946. "Science as a Vocation" [originally a speech at Munich University delivered in 1918]. From *Max Weber: Essays in Sociology*, edited by H.H. Gerth and C. Wright Mills. New York: Oxford University Press, 129-156.

Williams, William Appleman. 1962. *The United States, Cuba, and Castro*. New York: Monthly Review Press, 1-3, 168-175.

Zeitlin, Maurice. 1969. "Cuba: Revolution Without a Blueprint." *Transaction/Society*, Volume 6, Number 6, April, 1969, 38-42.

Zimbalist, Andrew and Claes Brundenius. 1989. *The Cuban Economy: Measurement and Analysis of Socialist Performance*. Baltimore: Johns Hopkins University Press, xiv.

Source and Original Title: "The Conscience of Castrologists: Thirty-Three Years of Solitude" in *The Conscience of Worms and the Cowardice of Lions: The Cuban-American Experience, 1959-1992*. Miami: The North-South Center/University of Miami, 1993, 15-35 pp.

24

Social Science as an Instrument
of Democratic Struggle

There have been three waves of social scientific migration to the United States in the twentieth century. The first, from Russia, was a fifty-year outflow of intellectuals—from Pitirim Sorokin to Vasily Leontief to Alexander Solzhenitsyn—as a consequence of the communist tyranny. The second was from Germany and Austria, a forced migration of the cream of Jewish social scientists—too numerous to list—as a result of Nazism. Among that group were the very greatest figures in the history of social science, from Sigmund Freud to Paul Lazarsfeld. The story of this European intellectual migration has been well told and needs no further elaboration—at least not in this context.[1]

The third great migration of social scientists in this century has been from Cuba. This story has been less well understood than the previous two, in part, because it is more recent. In some measure too, the participants have been uneasy in defining their own exile status.[2] Economists, social scientists, planners, lawyers, bankers, and business people who escaped the dead hand of Castroism after 1959 not only received asylum in the United States but gave in return a precious gift: the restoration of meaning and decency to social research. Cuban social scientists emerged at a time when our native crops of social scientists were least able to distinguish truth from partisanship, or compassion from passion, and hence when we were most in need of just such an infusion of reality. In this sense, providence seems to provide a special place for the United States of America. But the examination of the history and current status of social research is a story to be told elsewhere and in a context with different parameters.

In the front line of resistance to the distorted vision of North American social scientific writing about Cuba in the 1960s were journalists like Jules Dubois and Theodore Draper, and the "old fashioned" people trained in law, like Andrés Suárez. It was they who "took the hit" so to speak. They uniquely challenged a prevailing consensus that found solace in Castro and held animus for Kennedy, or more exactly, for the United States as such. Independent journalistic thinking has been a hallmark to this day, with people like Carlos Alberto Montaner, Ramón L. Bonachea, and Andrés Oppenheimer[3] setting forth critical opinion, albeit from differing vantage points, charting paths for the social scientists to examine in depth. Without these journalists, who were actually the first to review events and observe the regime without rose-colored glasses, I seriously doubt that social scientists would have been bold or forthright.

Beyond the journalists are three primary groups of Cuban social scientists in exile. The first phalanx of social scientists was recruited largely from people trained in practical economics, bankers and businessmen who adhered to revolutionary principles. When their principles were perceived as betrayed by the Castro regime, they retained a lively sense of economics as a science. Next echelons were those trained in law. Upon their arrival in the United States, they drifted into international relations and then political science as such. A third group was recruited from liberal arts and humanistic backgrounds. They were often second generation and found in sociology a mechanism for looking at social issues within Cuba, for subjecting to analysis what too readily had been taken for granted in areas like health, welfare, literacy, religion, education, and race and class composition.

It is an anomaly that overseas analysts of Cuba, both supportive and critical, reside in the United States, Latin America, and

Europe. This culture, the culture of social science, has shaped debates about Cuba. It is probably true that neither ideology nor utopia will ever be entirely transcended. Karl Mannheim staked his hopes in a *freischwebende Intelligenz*. But such freewheeling, uncommitted intellectuals have been in extremely short supply since the salons of Paris, the beer halls of Berlin, and the coffee houses of Vienna were overrun by totalitarian rulers. Once in power, they found little use for deracinated individuals, except as window dressing. In such a world, the social sciences offer the best opportunity for finding the truth about social systems and political leaders. It was the genius of the Cuban exiles that they understood how precious a tool social science was, or could be, in their struggle against the tyranny of Castro.

While the special conditions within the United States have shaped the forces of research about Cuba, particular individuals and disciplines have played central roles. And it is perhaps the best course of discovery to see the exiles as intellectuals in terms of their respective disciplines. This will tell us much about the nature of the people involved and the causes they advocated. We are dealing with individuals who, for the most part, started their careers in support of the Cuban Revolution of 1959. Like their compatriots throughout the hemisphere, the tradition of university radicalism was real and thoroughgoing. They shared hatred of tyranny and deep hopes that the world of learning was a pathway to reform of the political system. Their tradition of learning was deeply European—where specialties were embedded in the larger humanistic culture. It was a world fashioned after the reform suggestions of Ortega y Gasset in *The Mission of the University.* These were suggestions that made the intellectual class of exiled Cubans profoundly cognizant of their linkages to a larger cultural community of Latin American democrats. Let us see how this plays out in the world of social science.

The training of economists, by far the largest single bloc of Fidelistas, and ex-Fidelistas, extended beyond the bureaucratic and administrative. Even those involved in tasks such as banking and commerce held strong convictions about a democratic order in the new Cuba. When the new democratic order was not forthcoming, their sense of disillusionment was profound. This first wave of social science migrants to the United States may have come for a diverse set of reasons, but they shared in common democratic rather than authoritarian premises. Operationally, that meant a sense of civic culture was embedded in the economic and social analysis they came to advocate. In terms of academic progeny, this further meant identification for Keynesian and post-Keynesian monetary reforms rather than Marxist-Leninist notions of total systemic overhaul. Indeed, the early years of Fidelismo inured them against categorical imperatives at the policy level.

It was not so much that their economic premises were identical, but rather that their sense of reform had been betrayed by the dogmatism with which Castro approached problems of the Cuban economy. Instead of economic diversification, there was intensified dependence on a single crop. In place of economic independence, there was growing dependence on Soviet power. And in place of a notion of a council of economic advisors, there emerged a *partinost* concept of science, exemplified by the leading role given to Ernesto Guevara in the reformation of the national bank. This may have been a popular move within the communist cadre, but it was a sure signal that political rather than professional appointments and decision-making were to be the order of the day. I suspect that it was this latter turn toward fanaticism that led the leading younger economists to seek exile rather than continue with the regime in power.

A second prominent group was the political scientists, or better, the lawyers. The fine lines crafted in North American universities were far cloudier in Cuban university life. There, faculties of law trained international specialists, and the notion of political science was infused by the rule of law. Indeed, one must note that if the economists were turned off by the process of politicizing, this was even more nearly the case for political scientists. For in the early 1960s, when the functions of party and state were merged in true communist fashion, so too were the functions of law subsumed under the needs of Cuban policy.

The Andrei Vyshinskii or neo-Stalinist model became the Cuban model of law. Prospects for an independent political science and an autonomous judiciary were dissolved in the heat of orthodox Stalinist partisanship, in the fusion of state and party functions.

Many political scientists were from a younger cohort. They completed their graduate studies in major American universities, which greatly influenced the course of their development. The works of Harold Lasswell, V.O. Key, Hans Morgenthau, Daniel Lerner, and later Samuel Huntington became integrated into the older juridical traditions of international law as they were taught in the pre-revolutionary University of Havana. Several critical individuals came to political science from the historical sciences; in a Cuban context, this meant the human sciences writ large.

The lines were not drawn sharply, and the sense of overlap was substantial. One would have to say that historians, within what we would today see as a liberal arts orientation, formed the third part of the triad that gave substance to a Cuban-American social science paradigm. People like Luis Aguilar and later Jorge Dominguez[4] provided analysis of Cuba in the first half of the century that enabled researchers to establish a reasonable measuring rod for examining the Castro epoch. This was especially true in areas ranging from constitutional reform to linguistic corruption of the Spanish language by the totalitarians.

The historians were crucial in establishing the baseline, the source, of Cuban democracy. They reminded one and all that Castro was like a modern-day Robespierre, someone who wanted to begin the world anew, to start the clock from zero. The historians showed us that this effort was largely fiction, doomed to tragedy and failure. Cuba had a democratic as well as an autocratic tradition. To be sure, historians of the stature of the great encyclopedist and geographer Levi Marrero, by reconstructing the history of Cuba, reminded the research community that older autocrats were mild compared to the fate that had befallen post-1959 Cuba.

There were other social scientists. These men and women often came later and were products of higher education in North America. It is from this pool that the sociologists were drawn, and they added a dimension of considerable consequence. For in a context that was extremely difficult, in departments filled with excessive radicalism and antagonism toward the United States for what was seen as an unjust war in Vietnam, the new Cuban intellectuals learned much from the tradition of classical and modern sociology and applied these lessons, albeit sotto voce, to the situation in Cuba.

While these younger sociologists are perhaps less broad in intellectual scope than their elders, they were also far better trained. Hence, their critical analysis, while much "cooler" in rhetorical terms, nonetheless has served to enrich the ethnographic tradition as well as the analytical tradition derived from North American sociology. The study of deviant youth, of military mobility, of the character of the health system, while not always on target, has provided nonetheless a much-needed base in social analyses that has made Cuba subject to investigation like no other society. Such cool analysis went beyond the ballast of ideological Marxism, into a clear-eyed set of statements of what Cuba under Castro actually had accomplished. And as the regime bared its claws, this line of sociological investigation became sharper and more pointed. Once again, it carried the critical tradition into the next generation of Cuban exile scholars, becoming a counterpoint to a point, a way of viewing Cuba that provided powerful amplification of the subjective, anti-human side of a totalitarian society.

In recent years, the Cuban exile community and its social scientists have broadened their analytic scope with greater sophistication and meaning to all students of development and political culture. They have done so, until recently, with remarkably little institutional and foundation support. Indeed, one might fully expect that, when the Castro tyranny is over and done with, the theoretical accomplishments of these exiles will stand—all the more astonishing for their being given so little support or encouragement for so many years.

At a time when scholarship in Cuba proper simply dried up or turned parochial, a new generation of Cuban American scholars like Luis Aguilar, Pérez-Firmat, Edward González, and Carmelo

Mesa-Lago developed a variety of comparative frameworks that involve Eastern Europe, the Middle East, and Russia, as well as more conventional North-South linkages. Cultural studies conducted by Marcos Ramos and Carlos Ripoll have made it perfectly plain that such interests remain very much alive inside Cuba. The very notion of the North-South Center is an offshoot of the Cuban Studies Center. It is predicated on a notion of cultural identity and physical Diaspora. While the amplification of this extends far beyond Cuba, we must see this idea as originating in Hispanic regionalism, a kind of Bolivarism without the ultra-nationalism that came before.

One could well cite other illustrations. But these must suffice to show that Cuban intellectuals in exile, far from being parochial, limited, or narrow, are, in fact, the third great wave of social researchers to these shores in the present century. They share with the Russian migration a deep disdain for totalitarian solutions. They share with the German-Jewish migration a feeling for the universal nature of political issues. But they are also different. They have stayed focused on Cuba and the hemisphere. Unlike the Frankfurt school, for example, they have not forgotten their national and linguistic roots. They do not cling to the illusions of democratic socialism, or a Stalinism with a human face, although many were, and some remain, dedicated to social democracy.

Because for the most part they were not accepted in the major U.S. institutions of higher learning, as were the Sorokins, Marcuses, and Lazarsfelds, Cuban migrants became a critical force enriching the land grant universities; often public agencies were more responsive to the Cubans' needs as refugees. Hence, a certain unique dimension took place—a symbiosis of old and new. Rather than a presumptive insinuation that anything from German culture was better than American civilization, the Cubans took up the study of social science in a highly pragmatic way. They took what they felt was important, whatever its points of origin, and applied it creatively. In so doing, they enlarged the range of possible applications of social research to quite new and different circumstances. In this, they were closer to the grain of actual American experience. They insisted, for better or worse, on criteria of relevance as well as accuracy.

Most important, Cuban social scientists had a keen sense of the need for a research design well integrated into the policy process. By their incessant demand for a Free Cuba, they became plugged into congressional committees, journalistic activities, and institution building at university levels that were disdained by older European immigrant intellectuals. Indeed, the tradition in advanced societies of providing annual yearbooks of social and economic performance has been maintained by Radio Martí in its landmark series on *Cuba Annuals*. In this regard, the work of José Alonso and his team can hardly be exaggerated.[5] For the past decade, the sifting and distilling of information on and about Cuba that has lasting significance has been in his charge. And what, in other circumstances, might enlist the efforts of hundreds of people has been performed with distinction by a handful of dedicated people. A free society is an information society, while a totalitarian society is a misinformation society. The existence of *Cuba Annuals* in the United States points up this irony with stunning impact. Typical of this group of government-oriented social scientists is an individual mentioned earlier in another context, Ernesto Betancourt, who spent 16 years at the Organization of American States before becoming the first director of the Radio Martí Program of the United States Information Agency. Others, like Jorge F. Pérez-López, went to the Bureau of International Labor Affairs in the United States Department of Labor. While yet others, like Peter J. Montiel, spent many years at the World Bank and the International Monetary Fund.

These are outstanding individuals who, lacking broad institutional support, managed to convert their policy activities into research environments. They were typical in their administrative work environments but atypical in their high level of intellectual productivity. Ernesto Betancourt, for example, is the author of a fundamental treatise on the nature of revolutionary violence, one that perhaps marks the first major step beyond the formulations of Crane Brinton's "natural history of revolution" in the

1930s. The work of Pérez-López on *Measuring Cuban Economic Performance* provided a breakthrough mechanism for translating communist fictions into economic facts. And the efforts of Peter J. Montiel have been directed at comparative analysis relating macroeconomic models in developing countries to policy efforts aimed at reducing inflation in such places as Argentina, Brazil, Israel, and Eastern Europe.

This group of Cuban American economists, with a government-based set of linkages, has a high interest in connecting policy analysis and macroeconomic change in developing areas. At the substantive level, their interests are in saving, investment, and growth; while at the comparative level, in the performance of free market and planned market systems. They were and remain the quintessential Schumpeterians. Perhaps this emphasis on economic models of growth helps explain why Cuban American scholarship remains interested in improving accuracy in data presentation and retrieval, with a special emphasis on modeling and data accountability. The absence and complete breakdown of such safeguards in Cuban statistical information has prompted such interests. We forget that strong ideological positions sometimes provoke, as well as prevent, the need for a high information profile. In any event, they typify a special contribution of Cuban scholars to the life of America and to the lifeblood of the social sciences.

If the Cubans are known rightfully as the Jews of the Caribbean by virtue of their industry, innovation, and entrepreneurship, the Jews themselves are with equal justice known as the people of the book. The Latin American landscape in the past half-century has been enlarged and enriched by their analytic, and at times, their physical presence. Indeed, no people has more enriched—even transformed—the study of Latin America than have the Jewish intellectuals. They have given theoretical hope to empirical research and have converted the study of the region from a desultory variety of history as pure dynastic narrative into a centerpiece of analysis, criticism, and policy. Nowhere is this more evident than in the study of Cuba.

The worm within the apple, however, is Jewish intellectual response to the Cuban Revolution and its aftermath. This is hardly a theme for polite society. But rather than whisper about such matters, it might be time to bring it front and center. I have written elsewhere and often on the dual nature of Jewish intellectual conscience. It is bifurcated along a dual axis of a search for freedom on the positive side and hatred for totalitarian modes of rule on the negative side. It is little wonder that this split intellectual personality reflects itself most directly—and bitterly—in the social sciences.

The line-up is painfully revealing: Richard Fagen, Maurice Zeitlin, Sandor Halebsky, Leo Huberman, and John Gerassi have argued the case and cause of Castro's Cuba; and Elliott Abrams, Bernard Aronson, Mark Falcoff, Rhoda Rabkin, and Linda Klein among others have made the case for the prosecution.[6] Cuba provides a painful example of a continuing pattern: one group of American social scientists of Jewish extraction taking a strong leadership role in an effort to sanitize and sanctify yet another dictator promising moral redemptions and economic rectifications, and another group attempting to make plain the disastrous consequences for democratic outcomes of such a dictatorship.

The appeal to social justice is strong within Jewish tradition. And among Jews without Judaism, those who have secularized the search for divine redemption into earthly equity, interest in communist regimes remains a strong component. When one thinks of the significant Jewish component in the origins of every movement from international psychoanalysis to international communism, one is reminded of that unquenchable Jewish optimism. Jews cannot easily relinquish a belief that the law giver as dictator somehow will provide new light onto the suffering souls of the world. But in truth, the Jewish tradition is too rich in irony, too close to the marrow of real-world events, to fall prey easily to the murky universalism dished out by dictators.

This was especially the case for Cuban exiles of Jewish extraction, who watched a thriving Jewish community of twelve thousand at the time of the Cuban Revolution; dwindle to a group of fewer than one thousand at present. I dare say that the lapse into silence on the part of some social scientists of Jewish extraction with respect to Castro's Cuba has been as much motivated by the single-minded anti-Semitism of the regime, and the consistency of its support of Yasser Arafat, Muammar Qaddafi, and Saddam Hussein, as by its internal programs and policies. To be sure, there is not a regime in the world where the practice of anti-Semitism has been brought to a higher pitch than in Castro's regime. Among Cuban exiles who turned to social science, there is a noteworthy group of individuals of Jewish ancestry, foremost of who is Jaime Suchlicki. It must be said frankly that the empirical reality of dictatorship rather than the longing after utopia obviously, if somewhat belatedly, gained the upper hand in Jewish thought. The social sciences became a tool neither of ideology nor utopia but of analysis and struggle. And it became such, and remains such, within the Jewish community.

I do not wish to deny or minimize the role played by non-Jews and non-Cubans alike. To be sure, the work of Hugh Thomas and John Plank offer towering evidence of broad interest. Yet, it remains the case that we are dealing with an ethnic drama of no small consequence, a search for social scientific analysis wrapped in a gnarled bundle of ethnic and religious twine. Those in the exile community who are bitter at the number of Jews found in support of the last great tyrant of the Western world should remember errors in estimates notwithstanding, that they were motivated largely by the universal search for justice that has long propelled Jewish life and letters. It must also be recorded that the growing numbers of Jewish intellectuals found in opposition to the tyrant and in defense of freedom is a tribute to that same longing for universal justice. We have a play within a play, a theology within a sociology. Dictatorships have a way of eliciting complex responses from the sensitive and the scientific.

In speaking of the Jewish factor, it is intriguing to note a fusion of regional as well as professional factors: a fission of ethnic and religious tribes. For the Jews and Cubans uniquely give distinctive character and flavor to Miami. They mutually reinforce each other's sense of commerce, industry, and intellect in an enclave area. Whether one calls this a geist, esprit, or espiritu, its presence is felt clearly. The two groups fuel this city; they give it an identity all its own. Indeed, they even import old-line Protestants to give the city that certain Mayflower flavor. That the social scientific world has become an intrinsic part of this special city is nothing surely to neither disguise nor disparage. Such a special blend of ethnic, religious, and national factors is the stuff of growth and helps to explain why the social sciences have been powerful tools for two diverse groups for whom the search for truth preempts the truth of searches. Cubans and Jews, Cuban Americans and Jewish Americans have in common a stubborn belief that real information transforms people and heals nations. They are the source of plans, practical and utopian, for the remaking of Cuba in a democratic fashion.

This special set of circumstances has eased the flow of a unique symbiosis of social science to both the larger society of Cuban exiles and the somewhat smaller society of Jewish migrants from other parts of the United States. Unlike the typical European experience, in which the ethnic population and the scholarly community were at loggerheads in the New World, or at the least, indifferent to one another's concerns, the Cuban community has always taken a lively and positive interest in the activities of its social scientists. That sense of support gave to the social scientists an aura of practicability and responsibility to a larger body politic that is often absent in émigré social science research from older sources. This has a weakness to be sure—perhaps an overzealous desire to accommodate. But such tendencies are more than offset by support in fiscal and intellectual terms. Doubtless, when the tyrant in Cuba is overthrown, relationships of intellectuals to other segments will be "normalized," but for the past 33 years, it has been a unique symbiotic relationship. The social research personnel have drawn inspiration from the needs of the exile community, while the exile community has been consistent in supporting the tasks of social scientists, even when these may have appeared remote.

Such a wide array of participants has sometimes resulted in a cacophonous rather than harmonious set of intellectual relations.

This is evidenced in the policy field, where there seem to be nearly as many points of view and recommendations for a post-Castro arrangement as there are commentators. This might fit well with the contentious if not combative nature of Cuban intellectual life, but it does blunt the edge of speaking against the still-reigning tyrant with a single voice. This should provide small comfort to the dwindling days of the Castro regime. For in their very diversity, the voices of democracy assert their priorities and claims over Cuba.

As a result of their geographical proximities and social scientific proclivities, researchers of Cuban extraction have remained concentrated geographically and in greater personal contact than the Europeans who preceded them to these shores. The social scientists of Cuban descent were less absorbed in older disciplines and more involved in bending those disciplines to newer tasks. In short, the indebtedness of our nation to social scientists from Cuba was and remains enormous, yet still largely unacknowledged—mired in the hatred of those for whom Fidel Castro remains either a heroic figure or an embarrassment. This contribution is part of the experience of Cuban visions and American vistas. It has been an amazing cross-fertilization. The struggle for a democratic Cuba involves the recognition that truth itself is a weapon in this effort. In consequence, serendipitous and unintended thought it might have been, the soul of social science itself has been given new life and renewed vindication by the Cuban-American experience.

References/Notes

1. See Donald Fleming and Bernard Bailyn, editors, *The Intellectual Migration: Europe and America, 1930-1960.* Cambridge: Harvard University Press, 1969, 748 pages. See also Ilja Srubar, editor, *Exil, Wissenschaft, Identitat: Die Emigration deutscher Sozialwissenschafter,* 1933-1945. Frankfurt am Main: Suhrkamp Verlag, 1988, 383 pages.
2. Among the previous efforts to summarize Cuban Studies in the United States, one can mention Nelson Valdes, "Revolution and Paradigms: A Critical Assessment of Cuban Studies" in *Cuban Political Economy: Controversies in Cubanology,* edited by Andrew Zimbalist. Boulder: Westview Press, 1988; Enrique Baloyra, "Side Effects: Cubanology and Its Critics" in *Latin American Research Review,* Volume 22, Number 1,1987; and Car-

melo Mesa-Lago's "Three Decades of Studies of the Cuban Revolution," (mimeographed), 58 pages. These examinations, from differing perspectives, have in common a strong defense of social science accompanied by the expected critique of communist partisanship.

3. Andrés Oppenheimer's work at *The Miami Herald* and *The Journal of Commerce* has netted him wide attention. His new activity, writing editorial commentaries, indicates a level of analysis of Cuban affairs beyond any other being offered in a newspaper context.

4. The work of Jorge I. Domínguez has provided researchers with a remarkable chronicle of Cuban foreign policy in the fulcrum of its history. See especially, *Cuba: Order and Revolution*. Cambridge: Harvard University Press, 1978, 683 pages and *To Make a World Safe for Revolution*. Cambridge: Harvard University Press, 1989, 365 pages.

5. *Cuba Annual Reports* are prepared by the Radio Martí program, initially as quarterly reports on Cuba issued by the Voice of America of the United States Information Agency. From their inception, in 1985, these have been published by Transaction. A great deal of credit must go to Ernesto Betancourt and now Rolando Bonachea—the past and present directors of Radio Martí—for instituting this service and making it available to the American public. It should be noted too that prior to the 1959 Castro revolution, Cuba had the most advanced *Anuarios* in Latin America.

6. I have checked through the current edition of my anthology on *Cuban Communism* (New Brunswick and London: Transaction Publishers, 1989, seventh edition) and identify no fewer than twelve who are of Jewish-American and/or Jewish-Cuban ancestry. Just mentioning their work does not do proper credit to them, but at least it makes the point of this segment of the paper unqualifiedly. They are, among others, Alan H. Luxenberg, Leon Gouré, Rhoda Rabkin, Linda Klein, Mark Falcoff, Vladimir Tismaneanu, Jaime Suchlicki, and Susan Kaufman Purcell. One should look at Rhoda Rabkin's fine dissertation on *Cuban Politics: The Revolutionary Experiment*. Westport, Conn.: Praeger, 1991, 233 pages.

Abrams, Elliott. 1990. "Comment." *Cuba in the Nineties,* edited by Frank Calzon. Washington, D.C.: Freedom House, 23-24.

Aguilar, Luis E. 1972. *Cuba 1933: Prologue to Revolution.* Ithaca: Cornell University Press, 256 pages. For his more recent work, see "Castro's Last Stand: Can Cuba Be Freed without a Bloodbath?" *Policy Review* (Summer) 1990.

Aronson, Bernard. 1991. "Statement before the Subcommittee on Western Hemisphere Affairs." *Cuba in a Changing World: The United States-Soviet-Cuban Triangle.* Washington, D.C.: U.S. Government Printing Office, 89-135.

Betancourt, Ernesto. 1991. *Revolutionary Strategy: A Handbook for Practitioners.* New Brunswick and London: Transaction Publishers, 203 pages.

Bonachea, Ramón L. and Marta San Martín. 1974. *The Cuban Insurrection, 1952-1959.* New Brunswick and London: Transaction Publishers, 451 pages.

Díaz-Briquets, Sergio. 1983. *The Health Revolution in Cuba.* Austin: University of Texas Press, 227 pages; and more recently, *Cuban Internationalism in Sub-Saharan Africa.* Pittsburgh: Duquesne University Press, 1989, 211 pages.

Draper, Theodore. 1962. *Castro's Revolution: Myths and Realities.* New York: Praeger, 211 pages; and also his more popular effort on *Castroism: Theory and Practice.* New York: Praeger, 1965, 263 pages.

Dubois, Jules. 1959. *Fidel Castro: Rebel.* Indianapolis: Bobbs-Merrill Publishers, 391 pages.

Fagen, Richard. 1964. *Cuba: The Political Content of Adult Education.* Stanford: Hoover Institution Press, 77 pages; *Cubans in Exile.* Stanford: Stanford University Press, 1968, 161 pages; and *The Transformation of Political Culture in Cuba.* Stanford: Stanford University Press, 1969, 271 pages. It is not without interest that Fagen's writings on Cuba ceased at this time—just when things were getting interesting.

Fernández, Damian. 1990. *Central America and the Middle East: The Internationalization of the Crisis.* Miami: Florida International University Press, 239 pages.

Gerassi, John. 1973. *Fidel Castro: A Biography.* Garden City, N.Y.: Doubleday & Company, 137 pages. It is instructive to contrast this potboiler with the work of another Jewish commentator (and socialist) Leo Sauvage. *Che Guevara: The Failure of a Revolutionary.* Englewood Cliffs, N.J.: Prentice-Hall, 1973, 282 pages.

Gonzalez, Edward. 1969. *The Cuban Revolution and the Soviet Union, 1950-1960.* Los Angeles: University of California (Dissertation), 659 mimeographed pages. The major work of this author is *Cuba under Castro; The Limits of Charisma.* Boston: Houghton-Mifflin, 1974, 241 pages.

Halebsky, Sandor, editor. 1985. *Cuba: Twenty-Five Years of Revolution, 1959-1984.* New York: Praeger, 466 pages; and the more recent edited effort, *Transformation and Struggle; Cuba Faces the 1990s.* New York: Praeger, 1990, 291 pages. For a rather different treatment on a broader canvas, see Mark Falcoff and Robert Royal, editors. *The Continuing Crisis; U.S. Policy in Central America and the Caribbean.* Washington, D.C.: Ethics and Public Policy Center, 1987, 555 pages.

Huberman, Leo. 1968. *Cuba: Anatomy of a Revolution.* New York: Monthly Review Press; and *Socialism in Cuba.* New York: Monthly Review Press, 1969, 221 pages.

Jorge, Antonio. 1991. *A Reconstruction Strategy for Post-Castro Cuba.* Miami: The North-South Center, University of Miami, 38 pages.

Mannheim, Karl. 1954. *Ideology and Utopia.* New York: Harcourt, Brace and Company.

Marrero, Levi. 1950. *Geográfia de Cuba.* New York: Minerva Books, Ltd., 707 pages. But the major work and simply astonishing effort is the multi-volumed *Cuba: Economía y Sociedad,* published in Madrid by Editorial Playor, 1985 *et passim.* The testimonials offered to this effort, the equivalent of Joseph Needham's *Science and Civilization in China* (and still not available in English), by people such as J.G.A. Pocock and Ernest R. May, are entirely deserved.

Mesa-Lago, Carmelo. 1979. *Cuba in the World.* Pittsburgh: University of Pittsburgh Press, 343 pages; *Cuba in the 1970s: Pragmatism and Institutionalization.* Albuquerque: University of New Mexico Press, 1974, 179 pages; *The Economy of Socialist Cuba; A Two-Decade Appraisal.* Albuquerque: University of New Mexico Press, 1981, 235 pages; and *The Labor Sector and Socialist Distribution in Cuba.* New York: Praeger, 1968, 250 pages. Mesa-Lago has uniquely charted the economic forces in Cuba since the inception of the Revolution. Much of his work now appears in journal format, but he has continued with this task—enlarging its scope to include more comparative examples and frameworks.

Mesa-Lago, Carmelo and Carl Beck, editors. 1975. *Comparative Socialist Systems.* Pittsburgh: University of Pittsburgh Center for International Studies, 441 pages. This theme was first enunciated by Mesa-Lago in his dissertation on *Unemployment in Socialist Countries: Soviet Union, East Europe, China, and Cuba.* Ithaca: Cornell University (dissertation), 1968, 569 mimeographed pages. After ten years of publishing on Cuba in journals, Mesa-Lago has written a new book, *Cuba After the Cold War,* to be issued by the University of Pittsburgh Press.

Montaner, Carlos Alberto. 1985. *Cuba, Castro, and the Caribbean: The Cuban Revolution and the Crisis in Western Conscience.* New Brunswick: Transaction, 116 pages; *Fidel Castro and the Cuban Revolution.* New Brunswick: Transaction, 1989, 214 pages; and his earlier effort on *The Secret Report of the Cuban Revolution.* New Brunswick: Transaction, 1981, 284 pages.

Montiel, Peter J. 1992. *Informal Financial Markets in Developing Countries: A Macroeconomic Analysis* (with P.R. Agenor and Nadeem Haque). Oxford: Basil Blackwell Ltd.; and *Macroeconomic Models for Adjustment in Developing Countries* (with M. Khan and N. Haque). Washington, D.C.: International Monetary Fund, 1991.

Mujal-León, Eusebio. 1988. *The Cuban University Under the Revolution.* Washington, D.C.: Cuban American National Foundation, 70 pages.

Ortega y Gasset, José. 1991. *Mission of the University* (with a new introduction by Clark Kerr). New Brunswick: Transaction, 120 pages.

Pérez, Lisandro. 1989. *The Cuban Population of the United States.* Miami: Florida International University, 22 pages.

Pérez-López, Jorge F. 1987. *Measuring Cuban Economic Performance.* Austin: University of Texas Press; "Bringing the Cuban Economy into Focus." *Latin American Research Review,* Volume 26, Number 1, 1989, 17-53.

Pérez-López, Jorge F. 1992. *The Cuban State Budget: Concepts and Measurement.* Miami: The North-South Center, University of Miami, 168 pages.

Ramos, Marcos A. 1989. *Protestantism and Revolution in Cuba.* Miami: Institute for Interamerican Studies, University of Miami, 168 pages.

Ripoll, Carlos. 1985. *The Heresy of Words in Cuba: Freedom of Expression and Information.* New York: Freedom House, 55 pages.

Ripoll, Carlos. 1990. *Los Fundamentos del Estalinismo en Cuba.* New York: Granada Arts Services, 50 pages.

Roca, Sergio. 1976. *Cuban Economic Policy and Ideology.* Beverly Hills: Sage Publications, 70 pages; *Economic Structure and Ideology in Socialist Cuba.* New Brunswick: Transaction, 1975; and *Socialist Cuba: Past Interpretations and Future Challenges.* Boulder: Westview Publishers, 1988, 253 pages.

Salas, Luis. 1979. *Social Control and Deviance in Cuba.* New York: Praeger, 398 pages.

Suárez, Andrés. 1967. *Cuba, Castroism and Communism, 1959-1966.* Cambridge: Massachusetts Institute of Technology Press, 260 pages.

Suchlicki, Jaime. 1969. *University Students and Revolution in Cuba.* Coral Gables: University of Miami Press, 177 pages; *Cuba, Castro, and Revolution.* Coral Gables: University of Miami Press, 1972, 250 pages; *Cuba: From Columbus to Castro.* New York: Scribner, 1974, 242 pages; and most recently, *Historical Dictionary of Cuba.* Metuchen: Scarecrow Press, 1988, 368 pages.

Thomas, Hugh. 1971. *Cuba: The Pursuit of Freedom.* New York: Harper & Row, 1696 pages; and *The Cuban Revolution.* New York: Harper & Row, 1977, 755 pages. In this same connection, a decent and fair-minded early compendium was the one edited by John Plank, *Cuba and the United States.* Washington, D.C.: The Brookings Institution, 1967, 265 pages.

Vyshinskii, Andrei Y. 1948. *The Law of the Soviet State.* New York: Macmillan Company, 749 pages. It is not without irony that this unadulterated Stalinist effort was sponsored by the American Council of Learned Societies in its series devoted to humanistic studies.

Source and Original Title: "The Conscience of Worms: Social Science as an Instrument of Struggle" in *The Conscience of Worms and the Cowardice of Lions: The Cuban-American Experience, 1959-1992.* Miami: The North-South Center/University of Miami, 1993, 37-55 pp.

25

The Cuban Revolution: The Myth of Theory and the Theory of Myths

In Juan Rulfo's now-classic 1955 novel, *Pedro Páramo,* one follows a dusty road to a hallucinatory town of death. The following dialogue occurs: "Up and down the hill we went, but always descending. We had left the hot wind behind and were sinking into pure, airless heat. The stillness seemed to be waiting for something. 'It's hot here,' I said. 'You might say. But this is nothing,' my companion replied. 'Try to take it easy. You'll feel it even more when we get to Comala. That town sits on the coals of the Earth, at the very mouth of Hell. They say that when people from there die and go to Hell, they come back for a blanket.' I asked, 'Do you know Pedro Páramo?' I felt I could ask because I had seen a glimmer of good will in his eyes. 'Who is he?' I pressed him, 'Living bile,' he replied."[1]

And so it is. Our excursion into the mouth of the Castro phenomenon requires a sense of the surrealistic, of living bile. If I may be permitted a take-off on a famous quip by Marx: What first appeared on the scene of history as paradise reappears in contemporary Cuba as paradise lost. That descent into Hell taken, it is an appropriate time to summarize what we have learned—if anything—about the nature of the political and social process called, for want of a more artful phrase, "Castroism." Our learning curve takes us between the myth of theory construction and the reality of myth-making. From the rubble of this regime, there is much to be learned; whether the intellectual class is willing to do so is quite another matter.

Thirty-three years of Castroism helps us to appreciate the distinction between classical myth and political myth—that is, between a harkening back to a time that was magical and beatific, to a denial of time as tradition, to asserting that everything is in front of us, and nothing of value is behind us. The political myths developed by Castro and his acolytes pertain to expectations of what shall occur rather than reflections upon what has occurred. Let us discuss the contributions to political mythology by Fidel Castro and the Revolution which he fashioned.

The Myth of Eternal Development

Castro built his regime on the Marxist-Leninist doctrine that socialism is the inevitable and imminent consequence of capitalism. Furthermore, it is a superior system in terms of delivering goods and services. A parallel vision is that socialism guarantees autonomy and sovereignty. This is the master myth of communism in power, since in empirical terms its actual ability to compel economic development through change in political regimes is highly suspect.

It is clear enough that changes in the real world are neither unilinear nor unidirectional. In contrast to Marxist doctrine, social change moves in all sorts of directions, down as well as up, and most often laterally. What we know as Brownian movement in biology is also the case in economy. To speak of "laws" of development in which vast social systems, the world over, move from primitive communism, to slavery, to feudalism, next to capitalism, and finally to communism at a "higher stage" is little more than the myth of the eternal longing for paradise dressed up as a "law" of society—nothing short of a scientific canon.

There are regularities in social and political life. There are relationships between prices, wages, and profits that tend to stimulate growth and depression. But these all take place at a "middle range," that is to say, at a range of reality in which one can identify the major variables and hence manipulate and manage them. So much writing on communist regimes has been framed by eighteenth-century political economy that the critical importance of twentieth-century political psychology has been either neglected or seriously downplayed. In Castro, we are dealing with a personality who has ruled over a long stretch of gubernatorial time. Hence, patterns of behavior, more than forces of history, are decisive.

Castro illustrates well the myth of Cuban development in action. Confirmed Marxist and Communist that he claims to be and has been he is yet able to tell us in 1992 that Cubans should count their blessings that the nation is in the grip of a terrible fuel and food crisis. His response is intriguing. Instead of expressing even a modicum of concern that development is dependent on those fuels that drive the new technology, something Castro clearly must know, he makes no effort to seek mechanisms to relieve his people of the burdens imposed by his own political arrogance. Instead, he reverts to a solution predicated on the return of Cuba to primitive agrarianism.

Waxing elegiac, Castro notes, "We are back to the ox—the noble ox. If the earth is wet, tractors are useless, and oxen are thirteen times as productive." Castro takes as a given that the fuel shortage seriously has impaired production of foodstuffs in Cuba. He goes beyond this, however, and converts fact into virtue. Fidel does not tell us that tractors are a hundred times more productive than oxen on dry days! He takes the same approach toward cuts in transportation services. Necessity becomes a virtue. "We are going to the bicycle. We distributed a million bicycles in 1991."[2] Again, there is not a word about the waste of human energy in getting to and from work or the drainage this entails in performing work.

Beyond what has been widely reported—the indifference of the Cuban regime to the worsening quality of national life in stark contrast to the effort to attract tourists from Europe, Canada, and Latin America, and gratifying their expectations[3]—is a more protracted significance: Cuba is on an intense downward spiral. So-called laws of development have simply been abandoned. Further, suffering as such is presented as something of a virtue, stimulating self-sacrifice and dedication to basic needs.

We sometimes forget that Stalinism has two sides. One is an excessive faith in laws of development through which communism triumphs over its capitalist foes and moves into a world of happiness—what Joseph Stalin often referred to in the last years of his life as the fourth law of socialism. The other, darker side of Stalinism is a belief in the blessings of sacrifice, and if necessary, mass death. Much of the Soviet Union's terrible suffering was cast by Stalin in generational terms: Future generations will benefit from sacrifices of the present generation. Needless to say, specifications as to the time needed to bring about such a great instauration were not provided. It seemed enough to assert that the task of the revolutionary shock troops was to suffer now for a better tomorrow. This same dark side in the theory and practice of Stakhanovism is now evident in Castroism. In the absence of the optimistic descriptions of the blessings of the new regime, we have moral purification of a regime in economic disarray.

In place of the myth of development, we end up thirty-three years later with the reality of reverse development, or worse, downward economic mobility for the entire infrastructure. It is a phenomenon we saw take place in the Middle East, specifically in Iran after the overthrow of the Shah, and it is now clearly the marching order of the final stage of communism in Cuba. The difficulty that Castro has had to face is that, unlike the various Ayatollahs, he cannot claim the virtues of traditionalism and the vices of modernization. He has to live with a self-proclaimed doctrine of eternal progress in face of social facts that belie such gratuitous claims.

The Myth of the Revolutionary Will

The history of Marxism and socialism alike has been plagued by the philosophical dilemma of determinism. If all events are determined by a series of laws, and if people are subject to law-like behavior, just what is the role of the individual in determining his or her own fate? In other words, if every event is part of a larger intertwined pattern or mosaic written in the stars, why not sit back and let the revolution take its course?

The problem is that the so-called inner contradictions of capitalism either have never materialized, or when they did, have yielded a
wide variety of outcomes—few of which could have been, or were,
predicted. Simply put, an economic depression, such as that which
gripped the world in 1929 and the following decade, resulted in a
variety of outcomes: fascism in Germany, militarism in Japan, so-
cial-welfare New Dealism in Scandinavia and the United States,
and a hardening of the communist regime in Russia.

These larger themes have been well covered and need not be
repeated here. Sidney Hook said it best: "Every contingent fact
makes a break in a web of historical relationships that determines how far it shall fall. All that we need to vindicate here is
the fact that the web is often broken, and that a great man may
be one of the contingent phenomena that break in."[4] Implicit in
such an analysis of the role of the great man, of human will as
it were, is the need to focus upon subjective as well as objective
factors; for it is the combination and permutations of Friedrich
Nietzsche and Karl Marx that uniquely characterized the rise of
Castro to power in Cuba.

The July 26th Movement began with a set of premises about
human will characteristic of the Franco-Italian or Sorelian response to orthodox Marxism. In this belief system, leadership
and will, mobilization and charisma, are at least as important as
history and economy.[5] Indeed, discussions about Castro's "early
Marxism" are essentially silly, since the exact date at which he
became a communist or a confirmed Marxist is far less important
than the set of convictions with which he approached the tasks
of revolution-making. It is the character of his fervor rather than
the nature of his ideology that was decisive.

The kernel of truth in the myth of revolutionary will is the
huge role of personality in the progress of the Cuban Revolution. Castro took Stalin's personality cult to another level. Stalin's
presumed greatness in all things from linguistics to philosophy
was attributed to his special understanding of objective history.
With Castro, it was the subjective side of Stalin—the variety of
his psychological characteristics from pragmatic flexibility to

iron determination in the face of adversity—that were deemed crucial by Castro and his propagandists of the soul.

Many things were important to the success of the Cuban Revolution: willingness to give history a nudge as well as impatience with situations the way they were. Castro applied the lessons of decision theory more than economic laws. But the Achilles' heel of this approach is that it overlooks external circumstances in the world at large. Conversely, it is an approach which gratifies ego more than copes with others. A prosaic illustration will suffice here: The essential indifference—indeed, at certain levels, even support—of the United States to Castro's revolutionary movement led to a specific erosion of will on the part of Castro's political opponents. Couple this with a tradition of caudillismo that was harnessed to revolutionary slogans, the advanced state of communications and transportation in Cuba, and the oft-cited unique topography of Cuba which gave cover to guerrilla warriors, and the special circumstances which made the Cuban Revolution a reality can be readily explained—not as an immutable law of nature but as a specific moment in national time and place.

One must look at the prosaic history of Cuban-American relations to grasp the significance of lack of will on the part of the Eisenhower administration as opposed to the will power of guerrillas in the mountains. The following from Paul Johnson's *Modern Times* should help to clarify the point: "William Wieland, in charge of the Caribbean desk, had hitherto taken the view, 'I know Batista is considered by many as a sonofabitch ... but American interests come first ... at least he is our sonofabitch.' Now Wieland changed sides. Earl Smith, appointed Ambassador to Havana in 1957, was told: 'You are assigned to Cuba to preside over the downfall of Batista. The decision has been taken that Batista has to go.' Wieland sent him to be briefed by Matthews, who told him 'it would be in the best interests of Cuba and the world if Batista were removed.' Roy Rubottom, Assistant Secretary of State, was also pro-Castro, as were the CIA in Havana."[6] Not until 1979, in Iran, would another United States administration deliver a head of state to the lions in favor of a radical regime.

What this demonstrates is that political processes are essentially voluntary, the product of human choice, and thus subject to reversal and variation. But this self-evident truth, when combined with dogmatic Marxism in place of real social science, gave way to a new determinism: the dangerous myth of the *foco*.

The very ease of Castro's success, despite a series of near-riotous and near-calamitous mistakes in the period of 1953-1959, again fully documented in the literature, created a problem for Castro. The myth of the *foco* was such as to be enshrined as a virtual "law" of socialism by people like Regis Debray. Despite this, the thought that the victory of the Cuban Revolution was any less determined than that of the Russian Revolution as such was intolerable to the totalitarian mind and the closed heart.

One might take a diabolical view that the adventures of Che Guevara in Bolivia were programmed for failure, and by no means a function of historical laws. Some of his diary notations indicate as much. The larger theme that Nietzschean Will can overcome all resistance of the popular will to the revolutionary exercise overrode all sense of possibilities and limitations. There are no fortresses that the good Bolshevik cannot conquer, according to Lenin. Armed with such slogans, Castro sent many men into battle, with a calamitous consequence. Indeed, he has admitted that all of 1988 was so taken up with the Angolan adventure that no time was left for the conduct of domestic affairs.[7] This reminds one of the Hitlerite decision to move Jews to the death camps as a higher priority than moving troops to the Russian front in the fatal year of 1943. The same rationale was in play: the superiority of moral purpose over empirical need.

The foreign adventures of Castro, long before Angola, were a series of failures of cataclysmic proportions. Not only was there a loss of leadership in Bolivia, but a loss of innocence concerning the automatic character of popular or peasant support. Similar adventures from Guatemala to Venezuela punctuated the early history of Castro's regime. Finally, in place of a doctrine of revolutionary will, we end up with a policy of trouble-making as an end in itself. This may well have been a function of another myth—that of Communist Cuba as a world-class actor. By the present decade, the exhaustion of the regime is, in part, a consequence of the end of ideology, or at least a specific ideology, in which communist will is indomitable and capitalist will negligible.

Perhaps the last hurrah in the myth of the *foco* came with the Angolan adventure. A decade of military involvement in that complex African nation ended with Cuba not even being invited to the peace process—and with all sides convinced that it was best for the Cuban troops simply to leave. It became a precondition of reconciliation in Angola. The internal consequences for Cuba are yet to be known fully, but the loss of many troops, the coming of the AIDS epidemic to Cuba, the turn from militarism as a populist slogan; all were rooted in the collapse of the "fraternal" efforts of Castro to bail out a communist regime in the Southern Cone of Africa. This campaign, far from establishing Cuba as an independent player in world affairs, was the denouement of Castro's global pretensions, the last card in the theories of revolutionary momentum put in motion by the Tri-Continental Conference in the mid-1960s.

The use of foreign adventures as a form of policy-making is hardly unique to Castro's Cuba. What is novel, what indeed is mythological is the elevation of such adventures to a law of socialism; they become, for Castro, a kind of "jump-start" for history itself. Real history condemned Castro on this decisive point. His foreign adventures contributed heavily to Castro's isolation in the hemisphere, as well as his inability to perform as a world-class actor, and took a heavy toll upon his people. The real lesson is clear enough: The use of a single victory as a model for behavior is risky, and the assumption that anyone path to national change is the correct path is ludicrous. Yet, this myth persists and will persist as long as no idea of legislative or juridical checks and balances can be imposed tolerably on the exercise of raw power.

The Myth of National Liberation

One of the great declarations of Castro at the onset of the Revolution of 1959 was that capitalism equals dependence on major powers and communism equals independence from them. To be sure, he was clever enough to exclude the Soviet Union from this simplistic analog. This myth was a byproduct of the Stalinist theme of self-sufficiency. Given the size and structure of the old Soviet Union, this myth was sustainable, though it required a huge loss of human life. The enlargement of the themes expressed in Lenin's *Imperialism* resulted in a corollary—that smaller nation states are wholly subordinate and dependent upon the great capitalist powers. To break the cycle of dependence, of colonialism, requires a socialist revolution.

As with all myths, this one too had a grain of truth. Imperialism was real, and the force of the United States was not always used for the common good of the Cuban people—to put matters mildly. But moving even further back into time, Cuba's history was also intertwined with Spanish colonial adventures, which were scarcely exercised to enhance the lives of the Cubans. To be sure, as Carlos Rangel noted, the sustained process of modernization was a feature of American and Northern European development. But Latin America, instead, was colonized by Spain, a country that refused for many years to embrace the premises of the free market or the free society. These tendencies were reproduced—and even reinforced—in Cuba, which suffered a strong brake on development in the nineteenth century but also a powerful impulse to development in the first half of the twentieth century.[8] Still, despite a certain advanced status within the Caribbean Basin, the sources of popular resentment for colonialism were real enough. The revolutionary act, whatever its consequences, was seen as a unique ability to throw off the past, to eliminate a tradition of dependence upon foreign powers. This was heady wine.

The problem was that imperialist powers come in all sorts of sizes and shapes. They include communist states and capitalist states. In order to derive the benefits of trade and aid advantages, Cuba was not only compelled to remain a dependent state, but it became locked into a syndrome of backwardness that depended upon continuation of the single crop economy, with ancillary potential in nickel, petroleum, and tobacco. One might argue that this was simply an illustration of an old axiom: The more things change, the more they remain the same. Yet they did not really remain the same; they moved backward. Soviet imperialism was even less capable than Spanish colonial imperialism.

For years Castro argued vehemently against the idea of Soviet dependence. He claimed that, in nearly every case, Soviet trade was advantageous to Cuban interests. He simply could not accept the idea of his own dependence, nor could he accept the notion of communism as a higher level of imperialism. As a result, he built a series of new self-deceptive sub-myths: Soviet aid was friendly and benevolent; Soviet aid was, if anything, so favorable to the Cubans that it set in motion new levels in moral and legal behavior between friendly big powers and fraternal small powers. Castro further argued that Soviet aid was in no way pegged to actual Cuban political actions or decisions. It became a higher law of dialectics that Soviet aid was granted without strings, in marked contrast to U.S. aid given to earlier regimes. These were but a few of the rationalizations offered over the years to prop up the myth of independence.

The problems with such theorizing became manifest as the regime advanced in years if not in wisdom. There were a series of political actions, as exhibited in voting preferences at the United Nations. Cuban support for the suppression of the Czechoslovakian Revolution of 1968 and the opposition to United Nations resolutions on terrorism and unwarranted use of force made it clear that a high political price was extracted for modest economic concessions. There were also a series of military adventures after the Tri-Continental conference: direct military support for the Syrian armed forces against Israel in the 1973 War and the extraordinarily high degree of participation by the Cuban armed forces in the Angolan Civil Wars of the 1980s.

It has been argued, with some persuasion, that Castro's participation in conflicts far beyond the Caribbean region was not inspired by Soviet demands, that, in fact, it exceeded and even compromised Soviet requirements. The degree of independent, Cuban-inspired support for native communist regimes and insurgency movements may not be known for a while, but it is clear that absolutely no actions were undertaken by Cuba that could be viewed in any way as contrary to Soviet interests. Thus, even if direct Soviet sanctions were not present for specific Cuban policies, it is clear that the overall political proclivities of the Soviet Union were followed slavishly to a degree that was unparalleled by nations of Central and South America that presumably were client states of the United States.

To be sure, the special relationship of the Soviet Union to Cuba was a case study in dependency. Such dependency was not reduced by the adoption of the USSR's social system. It was, in fact, exponentially increased. I would argue that the virtual failure of the Cuban Revolution to be exported to other nations of the hemisphere is far less a function of North American vigilance or intransigence than of the actual Cuban experience with Soviet power. For not only did dependency increase; there was no serious incentive for Cuba to link up with a major power, such as the Soviet Union, whose inability to advance, even minimally, the needs of the indigenous population was transparent.[9]

In that sense, Castro's myth of independence turned into a broad-ranging reevaluation of the realities of dependence. It also led to the collapse of dependency theory as a measure of North-South relations. For during a thirty-year span in which American military involvement in Latin America lessened dramatically, and American aid and trade took on bilateral forms of a sort that gave to recipient nations as good as they got in terms of concessions in doing business, the Soviet Union was seen to increase its dominance over the Cuban economy in every sphere. Moreover, the political and military arrangements it enforced locked Cuba into a backward syndrome from which it has not, and arguably cannot, recover—short of another revolution.

The Myth of Social Transformation

A characteristic of revolutionary regimes, since the French Revolution, in particular, has been the notion that the world is transformed essentially by the revolutionary act itself. The revolution becomes the demarcation between past and present. The hatred of Castro by those who oppose him derives from more than the usual sources of imperial fear and class hostility. Rather, it has to do with the idea that less-than-people—worms in human form, to be exact—roam the earth. They dare to remember the past and prefer it to the purified present.

A key element in Castro's survival has been the myth of the social revolution. The idea has been promulgated that, before the 1959 Revolution, there was nothing but colonial pretense and abject surrender of sovereignty. After the revolution, we are told, all this changed: Health, education, and welfare are said to be greatly improved; the awful consequences of dependent capitalism, such as gambling and prostitution, are said to be eliminated. Of course, in the fullness of hindsight, and in the knowledge of Castro's push for tourism as a way of life, we now know that prostitution has returned to Cuba; certainly discussions of casino gambling in hard currency are well underway.

Once again, the character of myth limits the impact of empirical events. The emphasis on medicine and literacy has been so effective that even hardened opponents to the regime have come to accept this as the one area in which Castro has achieved notable successes. Public health and medical services have never been more widespread and, we are told, education is likewise so broad as to eliminate illiteracy. Again, this myth is presented in opposition to the situation in advanced capitalist nations, in which medical costs are indeed high, and in which coverage is not universal. Similarly, Castro argues that capitalism provides different streams of education—private for the wealthy and public for the poor—whereas communism does away with such artificial distinctions.

Without denying in any way that real and serious problems do exist in the health and educational systems of advanced capitalism—none more so than in the United States—one needs to examine the myth of Cuban social progress nonetheless. For again, such goods and services have perhaps the greatest appeal to people outside Cuba and the most enduring value to people within Cuba.

Without laboring points that others have taken up in a variety of contexts, there are two fallacies here: First, Cuba had a very advanced infrastructure in the social sector prior to 1959, and second, when one examines the actual content of medicine and education in present-day Cuba, one finds a near-calamitous condition. Because we search for causes of revolution in the immiseration of the masses, we tend to superimpose a myth of our own on the realities of the world. We want to find a horrid state of affairs before the revolution in order to justify the revolutionary act. This myth is not unique to those examining the Cuban Revolution of 1959 but common to those who have examined previous revolutions as well.

Recent data on the quality of medical services indicate a near-crisis: Necessary drugs are absent; equipment is poor; training of surgeons for serious health emergencies is inadequate.[10] Indeed, if there is one area in which the myth of the Castro regime has been punctured, it is certainly in the area of medicine and health. Castro responds with claims that the U.S. embargo has put a crimp in Cuban medicine. But even were that so, which is hard to sustain since Cuba manages to buy around in many other areas of strategic importance, the growing charges of stratification of services for political elites as opposed to the rest of the country cannot be blamed on external embargoes.

In the educational sphere, the issues are slightly different. They do not pertain to universal education or to the absence of illiteracy, since pre-revolutionary Cuba scored well in these areas. Rather, the issue is the content of the educational process. From the outset, Castro recognized the importance of propaganda, and hence, educational curricula were filled with paeans of praise to the regime, its leadership, and its purposes. The issue of illiteracy was a smokescreen to avoid analysis of the contents of education or of the uses of literacy to sustain myths rather than to explain events or advance cultural life.[11]

From the outset, the higher culture was harnessed to the regime's needs: Novels, films, television, even science and criticism were harnessed to the requirements of the State. The Castro regime adopted the East German communist model of mobilization in sports. It remains dedicated to the collective benefits of sportive events at all age levels. What took place was gigantic

social mobilization, again at the expense of political mobilization. The myth of rejuvenation and regeneration replaced the
political slogans of an earlier revolutionary time, but always
with the foreknowledge that the revolution made possible such
good consequences.

No regime can sustain a myth without mythmakers. And the
cultural apparatus in Cuba was mobilized for such ends. Major sports
figures from baseball to track and field and boxing became the demonstration of the myth—willing participants to an illusion of success.
As in the Soviet cultural apparatus, writers and scribblers became the
shock troops of cultural wars. With the loss of prestige of the regime,
these cultural figures have put some distance between themselves
and the regime, with articles appearing that do not extol the regime
or its leadership and films that have no obvious ideological message.
Nonetheless, the social myth remains the most powerful weapon in
Castro's arsenal, the one area in which large numbers of communist
cadre can participate in world culture with a telling impact.

The Myth of the Moral Man

From the outset, the Castro Revolution argued that if capitalism is an unmitigated evil and socialism a pure good, then such
opposite properties would manifest themselves in the realm of
personal behavior. Specifically, Castro bought the Stakhanovite
package from the Soviet Union, claiming that the Communist
Party, and before that the July 26th Movement, were made up of the
best and the brightest. That translated into those precious people
whose behavior transcended economic utilitarianism. It was an
ethic driven by self-sacrifice, social understanding of the laws of
history and total fusion of the public good with the private will.

Operationally, this first translated into a sixth day of work without compensation. Later, certain nuances were added: willingness
to perform shock troop work whenever needed, unquestioning
willingness to serve the regime in whatever emergency military
or paramilitary tasks were required, placing state above citizen
in confronting possible acts of sabotage. In short, through

the Committees for the Defense of the Revolution, a political component of sacrifice was added to the earlier, less advanced, economic varieties.

To this day, Castro esteems the purity of self-sacrifice, and almost (but not quite) to the point of the Christian notion of sainthood. The party cadre may not always be sanctified, since sometimes they are called upon to engage in violent acts. But in their devotion to party, state, and nation, the Communist Party member is the apotheosis of what the Cuban society as a whole was to become under socialism. Cuba was to be the showpiece for the hemisphere and ultimately for the entire developing world. Indeed, many claims to leadership in the Third World came to rest on this quite special concept of moral man.

The ideal of personal immolation was enshrined as a social myth with the death of Guevara. If in life he was presented as the living embodiment of Bolivarism in the twentieth century—an Argentine who dedicated his life to the cause of Cuban communism—in death he became more than that. First, support of guerrilla insurgency in Bolivia was presented as an international obligation, fulfilled only by the highest of the high, the most ethical of the ethical. But Guevara's death took on the trappings of a mid-twentieth-century crucifixion. The resurrection was to take the form of one, two, three Cuban Revolutions in the hemisphere. That the actual career and death of Guevara was a sordid affair and that the promised further revolutions in the hemisphere did not take place hardly scratches the surface of the myth. Indeed, in death, the myth of sacrifice was enshrined permanently in Che, who played Paul to the church of communism.

The problems with the myth of moral man turned out to be somewhat larger than the myth itself. To start with, the population of Cuba immediately perceived that, far from being an ethical imperative, the concept of moral man was an economic imperative, an effort to extract a high proportion of unpaid labor time from workers. And in the context of Marxism in which "surplus labor" translated into unpaid work, the use of the extra hours and days of unpaid labor were part of the capitalist inheritance rather than the communist future. Add to this a situation in which even paid labor could not be translated into purchases of needed or desired goods and services, and this particular myth was, if not punctured early on, necessarily modified.[12]

But such modifications as were brought into play by Castro later in the Revolution were done to strengthen and not weaken the myth of the moral man. First, there was a broad assertion that rural living was superior to urban life. Second was the claim that the smaller centers outside Havana contained the seeds of regeneration for the nation. Third came the effort to instill peasant virtues by moving the denizens of the major cities, especially Havana, to rural regions for crop harvesting. But whether measured in terms of days or weeks, the same assertion that a moral imperative was involved remained intact. Not profits but purification presumably was the goal.

The terrible irony of Castro's mythmaking is that the very goals it aims at are subverted by the instrumentalities employed. Thus, the drive for foreign tourism, with its goal of increasing hard currency, stimulates precisely a level of venality that is reminiscent of the worst days of Havana in the pre-revolutionary epoch. Just about all journalistic reports indicate that the medium of economic exchange is the U.S. dollar. Social life is divided between discos and dance clubs run by the Union of Young Communists and the cheap, one-hour hotels called *posadas* to which the ordinary youth of Havana must turn for moments of privacy. Prostitution, that great capitalist scourge that was presumably eradicated early on, is now institutionalized. One writer has observed that "the system has spawned a form of commerce in which Cuban women have been known to give male tourists a night of their time for access to the good life."[13] In short, the myth of the moral man is punctured by the very regime that considers itself beyond moral reproach.

It is interesting to speculate on an equation: The higher the claims of morality, the lower became the activities of polity. That is to say, as the Castro regime hardened, and as one sector of society after another was stripped of autonomy and authority, claims for a higher moral purpose grew in size. At the same time, political participation began to dwindle. Any sense of ideological opposition was destroyed with the brutal suppression of every voluntary association. As a result, even the notion of a moral man became threadbare to the point of mirth and derision; it, nonetheless, eliminated even a shred of political opposition or social independence.

We tend to operate within Aristotelian categories in which the political is the stepping stone to the ethical. But this Western legacy was reversed with the Cuban communists. For they transformed the notion of the moral man into a concept of the loyal man, and it was an unthinking, Orwellian loyalty at that. Such loyalty to regime and leader made the need for active political life superfluous, even dangerous. As a result, when all else fails— as it has—the myth of the moral man remains a way to mobilize people into economic activities, even as a general demobilization takes place in the political realm.

There is a corrupted Machiavellian dimension to all this. The myth of the moral man has enabled Castro to extend his longevity in office. Appeals to electoral politics fall on deaf ears, indeed are increasingly vilified, in part because Castro is not cast in the mode of a political leader any longer. Rather he is the leader of a moral crusade. However long it takes to achieve, this crusade preempts the mundane world of political combat or opposition. Thus at the very time the regime is suffering from terminal cancer, it claims the loyalty of the citizens. With all due respect to Castro's acumen at eliminating potential enemies and purging the regime of opposition forces, the larger truth is that his support base rests on a shared sense that the myth of the moral man remains operational—not despite, but rather because of, adversity. The resilience of totalitarianism in the twentieth century, a century in which heroes are suspect and expectations have turned sour, inheres in the ability of leaders such as Castro to convince the masses that suffering is divine while affluence is sinful.

Conclusion

If these myths are so transparent, what has sustained the Castro regime over such a long time? The answers are not readily apparent. We need to look closely at the Sorelian conception of the political myth as formulated at the start of the century better to appreciate the staying power of the Castro regime. To start with, Sorel pointed out that the actual empirical potentials of socialism are so paltry that without the political myth the idea of socialism would collapse. As a result, it is the mythic properties of socialism, of ideas of equity and ideals of justice that uniquely sustain the regime.

Even now, despite awareness that communism took twice as many innocent human lives as Nazism (to be sure, it had four times the number of years in which to perform its damage), the attitudes toward the two main varieties of twentieth-century totalitarianism differ. In large measure, and again with a bow to Sorelian wisdom, the socialist ideal is close in spirit to primitive Christianity, to those religious traditions which have sustained people of good will in the face of systems of evil deeds.

Increasingly, as the gap between empirical reality and mytho-logical utopia grows wider, Castro has fallen back on this proximity of the ideas of communism and Christendom. The Church has once again become a central factor in Cuban life; Protestantism and Catholi-cism have grown substantially since the early anti-religious phase of the regime, and, of course, the Santeria phenomenon is not to be denied its due as a vital factor in the private lives of many Cubans.

As confidence in secular institutions, such as the armed forces and the administrative cadre of party and state, has declined, religious fervor has grown. Church attendance is higher than it has been in the past, and Castro's tolerance likewise has expanded from a time when priests were rounded up and expelled from Cuba. It is now the case that, when forces of potential opposi-tion to Castro are cited, the Church is increasingly mentioned, although there is slender evidence of a clear line of opposition.

We must also factor into account the revolt against modernity. Asceticism as an ideology, and increasingly as a fact of Cuban life, has increased with every denial in material goods. While Castro does not have the capacity to perform as an Ayatollah or Imam, he does have the capacity to call into play notions of sacrifice and visions of again being surrounded. In other words, as the material conditions deteriorate and appeals to real his-tory dissolve, the spiritual conditions and appeals to teleology are then accentuated.

In a capitalist society or free-market environment, the myths would have long ago caused the breakdown and collapse of the Castro regime. In Cuba they are themselves factors in the sustenance of the regime, at least in the short run. We tend to presume that negative indicators in matters of economic growth and social welfare automatically translate into an inability to continue in power. In the long run, this is undoubtedly the case, but in the short run, this is not so. Just what constitutes a long and a short run is itself a subjective measurement.

While myth will continue to drive politics, some myths lose their potency. The best-case scenario with respect to Cuba is that the distance between reality and utopia is so great at this point that the totalitarian rubber band simply will snap—and it will be time for renewal and restoration. This deterioration in the mythmaking potential of Castro is captured beautifully in Georgie Ann Geyer's recent biography: "In the beginning, the Cuban people had called him 'Fidel' in adoration, in salvation, in love; like a Spanish woman with her husband before marriage. After the magnificence of the *Triunfo,* they immediately began calling him 'Castro' in sobriety, in respect, in fear. In the end, they called him only *'El'* or 'He.' For he had become finally not one of them but a differentiated creature away from them; that sun so hot that it burned to come close."[14]

Even harsh lives, disappointed lives are composed of dream-like elements. And dreams are not constrained by empirical substances—unless and until they are analyzed. I am sobered by John Maynard Keynes' warning that "there is no harm in being sometimes wrong, especially if one is promptly found out."[15] It has been my purpose and pleasure in these lectures to engage in an act of self-analysis as well as social analysis. I shall leave for others policies for the American present or programs for the Cuban future. Doubtless, to the extent that I have been in error, I will be found out. To the extent that I have been right, it will be sufficient reward that I will know this to have been the case. Not history, but compassion, absolves us. I suspect that it will be only at the very end of his political journey, if then, that Fidel will make this discovery.

References/Notes

1. Juan Rulfo, *Pedro Páramo*. Translated by Margaret Sayers Peden. Evanston: Northwestern University Press, 1992.
2. John Newhouse, "Socialism or Death" [A Reporter at Large: Cuba]. *The New Yorker.* April 27, 1992. 52-83.
3. Anne-Marie O'Connor, "Fidel's Last Resort," *Esquire.* Volume 117, Number 3, March, 1992. 102-104, 156-157.
4. Sidney Hook, *The Hero in History: A Study in Limitation and Possibility.* [1943]. New Brunswick and London: Transaction Publishers, 1992, 88-96.
5. Irving Louis Horowitz, *Radicalism and the Revolt Against Reason.* London and New York: Routledge & Kegan Paul Ltd., 1961.
6. Paul Johnson, *Modern Times: The World from the Twenties to the Nineties.* London and New York: HarperCollins, Inc., 1991, 621.
7. Maurice Halperin, *Return to Havana.* Unpublished manuscript [1992]. Chapter IX, entitled "Out of Africa" (66-74), offers a keen insight into Castro's willingness to risk everything for his African adventure.
8. Carlos Rangel, *Third World Ideology and Western Reality: Manufacturing Political Myth.* New Brunswick and London: Transaction Publishers, 1986, 193 pages; and *The Latin Americans: Their Love-Hate Relationship with the United States.* New Brunswick and London: Transaction Publishers, 1987, 322 pages. For an excellent summary of Rangel's analysis of the impact of Anglo-American versus Spanish-Portuguese involvement in Latin America, see Gianfranco Pecchinenda, "Considerazioni sulla sociologia di Carlos Rangel." *Modernizzazione e Sviluppo,* Volume 2, Number 1-2, 1991, 57-62.
9. Yuri Pavlov, *Russia and Cuba.* Unpublished manuscript [1992]. We have it on the authority of a former Soviet diplomat, directly concerned with Cuban affairs, that this relationship was one of dependency and not equality. In the same vein, from an American vantage point, see Robert A. Packenham, "Cuba and the USSR since 1959: What Kind of Dependency?" in *Cuban Communism* [seventh edition], edited by Irving Louis Horowitz. New Brunswick and London: Transaction Publishers, 1989, 135-165.
10. Cuban Communist Party, *A Public Survey on the Quality of Health Care in the Province of Holguin, Cuba* [mimeographed version, released by The Cuban American National Foundation] June 1988, 36 pages.
11. Roger Reed, *The Cultural Revolution in Cuba.* Geneva, Switzerland: Latin American Round Table, 1991, 268 pages.
12. Antonio Jorge, "Ideology, Planning, Efficiency and Growth: Change Without Development" in *Cuban Communism* [seventh edition], offers a keen summary and critique of the "moral economy" in Castro's Cuba.
13. Vernon Silver, "Privacy, By The Hour Only," *The New York Times.* November 8, 1992. section 9.3.
14. Georgie Ann Geyer, *Guerrilla Prince: The Untold Story of Fidel Castro.* Boston: Little Brown & Company, 1991, 394.
15. John Maynard Keynes, *Essays in Biography.* New York: Harcourt, Brace & Co., 1933, 318 pages.

Cuban Communist Party. 1988. *A Public Survey on the Quality of Health Care in the Province of Holguin, Cuba.* [Mimeographed version, released by The Cuban American National Foundation]. June, 36 pages.

Geyer, Georgie Ann. 1991. *Guerrilla Prince: The Untold Story of Fidel Castro.* Boston: Little Brown & Company, 394.

Halperin, Maurice. [1992]. *Return to Havana.* [Unpublished manuscript]. Chapter IX, "Out of Africa," 66-74.

Hook, Sidney. [1943] 1992. *The Hero in History: A Study in Limitation and Possibility.* New Brunswick and London: Transaction Publishers, 88-96.

Horowitz, Irving Louis. 1961. *Radicalism and the Revolt Against Reason.* London and New York: Routledge & Kegan Paul Ltd.

Johnson, Paul. 1991. *Modern Times: The World from the Twenties to the Nineties.* London and New York: HarperCollins, Inc., 621.

Jorge, Antonio. 1989. "Ideology, Planning, Efficiency and Growth: Change Without Development." *Cuban Communism* [seventh edition]. Ed. Irving Louis Horowitz. New Brunswick and London: Transaction Publishers.

Keynes, John Maynard. 1933. *Essays in Biography.* New York: Harcourt, Brace & Co.

Newhouse, John. 1992. "Socialism or Death" [A Reporter at Large: Cuba]. *The New Yorker,* April 27, 52-83.

O'Connor, Anne-Marie. 1992. "Fidel's Last Resort." *Esquire,* 117, 3(March), 102-104, 156-157.

Packenham, Robert A. 1989. "Cuba and the USSR since 1959: What Kind of Dependency?" *Cuban Communism* [seventh edition]. Ed. Irving Louis Horowitz. New Brunswick and London: Transaction Publishers, 135-165.

Pavlov, Yuri. [1992]. *Russia and Cuba.* [Unpublished manuscript].

Pecchinenda, Gianfranco. 1991. "Considerazioni sulla sociologia di Carlos Rangel." *Modernizzazione e Sviluppo,* 2, 1-2: 57-62.

Rangel, Carlos. 1986. *Third World Ideology and Western Reality: Manufacturing Political Myth.* New Brunswick and London: Transaction Publishers.

Rangel, Carlos. 1987. *The Latin Americans: Their Love-Hate Relationship with the United States.* New Brunswick and London: Transaction Publishers.

Reed, Roger. 1991. *The Cultural Revolution in Cuba.* Geneva, Switzerland: Latin American Round Table.

Rulfo, Juan. 1992. *Pedro Páramo.* Trans. Margaret Sayers Peden. Evanston, Ill.: Northwestern University Press.

Silver, Vernon. 1992. "Privacy, By The Hour Only." *The New York Times.* November 8, section 9.3.

Source and Original Title: "What Have We Learned From Thirty-Three Years of the Cuban Revolution? The Myth of Theory and the Theory of Myths Revisited" in *The Conscience of Worms and the Cowardice of Lions: The Cuban-American Experience, 1959-1992.* Miami: The North-South Center/University of Miami, 1993, 57-80 pp.

26

Consequences of the American Embargo

The purpose of my statement is to provide a game theoretical framework for the analysis of current political and ethical issues involved in a reconsideration of American foreign policy toward Cuba. It is clear that while few celebrate the character or structure of the Castro regime, a debate is emerging as to the policy toward the regime in light of his continuing staying power.

Political issues turn, therefore, not so much upon different appraisals but changing policies toward Cuba. Ethical issues turn on what policies are best calculated to cause the people of Cuba the least grief or despair without giving sustenance to the dictatorship. In this multi-layered situation, policymaking becomes freighted with extrinsic considerations that make this a special moment in the near 35-year history of Castro's Cuba.

The paper reviews the arguments currently being put forth for a lifting or a continuation of the embargo and also asks whether the embargo is intended to be an effective economic mechanism or a symbolic statement of United States foreign policy. The position taken is that demands for policy change are being made without clear regard for what, if any, fundamental changes are taking place in the Castro regime.

The analysis thus concludes with a reaffirmation of the causal sequence outlined by present and past American administrations: first, democracy; second, elections; third, policy alteration and reconsideration. These can occur in rapid succession and almost simultaneously. But in an environment where one "side" is rigid, the prospects for flexibility on the other "side" are limited. Thus, one can expect a moderate tactical thaw in relationships but little in the way of immediate basic policy shifts.

To start with, we require an appreciation that an embargo is a policy seeking to achieve certain ends. It is not an act to be taken lightly. Nor is it an act undertaken by friendly nations in dispute. An embargo represents a termination, in whole or in part, of goods and services by one nation to a second nation deemed hostile and demonstrably unfriendly. An embargo, however, is a far cry from an act of war or invasion of the territory of another nation. Nor does it represent the cessation of all contact between the hostile nations. As in politics generally, an embargo has both real consequences and symbolic significance.

The act of embargoing is very much part of a game theoretical environment: (a) it involves a situation in which two or more nations or individuals are involved; (b) it involves a decision in pursuit of the objectives of at least one player; (c) it involves a decision making scenario of one option over others that may be available; (d) it involves an expected utility payoff, that is, the success of a policy; (e) and finally, its aim is to change the political behavior of the opponent, or failing that, the removal of an opponent in favor of one more interested in a new consensus rather a continuation of the conflict.[1]

The American embargo of Cuba, which reached its apex in The Cuba Democracy Act of 1992, is as powerful and forthright an example of the above description of the game theoretical environment as any currently practiced by the United States. Clearly, as the testimony and discussion have made evident, this has been a contentious policy.[2] Its consecration in law took place rather late in the policy game, so that the de jure policy came considerably after the de facto state of conflict that exists between the United States and Cuba. To further complicate matters, and in our rhetoric at least, the players changed with the election of William Clinton, a Democrat, replacing George Bush, a Republican. This signaled a potential for change in policy approaches.

It should be added that on the other side, the key player, Fidel Castro, continues in power entering his thirty-fifth year, and clearly, is an individual with a staying power far in excess of the expectations of his critics worldwide. And while Castro modestly welcomed the change of players in the United States, to date no substantial change in Cuba's internal policies, leading to the imposition of the embargo to begin with, have taken place. For example, there have been only slight shifts toward a market or free economy, no lessening of control of the police and armed forces in the everyday domination of Cuba, and no movement toward popular elections or a multiparty system each of which might be taken as signs that the initial decision to impose the embargo would be subject to review.

Hence, such a discussion is less a matter of studying changes in the structure of Cuban domestic or foreign policy, although these are underway, but more, whether the embargo works, the political question, and also whether it is a "good," the ethical question. That is to say, the discussion over the American embargo takes place during a time in which the behavior of the "other side," Cuba, is essentially a constant. This is a debate not on the political efficacy or personal decency of Fidel Castro, as it is uniformly understood that his days are numbered and the worth of his regime permanently tarnished by authoritarian practices. Rather, this debate is on the best ways of ridding the Cuban island of Castro and assisting its people in the process. I shall now turn toward just such considerations.

The great victory of what can be termed the orthodox position, the one held by the Cuban American National Foundation, was the signing into law of the Cuba Democracy Act. In one fell swoop, this piece of legislation tightened the United States' embargo and held out the promise of a loosened communications framework. However, by virtue of its strong linkages to both the Reagan and Bush administrations, the Cuban American National Foundation has lost a substantial amount of its insider cachet. But not entirely. It was strong enough to void the appointment of Mario Baeza as Assistant Secretary of State for Inter-American

Affairs, and it was also a powerful force in the continuation of support for Radio Martí, although this umbrella did not extend to Television Martí. The House Appropriations Committee refused to authorize funds for the station's broadcasts to Cuba, and it is clear that the White House made scant efforts to overturn congressional decision making.

On the other side, a plethora of organizations have emerged to urge some form of reconciliation between the United States and Cuba. These include groups such as Cambio Cubano, headed by Eloy Gutierrez Menoyo, and various socialist parties such as the Cuban Democratic Party and the Christian Democratic Party. The position taken by these rather feeble groups is essentially that with the collapse of the Soviet empire, Cuba is not an international threat, and with the loss of revenues from sugar and tobacco crops, Cuba is not much of a hemispheric threat either. They are hoping for a cancellation, in part or in full, of the embargo. Such a view is described by former Ambassador Wayne Smith as "A Pragmatic Cuba Policy."[4] At the least, these domestic support groups expect the United States to condemn any illegal activities emanating from this country, such as the May 1993 effort by Alpha 66 to deliver automatic rifles and explosives to Cuba from American shores, or the hijacking of air craft. But it should be kept in mind that the Bush administration also adhered to a position of strict nonintervention into the internal affairs of Cuba.[5]

The debate is far less one of ideology than strategy. For example, two people, strongly identified with conservative politics in general, and quite specifically on Cuban affairs, William Ratliff and Roger Fontaine, have urged a deep reconsideration of the embargo policy. The importance of this break in conservative ranks warrants a direct quotation from their op-ed piece: "Clinton must facilitate the exchange of people and ideas. Yes, exiles and others who visit Cuba will take in some foreign currency. But despite Castro's efforts to segregate them with his own form of tourist apartheid, their presence, and the news they bring with them, will testify to the superiority of democratic free market economics over Fidel's despotic socialism. The end of the embargo and these exchanges will show that the United States is not hostile to Cubans in general, and they will stimulate the growth of alternatives in Cuba's stunted civil society. U.S. policy must show that Castro's warning of `aprs Fidel, led,luge' is self-serving propaganda."[6]

The influential Gannett flagship paper, *USA Today*, has also called for a changing of political course. Its editorial argues, "Cuba shouldn't get tougher penalties than Chile or Brazil, enriched by U.S. aid despite rights violations, or China, which enjoys normal U.S. trade despite Tiananmen Square." The editorial adds that the embargo has worn thin in the international community, and besides, "Lifting the embargo makes economic sense. It would reap for the U.S.A. about $223 million of the annual trade now flowing to Europeans entering the Cuban banking and tourist markets."[7] Such influential Cubanologists as Jorge Domínguez have echoed and amplified such sentiments. He noted that "doing something like this would be a bold political risk in the American context, but would produce a Cuba very different from anything we have ever seen: something that looks and feels like a market economy."[8]

It is evident that Castro has understood the importance of this sea change in Cuban American and Native American thinking. He has taken three admittedly small measures to improve relations: a willingness to discuss U.S. property embargoes in the early 1960s now worth roughly $6 billion; a reduction in the size of the swollen Cuban armed forces; and the use of dollars in tourist stores. Of course, the problem with these concessions is that Cuba is a country on the verge of bankruptcy with hardly any cash reserves. Thus, even if Castro admits to obligations, they are not likely to be fulfilled. And by the same token, the diminution of the military is a function of a country in which shortages are enormous, and the ability to reward the military no longer exists. In any event, it might well be argued that a reduced military is a reduced threat to Castro's personal rule. The Ochoa affair is, after all, only five years old and remains etched in the minds of those who might contemplate a golpe de estado from above. The infusion of a dollar economy carries the risk of separating the small elites from the masses of Cubans living on substandard wages. Such hard currency stores hardly helped Eastern European communism, and their potential for helping the economy of Cuba is not much better.

The responses to the new aperture have not been long in coming. Perhaps the most typical of the orthodox views is by the dynamic Republican member of the U.S. House of Representatives, Ileana Ros-Lehtinen. Essentially, her position is that the United States "should not betray Cubans now by letting Castro get what he needs to keep his regime afloat" She goes on to add, that "deprived of Soviet subsidies, Castro no longer has the oil to power his tanks, he no longer has the power to run his searchlights, and he no longer can buy the very goods that he denies to the Cuban people. What is needed now is a clear focus on the ultimate prize of a free Cuba, and not to allow an aging dictator to further delay the advent of democracy."[9]

And mainline conservatives' voices have also begun to speak out on the question of lifting the embargo. The position of syndicated columnist John J. Farmer is rather typical. "How will Fidel's finish occur? One hopes not as violently as Nicolae Ceausescu. But like the Romanian tyrant's, his will probably be an inside job too, either by military coup or popular [up] rising or some combination thereof. But just as there is no reason for the West to help Castro, there is even less to take a violent hand in hurrying him into history. He is not even a minor menace anymore. It is best to let the Cubans decide when the have had their fill of Fidel."[10]

Here then, we have an outline of positions on an American debate on Castro's Cuban early 35 years after the assumption of power. This is hardly a world shattering debate, but it does serve as a bench mark for the Clinton administration and its foreign policy. Curiously, early examples of Democratic administration responses have been extremely careful. Essentially, it is a cause-effect sequence that is at stake: if free and untrammeled elections, then the removal of the embargo. If there is a restoration of an internationally recognized human rights policy, then there can be a withdrawal from Guantanamo. If the establishment of free market rights, then negotiations for new trade and aid. This cause and effect sequence is clearly within the rights of a big power and enforceable due to the repressibilities of a small power. Clinton has demonstrated an adroit ability to play power politics on a global canvas. His position also reveals an acute sense of domestic pressures and counter-pressures.[11]

Signals have been mixed: a passive executive permitting an activist legislature to cut Television Martí from the United States Information Agency and substantial reduction in the budget of Radio Martí. However, the administration has also moved to cut telephonic transmission from the United States to Cuba via Canada, once Castro made it his policy to curtail sharply direct telephonic communication. Prosecutors in the U.S. Attorney's Office have drafted a proposed indictment charging the Cuban government with being a racketeering and drug dealing enterprise.[12] Thus far, such an indictment has not been issued whether for lack of hard evidence or political caution is hard to determine.

On the Cuban side, too, there is ambivalence: reopening direct forwarding of monies and goods from Miami to Havana has been proposed but not implemented, on the ever-present humanitarian grounds. In the larger picture, private sector initiatives sometimes legalized other times not sanctioned have sprung up. At the same time, Sunday drills against the coming mythic invasion from the United States continue to be held.[8] So an uneasy truce remains in place. The initiatives have been shifting from "hawkish" to "dovish" impulses, initiated by people like Wayne Smith, Washington's senior diplomat in Havana from 1979 to 1982, and a cluster of retired army and navy officers visiting Cuba with the ostensible purpose of "easing tensions," which translates into some sort of higher profile recognition for the Castro regime.[13]

We come now to the policy recommendations toward Cuba that has been offered in the fulcrum of a new American administration. The installation of a new administration in Washington does indeed propel the idea of a different set of relations between Castro's Cuba and our country. Talk has already begun to the effect that after a respectful period of time, the Clinton administration might seek the path of reconciliation with Fidel's dictatorship. For the moment, the administration's public signals are mixed: sanctioned, but informal trade missions to Cuba; proposed total withdrawal of funds from the North-South Center; putting a career officer without an ideological commitment to the exile community in charge of the Latin American desk at the Department of State; yet leaving funds intact for Radio and Television Martí this at a time when there is a decision to dismantle Radio Free Europe and Radio Liberty.

There are those who would counsel renewed effort at reconciliation and accommodation between the Castro regime and the United States. The argument essentially proceeds as follows: (a) the diplomatic isolation of Cuba serves no useful foreign policy end; (b) with a new administration in Washington, the United States has the opportunity to wipe the slate clean; and, consequently, (c) such a restoration of economic and political relations would signal the eventual democratization of Cuba. To be sure, there are variations on this scenario, depending on the audiences whose support is solicited. Hard-liners are told that such an aperture would hasten the departure of Castro from power, while liberals are encouraged to believe that this opening would encourage a renewed human rights posture on the part of the communist officials in Havana. In its remarkable and singular assault on a piece of U.S. congressional legislation The Cuba Democracy Act of 1992 the United Nations General Assembly has already signaled its desire for a policy shift to a softer line on the part of the United States. And recent statements by Castro indicate that he sees repudiation of this piece of legislation as a central goal of his government's foreign policy.

The problem with the drumbeat for policy change inheres in the assumptions being made: above all, the assumption that the fault in present United States relations with Castro's Cuba is uniquely that of the former; similarly, the ideas that Castro's intentions were badly misunderstood to start with and that given an opportunity to mend his ways, Castro would become an excellent hemispheric citizen seem strained. Finally, there is the suggestion that with the collapse of the Soviet empire, communist Cuba is a minor irritant, one that a benevolent world power such as the United States can readily afford to treat in a benign rather than punitive manner.

Those who argue for reconciliation have been heard fully and fairly. Indeed, such advocates have been given a better hearing than they usually grant those who stand in firm opposition to such a turn. What is wrong with such an argument for benevolence? To start with, a policy of accommodation with the Castro government is not consistent with United States policy toward tyrannies. For the United States to stand on moral principle when it comes to "friendly tyrants" in the Middle East or Asia, but embrace Castro on pragmatic grounds would be a curious turn. It would grant Castro the fruits of his aggression, providing him with diplomatic succor the United States have accorded neither to Kim Il Sung of North Korea nor Saddam Hussein of Iraq.

Such a policy would also deny the realities of 34 years of implacable opposition by Castro to any and every democratic regime in the Western Hemisphere. As Abraham Lowenthal noted in a recent review of Latin America in Foreign Affairs, democratic regimes in Latin America are far shakier than one round of popular elections admits to.[14] Such a policy turn would hold Castro blameless for adventures in Angola that did nothing to insure the democratization of that nation, and de facto would legitimate his principle of military intervention by an armed praetorian force throughout the world. The enthusiasm with which Castro and his revolution have been supported by ultra radical elements in the United States has had less to do with the terrible loss of lives and destabilization of democratic regimes inspired by Cuba than with Castro's posture of anti-Americanism, a posture that continues to link the enemies of freedom the world over.

There is also the simple reality that such overtures have rarely been effective in modern diplomacy. The capitulation of Neville Chamberlain at Munich did not insure peace in his time but only hastened the hard-hearted march of Hitler through the whole of Europe. The Molotov-von-Ribbentrop non-aggression pact between Germany and Russia did not forestall or terminate the forces of aggression or even buy very much time for Russia to arm. It simply hastened that dark day in June 1941 when Hitler extended the war to Russia. On the other hand, it must be acknowledged that Nixon's opening to China did have positive consequences although as we saw with Tiananmen Square, this opening did not so much insure democracy in China, as it encouraged economic stability in that country. Clearly, there is a serious question as to whether a softening toward Castro might weaken democratic elements throughout the Caribbean region especially in shaky places like Nicaragua, Haiti, and El Salvador. If it did, for this reason alone, it would become an extremely risky proposal.

Some might object that analogies of Castro with Hitler, Stalin, or Mao are inherently fallacious, that Castro is not remotely capable of such exercises of world or regional power. That may well be true, but hardly as a result of the soft-liners. Castro's record of 34 years of implacable opposition to democratic norms, indeed, his continuing assaults within Cuba against the smallest signs of opposition indicate that the analogy of one police state to another is quite appropriate. And one must still reckon with a bloated Cuban armed force entirely capable of regional trouble-making should the occasion arise. The argument that Castro is now powerless and, hence, need not be opposed subverts any claims to moral superiority for Western democratic forces. If one argues American policy making should only act against tyrants when there is potential for naked aggression and the United States is directly threatened, there is no room for action when democratic institutions are threatened, whether by big or small totalitarian states.

There is nonetheless a need to rethink the basis of current American policy toward Castro's Cuba. For much of our policy has indeed been based on premises that are in need of sharp revision in the light of the collapse of the Soviet empire. Such a policy revision may not necessarily comfort the friends of democracy. Indeed, behind so-called efforts to "normalize" relations between the United States and the present-day rulers of Cuba lies an effort sometimes conscious, but mostly unconscious to deny the totalitarian character of today's Cuba.

There is a remarkable congruence of opinion from eyewitness sources on the economic collapse of Cuban communism. The work of Spencer Reiss in *Newsweek*, Tim Golden and Jo Thomas in *The New York Times*, Andres Oppenheimer in *The Miami Herald*, John Newhouse in *The New Yorker*, and Anne-Marie O'Connor in *Esquire*, underscore the remarkable ability of on-site observers to see better and further than the social scientists turned Castrologists that I reviewed in *The Conscience of Worms and the Cowardice of Lions*.[15] There is little purpose in repeating what this sextet of reporters has so forcefully and brilliantly written in their accounts of present day Cuba. But one should examine the underlining meanings shared by these commentaries for the light they shed on the fundamental theory and practice of international relations.

The collective journalistic portrait yields five interrelated propositions: (1) There is a virtually irreversible revolution of fallen expectations in Cuba. (2) There is a movement from development to underdevelopment in slow stages. (3) For most Cubans, non-participation rather than direct opposition has become a buffer against the worst infections of the regime. (4) Cuba has become a land without hope, but without the tools or infrastructure for rebellion. (5) Emigration as a safety valve for Castro, or as a mechanism to avoid protest, has just about dried up. The relative weight of these elements can be challenged, but not their presence in the Cuban mosaic of 1993.

The famous formula of a revolution of rising (or falling) expectations must now be modified to take into account the situation in Cuba, where we have the revolution of fallen expectations. When a society converts from automobiles to oxen, when capitalist evils return in an enhanced form as socialist virtues, i.e., class division, prostitution, foreign tourism (already twice that of 1958, the last year prior to Castro's golpe), and literally from light to darkness, then elimination of the extremes of social stratification which the Cuban Revolution sought to alleviate, if not entirely overthrow, are fast being restored.

Castro has insured himself a unique position of power by clever, indeed brilliant, dismemberment of all sources of opposition from the bureaucracy to the military. What he cannot insure himself against are the ravages of time and biological fate. The revenge of nature, not politics, may ultimately overcome the dictator. Whether it is a political or direct mass struggle, an assassin's bullet, or a palace coup d'etat, the regime will come to termination. The question is only how it will end.

Even if elements of the social and political process conspire to permit one or two more years of grace, Castro must still face the unbending will of time itself. History may not absolve Fidel, but biology surely will not overlook him. He may survive one more mistake, one more tactical blunder, one more episode of forgetfulness, but the dictator will fall. And on that judgment day, those who stood firm against this long night of tyranny will be able to relent, to relax, and some will return. Some envision a transfer of power from Castro to a younger individual or cohort, but this supposes a transfer of charisma as well.

Undoubtedly, Castro has benefited from the unique circumstances that permitted more than a million of Cuba's best and brightest to immigrate to the United States. This may also have been a bonanza for the United States, for the talents and creativities of the Cuban people had made their country one of the region's most innovative. But the emigration also permitted Castro to rid himself of a permanent base of opposition in class and occupational terms, if not direct military opposition. It is simply hard to believe that Castro would have long survived in the absence of such a mass migration.

On the other hand, it is equally difficult to imagine a firm United States policy toward Castro without a Cuban exile community. We tend to emphasize, *sotto voce* to be sure, the costs of the exile community to the advancement of democratic norms within Cuba. But it must be said that the Cuban communities of Miami, parts of New Jersey, and elsewhere, have done something easily overlooked: They have provided a spiritual and at times material haven for people in similar dire straits from other places.

The Nicaraguan exile community in Miami readily became part of the Latino influence and was permitted a base of opposition to the Sandinistas one that met with considerable success.

It has sometimes been said that democracy flourishes in small states. While this may be the case, it is also correct to point out that dictatorship may also flourish in small states; Cambodia, Haiti, and North Korea come readily to mind. In the case of Cuba, control has been ironclad because of the ease with which surveillance is possible, movement of citizens monitored, and opposition thwarted in early stages. Cuba is not simply a small state, but an island state and this increases a potential for isolation that is clearly far beyond anything feasible in Eastern Europe in the past or the Far East in the present. We have become so enamored of political and/or economic determinism that even the rudiments of geographic variables have been lost to our generation.

But all these points have been made by others as well as myself in the past. The fact remains that while conditions for revolution are extant, the capacities for revolution are not. In part this is simply a function of Fidel's perfection of the tools of tyranny. In part, this is also a reflection that revolutions of falling expectations are as real as revolutions of rising expectations. Survival is quite possible in a lower order of economic well being. The Cuban regime no longer makes participation mandatory, so that non-political life or, better, depoliticization, is taking place on a massive scale. Nor should it be forgotten that while the rest of Latin America may have spurned the Castro road to domination, many still maintain cordial diplomatic relations and provide a framework for regime legitimation that was absent in Eastern Europe.

Castro will fall as surely as his regime has failed in its purposes. Indeed, he himself now speaks of being out of power in five years. Of course, he means by that a removal of his person from power but not dismemberment of the Communist Party of Cuba. So the struggle has shifted from personal rule to regime continuation. Castro knows as much. It is a sobering thought that so many predictions of Castro's failure and collapse from Fulgencio Batista's to George Bush's were broadly and badly overstated.

My remarks describe a bifurcation in the studies of communist Cuba: a Native American intelligentsia enthralled with Castro as the shining path of anti-Americanism, and a Cuban exile group who saw in the theory and practice of social science the ultimate and irrefutable rebuke to the tyranny imposed on Cuba after 1959. In some curious way, that same split remains today. Indeed, even the rhetoric harkens to an earlier period. Only a few North Americans have come to appreciate the power of critical social analysis, while scarcely any Cuban exiles have succumbed to the siren calls of anti-American ideology.[16]

The struggle remains the same running like a dorsal spine through the last 34 years of hemispheric relations and world ideologies, and no less from 1933 to 1993 within Cuba. Even if Castro's stay in power has turned out to be more protracted that I, for one, ever imagined, his long denouement has taught us the process of definition. The bifurcations spoken of have come to define the best and the worst in the American and Cuban political landscapes. The process of democratization may be slower than anticipated, even thwarted at times. But the values inherent in that process remain strong and true. In his March 23, 1993, press conference, President Clinton, in defending the Cuba Democracy Act, put matters succinctly and in proper causal sequence: first democracy, then elections, followed by policy reconsiderations. Whether the president can adhere to such an ordering of priorities under the constant battering of extremists on both sides remains to be seen.

References/Notes

1. For an excellent presentation of the theoretical approach herein taken, see Roger B. Mikes, *Game Theory: Analysis of Conflict*. Cambridge: Harvard University Press, 1991. 568 pages. The work is written with particular relevance to social scientific analysis.
2. Unless otherwise indicated, the references in my article will be drawn from Consideration of the Cuban Democracy Act of 1992. These Hearings before the Committee on Foreign Affairs of the House of Representatives (H.R. 4168 and H.R. 5323) summarize more than the debates; they include relevant data in the formation of the legislation. Washington, D.C.: U.S. Government Printing Office, 1993. 563 pages.

3. Howard W. French, "The End Has Begun," *The New York Times* (August 8, 1993) (section 4:4).
4. Wayne S, Smith, "A Pragmatic Cuba Policy," *Foreign Service Journal* (April, 1991) 153-157.
5. Larry Rohter, "In Miami, Talk of Talking With Cuba," *The New York Times* (June 27, 1993) 16.
6. William Ratliff and Roger Fontaine, "The End Game," *The Orange County Register* (December 27, 1992) 19.
7. *USA Today*, "Ease the Trade Embargo on the Cuban People," (June 18, 1993) 12A.
8. Jorge I. Domínguez, "Secrets of Castro's Staying Power," *Foreign Affairs*. 1993. 72 (2), 97-107.
9. Ileana Ros-Lehtinen, "Keep Pressure on Castro," *USA TODAY* (June 18, 1993) 12A.
10. John J. Farmer, "U.S. Need Only Wait for Castro's Cigar to Go Out." *The Star-Ledger* (June 17, 1993) 22.
11. Linda Robinson, "Capitalism Comes on Little Cat Feet: The Economy is the Issue in Castro's Cuba," *U.S. News & World Report* (July 28, 1993) 42-45.
12. Donald E. Schulz, "Can Castro Survive?" *Journal of Interamerican Studies and World Affairs* 35 (1) 113-114.
13. Larry Rohter, "Unofficial U.S. Military Group Will Visit Cuba," *The New York Times* (June 29, 1993) A9.
14. Abraham F. Lowenthal, "Latin America: Ready For Partnership?" *Foreign Affairs* 1993, 72 (1) 74-92.
15. Irving Louis Horowitz, *The Conscience of Worms and the Cowardice of Lions: Cuban Politics and Culture in an American Context*. Coral Gables: University of Miami, North-South Center and New Brunswick and London: Transaction Publishers, 1993.
16. See the recent exchange, Jesse Jackson, "Presiones de la CIA y los ultra-derechistas", and Frank Calzon, "La oposición representa el futuro" in *El Nuevo Heraldo* (December 29, 1993). p. 7A.

Source and Original Title: "Ethical and Political Consequences of the American Embargo of Cuba." *Investing in Cuba: Problems and Prospects* (edited by Jaime Suchlicki and Antonio Jorge). Conference sponsored by The Canadian Institute of Strategic Studies. New Brunswick and London: Transaction Publishers, 1994, pp. 1-16.

27

On Socialist Economics and Communist Politics

The commentary by Carmelo Mesa-Lago on my writings on Castro's Cuba is so fair-minded at the expository level that he leaves little to add except a deep appreciation. To have such a level-headed colleague in an area known for its explosiveness and damaging allegations at personal levels is no small statement of the worth of scholarship—or for that matter, just how the democratic imagination works at its highest levels. Our differences however remain real and worth exploring.

Such differences start with the very title of his piece: I categorically deny that the phrase "socialist Cuba" is an exact reflection of the system that has been put in place by Castro for the last thirty-five years. In this matter, Ernesto Betancourt's views are far closer to my own; we are dealing with a traditional caudillo type who builds a cacique system, and then enshrines this travesty with the rhetoric of socialism. In addition, he draws inspiration from the worst totalitarian features of Soviet dictators to give his regime a muscle and a staying power that could only be the envy and joy of Latin American dictators who came before him.

Carmelo is the veritable *decano* of Cuban studies. He sees it as part of the corpus of social scientific, especially economic, examinations of the Castro regime from its inception to the present. Indeed, he epitomizes the extraordinary ability of émigré Cuban scholars to use social research in ways that illustrate the potency of honest work on a dangerous subject, and to do so without rancor or bitterness. Against the shouts and screams of ideologists, Carmelo has always upheld the honor of science by simply demanding that truth must preempt passion in the conduct of our affairs. Indeed, it is such a search that distinguished the life of the mind to begin with.

It is fair to add that Carmelo from the outset operated within a university context far removed from the bastions of Cuban émigré geographical strength, and, as a result, faced a good deal more wrath than those who criticized him for being less than thundering. Raised fists may work in Miami, but it takes a good deal more persuasive tools to work in Pittsburgh. I might add a personal appreciation that Carmelo never treats Cuba as a professional vocation unto itself. He has studied Eastern Europe in great depth, as well as other parts of Latin America. It is the nature of command and market economies and how they impact the social fabric that is at the heart of his work—and I would add, at the soul of his commitment to democratic values.

So there is little need to dwell further on the huge areas in which our thought overlaps. Let me rather address candidly those frames of reference in which we do not share a consensus. At the core of our differences, such as they are, are three areas: first, a difference in emphasis of economic and political factors in the malaise of Castro; second, a different reading of historical and causal sequences; and finally, a different view of Castroism as an ideology. Rather than labor those areas on which we have a strong agreement, I would like to emphasize, admittedly in far too brief a span, those areas that divide us on the meaning of this long-lived tyranny.

Carmelo is of the opinion that the economic malaise in Cuba, caused most recently by the collapse of the Soviet Union and the special role that nation played in the survival of Castro's Cuba, is at the root of the increased political repression within the island. Indeed, it is hard to deny that the end of Soviet aid, and the relative isolation of Castro in economic terms, has been a big factor in the sickness of its economy. Nor can one deny that hardships have increased in the recent years. But I maintain that Carmelo has his sequencing wrong. The political repression predates the economic malaise by several decades!

The fact that I could write an essay for *New Politics* entitled "The Stalinization of Cuba" as early as 1964 indicates how far advanced the machinery of repression became independent of economic hard times. Indeed, one might well argue that Castro's incredible megalomania was fueled by early economic successes, that he saw the prospects for further economic development through political consolidation. After all, Fidel was under the influence of the Stalinists—especially the sort of thinking put forth by Paul Baran and Leo Huberman in those early halcyon days. Carmelo still waffles on the issue of Stalinization. It serves no serious end to say that we stand together on the major points of my analysis, and then claim that the objections to my theses have merit on the minor points.

This is no small matter, since the idea put forth by Carmelo in his recent work *Cuba after the Cold War* (1993) would indicate that economic troubles caused political repression. I would say that the regime from the outset was repressive. This was understood first subjectively, by the flight of hundreds of thousands of refugees, especially from the professional and commerce, and only later appreciated by the scholars. The former were interested in new lives and careers, only the latter were interested in squaring old ideologies with new realities.

The underestimation of the totalitarian nature of the Castro regime was partially a consequence of the overestimation of the socialist character of the economy. Carmelo did not fully factor in the traditional cacique elements in Fidel. The labels were different, but the bottle contained similar equations: a strong military faction, rule by political decree, constant major decision making by the leadership—in short, whether we are looking at rightist or leftist regimes, we see precisely the absence of democracy that would have eased Cuba's burdens, or that could have led to a normalization of relationships with the rest of the world once the communist bloc disintegrated.

It was this inversion of the economic and the political that led to a series of blunders even among stalwart opponents of tyranny. The attempt to establish bilateral relationships between the University of Pittsburgh and the University of Havana—which Carmelo after all championed, signing the formal documents establishing this special relationship—was performed in hothouse isolation of larger political realities. The effort at normalization even at micro-levels, while well intentioned, only exposed the political impotence of the oppositional forces in Havana. It was this misreading of the nature of Stalinization that informed Carmelo's faith in some sort of rapprochement long after many others writing on the subject felt it appropriate to do so.

I raise this not to blow bubbles at Carmelo. His motives in seeking some sort of normalization were pure of mind and heart. Alas, he did not have a signal from Fidel along the same lines. And this was not a function of economic malaise, but of political rigidities of the Cuban Stalinists. They could not back away from their ideological commitments, and yet could not sustain them in the face of post-cold war environment. As a result, Castro is part of a series of terrible contradictions: to build an infrastructure of hotels for foreigners while keeping these off limits to Cubans, establishing supermarkets where only hard currency could be spent, and thus encouraging the very black market and collapse of the native currency he desperately sought to avoid, permitting the resurgence of gambling and prostitution and deviance among the youth, while maintaining strict adhesion to a puritanical version of Marxism-Leninism.

In short, the unraveling of the regime was not primarily a function of the collapse of Soviet and East European communism, but of a series of policy decisions by Castro driven by ideological commitment and cultural closure. Even the hint of private sector, free-market solutions sent Fidel into a frenzy. For that matter, overtures toward rapprochement with the rest of Latin America or the United States were always based on ridiculous premises that the rest of the hemisphere must make concessions to him. This one-way traffic across a bridge that had little to offer on the other side is what doomed Castroism—and not the economy.

But this is jumping the gun, as it were, moving to a contemporary framework. I admit that Castro attempted to play a world role long after the failed adventures in other parts of Latin America. Surely the Angolan adventure demonstrates as much. But this proved to be such a dreary flop, and so short-lived, that agreements involving settlement in Angola that took place in London did not even involve Fidel. Indeed, my point that Fidel was a Stalinist who mistook Cuba for Russia stands. And the events of the last five years confirm as much. I appreciate Carmelo's point that Castro at times acted independent of his Soviet sponsor, even in contradiction to its wishes. But this was because, according to Fidel, it was Soviet "revisionism" that failed to seize proper military and political initiatives. That is to say, the Stalin-Lenin line was carried forth by Fidel, not Gorbachev.

I am not certain what Carmelo's disagreement is with my work on the militarization issue. Indeed, every ounce of data he adduces relates to the exponential growth of the armed forces in recent years, all of which tends to confirm the Stalinization hypotheses. But I suspect that his faith in socialism is far greater than mine—certainly when it comes to Cuba, whether we are talking of past or present decades, this charade must be stripped away as a necessary prelude to serious analysis. It is not a mat¬ter of whether Carmelo and I agree or disagree on a specific point, but rather what is to be the overall characterization of the regime. It is this I miss in Carmelo's own work, no less than his critique of my formulations.

Carmelo's problems are magnified by again drawing attention to the notion of regime institutionalization. My argument was predicated not necessarily on the charismatic nature of Castro, but the inability of a regime such as this to achieve even non-democratic institutionalization. In part the point is moot. But one would have to believe in tooth fairies to assume that a post-Castro epoch would simply maintain the "socialist" character of the Cuban regime intact. And yet, again I find him taking the Soviet post-Stalinist model as viable, much less typical.

I would claim that the collapse of the Soviet empire indicates precisely a failure of non-democratic regimes to institutionalize. To speak of institutionalization a la Soviet Union between 1971 and 1985 may save a theory, but it does little for reality. Why, for example, does this process cease in 1986? Why is the rectification process introduced precisely at a time when institutionalization should have been enhanced? Why does Fidel retake control of the economy? Certainly not out of fear of a decimated bureaucracy or administrative apparatus. Could it be, my friend, that he never relinquished personal authority to start with?!

In discussing political issues, one notices that Carmelo shifts dates so that the keys become 1970-75 and then 1975-89. In short, Castro's global strategies seem to reveal little correlation with his economic policies. If he were to take less seriously the words of Fidel, and more the deeds, at least some of the differences between us could be better resolved. And we could get beyond a laundry list of agreements and disagreements into a fundamental characterization of the regime. Again, this is absent in Carmelo's analysis—a balanced appraisal of an unbalanced regime is no solution.

It is true that my attitude toward normalization changes over time. The United States lives in a world of different social systems, even now, and cannot demand adhesion of social systems as the price of diplomatic recognition. Certainly, I felt that the Bay of Pigs invasion was a disaster, and the potential for rapprochement set back as a result. However, the changes duly noted in my position are not a function of whimsy, but of changing approaches by Castro. Military intervention by Cuba in all parts of the world made normalization virtually impossible. My reading of events was not a function of a growing exile community in Miami, but a growing desperation in Havana.

It is not my stand against normalization, it is the Castro government's inability to accept any sort of reality check on its potencies that compelled me to take a harder stand on normalization of diplomatic relations. Indeed, the fact that Castro's position was repeatedly denounced within the last stages of the Soviet Union as adventurist and dangerous, indicates that the changes were not in the American analysis of Castro, but in the policies of the Cuban government.

We are now in the final stage of Castro's regime. As I have indicated elsewhere, the first part of the discrediting of Castro has already taken place. He simply is no longer feared by his people, and no longer the archangel of Marxism-Leninism. But in the absence of opposition, or better the vacuum created by the decimation of the civil administration bodies and the military forces alike, we are left with a huge political black hole waiting to be filled. All of this, Carmelo knows well—probably better than I. No one wants to see needless suffering, certainly not of the Cuban people. The issue becomes how best to curb such sufferings by massive aid to the Castro regime, or a continuation of the present policies intended to force him from power and permit something better to take its place.

In summary, I find the "balance sheet" approach to my work on Cuba to be only partially successful. One could just as well make the same sort of bookkeeping set of trial balances on Carmelo's work. Indeed, he does this to himself and in this very essay-shifting moods as well as assessments paragraph by paragraph. The key remains structural analysis. From the opening sentence to the very last sentence of his chapter, speaks of "Cuban socialism." I speak, and have spoken, of "Castro's Stalinism." These may overlap in certain areas. But from this distinction flows considerable differences in analysis and opinion. But from such dialectical exercises we may arrive at greater truths about the agonies of the past thirty-five years. We may even end up with ways to avoid such quagmires to begin with. And on this Mesa-Lago and I stand shoulder to shoulder.

Source and Original Title: "Critical Responses to Friendly Cities." *The Democratic Imagination* (edited by Ray C. Rist). New Brunswick and London: Transaction Publishers, 1994, pp. 554-560.

28

The Jewish Experience in Cuba

The amazing part of the Jewish experience in Cuba is not its travails or tribulations, but that the sense of community has survived sixty years of tyranny, neglect, mocking humor, and direct efforts to extinguish it. When one considers the sad fate of Jewish community life in the Middle East, and here I can claim a first hand observation of Egypt, the contrast becomes startling. One can read Robert Levine's book as the history of a community that descends from a vibrant to a vestigial status, but it can just as readily be seen as an example of tribal resistance to a hostile nation state. The size of the community has shrunk from approximately 12,000 at the time of Castro's assumption to power in 1959 to a rump group of roughly ten percent of that, 1,200; but recent news from Havana is that Jewish community life, far from perishing, its devotees are actually undergoing a mild renaissance.

In tracing the Jewish experience in Cuba, Professor Levine, of the department of history at Miami University, provides some clues, and perhaps leaves undeveloped a few others, as to how this capacity for survival in adversity came to pass. It is clear that Professor Levine is intrigued by his subject—not as a case study in the rise and fall of a religious minority in a Latin Catholic culture—but as an illustration of the special nature of the Jewish experience in the century as a whole. Indeed, the *SS St. Louis* Incident, to which is given over the largest chapter in the book, well demonstrates the tangled web of global politics entwining Jewish life and exile politics during the period of Nazi German dominance in Europe. There have been books and films on this "incident," but only Professor Levine can properly lay claim to placing such events on Cuban soil and in Cuban-American history.

Cuban twentieth century history offers a mini-capsule of Jewish ambiguities no less than survival capacities: Levine gives us a vivid picture of the Jew as bourgeois—we are told for instance that 75 percent of the Jews on the eve of the Castro takeover were engaged in small scale retail trade, 15 percent owned large stores, and ten percent engaged in the production of consumer goods. Yet, true to the Jewish Beruf, this did not translate into conservative politics. Many of the Jewish immigrants were communists. Indeed we are told that it was a chemical engineer and elderly Zionist socialist was one of two men who financed the purchase of *Granma*, the boat that took Castro and some of his followers back to Cuba from Mexico to begin his guerrilla campaigns in the mountains. At the same time, Levine documents the ambiguity on the other side—the constant tensions and strains in the Cuban revolutionary attitudes toward the Jews—attitude that drifted from a special positive status with respect to houses of worship to some of the most vicious propaganda found in the West since the Protocols of the Elders of Zion.

Only when Cuba fell under the spell and orbit of Soviet foreign policy did the Jewish condition in Cuban politics become utterly hopeless. And as I noted in my Bacardi lectures of 1992, published as *The Conscience of Worms and the Cowardice of Lions*, this same series of ambiguities was repeated and recreated within the confines of American Jewish intellectual life. In short, it is no exaggeration to say that Levine's book offers a microcosm of more than a tribal community surrounded by larger ethnic and national forces. It mirrors the amazing pulling of the major powers—East and West, Fascist and Communist, Democratic and anti-Democratic—exert over smaller nations like Cuba. In this sense, Castro was as much hostage as Batista to the great nation syndrome. The loyalties shifted, but the dependencies remain a constant. For the Jews, the situation deteriorated because the old loyalties to Latin America were at least covered by a patina of democratic sentiment and middle class goals. The new loyalties of the Fidelistas had no such support base. Little wonder then that ninety percent of the Jewish community came to the United States—indeed, as Levine makes clear, under the dubious cover of being political refugees from Castro's tyrannies, the Jews were again forced into a "wandering" modality.

A serendipitous finding of Tropical Diaspora is how well the Catholic and Jewish cultures managed to get along when left to their respective devices. Levine tells a story of nationalist immigration laws under the Machado reign of terror in the early 1930s, benevolent bribery and blackmail during the Batista era, the public display of Nazi symbols and values by native Falangists, utter cowardice by President Laredo Bru during the *St Louis* incident, and finally, the decimation of the Jewish community of Cuba during the early stages of Castro. What makes the story so grim is how one small island nation in the Caribbean was held hostage to global patterns of anti-Semitism and racism. Fascism, Falangism and Communism—translated into German, Spanish and Russian interventions in Cuban affairs took turns in scapegoating the Jewish community. As a result, the tragedy of this small tribe was played out on a huge canvas, not infrequently, with the willing participation of the victims.

If there is a lesson in this it is that Jews were simply the advance guard of Cuban victims. Without grotesque ideological distortions and political entanglements, Jews would not only have had a safe harbor, but would have played a vital role in the further evolution of Cuban society in general. Levine, while frank about the politics of underdevelopment, and its capacities to emasculate a people, is even blunter in making clear the weakness of a Jewish community that thought it could achieve with payoffs and accommodation what it could not create in open political discourse. Indeed, there are occasions when the book even adopts a mocking tone toward Jewish retailers—as if they were different than retailers the world over—giving customers what they wanted! But in the larger picture, Levine is correct: the Jews of Cuba participated in their own destruction as a result of over-identification with communist causes, and their under appreciation of the democratic spirit.

The Jewish experience in Cuba was different than its contact with the Enlightenment in the nineteenth century. For starters, the Jews could hardly integrate into a culture it felt was lower than itself, yet it did not have the wherewithal to create cultural artifacts to withstand such blandishments. It is the strength of Professor Levine's study to make plain this tension within with Jewish life—one felt keenly by Jews in every part of Latin America, and that certainly did not endear them to the Cubans, who felt that they had achieved a high culture prior to the entreaties of the new dictator. In this, Professor Levine is even handed—perhaps to a fault—seeing the Jews as the agents of their own stereotype. Still, one senses that Levine is correct to note that orthodoxy within either the Ashkenazic or Sephardic traditions did not have sufficient clout to ward off the beasts of secular authoritarianism.

Levine tells a story of two unusual peoples: the Cubans—often called "los Judios de la Caribbean" and the Jews as such—often called much worse by their ostensible saviors. And yet, as the will to be free of tyranny has grown strong in recent years—within Cuba no less than in the exile communities, there is cause of optimism. One suspects or at least hopes that the Tropical Diaspora will need considerable updating in the years to come. This is one time that the story of a Jewish Diaspora has not simply come to an abrupt halt—despite every expectation that this would have occurred. I imagine that the prospect for a different ending than the one provided, i.e., "Cuban Jews came to Miami and to New York as Cubans, not as Jews" will not prove unpleasant to Professor Levine. For one can well imagine, that the Cuban Jews will return to Havana—both as loyal Cubans and as dedicated Jews.

Source and Original Title: Tropical Diaspora: The Jewish Experience in Cuba (Robert M. Levine). *The Americas: A Quarterly Review of Inter-American Cultural History,* Vol. 51, No. 2, (October 1994), pp. 286-288.

29

Castro and the End of Ideology

Economists talk about numbers. Political scientists declaim about power. Sociologists pontificate about ideology. The trouble with this division of academic division of labor is that if the economists were entirely right, the Castro regime would have fallen long ago. If the political scientists were on target, Fidel Castro, given his huge concentration of authority, would never fall. As a result, it is left to those in the softest of the soft social sciences to muddle through with some explanation for the current state of affairs in Cuba 35 years after a revolution of fallen expectations.

We should begin at the beginning in order to get a sense of the end. The dubious honor of running the longest existing dictatorships in the world belong to Kim Il-Sung of North Korea, and Fidel Castro of Cuba. The combined total of premiership and presidency of the former started in 1948, the leadership of the latter started in 1959, and continues uninterrupted through to the present. Both managed to take perfectly viable societies to an economic dead-end without relinquishing authority.

Dictators see as their great strength longevity—ruling with the immodest presumption that they are uniquely endowed with special talents that only that wonderful and ubiquitous phrase, "the people" will or can properly appreciate. How, in the absence of free elections or referenda, such determinations are made is based on another strange magical phrase: "feeling the pulse of the people." Medical doctors view the pulse as belonging to individuals, whilst political fanatics view the pulse as some sort of collective spirit.

Since that pulse is backed by the direct power of life and death lodged in the hands of a single person, group or party, the outcome of such medical analogies are hardly ever in doubt. The fly in the ointment of such a nifty, Orwellian play on language, is the hardening of arteries of such leadership structures. Longevity without legitimacy tarnishes the imagery of a vibrant, youthful regime. And nowhere does this phenomenon appear in a more grotesque form than in the realm of ideology.

Here we are justified to invoke the statement of Daniel Bell, in his afterword to a recent edition of *The End of Ideology*, "Ideological discourse tends to obscure that few movements are monolithic or can sustain uniformity for long. There are first the structural rigidities that breed pressure for change: the increasing inability to operate a large, complex modern society from a narrow base of power, either for economic management or political direction, so that widening the arena of decision-making, providing for some decentralization and individual initiatives, becomes necessary if a society is not to sag or stagnate."

What we have in Castro's Cuba is a perfect illustration of this condition. Therefore, we are justified to speak of the end of Castroism as ideology, even though he continues to sit uneasily on the final throne of communist power in the hemisphere. The death of a regime is sometimes made evident by dramatic events: mass uprisings from below or regicide from above. But other times, as in the case of Fidel, it is made evident by the exhaustion of ideology.

Now there are two streams that enter into this process: external and internal. In the external category there is the diminution of Castro's global authority over the 35 years of his rule: from a potentate of Third Worldism (along with people like Tito, Nasser and Nehru), he became the spearhead of guerrilla insurgency movements. The Cuban Revolution of 1959 became the disastrous "model" for similar excursions—most notably in Bolivia,

Nicaragua, EI Salvador, Peru, Venezuela and other nations of the Caribbean and the Americas.

When this came to an end—starting with the Guevara fiasco in Bolivia in the 1960s and concluding with the demise of Sandinista rule in Nicaragua in the late 1980s—the model itself finally and rightfully became suspect. While a last hurrah of this globalist pretension was fought out in Angola, the costs became so apparent to the Cuban people—in everything from material deprivation to medical catastrophe, such as an AIDS epidemic carried by returning Cuban troops—that the world historic quickly became reduced in size and substance. Castro as an "ism" became a foot note to a variety of power relationships—staring with the removal of Soviet missiles in 1962 and ending with a settlement of the Angolan War—all without the input or direction of Castro and his ism.

Thus, we are dealing with Castroism as an internal or national affair. It is within Cuba that the ideology took root, and within Cuba that the roots have finally dried up. Castro's source of energy from the get goes was anti-Americanism. The ability to finally close a chapter of national humiliation and exploitation that began in 1898 ended in 1958. The national euphoria that ensured is evidenced by the fact that so many of the leaders of the opposition to Castro were themselves heavily (and proudly) involved with the manufacture of the revolution to start with.

Castroism to this day is debated in terms of orthodoxies with or breaks from Marxism-Leninism. But other than its importance in biographical terms—of determining the truth or falsity of Castro's self-proclaimed notions—these are insignificant. What is significant is the employment of the totalitarian model of rule by Fidel: the collapse of the State into the Party; the fusion of civil and military rule, the crushing of all forms of political opposition. That such measures were undertaken in the name of the anti-imperialist and anti-capitalist crusade did not make them less draconian or of lesser repressive consequence.

But as emergency measures hardened into fixed policies, and as friends became enemies and all forms of independent action became suspect, the end of ideology appeared on the scene. This was heightened by the events from 1989 through 1991 that saw the collapse of communist power in Eastern Europe, and then the end of the Soviet Union itself. Like mystical belief systems in general, ideologies are sustained and nourished by the myth of total victory. In the case of Castro, he could offer neither victory in the functional sense, nor a model in the ideological sense. As a result, he must stare at the reality of total defeat on a daily basis.

One will quickly then ask: Why does Castro survive? And the answers are many and reasonable—ranging from the liquidation of the middle and industrial classes as a functional entity; the purging of the armed forces and hence their dismantling as source of opposition; the conversion of the administrative bureaucracy into political activists rather than economic actors—to the power of repression as raw power, whether or not embossed by an ideology.

Hence, the actual meaning of the end of ideology as we speak is as a prelude to the end of the communist rule as such. But this is not to be seen as automatic, or as simultaneous happenings. Indeed, we have here a case of the exhaustion of ideology and the turn to raw power as a mechanism for continuation of rule.

The problem is that every effort at justification for Castro becomes self-contradictory. The infusion of foreign capital to build luxury hotels or the establishment of select stores for purchasing overseas foodstuffs and tape records comes upon the exaggeration of a society of haves and have-nots. And that points up the collapse of an ideology of extreme egalitarianism. In other words, the end of ideology announces the end of the regime not just abstractly, but concretely in the behavior of the people and in the silence of the leadership in the face of such clear incongruities.

This is further enhanced by the decomposition of the social fabric and economic infrastructure: again from the breakdown of rules governing work to the erosion of what was early in the regime heralded as a great hospital and medical system, the regime is unable to deliver on its ideology. Indeed, it becomes plain that the system worked imperfectly with external support from communist powers. In the absence of such powers, much less support from abroad in direct monetary or mineral impute, the bankruptcy of the ideology became complete.

How do we know this has taken place? Aside from eyewitness reports to the above, there are telltale signs in the culture: the revival of religious life from Catholicism to Judaism to the growing power of the *Santerías* in privatizing belief if not predicting collapse. Further, the organs of culture begin to take an anti-political form: literary publications begin to operate in an autonomous way. The obsequious bows to the majesty of the Communist Party or to Fidel Castro specifically, are replaced by darker hues of cultural analysis by the intellectuals on one side and grim humor by the populace on the other. Young people in particular begin to drift from received doctrines. Music and social athletic clubs take on autonomous forms.

In short, the end of ideology is followed, not by an immediate end to the regime, but by an erosion of authority within the regime. This is admittedly a long, drawn out process, in which individuals suffer imprisonment and others ostracisms—but the three-step process as such is not to be denied: first an end to ideology, second, the end to politics (and that means mass mobilization and or participation), and third, an end to the regime itself. I submit that we have now entered that third and final stage.

Neither myth nor miracle can save the regime from destruction. Tragically, those who rule prefer not to see this. But then again, whoever accused long-standing dictators of having a sense of vision? History will not absolve Castro. It will punish him for the torments inflicted on the people of Cuba. One hopes that such a search for retribution and justice will not prolong Castro's stay in power, or the sufferings of the Cuban people. But my mission on this day is not to prognosticate or predict, but simply explain how, through the life of a totalitarian ideology one gets to the death of a totalitarian regime.

Source and Original Title: "Castro and the End of Ideology." *North-South*, Vol. 3, No. 4, December 1993-January 1994, pp. 6-10.

30

Military Autonomy and Dependency
in Castro's Cuba

Perhaps the most astonishing aspect of the subject at hand, i.e., the role of the military in contemporary Cuba, is how important it is to understanding the entire history of Castro's regime, and correspondingly, how little attention the subject has been given by the social science and international relations communities. Were it not for the excellent efforts by a hand full of political scientists, and an equally small cluster of foreign correspondents with long track records in Cuban affairs, our knowledge of this area could well be so limited as to place in jeopardy American national interests; or at least, proper assessments of a volatile nation-state.

If one reviews monographs and texts on the Latin American military, from the inception of the Castro Revolution of 1959 to the present, the absence of Cuba is more than noteworthy. It is scandalous. Volume upon volume discusses everything from the structure of Latin American soldiering to United States foreign aid in the military arena with nary a nod in Cuba's direction. Thus we have books on the bureaucratic-authoritarian model in Latin America with no mention of Cuba, and books on the foreign aid component of weaponry and manpower with no mention of the late Soviet Union.

Here we have the first major clue as to the reasons for this analytic vacuum: the overwhelming academic sociological and political science commitment to see the military of Latin America as a creature, if not downright creation, of the United States. A prototypical example is a collection which appeared in 1994 (not 1964 I hasten to add, when such analysis might have had a sensible component) in which no fewer than nine of eleven chapters address United States interests in military affairs, in a volume dedicated to security, Democracy and Development in U.S.-Latin American Relations. And of these only two have the decency to make plain the huge decline in foreign aid from military goods to civilian requirements.

More to the point, in a volume emanating from the Miami based North-South Center, and dedicated to examining security and military problems in United States Latin American relations, there are exactly two passing references to the "Cuban Revolution" and not a line devoted to the simplest facts that (a) the budget for the military is higher in Cuba than any other hemispheric nation; (b) the external, overseas involvement of this military from the Middle East to Africa made its military a praetorian guard of near-Prussian dimensions; (c) this military, with structural characteristics not unlike other totalitarian regimes such as Paraguay under Stroessner, was fully and totally supplied by the communist bloc, primarily the Soviet Union; (d) the Cuban military, by self-admission of the regime, was a critical pivot in the drug trade to North America and Europe; and finally, (e) on occasion, the military created by the Castro government performed the classic Latin American repressive police functions aimed at its own people.

This is by no means to single out what is, by and large, an even-handed text, at least in effort. It is to note that the myopia is so deep and pervasive that even in Miami, where sensitivity about Cuba runs high, books on the subject of the armed forces of Latin America appear as if Cuba does not exist. To do otherwise, would mean the abandonment of theories in which the United States becomes the enemy: the source of the "interventionist impulse" in one scenario, and the heart and soul of the "war system" in another. And it is easier to surrender realities than theories for those smitten by anti-Americanism as a way of intellectual life.

That this should be the case indicates some profound problems in the social scientific community essentially the construction of "models" that have not the slightest relationship to facts, and in mortal fear of genuine comparative analysis, lest notions of global dependency on the United States be shown as sham. Indeed, to save the "dependency" model and its correlate, the "bureau-cratic-authoritarian regime" model, Cuba had to be ignored, or cause great damage to faulty theorizing. The journalists, bless them, unconcerned with grandiosities and pomposities, but simply reporting the newsstand that included troop deployment and weapons acquisitions became the sole source for accurate information to the larger public.

So it should be noted that the study of the Cuban military, in the context of its Latin American framework (with some noteworthy exceptions, as in the work of Leon Goure, Phyllis Greene Walker, Christopher Whalen, and Jay Mallin) is a virgin subject at the very point in time when the Castro regime is ancient and decaying. To guide us in this effort we most fortunately also have the work of a few younger scholars such as Robert H. Dix who notes that "we may well be witnessing the emergence of a more institutionalized form of military involvement than in the past, a kind of hybrid regime that entails an explicit, albeit delimited, role for the military that both preserves military autonomy, and grants it a certain defined political voice within otherwise democratic politics, yet falls well short of direct military rule, or of mere facade democracies."

While this formulation comes closest to capturing the current state of affairs in the Latin American military broadly speaking, the need to account for the special features of the Cuban armed forces remains a critical task. For what we have in Castro's Cuba is the only global military force. In terms of troop movements from the Middle East to Africa no less than other parts of Latin America, in terms of the coordination of this military force with the larger ambitions of the late and unlamented Soviet Union, in terms of the size and sophistication of its hardware components, Castro's Cuba did more than preserve military autonomy, he expanded its international role beyond that of any other nation in Latin American history. Indeed, its very scope created special contradictions in the Castro regime.

I should like to explore this theses in light of the Cuban experience, both what has been, what is, and what can be expected in the near future post-Castro system. In this sense, developments in places with comparable patterns of military intervention from Paraguay to Columbia and Venezuela are not without meaning, although such comparative details go considerably beyond the task at hand.

The key to what has been: a double legacy of guerrillas at war; and on the other side, a Leninist-Stalinist legacy of the professionalization of the armed force (conspiracies, assassinations, distrust, arrests). This contradiction is so pervasive loyalists and defectors alike are at odds in making serious determinations of future military behavior. In the absence of a clear sense of loyalties in the post-Ochoa period, it is virtually impossible to know if or when a showdown were to take place, whether the loyalties of the military would be with the party or the people, or for that matter, if the armed forces would act as unified agency.

The key to what is: a double legacy of an armed force which serves as the praetorian guard of the Communist Party of Cuba and no less a potential source of a golpe de estado against the Castro regime. This can best be described as a split between security and defense, or a division between MININT and MINFAR. Again, we are looking at a regime that has created a certain balance of forces aimed at holding in abeyance any effort at the overthrow of the regime. In developing this model however, a certain stress within the holders of hardware has developed. One can see this in the riots of early August 1994 in which the regular armed forces essentially remained passive, while Castro had to call out special units with special training loyal to his command.

The key to what will be: a double legacy of military loyalty to Castro, while also a hatred for the demoralized state of the military that followed the execution of senior officers. Beyond the Ochoa affair, is an armed force we know from those have defected, that is divided along the lines of rank, command, and even race. The reward system of an earlier period is also less in evidence, since the black market activities have bypassed normal channels whenever necessary.

In this connection, the current stage of the domestication of the Cuban Armed Forces, its incapacity to function outside of Cuban borders, only heightens contradictions between the military and the polity. Military dreams of world roles have shriveled in the present decade of the 1990s, accelerated with the collapse of the Soviet Union in 1989. But again, it is hard to measure demoralization outside the context of battle situations. Behavior is determined by all sorts of external events, and not simply the inner condition of the present moment.

Let me enlarge upon this tripod of a double legacy, if one may be permitted to mix terms in the hope of clarification. While each pairing has unique elements meriting microscopic examination, these three sets of contradictions are unified in their macroscopic consequences, ultimately to devitalize (but not in itself topple) the regime.

A Note on Surveys and Scenarios

It is exceedingly difficult under normal circumstances to secure accurate and useful information on foreign armed forces. This is especially true when such regimes are thoroughly hostile to American interests at one end, and true in general when access to members of the armed forces are virtually impossible through regular, normal channels, such as joint military exercises or organizational linkages that bring members of the armed forces into direct contact.

In the case of Cuba, both factors inhibiting exact information exist. However, starting with Mariel in 1980, continuing through the decade with a series of high level defections from FAR, and now again with the Cojimar boat lifts of 1994, the United States is in a position to gather exact data of a powerful sort. Indeed, one can surmise on a random basis that hundreds of men now awaiting processing at Guantanamo are either currently serving in the Cuban armed forces, or have been recently past participants. Reliability of such informants is always an issue. But the risks in such exaggerations can be readily offset by cross-checking and verifying data provided.

Direct interviews with these individuals could, and in some measure already have, yielded a collective profile of military morale in Cuba that provides a special dimension to this project. This may well have been explored already. If not, it certainly should be. Of course, the essential caveat here is that those who chose to flee Cuba represent a special stratified sample already, and hence, the judgment of such individuals must be filtered through the evaluation process carefully. Nonetheless, the risks involved notwithstanding, prospects for confirming general impressions with specific interview data should not be missed.

What then have we learned on an authoritative basis? The latest and in my view entirely reliable data, suggest the following linked developments: (1) The fusion of party and military, institutionalized on a daily basis by their joint utilization in agricultural and construction projects that aim to benefit the population. (2) Special privileges to the military, such as plots of land as a mechanism to sustain families of the armed forces. (3) Assignments to the armed forces in the tourist, industrial and construction sectors; in effect recreating the "middle class military" phenomenon known widely in Latin America. (4) Finally, quasi-bribes, such as monthly allotments of consumer goods that the average population does not receive.

The two edged sword of the Cuban military its service as the praetorian guard of Castro's overseas adventures, and its deep and abiding sense of service to the nation as such makes it very difficult to offer serious predictions or prognosis in the event of a political crisis of the regime. My own surmise is that the armed forces would serve as a passive rather than active agent in any concerted uprising. That is to say, in the event of any sort of mass uprising, the armed forces would resist slaughtering its own people; but could not be counted upon as a force to stimulate such basic regime changes.

The distinction between communist and nationalist elements in the Cuban armed forces were evolving rapidly in the late 1980s. But the "Ochoa Affair" and its outcomes whether by design or accident has thwarted such a natural evolution. However one might well imagine a series of brush fire skirmishes between the popular sectors and the party forces in which the armed forces played a passive role.

This would leave the security forces free to act, but it could also create the basis of bringing to the fore long simmering animosities between military and police functions within the Castro regime.

While speculation, labeled as such, is warranted, we need to rule out analogical reasoning that is structurally flawed. For example, a number of analysts have put forth the idea that the Cuban armed forces are in a similar situation to that the Spanish armed forces in the final years of Francisco Franco. While this is superficially attractive, the actual parameters of Cuba in 1995 and Spain in 1965 are dramatically different. Cuba lacks a monarchical tradition. Spain had a Pretender to the Throne in waiting; thus providing the sort of legitimacy during a transitional period that made possible an order succession. In fact, it is the near total dismemberment of civil society that in its own way curiously impedes the military from performing a constructive oppositional role. In a world of party-military alliance, prospects for a gradual return to civil society are hard to conjure up. So much for analogues drawn from two discrete cultures held together by a common language.

My own deepest impulse is to see the Castro regime as increasingly similar in function and structure to classical golpista regimes elsewhere in the hemisphere. In that sense, Cuba is the backwater of Latin American tendencies toward democratization. And I do not believe that Cuba can long hold out against such winds of change. But this is not to claim that the armed forces will act as a unified phalanx either in opposition or in support of the Fidelistas. Thus, if one is thinking in terms of scenarios, or policies that can be linked to expected states of change, it is best to realize that the armed forces of Cuba will neither serve as the saviors of a democracy yet to be, nor the firm defenders of a dictatorship that still remains. This is admittedly a non-dramatic view of the situation. The construction of alternative scenarios is a perfectly reasonable activity in which to engage. However, we must always allow for the possibility of emerging factors that are not easily anticipated. This is especially the case with Cuba, in which spontaneous and unanticipated events play such a large part in the development of oppositional voices of protest.

The most creditable view we have available of the Cuban armed forces, made at some remove from the current scene, and with limited information of the daily operations of the armed forces of Cuba's tightly controlled regime, is of a force that poses little external or regional threat to other states in the region. But at the same time, the same must be said with respect to the communist regime: it poses little internal threat to the continued rule of the Communist Party and the Castro family. The mouse that roared: in Latin America in the 1960s, in the Middle East in the 1970s, in the Southern cone of Africa in the 1980s, has been reduced to a mouse that squeaks at home.

Nor is this condition simply a function of the collapse of external adventurism. It must be understood that as the last bastion of Marxist-Leninist orthodoxy, the Cuban military adhere to a code of professional conduct that is quite similar to what one finds in the western powers: its defined tasks are to defend the national purpose as that purpose is defined by the party in power, but not to run the state as such. In this, Cuba's armed forces are unlike most of the classical military structures elsewhere in the hemisphere. Cuba may be a highly evolved military dictatorship, but it is no less a highly refined professional military. This serves to inhibit the organization of a golpista group or even a conspiratorial mentality. Were this not the case, the response to the Ochoa executions would have been far more explosive; instead the outcome was seething quiescence.

How the United States elects to respond to this military impasse—through easing sanctions or by tightening the current embargo policy posture—goes beyond the confines of this exercise. That oppositional elements to the present regime continue to expect so much, and have so little to show from the Cuban armed forces, is itself a dramatic illustration of how ably Fidel Castro has bridled military power through a combination of guile and bile, or better yet, intimidation and ideology. He has managed to perform this complex effort whilst crushing civilian authority and possible alternative sources of opposition. One must begrudgingly credit Fidel Castro with a neat sort of legerdemain, albeit with terribly tragic consequences for the Cuban people.

References/Notes

Alonso, Jose F., "The Ochoa Scandal," in Cuba Annual Report: 1989. [Office of Research and Policy, Radio Marti Program. United States Information Agency]. New Brunswick and London: Transaction Publishers, 1992. pp. 285-377.

Bloomfield, Richard J., editor. *Alternative to Intervention: A New U.S Latin American Security Relationship*. Boulder: Lynne Rienner Publishers, 1990.

Dix, Robert H., "Military Coups and Military Rule in Latin America," in *Armed Forces and Society*. Volume 20, Number 3, Spring 1994. pp. 439-456.

Falk, Richard A. and Samuel S. Kim. *The War System: An Interdisciplinary Approach*. Boulder: Westview Publishers, 1980.

Goure, Leon, "War of All the People," in *Cuban Communism* (eighth edition), New Brunswick and London, 1995.

Horowitz, Irving Louis, "Military Origins and Outcomes of the Cuban Revolution," in *Cuban Communism* (seventh edition), New Brunswick and London, 1989. pp.545-573.

Mallin Sr., Jay, *Covering Castro: Rise and Decline of Cuba's Communist Dictator*. Washington D.C.: U.S.-Cuba Institute Press, and New Brunswick and London: Transaction Publishers, 1994. esp. pp.97-111.

Martin, Marta San and Ramón L. Bonachea, "The Military Dimensions of the Cuban Revolution," *The Cuban Insurrection*, New Brunswick and London: Transaction, 1974.

Planas, Ricardo, "Cuba's Search for Stability: Castro's Agenda for 1995 and Beyond". Unpublished report prepared by the Office of Research, Radio Marti Program, United States Information Agency, January 1995. 18 pp.

Schoultz, Lars, William C. Smith, and Augusto Varas, editors. *Security, Democracy, and Development in U.S.-Latin American Relations*. New Brunswick: Transaction Publishers, 1994 (a publication of the North-South Center of the University of Miami).

Stepan, Alfred, *Rethinking Military Politics*. Princeton: Princeton University Press, 1988

Walker, Phyllis Greene, "Political-Military Relations Since 1959," *Conflict and Change in Cuba*, edited by Enrique A. Baloyra and James A. Morris. Albuquerque: University of New Mexico Press, 1993. pp. 110-135.

Source and Original Title: "Cuba's Military: Autonomy or Dependence?" *Freedom Review,* Vol. 26, No. 4, July-August 1995, pp. 13-16.

31

Cuban Models and Democratic Choices

The title of my remarks is perfect as an after-dinner topic; or in this case, after lunch. Whether they deserve to be dignified with the notion of *un almuerzo de trabajo* is something else again; depending on how exhausting the process of eating turns out to be. Since the subject at hand—models of capitalism and democracy—fills libraries, I can only hope that your good nature will prevail, and you will permit me to indulge in a form of speculation that may or may not be relevant to the specific subject of this special conference on The Transition to Democracy and Lessons for Cuba. In the words of W. Somerset Maugham: "I only want to set down what I know of my own knowledge." I appreciate your further indulgence in permitting me to speak in the English language—one rationale for doing so, other than an ease with my mother tongue, is that so much that is useful (not to mention so much that is useless) first appears in this language.

We start with a gigantic anomaly: for most of the century, the talk of models of development entailed a concept of transition from capitalism to socialism, and for the less sentimental and more "advanced," the transition from formal democracy to the supposed real democracy of the dictatorship of the proletariat. But if there is a single "model" that has been discredited, that has been consigned to the ashes of modern history, it is the infallibilist, deterministic idea of an inexorable movement from capitalism to communism—with an interminable stop-over at socialism. Given the monumental nature of the collapse of this model we need to ask ourselves what went wrong. For in the crucible of every day life we must learn to discard models, as well as create them.

In my opinion, the deep source of the problem is the relationship of democracy to capitalism as such, or if one prefers, the relationship of politics to economics. By use of a phrase like "political economy" we have managed to paper over a problem as serious in social science as we find in the physical sciences: namely a kind of Heisenberg Effect of being unable to chart or predict the behavior of waves and particles at the same time or within the same frame. We can give rather satisfactory definitions of democracy and we have an abundance of information and literature on capitalism. What we seemingly have a hard time doing is to offer a sensible analysis of the two words in tandem—that is the exact relationship of capitalism and democracy. We have an even harder time making predictions as to the preconditions for linking them in the future.

There is scarcely any division of opinion between conservatives and liberals on this matter. If we examine recent conservative analysis we see a full range of views. Irving Kristol offers two cheers for capitalism as the source of democratic behavior, while Russell Kirk offers dire warnings that capitalism is the source of sheer anarchy not democracy; democracy leads to a collapse of moral order and an endless cacophonous sound of complaints. Democracy leads to a sense of rights without obligations, he says, of law without justice, and of power without reason. Liberal opinion echoes similar divisions of opinion. John Kenneth Galbraith sees capitalism as a military industrial complex whose countervailing springs of rule have run amuck. Robert Heilbroner increasingly sees capitalism as a self-correcting and self-renewing instrument of modern democracy.

Whatever the merits or demerits of a general theory or broad models about the relationships of capitalism and democracy, the question cannot be settled by appeals to logic. All of these figures represent a wealth of talent and prestige, and many other estimable people have also written on this subject—from Michael Novak to Gunnar Myrdal. All have stared down this problem, and they have come up with a variety of ways to fine tune the relationship of democracy to capitalism. Yet we persist in seeking better models and clearer solutions than those currently available. I submit that we do so because the very concept of "models" is suspect. Blueprinting futures is risky. One can do so in controlled environments in which experiments on animals or organic matter are conducted. But the same sort of theorizing collapses in the face of wide open environments and thinking, calculating individuals.

One is tempted to add that a great problem, a weakness of dictators is their penchant for model construction. Indeed, Marxism-Leninism is the first major effort to micro-manage social change by planning to destroy one system and install in its place another. This very goal is somewhat akin to the attempt to genetically manufacture perfect children—and I daresay, it has met with the same trepidation and concern from ordinary people. The intervening variables: from national aspirations, geographic differentiation, ethnic and racial competition, levels of industrial development, and character of linguistic clusters are all so different that efforts to manufacture of general models has received well deserved skepticism. And when we add to these sociological factors those of a more intimate, psychological sort, the task of prediction becomes—to put it mildly—formidable.

No more than thirty years ago a broad social science consensus confidently spoke about the transition of the Americas from civil to military societies. Now we seem to be speaking with equal assurance of the transition from dictatorship to democracy. We need to remain modest about our predictions. The track record of social science on such matters ranges from poor to awful. As the famed historian Walter Laqueur has reminded us, intelligence is just what the intelligence community has lacked. Its predictions about Soviet power made as recently as 1988 seem absurd in 1993. One must also say in all candor that those who have annually predicted the collapse of Cuban communism have been forced into ad hoc reasoning as to why this event, certain to happen, still remains in abeyance. Modesty in the face of reality is the only proper posture for social science prediction.

Such modesty must start with a sense that all models are subject to decomposition, and no model perfectly fits any society. And we must end with a similarly appreciate that social systems are also subject to disintegration, and no system perfectly fits any individual. This does not mean that we live a in a wide-open, chaotic universe. It simply means that efforts at prediction come upon the imperfect nature of implementation. Human beings plan their future, but they carry rabbits' feet in their hip pockets in the full knowledge that disasters—natural and human alike—lurk behind every model. But between chaos at one end and perfect models at the other is a wide net—and the ability to live within that great expanse is what we need to focus on. At least, that is what I intend to focus upon in my remaining time today.

A second key element in our thinking requires that we get beyond the bizarre notion that leader must "solve" the material problem first and then address the political concerns second. This artificial causation is based on the idea that the stomach is causally prior to the mind. Few theories have caused greater pain and suffering—in the name of alleviating pain and suffering. This sort of approach has been used not only as a foundation stone of developmental theory, but as a disguise for dictatorial practice. A democratic approach cannot arbitrarily determine whether food comes before books. Rather, it must see to it that the human person has access to both. Otherwise, the business of satisfying the "material conditions" becomes a destructive mechanism for destroying the human person in the name of advancing those abstract material conditions. So this piece of Marxist-Leninist casuistry must be laid to rest with the system it permitted in the first place. Democracy does not choose between mind and body; it advances the cause of the human being as such.

Let us now briefly review the twentieth century and see in broad measures what has ended and what has arisen. In terms of social class, the peasantry and the proletariat are both shrinking.

The very notion of development entails a sense that of movement from rural to urban, farming to industrial bases of society. At the other end, the bourgeoisie as a pure class has also diminished in size and importance. The ownership structure of modern capitalism has shifted from being individual to corporate in character. This was already well charted by Berle and Means in the early 1930s—and it is a process that has accelerated as the century comes to an end.

What have grown over the course of the century are a managerial class in the private sector, and an administrative class in the public sector. Managers and administrators have much in common with each other whatever sector of the economy to which they are linked. They share a passion for efficiency and rationality, and a disdain for ideology and teleology. They comprise not only a huge portion of the technically able. They also cross over from public to private sector activities (and vice versa) with astonishing ease. The students in our classes are not working to become either captains of industry or workers in the vineyards. They are equipping themselves with technical competencies that will permit them to participate in a modern society: as doctors, lawyers, accountants, engineers, militarists, they will be specialists in service rather than generalists in analysis.

There is little purpose in bemoaning this development, in labeling it a dangerous consequence of positivism or worse. It is the raw stuff of reality. Democracy begins with the clang of professional life; and capitalism begins with a professional market as much as a free market. Indeed, the shape of class struggles to come is between those who have access to the means of information and communication, and those who are not so equipped. The very notion of literacy has shifted from reading and writing to those who compute and manipulate data. In such a world, nineteenth century models of capitalism are hardly more serviceable than a twentieth century notion of communism The shape of the twenty first century is making much of our economic inheritance obsolete. And as in so many facets of our lives, change does not come about as a result of intentions but through a process of discovery that brings with it unintended consequences—some good, some evil.

In this equation, not only does the market change its face, but so too does democracy and its meaning. The issues which democracy must resolve are less about the nature of political rule and more over private rights. Democracy comes to be defined systemically not simply as the right to participate, but also as the right not to participate, and not to suffer negative consequences as a result. We are all creatures of inheritances, and as social scientists, models are our inheritances. Democracy is more than a system of formal governance. We need not abandon our inheritances, but we must build upon it. It is a style of life that permits one to make mistakes and not suffer fatal consequences for doing so. Democracy is also a system that allows for a change in direction and emphasis, again without suffering murder, exile or excommunication. The very flexibility of democracy as a political order distinguishes it from dictatorship and its rigidities. In short, democracy, like capitalism, is a culture not a model. It is a way of life and a normative set of routines.

The people of the Americas are no longer infatuated, if they ever were, with labels about big words. They share a sense of adventure not a need for uniformity. If we really want to see continued strength for democracy and capitalism, we would be well advised to keep our eyes and minds on the third sector, the huge world of voluntary associations, from churches to foundations. These are the individuals and agencies that keep the word "free" in free markets and who prevent democracy from becoming a legal formalism. At this very moment, not a city or hamlet in America, not a hotel from one end of North American to another is without a meeting, a gathering, a conference such as the one we are holding. In that act of communion, of coming together voluntarily for shared purpose, lies the best hope for a living democratic society embodying free market and free thought principles.

If we look at Cuba for a moment, what do we see? Certainly no lack of public sector management. Indeed, that management has led the Cuban regime to the brink of disaster and perhaps to civil conflict. But we also see a gray market and a black market, a free enterprise zone emerging (without official sanction) to satisfy the everyday needs of ordinary people. This development may be hailed, but it is also fraught with dangers. The underground economy is always risky. It includes those who are sharp and even ruthless, as well as many for whom legality and decency still has some meaning. Dictatorships can, and often have, controlled the private sector. Indeed, Nazism offers tragic evidence to this end. What we do not yet see, and what we need to see, is the plethora of voluntary associations—from Rotarians to Philatelists—that give meaning to the market in stimulating a renewal in democracy.

The first half of the post-Castro revolution in Cuba is well underway: the dissolution of the machinery of repression, the end of the cult of personality, and the mass disdain for totalitarian solutions. The second half, the implementation of voluntary associations from open political parties to unfettered social-athletic clubs, remains to be undertaken. Not the model, but the anti-model will come to define the next Cuban revolution. The end of the long night of multiple tyrannies lasting from 1933 to 1993, which began with small corruptions and ended with huge distortions. will be signaled less by fierce military battles than by people going about the business of working and living without the need to respond to the grandiose demands of megalomaniacal leaders.

Democracy will be observed in the restoration of private lives unwatched and unsupervised, and by public lives dedicated to human enhancement and cultural enjoyment. Like the rest of the western hemisphere, Cuba does not need more models; it needs freedom from model builders. It needs end of political dictatorship and a closure to economic communism. Given those two parameters of development, the people of Cuba will take care of themselves. Political economy, or if you prefer the fusion of democracy and capitalism, will come together, when they come together. They will be evident not in abstract slogans, but in concrete lives. This will be observed in the internalization of a sense of obligation to the common good no less than a feeling of entitlement.

The Cuban people will know the real thing when they have it, not only because they will have Coca-Cola once again, but because they will have a choice of beverages from Russian vodka, French wine, to Cuban distilled Bacardi rum.

The Cuban people will know that they have a free economy not because they have jobs, but because they can buy what they want, when they want it, and how they want to buy it.

The Cuban people will know freedom, not because it is shouted from the rooftops by agents of the Committees for the Defense of the Revolution, but because they will no longer be spied upon by friends or neighbors.

The Cuban people will know democracy not simply because they go to the polls to vote, but because they can stay home and not vote without feeling the wrath of the State and without fearing condemnation from the authorities.

The Cuban people will know who they are when they are at liberty to travel about, when travel is in jets not on rafts; and when a trip is once again a vacation from every day life, not an irreversible process of self-exile.

By such small details in everyday life rather than grandiose models do people the world overcome to know the meaning of political economy and the values of unfettered democracy. In development theory, we use a concept called "the advantage of coming last." Hopefully, the new Cuban State will make use of it. For what we have learned, after centuries of torment and turmoil is that a free market and a free society is more a process than a system, more an interaction than a model, more a set of moral decencies than an ideological persuasion. This is precious little to have learned for our troubles. But they are worthy of our respect and our passion.

Source: Conference on Capitalism and Democracy, University of Miami, Center for International Studies 1995.

32

Endless Celebrations for an Old Dictator

The beginning of a New Year is special event for everyone: a moment of optimism for a future with unforeseen options, and a time of reflection on what could have been. But given the date of the guerrilla seizure of power in Cuba, January 1, 1959, the start of the year remains a bitter sweet reminder for Cubans at home and abroad of a revolution that failed but that persists. It is as if the normal rhythm of political history, the rise, collapse, and occasional reform of states, has passed by Cuba. Instead, the uniform consensus is of a State exhibiting near-total stagnation from within, and a loss of power and prestige on any larger geopolitical canvas.

After 37 years, Cuban leadership has even lost the capacity to distinguish the popular will from party ideology. Illustrative of this is a demand by the Bishop's Council that the government cease ridicule of and discrimination against believers. This resolved itself in an order by the government not to interfere with individuals from purchasing Christmas trees, but prohibiting all government offices from displays of religious ornamentation. In a land where options are tantamount to counter-revolution, score a small victory for the free expression of ideas.

The symbolic result is the further estrangement of people from the state. This terrible alienation, in which a people have become a nation without politics, characterizes Cuba as it enters a new year. The sources of public estrangement are deep in the marrow of Cuban society. They include a series of unresolved contradictions that threaten to become more severe as the New Year progresses. Deciding whether they are sufficient to topple the regime is, however, less important than appreciating their consequences to date.

First, there is festering unhappiness within the armed forces to the Communist regime. While the Ochoa Affair of 1989 suppressed any show of manifest resentment, the fact remains that there are still numerous retention centers in Cuba for former members of the military. In addition, the new economic role of the military is not entirely to their liking. The mission of a once proud and efficient military is now reduced to managing enterprises and producing food for themselves and the population at large. It is unlikely that the divisions within the armed forces will heal, and this signifies a latent source of opposition far more dangerous than the Cuban government dares acknowledge. The golpe or elimination of the Castro brothers remain as a possibility for avoiding a blood bath on the island, while restoring the nation to normalcy, albeit in a traditional Latin American guise. The dilemma here is that upper echelon cadres are frequently rotated and military command structure is divided along a tripartite geographical axis precisely so that Castro can ferret out and control conspiratorial plots and plans. At the same time it makes the military a force for nation-building or consolidation nearly impossible to carry out.

Second, paradoxically, the monolithic Miami-based opposition to the Castro regime is weakening. This emergence of pluralization is evident. The Cuban American National Foundation is no longer the sole source for opinions and ideologies. Indeed, CANF is suffering a generational crisis, with its roots and appeals in and to the older generation of Cubans living in America. But in this situation, the myth that any overthrow of Castro would mean the imported solutions to domestic Cuban problems would be imposed has been severely weakened. Even conservative Cubans in Miami have been careful not to oppose attempts to develop some sort of common anti-Castro front comprised of diverse political viewpoints; they realize full well that revanchist claims can only needlessly postpone the coming of inevitable changes in Cuban governance.

Third, while Cuban sugar production may rise slightly in 1996 to perhaps 3.5 to 3.8 million tons, this increase is entirely insufficient to offset the cost of interest on loans made to purchase new harvesting equipment, much less pay back the principal on the loans themselves. And as Castro is learning, hard currency countries drive hard bargains when doing business. Thus, unless a minor miracle occurs and the world price of refined sugar rises dramatically, the long term economic crisis within Cuba is likely to further deepen in the absence of any fundamental restructuring of the Cuban economy.

Fourth, the Cuban monetary system is on a collision course with the Cuban people. The division between those who have and those who do not have the ability or right to traffic in hard currencies, especially dollars, has left Cuba with a small class of "wealthy" individuals and a large class of poor individuals. Worse still, the beneficiaries of economic opening so far have been precisely those groups who have traditionally been hostile to the Castro Revolution, and those punished by the new economic opening are precisely those who in past years were supportive of the Revolution. And yet the Castro regime is unable to reverse tendencies toward a "second economy" without inviting a total and immediate economic breakdown and an increase in popular discontent.

Fifth, to be sure, Castro himself seems well aware that the course he has pursued may be irreversible. He went to China to make clear his intention to hitch a repressive political apparatus to a limited market opening. Cuba has adopted the worse features of the "Chinese Way" of economic openness and statist closure, and Castro went to china to make that symbolism public. Of course, in back of the symbol is the need for cash. And in this the Chinese authorities came up empty. They in effect offered Castro a gratuity rather than loans or outright grants. That Castro anticipated that the trip would yield greater benefits is a testimonial to his own grandiose myopia. His denunciations of Mao in earlier periods as "revisionist" and "nationalist" can hardly have been forgotten. The Chinese are renowned for elephantine memories, an ailment that cannot be said to have afflicted American politicians and publicists.

Sixth, the only economic hope left for Fidel is either the return to full power of the Communists in Russia, and a massive influx of aid to Cuba, or a U.S. lifting of its travel ban to the island, which would bring an immediate infusion of cash to the Castro strapped economy. But even should change occur in Russia, and this is by no means a certainty, Cuba will be a low item on the agenda of Russia's Communists, much less that of everyone else. Given the electoral climate in the United States and the continuous refusal of the Castro regime to provide serious economic and political changes in the island, and Castro's recent renewed harsh criticism of the United States, it is unlikely that U.S. policy will change much in 1996.

Seventh, the Cuban infrastructure can no longer endure further disintegration. With construction being centered in hotels and agencies catering to foreign tourists and investors, the ordinary public needs for road repair, school construction, hospital improvements, in short, social reconstruction, remain stalled and idle. What this also does is defeat the long wave ideology of the regime, the notion that sacrifice is a benefit that will be reaped by the young generation. The young generation has grown to maturity disillusioned and alienated, having seen earlier gains dissolve rather than be enhanced. Hence, the potential for mass mobilization has now dwindled to zero.

Eighth, the essential contradictions within Cuba have reached a point in which the cultural apparatus no longer believes in the communist system. In all the major cultural productions, everything seems fair game for discussion from French Dadaism of the fin the Šiecle to the worth of Cuban ballet in the 1920s. Abstract art has replaced socialist realism in the pages of artistic and cultural publications. What is missing, even in the rare article on materialistic philosophy, is any mention of Fidel Castro or his leadership. To be sure there is no criticism whatsoever of

Castro, but the silence is deafening. Partinost has given way to partyless. And as Georgie Anne Geyer observed several years ago in her biography of Castro, he has become simple "El" or "He" an amorphous, shadowy figure. beyond comedy, but transcending tragedy as well.

Ninth, much of the exile community is in a state of despair, an understandable consequence of repeated fantasies turned into prophesies of regime failure. Signs of such despair are everywhere. [Not the least is the bitter disputes within Radio Marti that have rendered that "program" the most contentious and least predictable element in the United States Information Agency efforts at global outreach.] The march of events in Cuba has never moved in lock step to either well wishers or enemies of the regime. There is no reason to assume that this will change in 1996. However, the despair felt by those who for years have prognosticated a collapse of the Castro regime, may be premature rather than incorrect.

At the end of the day, or better, the start of a new year, what we observe in Cuba is a silent revolution eon, one based in part on wish fulfillment but also on a denial of legitimacy to the Castro regime. In operating as if there is no Fidel Castro, and as if the dictatorial regime lack bite, the people of Cuba have managed to achieve a state of normalcy. Even if this rationality is based on a denial of political alternatives, it has beneficial consequences: fear is diminished, the need to scrutinize every pronouncement of the tyrant is dissolving, and the ordinary pursuits of daily life are being carried out with a semblance of dignity and decency, the agents of the regime and party cadres notwithstanding. Cubans are a sophisticated people. They teach us one way of response to tyranny; it requires no grand design, only personal resolve and resourcefulness coupled with a good sense of humor.

Source and Original Title: "Cuba 1996: The Last Caudillo" (with Jaime Suchlicki). *Freedom Review,* Vol. 27, No. 2, March-April 1996, pp. 18-21.

33

Reality Avoidance and Political Pilgrimage

Political pilgrims have been a special part of the Cuban landscape ever since Fidel Castro came to power in January 1959. It started with Herbert L. Matthews' dispatches from the Sierra Maestra, and came to fruition with his March 8, 1959 interview published in *The New York Times Magazine* in which Matthews declares that "no one ever calls him anything else [but Fidel] in Cuba" since he "obviously arouses all the maternal instincts in women a subject on which Mr. Matthews presumes to have been well versed." In 37 years since then, the iconography has hardened into dogmatism, while the idolatry has gone from bad to worse.

How can it be that professional people of ostensibly sound mind and firm moral principles are able to tender their support for the longest running dictatorship in the world? I have in mind those political pilgrims, who still manage to sing paeans of praise for Fidel Castro and his Cuban regime after 37 years of demonstrated tyranny, while bemoaning the fate of militarism and the loss of civil liberties in other nations of the region. That such individuals are able to do so, not only in the face of overwhelming empirical evidence of a singularly failed government, but a century of turmoil and tyranny identified with communism throughout the world, is for me at least, less a matter of failure to face facts than an embrace of fantasy psychological and sociological illusions that persist despite evidence to the contrary.

I

In late March of 1996, the Central Committee of the Communist Party endorsed a hard political line. It declared that the
limited opening of the economy had created a class of Trojan
horses, parasites and fifth columnists in its midst. Raúl Castro,
in his plenary report argued that Cuba, must at all costs avoid
reforms of the type that undermined the Soviet Union and other
socialist countries. Deviations from Communist Party norms were
assaulted at every level from demands for wage increases by labor
unions to cautions statements about further openings of the economic system to reforms by research institutes. The tightening of
the Party grip came along with the usual pathological calls for vigilance against the "diversionary roles" of class enemies and "those
falling into the spider's web spun by Cuba experts abroad." But
renewed evidence of the Stalinist persuasion of Cuba's maximum
leaders makes little impression on apologists for the regime.

Apocalyptic and prophetic movements of all sorts demonstrate this deep gap between lofty utopian ambitions and desultory
actual performances. There is a rich literature created over time
by those who study religious and political movements. Indeed, the
singularly monumental efforts of Paul Hollander in *Political Pilgrims*
and *Anti-Americanism* give us just the sort of analysis that makes
"sense" of human attachments to political extremisms, as did Sigmund Freud nearly a century ago in studying the enormous power
of illusion in the conduct of our private affairs. In this sense, utopian
longings function as the equivalent of sexual fantasy. It matters not a
whit that dictatorial rule has been in effect in Cuba since 1959. The
survival of the totalitarian regime is considered prima facie evidence
of the moral worth of the regime, while any of its weakness are attributed to foreign interference or external enemies.

The political pilgrim is not your ordinary, garden variety tourist seeking fun in the Cuban sun. Rather, he or she is an individual
identified and singled out by the totalitarian host regime as
pliable enough in convictions and sufficiently influential in connections to warrant the costs of an all expenses paid short-term

excursion; one in which the great dictator (or his representative) speaks intimately and lovingly of the regime's deep and abiding affection for the American people always making clear that they differ from the American system. The political pilgrim does not have to be either Left or Right. He or she can be drawn from the ranks of labor leaders or captains of industry. Party identification is not required; the lack of affiliation may be an asset, since the search is for those articulate enough to identify with the regime while giving the appearance of remaining a "mainstream" voice. Once the regime eliminates from consideration those shriveled ranks still willing to join a brigade for a summer outing in sugar cane cutting, the actual selection of the political pilgrim becomes an art of no small merit for the regime.

My purpose is not to re-examine what has been ably done by others in a European context. Nor for that matter, is it my aim to study the fascination of democratically minded people with specific types of dictatorial regimes and leaders. Rather, I would like to examine the specific dynamics of support for Fidel Castro as it persists in the present climate of American elite opinion. Before I begin, let me preface these remarks with some brief references to personal history, and then move on to variations on an old theme: the social-psychological sources of support for tyrants.

My first personal contact with a political pilgrim was the late C. Wright Mills. In the first year of the Castro Revolution of 1959, he took a one month tour of Cuba, and with more than modest guidance from Carlos Franqui and the staff of Revolución, produced in one more month *Listen Yankee* perhaps the best selling book on Cuba immediately after the revolution, and certainly one that solidified Mills' image as a man of the Political Left. Having examined this phase of Mills in my intellectual biography of him published in 1983 *C. Wright Mills: An American Utopian* I will spare you further analysis of this scholar and his successful efforts to bring the Revolution to the forefront of the North American consciousness.

When I read *Listen Yankee* in manuscript form, I raised many questions and concerns from the superficial sense of Cuba's pre-

1959 history to its strange, cleansed pragmatic view of Castro. Few of my concerns were taken seriously. But after publication, when a debate on the book was scheduled with another scholar and politician, the late A.A. Berle, Mills asked me to assist him in researching the background of Cuba. In truth, he was far less interested in studying Cuba, than in finding the weak spots in Berle's career that he, Mills, could use in the television debate. The dedicated pilgrim is less concerned about the truth of his own formulas than finding error in the ways of his opponents.

The 1961 debate itself never took place. Mills perhaps felicitously suffered a heart attack days before the scheduled television debate. (Mills himself died of another heart attack in March 1962). But lesson number one became evident; those dedicated to a cause or a movement see criticism not as evidence of regime weakness, but of shortcomings in the character of those in opposition. The tendency to see opponents as enemies is an essential, permanent characteristic of those who remain dedicated to the cause of Cuban Communism.

The next phase in my learning process took place with the 1964 publication of my essay "The Stalinization of Castro." Knowing full well that people on the Left viewed me as heir apparent to Mills, and wishing to minimize any hostility from those who might view me as betraying that legacy, I published the paper in *New Politics*, Julius Jacobson's successor journal to Dwight Macdonald's *Politics* a publication for which Mills wrote and had great affection. But the critical character of my assessment clear enough from the title could not spare me furies that come with a political break. The article was a subdued but detailed account of how events in Cuba indicated a morphology common to communist regimes the world over. I remain very proud of the characterizations made in that article, and in retrospect would not change that early essay one jot or tittle.

Once more I experienced the phenomenon of the political pilgrim. A Canadian political scientist, Ian Lumsden, took it upon himself to expose my errors. Those "errors" included my observations that in Castro's Cuba as in Stalin's Russia there was already (1) subordination of society to Party and State; (2) leadership purges that made Castro and a small coterie the exclusive voice of party and regime; (3) the communist curse of inner party struggle replaced and substituted for class struggle; (4) Cuba was subjected to civics, not politics, i.e., demand for regime loyalty; (5) Castro had halted discussion about alternative paths to development, settling on single-crop communism; and (6) Castro had sealed off Cuba from the rest of the hemisphere and the world, a task made relatively simple in an island economy and special geography. I must add that I was still writing from inside a strong Left commitment or so I thought. But this did not help. Indeed, it may well have exacerbate my problems, since cries of Trotskyism and Treason were raised not just by a Canadian critic but the Moscow-based World Marxist Review, the Comintern organ which saw fit to excoriate me.

The most revealing aspect of Professor Lumsden's attack is not his illusion, still widely held, that "Cuba continues to make progress toward a socialist democracy", but the insidious belief that in the face of disquieting truths one must maintain disciplined silence. The retreat to silence about regime shortcomings has become a theme of fanatics in this century. It was held that my article offers "more to aid the enemies of the Revolution than to facilitate its comprehension." And that "in the face of inadequate information one would have expected Horowitz to have given Castro the benefit of the doubt rather than subject it to an analysis which draws parallels with the most savage regimes known to mankind." Here we come to a second characteristic of the new political pilgrim: when in doubt say nothing, or give reality a special spin that will save the regime from criticism. This is a corollary to the first characteristic mentioned earlier: if shortcomings are raised and cannot be avoided, describe them as transitional features of a revolution in exceptional circumstances, negative aspects which will dissolve over time.

I shall pass over the next thirty years rather quickly. The second of the Bacardi lectures which I delivered at the University of Miami in 1992, which were published under the title of *The*

Conscience of Worms and the Cowardice of Lions was devoted exclusively to critical examination of "The Conscience of Castrologists." I therein describe a sad story of repetition of pattern of apologetics for dictatorship found among Nazi supporters of the Hitler regime in the American First Days, and among supporters of the Soviet regime during the halcyon days of the Stalinist epoch. It is a pattern marked by a tragic confusion of anti-Americanism with intoxication with the rhetorical claims of communism.

What became clear is how much more susceptible intellectuals are to demagoguery both receiving and extending it than are ordinary mortals. In part this results from their unique sense of "history" or in truth meta-history, claims about the future that rivaled and exceeded theological claims as to the wondrous state of paradise that awaits all true believers in the next world. I summarized this intellectual long trek to nowhere in quite the same terms that Walter Laqueur and Richard Pipes later defined the pseudo-science of Sovietology. What I wrote in summary in *Conscience of Worms and Cowardice of Lions* does warrant repetition. It is a prelude to the strange present ideological moment, which will occupy the remainder of these remarks.

"What all is said and done, error and truth and both part of human nature. And in the case of the history of social scientific prognostication, error is perhaps the greater part of human nature. As a result, error can, and within a democratic society must, be forgiven explained rather than punished. What cannot be forgiven, and what characterizes Castrologists, the step-children of Kremlinologists, as a group, is the sin of pride, the hubris of self-righteousness, and the animosity toward those with whom they disagree. Their motto inheres in their methodology: Deny all wrongdoing; attack those who have raised objections with ad hominem assault on their motives; demand levels of evidence beyond even the proverbial smoking gun; and as a last resort, when the intellectual game is up, lapse into permanent, sullen silence. To the best end, and perhaps after the end, we are faced by a group of self declared experts daring to use the work 'science,' for whom the only issue is Right or Left instead of right or wrong."

II

We turn now to three examples of political pilgrims turned apologists, these are a mere handful of those who fit the profile herein described. They suggest a disturbing trend in which the dictator defines the policy goals of the regime, while preparing the pilgrims to serve as point guards for such policies. It is clear enough that Castro has made it a cardinal goal to secure the lifting the embargo, and the defeat of all efforts to increase Cuban economic isolation. Today's political pilgrims are frontline troops in this effort. They no longer confine their remarks to the lofty purposes of the regime, but enter the policy discussion overtly and unabashedly. Indeed, were it not for the fatal blunder by the Cuban regime in shooting down the two civil aircraft that fly near Cuba, this campaign might well have succeeded in forestalling the passage of the Helms-Burton Bill, if not toppling the earlier Torricelli-sponsored effort at legislative isolation of Cuba from the rest of the hemisphere. Indeed, even with the shoot-down, the campaign to topple American foreign policy aims in the region has not abated. If political pilgrims are not easily dissuaded by 37 years of dictatorship, they are even less likely to be disabused by a singular incident.

My first example is Wayne Smith, the former diplomat to Havana during the Carter Administration. Here we have the example of a public servant turned advocate. His writings have become synonymous with support for Castro located in Washington, D.C. circles. In his most recent utterance in Foreign Affairs, Smith goes beyond even his former sycophantic self. He depicts Cuba as a nation moving gradually toward social democracy under the guidance of Fidel Castro. The Supreme leader period now marching toward its fortieth anniversary is viewed as a mere interregnum. Grudgingly, we are informed that Castro is still not quite ready for social democracy. But if the embargo were to be lifted, he would become more likely to follow the path of reform.

Wayne Smith has his earlier counterpart in the late Joseph E. Davies, who reported on the Moscow Trials of 1938. In the face of overwhelming evidence of a fraudulent series of trials cum purges, he reported back in Mission to Moscow that the trials were fair. In the words of Freda Kirchwey, then editor of *The Nation*, such issues as fake trials and purges of innocents followed their execution after abject confession, were secondary to the moral stance of combating the evils of fascism. As TRB shrewdly observes in *The New Republic*, "Wayne Smith has emerged as a moralist against America, but a relativist toward Cuba."

Smith is certain that "Castro is not on the way out anytime soon. In fact, he may be the best guarantor of Cuba's peaceful transition to a market oriented economy and more democratic government." This at a time Castro is closing out small enterprises as rapidly as they open for business, and imprisoning political opponents as quickly as they surface. The real enemy for Ambassador Smith is America, specifically the Cuban exile community. We are assured that Castro will survive "obviously flawed instruments as the Helms-Burton bill. The new Cuba will be a society based on Cuban realities." But the idea that such "realities" exclude Castro, or for that matter include the overseas and exiled Cubans, is not entertained. The new political pilgrims have grown sharp teeth and fight with jagged razors.

Smith's autobiography-cum-travelogue, *The Closest of Enemies*, reveals the vanity of the diplomat, his proximity to power abroad and his relative remoteness from a power base at home. His embarrassingly puerile account of his service in the U.S. Embassy in Havana between 1958 and 1961, and again as chief of the U.S. Interest section there from 1979 to 1982, in which he seemed preoccupied with being photographed with the great dictator or, in front of monuments of past dictators, and with family album photos, all reveal a special sort of political pilgrim, the heady wine that comes with being a force overseas, far more than that at home. I am reluctant to take recourse in psychological examination, but to avoid this aspect of the new political pilgrim is to miss the nuances in the role of apologist for totalitarian rule. The diplomat as apologist is like the anthropologist turned native a phenomenon of over identification obviously strikes policy people no less than social scientists.

A second type of political pilgrim who has his counterpart in apologists for Stalinism is the religious personage. In the case of Cuba, there is Edward T. Walsh writing about "the devastating impact on Higher Education in Cuba" not of the dictatorship, (but you guessed it) the Embargo! The Reverend Walsh, a self-described former chaplain at North Carolina State University and a member of the Ecumenical Project for International Cooperation and of the Baptist Peace Fellowship of North America, puts to shame the Very Reverend Hewlett Johnson the most extreme clerical apologist for Stalinism during the Nazi-Soviet Non-Aggression Pact period of 1939-1941.

Walsh tells us through the pages of *The Chronicle of Higher Education*, that "although the current situation is difficult, it in no way compares with the poverty of the past." Citing high college enrollment, but ignoring what is being taught, the Reverend concludes that the sole source of the problem is our insane embargo. Waxing philosophical, he instructs that "human experience should have taught us that contact and dialogue with 'the enemy' break down barriers and false stereotypes among all parties to dispute." It turns out that the enemy is really at home. "It is about politicians from both parties, accepting campaign donations from extremely well organized and well financed Cuban-American political action groups." It never dawns on Reverend Walsh that the source of the devastating situation in Cuba's higher educational system is the dictatorship as such. As it turns out, the voice may be the Reverend Mr. Walsh, but the vituperation is that of the maximum leader, Fidel Castro.

Finally, there is the voice of policy-maker turned academic. Cole Blasier, well known from Pittsburgh to Miami, but once again, a Beltway insider. He spoke after, not before, the downing of the private aircraft from Florida. Blasier offers not an ounce of solace about the murder of innocents, who were condemned directly from the office of Fidel Castro. Instead, we are told that "Most Americans know and care little about Cuba" (needless to say this statement is made without evidence from public opinion surveys). However, Blasier is certain that a policy based on Castro's overthrow "is not an appropriate basis for United States policy." What then should be the basis for such a policy? It turns out to be that "the United States has had economic interest in Cuba. Some United States traders want to trade, and investors want to invest. Cultural exchange interests should not be ignored, either. The debate on Cuba needs to be recast" But how one might ask. Blasier's answer is simple: "Let's think first of what's good for the United States, not what's bad for Mr. Castro."

The clear implication is that there is a disjunctive between what is good for America and bad for Cuba. It never dawns on him that the parallel might be authentic. That what is good for the United States is precisely what moves toward the termination of the Castro dictatorship. Even the use of such language as dictatorship or tyranny is disallowed by Blasier. The clever juxtaposition of the United States and Cuba is so utterly transparent, that one is led to conclude that anything short of the bombing of Miami would not command even a mild rebuke of the Castro regime much less a strong censoring, by Blasier.

III

The movement by a political pilgrim from scholar to ideologist becomes a natural evolution; one reinforced by the character of area studies organizations to the composition of university departments in history and the social sciences. In part, the longevity of the Castro regime gives it legitimacy, strength in the minds and hearts of people like Smith, Walsh and Blasier. The political pilgrims of an earlier period started with a profound belief that social betterment for the masses that can be brought about by revolution. The political pilgrims of the present era reveal few such illusions about the regimes they support. They know full well the despotic character of the leadership they support. In this sense, the collapse of the Soviet empire has had a transforming impact on political pilgrims subjecting their aims to more confined purposes.

The new, hard-nosed pilgrims have big fish to fry: starting with the American commitment to democratic government. Of the three principles on which both parties are in full agreement free elections, free parties, and free economic choice the one deemed most vulnerable is the last; since it is interpreted that the embargo inhibits just such economic expansion. The political pilgrims do not, in short, collapse in the face of simple policy imperatives. They merely reinterpret them into useable parts. But when the dictatorship itself finally expires of one thing we can be certain: these same self-serving clarions of the people will either find new despotisms to support, or lapse into a permanent silence. The choice is not enviable, but then again the type with which we are dealing is not admirable.

Ultimately, but often unstated, the illusion of socialism unsullied by communist power still serves to sustain the political pilgrims. The myth of that system is at the heart and soul of the inability of good people to come to terms with dictatorship and tyranny. This was brought home to me in the Festschrift honoring my work. *In The Democratic Imagination*, Carmelo Mesa-Lago employs an entire group of students to survey all of my writings to minute and detailed scrutiny. I will not burden this with either the commentary or response, both are readily enough available, and I should add, entirely courteous. Nonetheless, I was struck by how the language, the rhetoric used to describe the regime differs sharply amongst scholars with the best intentions.

For me, and I suppose, severe critics of the regime, we see in Cuba a communist dictatorship. Indeed eight editions of *Cuban Communism* repeatedly attest to the centrality of this belief. But for the new political pilgrim, the reference is never or rarely to communism. It is rather to socialism and democracy. Indeed, to simply repeat what Castro has stated on innumerable occasions, his allegiance to communism as a political practice and a moral faith is enough to cast suspicion on one daring to repeat the obvious. For most political pilgrims, Cuba under Castro is not quite a full bodied socialism, not quite on the high road to democracy, but close enough to warrant support and bask in the warm glow of pleasant touristic rhetoric. The Church Historic can make mistakes; the Church Triumphant can never err. So after all the encomiums are passed out, and all of the criticisms pissed forth, the chasm remains between those see totalitarianism as a function of communism, or communism as some sort of dim and distant consequence of socialism.

The source of the new political pilgrimages is located precisely in this chasm, in the polarity between those who see the history of communism as a twentieth century catastrophe ending up logically, and even necessarily, in the triumvirate of Stalin, Mao and Castro; and those who see this same history as a long, tortuous road to a higher democracy and an end to the evils of capitalism as a system in which the United States serves as an exemplar of world leadership. Paul Hollander came close to making this discovery on his own and as a general axiom. But he was writing on the subject before the final decade of the century, and assumed that the fall of European communism would result in a possible low-point in Anti-Americanism. He could hardly be faulted for failing to appreciate that political pilgrimage reaches its desultory abyss only with the last remaining pure case of communism, Castro's Cuba.

The nature of Revelation is to both announce the arrival of the savior and outline the characteristics in the search for perfection. And as Leo Gershoy and Frank Manuel long ago pointed out in terms of the makers of the French Revolution, it is in the nature of revolutionary leaders to do likewise; and in the process, cast out and destroy what is held to be old or imperfect. Fortunately, the empirical basis of politics, unlike the spiritual basis of theology, makes it far more difficult for tyrants to sustain terrible illusions of post-modernity. The loss of innocence is quickly followed by the end of legitimacy sadly, at a terrible price in terms of human life and collective well being. The Cuba lobby of the past has been transformed into the Cuba support network of the present. The singular task of our social science and the honest study of international policy is to make sure that such illusions are exposed, and correspondingly the tasks of democracy are aided and abetted, not undermined by honest research. Political pilgrimage is with us, probably for the duration of the modern epoch in which demigods have at their disposal the capacity to define the collective vision of the good. But so too is social science, which subjects propagandistic notions of the good to the test of the right.

References/Notes:

Alpern, Sara. *A Woman of The Nation: Freda Kirchwey.* Cambridge: Harvard University Press, 1978. pp. 118-119.

Blasier, Cole. "U.S. Fixation on Castro May Do Us No Good," Letter to *The New York Times,* March 1st, 1996.

Castro Ruz, Raúl, "Informe del Buro Politico sobre la situation politica y social del pais..." *Granma* (March 23) 1996.

Davies, Joseph E. *Mission to Moscow.* Zurich: Steinberg, 1943.

Deutscher, Isaac. *The Prophet Outcast: Trotsky, 1929-1940.* New York and London: Oxford University Press, 1963. pp. 257-355. For a current, more critical assessment, see Dmitri Volkogonov, *Trotsky: The Eternal Revolutionary.* New York: The Free Press, 1996. 524 pp.

Franqui, Carlos, *Diary of the Cuban Revolution.* New York: Viking Press, 1980. 546 pp.

Franqui, Carlos, *Family Portrait with Fidel: A Memoir.* New York: Random House, 1984. 262 pp.

Gershoy, Leo. *The Era of the French Revolution, 1789-1799: Ten Years that Shook the World.* Princeton: Van Nostrand, 1957.

Hollander, Paul. *Political Pilgrims.* New York and London: Oxford University Press, 1981.

Hollander, Paul. *Anti-Americanism: Irrational and Rational.* New Brunswick and London: Transaction Publishers, 1995. See esp. the new Introduction, 85 pp.

Horowitz, Irving Louis. "The Stalinization of Castro", *New Politics,* Vol.4, No.4 (1965).

Horowitz, Irving Louis. "Castrologists and Apologists: Science in the Service of Sentiment", *New Politics,* Vol.5, No.1 (1966), pp. 27-35.

Horowitz, Irving Louis. *The Conscience of Worms and the Cowardice of Lions: Cuban Politics and Culture in an American Context.* Miami: North South Center, and New Brunswick: Transaction Publishers, 1993. pp. 15-36.

Horowitz, Irving Louis. *C. Wright Mills: An American Utopian*. New York and London: Free Press-Macmillan, 1983.

Horowitz, Irving Louis. "Are the Social Sciences Scientific?", *Academic Questions*, Vol.9, No. 1 (1995-1996), pp. 53-60.

Klehr, Harvey, with John Earl Haynes, and Fridrikh Igorevich Firsov. *The Secret World of American Communism*. New Haven: Yale University Press, 1995. pp. 299-301.

Lane, Charles. "Fidel and Mr. Smith", *The New Republic* (March 25) 1996. p. 6.

Laqueur, Walter. *The Dream That Failed: Reflections on the Soviet Union*. New York and London: Oxford University Press, 1994. p. 112.

Lumsden, C. Ian. "On Socialists and Stalinists: A Reply to Irving Louis Horowitz," New Politics, Vol.5, No.1 (1966), pp. 20-27.

Manuel, Frank. *The Changing of the Gods*. Boston: University Press of New England, 1983. 216 pp.

Matthews, Herbert L. "An Intimate Lunch With Fidel." First published in *The New York Times Magazine* (March 8, 1995), and reprinted in *The New York Times Magazine* (April 14, 1996). p. 104.

Mesa-Lago, Carmelo. in *The Democratic Imagination*, edited by Ray C. Rist. New Brunswick and London: Transaction Publishers, 1995, pp. 305-332. See also my response on pp. 554-560.

Mills, C. Wright. *Listen Yankee!* New York: McGraw-Hill, 1960.

Pipes, Richard. "Misinterpreting the Cold War: The Hard Liners Had it Right." *Foreign Affairs* (January-February) 1995. pp. 159-160.

Smith, Wayne S., *The Closest of Enemies: A Personal and Diplomatic Account of U.S. Cuban Relations Since 1957*. New York: W. W. Norton, 1987. 308 pp.

Smith, Wayne S. "Cuba's Long Reform", *Foreign Affairs*, Volume 75, Number 2 (March-April) 1996. pp. 99-112.

Walsh, Edward T. "An Embargo's Devastating Impact on Higher Education in Cuba", *The Chronicle of Higher Education*, (March 22) 1996, pp. B1-B2.

Source and Original Title: Cuba: Political Pilgrims and Cultural Wars (with Mark Falcoff and Raúl Castro Ruz). Washington, D.C.: Freedom House, 1996, 44 pp. [monograph] "Political Pilgrimage to Cuba, 1959-1996." *Humanitas*, Vol. IX, No. 1, 1996, pp. 52-64.

34

Three Points of Light: Long Term U.S. Policy Responses to Cuba

When the dust of controversy settles, as it inevitably must, the most salient point to note about American perceptions and policies toward Cuba is the consensus that has developed over the past nearly forty years of the Castro Revolution, as to the nature and goals of the regime. The dissensus which obviously also exists relates simply to what should be done about this regime, presumably in its final stages and denouement.

The disjunctive between fact and value is now minimal. In plain language, awareness of the despotic and totalitarian nature of the Castro regime is widely shared among liberals and conservatives, Democratic and Republican voters, and across various divides of race, gender, and age. What is now being argued, and vigorously, is how to respond to this unique despotism. No one seriously believes we are dealing with a democratic regime susceptible to reform. Indeed, if there was a shred of doubt left on this score, it was dispelled by the Fifth Congress of the Communist Party of Cuba held in October of this year. The oft-critical *Miami Herald* dubbed Fidel Castro's seven-hour marathon "the Yadda, yadda, yadda affair in Cuba."

This is well reflected in the bipartisan sponsorship of legislation with respect to the economic embargo of Cuba and the

equally shared concern for expanding person-to-person relationships on a non-governmental level. Senator Jesse Helms* is
indeed a major Republican spokesperson, but so too is Robert
Torricelli**, a major Democratic figure, whose success in New
Jersey in no small part is due to the broad based support he
receives from his Latin constituencies. It might be argued that
political passions rather than human rights drive various strategic approaches to Cuba. But this is hardly news, or a situation
unique to Cuba.

What is unique, what cannot be ignored or forgotten, is the
special role Cuba has played in hemispheric affairs over the
nearly forty years of Castro's rule. Policy forecasting is one thing.
Historical events are quite another. We have witnessed Cuban
military incursions on the sovereignty of other nations on an
almost routine basis: starting with adventures in the 1960s in
Guatemala, Venezuela, and El Salvador. These guerrilla incursions became the military norm in the 1970s. Indeed, one might
well say that Cuban participation in the Sandinista movement
in Nicaragua was its crowning, if temporary, achievement; just
as earlier Cuban incursions into Bolivia (with the larger aim of
destabilizing Argentina) was its most noticeable failure. But success or failure never deterred the Castro government from its
self-appointed mission to seize upon every discontent, legitimate
or otherwise, to facilitate armed struggle.

Whether in Angola in the dim past or Mexico in the grim
present, the answer to strife, to inequities, to legitimate differences, the Castro government offers was and remains always
the same: armed insurrection. Whatever the internal problems
within Cuba whether of declining levels of production, backward
technologies, or deterioration of its urban infrastructure, all of
these have taken a back seat to an interventionist foreign policy.
To be sure, were it not for the dogmatism of communist rulers
in Havana, the United States would have found it far more difficult to maintain consistent support for its own foreign policy.
While overt Cuban military incursions have sharply declined
during the current decade, in part through the exhaustion of

the armed forces itself, and in part as a function of the collapse of the Soviet Union, the military apparatus, even in its reduced status, remains a potent force for mischief. It has not so much dissolved as turned inward, a force directed at the further political demobilization of the Cuban people. Never once in his long despotic rule has Fidel Castro ever expressed regret over these incursions; only a surly admission that he was not the player on the world stage he imagined himself to be.

This is not said to justify the blundering, half-hearted, military adventures of the United States at the Bay of Pigs in 1961 or the early idiotic efforts to rid Cuba of communism by attempting to assassinate Castro. It was absurd to think that in doing so, problems that led to the Cuban Revolution of 1959 would also have disappeared. But it would be ludicrous to claim a causal linkage between American diplomatic failures under the Kennedy administration and the extraordinarily rigid behavior of the Castro government over the following 37 years. If blame must be placed, it should be with Marxism-Leninism, and its unyielding belief that capitalism will strangle itself with a little tug at the rope, permitting communism to emerge full blown in all parts of the Third World.

Cuba's military incursions by an armed, Praetorian Guard increasingly functioning as a Prussian-styled elite, rather than a peasant movement of the oppressed, has met increasing hemispheric resistance. This is far less a consequence of U.S. foreign policy than broad recognition that neither Latin America nor the Middle East nor Africa are playgrounds for testing crude theories of guerrilla insurgency. Nonetheless, in light of such consistent Cuban belligerency having little if anything to do with North American intransigence and much to do with communist ideology to advocate lifting the embargo or sanctions is simply to advocate a policy of appeasement. It is to presume, against all historical evidence to the contrary, that aid, trade, and a blind eye to human rights violations, will somehow result in normalization and democratization of relations between the United States and Cuba.

Many of those who advocate lifting the embargo point to a profound inconsistency between United States trade and aid policies toward Communist China and Communist Cuba arguing in effect that this calls for a revising of, or better, a rescinding of the embargo. While it is clearly the case that inconsistency is the diplomatic norm, there are serious problems with this line of ana-logical reasoning: first, it assumes that consistency is somehow the same as virtue; and second, that U.S. policy lacks flexibility. Neither is, nor has been, the case with respect to Cuba.

Nations differentiate policies on a wide series of variables: ranging from the critical importance of another nation in the world scheme of things, to a perception of immediacy of threat or danger posed by the other nations. On such a dual axis it is evident that American foreign policy is based on the idea that China is an opportunity whereas Cuba is a risk. Put more crassly, it is not possible to treat China with the same negativity as the U.S. government can treat a belligerent such as Cuba. The issue should not be reduced to treating China in economic terms, while treating Cuba ethically. Rather, we must evaluate the prospects of moving each nation in terms of American national interest. While this may not be the ideal arrangement, it is hardly unknown in the annals of diplomacy. Indeed, one might argue, as did the late Hans Morgenthau, that such calculations are the very essence of foreign diplomacy.

There is another line of reasoning that merits consideration. It is rarely if ever heard from those who advocate the end to the embargo. Perhaps the United States should treat China with the same vigorous containment as it applied to Cuba. People as different as William C. Triplett, former counsel for the Foreign Relations Committee (*Washington Times*, September 12) and A.M. Rosenthal, feature editorial writer for *The New York Times* (September 23) have argued that everything from most favored nation status to sanctions for human rights violations should apply to China. Indeed, they assert that everyone from Mao Zedong, to Deng Xiaoping and now Jiang Zemin come to the diplomatic table with hands bloodied by the corpses of millions, and this should be the cornerstone of American response, not the advantages of doing business in an expanding marketplace of one billion people.

By extension, this argument acknowledges that the policy toward Cuba is correct, and that what is incorrect or improper is the policy-making approach toward China. Viewed in this way, inconsistency in United States foreign policy is recognized, but resolved in the triumph of ethics (or human rights) over economics (or market shares). An argument of this sort need not be dismissed out of hand. Indeed, it would clearly uphold principles of democracy and serve as a model for the treatment of totalitarian regimes large or small, near or far.

In this way, the Helms-Burton Act, and the Toricelli-sponsored legislation on democracy in Cuba would be seen as models for other outlaw states that transgress ordinary civilities between nations. Such a model would punish the propensity of nations to provoke military confrontation that could entail U.S. participation whether we are talking of a possible invasion of Taiwan or overrunning Guantanamo Bay. In short, the argument for consistency cuts both ways and not always to the discomfort of those urging continuing or even strengthening the embargo.

That said; discussion of the embargo of Cuba should not be reduced to a discourse in syllogistic logic; or even whether food and medicine from the United States can be smuggled into Cuba via third party sources. The plain truth is that American policy toward Cuba is and has been nuanced; especially in the past five years. The United States has offered several windows of opportunity to Cuba ranging from an opening for larger numbers of Americans and Cuban American visitors to the island to greater linkages at the communication level. In each instance, such essentially diplomatic probes have been rebuffed by the Castro regime.

The overall regime response has been severe constraints on private sector growth, coupled with even more vigorous recourse to intimidation and imprisonment of even modest opposition. To be sure, even that handful of companies in Canada and Europe anxious to defy United States sanctions, such as Sherritt International, come hard upon a hostile investment climate in Cuba. One might well claim, on empirical grounds, that it is less fear of Washington retribution than Havana resistance to an open marketplace that has made Helms-Burton a relatively successful piece of legislation. In this same connection, the idea that increasing tourism would dissolve Castro's rule, ignores the nature of tourism: the ease with which tourists are isolated from the major arteries of Cuban society. Again, the general hostility of the regime to an open marketplace is hardly likely to induce widespread growth in an already overdeveloped area of the tourist industry. People do not take vacations in order to incite rebellion, or for that matter, incur the wrath of regimes. Such thinking on the part of opponents to the Castro regime reflect more the frustration with a regnant government, than a sensitive reading of events.

To adopt a Chinese Confucian metaphor: the policy of the United States can be synthesized as "the three frees": Free Enterprise. Free Parties. Free Elections. China is at least one third of the way there! Cuba fails the test of "the three frees" on all counts. I am not calling for interventionist policy by the United States. I am not asserting the need for a government in exile in Miami. I do not think there is a prospect or need for insurrection within the island. The "three frees" should simply remain the bedrock, the cornerstone of American foreign policy in distinguishing friends from enemies. Let those who insist upon a fundamental revision of this policy ask themselves if they are really motivated by a desire to enhance democracy or by one that would by indirection justify dictatorship in Cuba. For that is the touchstone by which the American people should assess, and properly so, all demands for changes in foreign policy including proposed redirection of U.S. approaches to Communist Cuba.

Being centrist is not the same as being neutral; and being inconsistent is not the same as being wrong. It is my considered judgment that American foreign policy toward Cuba during the Clinton administration, while hardly the model of clarity either advocates or detractors would wish, nonetheless is a serviceable approach. It distinguishes claims of the Cuban people from posturing by its present rulers. It also remains open to any serious overtures by the Castro regime to face "the three frees" with an openness that the situation demands. The issues confronting United States Cuban relations are rooted in the stuff of national currency: legitimacy. That is what nations bestow on each other. That is what the United States is not prepared to traffic in as long as the Castro regime maintains its stubborn animosity to "the three frees."

References/Notes

*   The Helms-Burton Bill is the name Congressional sponsors attached to The Cuban Liberty and Democratic Solidarity Act. The most controversial aspect of the legislation is a provision which denies United States visas to traffickers in stolen U.S. property. Any agreement to rescind such a penalty requires a mechanism for the resolution of U.S. property claims without rescinding a waiver of Title IV regarding the general rules concerning confiscated properties. See Juan J. Lopez, "Implications of the U.S. Embargo for a Political Transition in Cuba" (unpublished paper delivered at the seventh annual meeting of the Association for the Study of the Cuban Economy, Miami, August 7-9, 1997, 48 pp.; and Joaquin Roy, "The Helms-Burton Law: Development, Consequences and Legacy for Inter-American and European-US Relations", *Journal of Interamerican Studies and World Affairs*, Vol. 39, No. 3., Fall 1997. pp.77-108.

**   The Torricelli Bill is the name Congressional sponsors attached to The Cuban Democracy Act of 1992. Key features of that legislation involved support for a peaceful transition to democracy in Cuba. The most controversial aspects involved tightening the 1975 provision of the U.S. embargo to prevent illegal dealings; increasing direct communications between American (especially Cuban-Americans) and Cuban peoples bypassing the Castro government when feasible. See K.S. Wong, "The Cuba Democracy Act of 1992: The Extra-Territorial Scope of Section 1706(a)," University of Pennsylvania Journal of International Business Law, Vol. 14, No.4., Winter 1994. Pp. 651-682; and Irving Louis Horowitz, "Ethical and Political Consequences of the American Embargo of Cuba Investing in Cuba: Problems and Prospects," edited by Jaime Suchlicki and Antonio Jorge. Canadian Institute of Strategic Studies Transaction Publishers, New Brunswick & London, 1994. pp.1-16.

Source and Original Title: "Three Points of Light: U.S. Policy Responses to Cuba." *Cuba 1997: The Year in Review.* Washington, DC: Center for a Free Cuba, (Winter) 1998, pp. 13-16.

35

Cuba Lobby Upgrade: *Plus ça Change, Plus C'est la Même Chose*

One of the great myths about Castro's nearly 40-year reign in Cuba is that U.S. opposition to his rule has been undivided, implacable, and inflexible. This myth is wrong on several counts. First, those who oppose Castro's rule—whether they are part of the Cuban-American community or the wider society—are as divided as any other single ethnic group in the United States on any other issue. Second, mass support for the regime of the Cuban dictator has been either absent or ineffectual. In contrast, one would have to say that the Cuba Lobby is alive and well. It is as single-minded in its limited aims as the opponents have been divided in their more ambitious concerns. What restrains the Cuba Lobby, or at least limits its effectiveness, is the vast majority of ordinary Cuban Americans, citizens clustered in such strategic voting blocs as South Florida and North New Jersey, who remain essentially opposed to extending ties to Castro. On the other side, elites supporting Castro are clearly well positioned and well funded. They emphasize select policies rather than mass politics.

The Structure of the New Cuba Lobby

Four component parts of the Cuba Lobby as it now is constituted can be discerned: (1) intellectual-academic; (2) business-commercial, (3) political-policy, and (4) foundations and grant-making agencies. The extent of their interlocking characteristics is hard to determine, but one can assume by the cast of characters involved there are at least informal connections. This is not necessarily conspiratorial or negative. It simply reflects a presumption that birds of a feather do indeed flock together. But each of the four wings has different strategic objectives. Their common link is denunciation of the embargo; they often overlap regarding to whom they appeal for fiscal support.

1. The intellectual-academic wing is represented by five groups (who often do work together): The Science and Human Rights Program of the American Association for the Advancement of Science; The American Association of University Professors; The American Association for World Health, The American Physical Society; and the ever militant Committee of Concerned Scientists. They have as specific agenda items changing United States travel policy toward Cuba (and as a bow to evenhandedness, Cuban travel policy toward the United States); expanding academic and scientific exchanges between the two nations; treating the right to travel as a human rights issue, with specific emphasis on restrictions on U.S. and Cuban scientists; and expanding contacts for further scientific and academic collaboration. On a wider front, these organizations emphasize the impact of the U.S. embargo on health and nutrition in Cuba.

The overriding problem in this academic agenda is precisely the notion of evenhandedness: as if Castro's dictatorship somehow has as its moral equivalent the United States democracy. This academic agenda equates the character of University life in a repressive regime with that of University life in the most free-wheeling of academic environments. In 1978, academic sectors of the Cuba Lobby were content to establish some level exchanges of personnel between places like the University of Pittsburgh and the University of Havana. In 1998, nearly forty years after the establishment of the regime, the Lobby is far more global in its outreach. The absence of historic memory about the Castro regime makes it appear that there is a *prima facie* need for coop-eration between scholars and scientists in the two nations. There is the further presumption that academic individuals speak with equal weight for themselves, and implicitly, not for their govern-ments. The academic agenda is set in such broad terms, that only the most "illiberal" scientists or academics could possibly object. This wing of the Cuba Lobby is prepared to examine everything save the nature of the system of governance in Cuba.[1]

2. A variety of business interest lobbies seek to expand trade and aid to Cuba—especially the former, in areas ranging from livestock manufacturing to tools for improving transportation and communication. By self-definition, organizations like the U.S.-Cuba Trade and Economic Council are "the first and only organization within the United States to have established rela-tionships and received the written support and cooperation of the Chamber of Commerce of the Republic of Cuba." Not only do these wired trade associations emphasize the benefits of ex-panded trade to the fiscal bottom line of American corporations, they also show how such trade can materially aid key congres-sional districts and business organizations. Major umbrella or-ganizations such as the National Association of Manufacturers and the United States Chamber of Commerce, have become increasingly convinced by such blandishments. Specific target groups, such as Americans for Humanitarian Trade with Cuba, and Alamar Associates, provide consulting services to Ameri-can companies interested in doing business in Cuba. The same approach is characteristic of the American Business Council on Cuba, USA Engage, which is openly dedicated to moving foreign policy toward lifting the embargo.

On overview, it is apparent that the strategic approach of the business wing of the Cuba Lobby, now as in 1978, is hard-headed. That translates into ignoring the Cuban dictatorship, and basically asserts that it is time to get on with the business of business with Cuba. Analogies are frequently drawn with the United States' ability to conduct normal trade relations with the old Soviet Union, and more emphatically, with present-day China. Indeed, several organizations point out that although China has roughly one hundred times the population of Cuba, it can boast little more than twice the anticipated amount of impact on American business. The Cuban regime has welcomed business initiatives, although it has been circumspect with respect to what changes it is prepared to make to accommodate everything from labor practices to ownership structure.

The frequency of comparisons of China and Cuba requires further examination: aside from the fact that Cuba has rejected a Chinese model built on expanded consumer orientation in product lines and private firms in areas ranging from housing to computers, there is Cuba's dismal economic performance during Castro's nearly forty years of rule. In a recent report estimating the cost of communism in Cuba, Peter Brimelow and Edwin Rubenstein assume "that Cuba's current per capita output should be about the same proportion of Florida's output as it was in 1959. This gives us a current figure of $4,169, more than three times higher than Cuba's actual output of $1,300.... Even troubled Mexico's per capita GDP has closed with that of the U.S. quite considerably over the last four decades—from less than an eighth in 1959 to about a third recently. Still, our modest estimate suggests that the shortfall in Cuban GDP as a result of Castro was a hefty 31.5 billion in 1995. In the language of takeover artists, Cuba is an under performing asset."[2] This is a rather quaint way of referring to a socialist economy which its prime leaders extol as being uniquely predicated on the moral superiority of its vanguard ideology.[3]

3. The political wing of the Cuba Lobby is amorphous, ranging from the anti-Castro Cuban Committee for Democracy, which bills itself as "the voice of reason in the Cuban-American community," and urges lifting the embargo and a dialogue for gradual change in the regime. While this wing has few illusions about the economic worth of Castro's Cuba, they share with the Cuban leader the apologia that the situation would be different

in the absence of the embargo. This is the essential line taken by Cambio Cubano, a moderate group of decent people aiming for a direct appeal to the exile community of Cubans in the United States. Other elements in the political support groups are indeed just that, support groups for the Castro regime. The most long-standing and active is perhaps the Center for Cuban Studies, and with a milder rhetorical posture, the Center for International Policy, which boasts the support of former ambassadors and officials of the United States with a long continuing interest in Cuba. Quite a few elements of this wing have Cuba as a critical agenda item, but not, an exclusive concern. Such groups as the Council of Hemispheric Affairs, The Cuba Program of the Georgetown University Caribbean Project, The General Services Foundation, and the Interreligious Foundation for Community Organization all promote peace through reconciliation. The basic pitch is humanitarian.

The anomaly within the political wing of the lobby is a certain confusion as to whether the end of the embargo is a goal unto itself or the first stage in the revision of American foreign policy to include a strong socialist and social justice component. Indeed, some political groupings are clearly more concerned with changing the direction of American foreign policy in general than with any specific interest in the Cuban condition. This wing offers a porous umbrella—under which everyone from anti-Castroists and advocates of the regime cooperate. Clearly, for some groups lifting the embargo is the first and necessary condition for the democratization of the island, while for others the same action by the United States would serve as an endorsement of the Castro regime itself. The political wing also brings into contact secular and sectarian organizations, often working at cross-purposes, or at least in uncertain alliance Thus one can find both the ruggedly individualist and conservative Cato Foundation and the just as rugged social-mission-oriented World Council of Churches arguing the absurdity of the embargo—but with little else in common. As a result of the intransigence of the Castro regime, direct political lobbying has probably been the best funded but least effective cluster within the Cuba Lobby. [4]

4. The fourth wing of the Cuba Lobby consists of foundations dedicated to activist agendas of one sort or another. This is the most amorphous portion of the Lobby. Granting agencies that have supplied considerable funds to the analysis of Cuba range from the highly pro-Castro partisan Arca Foundation (which over a three-year period, from January 1994 to December 1996 awarded close to two million dollars for these purposes), to the Ford Foundation (which during the same period awarded $1,779,000 in matters related to Cuba, but without a specific focus or agenda, other than expanding contacts and understanding)—a role that the Ford Foundation has conducted as an NGO in a variety of fields. Also there is the John D. and Catherine T. MacArthur Foundation (which for the years 1993 through 1995 gave to Cuba related issues a total of 2,483,687). There are a variety of smaller foundations, including the aforementioned General Services Foundation, that fall into the category of those urging a new situation and relationship between the two countries, but which are indefinite on what would be expected from the "other side."

The actual research results of foundation efforts remain to be determined. Programs with the ever popular theme of environmental protection provide a bridge between scientists and social scientists in Cuba and the United States. But the suspicion, hardly unwarranted, that such funding is less oriented to research than to results can hardly be disabused, at least unless and until solid research results begin to emerge. Foundations often serve U.S. interests in environments that are complex and difficult for the government itself to take a stand. But they also legitimate policies that may work at cross-purposes with the government as such. For now, these foundations are so remote from the ordinary experiences and activities of Cuban-Americans as to be less effective that the other wings, in which the mission is clearer. Charges of elitism have always haunted foundations in every area, and never more so than in their efforts to address and change policies concerning Cuba.[5]

The number and variety of organizations involved in influencing the federal government to lift the embargo is truly impressive—far exceeding in scope that of the Cuba Lobby twenty years ago. But they often include overlapping personnel. And despite a big push to broaden its appeal, the Lobby still has minimal Cuban-American participation. Ultimately, the problem for this mélange of organizations that comprise the Cuba Lobby is the Castro government itself: Castro is an intransigent leader earnestly convinced of the superiority of communism over capitalism, of Latinos over Yanquis, and not incidentally of Cuba over the United States in moral and cultural terms. His convictions, translated into policy in Cuba make the goals of the Cuba Lobby (to fundamentally reconfigure U.S. policies) at least as difficult as they were twenty years ago. In addition, there is the disquieting fact that a dictator in power for forty years is not necessarily a kinder or gentler species of ruler.

One can expect the Cuba Lobby to continue to focus on short term goals—especially lifting the embargo—while assiduously avoiding analysis of the regime's performance in economic, and political sectors, or for that matter, areas of medicine and education. At the empirical level the consensus that Castro's communism is an unmitigated disaster remains incontestable. This is the elemental fact around which the Cuba Lobby in its soft or hard versions cannot end run or find a palatable solution. It is silence on the issue of dictatorship, of totalitarianism at work, which leads one to expect little in the way of change—either in the United States' insistence on bilateral initiatives or in the actual structure and function of the Castro Communist stranglehold on its own people. The appeal to human rights by the Cuba Lobby is bizarre—coming as it does from a variety of business people who could scarcely worry less about such niceties, and from political pilgrims for whom human rights abuses are minor blips on the screen of world revolution.

Foundation support for the Cuba Lobby raises larger issues. The bias, the unmitigated sense of partisanship, is evident in funding of agencies with a history of anti-American biases of one sort or another. With respect to Cuba, such agencies are dedicated to a simple goal: the removal of the embargo. Castro's problems are blamed on the actions of Washington, DC. Political pilgrimages are offered to politicians, professors, theologians, businessmen—any group whose presence in Cuba might be translated into public pressure to change the course of foreign policy. Foundation grants range from direct action challenges to U.S. restrictions on sales to Cuba, to those supporting publications and position papers that argue the case for lifting the embargo and establishing direct relationships between American and Cuban elites, to creating special advantages for Castro in his dealings with the United States.

There is a wonderful Orwellian dimension to much of this effort. For example, the Center for Public Integrity in Washington, DC is given money to "prepare a report on how private money is spent to influence U.S. policy toward Cuba." Indeed, was such a report to be undertaken in a serious way, researchers awarded money would need to turn a sharp searchlight on themselves. But that is extremely unlikely. The Cuba Lobby has learned a great deal since 1978. It has learned how to manipulate every lever of power, every sector of influence, to gain its ends. It has learned to be wary of dealing with Cuban life as such. Only the solidly entrenched mass opinion of the exile communities, who know that Castro is a tyrant who has transformed Cuba into a prison house, restrains their impact.

The Cuba Lobby: 1978-1998

The overriding characteristic of the Cuba Lobby in 1998, in contrast to 1978, is disregard for the internal character of the Castro regime.[6] Most wings of the Lobby pay little if any attention to the nature of the dictatorship, the pattern of widespread abuses of civil liberties, the operational norms of the Communist Party which insist upon discipline and solidarity, or the harassment and, when required, imprisonment of opposition. In short, all reasons to struggle against the dictatorship are ignored. What the new lobby emphasizes instead is the need for consistency in American foreign policy as a goal in itself.

In this regard, comparisons are nearly always made between China and Cuba. How can it be, asks the Cuba Lobby in tireless unison, that the Communist regime of China is treated so radically differently from the Communist regime of Cuba? Indeed, the United States' recent decision not to support the annual United Nations condemnation of human rights abuses in China is cited as evidence that our policy toward Cuba is biased and hypocritical. The size of the Cuban opposition to Castro in Florida or the relative feebleness of Fidel's regime is contrasted with China's vast economic and military might. Instead of arguing the need for stronger sanctions with respect to China, the Cuba Lobby now simply argues that U.S. policy toward Cuba should be consistent with policy toward China.

The new Cuba Lobby contains many of the players as it did two decades ago. Its positions draw power from changes on the world scene. (1) the collapse of the Soviet Union and East European Communism; and the corresponding view that Cuba is no longer a military danger to the United States; (2) the sense of a need to create a consistent foreign policy that treats China, Cuba, and communist remnants in identical or similar fashion; (3) Cuba's inability to act as an aggressive power overseas, unlike its situation in the 1970s; (4) the sense that a new turn in U.S. policy will create a corresponding set of initiatives by the Cuban regime; and finally, (5) the embargo's greater effectiveness hinders and hurts ordinary Cubans and leaves unscathed the Party elite, raising human rights considerations. I believe that these five elements accurately summarize the new Cuba Lobby position.

A fascinating characteristic of the Cuba Lobby is its fusion of old and new organizational formations. For example, Americans for Humanitarian Trade with Cuba favors easing the 36-year-old economic embargo against Cuba. In turn its key personnel are linked with the Washington-based Center for International Policy. A key figure in the Americans for Humanitarian Trade is retired General John J. Sheehan, former NATO Supreme Allied Commander, who recently returned to Cuba aboard a Cubana

Airlines charter flight. After saying that he was once assigned to the naval base at Guantanamo Bay, he remarked "now ... I am on this side of the fence" [meaning Fidel's side. ILH]. The members of the general's delegation included Claiborne Pell, former chairman of the Senate Foreign Relations Committee, and Kurt Schmoke, the mayor of Baltimore.[7] The Cuba Lobby makes up for its lack of popular support by the visibility of its elite figures. Despite some softening and disaffection in the ranks of the political opposition to the Castro regime, the Cuba Lobby remains essentially estranged from a mass base. It is a problem that a few segments of the Lobby are starting to address, especially those groups closest to the Cuban American community as such.

President Clinton's proposed modifications of the embargo include direct wire transfer of funds from the United States to Cuba (in limited amounts), unrestricted flights to Cuba by humanitarian groups, and fewer restrictions on shipments of drugs and foodstuffs areas. These initiatives have certainly intensified focus on the issue of American policy to Cuba as a whole. However, President Clinton himself has cautioned against viewing these limited unilateral initiatives as anything more than a response to human rights concerns expressed by the Pope on his January visit to Cuba. Undoubtedly, U.S. policymakers along with the Pope imagine that softening the embargo will bring about a corresponding shift in Castro's policies toward the United States. However, to date no ground-breaking changes seem to have taken place. Indeed, Cuba has insisted that it would treat the visit of the Pope as an encapsulated event, and not one that required any alteration in Communist Party tactics or goals.

Not every voiced opposition to the long standing embargo against Cuba, or to more recent legislation extending trade and aid restrictions, is a consequence of the Cuba Lobby's efforts. For example, both Mark Falcoff[8] and James K. Glassman[9] of the American Enterprise Institute and earlier, William Ratliff of the Hoover Institution at Stanford University, Roger Fontaine of the Center for Strategic and International Studies,[10] and Jorge I. Domínguez[11] coordinator of the Inter-American Dialogue Task

Force, have all shifted ground. They now urge modification rather than lifting the embargo.[12] These courageous policy and academic personnel are scarcely agents or agencies of the Hard Left; nor can the authenticity of their manifold concerns be lightly dismissed. Their arguments are based on a variety of grounds: the assertion that trade is a human rights issue, i.e., the embargo hurts the wrong people; the position that lifting the embargo is a mechanism to force change in Castro's Cuba, denying Castro a scapegoat for his disastrous economic performance in nearly forty years of Communist party rule; and finally, the assertion of a need to restore some consistency in American foreign policy with respect to unfriendly nations. And of course those who take the Papal visit to Cuba as a policy shift, such as Richard John Neuhaus, the conservative director of the Institute on Religion and Public Life, now hesitatingly "believe a convincing case can be made that the embargo should be lifted."[13]

* * * * *

This statement is not intended as a general reconsideration of the embargo situation. Indeed, I offered my own position at a United Nations Association conference in Miami held late in 1997. I frankly see no compelling reason to change my position at this time. Unilateral initiatives with respect to Castro can just as easily be viewed by the Cuban people as a demonstration of American lack of concern or resolve as they might result in changing attitudes toward a more positive outlook on American society generally. Embargoes are essentially political, or if you will, symbolic. They rarely result in the sort of economic crises that can bring a regime to its knees—certainly not in a world all too ready to take up the slack if the United States proves reticent to trade with its foes.[14]

Events have a way of forcing departures from long established norms. That holds for Castro's Cuba as well as Clinton's United States. The death of Jorge Mas Canosa has fueled widespread efforts to change attitudes within the Cuban community of Miami. Imagine what changes might be inspired by the death or simple incapacitation of Fidel Castro in Havana. This is not said to urge others to accelerate the biological process by military or covert means. It is a reminder that one needs to distinguish between tactics, policies and principles. The Cuba Lobby as presently constituted conflates these three items. Better yet, its "principles" seem to be little more than the customary denunciation of American aggression in Latin America; a position far better suited for the first than the second half of the twentieth century.

To be sure, the Cuba Lobby of 20 years ago and now are quite different in their appraisals. Twenty years ago it was still (barely) possible to defend the Castro revolution as a beachhead in the hemisphere for a broad scaled evolution of socialist styled revolution. The dismal performance of Castro in the economic and human rights realms, have taken that approach off the policy table. The increasingly prominent economic wing of the Cuba Lobby simply seeks their share of the small Cuban pie; and could hardly care less for the evolution of socialism on the island.[15] This difference between the older militant lobbyists and the newer pragmatic lobbyists make it an uneasy and unstable coalition. Perhaps the best argument that can be mustered for an end to the embargo is that it might conceivably knock the props out from under this coalition of angry, marginalized policy-makers and business people in search of the next dollar. Whether the removal of such a Lobby is worth the price of a change in American policy toward Cuba remains questionable. Indeed it is even a dubious premise that the end of the embargo would slow down, much less close down, the Cuba Lobby. Anti-Americanism has a way of finding new objects of animus, as does the search for profits, without regard to larger policy considerations.

Whatever the cogitations and agitations in the United States' political and business circles about the embargo, the fact remains that the course of the Cuban Revolution is little dependent on either the embargo or its removal. The intrinsic mechanisms of the regime are playing out to a disastrous conclusion. As I have said on several occasions, biology trumps sociology. We can expect large scale changes in Cuba in the near future. These will not occur because of discourse on embargoes, or presumptions about lobbies. They will take place simply because the biological clock is ticking. Not even claims for the immortality of the regime or the system can be transferred to the immorality of the person or the leader. "God does not play dice with the world. The Lord God is subtle, but malicious he is not," Einstein is reputed to have told his biographer. But this observation apparently does not include the games that political individuals play, which are indeed the haven of malicious gamblers. Cuba is hardly exempt from providential constraints or human foibles.

In October 1997 I observed that the policy of the Clinton administration toward Cuba was one of the few examples of a statement of principles that could claim to be acted out in policies. At the risk of repetition, let me excerpt that conclusion: "Being centrist is not the same as being neutral, and being inconsistent is not the same as being wrong. It is my considered judgment that American foreign policy toward Cuba during the Clinton administration, while hardly the model of clarity either advocates or detractors would wish, nonetheless is a serviceable approach. It distinguishes claims of the Cuban people from posturing by its present rulers. It also remains open to serious overtures by the Castro regime to face 'the three frees' [free elections, free trade and free parties] with an openness that the situation demands. The issues confronting United States-Cuban relations are rooted in the stuff of national currency: legitimacy. That is what nations bestow on each other. That is what the United States is not prepared to traffic in as long as the Castro regime maintains its stubborn animosity to the 'the three frees.'"

Now this too threatens to become, in the words of diplomacy, a position waffled. It joins a growing list of confused orientations from the Clinton administration—ranging from manifest support for African dictatorships in the name of dubious democratic claims, to the maintenance on a nearly permanent basis of American troops in Bosnia in the forlorn hope that our military presence will somehow magically dissolve one thousand years of animus. Cuba once again has become a place in which United States initiatives for an opening are met by a combination of derision and condescension. The new U.S. initiatives have received the following response from Roberto Robaina, Cuba's foreign minister: "This is a cosmetic operation that does not go to the heart of the problem... The White House continues blindly in its attempt to impose on Cuba changes which Cubans alone should decide."[16] This is hardly the stuff of generous policy response to the unilateral initiatives of the American government to modifying the embargo. There is a clear dichotomy between how U.S. lobbyists see the impact of the embargo, or its removal, and how Castro sees the same phenomenon. What for the Cuba Lobby is the central thrust of its operations, repeal of the embargo; remains a rather modest agenda item for Fidel, except when reporting on crop and harvest shortfalls; in which case, the embargo is trotted out as the culprit rather than the system of repression under which the Cuban people labor.

The short-term consequences of this policy shift have been to roil the Cuban-American community into a protracted debate on the lifting of sanctions, and to break the will, the spirit, of an exiled people in its ongoing efforts to overthrow a tyrant. This is not to say that the Cuban overseas communities have acted with uniform intelligence. Indeed, they can be faulted for a wide variety of sins: ranging from adolescent conspiracy theories to abortive raids on Cuba that could be and were provocative and doomed to failure. But a sense of common purposes—the restoration of democracy—was never debated. Now at the moment of Castro's final hours, of desperation at the sense of political malaise, in a Cuban economy wrecked to the point of no return without systemic reform, at this moment we are bullied by a small corps of disenchanted elitists to adopt a unilateral mode of action. Moreover, it carries with it scarcely any possibilities of corresponding weakening of the leashes on the Cuban people by their communist handlers.[17]

In the way of a Greek tragedy, U.S. policy probably had to come to this point of decision. It is neither a pleasant nor an easy moment. Friends are pitted against friends—never a pleasant condition in politics or in private lives. One can hope that such differences can be repaired, and indeed, that they do not lead to yet more serious ruptures among all the legions of honest people struggling against the Castro tyranny. I personally take small comfort in the fact that the "moral" opprobrium has presumably shifted from Clinton to Castro. This may be a theological high point in forty years of opposition to a vile dictatorship. But it is also a political low point, and should be recognized as such. Neither the *realpolitik* of advanced policy making nor the theology of partisan purpose can erase the fact that in its magnanimous gesture toward the Cuban dictator the United States performed a dubious service toward the Cuban people.

Let me conclude by pointing out what is too easily forgotten. Whether the embargo is sustained, modified or repealed, or even whether its advocates or critics turn out to be correct in assessing the rewards or damages created by the various congressional and presidential initiatives, the fact remains that the primary source of the impoverishment of the Cuban people is the Communist system of government imposed on them by the Castro regime. In the name of establishing a Robespierre-like reign of virtue, Castro has taken the crown jewel of the Caribbean and converted Cuba into a prison house. If the embargo were to be removed tomorrow that ineluctable fact of an entrenched totalitarian regime would still be in force. Each corporation, each politician, each intellectual, and each citizen, must continue to determine whether to support or offer succor to the tyranny. The struggle against this last hemispheric bastion of totalitarianism will hardly dissolve as a result of changes in American policy and strategy. On that ultimate issue I have no doubt that the American people stand in solidarity with the Cuban people. Any action or policy that would extend this nearly forty-year-old absolute dictatorship must be viewed for what it is: a collapse of political confidence and a denial of moral nerve.

References/Notes

1. The intellectual-academic wing of the Cuba Lobby is orchestrated by The Science and Human Rights Program of the American Association for the Advancement of Science. Its newsletters and promotional literature speak of being "in collaboration with The American Association of University Professors; The American Association for World Health; The American Physical Society; and The Committee of Concerned Scientists." This is a formidable array of organizations and individuals by any quantitative or qualitative standard. It needs to be noted that such activist commitments are usually grounded in the decisions of key staff members, and do not always represent the will of the membership.

2. Peter Brimelow and Edwin S. Rubenstein, "The Cost of Castro." *Forbes*. March 23, 1998. p.80.

3. The business-commercial wing of the Cuba Lobby include the United States Association for International Business and Trade; National Association of Manufacturers; United States Chamber of Commerce; the United States-Cuba Foundation; and the United States-Cuba Trade and Economic Council; and USA Engage. These tend to cluster in the New York and Washington areas. They draw representation from a variety of major corporations, ranging from Caterpillar to Archer Daniels Midland, that is, firms manufacturing or distributing the sort of equipment and providing the kind of services that could be utilized by Cuba.

4. The political and policy wing of the Cuba Lobby is largely centered in Washington DC, and includes Inter-American Dialogue; Institute for Policy Studies; Human Rights Watch; Global Exchange; Cuban Committee for Democracy; Cuban American Committee Research and Education Fund; Council of Hemispheric Affairs; and the Center for International Policy. Many of these types of organizations are staffed by former members of the Senate and the House of Representatives; including former aides and staff members. Cambio Cubano is noteworthy for being one of the very few such organizations with former leading Cubans in leadership roles.

5. Perhaps the most surprising is the degree of involvement in Cuban affairs by grant making and foundation agencies. Alamar Associates provides not only funding but consulting to a variety of firms; The Arca Foundation, as its name implies has indeed been a treasure chest of support for Cuban causes; The Ford Foundation, once known as a conservative bastion, has been active in opposition to the embargo; another old line agency, The General Services Foundation, has been equally active in grants for Cuban causes; and the John D. and Catherine T. MacArthur Foundation, in keeping with its general ideological proclivities, is also a major supporter for a rapprochement in American-Cuban relations.

6. Irving Louis Horowitz, "The Cuba Lobby: Supplying Rope to a Mortgaged Revolution." *The Washington Review of Strategic and International Studies*. Volume 1, Number 3. July 1978. pp. 58–71.

7. Pascal Fletcher, "Policy Makers Greet Allies from U.S.," *Financial Times* (London). March 17, 1998.
8. Mark Falcoff, "Is It Time to Rethink the Cuban Embargo?", *American Enterprise Institute for Public Policy Research.* March 1998. p. 4.
9. James K. Glassman, "No Sanctions, No Castro." *American Enterprise Institute for Public Policy Research.* March 1998. p. 2
10. William Ratliff and Roger W. Fontaine, "Liberate Cuba, Liberate Us, Lift the Embargo, Now." *The New York Times.* February 17, 1994, p.A-23.
11. Jorge I. Domínguez and Sally Cole, "Cuba and the United States: Recommendations for Building a Framework for Cooperation on Environmental Matters" in *The Environment in U.S.-Cuban Relations.* Washington, DC: Inter-American Dialogue, January 1997, pp. 1–12.
12. Stephen Erlanger, "U.S. to Ease Curbs on Relief to Cuba and Money to Kin." *The New York Times.* March 20, 1998. p. 4
13. Richard John Neuhaus, "The Cuban Revolutions." *First Things.* Whole Number 83. May 1998. p. 28.
14. Irving Louis Horowitz, "Three Points of Light: U.S. Policy Responses to Cuba." *Cuba 1997: The Year in Review.* Washington, DC: Center for a Free Cuba, 1998. pp. 13–16.
15. This shift is even the case for earlier supporters such as Wayne S. Smith, "Wanted: A Logical Cuba Policy," *International Policy Report.* February 1998; and even more, his earlier comment on "The U.S.-Cuba Imbroglio: Anatomy of a Crisis," International *Policy Report.* May 1996 (both reports issued by the Center for International Policy).
16. Pascal Fletcher, "Low-Key Cuba Welcome for Relaxed U.S. Embargo," *Financial Times* (London). March 23, 1998.
17. Jaime Suchlicki, "The U.S. Embargo of Cuba: Important Considerations." *Cuban Studies Association Document Series.* No. 3, March 1998.

Source and Original Title: "The Cuba Lobby: Then and Now." *Orbis: A Journal of World Affairs*, Vol. 42, No. 4, Fall 1998, pp. 553-565.

36

The Cuban Embargo and the American Interest

This set of hearings has been called ostensibly to assess the impact of the Pope John Paul II's visit to Cuba fifteen months ago. And I will try to address that issue, albeit somewhat elliptically, and perhaps in a less narrow manner. It is important to remember the many criticisms Pope John Paul II enunciated about the moral and spiritual disintegration of Castro's Cuba. Ironically, his call to remove the boycott of Cuba has become one of the main issues driving the United States toward a more moderate policy position. The Pope's statement had been the core of the earlier round of hearings of the International Affairs Committee, and I dare say, will be this case in the present round as well. We are in the midst of a struggle. It is not only about whether the embargo helps to sustain Castro in power or whether it is the last best hope in weakening the regime in Havana and compelling at least a few economic reforms. It is also part of a much larger struggle over the soul of American foreign policy. More specifically, we are in a great debate as to what constitutes the American national interest and whether commercial private interests should drive it solely or primarily.

The United States has already attempted to soften the impact of the embargo on Cuba in a series of small steps and trial balloons. It has expanded telecommunications between the two nations; increased direct contact between political, cultural, academic and business personnel; and most important, limited still further what goods can or should be embargoed. These actions by the Clinton administration have been greeted with a series of stinging rebukes. Castro and his spokespersons have described such unilateral initiatives as little more than insults and interference with Cuban sovereignty. Yet at the same time he continues to claim that the embargo is the cause of all the miseries of the Cuban people. In the same breath he proclaims the embargo to be a hopeless failure in preventing Cuba from marching into the socialist future.

The internal political situation in Cuba has been far worse after such overtures than before—and that is saying a great deal. The legal apparatus of the Castro government has been mobilized to squelch even the most modest forms of criticism and to frighten the non-committed and the non-political into some sort of revitalized mass mobilization. Castro's response to a weakening internal situation is tightening the totalitarian vise, and thereby insuring that any transition period will remain autocratic and dynastic—not unlike the communist model used in the succession from father to son (in the Cuba case, from older brother to younger brother) in the case of North Korea. Such steps have seriously compromised the efforts of the Cuba Lobby to "normalize"relations between American democracy and Cuban dictatorship However, real world events do not seem to prevent the Cuba Lobby from continuing its campaign to invalidate or at least demonize, the Helms-Burton and Torricelli bipartisan legislation, as well as earlier, long standing legislative safeguards.

On the Cuba Lobby, its organization base and financial support, I will spare this committee any lengthy discourse, and with your permission, simply place in the record two articles I wrote twenty years apart. The first appeared in the *Washington Quarterly*, and more the recent one in *Orbis*. Both articles provide ample evidence of the existence of a well-financed lobby, the continuation over time of such a lobby, and finally, its policy aims. The renewed impetus of this lobby after the papal visit has not yet succeeded in changing the political structure of American-Cuban relations to any substantial degree, because the Castro regime has been intransigent to a fault. Indeed, were it not for its Marxist-Leninist fanaticism, and the sheer lack of flexibility and professionalism in Cuban foreign policy, the United States in its present conciliatory administrative temperament might well have seized any opportunity to overturn the embargo and move to a higher ground.

As matters stand, the continuation of such a conciliatory posture remains impossible for a variety of reasons. The essential position of the Clinton administration and its predecessors has been unusually consistent as well as resilient. It is best articulated in what I have elsewhere referred to as the three core principles of American policy toward Cuba: free parties, free elections, and free trade. Though many Cuba lobbyists have gleefully noted an inconsistency in U.S. policy towards Communist China and Communist Cuba, the Clinton administration has properly, if somewhat cautiously, noted that China has moved very far on the free trade and free enterprise fronts—which is at least one-third farther along the road toward global normalization than contemporary Cuba.

What is important about the current debates regarding the embargo is that they are essentially internal American debates—very weighty ones indeed, between economic forces on one side and political forces on the other. I would further argue that the contemporary debate in respect to Cuba well illustrates the premise I recently outlined in my new book *Behemoth*: that the end of the twentieth century witnesses a growing struggle between the commercial and business community at one pole, and the government policy apparatus on the other. This is a weighty struggle, with many tangential elements. It is an unanticipated development in the evolution of large-scale businesses and equally large-scale political interests. The wide-ranging debate over our Cuba foreign policy indicates that different interests are served by different forces and underwritten by different constituencies.

In the case of Cuba, we have a strange alliance between conservative business forces and radical intellectual elements. For
quite different reasons, both are anxious to restore and normalize
relations. Business interests wish to do so as an illustration of a
new coda: that the bourgeoisie has no political party allegiance,
only an allegiance to the bottom line and to unimpeded trade.
The cadre of intellectual devotees of Fidel for the past forty years
simply wants to provide legitimacy and cover to the Communist
regime of Cuba. These bedfellows are so strange, that institutions
like the Council on Foreign Relations have sought to provide a
patina of respectability to this alliance of convenience by enlisting
the support of such outstanding luminaries as Bernard Aronson
and former secretary of state William Rogers to serve as legitimating figures. And organizations such as the Latin American Studies
Association have long served as forums that bring together Cuban
university officials and their North American counter-parts—with
a corresponding marginalization of Cuban American academics
who stand in opposition to the Castro regime.

Those who uphold the embargo and the various pieces of
legislation aimed at containing Castro's Cuba—at least until
he is brought to heel on issues ranging from rights to reparations—are equally strange bedfellows. This is one of the few areas
at the moment in which there is a firm coalition of Democratic
Party and Republican Party representatives, senators, governors
and mayors, united in their opposition to breaking the embargo.
That there may be a directly political element, the voting blocs of
Cuban Americans in Florida and New Jersey, does not obviate the
fact that the mainline opposition to accepting Castro in the family
of American nation-states has held firm, through thick and thin
over the course of many presidencies. Those for whom American
democracy is anathema seize on this broad-based coalition as
proof positive that Castro is right and Clinton wrong.

But such is not the situation. To start with, the weight of
empirical evidence as to the tyrannical and dictatorial nature
of Castro is so overwhelming, that even those who advocate a
lifting of the embargo are compelled, often grudgingly, to admit

that the issue is one of tactics and logistics, not principles. Even opponents of current American foreign policy dare not make fatuous claims about the Castro regime as it enters its final and desperate years. Instead we are told from the side door, from the Aronson-Rogers commission, that we should recognize Cuban interests because not to do so is to undermine Cuba's movement toward "a still fragile civil society which is struggling to take hold in Cuba" and a new alignment of political and economic forces. Not surprisingly the Castro regime always manages to come to the rescue of those who oppose lifting of the embargo by its own stony and unyielding rhetoric, not to mention legal repression. Those awaiting Castro's movement toward a civil society have had a long, forty-year wait, and the end is not in sight. Alas, tendencies toward democratization seem further from rather than nearer to realization.

Debate on what should be American policy toward Castro's Cuba is in fact a debate for the soul of American foreign policy as such. This is a debate in which the national interests of the state and its people are juxtaposed against the private interests of some elements of the commercial and industrial sector. U.S. relations with Cuba are a major policy issue, not an issue to be resolved simply by legislative act or executive order. This debate goes to the heart of who rules the United States, on whose behalf, and at whose behest. That we are even having such a debate at this point in time does not result from changes in Cuban political affairs. It reflects instead extraordinary changes in the coalition of social and economic forces that determine American foreign policy. The expanding globalization of business interests has made them increasingly impervious to old-fashioned political appeals. Indeed, such interests incorporate real politics into their relationship with their own government and those of other nations. The corresponding increase in the concentration of government services at the national level has made the federal bureaucracy a force that is also more powerful than ever before. Thus we have in the debate on Cuba nothing less than an encapsulated version of the shape of the new politics of the twenty-first century, one in which big confronts big more frequently than right confronts left.

The business community, once as divided in practice as it was on the Cuba question in principle, has shown an increasing willingness to flex its muscles and put money behind every effort by every group to remove the boycott. It wants a business-to-business relationship with Cuba, arguing that this will fuel political change. The ineluctable problem is that Castro and his Communist Party militants will not play the game according to bourgeois rules. They are willing to have a connection with U.S. business, but only so far as it strengthens the Cuban government's control of all enterprises of any kind. Beyond that, the communist regime is not in any mood to discuss reparations for businesses confiscated soon after the seizure of power in 1959.

Fidel Castro has made plain his opposition to private enterprise in a series of actions—from shutting down efforts at small light industrial growth in private hands to resisting even a semblance of the equitable distribution of funds from a scheduled exhibition baseball game. No event goes unsponsored, and no handling of Castro's effort at people-to-people contact goes unnoticed. The United States insisted that no money go to the Cuban government, while Cuba pushed to donate the proceeds to victims of hurricanes in Central America. A compromise was reached that permits the funds to be used to promote sports activities, anything but an acknowledgement of real needs of real Cubans. Unlike Ping-Pong diplomacy, baseball diplomacy illustrates his tendency to resist any aperture or opening to the United States. Every effort at normalization of relations is interpreted as a sign of a lack of American resolve, and has thus been met by everything from shooting down civilian aircraft to arrests and prosecutions of even the mildest human rights critics of the regime.

I do not argue that we should simply maintain our policy of partial embargo until we have concrete evidence of real change in political direction or in administrative rule within Cuba. Even were there no legal embargo it would still exist on the ground in practice. The Castro administration is congenitally unable to move away from the most backward precepts of Communist Party rule—even as large Communist regimes like China and small ones like Vietnam make just such an effort to do so. In 1964, I wrote about the early days of what I called the Stalinization of Castro's Cuba. In 1999 I must sit here and confirm the completion of this awful process. Castro has smashed an independent administration, an independent banking system, an independent press, an independent labor union movement, and an independent military. What remains is the dried husk of what was once a promising beginning.

The good news is that Stalinism is an unstable form of government even within communist rules of the game. The bad news is that in the short run, the Cuban people must suffer such a tyranny. They suffer not as a consequence of United States initiatives to prevent Castroism from spreading its cancerous forms elsewhere in the world, as it did in the past from Africa and the Middle East, not to mention Latin American and the Caribbean. The cause of immiseration of the Cuban people over the past forty years, their decline from the most advanced nation in the Caribbean basin to one of the most impoverished and backward, is the Castro regime itself. The ideological eyewash that the Cuba Lobby has served up can neither refute nor rebuke what democratic peoples from the Hudson Bay to Tierra del Fuego know full well. Thank you.

*** *** ***

Question from the Chair: In a recent report by several former Members of Congress who visited Cuba they wrote "political dissidents, independent journalists and NGOs all express concern about the way Washington rhetoric links the construction of civil society in Cuba with the removal of Castro, especially as it is stated in the Cuba Democracy Act and Libertad Act." Is this a real concern and does it in fact expose these groups to charges that they are engaged in subversion of the regime?

Horowitz Reply: With the best of intentions, the Council on Foreign Relations Task Force Report on U.S.-Cuban Relations in the twenty-first century attempted to assuage such fears and concerns. Bernard Aronson and William Rogers, directors of the report, did so by speaking of the present day Castro Regime as moving in the direction of a civil society. I confess not to share this faith in Castro's capacity to conduct such an orderly transition. Cuba is a communist state, whose apparatus is underwritten entirely by military force are quasi-military party cadre.

The issue is neither the removal nor celebration of Castro, but the repressive nature of the regime as it has evolved and continues to function. Executive and even more forcefully, Legislative leaders on hemispheric affairs have repeatedly made clear that the movement toward civil society would be met by enthusiastic corresponding steps toward diplomatic normalization on the part of the United States. Thus far, steps toward civil society: free political assembly and expression; unfettered elections in which more than an official party can participate, and a free and open marketplace in goods, services and ideas can take place, are noticeably absent.

Opposition to the Castro regime within Cuba is not proof of dissident subservience to the United States, but simply a demonstration, however limited, that some beginnings to a civil society are feasible. That even the most modest, apolitical opposition to Castro is viewed as "subversion" says all that needs to be said on the fiction of this communist movement toward a civil society and a market economy. If and when such movement does take place, as it has in other parts of the old communist empire, the current status of American foreign policy toward Cuba can and should be reviewed, and if need be, revised. But to implement broad policy shifts unilaterally would be a sign of American ambivalence at a time when the Cuban people require American resolve.

Source and Original Title: "Searching for the Soul of American Foreign Policy: The Cuban Embargo and the National Interest", Testimony prepared for delivery on March 24, 1999 before the House Committee on International Relations, Subcommittee on the Western Hemisphere, Washington D.C.

2000s: Dissolution of Political Power

While the current decade is one in which it has become evident that the long night of dictatorship cannot be continued, this is an uneven march to the end. The Last Hurrah may be apparent, but it is rarely taken in which the dictator goes gently into that night. Several events took place that buoyed the faltering regime: The victory of Hugo Chávez Frías in Venezuela, which gave Cuba a restored lifeline to cheap and subsidized oil imports—and a fellow dictator with shared values a stone's throw away. The election of Luiz Inácio de Silva (Lula) in Brazil, which at least at the outset seemed to denote a huge shift to the Left in hemispheric politics; the victory of Juan Evo Morales Ayma in Bolivia, which while of little immediate economic importance, gave Castro an enormous sense of triumph. This was, after all, the nation where Che Guevara had been sent on a guerrilla mission and been destroyed by a less than brilliant military cadre. Indeed, despite certain drifts to the Right in Mexico and to the Center in Chile, the overwhelming theme through Latin America was nationalism and resistance to economic pressures—real and imagined from the United States. The steady drum beat of opposition to Castro remained contained and even quiescent for most of the first decade. In short, dissolution at home was muted by presumably favorable events abroad.

But the truth seems to be that such overseas events could not cover up the inevitable march of biology over politics. The entire decade hinged on the failing health of Fidel Castro, his passing of everyday power to his younger brother Raúl (no youngster himself!), and a constant flood of weekly reports on world events —ranging from stock market problems with the sub-prime to the troubles of the United States in Iraq. Castro has his own policy solutions, ranging from the best candidates that the Democratic Party could field in the 2008 election to a steady stream of advice for his Venezuelan fellow dictator and equal invective for the Spanish Royal family. The major problem is that the dictator can attempt to transfer power to a trusted partner, but he has no way of insuring that the policies advocated in the past will be carried out in the future. Indeed this is a critical problem with dictatorship itself: transitions are very hard to manage. The single Party State can be retained—as with China—but not the single person preferences. Political parties have a way of generating schisms, rivalries, and antagonisms. At times, these single party states reveal greater bitterness and hatreds than the multi-party systems that they attempted to displace.

So at the close of the current decade, a certain political vacuum exists, one that Fidel Castro has himself come to recognize by not only the transfer of power but also indicating to the Cuban people that he would not stand in the way of a younger cohort of party officials and officers from exercising power. Indeed, the current situation indicates that the rule of Fidel Castro has come to a close —not with an administrative bang, but with a hospital bed. The rise of opposition to the present system, within Cuba no less than outside in the Cuban-American community in the United States is itself an augury of things to come. The question of moment is what will be left of the Castro legacy in the period ahead? How will the nation, its people and leaders, respond to a world without Castro as its supreme leader? While there is a great deal of writing and research on this topic—much of it speculative—the sense that an era is not about the pass, but has already passed is apparent. The Cuban people are not fearful of the ghost of Castro, and the nations that have endured his taunts and tirades are unafraid to say ask for his silence.

37

The Two Cubas of Elián González

"God brought him to us for the hope of Cuba" opines a young man by the name of Jimmy Farfan outside the residence at which Elián González is living. Whether it is God, the infant Moses, or the baby Jesus, or none of the above, it is evident that an event tantamount to a national crisis is playing out in Miami. The child—brought out of Cuba in late November of last year by his mother who perished on the treacherous voyage to the United States—survived unattended for six days on the high seas before being rescued and delivered to relatives in Miami. In the meanwhile, the Cuban government, representing the interests of six-year-old Elián González's father, demanded the immediate return of the boy. The wish to be reunited has clearly been stated by the father and the remaining family members' back home. The story of the two Cubas could hardly be etched with greater simplicity.

Whether Elián González should remain in the United States or be returned to Cuba, whether he has been liberated or captured, whether his situation is a personal trauma or a political trial, has roiled Cuban-American relations to a fevered pitch hardly imaginable even three months ago. It is as if all sides realize that something quite beyond the fate of one boy is being determined. More nearly, it is the fate of one people living in two distinct communities under radically polarized conditions. In all the tons of scenario building and design engaged in over the years by those presumably knowledgeable about Cuban society, I know of none that linked the fate of the Cuban dictatorship—and for that matter, a little bit of American democracy—with that of a six-year-old child who lost his mother and is without his father, and whose future is rooted in the affairs of nation-state politics.

The *New York Times* has leapt into this agonizing affair with its customary assuredness of liberal purpose. Its reporting sheds light on the greater whole—if one can speak of the Elián González matter as having such a metaphysical whole. One would imagine that 40 years of hindsight regarding the nearly shameless propagation of the Castro faith by the *New York Times* (starting with Herbert Matthews' series of interviews in 1958 that brought the Cuban dictator to the attention of the outside world) would reduce that august newspaper to at least quiescence. Nothing could be further from the truth, quite the contrary, the more exposed the totalitarian character of the Cuban regime, the higher that newspaper ratchets up its powerful convictions that the boycott against Cuba should be lifted, unilateral "normalization of economic relations should commence," and political contacts should be elevated to what exists amongst friendly states. So blatant is the position of the *New York Times* that even readers of sister liberal papers such as the *Washington Post* and the *Los Angeles Times* must be uncomfortable. Indeed, on March 5 the *Washington Post* editorialized that the Elián González affair represents "an emotionally and legally charged drama," and noted that in terms of the political situation in Cuba, it is "a sideshow, which is probably why Fidel Castro milks it for every ounce of propaganda effect he can."

But it is the *New York Times* of April 1 that takes the prize in blurring any distinction between news and editorials, between factuality and ideology. Having failed miserably in its attempt to portray the position of those in Miami who wish to secure a six-year-old refugee boy's status as a permanent resident as that of right-wing extremists, and watching with dismay the forging of a broad coalition within Miami of a rejection of his return to

Cuba, the front page of the newspaper of record in this country features an article by a Rick Bragg arguing that the situation "Highlights a Virtual Secession of Miami." Even the quotations presented by Bragg as representing extremist positions hardly add up to anything more than a defiance of the Department of Justice's peremptory rulings that the boy should be returned to his father. There has not been a single slogan raised of secession. Indeed, the defenders of Elián argue the reverse, that it is only within the bosom of the United States that the boy can expect some semblance of normality. Not a single voice has been raised in support of violence within the Cuban American community, other than the violence that ensues from a Martin Luther King defense of the free conscience.

The article features statements intended to portray a secessionist and law-defiant mood in Miami. To that end, Lisandro Pérez, head of Cuban Research at Florida International University, argues that "this is a city that is separate. We now have our own local foreign policy." Indeed, Miami is different. It does have a special local culture that is distinct, but no more so than New Orleans, or for that matter, Berkeley, California. These differences at time do pit city against state—and even against nation. But unlike calls for separation from the United States by the white supremacists in Alabama, they simply never rise to the level of secession in intent or ideology.

To deal in such rhetoric is to invite federal intervention into the affairs of a small community. The interview with David Abraham, professor of immigration law at the University of Miami, does just that. He makes the thrust of this assertion of secession quite plain: Drawing a parallel with the defiance in the 1950s, symbolized by the resistance to school integration in Little Rock, Arkansas, Professor Abraham notes that: "It may regrettably take an overwhelming display to prove South Florida is part of the United States." The struggle over Elián's fate, involving jurisdictional as well as moral concerns, is not an effort to subvert U.S. law, but to demonstrate just who it is that defines and carries out such law.

The final piece of the puzzle is the demonizing of the Cuban community of Miami for its anti-Communist posture. It would seem that far from being a bona fide part of the American experience in the twentieth century, the "Miami Mafia" is now pictured as the enemy, the outsider, precisely for the vigor of its position. Again, Lisandro Pérez at least has the merit of defining the issues sharply. Arguing that the position of the Cuban American community "will have a negative implication" to those sitting in Middle America, he goes on to state that: "They have been spoiled by the U.S. government in the past. Look at the record. They've gotten television stations, radio stations, to broadcast their message to Cuba." But that message is simply the same as what was broadcast through Radio Free Europe: a message of hope to those trapped under the yoke of communism and a warning that Americans can be counted upon to support the cause of democratic rule. As the Elián González issue evolves "in the trenches" it becomes increasingly clear that the Cuba Lobby and its strange band of congressional supporters and leftist apologists simply want business as usual with Castro. They see this as an extraordinary opportunity to drive a fatal wedge between the Cuban community—the most successful Latin American group in North American society—and the American people. The goal of Fidel clearly is to make Elián not just a victim but to destroy the delicate sense of community that has tied the Cuban Americans to their new land these past forty years.

The orchestration of front page and editorial page in the *Times* is hardly more obvious than in Anthony Lewis' comparison of Little Rock in 1957 and Miami in 2000—talking about "howling mobs confronting federal marshals as they carried out the law" and asking "are we going to see that again in Miami?" This bit of rhetorical flim-flam disguises the more obvious connection of Miami today with Birmingham of the Reverend Dr. King in 1960s. "The idea of law" that Mr. Lewis is so concerned with has limits. The marchers in Birmingham tested those limits. It might well be that this is another occasion in which the limits of law are tested and found wanting. After all, it is an unusual situation on the face of it when a mother takes a son into perilous waters, loses her life in the process to escape tyranny, and then the boy survives—only to have the government pontificate about "father's rights"—as if this were a routine matter of family and gender issues. Fanatics who in the past could barely raise a whisper about paternal rights are now singing the song of gender equity! The law may be clear, but the specific situation is not.

The use of a child as a political pawn is a grave personal catastrophe. The denial that he is such a pawn would be a political blunder on the part of all concerned. The fate of Elián González is a sad item in the mosaic of everyday life. But it is just such quirky details that give meaning to the phrase symbolic politics. The return of a child to a surviving parent is indeed "the rule of law." But laws are modified, changed and fine-tuned precisely by exceptional situations. And the death of a mother along with others on a desperate voyage to escape tyranny and the survival of that child on the same voyage of the damned is certainly exceptional. Add to that a condition of return of the child to the father signifies his return to the Cuban dictatorship, a nation barely recognized in diplomatic terms by the United States, and a father who is under strict supervision of that foreign power, and you have an extraordinary no less than exceptional condition. The English language makes a sharp distinction between "law" and "morality" in recognition that the foundation of law is the codification of ethical principles and premises. Were law to be an end in itself it would soon stagnate and become its opposite the practice of lawlessness by those who exercise raw power. In this sense, the Elián González "case" is a reminder, much needed at this point, of how nuanced the rule of law is in democratic practice.

The Cuban American community understands well such distinctions between the legal and the ethical. Hence it appreciates this struggle over the fate of a single child as a defining moment in its strange encounter with a benevolent new homeland, one with a history of isolationism and anti-immigration views as well as providing a welcome mat for immigrants and dissidents. To be

sure, Miami has probably has done a very poor public relations
job in educating the rest of America as to the meaning of the
Elián González affair. That said this remarkable community of
unusual solidarity and high economic and educational achievement is not a "mob." In no shape or form is it dedicated to
secession from the United States. The Cuban Americans are
not a group dedicated to overturning the rule of law. What it
is, and why it has banded together, is a community that recognizes that it has a special relationship with the Cuban dictatorship. Accordingly, the Cuban American community has
a special need to resist Castro's attempts to crush its demands
for legitimacy and normality—despite 41 years of a heartless
and cruel dictatorship.

Communities, no less than individuals, are always free to
choose their battles or their battlegrounds. It might well be that
Elián González is returned to the isle of sorrow known as Cuba.
It might well be that the rule of American law is understood to
apply to all citizens, including Cuban Americans—oddly enough,
perhaps the most law abiding element in a city not noted for
such niceties as respect for others. If this comes about through a
massive federal intervention into the affairs of Miami, then it will
be reminiscent of the many such interventions of the American
past that imposed the rule of law at the expense of the rights
of individuals. The parallels made will be with trade unionists
on strike in Colorado mines, political radicals in search of free
speech during the Palmer Raids, and yes, with Birmingham's Bull
Connor and his use of police dogs in the futile effort to impose
the rule of law as an entity that stands over and above our sense
of justice and compassion.

The overwhelming power of the federal government will
doubtlessly win the custody battle in the short run. When Elián
becomes a man and the nightmare of Castroism is a long dark
cloud on an earlier epoch, he can determine for himself where
he wants to live and with whom. But to return Elián González
to Cuba under the threat of American arms may do little for the
rule of law; it will certainly do much for the force of arms. The

Cuban exile community has proven itself worthy successors to previous waves of loyal immigrants to America. To satisfy the cynical agenda of a dictator who has seized a strategic opportunity to drive a wedge between Cuban Americans and all others would be a far reaching tragedy—one that I cannot personally see this or any other administration endorsing. However, it is a tragedy in the making. The incapacity of the Cuban American community to mobilize the American people as a whole to its cause, and the determination of the American president and the head of the Department of Justice makes such an outcome just about certain. The long run consequences of this standoff remain far from certain.

Source and Original Title: Demonizing Miami: The Two Cubas of Elián González. This article was written prior to the events leading up to the seizure of the child from the home of his Miami relatives by federal marshals and his return to his father on the Saturday morning of April 22, 2000.

38

Cuba after Castro: The Historical Limits to Dictatorship

Speaking of the year "1953" in his *Memoirs,* Andrei Sakharov, *Memoirs* describes the Stalin Era in terms that strike me as entirely appropriate to the Castro Era in Cuba. "How can one speak of symmetry between a normal cell and a cancerous one? With its messianic pretensions, its totalitarian suppression of dissent, and its authoritarian power structure, our regime resembles a cancer cell. The public in our country has no control whatsoever over vital political decisions, foreign or domestic. We have lived in a closed society in which the government concealed matters of substance from its own citizens. We have been closed off as well from the outside world, and our citizens have been denied the right to travel abroad or exchange information."

A theme of growing importance to the Cuban American community, and to American specialists dealing with the current regime is wrapped up in the phrase: prospects for transition to democracy from the current dictatorship. Indeed, this has been a staple in the arsenal of Cubanologists for so long that the wonder is that it has not gone away in the debris of failed prophesies Few among us can honestly claim a belief that the Castro regime would still be with us months shy of the fortieth anniversary of the 1959 seizure of Cuban State power. What must be explained is not simply an anomaly, but why the faith in some sort of changes in state power remains a serious agenda item. In accepting the challenge of this keynote I agreed to address this issue of transition head on. I do so in the spirit of trying to understand the ubiquitous nature of Cuban history under the present tyranny more than the prospects for a future Cuban society. So let me proceed with the task at hand in the full appreciation that the examination of closed societies from afar must always remain problematic.

Forty years of dictatorship represents a tremendous hurdle to overcome. The corrosive features of the communist economic system are such that even after a decade of German reunification, the East German area lags far behind West Germany in economy and life style. And even with massive aide and assistance from the West, the remnants of communist style and substance remain. Indeed, East Germany stands as a testimonial that five hundred years of the German Protestant work ethic could be dramatically eroded by less than fifty years of German Communist rule. Given an even greater series of social hurdles to overcome, it would be dangerous and foolish to expect Cuba to immediately enter the front ranks of Western hemispheric nations, even with massive assistance from the Florida-based Cuban community.

The idea of a "transition to democracy" ballooned frequently and easily in Washington circles represents a mechanistic way of thinking. Democracy requires in place a number of characteristics in order to be operative: some are available in Cuba, others not. A creative and innovative people capable of repairing and modifying just about any artifact do exist. A people schooled in a computer environment, with sound work habits do not exist. Like all communist regimes, an information-communication world without borders is perceived as a threat to the stability of the social system itself. There are perhaps fewer fax machines in all of Cuba than in one square block of the Miami business district.

Totalitarian regimes have a way of being self-contradictory: They want production, but have no mechanism to fairly distribute the results of production—that is the failure of planned systems and the success of market systems. They want regime loyalty and promise low unemployment, but they have no way to ensure the former or avoid the latter save for bribery, corruption, absenteeism, and sheer indolence. In such circumstances, the first steps will be to change the moral climate of the workforce. This sort of transformation takes many years, even decades to create. It is a sad fact that ethical transformations are far slower to evolve than technological changes.

Keep in mind too that Cuba before 1959 was, for all its charms, hardly a model of democratic order. The existence of multiple parties does not in and of itself ensure against strong-armed dictators, military caciques, electoral; frauds, etc. Thus, in speaking of a "transition to democracy," it is significant to note that unlike say, Czechoslovakia between 1918 and 1938 (when the Hitlerites overran that country) and 1945-1948 (when the Stalinist coup erased this brief springtime of freedom); Cuba has a far less enviable record of democracy. In short, Batista was no Masaryk. The need to examine the first 59 years of the century in light of what has taken place in Cuba over the past 40 years is a high order of historical and sociological business.

Too much scenario building goes on in an historical vacuum; as if game playing can somehow predict real world outcomes. That such a discredited notion can come back into style after the utter fiasco of war gaming and civic reconstruction that became the Washington mode during the early stages of the Vietnam War is simply incredible. Without lapsing into a historical or biological determinism, it remains a truism in social life that human beings cannot simply start the world anew, as if no past record of success and failure existed. The French Revolution is the perfect model of such a theory of starting fresh, and ended after four years in a disastrous reign of terror; all in the name of democracy and the rule of the people.

Democracy is essentially a civil process—involving a balance of executive, legislative and judicial functions, all responsible to a larger public. Cuba under Castro, and some time before that, has been a militarized regime operating under the cloak of socialism and communism. Hence, before any transition to democracy is possible, there needs to be a transition from military to civilian controls of the organs of State power. This can be a long or short process. Given the experience of other nations with similar backgrounds, one can anticipate a return to civilian government, but continuing a pattern of strong top down leadership with all that implies. Thus, while all democracy implies a civil process, it is not the case that all civil processes are necessarily democratic.

The transition process, democratic or otherwise, will feature new forms of struggle that were quiescent prior to 1959, and they threaten to be tremendously disruptive. The key struggle will be racial in character. For both the Batista and Castro dictatorships, Cuba served as a model of interracial and inter-ethnic harmony. This fictional view of race relations served well the interests of the dominant white majority. But that majority was slim prior to 1959, and with the exodus, perhaps even narrower at present. One must expect the rising tide of Afro-Cuban expectations to burst on the political scene with the end of Castroism—and this can serve as a disruptive element in any transitional form of government, especially one intent on building up the economic and class infrastructures on the island. Castro's recent courting of the English-speaking, largely black regions of the Caribbean, is a back-handed appreciation that race no less than class matters.

The transition process must take seriously the Leninist-Stalinist character of the present Cuban state. Too often, Cuba is perceived as a Latin American or Caribbean nation that somehow went awry. But its patterns are now quite distinct: far from being a nation of revolving dictatorships, with little character and fewer roots, Castro's Cuba features the longest running communist dynasty—rivaling that of North Korea (and with equally disastrous economic impact). Thus, in any appraisal of regime changeover or makeover it is critical to take into account the special circumstances in ideological no less than economical terms, or in structural no less than regional terms. Again, even a brief appraisal of Eastern Europe and Russia after the fall of Communist rule indicates the continuing strength of totalitarian parties and ideologies. It would be dangerously naive to think that Cuba after Castro would be bereft of a Communist movement of potency for some time to come.

Any serious discussion of transition in Cuba must reckon with our host: the way in which the Communist Party and its supreme personality as well as its leader, Fidel Castro, pass into history. There are enormous differences between a regime termination

that is announced by exile rather than liquidation of the leadership, in states that have pseudo-dynastic properties, by a gradual
conversion into a multi-party state rather than a violent lurching
into a new state. This of course has a tautological dimension. But
far from being a syllogism of governance, we have ample evidence
from Eastern Europe to know that how the old order goes into
the night is a crucial element in the evolution of a new order.

Having argued a case for caution and conservatism in evalua-
tive and methodological terms, it should be noted that this is not a
brief for extreme relativism in looking at the prospects for democratic transition in Cuba. Rather, the trick (if that be the proper word) in
all serious efforts at future prognosis is looking backward, that is, at
the history of Cuba and its people. For in some sense, what binds us,
what brings us together in our convictions, is a deep appreciation
that history is absolutely not on Castro's side, that his fatuous claim
is an act of intellectual bravura mixed with bad consciousness. He
is lead to invoke the muses of the past because of his failures in the
present. One does not require a perfect scenario to predict the total
and ultimate demise of his person and his system.

The process of national transition is a personal, moral redemption, no less than a public, political transformation. Prisoners in
Cuba continue to remind us that: "The system maintains its political control principally through self-repression. Each Cuban has a
built-in policeman." Yet the slogan at the time of the Papal visit was
"no tengáis miedo"—have no fear. The Cuban process of transition
may come to rest on how this 40-year-old personal contradiction
between self preservation and self sacrifice plays itself out. Biology
trumps politics at the level of dictatorial leadership, so too does
psychology trumps sociology at the level of quotidian life. Talk
of systemic change notwithstanding, individual responsibility for
national revival will largely determine political outcomes. On these
bedrock set of assumptions about the human nature of the human
sciences we must ultimately come to rest and to hope.

Source and Original Title: "Eleven Theses on Cuba after Castro."
Studies in Comparative International Development. Volume 34,
Number 4, Winter 2000, pp.3-6.

39

Humanitarian Capitulation

The Council on Foreign Relations is a strange and wondrous arena for policy-making. On one hand, it issues self-righteous bromides on *Humanitarian Intervention*,[1] from which even its ardent participants feel compelled to dissociate themselves. In the words of one of them, Dov Zakheim: "Let us be honest with ourselves. The criteria for intervention have had less to do with the nature of any particular humanitarian crisis than with much more mundane concerns such as power balances, state interests, and military feasibility." Paradoxically, the Council has also become the fulcrum and spearhead of the Cuba Lobby—those seeking the establishment of normal diplomatic and social relations with Communist Cuba. One might describe these as advocates of humanitarian capitulation. The contradiction between an activist military posture in Yugoslavia and a pacifist civil approach to Cuba remains an inexplicable contradiction in American foreign policy.

Heading the group advocating normalization with Cuba are two distinguished public servants: Bernard Aronson, who served as assistant secretary of state for inter-American affairs between 1989 and 1993 in the Bush administration, and William Rogers, secretary of state from 1969-1973 in the Nixon administration. The fact that both are, presumptively at least, Republicans, underscores a point repeatedly made in the reports of this working group: their bipartisan character. Despite this however, judging by the political positions of many members and observers, more Democratic than Republican figures are represented. In the world of political flimflam, political allegiances are not incidental to those in search of fame. The draft of the second report of the Aronson-Rogers commission of the Council on Foreign Relations, entitled "U.S.-Cuban Relations in the 21st Century"[2] continues proposals earlier issued in January 1999 as a Report of an Independent Task Force of the same name, one also sponsored by the Council on Foreign Relations. The 1999 report was a nervous effort to find common ground in liberal and conservative views on Castro's Cuba, and was issued with the obvious goal of changing U.S. policy. This new effort is far more assured and outspoken in pursuing of an accommodation between the two nations. Underlying its assumptions is the belief that Castro's Cuba, given half a chance, will march down the road of democracy. In congressional testimony as well as other publications, I have addressed my reservations fears about the accommodations made in the initial report.[3] Here I focus my discussion on this revised effort—one dedicated to sharply altering the course of American foreign policy toward Communist Cuba.

My expressed concerns as to the purpose of the 1999 report have been entirely confirmed by this "Follow-On Report." If not for the sponsorship of the Council on Foreign Relations, I seriously doubt that this report would receive even casual attention in policy-making bodies of government despite its pretentious rhetoric. But that organizational legitimacy, matched by the qualifications of the members and observers associated with this independent task force, compel serious review of its contents. I should add that as a member of the Council on Foreign Relations for more than 30 years, I feel not just a right, but an obligation to enter a dissenting opinion.

This "Follow-On Report" spells out policies more or less unstated in the 1999 Report. Like all documents aimed at policy-making through consensus building, this one rests on a series of metaphysical presuppositions. These must be examined.

The first assumption is that a shift in American foreign policy requires only bipartisan agreement on procedures not changes in actions by the other side. In the words of the report: "the spread of information, new ideas, and fresh perspectives, through expanded human contact, can help break the isolation of, and expand engagement in, Cuba." The second, even more disastrous assumption follows from the first. It is that unilateral policy making by itself can change the situation on the ground in Cuba. The document ignores Castro's current foreign and domestic policy, or treats it in such broad generalities. It conveys no awareness that in Castro the United States is dealing with an unyielding dictator determined to bring the major world power to heel.

Given the substantial dubiousness of the document's metaphysical domain assumptions, the four "baskets" of recommendations that follow can best be seen as a wish list developed in Washington, D.C. with little or no regard to actual current events in Cuba. Indeed, the report has a "Wizard of Oz" sensibility, prepared in isolation of Cuban realities. This is both disconcerting and disheartening. An essential premise of diplomacy, in all negotiations between rivals whatever at the personal or national level, is a trade off of interests. Both parties must make accommodations to achieve new advantages that could not otherwise be gained. In the absence of even a remote sense of the empirical conditions that prevail in Cuba, the wish becomes father to the act. The limited prospects for policy revisions in the face of Castro's determined opposition to the United States and all that it stands for in the policy arena are simply disregarded or purposely overlooked.

The Report plays a peculiar shell game. On one hand it advocates near total overhaul of American foreign policy toward Cuba. On the other hand it makes no effort to define the terms by which new policies might be evaluated. The assumption is that all of the recommendations proffered will immediately result in a more benign dictatorship, and ultimately lead to the fall of the regime under the evidence of its own cruelties in made clear by American benevolence. The likelihood that the unilateral implementation of the report's four baskets of recommendations would further entrench Castro's more than 40 years of rule is not even considered, let alone debated. In a bizarre outcome, the most powerful nation on earth throws a series of lifelines to the world's longest-standing communist dictatorship on the assumption that good things will happen. If such unstated assumptions and suppositions were forthrightly presented, one might be tempted to take the Aronson-Rogers report seriously. Because they are not, one must explore the probable consequences of their cogitation.

The Aronson-Rogers report is divided into four "baskets." The first consists of proposals involving family reunification and migration. With each "basket" the United States is the donor and Cuba the recipient. For example, ending restrictions on family visits entails ending restrictions on visitations of Cuban Americans to Cuba; it does not posit that in turn Cubans will be allowed to visit the United States. This basket also advocates lifting the ceiling on remittances to relatives by U.S. citizens, leaving such matters in the hands of individuals. It provides no safeguards that remitted monies would actually end up in the hands of family members or escape "taxation" by the Castro government.

Couched as they are in humanitarian language, these proposals would allow island-resident Cubans to be claimed as dependents for U.S. income tax purposes, and permit Cubans to visit the United States to take unimpeded advantage of the opportunity of seeing their relatives. The proposals call for increasing legal immigration from Cuba; a review board for assessing potential migrants; expanded consular services; and it urges the prosecution of alien smugglers who facilitate illegal immigration. Finally, the Report urges that migration becomes routinized, that is to say a fixed number of people to gain admittance each year. These proposals seem innocuous enough, save for the fact that they are proffered with absolutely no requirement for reciprocity on the part of Castro. Indeed, every proposal indicates a decidedly indifferent view toward genuine reciprocity. Fidel might welcome an infusion of money; he would not welcome the sort of free market society implied by such recommendations. Behind the veil of humanitarianism is the arrogance of power, exercised unilaterally, and prospects of Cuban society getting beyond Castro.

The second basket concerns the spread of information and new ideas. Operating under the presumption that the free flow of ideas alone will produce contagious results, the task force advocates issuing a general license for travel to Cuba by all Americans, making federal funds available for people-to-people exchanges to promote growth in non-governmental institutions in Cuba, and direct commercial flights and ship service between major American cities and Havana, Santiago, and Camagüey in Cuba. At this point, there is a subtle shift in baskets (clusters of issues) from human rights concerns to an entire revision of U.S. foreign policy. The assumptions are startling. The Cuban government is presumed to be willing to open its small cities as well as Havana to free travel, and even to permit its citizenry free access to the Internet and other forms of the new information technology. All evidence indicates the reverse to be the case—Cuban policy in these areas is to restrict communication and travel alike. Levels of repression have increased, not decreased, in the past several years.

Beyond the absence of any requirement of reciprocity is a leap of faith: the assumption that dictatorship will evolve into democracy as a consequence of open exchanges. Castro's continued insistence on a single leader, single party and managed economy argues against such undue optimism. One should assume that Castro would accept all sorts of arrangements with respect to expanded travel and yet continue the monolithic power he has exercised for 40-plus years. A basic flaw in the Report's assumptions is the notion that there is an inexorable transition "from communism to democracy" once any changes is initiated. It is true that this has occurred on a selective basis in Eastern Europe, with mixed results, especially in Russia. The Chinese case is more instructive. Indeed, the Chinese model, studied so vigorously by the Cuban leadership, allows for just such "open windows" at the economic level, while maintaining tight controls at the political level. A more accurate representation of the *optimal* changes in

the short run is a transition from dictatorial to civic—or civilian—rule. There is a large jump from dictatorship to civic society,
but an even larger one between civic societies organized along
authoritarian lines and those with democracy as a goal. Given
the fact that Castro's Cuba has repeatedly and unambiguously
rejected even modest accommodations toward civil rule, the
unstated expectations of the Aronson-Rogers Report can most
generously be described as utopian.

The third basket offered in the Report pertains to security.
More directly, it concerns the role of the military in "moving
down the road to civilian control in a future democratic state."
If the second basket is best viewed as utopian, this third basket
can only be described as incredibly myopic. The idea that the
Cuban military can assume such an independent political role
ignores everything from its origins as the guerrilla movement, to
the ideological cleansing of its armed forces following the Ochoa
affair, in the late 1980s. The Ochoa affair resulted in the breakdown rather than an extension of professionalization within the
Cuban armed forces. Over time, the armed forces have become
more, not less, allied to the dictatorship. In essence they are the
Praetorian Guard of the Castro regime.

This third bundle of goodies is divided into a simple triad:
military-to-military contacts, the continuation of counternar-
cotics contacts, and cooperation on mutual interests in regional
security. Each of these proposals is so preposterous that it would
take a man from Mars not to recognize them as such. To start
with, military-to-military contacts, even if they were permitted,
would be extraordinarily dangerous without the total commitment to such a project by Castro and the party leadership. This
is unlikely not only because of continuing U.S.-Cuba hostilities,
but also the strong opposition of the Organization of American
States (OAS) to Cuban expansionism and adventurism in the
hemisphere over the years. Any Cuban officer seeking to establish
direct contact with the U.S. military would more likely be shot
for treason by Castro rather than celebrated for his forward-
looking vision.

If one takes the Ochoa affair at face value, it appears that major figures in the Cuban armed forces were themselves deeply immersed in narco-trafficking. The possibility that Castro himself has been involved in the narcotics trade makes the Cuban armed forces an improbable partner in the hemispheric struggle against drugs trafficking. As for mutual interests in regional security, this depends on whose security the Aronson-Rogers Report has in mind. At the moment, the Castro government sees its "security" as allied with the new dictatorship of Hugo Chavez in Venezuela. Both consider the guerrilla movements in Colombia and Peru that threaten stability and civic rule in both countries as potential allies. It has always been the dream of Fidel to build a revolutionary alliance along the northern tier of South America, a modern-day Bolivarist united front against the United States and its Monroe Doctrine. To put forth as a serious proposal the idea of Cuban participation in a common front of "friendly nations" that would provide regional security—against the longstanding allies of Castro no less—is at best naïve, and at worst dangerous. This is an astonishing example of disconnectedness between the Report's policy proposals and the empirical realities in the outside world. In this report the two never meet.

The fourth (and happily) final basket pertains to trade, investment, and property and labor rights. Here, one must acknowledge that here a degree of realism filters through the cloud of ideological baggage. Certain humanitarian measures have already been implemented, such as the termination of sanctions on food and medicine exports. The second element, the export of informational products such as books, diskettes, and intellectual property in general, is, as the report acknowledges, already part of American foreign policy. Existing regulations are minimal on the part of the United States. The major limitation is impediments to the free distribution of information in Cuba. Even the establishment of private libraries has become an issue throughout Cuba. Castro has been bitterly resistant to any show of an open society, as evidenced by his monitoring of information allowed to enter Cuba, and the arrest and detention of foreign nationals for so much as collecting or disseminating information. Once again as throughout the Report, its authors failed to appreciate the host, in this case, the recalcitrant ruler of Cuba, Fidel Castro. The problem with Cuba is not training in high technology but access of its people to any technology.

The final point, resolving expropriation claims, is well articulated and judiciously stated. The Report is correct: a forward-looking strategy is the best. For rather than require reimbursements for expropriations and brand-name piracy as a requirement by the Cuban government, it is far wiser to develop a plan that permits Cuba to earn the money needed to satisfy U.S. claims through future business activity—both within Cuba and on a worldwide basis. Whether property settlements are made on a company-to-company basis or a government-to-government basis is less important than the presence in Havana of a regime that is willing and able to support such negotiations. The elements of dialogue being proposed—extending from licensing American business activities to enlarging the rights of the Cuban workers—are certainly negotiable. The question is, with whom?

It is evident from the sheer space this basket of recommendations is given in the Report that the Aronson-Rogers group sees the business community as the soft underbelly of American policy. The desire to expand and grow is a universal commercial trait. It is not surprising that the Report devotes so much attention to business ends. Efforts to enlarge the rights of laboring men and women and people of color are within the framework of business goals as is the proposal to have American universities establish management training and labor rights institutes. One fears however, that such proposals would make sense only in a post-communist and post-Castro situation. The idea that Castro—the last great ideologue of Communism—would sanction advanced training in business management, should bring a wry smile to the faces of those members of the Council on Foreign Relations commission who have any awareness of the regime over the last 42 years.

That brings the discussion back to square one: how should the United States deal with the Castro regime? The Report supports the Cuban observer status at the World Bank and the Inter-American Development Bank. Its one sign of opposition to a capitulation is the recommendation that membership of Cuba in the Organization of American States be withheld. The underlying question is how long the Castro dictatorship as such will continue to exist. Castro's Cuba is not simply a communist regime doggedly determined to survive in a sea of capitalist opposition, but one that continues to believe that the United States and Western democracy will collapse. Castro continues to assert that communism represents the future—the end of the USSR and the rise of capitalist regimes in Eastern Europe notwithstanding.

Whatever the sources of Castro's vision: ideological rigidity, long-standing animosity for the United States, or belief in the political value of his position, the plain fact is that he offers a unilateralist policy posture. There is to be no trade-off, bargaining or bartering with the United States. Sanctions are to be terminated and the embargo lifted without even a semblance or appearance of a quid quo pro. The Aronson-Rogers reports simply accept these premises, one that requires no action on the part of Castro either in the field of free elections and parties or in the simpler terrain of the free market. There is more than the faint whiff of the Neville Chamberlain approach to Adolf Hitler and Nazi Germany at Munich in 1938: acquiesce in the demands of the dictator and he will soften his stance and see the values of reason and rejoining the community of civilized nations. While far less is at stake in 2001 Cuba than 1938 Germany, the same presumptions of rationality and civility obtain. And while this might buy short term pacification of the region, it does little with respect to long range goals of the United States, or for that matter immediate aims of the Cuban people for a democratic society. In warming relations with the Castro dictatorship, the Aronson-Rogers approach is freezing the situation with the Cuban nation.

No doubt the Aronson-Rogers group has received a plethora of private assurances from Castro and his cohort that these proposals would be fairly received if proffered by the American government. But so too have a myriad of groups through the last four decades received similar private assurances. What remain in place are the public utterances, and the political mobilization demands of the Castro regime. What is said in public at high noon in public squares and not at private parties at post-midnight soirees is the ultimate test of how to judge the credibility of a regime in sorrow as well as in opposition, one can only say that the record indicates this Report, the latest and perhaps most powerful assault on American foreign policy toward Cuba over the decades, can go nowhere It will prove an embarrassment to its sponsors, and to those who signed on to this document and should know better.

References/Notes

1. Alton Frye (project director), *Humanitarian Intervention: Crafting a Workable Doctrine*. New York: Council on Foreign Relations, 2000, 94 pp.
2. Bernard W. Aronson and William D. Rogers (co-chairs), *U.S.-Cuban Relations in the 21st Century: A Follow-Up Report of the Independent Task Force on U.S.-Cuban Relations* (draft report first issued on October 10, 2000, public announcement made on November 29th, 2000).
3. Irving Louis Horowitz, *Searching for the Soul of American Foreign Policy: The Cuban Embargo and the National Interest*. [Testimony delivered before the House Committee on International Relations, March 24, 1999.] Published in the Occasional Papers Series, Institute for Cuban and Cuban-American Studies, University of Miami, September 2000).

Source and Original Title: "Humanitarian Capitulation: U.S.-Cuba Relations According to the Council on Foreign Relations." *The St. Croix Review.* Vol. XXXIV, No. 1, February 2001, pp. 46-52. Published simultaneously as "Humanitarian Capitulation: U.S.-Cuba Relations According to the Council on Foreign Relations." *Vital Speeches of the Day.* Volume LXVII, Number 11, March 15, 2001, pp. 329-332.

40

One Hundred Years of Ambiguity: U.S.-Cuba Relations in the 20th Century

Henry Adams in *The Education of Henry Adams*, wrote in 1905, more than a century ago, that "double standards are inspiration to men of letters, but they are apt to be fatal to politicians.... Modern politics is, at bottom, a struggle not of men but of forces. The men become every year more and more creatures of force, massed about central powerhouses. The conflict is no longer between the men, but between the motors that drive the men and the men tend to succumb to their own motive forces" (Chapter XXVIII).

What brings this to mind is the seemingly endless discussion and ink spilled to determine whether Fidel Castro was a Communist before his seizure of power in 1959, or whether he became one at some later date. While the results are inconclusive, what is certain is that Castro was a Cuban nationalist long before the triumph of the July 26th Movement. Understanding Castro's Cuba therefore requires examination of that nationalism—its historical roots and its political consequences—as much or more than examination of Castro's communism. This, in turn, obliges us to study the imperfect origins of independence in Cuba itself. Such study requires a century-long retrospective, not just a look at the 42 years in which the Castro regime has held political power.

Two dates stand out in the American-Cuban relationship: 1898 (the year Spain surrendered Cuba to the United States following the Spanish-American War), and 1959 (the year the Soviet shadow to the Cuban Revolution ended any chance of resolving the contentious issues dividing Havana and Washington). There are other critical dates in Cuban internal political dynamics, such as 1925–33, the period of the Gerardo Machado dictatorship, and 1934–59, the populist-militarist era of the Fulgencio Batista dictatorship. But they do not matter nearly as much as 1898 and 1959, which is a sad reflection of the fact that, unlike most other countries, Cuba's political history has been marked by popular passivity and hence a tendency toward largely undisturbed military and then totalitarian rule.

Despite the importance and drama of the Spanish-American War, 1902 is a better starting date for this narrative than 1898 because it was only after the four years of American colonial hegemony that Cuba could begin to define its status as an independent nation. The four-year interregnum between 1898 and 1902 demonstrates the simple fact that real liberation, much less democracy, cannot be given—certainly not by the armed forces of an occupying power. National independence must be earned; it must be won against opposition. What the United States was able to provide, and the wisest thing in its power to grant, was schooling in the practices of a free and autonomous society. The Cubans were allowed to act as if they had won and created some of the basic rights and duties of a democratic nation. The immediate consequence of this was to heighten a note of ambiguity in a political situation already less than clear-cut.

As it happened, Cuba has been unable, ever since 1902, to clarify its status *vis-à-vis* the United States. This was not entirely the fault of Cubans. The native Cuban regime in 1902 was established under the ostensible protection of the Platt Amendment, which was terminated only in 1934 as a part of the Good Neighbor Policy. Thus, in 1902 and 1934, not much less than in 1898 and 1959—and, of course, in October 1962—external forces rather than internal actors determined the course of Cuba's national existence. Around these dates one may plot, so to speak, Cuba's one hundred years of ambiguity.

Cuba has never been the master of its own fate in its independence struggles. Without minimizing the bitterness of the Cuban popular classes against Spanish colonial rule—or, for that matter, the bravery of the Cuban guerrillas who fought the best troops of the Spanish empire—the plain fact of the matter is that the United States and Spain set the terms of Cuban independence. Native forms of national struggle were not entirely absent; indeed, by 1897 it became evident that the Spaniards were unable to impose a purely political or legal solution on the island, and that raw military force was required. In such circumstances, the indigenous resistance in Cuba could not hope to achieve more than a military stalemate—at least in the short term—without external intervention, whether the resistance wanted it or not.

In such a vacuum of power, the United States was able to extend as well as to impose its Monroe Doctrine over a Spanish colony. It did so first by insisting on a pacific solution that did not require outright subjugation of the native peoples and then, when it became apparent that Spain did not have a civil administrative infrastructure that could impose such an outcome without using military force, moved to intervene directly. Spain's frailty thus allowed President McKinley to move into the power vacuum in fairly simple fashion—something that his predecessor, Grover Cleveland, resisted doing. But nothing has been simple since. In 1902 Cuba became a relatively independent nation, modeled after the United States in its formal apparatus of government. The arguments over the one hundred years since 1902 confirm the use of the term "relative." Radicals argue that "relative" means that Cuba enjoyed little true independence. Conservatives claim that all sovereignty, especially for a small nation with a single-crop economy, is necessarily relative.

One of the few scholars writing on Cuba who deeply appreciated this ambiguous legacy is Hugh Thomas. In an essay focusing on the Batista era, he stated the historical situation frankly:

Cuba was not China or Nicaragua. It was a state whose independence from Spain in 1898 was in effect secured for it by the United States as a result of the Spanish-American war. As such, Cuba's freedom of action was limited for 30 years (1902–34) under the Platt Amendment, enabling the United States to intervene legally in the island's internal affairs under certain circumstances. Such intervention occurred several times—in 1906, 1912, 1917, and 1933. Although after 1933 the country's industries and services were increasingly "Cubanized" by local entrepreneurs, much of the aura of the old days still hung about U.S. Cuban relations in the 1950s.

Thomas goes on to note that "Cuban national history read by students at the University of Havana revived memories of the early part of the century, when U.S. business involvement promoted the rapid economic development of the island and at the same time put a damper on the rhetorical romantic Cuban nationalism articulated by José Martí during two ruthless wars against Spain (1868–78 and 1895–98)."[1] Castro was indoctrinated by this special reductionist reading of Cuban-American history—that U.S. domination repressed Cuban national aspirations.

The problem for Cuba, after securing its independence, was the ambiguity of the outcome. It achieved a result that it desired without devising a method for accomplishing it. The result was that regimes in Cuba from 1902 through 1959 wrestled with a dilemma that they could not resolve. A group of democratic reforms introduced in 1933 was identified with Machado and represented a step toward securing greater autonomy, for on their account the Platt Amendment was soon lifted. But the reforms fell prey to a series of coups and were weakened further by the illegitimacy of the Batista regime. Instead of resolving matters either with regard to Cuba's political culture or relations with the United States, the Batista dictatorship was halfhearted and inconclusive, like so many earlier regimes. Into such a situation Fidel Castro came to power—not as living vindication of Marxism-Leninism, but as part of an effort to move Cuba beyond ambiguity and to nationalist closure, and, in consequence beyond the suffocating sphere of American influence.

The absence of closure before 1959 clearly helps to explain the ferocity of Castro's resentment of the United States. This resentment is not simply a consequence of generic factors (big power versus small power, or Anglo versus Hispanic cultures). Rather it is a result of the specific history of Cuba and its intersection with the United States from 1898 to the present. In a nutshell: the United States invaded Cuban soil and, no less, liberated it from the Spanish empire. Castro's May Day speech of 2001 indicates his unbending hostility toward and suspicion of the United States. He denounces hemispheric trade agreements as "annexation." He says such a free trade "would mean more neo-liberalism, less protection for industry and national interests, and more unemployment and social problems. National currencies would disappear to be replaced by the dollar, and all monetary policy across the region would be dictated by the U.S. Federal Reserve."[2] The distant echo of the Platt Amendment can be heard in his remarks. It is not simply a policy difference, but a psychological distance that is reflected in Castro's words. How this came about is worth reviewing.

Pivotal to any analysis of this history is the fact that in the year 2002—one hundred years after Cuba's acquisition of independence and more than 42 years after the imposition of Communist dictatorship—one can still speak of Cuba in terms of a single-crop economy, although the sugar crop is sweetened by other revenue streams. However one feels, or better said, to whatever one ascribes the causes, the fact is that Cuba is an economy dominated by "dollarization", and tourism is a major source of income. The classical situation of small nations of the Caribbean—still extant in Cuba—is indicative of the hard truth that the politics and ideology of Marxism-Leninism comprise a sort of fool's gold, a fantasyland of autonomy. The Castro regime is strong enough to goad the United States but weak enough to require appeals for aid to other Western powers. The writing of this scenario was already on the wall with the Cuban missile crisis, which was precipitated as well as settled by the major contestants in the Cold War. The turf may have been Cuban, but the decision-making had distinctly Russian- and English-speaking voices. Listen to the analysis of Adam B. Ulam, perhaps the sharpest Sovietologist of his time, of the events of October 1962:

> Riding Russian coattails brought security rather than solution for the Castro dictatorship. It created a transitional equilibrium that became permanent more through inertia than design. And so it was with the Cuban Revolution of 1959. That cataclysmic event finalized the resentment and focused the animosity toward the United States for its involvement in Cuban affairs. It did not provide a solution in 1902 that satisfied either democrats or autocratic landholders within Cuba, nor did it bring to closure the sense of solitude and isolation that Marxism promises in theory, but that Leninism-Stalinism took away in practice.[3]

Left-wing scholars take the view that if there had been no U.S. invasion or occupation, Cuba would have ridden the coattails of the 1895 uprising toward full autonomy. In this view, the sinking of the U.S.S. *Maine* in Havana Harbor on February 15, 1898, with a heavy loss of American lives, provided President McKinley with a pretext to intervene in the conflict. The demands were for Spain to terminate its concentration camp policy, offer an armistice to Cuban rebels, and accept the United States as a final arbiter between the parties. Cuban independence was not mentioned. Benjamin Keen and Mark Wasserman develop an interesting view—one that parallels Fidelista historiography:

> The ensuing war was short and nasty. American commanders ignored their Cuban counterparts, excluding Cuban generals from decision making and relegating Cuban soldiers to sentry and clean-up duties. Incompetence was the dominant feature of both the Spanish and American war effort. American military actions were incredibly ill prepared and badly led. The only major land battle of the war, the famous charge up San Juan Hill, which helped to catapult Theodore Roosevelt to national prominence, was very nearly a catastrophic defeat for the United States. Spain, to some extent, defeated itself, for its generals believed the war lost from the beginning and sought above all to minimize their losses. Thus, in a bizarre little war, the United States Army, wretchedly led, scandalously provisioned, and ravaged by tropical disease, swiftly defeated a demoralized, dispirited Spanish army and snatched the fruits of victory from the Mambises, the Cuban guerrilla fighters who had fought gallantly in a struggle of three years duration. The

exclusion of Cuban leaders from both war councils and peace negotiations foreshadowed the course of Cuban-American relations for the next sixty years.[4]

The unspoken assumption in this account of events, in which Spaniards—and especially Americans—marginalize Cubans, is that Castro put an end to such humiliation. But he did no such thing. The negotiations between the United States and the USSR over the missile installations aptly demonstrated that Castro had no more input in the solution than the Cuban guerrilla leader Antonio Maceo had in the settlement between the United States and Spain. The further presumption is that, if left to their own devices, Cubans would have put an end to Spanish rule. Such an outcome was certainly the wish of José Martí, Antonio Maceo and Máximo Gómez, but whether that wish would have become reality is problematic. Under the direction of General Valeriano Weyler, Spanish military policy shifted to anti-guerrilla tactics. The Spaniards then drove back the Cuban revolutionists to the eastern end of the island. All seemed lost until the U.S. military bailout. What we do know for certain is that the interregnum ended in May 1902 with the voluntary departure of the U.S. military and the declaration of a free and sovereign Cuba.

A quite different, conservative reading of the same events comes to us from Milton Eisenhower, the brother of Dwight D. Eisenhower and a diplomat and educator in his own right. Milton Eisenhower viewed the American intervention as an appropriate response to Spanish imposition of taxes and other restrictions on direct trade in sugar and tobacco between Cuba and the United States. He saw this as parallel to the American pre-Revolutionary War slogan of "no taxation without representation." Indeed, Eisenhower goes so far as to declare Spanish cruelties as "forerunners of Hitler's mass executions in World War II." In this situation, Cuba "seemed a natural ally if not a dependency of ours." While there is a big gap between an ally and a dependent state, and while trade irritants hardly seem sufficient cause for an invasion, it is worthwhile listening to this voice of American rationalism:

For four years following the victory over Spain in 1898, the United States maintained military rule in Cuba. This seemed essential, for the former colonials had had no experience in self-government. Our military control was honorable. Local governments, the courts, and other public agencies were improved. Progress in agriculture, education, health (especially in the campaign to eliminate yellow fever), transportation, trade, and general living standards was noticeable but not notable. There was little if any serious thought given to changing inherited social customs. The Cuban people themselves did not then seek such change. Most of them wanted independence—only large landowners objecting—and they got it, with qualifications in 1902. The limitation on independence was the Platt Amendment to our treaty with Cuba. In the ensuing years of quasi-independence, Cuba suffered the indignity of numerous interventions by the United States, saw most of its own Presidents promise honesty and reform only to fatten their own pockets, lived in fear of slaughter by military and guerrilla leaders, and came to accept betrayal as an inevitable condition of government.[5]

The range of professional opinion across the political spectrum, then, confirms this uneasy sense of ambiguity in Cuban national life. All recognize that the United States served as both colonial master of the Western Hemisphere and also democratic liberator from colonialism. Fernand Braudel sees this duality as a function of the "degree of isolationism that has been a basic feature of the United States."[6] Carl Becker, while bemoaning the less-than-sterling conduct of American intervention, nonetheless sees such behavior in terms of a defense of "democratic institutions to which America was committed" and opposition to "the extension of the European political system [Becker's italics] to this continent."[7] Raymond Aron considers the United States guilty of "a great power policy, even an imperialist policy in the ordinary sense of the term." This classical colonial policy was followed by a more recent policy of benign, or not so benign, neglect of Latin America. Aron goes on to say that "a sense of geography and memories of the past are at the root of these [American] feelings and this behavior."[8] More recently, Henry Kissinger noted that, by the start of the twentieth century, "America found itself commanding the sort of power which made it a major international factor, no matter what its preferences." In short, from the Monroe Doctrine to the Platt Amendment, the United States was pursuing a policy of "national interest" and not just "remaining un-entangled" in its immediate neighborhood.[9] Each of these statements is a variation on the same contradictory theme: America simultaneously as dictator and liberator.

Clearly, in these two views the moral glass of American power is seen as half empty on the far Left and more than half full on the conservative Right. Perhaps no one caught the spirit of ambiguity more ably than Hubert Herring, who in his great History of Latin America wrote that the Cuban Republic from 1902–34 "was now free—but not free to make her own mistakes."[10] He added philosophically that "a clear lesson on the education of nations, as of children, [is] that none learns to order its life unless granted the privilege of going wrong as well as of going right." Projections of what might have been notwithstanding, it are a fact of history that Cuban independence was granted and not earned. This may be viewed as a bitter fact of island history, or a tribute to a people on a small island navigating colonial forces far larger than itself. What is no less evident is a Cuban Revolution of 1959 that saw itself as settling accounts with the legacy of 1898–1902. Castro's strength is less a function of the authority of Marxism-Leninism as an ideology than of an unrequited nationalism as a mobilization tool.

From the outset, Castro had an image of Cuba as larger than life as, certainly larger as the life of the island. From the start, Castro's self-image was that of Simón Bolívar in an era of communism. He sought to bring the future to the entire hemisphere—if not on horseback, like Bolívar, then as a foot soldier in the mountains. Castro was and remains the embodiment of nationalism tinged by a greater, if ultimately counterfeit, internationalism. The fusion of the two was solidified by the ideology of Marxism-Leninism in the form of the tradition of the

Comintern—centered in Havana rather than in Moscow. In each decade, from the Tri-continental in the 1960s through a variety of conferences over the next 40 years, Castro maintained that his position was properly in the vanguard, not the backwater, of revolutionary consciousness. So while foreign intervention and great-power intrigue pockmarked the history of Cuba from 1898 to 1959, the history of Cuba after 1959 was supposed to turn this around and make Cuba a world political actor—militarily, diplomatically and otherwise (such as through its international medical teams).

This effort has had modest results. On the one side, there was the removal of nuclear warheads from Cuba as a result of a Soviet-American deal, the embarrassment of Cuban troops participating in a losing effort in the Syrian Golan Heights, the humiliating defeat of Cuban troops in Grenada, the routing of the Cuban military presence in Angola and Namibia. These initiatives, aimed at reinforcing Castro's role in world affairs, failed in frustration and loss of prestige. But on the other hand, Cuba has had a tremendous impact on hemispheric affairs: for example, from the Venezuela of guerrilla Douglas Bravo to the Venezuela of President Hugo Chávez. Castro's impact on the Nicaraguan Left is widely recognized. Alliances have been forged with China for advanced military supplies, replacing those lost with the collapse of the Soviet Union. Training and arming Palestinians from the PLO forces is ongoing. There is scarcely a dictatorship in the world—from Kim Il Sung's in North Korea to Muammar Qadaffi's in Libya—that has not enjoyed the benefit of Castro's warm embrace. As the late Arthur P. Whitaker predicted as long ago as 1962, "although Cuba's ties with the Communist bloc make it difficult to appraise the difference between the two, Fidelismo is probably a greater potential threat as communism to the interests of the United States in Latin America. This is because Fidelismo expressed so well and for so long the rising Latin American tide of both continental nationalism and populism."[11]

However, what neither Whitaker nor Thomas could have anticipated was that national interests and populism would develop in Central and South America along an autonomous axis different from anything envisioned by Fidel Castro—or, for that matter, by Simón Bolívar. What has actually occurred, to Castro's obvious and public chagrin, is the development of international alliances at the political level, and regional and global market relations that extend far beyond the borders of nations in North or South America. Everything from telephone companies to oil drilling arrangements has changed the old system. Latin America is no longer a decidedly junior partner to North America. It is simply a partner whose size and scope depends upon investment prospects and corporate profits.

What has drastically reduced the significance of Castro as a player in global affairs is not a direct assault on Cuba's shores, but the sheer capacity of most other Latin American nation simply to bypass Cuba on its own road to a new twenty-first century. Henry Adams' "forces" are indeed at work. While Cuba remains a force to contend with, its xenophobic nationalism has institutionalized an economic backwardness that has in turn created a diplomatic impasse. Cuba is now isolated from the trends sweeping the region. Bolstered by revitalized democracies from Mexico to Brazil, Latin America is undergoing a degree of economic integration unforeseen by the allies of the United States and unnoticed by its enemies. Economic upheaval notwithstanding, the situation in 2002 is profoundly more favorable to the forces of hemispheric democracy than it was in 1961, or for that matter throughout the 1960s and 1970s. This illustrates Fidel's myopia as the century of ambiguity nears its end. Post-Castro Cuba will become part of an extraordinary hemispheric vitalization in which the fabled ogre of U.S. domination is absent. The problem of Cuban nationalism and jealousy for its sovereignty will be bound up in choices concerning hemispheric multilateralism, not obeisance to a new Platt Amendment. The long-term positive future of Cuba is neither utopian nor ideological. Rather, it is normalization in the best sense of politics, and rationalization in the best sense of economics.

References/Notes

1. Thomas, "Cuba, The United States and Batista, 1952–1958", in Irving Louis Horowitz and Jaime Suchlicki, eds., *Cuban Communism* (10th edition) (New Brunswick and London: Transaction Publishers, 2001), pp. 3–12.
2. Quoted in the *New York Times,* May 2, 2001.
3. *Ulam, The Rivals: America and Russia since World War II* (New York: The Viking Press, 1971), pp. 330–40.
4. Benjamin Keen and Mark Wasserman, *A Short History of Latin America* (Boston: Houghton Mifflin Company, 1984), pp. 408–9.
5. Eisenhower, *The Wine is Bitter: The United States and Latin America* (Garden City, NY: Doubleday & Co., 1963), pp. 296–7.
6. Braudel, *A History of Civilizations* (New York: Penguin, 1995), pp. 496–7.
7. Becker, *The United States: An Experiment in Democracy* (New Brunswick and London: Transaction Publishers, 2001), pp. 134–5.
8. Aron, *The Imperial Republic: The United States and the World,* 1945–1973 (Cambridge, MA: Winthrop, 1974), p. 185.
9. Kissinger, *Diplomacy* (New York: Simon & Schuster, 1994), pp. 37–40.
10. Herring, *A History of Latin America: From the Beginnings to the Present* (2nd edition) (New York: Alfred A. Knopf, 1962), pp. 401–16.
11. Whitaker, *Nationalism in Latin America: Past and Present* (Gainesville, FL: University Press of Florida, 1962), pp. 69–70.

Source and Original Title: "One Hundred Years of Ambiguity: U.S. – Cuba Relations in the 20th Century," *The National Interest.* Whole Number 67, Spring 2002, pp. 58-64.

41

The Conflict between Economy and Ideology in Cuban Communism

Long Term Perspectives

From the very outset of Cuban Communism, predictions of its demise were made—sometimes quietly, and at other times as a crescendo of self-declared expertise. But over and against what *should* have taken place, a countertendency emerged—since no such counterrevolution occurred, none *could* take place. Blaise Pascal, in his *Thoughts* (Number 332) caught the dynamic of the conflict between reality and utopia as it operates in dictatorship. "Tyranny consists in the desire of universal power beyond its scope."

In some measure such predictive extremes between the reality of the mundane and the utopia of the fantastic, were a reflection of the passions the Castro era has generated in his people. Hope replaced reason and passion displaced evidence. The polity itself was reduced to silence. In such an environment, the accurate measurement of events has been very difficult. Even if one believes, as I most emphatically do, that a free society is far superior to a totalitarian one, such a statement of values, however personally satisfying does not replace the need for careful, factual analysis.

However important the history, politics, economics and social structure of Cuba may be to the study of the present, it is also the case that the desire to know, nay predict, the future of Castro's Cuba remains a subtext in a great deal of analysis disguised as purely objective. The steady drumbeat of essays and articles on the "transition" of Cuba attests to precisely this brew of what exists and what we want to exist.

One of the grand luxuries of wealthy and large nations is their ability to develop a division of policy labors. As a result, we have an entity called "foreign policy" and another called "domestic policy" or sometimes "national policy." Small and dependent nations like Cuba really do not have such luxuries either of definitions or actions. When we look at Cuba today—the forty-fourth year of the Castro regime—what we observe is a mélange of events superimposed on one another. To some degree these are domestic policies driven by foreign exigencies, and in other instances, one finds foreign adventures that drive domestic affairs. Whatever the causal chain may be, the fusion and the interaction of domestic and foreign, national and international, is increasingly a hallmark of small nations, none more so than Cuba since 1959.

Indeed, it is a high irony of Castro that friend and foe alike harbor a certain admiration for his unwillingness to resign himself to such a sizing down. Yet, the wear and tear of trying to achieve grandeur in a context of small nationhood has finally proven too much even for Fidel. That he felt the need in mid-2002 to respond to the Varela Project—a modest effort to petition for a new referendum—by insisting upon a massive show of inflated support, attests to the prospect that time is running out on *el comandante*. The laws of entropy are greater than even his massive ego can resist. The establishment of 120,000 petition stations across Cuba, and the mobilization of seven to eight million people, or roughly one hundred percent of people on the island over 16 years of age, does little to reassure the rest of the world. More importantly, it does little to assuage the Cuban people themselves that this call for a constitutional amendment declaring Cuba's presumably "Marxist socialist" economic, political, and social system to be inviolable and unchangeable, is worth any more than the paper on which the petitions are printed. Underlining the present moment of regime desperation are economic circumstances over which Castro has little influence.

Cuba during 44 years of Communism has proven woefully unable to break the shackles of a single-crop economy. It has continued to rely on one crop, sugar, to supply other requirements for the society. Two main factors have limited the impact of such a policy: the continued plummeting of world sugar prices due to a glutted market caused by global overproduction, and of greater consequence, the severe deterioration of Cuban sugar mills themselves. Despite mobilization of the state apparatus, the sugar harvest is only slightly more than in previous years. Since the collapse of the Soviet Union, the sugar production of Cuba has plummeted from 8.1 million tons in 1989 (the last year of Soviet subsidies) to the present level of about 3.6 million tons. Cuba is now undertaking a program of closing 71 out of 156 currently operating mills. The breakdown of equipment, the inability of Cuba to maintain any sort of technological competition with other nations, has led to a situation in which falling production now reflects declining world prices. The limited ability to purchase oil with sugar has now reached crisis proportions.

To further complicate matters, the tourist industry that was to pick up the slack in sugar production, suffered greatly after the terrorist bombings of the World Trade Center and the Pentagon on September 11, 2001. For the first half of 2002, tourism to Cuba was off 14 percent from the same period one year earlier. Again, the problem is not simply the international decline in air traffic, but the relatively unattractive situation in Cuba with respect to tourist facilities. People on holidays are not looking for political slogans so much as pleasant personal situations for a limited time. The malaise of the national economy of Cuba feeds into polarizing consequences. The service sector displaces the production sector in the search for surplus. Indeed, in an effort to attract European tourists, the Cuban economic ministry has said it would allow the Euro currency to circulate alongside the U.S.

dollar. But even this has a cost to the regime. It heightens the already considerable gap between have and have not individuals, namely, those who benefit from foreign currency speculation and exchange from those confined to the domestic Cuban currency. The idea of a "Marxist" regime heightening the gaps between people in the economic and social realms is clearly an unanticipated consequence of the desperate search for new sources of state revenues.

A third element in Cuban life that both props the economy and unbalances any prospects for stability is the remission of considerable sums of money from Cuban Americans to relatives and families in Cuba proper. Such remittances, estimated by *The Economist* to total $800 million annually at the start of 2003, provide the regime with much needed hard currencies with which to make critical foreign payments and purchases. However, it also "dollarizes" the economy. As a consequence, the internal gulf between haves and have-nots is further exaggerated, making for a strain within the economic and social stratification of Cuban society that can hardly be addressed, much less resolved. Foreign currency remissions pushes further back what was once the primary goal of Castro's regime: the creation of an egalitarian society—even at low levels of earnings and opportunities.

As an indicator of how deeply global events have disrupted the national economy, one needs look at the Venezuela coup and counter-coup. Although Venezuela President Hugo Chávez has managed to retain state power, the dubious price of doing so was restoring some semblance of rationality to Venezuela's oil-based economy. Before the golpe, Venezuela supplied Cuba with more than 50,000 barrels of oil a day—about a third of the island's requirements. Much of this was to be financed at a two percent rate of interest over a 15-year time frame. One of the first pronouncements during the brief spell that Chávez was out of office was an announcement by Petróleos de Venezuela that the Venezuelan nation would immediately cease the shipment of petroleum to Cuba. While it was assumed that ideology would trump economy once again, and Chávez would restore shipments to Castro, the strikes and turmoil that have gripped Venezuela under its military dictatorial period frustrated such resumption. The Cuban government has confirmed that it has received few recent petroleum benefits from Venezuela. Moreover, it has been forced to turn to the spot market and spend "dozens of millions" of dollars in order to obtain oil. The instability of the Chávez regime at this point makes it difficult to predict whether any meaningful or permanent resumption of petroleum shipments from Venezuela to Cuba can take place.

It would be illusory to presume that economic reality will displace political despotism. Indeed, such "economic determinism" has continually been proven wrong in the past. Nonetheless, Cuba's current economic distress coupled with even modest political resistance and social disorder, makes the prospects for closure of the Castro era appear considerably closer at hand than at any time in the past 44 years. Certainly, it is now reasonable to consider a variety of scenarios for a transitional government after the termination of the Castro regime. The great strength of Castro has been a network of political organizations, from the block level to the women and youth brigades that owe a special allegiance to the regime for its central position in the society. But this depends heavily on some form of reward system—less than for the upper echelons of the armed forces, but still real—from privileges in newly constructed housing units to job favoritism working in industries that have contact with foreign, such as hotel waiters and bank managers.

But even if the system cannot readily be toppled by economic rationality, the problem for Castro and his associates remains real: how to maintain ideological fervor and street-level mobilization in a downwardly spiraling political economy. The limits of charisma should be sorely tested in the near term. Nonetheless, the failure to institutionalize the revolution, to move to a next generation of top echelon political leadership, does not necessarily spell the end of the regime as such. The emergence of dynastic communism, of a hierarchy built upon patronage and family ties, has proven resilient in places as far removed as North Korea and Syria, and is clearly what the Castro brothers envision for Cuba. It will hardly be the first time in history that personal vanity tinged by a sense of infallibility could result less in reform than in reaction, but this pattern of continuing dictatorship might itself also serve as a long-term trigger to rebellion and restitution of democratic norms. With the rest of Latin America serving as on-lookers to Cuba's collapse, rather than active supporters, the time for change in Cuba may actually be closer at hand than skeptics might imagine. In any event, the play of national and global forces has now reached a stage that can hardly be met, much less resolved, by manifestations of support or cooked-up signature drives to assure the great dictator that he still sits, albeit uneasily, on his proletarian throne.

The primary evidence for a necessary, if indeed insufficient, cause for such a systemic collapse is the woeful performance of the Cuban economy. Despite the regime's total dedication to maintain the peso as the currency of the nation, it declined 22.7 percent in 2001, with the same tendencies taking place in 2002. Indeed, the situation has worsened as a result of the decline in tourism from Europe and the deterioration of sugar revenues as mentioned above. A July 2002 report filed from Havana by Marc Frank on behalf of Reuters News Agency declares that "the dollar would be trading at 40 pesos to the dollar if not for a government imposed freeze on the exchange rate." The difficulty is that in the managed Cuban economy, the government is spending more money while declining revenues indicate lower solvency. It is evident that the return to solvency of the last decade has run out of steam in the present decade. As a result, it is hardly an exaggeration to say that Cuba is long in a protracted period best described as a crisis in the socialist state economy—that sector that employs more than 90 percent of the labor force.

The political contradictions within the Cuban system have become irrevocable. For the sham vote of 99.7 percent of Cuban people signing onto an amendment to the Constitution making the socialist system irrevocable, only served to highlight the brittle character of the regime. The imaginary support for Castro exceeds even the fantasies of Stalin's popular vote during the heyday of the Soviet terror. What this points to is an insoluble contradiction between Castro's evident desires to open the economy to globalization, while maintaining a closed political system at home. Thus it would appear that in areas where the United States embargo is simply not an operative factor, the contradictions of the socialist state appear manifest. Indeed, *The Economist*, in its first issue for 2003, estimates that the United States is already the tenth largest trading partner for Cuba, despite the retention of the embargo. But even these purchases for food create secondary contradictions, since other foreign trading partners dealing in credit envy the position of the United States, dealing with Cuba only in cash.

As the recent (2002) memorandum of European investors has made clear, there are a series of obstacles to doing business that are so prejudicial and egregious, as to deter even the most dedicated entrepreneur from going into present-day Cuba. A litany of complaints is cited. Customs and import charges, residence and work permits and visas, inflation of labor charges that bear no relation to actual labor performance or level of tasks needed, to a tax system that requires payment by foreign companies in dollars, while in reverse, offering Cuban pesos in payment of its outstanding obligations, and even the methods of charging payment. The fiscal system as a whole is rigged so that Cuban banks charge exorbitant fees without corresponding guarantees of payment. So it is that European commercial "good intentions" provide a road to economic hell rather than commercial parity.

Having provided this brief recitation of the current situation, it is important to reiterate that fiscal hardship and even crisis do not topple dictatorial regimes. The response of such regimes is to redistribute what wealth exists, so that there is essentially a parity of hardships—which itself reduces the risk to regime insolvency. And the regime of Fidel Castro has proven masterful at such management of scarce resources. The problem he and his government now face is how long such statist managerial techniques can keep the lid on the society itself. The redistribution of poverty is, after all, not quite the same as the distribution of wealth—and with the omnipresent dollar end of the economy, now reinforced by the inclusion of the Euro currency as a free floating element, the social pressures can only be expected to increase.

Recent Trends

As the first decade of the twenty-first century unfolds, several important international events are having a positive impact on Cuba and the Castro regime. There is the survival capacity of Hugo Chávez in Venezuela; the landslide electoral victory of Luiz Inácio Lula da Silva in Brazil; and the willingness of the Chinese to increase trade with and investments in Cuba. To this must be added the readiness of the U.S. Congress to liberalize the longstanding embargo of the island are encouraging Cuban leaders in their attempt to muddle through the difficult period following the collapse of the Soviet Union. These events, while not likely to alleviate Cuba's continuing economic crisis, may prove helpful to the longevity of the Castro revolution.

The Chávez presidency has proven highly significant for Castro. Initially Chávez tried unsuccessfully to incorporate Cuba into the San Jose Accord. This would have provided Cuba with Venezuelan petroleum at a discounted price. Mexican and other opposition prevented Fidel's younger comrade from achieving his goal of helping Castro. But the continued existence of the Chávez regime in Venezuela does provide a genuine, if modest source of raw materials at cheap prices. Of significant importance for Castro recently was the rise to power in January 2003 of President Luiz Inácio Lula da Silva in Brazil. A close ally of Castro in Latin America and one of the founders of the Foro de Sao Paulo, a group of leftist, Marxist and revolutionary leaders, Lula could provide Cuba with long-term, concessionary credits to purchase Brazilian food products. More importantly, perhaps, will be Lula's support for Cuba in international forums and in pressuring the United States to end its embargo of the island. The presence of Lula and Chávez in South America represent a formidable force in challenging U.S. policies with respect to the continuation of Castro's regime in Cuba.

Perhaps the most intriguing, if unanticipated, development in the past few years is the growth of Chinese investments and involvement with the Castro regime. The Chinese have built a variety of factories in the island and have invested in Cuba's biotechnology industry. But more important is the close military relationship that has developed between China's People's Liberation Army (PLA) and Castro's Fuerzas Armadas Revolucionarias (FAR). The PLA is providing Cuba with military spare parts, munitions, and technology. Raúl Castro and Defense Minister Chi Hao Tian have exchanged visits and a variety of Cuban military officers have spent time observing the Chinese economic and political experiment. China's establishment of an eavesdropping station in Cuba and its provision of equipment to interfere with Radio Marti as well as to monitor U.S. military and commercial transmissions are of obvious concern. After the release of the congressional "Cox Report" detailing Chinese espionage at a U.S. nuclear laboratory, it is hardly a secret that the Chinese are operating an extensive spy network in the Western Hemisphere. So it should be no further surprise that the Chinese might want an electronic espionage base close to American shores. China is not in the same league as the Soviets were in the 1960s or 1970s, but the People's Liberation Army hardly regards itself as a friend of the West. If it were, it would not have engaged in such potentially destabilizing practices as shipping advanced weapons to the Syrians and the Iranians. Indeed, Chinese foreign policy is patient and farsighted, In Cuba, the Chinese seem to be taking a calculated gamble: that the United States' complex relations with and economic interest in China will prevent the Bush administration from raising a big fuss over China's activities in Cuba. The shift from Russian to Chinese patronage is culturally significant, but the sense of Cuba as a client state of a communist regime appears as a constant.

Meanwhile U.S. policy toward Cuba remains under constant pressure. U.S. agricultural groups and states, interested in selling their products to any buyers, are pressuring the U.S. Congress to ease-up on trade relations with the island. During the past two years Congress has allowed for Cuba to purchase for cash U.S. agricultural products. Castro has responded by purchasing about $175 million worth of American products. It is the hope of the Cuban leadership that these purchases would entice American capitalists into providing Cuba with loans and credits to buy more in the U.S. market, further eroding the U.S. embargo.

Internally there have been several complicating developments in Cuba. Castro continues to cling to an outmoded economic model. Economic reforms of the mid-1990s, which indicated a mild opening toward the market, have been stopped and in several cases even reversed. Politically there continues to be Castro's opposition to even the most minimal opening. The visit of Pope John Paul II encouraged those who expected greater religious and political freedom. Neither has developed. As a matter of fact, at the beginning of a new century, the regime is increasing the persecution of dissidents and human rights activists. Cuba is undergoing a Chinese-type cultural revolution, albeit slower and less dramatic than in China, where an aging leader insists on purifying and rejuvenating "his" exhausted revolution before departing from this world.

The two operative words: Cuban and Communism have both lost substantial emotional steam over the course of these eleven editions. The rise of democratic politics and free market economics from Mexico to Argentina has reduced the blandishments of Castro's Cuba to bleatings. At the same time, the collapse of communism throughout Eastern Europe inducing the end of the despotism known as the Soviet Union, has further deprived Cuba of the pretension much less the reality of servicing as a Western hemispheric vanguard of a coming socialist sweep. As is usually the case, whenever events of cataclysmic proportions take place, longstanding political conventions and ideological proclivities are also changed.

What is often overlooked by those involved in everyday analysis of Cuba is how a remarkable consensus has been forged at the level of principles, which is to say in the overall characterization of Castro's Cuba. If at the start of the Cuban revolution of 1959 Castro and his small band of guerrillas were the harbinger of greater things to come throughout the hemisphere (and they had every right to think so), by the start of 2003 there was a widespread consensus that Communist Cuba is an isolated regime, drifting somewhere between limbo and the backwater. From left to right, liberal and conservative opinion alike now accepts the premise that the regime has little if any potential for establishing open economic markets, competitive and multiple political parties, or free popular elections.

Thus, in the midst of the heated debates that deal with the strategic issues of the U.S. embargo, there has now evolved a strong consensus that Cuban Communism is an antidemocratic ripple in the deep currents of changes that now characterize the hemisphere as a whole. As *Freedom in the World* reports: "Fidel Castro has shown no signs of loosening his grip on power, as cycles of repression, following harsh economic reforms, continued unabated." The very singularity of Cuba however makes it a nation of special concern and consideration for students and policymakers alike.

This said, in the past several years significant events have taken place in the Cuban infrastructure. The economic reforms initiated in 1994-95 have come to a halt; Castro has been clamping down harshly on dissident groups in the island and the revolution has lost its luster, particularly with the young on the island which seem alienated from the system and unwilling to follow the party's exhortations on Marxist rhetoric. As a result, a certain passive resistance has become the norm in Cuba. It underscores both the deterioration of Castro's infrastructure and a decline in participation in social and economic activities that could possibly carry the regime to a new plateau.

The Castro government has shown very few signs of making meaningful or durable concessions in the political and human rights arena recently or in the past four decades. There has been no indication that Castro intends to truly open up the island's political or economic system or promote a peaceful solution to Cuba's deepening crisis. History reveals various instances where strong and even autocratic political leaders have mellowed with age and softened their positions, but there is scant evidence that this is the case with Castro. On the contrary, as the Cuban leader has aged he has become more intransigent and difficult. At the Party Congress in 1997 he reaffirmed his staunch opposition to the U.S. and his unwillingness to relinquish personal power, statements he has often repeated.

During the past few years, Castro has mobilized significant resources to force the United States to lift the embargo and the travel ban. He has invited U.S. religious, political, business, and academics leaders to the island. He has reached out to moderate Cuban-Americans to begin a dialogue and to weaken Cuban-American opposition to a Cuba-U.S. rapprochement. He has even visited New York dressed in a business suit, rather than his usual military uniform, enticing American entrepreneurs with a vision of a major bonanza if Cuba is opened up. Castro's calculated moves were designed to gain time and to force the U.S. into unilateral concessions regarding the embargo and the travel ban. He hoped that U.S. and world opinion would force U.S. administrations to soften its policies and those U.S. attempts at subverting his revolution could be handled by Cuba's efficient security apparatus. His short-term tactically motivated actions did not envision the dismantling of communism in Cuba or weakening of his personal power over the Cuban people. On the contrary during the past few years Castro has become concerned with the continuity of the revolution once he disappears. He has been attempting to imbue the masses with a new sense of anti-Americanism through mass mobilizations and in the educational system. He also has been emphasizing the need for a smooth succession of power.

The Party Congress of last year reasserted Raúl Castro's position as the undisputed heir to Fidel Castro's dynasty. Both in the party's private meetings and in public, Fidel praised his brother and summoned the faithful to support him. Raúl's position as vice president, head of the military and second secretary of the party makes him the obvious replacement for Fidel. Clearly, the older brother wanted to make it clear to the party cadres and the population-at-large that the younger brother, as his anointed heir does, should be supported and obeyed and that his leadership would be best for the future of Cuba. The succession from dictatorial father to dictatorial son has been successfully concluded in Communist North Korea as well as in Syria and Jordan. It remains to be seen if the same or similar dynastic processes can be implemented in a Communist Cuba.

The Elián González case highlighted certain large-scale problems in American foreign policy toward Cuba's communist regime. Among the most telling of these is unease over immigration policy as a whole, providing a temporary alliance of residual left-wing support for Castro and rising nativist sentiments on the right. The case also revealed smoldering resentment toward the Cuban-American enclave in Miami, especially the sense of its economic gains and linguistic commitment to Spanish, again uniting diverse elements such as Haitians who felt slighted and those who dislike multiculturalism as a disguise for bilingualism. Finally, public opinion leaned heavily to the idea that a child should be united with a surviving parent, whatever the politics of that parent—even one loyal to the Castro regime. In microcosm, the fate of a single child indicated just how entangled domestic policy considerations could become with respect to present-day Cuba.

However, with respect to the structure of Cuban Communism as such, while this case accentuated the suspicions and hostilities that have been built up over four decades between Miami Cuban-Americans and Havana's Communist leadership, it does not necessarily change the parameters of the system as such. Indeed, it has been argued that the Elian Gonzalez custody battle was a diplomatic coup for Fidel Castro. At the same time, it can justifiably be claimed that this case has again focused attention on the character of the Castro regime in none too favorable a light even among those Americans who believed that a child should have been united with a surviving parent. So at year-end 2002, the most important "on the ground" factor is the continuing survival of the Castro regime, with allies throughout the Third World, but also with powerful critics in parts of the Third World, and not least in advanced democratic nations.

Policy concessions and constructive engagement did not work in the past. They are not likely to shake Castro's faith in a socialist future. Commitment to anti-Americanism, personal rule, and virulent internationalism, remain the cornerstones of Castro's policies. Faced with the approaching end of his life and his fear that once he is gone "his" revolution will change course and Cuba would end up as another friendly Caribbean island close to the United States, Castro is unlikely to open up either the economy or the political system to fresh winds of change. It might well be the case that impending better relations with the United States will be seen and feared by the Cuban leadership as an attempt to subvert the revolution and will lead to tightening political control.

Whatever may be the tactical considerations of the moment, on the basis of Castro's stated beliefs and recent actions, as long as Cuba remains under Castro's dominion, it will continue as a unique Communist project. Cuban Communism was undertaken in splendid isolation from and opposition to the course of history in the Americas-and for that matter, the rest of the contemporary world. This eleventh edition of *Cuban Communism* is thus offered at a time of economic crisis for the founding generation of the Revolution of 1959. Precisely how this new set of circumstances will play out in the short run is still difficult to say. Offsetting economic difficulties for the Cuban regime are political victories for hemispheric neighbors that feel powerful affinities for Cuban Communism. To modify the famous saying of John Maynard Keynes, in the long run we may not, after all, be dead, but the current regime of Cuba's aging dictator might be.

Source and Original Title: "Introduction to the 11ᵗʰ edition of Cuban Communism" in *Cuban Communism*, eleventh edition (co-edited with Jaime Suchlicki). New Brunswick and London: Transaction Publishers, 2003, xiii+ xxii pp.

42

Transition Scenarios for a Post-Castro Cuba: Speaking Loudly but Carrying a Small Stick

When the extraordinarily long history of the Castro regime finally bites the dust, the role of social scientists and policy analysts in exposing that dictatorship will be understood as pivotal. The exile community has produced a plethora of economists, historians, sociologists and political scientists equal in quality, and perhaps in even greater number, than that produced by exiles from Nazi Germany in the 1930s, and from Communist Russia in the 1920s and 1930s. Cuban intellectuals, in an uneasy alliance with a few North American colleagues (alas, too few) came to view honest social research as an unparalleled tool against Castro's regime. In the tradition of Enlightenment, the techniques, methods and approach of the social sciences were considered as in and of itself an arsenal of truth against the deceptions and fatuous claims of Castro.

This was all taking place at a time when domestic American social science retreated into a virtual cocoon of subjectivism, ideological thinking, and partisanship that is equally unparalleled for its vituperative critique of American society. It is as if the defeat of Soviet Communism was also the exposure of European Marxism, But instead of viewing this as an opportunity for a broad struggle against new totalitarian outposts in Latin America, Africa, and the Middle East, the claims of the most long lived and repressive regime ever to haunt Latin America became the chief cause championed by North American radicals turned social scientists.

As a result an anomaly took place with which we are still trying to work our way out of: a Cuban exile community and its offspring who view classical social science as the bastion of democracy and opposition to tyranny, in contrast to a North American community who view the classical traditions as inherently reactionary and against the will of the popular movements of our time. One outcome of this new radical orthodoxy is not only a failure to recognize the enormity of the achievement of the social scientists from Cuba, but a deep hostility and resentment to these upstarts, in a way that the giant figures from Berlin, Vienna, and Zurich in earlier generations rarely had to face. Indeed, the major figures were ensconced if not embraced in centers of learning at Harvard, Columbia, and Chicago. Even social researchers of less than perfect credentials who emanated from Russian and East Europe were sheltered from criticism. While there are some excellent Cuban scholars who were ensconced over time at such institutes of higher learning as UCLA, Pittsburgh, and Georgetown, its center of gravity was and remains the University of Miami—and hence a ready target to those for whom the very word Miami, and dare one add Florida electoral procedures, conjure up less than pleasant emotions.

The purpose of this contextual elaboration is not so much to give a capsule recitation of Cuban American intellectual life in the last half-century, or to even celebrate its achievements. Rather it is to indicate that the very deformities of the larger cultural educational picture has had ramification on Cuban scholarship in America, not simply of a positive, but also of a negative sort. For what we witnessed was both brilliant examinations of the interstices of Cuban life in all its parts—from medical to military—but the same exaggerations of the potentials of social science research that gripped those who participated in the Vietnam War prior and thought that they carried the magic messages from the academy to the polity to not only end the struggle, but create the conditions of victory over a hardened revolutionary foe. So it is this admixture of the sacred and profane elements of social research, of its capacity to reveal hard truths about social systems, and its exaggerated sense of self importance to establish conditions for the transformation of those social systems that characterize the present moment in time—a moment that is more than forty five year deep into the fabric of Communist Rule in Cuba.

Two works that have appeared in 2004 are prototypical examples of the contrary uses of policy science: its amazing capacity to identify social inequalities, political break points, and internal contradictions in the Castro regime, and no less, its astonishing conviction that it can build scenarios and designs for a post-Castro future fashioned out of this same evidence. The enlightenment fallacy reaches deep into the lives of Cuban-American intellectual life: the assumption that any rational person can present the evidence that would move other rational persons to abandon any pretense as to the worth of Castro's dictatorship. And for the non-believer, the social researcher has a barrage full of models, designs, and programs, scenarios, all rolled into a generational theory of transition from totalitarian to democratic rule. The result is a maximalist position on change, and a bilateralism emphasizing top down management—all well intentioned, all motivated by the highest goals of social science as planning, and alas, all with problems of a narrowness of vision that defeats the very social scientific qualities that led so many of these fine and truly wonderful people into social science research to start with.

As the independent Cuban Research Institute informs us, the politics of research is faced with one hundred thirty two organizations and outlets that have an expressed, targeted interest in Cuba and Cuban-American affairs. They range from Centers to promote human rights, to Centers dedicated to the idea that Cuba already has all the human rights anyone could ask for. Some are dedicated to strengthening the embargo. Others are simply trade outfits that seek to lift the embargo for commercial ends. Still others promote scientific and technical exchanges, while others use the same rhetoric to hustle a weekend of fun and games at the Copacabana. All the usual suspects are present and accounted for. Each party has political action specialists that seek to boost its image among the Cuban-American people. Many universities have programs on Cuba that vary from full-scale research activities (none more thoroughgoing than the Bacardi Center at the University if Miami) to summertime excursions (like the West Virginia University study aboard effort done in conjunction with the University of Havana). In short, what may have once been a modest effort to influence political opinion in the 1970s is now a full-fledged effort to insinuate definite policies, though the precise objectives differ broadly and at times diametrically.

This plethora of organizational formations that has led to new policy initiatives and developments U.S. policymaking toward Cuba, but the actual consequences has been modest. This may be because the sense of solidarity in popular life among Cubans has remained intact. Indeed, one could argue that the emergence of such a wide band of organizational formations is an example of the weaknesses as well as the strengths of those who aim to influence the political process from the top down. The pro-Castro lobbies want recognition of the Cuban dictatorship here and now. The anti-Castro forces emphasize transitional scenarios of a post-Castro future. Such organizational struggles attest to a point I made on "Ethnic Politics" in *The Encyclopedia of Nationalism*: racial, ethnic, and national minority politics have been mitigated in their impact in the United States by the existence of many varying and cross-cutting interests and beliefs. This helps to explain that although organizational efforts proliferate, and social scientists continue to present their ideas, Cuba remains "off the radar screen" for most of American political life.

Over time and multiple administrations, the dominant government position has remained simple and direct: essential changes in American policy will follow, not precede, a society in which free elections, free parties and free markets are established. With varying degrees of enthusiasm, Democratic and Republican leaders and officials have asserted a modest bundle of demands to Cuba's leaders. Whatever the distinction in attitudes toward lifting the embargo, the Helms-Burton measures, or increasing human and monetary exchanges between the two nations, both major parties have consistently identified the Castro regime as the source of the problem of the Cuban people, and hence its removal as the core of any solution. That position is seen much in evidence in the 2004 Government Report, more than 400 pages in length, on a post-Castro Cuba that was initialed and sanctioned by Secretary of State Colin Powell.

The consistency of American foreign policy toward Cuba is evident to the pro-Castro Cuba Lobby. Its response has ranged from denunciation of the colonial character of United States aims in the area to hectoring demands for a revision of this policy of the American policy of branding Cuba as a Stalinist pariah state in the hemisphere, and urging that the Castro regime be treated as a "normal" if mildly unpopular Latin American regime. For different motives and reasons, the Cuba Lobby has enlisted the services of far Left and far Right academic ideologies. The last Communist regime standing is buttressed by isolationist sentiments to avoid foreign entanglements, especially one that allows for unwelcome immigrants. At the fringes, there is now an emphasis on American interests as being served by support (usually tacit) for the Castro regime, and a new emphasis on American values as being served by the anti-Castro forces (often manifest). This represents, in my view, a qualitative shift from earlier efforts by pro-Castro Cuba Lobbyists in the past.

While these tactics are ideologically compelling, they take place at a time of weakened emphasis on Cuba in public opinion. With the American political struggles focused on the Middle East and the War in Iraq, several trends are evident: (a) a noticeable disinterest in issues related to Cuba; (b) movement toward moderate rapprochement with Castro under the guise of normalization of foreign relations; and (c) penetration of Castro emissaries in the cultural, scientific and academic agencies—at both government and non-governmental levels. In such conditions the pro-Castro lobbies have focused upon three areas of activities: American foreign policy troubles in the Middle East are held up as a good reason not to repeat the same mistake with respect to Cuba. So the fact that Cuba is not a central policy concern does not necessarily hamper those arguing for at least a tactical and diplomatic rapprochement.

First, they continue to lobby against embargo—with a new emphasis on a piece by piece breaking away of elite agencies such as the Council on Foreign Relations; and market agencies interested in promoting increasing trade especially in the farm states and those sectors of the economy especially hard hit by unemployment or downsizing in the American economy.

Second, they continue to urge dialogue within government sectors, i.e., military and diplomatic initiatives that would permit regionalization of the Cuban problem. This process of legitimating by common problem solving is evident in calls for common military and police interdiction of drug trafficking, goods smuggling, and what might broadly be called issued of terrorism, such as hijackings and bomb threats.

Third, they attempt to isolate the United States as a source of imperial designs on Castro's Cuba. While relations between Cuba and other nations are extremely uneven and reflect of the idiosyncratic nature of Castro himself (resulting in increasing tensions with Mexico and Spain, but closer ties with Venezuela and Brazil), the Cuba Lobby nearly uniformly emphasizing that American imperialism is the unique if not the sole reason for the lack of recognition of Castro's Cuba. In this way, human rights, central to the opposition, becomes muted, if not eliminated from the table.

The three objectives of the pro-Castro Cuba Lobby are to be accompanied by a new strategic turn predicated on identifying the enemy as Miami rather than Havana. Miami is portrayed as the foreign country within America, or as the exemplar of an unbridled capitalism. Growing Latinization of the city is disparaged. Widening opposition to bilingualism is yoked to resentment of the political power of the Bush family—governor and president alike. This provides a bridge to conservative concerns against bilingual and bi-cultural formations and liberal opposition to the reigning regime in Florida and Washington D.C. Widespread public opinion opposition to the embargo indicates that this "Left-Right" fusion is having its desired impact.

It would be imprudent to burden this presentation with further speculation about how best to respond to such a new turn in pro-Castro activities. A variety of organizations and individuals will have that collective task. But seen in this way, taking seriously the magnitude and the force of the opposition, will at least permit the Cuban American community and its allies in American political affairs to fashion responses to Castro's dictatorship that move beyond a series of transition scenarios of a post-Castro Cuba. Such approaches, good intentions and deep researchers notwithstanding, run the risk of utopian thinking; and even more, a static view of the domestic situation in the United States that presumes native American support. Whether the issues are the return of a child to his father in the aftermath of a successful escape attempt from Cuba, or the terrible fate of Cuban prisoners of conscience, such concerns remain remote and short lived in the memory of most Americans.

This in no way is meant to disparage or minimize the importance of such struggles for the conscience and public support of broad segments of American opinion. It is to note that opponents of Cuban democracy do not sleep in silence. A regime that has been in existence for more than 45 years, however despicable and desultory, achieves a certain legitimacy bestowed by longevity itself. Political scientists in particular have a proclivity to bestow legitimacy on the sheer act of one man or one party staying in power for an interminable length. The hope and biological prayer that this too shall pass, and the preparation of an endless sheath of papers to that effect, may accurately reflect what will eventually take place. But politics is a quotidian game. In this game, those who have fought long, hard and consistently for a democratic and independent Cuba must adopt strategically adroit tactics, if they hope to bring about in practice the principles so readily pronounced.

Policy researchers might be well advised to focus on present day iniquities within Castro's Cuba, to identify its regime with the worst examples of international repression, to continue to push hard for an American foreign policy that penetrates the veil of secrecy and isolation that characterizes the regime. The emphasis on transition scenarios, no matter how artfully they present a post-Castro national reconciliation has difficulties. It ignores the character of the present struggle, and assumes a democratic outcome that may not occur. One need not be reminded that the situation in the post-Soviet Union did not result in political democracy—pure or impure. One might well imagine anticipate a condition in which the same is true for Cuba.

The related problem with constructing scenarios for transition is that such designs are artifacts, well-informed constructs that are largely external in creation. They often implicitly compare democratic models in law and public administration for example with what presently obtains in Cuba, and presume that the transition will involve a trajectory moving from the totalitarian to the democratic in something akin to a straight political line. Highly qualified well-meaning scholars repeatedly inform us that the presumption of democratic outcomes and bilateral initiatives will carry the day. Such solutions are not commonly accepted, or for that matter feasible even within advanced political contexts and systems. But more than that, it must be recognized that transition scenarios about Cuba in 2004 and beyond, like game-playing scenarios about Vietnam in 1964, are manufactured utopias that must stand the test of time and space on native grounds. For example, few of the scholars seem willing to make plain that the strength of the Cuban economy in 1958, one year prior to the Castro takeover, did not bestow any corresponding legitimacy to the Batista dictatorship that ruled before Castro. It is true enough that Cuba has fallen on bad economic times. It is however not true that Cuba had good political times prior to the 1959 Revolution.

The idea that a totalitarian, or in its mild version, an authoritarian regime, is unacceptable as an alternative to Castro is attractive as political rhetoric aimed at Cuban-Americans, but it may fly in the face of reality. One can readily conceive of a non-democratic, even a military interregnum that lasts for some time, to replace and displace the Castro family and the regime it built. Such a non-democratic end product, however unappetizing, must be placed on the bargaining table alongside benign options that advocates of a post-dictatorship regime envision. We must be careful not to become victims of our own transition expectations. There is a risk that our efforts become objects of derision and mockery if they deviate from the utopian premises that are designed far beyond the Cuban shores. In short, our approach should be firm but also minimal: to advocate democratic ends and reassure Cubans of the three principles of free elections, free parties and free markets. But this should be done in a context that allows for flexible consequences—such as what we find in China, which has a unique but relatively open-ended economy and an absolutely closed polity.

After literally hundreds of proposals, recommendations, scenarios, and plans, covering everything from core institutions of a free economy, to modernizing the infrastructure and addressing environmental degradation, in both the government Commission Report and the non-government (but heavily funded USAID) report on a Democratic Transition, Jaime Suchlicki, director of the Institute for Cuban and Cuban American Studies at the University of Miami, lets the cat out of the bag. He courageously writes "one thing that has not come out and one thing that I am particularly concerned about is the role of the military in Cuba. The Cuban armed forces occupy a privileged position in society now, controlling some 60 to 65 percent of the economy and in any transition, whether it is slow or fast, they will a significant role. How do we reach out to the military? What do we do to co-opt the military? How do we influence the military?" (101). Those are indeed questions that require attention, and that challenge the brave new world of post-Castro Cuba. The so-called Powell report offers scant comfort, asserting simply that "among the most daunting challenges a transition government will immediately face are those that will pit popular demands for prosecutions of former Castro regime officials against the imperative of establishing a government firmly founded on the rule of law and due process" (171). Beyond the pomp and circumstance of such noble sentiments are the prospects of a civil war with a reasonable outcome at best, or a military takeover of Cuba in which Castro may be gone but the rule of law and due process have hardly arrived. Those who construct social science castles in the air would be well advised to read Machiavelli and Hobbes anew.

We live in a world of limited options. We may be faced with a Cuba without Fidel Castro but with a less than democratic regime for an indefinite period of time. To deny that prospect, or shunt it aside, to argue the case that under no circumstance can such a post-Castro Cuba emerge in which military leadership becomes dominant and mass politics maintains a Leftist caste, may serve only to lengthen the time in office of the tyrant.

Currently the role of the Cuban military in the economy is extensive and pervasive with the military managerial elite controlling, by some estimates, over sixty percent of the economy. The breath and depth of this military control of the countrys key economic sectors is astonishing. GAESA, the holding company for the Cuban Defense Ministry, is involved in all key sectors of the economy. Enterprises with innocuous sounding names such as TRD Caribe S.A., Gaviota, S.A. and Aerogaviota are all part of the vast economic involvement of Cubas Fuerzas Armadas Revolucionarias (FAR). There is every reason to expect that Raul Castro will continue to promote the involvement and monopolistic control of his armed forces in the economy as he has since the late 1980s and the collapse of the Soviet Union.

The period following the death of Joseph Stalin in the late Soviet Union witnessed the emergence of a series of Communist Party personnel. None of them, starting with Malenkov and exempting Gorbachev, would be invited to a democratic supper party. But within a half-century, the USSR crumbled; civic society and political parties returned to Russia, a limited but open economy took root, and the nation itself returned to the comity of world powers. But even now, Russia is ruled by a less than democratic figure, and its people themselves in a variety of public opinion polls are far more concerned with economic security than with political democracy. In a different fashion, one can ready envision a similar process and result in Cuba. Admittedly different, more positive, forces are at work in relation to a post-Castro Cuba than a post-Stalin Russia. At the same time, some factors move in a contrary, negative direction that cannot be overlooked. There remain Cuba's diminutive size, limited resources, wide spread impoverishment, its need for aid that is tied up elsewhere, and indeed its tradition of the anti-democratic now enshrined as tragic historical fact. A half-century mark is probably a good indicator of pro and anti-democratic tendencies in any nation of any size—from Russia to Cuba.

The pro-Castro Cuba Lobby is fully cognizant of this struggle between major political forces in Cuba. It is dedicated to maintain the dictatorship, and hope that over time, it becomes institutionalized as a thorn in the flesh of the Americas. Its great weakness is precisely its concern for turning American foreign policy rather than transforming Cuban domestic life. Its great advantage is that it represents a far cheaper approach to political change than the billions of dollars involved in transitional scenarios proffered on the presumption of a short-term restoration of a democratic Cuba. Anti-Castro forces must shift from future considerations to present struggles—not easy to do for social activists enthralled by the utopian vision of bringing about a quick end to tyranny. To dedicate its sizeable recourses and efforts to raise an awareness of the need to overturn the Castro dictatorship at all costs will require painful theoretical as well as practical readjustments. And that will be the task of such forces as the Center for a Free Cuba, the Cuba American National Foundation, Cuban Committee for Democracy, and countless other groups comprised of people seeking an end to the Castro tyranny and its displacement by something better—not perfect, but better. Latin America has entered a world in which technology moves at a dizzying pace, while moral postures still move in glacier like fashion. Policy makers whose mission is a free and democratic Cuba would be well advised to understand that practical politics is more akin to moral structure than technical change. This is not exactly a linkage that social scientists are easily prepared to accept.

References/Notes

Commission for Assistance to a Free Cuba: Report to the President. Chaired by Colin L. Powell, Secretary of State, Roger F. Noriega, Commission Coordinator, and Daniel W. Fisk, Chairman of the Working group Hastening Cuba's Transition. Washington, D.C.: United States Department of State, 2004. 423 pp

Humanitarian Aid for a Democratic Transition in Cuba. Seminar Proceedings, transcribed and edited by Eric Driggs González and Georgina O. Lindskoog, with a Foreword by Jaime Suchlicki, Director of the Institute for Cuban and Cuban American Studies, University of Miami, 2004. 123 pp.

A review essay is not the place for a historical review of pro-Castro sentiments in the United States since 1959. My own analyses of this policy variant of the totalitarian temptation are to be found in "The Cuba Lobby," *The Washington Review of Strategic and, International Studies*, vol. 1, no. 3, July 1978. Pp. 58-71; "American Foreign Policy Toward Castro's Cuba," *The Conscience of Worms and the Cowardice of Lions: Cuban Politics and Culture in an American Context.* Transaction Publishers/University of Miami North-South Center, 1993. Pp. 1-14; and "The Cuba Lobby: Then and Now," *Orbis: A Journal of World Affairs*, vol. 42, no. 4, Autumn 1998. Pp. 553-565. - ILH

Source and Original Title: "Transition Scenarios for a Post-Castro Cuba: Military Outcomes or Civil Prospects?" in *Human Rights Review*, Volume 6, Number 1, October-December 2004, pp 27-34. José Azel, "After Raúl, qué?". Focus on Cuba (Institute for Cuba and Cuban American Studies), Issue No. 94, March 17, 2008.

43

Castro's Corn: Petroleum and Globalization

A major development has taken place in Latin America during the early months of 2007. The Cuban dictator has risen from the ashes. Fidel Castro has written (albeit not spoken at public gatherings), about the emerging bio-fuels policy of the United States, and the forging of a functional, economic alliance with Brazil, the most powerful nation in Latin America. It might well be that this alliance is the greatest and least anticipated diplomatic victory for democratic pluralism in the region. If the development has been poorly understood, or at least little discussed in the American media, it has been fully absorbed throughout the hemisphere.

On the surface, the various statements reported in *Granma*, the official organ of the Cuban Communist Party, have announced the return of Fidel Castro to the ideological battlefield against his implacable foe, the colossus of the North. The statements include enough political fire and brimstone to indicate that the Cuban dictator has indeed been restored to his normal, frenzied rhetorical state, if not to the pink of health. But there are several implications of these statements that deserve attention: First, there are signs of a widening split between a nationalist, social democratic left headed by Brazilian President Luiz

Inácio Lula da Silva, and the old guard ideological left headed by President Fidel Castro of Cuba, with the active support of Venezuela's strong arm ruler, Hugo Chávez and Bolivian President Evo Morales.

For their part, the Brazilians have enlisted the active aid of the Ecuadorian government in the biochemical policy entered into agreements with the United States, involving the conversion of food sources, especially corn, into fuels for automotive and related energy needs. This alliance is a diplomatic and policy event of great moment. While the statements by Castro are primarily an assault on the United States, characterizing its "worldwide plan to develop ethanol from food sources" as "the globalization of genocide," the firm rebuke to Brazil for negotiating such an agricultural plan is the news behind the rhetoric. It suggests that Castro sees realization of the dreams of the Tri-Continental Movement of the 1960s in the twilight of his long term struggle against United States policies.

In these series of articles, published in the last week of March the first week of April, and appropriately enough, the first day of May, the Cuban ruler ostensibly focuses on United States energy policy. The *Granma* headline on March 30, doubtless approved if not written by the Comandante himself, reads "Condemned to Premature Death by Hunger and Thirst—More than three billion of the World." Never one for understatement, the article follows with the claim that "the sinister idea of converting food into combustible materials was definitely established as the economic line of the foreign policy of the United States." Castro's reasoning is based on a zero sum game: the more that corn is used to manufacture ethanol, the less the "hungry masses of the earth" can consume. But the heavy rhetoric of that *Granma* article was only a tune up for what came a week later.

The second statement, published in the first week of April provides an indication of how Castro intends to redeploy the ideological divide. He rhetorically asks: "From where and who is going to furnish the more than 500 million tons of corn and other cereals that the United States, Europe and the rich countries need to produce the number of gallons of ethanol that the big companies from the United States and other countries need as compensation for their substantial investments? Where and who is going to produce the soy, the sunflower and ripe seeds whose essential oils those same rich countries are going to turn into fuel? The five principal producers of corn, barley, sorghum, rye, millet, and oats that Bush wants to turn into raw material for the production of ethanol furnish the world market, according to recent data, with 679 million tons. In turn, the five principal consumers, some of which are also producers of those grains, at present need 604 million tons per year. The available surplus is reduced to less than 80 million tons."

In the third statement dedicated to this theme of oil, corn and globalism, Castro continues to beat the anti-American theme in terms of the energy situation. He critiqued U.S.-Brazilian cooperation in terms of the illusion of his presumed leadership of the fast evaporating Third World. "Insatiable in its demand, the empire has called on the world to produce bio-fuels to free the United States from dependence on imported oil." The funding for this bio-fuel approach is US and European capital, and such capital could even give support to Brazil and Latin America. Striking a note similar to that of Al Gore in the United States, the Cuban dictator speaks of "140 billion dollars every year without any concern whatsoever from the fallout in terms of climate change and hunger." The plain fact is that oil-poor nations such as Japan and land rich nations in much of Africa and Asia are in all likelihood going to be central players in the ethanol revolution. The imagery of development and underdevelopment is hardly credible under such circumstances. Of more intriguing consequences at the policy level is the potential for a formal split between Brazil and Cuba, or more realistically between an authentic national Left and seriously enfeebled internationalist extremism in Cuba.

It becomes a short hop from Castro's ludditism from "the annual consumption of their [U.S.] voracious automobiles" to President Bush's "intention to apply this formula on a worldwide scale, which means nothing less than the internationalization of genocide." It is an even briefer distance to celebrating his imagined friends. "China would never use a single ton of cereals or leguminous plants to produce ethanol. It is a nation with a prosperous economy that sets records of growth, where no citizen fails to receive the income necessary for his basic consumer goods, despite the fact that 48 percent of the population, which exceeds 1.3 billion people, works in agriculture." Never has Castro been more effusive in praise of capitalism! "China is intent on achieving considerable savings of energy by eliminating thousands of factories that consume unacceptable amounts of electricity and hydrocarbons. Many of the foods mentioned above [China] imports from all corners of the world, transporting them thousands of kilometers."

Castro assures us that "the worst may be still to come: a new war to ensure the supplies of gas and crude oil that will place the human species on the brink of a total holocaust." Castro, that great believer in "facts" sites anonymous "Russian press agencies, crediting intelligence sources" reporting that the United States prepared to go to war "more than three years ago." It supposedly started on "the day the government of the United States decided to totally occupy Iraq, unleashing an interminable and odious civil war." Further, with an oblique reference to the nuclear bomb developments in Iran, "to demolish every single Iranian factory is a technical task that is relatively easy for a power like the United States." The difficult part may come later, planning "a new war launched against another Islamic belief that deserves our total respect, as well as the other religions of the peoples of the Near, Middle or Far East, prior or subsequent to Christianity." Castro has his own vision of Armageddon.

But even if we discount the hysteria that underwrites Castro's claims, the devil must be given his due. The emergence of alternative energy sources predicated on the use of food crops does increase inflationary pressures. It is expected that crop demand may have just such a short term outcome, but it does not seem to have had more than a marginal impact to date. To start with, ethanol demands lead to the cultivation of new lands for easy to harvest crops, especially in places with currently uncultivated or poorly cultivated areas such as China, India, and Brazil. It might well be that ethanol production can actually have a leveling effect on those economies in which the gap between urban and agrarian sectors remain dangerously high. In addition, ethanol production provides a fiscal cap on natural fuels, thus reducing the price at the pump for automobile consumption. It is for example estimated that grain production dedicated to ethanol will roughly double in the United States alone (from 16% in 2006 to 30% in 2008), at current rates of consumption this can well result in deflationary rather than inflationary outcomes in a relative brief period. It could well be argued that a readjustment in the economy whereby the price of a gallon of milk is once more higher than a gallon of gasoline is a social benefit as well as providing the basis of a new global economic equilibrium.

At its deepest level, beyond dubious claims of Castro that ethanol production represents some atrocious genocide and his declared opposition to any effort to use food supplies to generate new modes of fuel reserves, represents an increasingly prominent coalition of the hard Left with forces of environmental control. Such forces of environmental reform are currently linked to the war against global warming on one side, in contrast to relatively open Western democracies, especially the larger and more powerful nations of the world (in which Brazil must increasingly be identified as a significant player), for whom issues of social development remain the driving forces in economic advancement. There is a growing realization that nations such as Brazil, South Africa, and Australia, along with Canada, Japan, China and India, are powers to be reckoned with. These new global powers, no less than the Big Eight, are the primary battleground of the struggle to reach a new equilibrium between the appropriate costs to be incurred in achieving development while recognizing risks to the environment in forging new energy and farm policies.

The world battle concerning the advantages and disadvantages of "globalization" have been moving in this direction through the first decade of the new century. Interest in finding alternatives to oil has achieved additional muscle, less through any empirical evidence of the shortcomings of globalization, so much as the growing fear of the oil rich Middle East nations. It is recognized that the elements that give it such great economic strength is a pot of liquid gold, but one that is exhaustible and subject to being side-swiped by new synthetic fuels. Even a suspected drop in oil usage by 20 percent as a result of ethanol use over the next several years would put a serious damper on conducting Middle East politics by petroleum means. It is little wonder that Fidel Castro's blast at the new accords between Brazil and the United States, elicited flowing words of praise from Castro's Middle East allies.

In this war of crowded words, the position of Brazil should not be overlooked. Marco Aurelia Garcia, the foreign affairs advisor to President Lula da Silvia, noted that Castro did not understand bio-fuels, and caused no problems for food production. "The world's problem is not a shortage of food but income." Lula himself, after signing the accords with Ecuador, said that "our countries are determined to promote this revolution of clean and renewable energy, which creates jobs and preserves our forests." And this position was reinforced by Brazilian foreign minister Celso Amorim, who simply and accurately added a postscript: "Chávez has oil, we have ethanol." The Ecuadorian President, Rafael Correa, simply added that "for us ethanol is a great opportunity." The political tone of the democratic left has been cool and respectful, but the implications for the western hemisphere are profound and wide ranging.

What we are looking at is a new coalition of forces defined less by images of Left and Right, than by a three-pronged attack on the Western alliance as such. The strange union of a Marxist dictator and Iranian demagogues indicates that Castro's ambitions for a world role have not diminished. His strategy is driven by three possibilities. First, there is the deep seated fear that the oil bubble could burst, leaving in its wake a shambles of so-called Third World alliances to whom Castro is entirely dependent for survival. Second, there is the question of how large nations function as economic barometers in contrast to how small communist nations are political vanguards of revolution in the Middle East, Africa, Asia and of course, Latin America. Third, there is the transformation of the struggle over globalization and its consequences for the economy and the culture into a much large struggle between authentic nationalisms within democratic impulses and ideological internationalism and its effort to liquidate the democratic option.

Designing scenarios is a two-way game. While the United States policy toward Cuba may be rooted in a desire for a neighboring society free of dynastic dictatorship and hoary dogma, the policies of Cuban communism are predicated on a new grand alliance, one that not only chains Venezuela and Bolivia to the Castro brothers' chariot, but also links up with a worldwide struggle against the democratic west. Even at the risk of losing Brazil as an ally, Castro sees an alliance that enlists an expanded Third World and engages the forces of China, Iran, and other diverse nations to reduce the United States from a world power to a cowering pigmy. Such an outcome is one that Premier Castro not only dreams about but can now taste.

The choice of issues selected by Fidel Castro from his sick bed is neither random nor idiosyncratic. They are rooted in unresolved issues of the free market and free elections that surfaced as critical pivots in hemispheric politics during the last century. The ethanol issue and the question of alternative energy sources in general, are linked to the latest "ism" craze of environmentalism, with its possibility of driving a wedge between Western nations and driving the West to the abyss, by causing it to doubt development and democracy as twin goals. But to juxtapose technology as a threat to peasant survival is not only a weak deck, but one that runs counter to the long-held Marxist belief in science as a magic carpet to social progress. Castro's two statements indicate an awareness of this dilemma, but offer no policy to reconcile such ideological differences.

A major ideological difficulty for Castro and his oil allies is that ethanol has, in the past, been an option embraced by the environmentally sensitive *Greens* the world over. Still, it would be dangerous for those engaged in bitter struggle to dismiss the terms of debate and discourse selected by Castro, or to see this latest rift in the hemisphere as anything less than a struggle to define the terms of a new century—both its alliances and its ambitions. For leaders of the totalitarian left to raise the issue of ethanol as a hallmark of those who would embrace genocidal prospects may seem bizarre, coming as it does from those who deny or cast doubt on real holocausts from Europe to Asia and Africa, but these are the terms of the larger debate. It is a debate that the West can ill afford to lose.

Source and Original Title: "Forging a Petroleum Policy without Petroleum: The Cuban Ideological Assault on Ethanol", *Cuban Affairs: Quarterly Electronic Journal.* Volume 2, Issue 3.

44

Rocky Shoals of Reform: Castro and the *Caudillo*

One of the singular moments in a dictatorship is its end point. And for Fidel Castro and Francisco Franco those points converge revealingly—indicating a possible future for Cuba after its *caudillo*'s demise. True, there are some notable differences, but ultimately their fates, or more specifically that of Francoism and Castroism, will more than likely prove that the issue is less when each leader dies physically, so much as when their ideologies perish politically.

The Convergence

In his day, Franco was heralded as the dictator who had held power for the longest time period: nearly 40 years. Castro is coming hard upon fifty years of rule. Both dictators assumed power after a preliminary period of armed struggle with a domestic enemy: Franco from 1936 to 1939, fighting against Juan Negrín López and the Popular Front; and Castro from 1956 to 1959, combating Fulgencio Batista and his Military Front.

Castro followed the trail blazed by Franco in the consolidation of power—the elimination of political opposition, the institutionalization of single-party rule, a repressive police system that created a groundswell of exile life when possible and prison life when unavoidable, and a cult of personality for maximum leadership. Castro fused government and political functions to a much greater extent than did Franco; yet, five years after coming to power, Franco combined the positions of head of state, prime minister and leader of the Falangist movement—and enjoyed sovereign legislative authority to boot.

Both Franco in the 1930s and Castro in the 1960s needed foreign allies. In 1939 Franco's Spain courted the pro-fascist Axis powers. And by 1961, Castro's Cuba had become openly aligned with the Soviet Union. The Soviet leadership did not much care for Castro, and the Nazi regime likewise took a dislike to Franco, but in both cases such antipathy had little bearing on the global scheme of policy decisions.

Economically, both Franco and Castro feared a free-market system and were dedicated to the principles of a command economy. They embraced national economic self-sufficiency, and both Falangism and Communism preached the idea of an organized working class.

Franco was remarkably adroit at fusing the working class into a common trade-union front, while nationalizing production and setting price controls for all goods. He allowed some entrepreneurial activities, but only as a mechanism to support the totalitarian state.

Indeed, being a far larger and more powerful nation with diversified resources, Spain could better implement a command economy than could Cuba.

The Divergence

For all of these similarities—and their significance to be noted below—the differences between the two dictators must also be duly noted because the comparison can provide important clues about Cuba's post-Castro direction. Whether it is a function of the orthodox military background of Franco, as opposed to the legal and guerrilla background of Fidel, is difficult to say, but clearly Castro wins the medal for sheer fanaticism.

The Franco regime maintained manifest neutrality even as the Nazi-Fascist Axis appeared to be winning. And later, as the Allied victories mounted, the ideological tone of the regime was muted. Franco became involved in a series of postwar diplomatic maneuvers aimed at restoring a sense of participation in the Western cultural milieu, and, significantly, displayed his ideological temperance through his succession plans—in direct contrast to Falangist suspicions of an empowered monarchy with democratic leanings. Indeed, it is this difference that distinguishes the likely legacies of Franco and Fidel.

In contrast to Franco the tactician, Castro displayed political zealotry at the Third World conferences he spearheaded, which took aim at Western power. His ideological commitment has been so pronounced that he has placed his philosophical proximity to pariah nations, such as Iran and Venezuela, over tactical advantage.

This difference in stridency will profoundly differentiate succession arrangements in Cuba. Franco's willingness to counter the Falangist consensus facilitated a royal succession, the best way to prevent Republican restoration. Thus, the royal family of Don Juan de Borbón, specifically his son, Juan Carlos de Borbón (Juan Carlos I), provided for an orderly, if uneasy, transition process.

Castro's notion of transition has never gotten beyond an emulation of a North Korean-style dynastic communism that shifts power within the family, rather than the party. Indeed, dynastic communism is a complete totalitarian system lacking the human face of monarchism. Of course, the heir apparent in Cuba is well-known and has parliamentary and party approval: Raúl Castro, Fidel's slightly younger brother. But the prospects of transition from Fidel to Raúl raise long-dormant issues regarding charisma, popularity, the armed forces and distinctive attitudes towards private property.

The Final Years

Despite economic stagnation, relative isolation from many Western European, as well as Latin American, nations and the emergence of scattered but real opposition, Cuba remained relatively stable in July 2006. Its alliances with Venezuela, Bolivia and, to a lesser extent, Brazil and Ecuador, as well as new trade agreements with China and a modest upswing in growth (despite widespread claims of statistical incongruities and ambiguities) have bolstered its stability. And as 2006 came to a close, news of Castro's various sundry ailments raised the possibility of political turnover as it became clear that change was in the wind. Still, no political crisis seems imminent.

A similar situation seems to have been in place in July 1974, when Franco complained of pain and swelling in his right foot. When it was determined that Franco was suffering from life-threatening abscesses, he was hospitalized in relative quiet. He received few visitors and made few public announcements regarding his illness. The image of an ailing dictator simply did not fit the robust military figure that had ruled Spain with fierce determination.

Franco's ailments multiplied: impairment of speech and depression became symptoms that were treated by psychiatric methods. Despite some disagreements with Franco's family members over his resumption of authority, Franco's inner circle, known as the "bunker" group, prevailed, and he continued in power and resumed many activities in the autumn of 1974. He began to meet with people, make small speeches and received salutes at the victory parade of the Falangist Revolution. At the same time, it became evident that Franco was suffering from Parkinson's disease and that his ability to maintain and exercise power was becoming increasingly tenuous. As one commentator at the time pointed out, "Despite personal anxieties, the resumption of certain state functions did not solve matters. Spain lives in a state of complete uncertainty and apprehension."

Socialists and social democratic politicians in Spain became more active. Along with the Christian liberal opposition to Franco, they sought to move beyond the crisis into a secular system, but were unable to muster the quorum needed for a purely civic solution. Through his ministers, Franco held out for the re-establishment of the monarchy, which appeared the best way to assure continuity, skirt secularization and address Basque terrorism and separatism. Franco was a firm believer in taking harsh measures against terrorism. He declared: "Either we finish these destroyers of society or they finish us."

The official and public activities that Franco resumed while he was obviously terminally ill had grave political consequences. Illness did not prevent him from signing decrees for the execution of terrorists—an unpopular decision, and one few would take under the risky circumstances. This was as late as October 1975, when his apparent illnesses could no longer be kept from the people. He was clearly suffering from heart attacks, and his ability to conduct even ceremonial duties of state was markedly impaired. In addition to Parkinson's disease, he suffered from myocardial arrest, stomach ulcers, renal failure, thrombophlebitis, bronchial pneumonia, toxic shock and irremediable heart failure.

With Franco's death the transition of power in Spain took place: a modern society to be ruled by a democratic Catholic monarch. To be sure, the rule of Don Juan Carlos held many surprises, not the least his encouragement of a rapid return to human-rights principles. The son, like his Bourbon father, was wedded to principles of fierce anti-totalitarianism.

Meanwhile, Castro's own "loyalists" (a half-dozen ministers along with Raúl) are surely the equivalent of the "bunkers" of Franco. And there is an eerie sameness in the medical ailments that have struck both Franco and Castro and their public portrayal: multiple sources of illness, mistrust of surgical repairs and operations that were less than satisfactory in their outcomes. If political ideology could determine medical diagnosis, then according to Castro's friends, his intestinal ailment is virtually an imperialist plot—or at least it was seen as such until the magnitude of the ailments could no longer be disguised.

There has yet to be a public disclosure of the illnesses Fidel suffers, only that he is on the road to recovery. But Fidel's absence from public functions and major gatherings speaks for itself. Every effort has been made to picture the transition process from Fidel to Raúl as smooth. The words of the hour are stasis and obedience to principle. While medical diagnosis seems hostage to ideological proclivities, one element is clear: For Cuba, it's business as usual.

Of Death and Dictatorship

While the transition in the mid-1970s from tyrant to monarch was unsettling to Spaniards and Basques alike, it was remarkable in its restoration of democratic norms. The situation in Cuba, while fluid, appears to be quite different. There is no instrument of political legitimacy that remains other than military authority. Democratic opposition remains fragmented both in size and outreach. There is doubt as to how the more than one million Cubans living in exile are to be treated in any new arrangement: Are their properties to be restored; are they to be welcomed back to the island; are they to be seen as interlopers who escaped during the dictatorship only to return as new masters of an ill-shaped national consensus? Thus, there will be an interregnum in which Castro will continue to live on—perhaps for the same two years prior to death in which Franco found himself. However, this interregnum cannot be resolved as it was in Spain.

Franco declared in his last will and testament that the "enemies" of Spain—or rather those opposed to his rule—were also the enemies of Christian civilization. But in an unexpected twist of national politics, the very royal family employed by Franco as a tool against political secularism and social pluralism turned out to be a major instrument for a relatively quiescent and peaceful transition towards democracy.

Despite some of the more prevalent predictions regarding Cuba, my own thinking is that Cuba will become neither benevolent democracy nor benign dictatorship in the near future. Instead, one can expect a return to the classical Latin model of military authority. The fact that Raúl Castro has been Cuba's defense minister since the early 1960s and has also served as a direct representative of Fidel in strategic policy issues provides a linchpin and continuum that may not be royal but is certainly dynastic.

The Cuban military, the only solid force in the nation other than the Communist Party, will indeed inhibit, if not dismantle, the current communist apparatus. At the same time, it will severely limit tendencies toward multiparty change. Even if Raúl Castro is open to some sort of power-sharing arrangement with others, his own strong links to the armed forces almost ensure his role as maximum leader. The transition from the charismatic Fidel to Raúl will be characterized by an elevated public presence of Cuba's armed forces.

The pivotal importance of the military in Cuba arises not from general theory—which states that the armed forcers were the praetorian guard of the working class—or from a Latin American inclination to champion the "man on horseback" in times of political malaise, but rather the decimation of all forms of Cuban civil authority: the virtual dissolution of an independent judiciary, the rubber-stamp, toothless nature of the legislative body, and above all, the Communist Party's assumption of executive powers.

The origin of the Cuban Revolution and its emergence as an armed struggle through guerrilla insurgencies and overseas adventures are a special feature of Cuban history. While in most other Latin American nations the military served internal police functions dedicated to the repression of popular movements, the armed forces in Cuba have not been seen as a comparable mechanism of repression. Its heroic image may have been tarnished over time by charges of corruption and even incompetence, but this was far more the case under the pre-Castro regime of Fulgencio Batista. The professionalization of the military under Castro's rule has created the unique basis for a post-Castro instrument of political transition.

The shattering impact of the Ochoa Affair of 1989—involving the trial and execution of a small clique of high-ranking military officials and heroes of foreign battlefields on charges of corruption and drug smuggling—did demoralize the military for a considerable time. But its reconstitution caused the Cuban armed forces to become increasingly professionalized—less a function of military choice than the level of punishment and reprimand.

One might reasonably argue that military authorities will yield to a civilian establishment predicated on liberal norms. But the special problems of Cuba will make this a very lengthy interregnum. The problems that the new regime must deal with are immense: racial strife between the large black minority and the white majority, a divide suppressed, rather than bridged, by Fidel; as well as a badly damaged infrastructure, from urban housing to medical facilities; to an educational system that is so rooted in ideology as to destroy scientific advances found elsewhere in Latin America.

The issue of private property is not simply one of establishing a healthy business climate, but the restoration of business and property to former ownership. This is an issue that extends into the relationship between the exile communities within the United States and the potential entrepreneurial forces within Cuba. Especially important will be the handling of the huge unrequited demand for new goods and services. In short, absent a fully operational civil-administrative state, which has been severely damaged by Castro, the armed forces, whatever their limitations, will in all likelihood be required to supervise such a national transformation.

The End of Francoism and Castroism

What I will forward with some certitude is that the same final judgment made by the fine historian Raymond Carr on the Spanish tyrant Franco will also await the Cuban tyrant, Fidel Castro: "His rule, he claimed, would be for life. And so it turned out to be. But 'the novel solution' could not outlast its architect. There was no Francoism after Franco." And so it will be with Fidel Castro: There will be no Castroism after Castro.

The common aspects of Francoism and Castroism limit their continuation. Both were driven by a cult of personality that becomes difficult to extend beyond the life of the person. And the sweeping repression so central to both dictatorships depends on an image of invincibility that is often undermined by the death of the leader. The reliance on foreign allies generally makes the dictatorship less tenable and the dependence on a command economy becomes unsustainable, particularly in the current Cuban context.

The expected death of Castroism becomes the ultimate irony and penalty of foisting upon a decent people a truncated Marxism-Stalinism, making endless appeals to personal sacrifice and metaphysical history, instead of governing through modest guidance and the presumption that human beings are quite capable of determining their own lives.

Source and Original Title: "Rocky Shoals of Reform: Castro and the *Caudillo*", *The National Interest*. Whole Number 89 (September-October, 2007). Pp. 66-71.

45

Cuba, Castro, and Anti-Semitism

Introduction

Karl Marx, in his brilliant historical study of The Eighteenth Bru-
maire of Louis Bonaparte, starts out by reminding us that "Hegel
says somewhere that all great historic facts and personages recur
twice. He forgot to add: 'once as tragedy, and again as farce.'"

With the holding in the year 2006 of the repeat meetings of
the so-called "Non-aligned Nations" that first met in Cuba 40
years ago, in 1966, we are reminded once more how little the Fidel
Castro regime has changed and how much the world has changed
in that time span. Nations like India that spearheaded the first such
meeting have developed amazing strides toward both democracy
and market enterprise, while others like Venezuela have gone
from a world that produced a democratic leader such as Rómulo
Betancourt to a military dictator like Hugo Chávez.

But the constancy of the Castro attachment to communism
remains as real in theory and as remote in practice now as it was
then. Part of this attachment was an emerging hostility to Israel and
overall contempt for the Jewish mini-Diaspora within the larger
flight of Cubans to the United States and other places where the
practice of free speech remains unimpeded. With new allies such
as Iran, Syria, and the Palestine Liberation factions in Gaza and

the West Bank, that hostility—fueled by decades of imbibing the Soviet legacy—has hardened into a primary credo. The remnants of the Jewish community in Havana, not-withstanding, Cuba is one more nation where anti-Semitism without Jews is a core belief.

In language strongly reminiscent of the Nazi epoch in German history and its main organ of propaganda, Der Stürmer, the Cuban Communist regime and its main organs of propaganda, Radio Havana and *Granma*, launched an unprecedented assault on the Israeli struggle against Hezbollah in Southern Lebanon. Characteristically for the Castro ideological machinery, Hezbollah was simply not mentioned. Instead, the conflict was pictured as an ongoing Israeli struggle—one that pits "arrogant Jews, armed to the teeth by the United States" against Palestine and Lebanon. The rubber-stamp Cuban National Assembly, even with ailing leader hospitalized, obediently expressed its condemnation of the "Zionist entity" as a "horrendous and shameless action, a genocide which challenges universal public opinion, laughs at the United Nations, and threatens to invade other countries, reminiscent of the era of Nazism."

There are unique dimensions to the vanguard role of the Cuban regime in its hostility to Israel. Not least is that Cuba is essentially a country lacking anything resembling a viable Jewish community. Indeed, estimates range from between twelve to fifteen hundred Jewish souls in a nation that in 1959, at the time of the Castro seizure of power, contained ten times that number, or between twelve thousand and fifteen thousand Jewish citizens. Therefore, by even a cursory examination of the Castro regime attitude toward Israel it is worth noting the special character of its Jews at home. Despite the attempt to downplay, even eradicate awareness of Cuba as an anti-Semitic environment, one hostile to Jews, it must be noted that until recently the American hard Left has continued to make distinctions between anti-Israeli from anti-Jewish behavior by the regime. Thus the mythological nature of this dualism requires at least a cursory examination.

The typical apologetic Leftist approach is to claim that the regime's anti-Zionist record "does not stem from anti-Semitic sentiment but from a purely self-interested approach to international relations." Indeed, the author of these words, Aleksandra Brikman, in a web site paper ironically entitled "Cuba: A Haven for Jews?," goes so far as to claim that "the Cuban government's position has always been and continues to be favorable and responsive towards the needs of its Jewish community." The sheer demographic facts of the Castro Era would tend to cast serious doubt on such a bromide. Ninety percent of the Jewish community left Cuba soon after 1959. Indeed, only in the mid-1990s was Cuba declared to be not so much an "atheistic state" but one open to multiple religious beliefs. This indicates a widespread contempt for religions in general, one that fell with special fury on the Jewish community. The very magnitude of the Catholic population inhibited, even if not prohibited, direct assaults on the majority faith in Cuba.

There are a variety of sources of anti-Semitism in Cuba, several of which predate the rise of the Castro regime. In the pre-Castro era, the most dangerous period for Jews was in 1938–1939, when German Nazi influence in Cuba was at its height. The crowning propagandistic moment in the period before the birth of Israel, was the refusal of its then President (Bru) and the Cuban government to permit the landing of the *S.S. Saint Louis* in Havana harbor in 1939. Nazi Minister Joseph Goebbels fabricated and hyped up the passengers' criminal nature, making them undesirable. Nazi agents within Cuba stirred anti-Semitism and organized protests, making the idea of an additional one thousand refugees seem to be a threat against Cuba itself. Negotiations for Jewish lives followed a pattern typical during the earlier phase of the Nazi era: fixing a price for the survival of each Jew. The most authoritative report at the time indicated that the Cuban government wanted five hundred dollars per refugee (approximate a half million U.S. dollars in total). It was said that this money was no more than the amount required for any refugee to obtain visa to Cuba. Negotiations by fits and starts broke down, the Cuban government finally refused any landing permits, and "The Ship of Fools" was denied entrance. A fate of death befell many on board and who were compelled to return to various European ports.

In addition to the Cuban government's venality and corruption, there was of course, the traditional animus toward Jewish refugees. This was especially pronounced in Catholic countries where the clergy was under the influence of the then less than supportive Pope Pius XII. Such sentiments were fueled by patterns of Jewish migration to the Americas after World War One. Immigration restrictions were tightened in the United States, especially after 1924. As a result, large numbers of Eastern and Central Europeans found their way to Cuba, on the unwarranted presumption that after one year of residency on the island, migration to the United States as part of the immigration quota would be routine if not automatic. This inability of these new immigrants to root themselves in the Cuban world was hardly a show of commitment in the new land, and this show of alienation was reciprocated with passivity, if not active hostility by the native population. While a small percentage of Jewish migrants did establish business and professional activities, the desire to reach the United States was clearly the dominant factor among the Jewish arrivals.

At the same time, the flow of Jews from the United States to Cuba, in the interwar period also contributed to something less than perfect relations between Jewish immigrants and Cuban hosts. Booms in gambling, casinos, and a variety of forms of deviance, including drugs and prostitution, had a Jewish component—sometimes greater in the imagination of the hosts than it was in fact, but nonetheless real. This also served to distinguish migrants and natives and served to inhibit Jewish participation in the Cuban political processes toward democratization that occurred in the 1930s. With such a lethal combination of immigration as a temporary transit point, criminal activity as a way of gaining a measure of security in a booming Cuban gray market, and traditional clerical hostility to alien religions at one level and political wariness to foreign nationals, including the United States, at another, the grounds of anti-Semitism were established before the seizure of power by Fidel Castro and his allies.

Cuba's Jewish Community has been described by Jay Levinson, author of *The Jewish Community of Cuba* in terms of "The

Golden Years, 1906–1958." The truth is that such a definition makes sense only in terms of Jewish organized life around its synagogues and burial grounds, but not with respect to terms of full participation as a national of the country. Indeed, such participation was absurd on the face of it, since the regime was essentially a dictatorship run by Fulgencio Batista, and could not be thought of as a regime open to democratic processes whatever the Jewish community might have preferred or desired. In any event, those so-called golden years soon turned to ashes. After Fidel Castro came to power, the overwhelming majority of the Jewish professional community left for the United States, Puerto Rico and other parts of Latin America, while its businesses were confiscated as part of the general anti-capitalist spirit of the new regime. Many of these businesses and people were transplanted to the United States, Florida in particular, with astonishing success. The Cuban people to start with were among the most advanced in terms of technological skills in the region. They wear with pride the designation: "the Jews of the Caribbean." Its Jewish component was simply an add-on to what already were a highly resourceful and innovative people—when given half a chance to be so.

Marxism–Leninism

The rise to power of the Castro government and transformation of a guerrilla movement into a source of organized State power brought this era of ethnic toleration to an end. The Cuban Revolution of 1959 was mediated by an ideology—Marxism–Leninism. This is not the place for a full-scale exploration of the place of ideology in the affairs of the Castro regime. But it is worth noting how the role of anti-Semitism plays its hand in its formation. When it comes to the place of communist doctrine in the world of Castro, it is not Marx's effort in *The Communist Manifesto*, and its egalitarian impulses, but his effort five years earlier in 1843 *On The Jewish Question* and its blatant and deep-seated animosities for religion, which merits our attention. "We recognize in Judaism" Marx notes, "a general anti-social element of the present time, an element which through historical development—to which in this harmful respect the Jews have zealously contributed—has been brought to its present higher level, at which it must necessarily begin to disintegrate. In the final analysis, the emancipation of the Jews is the emancipation of mankind from Judaism. The Jew has already emancipated himself in a Jewish way." Beneath Marx's Hegelian smoke was the anti-Semitic fire of the uneasy and uncertain family convert. For Marx, the Jew as bourgeois has "emancipated" himself in civil terms. The task was to eliminate Judaism itself as part of the effort at political emancipation from capitalism. In this scenario, one does not need Jews to stand in opposition to Judaism. Castro's Cuba without Jews fits the bill to perfection.

Nor is such theorizing a function of abstract theory. Castro had a long gestation period under Soviet tutelage—and that included the Stalinist legacy in which Jews were subject to special treatment: from the denial of their special victimization at the hands of the Nazi regime to a removal of Jewish scholars from the sciences and Jewish organizational life as a force unto itself, and a denial of emigration rights to Jews in particular. The frequent charge of "cosmopolitanism" in the xenophobic world of Great Russian chauvinism was a virtual code word for being Jewish, or better, anti-national. It permitted Soviet authorities to isolate and if necessary disgrace delegations and visitations from Israel.

The Soviet Press became a critical instrument in anti-Semitism, reaching a fevered pitch in identifying the Central Intelligence Agency of the United States with the Zionist Secret Service. In all such calumnies, not a single statement was ever uttered by the Castro regime in denial or rejection of such calumnies. Indeed, they were repeated faithfully and repeatedly in the propaganda organs of the Cuban Communist Party. The Soviets provided Cuba with the model of attacking human rights activities and organizations as a necessary extension of the Jewish Zionist conspiracy.

The fusion of Cuban foreign policy with the extremist regimes of the Middle East dates back to the ideological hardening that took place after the Tri-continental meetings of the mid-1960s.

The identification of Castro with forces dedicated to the destruction of Israel was made plain not only in proclamation, but also in practice. Direct military assistance was extended to Syria during the wars of 1967 and 1973. And while some question remains on whether Cuban troops were in the front lines in the tank corps, the advisory roles of Cuba is uncontested. Indeed, at the Havana 1966 meetings of the Tri-continental, the role of the Middle East as a bulwark against United States imperialism was reaffirmed. The Cuban position is that the war on terrorism is actually an example of "Liberation Imperialism." There is not a single reference to the repeated assaults on Israel, or the actual causes of the Middle East conflict—the denial of the right of Israel to exist as a nation-State in the region. Instead we are informed by the Cuban spokesman, Sabah Alnasseri, that "The war on Iraq broke an axis, which was in the forming between Iran, Iraq and Syria—and probably Turkey with its Islamic government—and which could have reinforced the position of Syria, Lebanon and Palestine in face of Israel."

In short, the struggle in the Middle East is between oil rich independent nations and the United States–Israeli effort to impose "neo-liberal conquest strategies of strong states and barbarized conditions on a world scale." While the rhetoric is far more in tune with classical Marxism–Leninism than one hears from Iranian or Syrian authorities, the consequences in terms of geopolitical alignments are the same: a denial of terrorism as a factor, and a rejection of the struggle against terrorist forces, as in any way acceptable, much less legitimate.

The Cuban Propaganda Machine

The ratcheting up of the Cuba propaganda machine is complex and at times tortured. It must display unflinching loyalty to the dictatorial regimes in the Middle East, whether secular or clerical, and also distinguish its position from those regimes by avoiding the over identification of Israel as a nation and the Jewish people as a world historic religion. Cuba's essential ploy in this regard is to identify the Israeli response to the Hezbollah forces in Southern Lebanon as itself genocidal. Thus Radio Havana in its July 1st message states that "not even the Nazis undertook a retaliation of such proportions against a civilian population." The response to guerrilla insurgency in the Gaza region is seen "as the army of Israel proceeding with its work of extermination" and identifies this struggle as "part of the fascist designs over the Palestinian people" (Mesa Redonda, July 28th). And finally, "the Zionist regime has shielded itself behind the kidnapping of an Israeli soldier to intensify their genocide of the Palestinian people" (Radio Habana, July 28th).

The Cuban organs of communication constantly identify Israeli actions with United States "flagrant complicity and perfidy... which guarantees the impunity of the aggressor regime." This statement released by the Cuban Ministry of Foreign Affairs on August 4th, follows from an earlier release on July 18th that "the real purpose are the hegemonic plans of Tel Aviv and Washington to dominate all the energy resources in the area." The emphasis on petroleum resources as the real source of the conflict in the Middle East accords well with the Marxist vision of economic determinants on all conflicts in which "imperialism" engages. Another statement of the Ministry of Foreign Affairs links Europe to American designs. "The armaments with which this genocide is being committed are supplied by the United States.... With rare exceptions, the European Union has served as an accomplice and has accepted the bland statements imposed by the Empire on the other side of the Atlantic." This linkage of Europe to America is seen as "the shameful and cowardly passivity of the European Union."

The Cuban propaganda machine, following the lead of Hezbollah and Iran, identified the cessation of hostilities by "the military hordes of the Israeli government" as a huge defeat for Israel and the West. "The myth of her invulnerability, fabricated by themselves and spread by their powerful allies, began in 1948, when they made the world believe that a militia of colonists installed in Palestine could defeat five Arab armies." And in a rare departure from distinguishing Jews from Israelis, the Radio Havana report of August 7th went on to note that "the legend grew when the arrogant Jews, armed to the teeth by the United States and allied with France and Great Britain, defeated Egypt in 1956." Increasingly, as the month long conflict unfolded, the Cuban information ministries and press ceased speaking of Israel and increasingly spoke the language of the Jihadist militants: of "the Zionist entity" and/or the "occupying power." This represents a significant departure from the previous Cuban position that was careful to distinguish the Jewish faith from the Israeli government, and indeed, unlike the radical Islamist states, continued to speak of Israel at least as a fact on the ground.

One great difficulty for the Marxist–Leninist regime is identifying the conflict in the Middle East in theological or apocalyptic terms. Itself a country largely Catholic in its population, Cuba was and remains hard put to see the "solution" of the issues in terms of the universal conversion of Christians and Crusaders into the Islamic faith. So what is missing in all Cuban analysis is the meaning of martyrdom, the immolation of warriors of Islam, and as one might expect, even a hint that any irrational element might be at work in the denial of the Holocaust or the effort to create a new Holocaust in the statements and actions of the Iranian sponsored terrorists in Southern Lebanon. The furious slaughters that are daily occurrences within Iraq between Shiites and Sunnis, between terror bandits and police, or assassinations of leaders attempting to force a legitimate government, likewise are seen as not fit for the propaganda radar screen. There is no mention of Hezbollah or Hamas, and just as telling, no sense of ongoing efforts to reach a pacific accommodation between contending forces.

The Castro government has in the past routinely cartooned Israeli figures in terms of hooked nosed caricatures dancing to the tune of Uncle Sam. But it tended to stay clear of outright assaults on Jewish sensibilities. That has now been replaced by a strong dose of anti-Semitism, of the sort common during the Stalinist era—in which Jewish interests are seen as cosmopolitan elements disloyal to the national interest of the people, whoever they may be. The sole reason given for Jewish existence is to participate in the imperial plunder of poor nations with rich mineral resources. The de-legitimating of Israel is now close to the official Arab extremist position. Israel is viewed as a nation without proper authority and one whose very right to exist is in grave question. It also accords with the strong adaptation of anti-Semitism as the official policy of Hugo Chávez and the oil-producing giant, Venezuela.

The strong allegiance demonstrated in the past by a heavily populated American Left intelligentsia has been left in tatters by the new developments in the Middle East. Once again, in Castro's Cuba, as in Stalin's Russia seventy years earlier, the fixation of belief in revolutionary utopias has been exposed as a terrible fraud with high risk consequences. This may be a small by-product of the recent war between Israel and Hezbollah, but in American terms, it is highly consequential. On a smaller scale, the emergence of a Cuban identification with an unsavory group of terrorists and true believers, blurs the classical gap between a communist left and a fascist right. The strong Jewish support evident in the emergence of the Castro regime has become silent, if not exactly repentant, of its past endorsements in the air and participations on the ground.

Anti-Semitism is so powerfully rooted as a cultural element in authoritarian cultures that even when, as in the case of Cuban Communism, it entails the tortured twisting of doctrinal elements within Marxism–Leninism, such as doctrinal claims about the "materialist foundations of society," its leaders will sacrifice the ideology to the reality. The fusion of Jihadist acts of revenge and terror, the instance on the supreme role of Islamist belief as a test of moral worth, and the virtual negation of popular rule as a test for regime worth, all become part of the common struggle against Israel as a nation and Judaism as a cultural tradition.

For a world that has witnessed the horrors of the Holocaust in Nazi Germany and the systematic decomposition of Jewish life in Bolshevik Russia, the new wave of warfare upon the singular democracy in the Middle East and the calumny heaped upon its people—even by European powers that should now know better—is a grim reminder that moral progress lags far behind technological advances.

References/Notes

The information gathered from the Cuba press and broadcasts is provided by *Cuba Facts* (Issue No. 24, August 2006), which is part of the Cuba Transition Project of the United States Agency of International Development and the University of Miami. The ongoing efforts of this service merit professional respect and appreciation as well as personal acknowledgment.

Source and Original Title: "Cuba Castro and Anti-Semitism" in *Current Psychology,* Vol. 26, Nos. 3-4, December 2007, 183-190 pp.

46

Semper Fidel

As Cuba moves closer to the half-century anniversary Fidel Castro and his political intimates' seizure of power, the number of books and essays trying to explain the man, the system and the nation seems to grow exponentially. While it may be small consolation, the writings are much better in the current period than in previous years. This is due in part to the exhaustion of those whose writings were characterized by celebratory tones. In the first ideological phase, voices from Europe and North America joined those from the Latin American Left in not only celebrating the Cuban Revolution of 1956–59, but in condemning the American Century that, while still in full force, was beginning to show the frayed edges of empire building. Vietnam in the 1960s, after all, could be viewed as the beginning of the end of an imperial vocation that started with Cuba and the Philippines in 1898. Such a view of interventionist power politics is the very driving force, now as then, of Castro's magical hold on his people. Whatever Cuban Communism's weaknesses as a social paradise or an economic exemplar, Castro can always trumpet his great success in keeping the colossus of the north at bay. And in politics, smoke and mirrors can rank high on a poor country's list of responses to guns and bombs.

Now that the sting of anti-American rhetoric has worn thin in Cuba, the background of those who write about Castro and his island has shifted from the ideologists and the sociologists to the journalists and historians. The results may not betoken a better life for the Cuban people, but at least it produces better judgment about the long night they have endured under the Castro regime. The three works considered here offer an interesting variety of efforts to chart Castro's personal and educational background. Castro's school days are the focus of an extremely well written and researched effort by Patrick Symmes in *The Boys from Dolores*. Symmes' book is followed by a critical but not tendentious examination of the prologue years of Castro's Revolution by Anthony DePalma in *The Man Who Invented Fidel*. Finally, there is Brian Latell's *After Fidel*, a report on the Castro of the moment, with an accounting of whatever we know (precious little, it would seem) of his brother and heir apparent, Raúl Castro. Taken as a group, the three books merit high marks. They provide a solid foundation for those who wish to know more about Cuba and have the patience to find out. More broadly, they also provide a critical look at what makes a dictatorship tick, and tick for so long a time.

The Colegio de Dolores, the preparatory academy where Fidel went to school, was hardly the sort of institution familiar in the annals of American elite education. Indeed, Patrick Symmes' description presents the place as a combination of a Jesuit-run institution, a boarding school for the less-than-privileged, and something of a holding pen for juvenile delinquents and assorted misfits. Misdemeanors were frequent, rules were stringent, and punishment was real albeit not brutal. We are told that behind the theology of the Church was the nomenclature of a military regimen. Fidel and his brother, along with many of his fellow students and their brothers (it seems that the company of brotherhood was a powerful factor in the organization of student life), were indoctrinated. By way of a series of interviews with people in Cuba and those in exile in Miami, Symmes offers a wonderful set of insights of this brotherly/military/church world. He argues that Castro's particular experience in growing up absurd provides clues to his character, behavior and even his ideology.

It is hard to deny the premise, but the problem, of course, is that while inputs were similar for all the boys of the Jesuit school, the outcomes were quite different. After all, the tale of Castro's early years can hardly explain how the conditions of his schooling yielded a ferocious dictator, when the same conditions yielded a kind and gentle historian with a subtle sense of humor and a commitment to democratic norms, as it did with Luis "Lundy" Aguilar. As we learn from George Orwell's *Such, Such Were the Joys*, harsh and punitive schooling gives to some of those who learn its lessons an eye to further implementation, but gives to others an impulse to reform, to rebel and to heal.

Symmes writes more about the context of a revolution than its contents—that is to say, about personal interactions and tendencies rather than political policies and ideological tendencies. While he is sympathetic to those who decided to make a revolution, he demonstrates an equal appreciation of those who rebelled against its excesses. Indeed, he has a pitch-perfect appreciation of what brought this motley crew together as youngsters. "The revolution against Batista was largely a phenomenon of class", Symmes reminds us, pointing specifically to the narrow stratum of the Cuban middle class:

> the professionals and technocrats, the engineers and lawyers. People like Fidel Castro. It was a revolution of lawyers, and of dentists. These were the people in Cuba who could literally afford to rebel, to risk things in pursuit of the better instincts of Cuban nationalism and democracy.

We have been so inundated with the myths of guerrilla insurgency—in which a rag-tag group of the downtrodden actually manages to take over the management of Cuban society—that the actual backgrounds of those involved have been misconstrued. In part, the Castro regime's rulers wish to erase their own past in the name of a muscular, quasi-military present. On the other hand, Castro's enemies would like to forget their own participation in a drama that destroyed one tyrant, only to see him replaced by an even more tenacious and evil "maximum leader." It would have been nice had Symmes made this point frankly, rather than ending on a note of understandable but ambiguous elegy; but one can't have everything.

Anthony DePalma, himself a correspondent and reporter for the *New York Times* for 20 years, has written a different kind of intimate narrative. His story is not so much of childhood colleagues, but of Herbert Matthews, another famed *New York Times* writer turned acolyte and supporter of Castro. By the time Matthews tracked down Fidel in the Sierra Maestra mountain range in 1957, he became not only a reporter but also a policy-maker among the newspaper fraternity. His heroic portrayal of Castro had a strong impact on American perceptions of Cuba and, by all accounts, contributed to the demise of the Batista regime. When the real ideological contours of the Castro regime became evident, the *New York Times*, then far more conservative than it has become today, made Matthews a scapegoat. His reputation and journalistic career foundered; he was accused of betraying his country.

At the time, the Gray Lady was still laboring under the shadow of Walter Duranty's whitewash of the genocidal slaughter of millions of Ukrainian peasants during the Stalinist first purge in the 1930s. DePalma rightly places the Matthews situation in that historical context, and he makes clear, as Robert Service recently noted in his own fine work, *Comrades: A History of World Communism* (2007), that Walter Duranty was a scoundrel and a thief—someone "who said anything that would prolong his comfort and commercial activity in the Soviet capital." What DePalma is less candid about is the place of political pilgrims and true believers, as opposed to professional scoundrels, in the celebration of totalitarian regimes. The history of continuing support for the Soviet tyranny by such figures as Edgar Snow, Joseph Davies and Hewlett Johnson—a skilled journalist, an ambassador and a Church divine—indicates that personal motives played little if any part in their belief system, just as with Matthews. Indeed, Matthews himself gave the final word on the honest reporter turned true believer: "Many of my stories harmed a cause in which my heart lay", he wrote, "but I have no remorse and no regrets."

Thanks to the Castro regime's success, at least in survival terms, such delusional sentiments were allowed to persist unchecked.

DePalma is a wise enough man to understand full well that, at the end of the day, Castro "possessed such an uncanny ability to survive that he would have managed to stay alive long enough to seize power whether or not Matthews had arrived at the moment when he and his revolution were utterly prostrate." So it seems too much to then claim that "Castro could have triumphed without Matthews, but then history would have been different." It simply is not true that Matthews "invented the image of Fidel Castro." That image was a collective portrait invented, or rather embellished, by all sorts of people, from Leo Huberman and C. Wright Mills in the United States to Régis Debray and Jean-Paul Sartre in France, with help from countless others from a variety of lands. Here DePalma misses a major opportunity to advance the moral ground of honest journalism. Instead of "thanking" Fulgencio Batista, Fidel Castro and Herbert Matthews for making his work possible, he would have done better to note that they represented a grotesque ideological amalgamation of ruthless rule and totalitarian pretenses foisted on a people who deserve better.

As an examination of a strange episode, of a moment in time and place in which one reporter's odyssey is examined, *The Man Who Invented Fidel* is a case study from which freshman j-school students could profit, not just by imitating its better qualities but by recognizing its limits. DePalma's brilliant chapter on Matthews' journey through the first part of his adult life illustrates the problem of reporting the truth and predicting the future. We learn of an education in romance languages at Columbia University, military service at the close of the First World War, life in Paris in the 1920s, and the Spanish Civil War. In Spain, Matthews' proclivities to support the republic reached a point of delusion in his refusal to believe that Madrid could ever fall to the Falangists, despite the confusions, errors and even outrages perpetrated by Republican forces on the Church.

The romance of revolution overtook Matthews in Spain (as it had another American journalist, John Reed, in Russia). As

Paul Hollander has insightfully analyzed in his notion of political pilgrimage, falling in love with the impossible makes a mess of a journalist's ability to know truth when he sees it. This is the painful problem DePalma knows well but addresses only in passing, ultimately leaving it to readers to figure out for themselves how Matthews' passions eroded his professionalism. Along the way, we learn a good deal about an America divided at the close of the McCarthy era and the emergence of a new generation, the American Camelot, who were convinced that they too were making a revolution—albeit a different, democratic one. Matthews was hopeful, even certain, that Castro would adopt that revolution, too, and guarantee a happy ending all around. But as in so many other cases of revolutionary activity, Castro's idealist rhetoric yielded to reality, a crude and brief proto-democracy to pure dictatorship.

By the time Matthews died in July 1977, ten years after his retirement, one would have thought that even he must have stopped expecting a happy ending. As it happened, however, Matthews wrote three books after his retirement, two of them about Cuba, one about Spain. In the two Cuba books, Matthews showed that he had learned little. He died unrepentant, still hoping, in effect, that his American wife and his Cuban mistress would meet, grow fond of one another, and then compete in showering him with gratitude and affection. Such things, of course, rarely happen, except in Hollywood films of its golden era of romanticism.

Brian Latell comes from another part of the policy forest. He has a forty-year background tracking the Castro dynasty that dates back to the Central Intelligence Agency in the 1960s, service as a National Intelligence Officer in the 1990s, and now as staff lecturer at the Cuban-American Center of the School of International Relations at the University of Miami. As befits a man with such a background, After Fidel is rich in detailed nuances of meaning. There are few people, if any, who examine every report, proclamation and change of personnel in Communist Cuba as deeply or in as much detail as Latell. As he is aware, everything that takes place in the political hierarchy of a dictatorship is replete with rumor, gossip and sheer speculation. After Fidel is less a study of the Castro brothers than an effort to make sense of changes taking place on the ground in Cuba now. The book contains many interviews with those who have served in military and administrative posts. But for that very reason the book merits skeptical review, since such people are often filled with a sense of self-importance, animosity, revenge and sculpted vendettas long in the making. Miami is, after all, less a community of scholars than a substantial and diverse world of exiles waiting for the fall of the regime and the restoration of something resembling a democratic order.

In its new paperback guise, *After Fidel* appears at a time when the younger Castro, Raúl, is in effect the leader of Cuba. Latell is wise enough to stay clear of scenario-building, instead simply emphasizing that Cuba is already in a de facto post-Fidel era. Reading Fidel's weekly report card (something like fifty "oped" pieces in 2007 alone) on everything from the dangers of ethanol to the horrors of the American stock market, one might think that Fidel is the last person on earth to know that his time is up. But his refusal to leave the stage of history is itself an intriguing aspect of dynastic rule, where the old fail to die on cue and the young wait with nervous patience for their turn to do their own damage. A dictatorship yields to no clear-cut interregnum. Rather, the new men of power assume a quotidian authority for which they lack juridical legitimacy.

Still, even operating as Number Two Brother, Raúl's political career, as Latell notes, includes long-standing direction of the Cuban armed forces, efforts at economic modification along the so-called China model (really, a Keynesian economic base built upon a Leninist political edifice), and details about liquidating supposed enemies of the people in a nation without legitimate courts. Some of these items are well known to the policy community, others may be presumed from secondary data. Latell handles them all in workmanlike fashion.

Where problems begin is with what might be called Latell's Shakespearean/Freudian line of analysis. In this realm, the behavior of a would-be medieval king (Raúl) is thwarted by a recalcitrant brother, who happens to be as charismatic as he is dogmatic (Fidel). The picture that emerges is of a Raúl who is less than enthralled by the rigors of El Colegio Dolores. He was not especially athletic and is modest in personal behavior, having been married to Vilma Espín, a cheerless ideological force in her own right, since 1959. Raúl has been decent to his children and to the Castro clan in general, to which he serves as intimate patriarch. The difficulty is that little more personal information is available about him. We know far too little to presume a psychological profile along Freudian or other lines.

It is, moreover, especially difficult to estimate the degree to which such factors actually encourage political behavior that might allow for liberalization of the economy, and with it some sort of a private sector rebirth in Cuba. Latell clearly finds hope in such a prospect, but the evidence for it strikes me as little more than wishful thinking, based only on Raúl's roles in administrating the military and economy. I suspect that Latell is right in observing that the traditional model of the "middle-class military" practiced widely in other parts of Latin America is an attractive one for Raúl. But there is no way to know if this is so because Fidel remains dedicated to the leveling policies of communism as the *sine qua non* of Leninist principles, and rejects the satanic ways of the United States. Certainly Latell's conclusion, that "Raúl likely plans to provide them [the Cuban people] with bread, rather than Fidel's revolutionary circuses", has yet to materialize—nor can it as long as Fidel remains on rather than in planet earth.

Then again, the picture of Raúl that emerges from the available fragments of a life is itself subject to critical review. Can the Raúl of the 1960s—who competed with Che Guevara "in killings and viciousness", who was notorious for his "cold bloodedness" in dealing with presumed members of the previous regime, and who morphed into a "repressed, manipulated younger Brother"—emerge as a man "with many exceptional leadership qualities—organizational and managerial skills, patience, the ability to delegate and institutionalize, as well as a certain methodical creativity"? The U.S. intelligence community has often had trouble dissecting the potential behavior of leaders-in waiting of whom they have limited information or knowledge. However bravely Latell attempts to inform and instruct, the actual information we have on Raúl cannot support such grandiose judgments. It is, of course, another matter entirely as to whether such data could in any event offer up anything useful on his potential future behavior in a post-Fidel world.

These three books nevertheless do indicate that the end of the dictatorship and the dawn of the post-Castro era are fast approaching. Much remains to be learned, and will be, once the archives of the regime are revealed—although much that has transpired seems to have been done through verbal command rather than written memorandum. But even in this strange transitional moment in Cuban affairs—in which a dying ruler rants and rails against his enemies from a private hospital bed, and a recalcitrant younger brother, himself no spring chicken, tries to fashion an administrative bureaucratic rationale for maintaining a communist regime in the island—certain things are apparent. A military regime with an ideology like that of Castro's Cuba offers little improvement over a military regime without an ideology. Indeed, while the Batista regime exposed a small elite's hatred of a large disenfranchised mass and a tourist haven for foreigners rooted in a depressing backwater for natives, Castro's Cuba does not offer much to emulate either. Each of these three books is in its own way offers a painful reminder of everything rotten with a twentieth-century military tyranny built in a beautiful place upon an imported nineteenth-century ideology.

Sources and Original Titles: The Boys from Dolores: Fidel Castro's Schoolmates from Revolution to Exile (Patrick Symmes, 2007) "The Man Who Invented Fidel: Castro, Cuba, and Herbert L. Matthews" of *The New York Times* (Anthony DePalma, 2007) *After Fidel: Raúl Castro and the Future of Cuba's Revolution* (Brian Latell, 2007). Review Essay as "Semper Fidel", *The American Interest,* Winter (January/February 2008)

47

Mi Vida: The Manichean Face
of Dictatorship

Fidel Castro is one of the few surviving Cold War enemies of the United States. He has witnessed as adversaries ten U.S. Presidents: Eisenhower, Kennedy, Johnson, Nixon, Ford, Carter, Reagan, Bush the Elder, Clinton, and Bush the Younger. Castro is certainly the longest running dictator in the Western hemisphere, and arguably in modern times. He certainly has an acute sense of history, or at least Cuban-American relations, as the ultimate measuring rod of the success of his regime. To be sure, this relationship remains his testing rod from start to finish. Exactly one year prior to the anniversary of his movement's 1959 seizure of power, he announced to a television audience that "In the morning, 49 years of the revolution will be behind us and the 50th year will symbolize half a century of heroic resistance. We proclaim our pride in this record to the world." His autobiographical potpourri, *Fidel Castro: My Life* is intended to both share the pride and give his version of events for the historical record. Longevity is indeed the acid test of legitimacy—as it is for all political structures.

There is a sense in which Castro's premature celebration of a half century of rule is quite accurate. For the year 1958 was one in which his guerrilla movement held increased ground in the sparsely populated regions of Cuba, and even more significant, a time in which the decay of the Fulgencio Batista regime became apparent. The entrenched political apparatus had been paralyzed and the Cuban military forces had become incapable of hard fighting. So the claim of the text of this work that it represents a half century review is justified, and should not excite historical purists who date the regime from the entrance of the guerrilla forces on the streets of Havana on January 8, 1959. Indeed the failed attack at the Moncada Barracks in 1953 is frequently used as the benchmark for the new era. But whatever the dates used by both friend and foe of the regime, this guerrilla group's seizure of political power must be surely recognized as a major event of the twentieth century—a movement with a rise that, as of this writing, is still awaiting its fall, a fall that Fidel Castro has sworn to prevent from happening.

It is assuredly an accident that the autobiographies of both Bill Clinton and Fidel Castro are entitled My Life. Even so and in both instances, the government changes they initiated have had a profound impact on the course of events. One must also note that Castro, like Clinton, has been clever enough to realize that makers of history operate in a climate of public acquiescence if not complete active support. That allows for the first and perhaps most significant observation about Castro's autobiography: his increasing awareness of the need to reshape the record of his half century into a response to populist aims and nationalist ambitions. Castro's thundering earlier rubbish that "history will absolve me" has been replaced by endless repetition in which Fidel assures his readers that in past and present, his only concern has been to satisfy the needs and desires of the Cuban people. Behind the absolute dictatorship of Castro family hierarchy lurks a mythic "public opinion" democracy of the people. This perhaps explains Castro's extraordinary claims that Cuba has never been a nation that harbored political prisoners or ever resorted to illegal measures to extract confessions, even as thousands languish in its places of incarceration. Then again, it was none other than Joseph Stalin in his own autobiography who announced as his primary achievements as absolute ruler of all the Russians (50 million plus deaths later) the arrival of a society based on the iron rule of happiness, the highest law of dialectical reasoning.

While it is the case that the Castro regime cannot be accused of killings in the massive scale of its Soviet and Fascist predecessors, and not by a long shot, it is still the case that Cuba has endured the horrors of authoritarianism—the weak but clear family relation to totalitarianism. The state led by Fidel and Raúl Castro is responsible for thousands of firing squad executions and extrajudicial killings. Even conservative reports indicate over one thousand deaths in prisons, police stations, or State Security offices, as well as dozens of civilians murdered while trying to escape by sea or seeking asylum in foreign embassies and at the U.S. Naval Base at Guantánamo. Pregnant women have been assassinated in political prisons, and religious leaders and minors have been executed by firing squads. Nine extrajudicial killings and five deaths of prisoners for lack of medical attention were recorded for 2007 alone. In short, a modest claim that Cuba has never been a nation of massive killing fields, as say Pol Pot's rule in Cambodia, is justified. However it should unreservedly be noted that neither has Castro's brand of communism been a utopian escape from physical and mental abuse. Cuba has received the lowest rating from *Freedom House* of more than 200 nations covered as "not free" from 1973 through 2006; and in the Heritage Foundation *Index of Economic Freedom* Cuba ranks next to last—sandwiched between Zimbabwe and North Korea. Those reading this apologia will readily appreciate the difference between outright deception and tacit rationalization. This distinction is a cautionary note for those reading this fascinating volume; especially since neither the *comandante* nor his interviewer seem to grasp the difference between first and last in the pantheon of free societies.

The fixation of dictators with self importance is hardly a recent phenomenon. But it is the case that figures as dissimilar in background as Adolf Hitler, Joseph Stalin and Fidel Castro have prepared autobiographical volumes, with varying degrees of success. It is probably the case that Hitler's statement at the start of his career was the most horrifyingly successful and Stalin's, which came at the end of his rule, was the clearest failure. Hitler's *Mein Kampf* after all predicted his rise to power and described the ideology and organization that would fuel it. Stalin's autobiography was in comparison, lifeless, wooden, and came at the very end of his career. Indeed it was such a shamed faced attempt at self-promotion that it was not even called an autobiography, but biography, although no one in the Soviet Union was taken in by such literary duplicities. Castro's autobiography falls somewhere between the two European despots of the past century. The interview format offers a modicum of honesty that the other two did not provide. His book was neither ghostwritten nor orchestrated by party loyalists; although it most certainly has been carefully edited. The interview format is straightforward and offers a note of authenticity that will be appreciated by readers of political memorabilia.

The weaknesses of the Cuban regime are seen through an extremely narrow window of Castro's strong criticisms of corruption, bribery, speculation, and money laundering. But Castro presents these not as problems of the regime, but as hangovers of the bourgeois system that preceded his rise to power. A half century of socialism has led, not to the moral society that he so desperately champions, but to the isolated and immoral society he has long feared. Castro attributes everything wrong with Cuba to American capitalism, habits of the social past, and his own small mistakes, such as allowing even a small private sector initiative to penetrate his island. He does not reflect on human nature to any degrees, and he certainly exhibits no willingness to discuss how extravagant notions of social equality in contrast to actual economic inequality might have been induced by the regime as it evolved.

What is intriguing is how Castro continues to see authoritarian solutions as a proper response to massive corruption and disaffections. For example, some 25,000 "social workers" are in effect brought in to assist block wide committees in support of the revolution (usually led by janitors and building supervisors) to form a vigilante group to identify those who do not report income or worse, oil and energy revenues, instead siphoning them into the hands of profiteers. Castro consistently invokes the amazing influence of the United States as the source of such excesses, but what he really offers is a vigilante threat presented as ethical options to a society in which theft of public property as a means to create any sort of private wealth has become pandemic.

In an interesting final pair of chapters, issues of macroeconomic dimensions are reduced to the personal history of the dictator—his past and present authority with respect to the Cuban people. However, anything resembling serious solutions is noteworthy for their absence. Other than maxims about the need for more and better education, and less inducements to private wealth, the *comandante* leaves his readers with little more than a series of platitudes about his past decisions and present authority. The Cuban people are promised a post-Castro period of economic socialism, and survival by virtue of the special "human capital" of the Cuban people. Castro has little trouble dealing with a general human culture, but his sense of actual developments in areas of information technology and economic rationalization of products and their uses, is virtually absent. Indeed, real changes in the structure of the international economy are reduced to "global liberalization."

The ultimate vision for Fidel is a united Latin America—along the lines of Simón Bolívar one must presume—by a common language, culture and ethnic mix. He then adduces how a united Europe, even with different linguistic clusters such as the Finns and the Hungarians, has managed to forge a distinctive entity. Of course, the roles of actual economic free enterprise and political discussion and action are simply not part of the Castro vocabulary. This myopia about differences in outcomes no less than inputs seems entirely genuine. Castro is trapped in the rhetoric of nineteenth century revolutionary romanticism. If his sincerity did not lead to such disastrous consequences, one might be tempted to appreciate and even applaud such honesty. But the thousand years of peace that Hitler promised Germany would follow his liquidation of religious and cultural enemies is not much different than the millennium of peace that Castro promises will follow the liquidation of economic and military foes to the north of Cuba. Because the means are fatuous, the ends are hardly likely to be given any chance at success. The age of ideology may have come to an end in the advanced societies of the West, but it remains the touchstone for decisions in the atrophied society of Cuba—and for this tragic outcome, Castro has no one to blame other than himself.

The formal structure of *My Life* is not without interest. There is an interlocutor who functions as a straight man, a foil for the wisdom of the great man. In Ignacio Ramonet, a self-declared personal friend of Castro, the maximum leader could hardly have a better literary companion. Not a single sense of criticism penetrates these pages. There is no doubt about the merit of the actions taken by Castro – including his African, Middle or Latin American adventures. The volume is billed as an autobiography, but Ramonet is not troubled by his parasitic role. He excoriates "those narcissistic interviewers who never stop attacking their interlocutor and are eager to demonstrate that they're cleverer, more intelligent and better prepared than the person they are interviewing" (17). One might think this is a fair enough statement, but not a word is said in rebuke of those who use the interview format as a means to fawn over the subject, or who function as an unrepentant straight man, totally devoid of independent judgment. Ramonet cannot quite escape his own conscience in this regard, so he launches into a panegyric of pathological proportions against "the dishonest and cowardly notion of the interview as a genre that allows the person interviewed to be stabbed in the back by the interviewer, under the pretext that journalism is free and 'objective' (on behalf of a perverted notion of freedom of the press) and allows the interviewer to do what he or she likes with the interviewer's statements." What is billed as "one Hundred Hours with Fidel" is in fact more like one hundred years of solitude.

With such a partisan in his corner, Castro does not need to be unduly concerned. On four occasions in different chapters, Castro amplifies and modifies his views on his mother, Lina, on Khrushev during the missile crisis, his views of Hugo Chávez, and finally, his moderating judgment on Saddam Hussein. To be sure, other than a few details, nothing of substance emerges in these pages despite claims that new observations "enrich the book enormously." Most of Castro's views have been reported earlier and often before this book became available. The one exception, arguably a ghostly premonition of what might well happen to Fidel in the docket of history, concerns his change of view on the deceased Iraqi head, expressed after the invasion of Kuwait. Now he says: "One does not judge a humiliated, humbled man so severely, not matter what he's done." Perhaps he identifies with a leader who imprisoned and tortured innocents who committed no crimes except opposition.

In such a stifling literary atmosphere, it pays few dividends to argue with Castro over anything from American political leadership to the evolution and hardening of the Cuban Communist revolution over time. Indeed, Ramonet anoints the tyrant as "a great Christian" —a designation that Castro shamelessly accepts "from the standpoint of social vision" (156-57). Rather, it might be more profitably to single out a few nuggets of realism that are allowed to penetrate the text and reach top soil. Autobiographies of tyrants are important not so much for what they reveal about the nation, as what they may inadvertently tell us about the personal leader.

Why do despots write or authorize such books? First, the need for justification: the very fact of longstanding dictatorial rule compels a need to explain why the rule of one is superior, even necessary, to the rule of the many. Second, the ruler must explain his identification with the needs of the ruled. He must be seen as giving expression to the deep felt sentiments of those less articulate and presumably less capable than the more articulate. Third, the leader must present himself not so much as the charismatic figure pictured by the sycophants and followers as the figure that history itself put forth as the only living obstacle to the system that existed prior to his domination. Fourth, the dictator must explain that the carnage, the tragedy of the coup d'etat itself was worth the price in terms of outcomes—whether it be the liquidation of the independent peasant as a means to feed the proletarian poor, or the total obliteration of the middle classes and professional experts as a means to create a new world where education for children and the health for the mature are quotidian occurrences. Finally, a dictator is not simply a person rooted in historical causes. The measurement of dictatorial success is the destruction of history as such, the liquidation of memory as a sense of continuation of culture over human space and time. This huge book does not disappoint in any of these multiple categories of absolutism.

The animosity of Castro for the United States is clearly genuine and total. Even when the liberation of Cuba from Spanish rule was under discussion, as in the period immediately preceding the American Civil War, Castro could speak only of the United States "which always wanted to devour our island." Poor Castro was led to speak of the Cuban flag as first "a symbol of annexation" introduced by Southern slaveholders modeled by the flag of Texas, and then he was led to view the flag as "a symbol of glory...the flag of the heroic struggles of our people"—not only during the national period but apparently the "socialism of today." Castro rails against the slavocracy in the United States, but then must admit that slavery was abolished in the United States in 1862, whereas it was not until 1886 that slavery was abolished in Cuba. Everything and everyone is measured by opposition to American annexationist policies. Actual changes in American foreign policy toward Cuba have little place.

Castro repeatedly excoriates any infringement on Cuban national sovereignty on the part of Yankee imperialists. Indeed, he even warned his colleague Saddam Hussein of the dangers and errors in invading Kuwait in the 1990 period. At the same time, he speaks with carefree abandonment of the carefully planned invasion and infringement on the sovereignty of African nations. The make-over is that such actions were on behalf of liberation and national health. And not once in his peroration about "Che" Guevara's mission to liberate Bolivia from the Bolivians did the idea enter that this might be perceived as infringement on the sovereignty of another nation. Latin America is one, and he is first among equals. Under Castro's personal orders a variety of adventurers and intellectuals were sent to Bolivia to soften up that nation for its eventual demise; and for an invasion of Guevara's beloved homeland, Argentina. The mythology of a heroic death is repeated, despite the evidence offered most recently by Humberto Fontova in *Exposing the Real Guevara* that Guevara surrendered in an abject way to the Bolivian Armed Forces, and with only half hearted support by either Aleksei Kosygin or Fidel Castro for Che's "impetuous" actions. The Castro myth is rooted in revolutionary romanticism, the Castro reality was national consolidation. The former wins out in this volume. In this latest version of the Guevara legend, a revolutionary must die as he lived: with nobility, without the slightest trace of weakness, an unflinching commitment to the cause. Heroes must be unblemished, while villains are without character.

The unmitigated egotism of Castro can scarcely be disguised amidst the face of transparent self-depredations. On speech writing he tells us that "Every time I've asked someone to write a speech for me, or at least a draft for me, it's been empty, ineloquent. I've had to rewrite it entirely." In contrast to his infinite modesty, were the "traitors": Carlos Franqui, Huber Matos, General Rafael del Piño, "opportunists" like Manuel Urrutia, "lapsed revolutionaries" like Carlos Aldana and Roberto Robaina. In conventional theological fashion, Fidel may have made unnamed mistakes, but never "errors of principle" like his enemies. Everything done was "for the good of the people" (580). Castro has no doubt that in the event of his demise, the next leader of Cuba "with absolute certainty" (620) would be his brother Raúl. Of course this too would be in the name of the people undertaken by the Cuban National Assembly. How such good deeds are to be measured remains locked in Castro's mind. That said, Castro demonstrates a populist touch that has stood him well over the years: His careful limitations of the cult of personality, his critique of extreme harsh measure on a grand scale, as those which characterized Mao Tse-tung and the Chinese Cultural revolution, are very much on his mind. One suspects that he can readily accept death, but not being forgotten.

Cuba is a *soft totalitarian* regime, without the brutal trappings of extreme *hard totalitarian* rule of a Pol Pot sort: there have been no assassinations on a mass scale, or concentration camps for the many, and a certain grudging toleration on the cultural front of the apolitical forces that are large in Cuban intellectual life. This is a consequence of a combination of internal elements and historical factors, and no less a large Cuban-American social structure in Miami that monitors Fidel on a daily basis. For the past half century I have described Castro in Stalinist terms —so why shift gears now and identify him as a "soft" rather than "hard" totalitarian? My response is admittedly not entirely persuasive. But as the regime aged, the totalitarian substance was weakened, perhaps more than softened. Cuba became a political regime more than touched by Latin American traditions of the *caudillo* and the *cacique*. We are at a stage in history when the liquidation of 10,000 human souls and the forced exile of over a million people are described as "soft". From Dachau to Darfur we have all become coarsened and perhaps dulled.

Above all else, in these pages Castro emerges as a man obsessed with illusions of high social development in Cuba, but not unaware of the shortfalls in every area of the economy: from crop and industrial diversification to the continuation of social deformations in the area of personal conduct and civil liberties. This compendium of orchestrated reflections and projects is a balancing act on a high wire of a dictator in his final stage of summing up, but not prepared to either admit defeat or to announce victory. Cuba remains a single party dictatorship, but it cannot exist only to obtain "privileges" for the members of that party. Cuba must continue on a path of moral righteousness, but it must not countenance opportunism and self-promotion. Fidel faces the problems of a Christian society without Christianity, of a supposedly advanced society without modernization, of a dedicated civil population, but one ruled by a military-police force that permeates every part of the system, in short of a civil society without civil rights.

There is a serious dilemma in books predicated on fatuous questions and tailored answers, especially when both have been scripted with care. This is not exactly a dialogue in the classical sense of Greek philosophy, in which major themes are opened for discussion among people of wit, difference and intelligence. Instead what we have is a summary of a life lived with absolute certainty and Manichean passion, a final summation that does not seriously question decisions taken during the past half century, and an unstinting continuing belief that the dialectics of history will "absolve" any and all decisions taken. Even a brilliant leader and courageous figure—and Castro is just that—must pay the price of his absolutism. This authorized autobiography proves that to rule for a half century, and to very rarely hear the word "no, you are wrong" or even "you may be right, but I have serious doubts," leaves an island of silent masses and even surly followers of the ruled. This is the logic of tyrants over the course of history. In this special sense, history has indeed absolved Fidel Castro.

Source and Original Title: Mi Vida: "The Manichean Face of Dictatorship" *Society*, Volume 45, No. 3 (May-June) 2008. Review Essay of Fidel Castro: *My Life.* By Fidel Castro and Ignacio Ramonet. New York: Scribner's Publishers, a subsidiary of Simon & Schuster, 2008. 724 pp. $40.00.

Index

For Product Safety Concerns and Information please contact our EU
representative GPSR@taylorandfrancis.com Taylor & Francis Verlag GmbH,
Kaufingerstraße 24, 80331 München, Germany

Batch number: 08153774

Printed by Printforce, the Netherlands